Counseling Based on Process Research

Applying What We Know

Edited by

Georgiana Shick Tryon

City University of New York

Allyn and Bacon

Boston • London • Toronto • Sydney • Tokyo • Singapore

Executive Editor: *Virginia Lanigan*
Editorial Assistant: *Erin Liedel*
Executive Marketing Manager: *Kathleen Morgan*
Editorial-Production Service: *Omegatype Typography, Inc.*
Composition and Prepress Buyer: *Linda Cox*
Manufacturing Buyer: *Julie McNeill*
Cover Administrator: *Kristina Mose-Libon*
Electronic Composition: *Omegatype Typography, Inc.*

Library of Congress Cataloging-in-Publication Data

Counseling based on process research : applying what we know / edited by Georgiana Shick Tryon.
     p. cm.
  Includes bibliographical references and index.
  ISBN 0-205-29827-3
1. Counseling.   I. Tryon, Georgiana Shick.
BF637.C6 C6355 2002
158'.3–dc21

                                             00-067552

Printed in the United States of America

10   9   8   7   6   5   4   3   2   1   06   05   04   03   02   01

Contents

Preface

Counseling and therapy are practiced in many settings with many different types of clients by counselors who subscribe to many different theoretical orientations. Yet there are common factors to each type of therapy conducted by every counselor with each client. This book addresses the common therapeutic factors by examining the counseling process research literature and relating it to what counselors and therapists do in actual practice.

Regardless of theoretical orientation, all counselors and therapists must engage their clients in therapy or the clients will not stay in treatment. All types of counseling are influenced by client expectations and resistance and the relationship between therapist and client. Counselors empathize with their clients in order to understand their problems and use certain verbal techniques and social influences to effect client change. All therapy progresses through stages, and some degree of client transference usually impacts the process. Most therapists, even those with considerable experience, receive some type of supervision, and all generally speculate about how each counseling session progressed. Finally, all therapy comes to an end. This book examines the counseling process research as it relates to each of these important issues.

The disciplines of clinical, counseling, and school psychologists have their foundations in the scientist–practitioner model. This model advocates the use of scientific research to inform professional practice. The current emphasis on the use of empirically documented techniques and treatments illustrates the continuing importance of the scientist–practitioner model. Yet, many practitioners complain that psychotherapy research is not useful to them. Many studies are conducted under such highly controlled conditions that the counseling they study bears little resemblance to counseling as practiced in the real world. The studies reviewed in this book were generally conducted in real-life settings and they address issues common to counselors and therapists of all orientations.

Each chapter of this edited volume reviews the counseling process research literature for a specific topic (e.g., engagement, working alliance, transference, termination) and translates research findings into suggested counseling practices. Good counseling process provides the framework for effective interventions by all practitioners regardless of theoretical orientation. Although there is a large body of process research with which to inform practice, most books for practitioners address counseling from a theoretical/clinical perspective rather than from a research base. This book integrates the science and practice of counseling. Each chapter is written by leading researchers in counseling process who describe their research and its application to counseling practices. Thus, the book addresses the frequent practitioner complaint that research appearing in scientific journals has no relevance to their work by directly connecting research to practice.

I would like to thank this book's reviewers: Connie Kane, California State University; and Christine Yeh, Teachers College, Columbia University.

About the Contributors

Ann Westcot Barich, Ph.D., is an assistant professor of psychology at Lewis University in Romeoville, Illinois. She teaches both at the undergraduate and graduate levels, and has clinical experience in a wide variety of settings. Her research interests are varied, including altruism, work–family conflict, gender issues in counseling, the multiple roles of women, counseling process and outcome, and critical thinking and the development of the self-concept. Her teaching areas include counseling theory, psychopathology, ethics, statistics, and research design.

Louis G. Castonguay, Ph.D., completed his doctorate in clinical psychology at the State University of New York, Stony Brook, a clinical internship at the University of California at Berkeley, and a postdoctorate at Stanford University. He is currently an associate professor in the Department of Psychology at Pennsylvania State University. His research focuses on the process and outcome of psychotherapy. He has received the Early Career Contribution Award from the International Society of Psychotherapy Research and the Jack D. Krasner Memorial Award from the Division of Psychotherapy of the American Psychological Association. He currently serves as the president of the North American Society for Psychotherapy Research.

Michael J. Constantino, M.S., is a doctoral candidate in the clinical psychology program at Pennsylvania State University. His main areas of research interest include the study of psychotherapy process and outcome, psychotherapy integration, and theories of the self. More specifically, his research emphasizes the impact on the therapeutic course (i.e., development of the working alliance) and outcome of the interaction between client–therapist interpersonal/intrapsychic process and the motivational properties of the client's self-system. He is also interested in how organizational properties of the self impact psychological adjustment and coping.

Changming Duan, Ph.D., is an assistant professor in counseling psychology at the University of Missouri at Kansas City. Her research interests include counseling process and outcome, cross cultural psychology, and stress coping of academic women.

Dr. Charles J. Gelso is professor of psychology at the University of Maryland, College Park. He received his doctorate in counseling psychology from Ohio State University in 1970. His theoretical and research interests focus on the therapeutic relationship within diverse theoretical approaches to therapy. He has published widely on related topics such as transference, countertransference, working alliance, and "real relationship" in psychotherapy. Dr. Gelso has served as associate editor and editor of the *Journal of Counseling Psychology,* and was recipient of the APA Division of Counseling Psychology's Leona Tyler Award in 1995.

Pilar Gonzalez-Doupe graduated from Wellesley College in 1991 in psychology and French literature. She completed her masters in marriage, couples, and family therapy at Purdue University in 1997. Currently a dissertator in counseling psychology at the University of Wisconsin–Madison, she expects to graduate in August, 2001. Her research focuses on group supervision in workplace settings.

Lisa E. Gordon is a doctoral student in clinical psychology at Miami University in Oxford, Ohio. She is currently assisting in the development of a psychoeducation program for inpatient adolescents at Mercy-Franciscan Hospital and is working on a dissertation focusing on metaphors used by cancer patients.

Martin Heesacker is professor and chair of psychology at the University of Florida. He has authored 67 scholarly publications, presented 65 scientific papers, and chaired 16 doctoral dissertations. A 1983 Ph.D. graduate of the University of Missouri, Dr. Heesacker has been an Early Career Award recipient in counseling psychology, a Fulbright Scholar, a Fellow of the American Psychological Association, and an Eli Lilly Foundation Teaching Fellow. He was honored by Florida TaxWatch with a Davis Productivity Award, received University of Florida teaching awards in 1993 and 1996, and has been UF Psychology Club's Teacher of the Year.

Elizabeth L. Holloway, Ph.D., is professor of counseling psychology at the University of Wisconsin–Madison. She is a Fellow of Division 17 of the American Psychological Association and Diplomat in Counseling Psychology of the American Board of Professional Psychology. She teaches workshops on her SAS model for supervision, coaching, and mentoring in United States, Europe, Middle East, and Asia. Her audiences have included psychotherapists, managers, teachers, and academics.

Dennis M. Kivlighan, Jr., former professor and chair, Department of Educational and Counseling Psychology at the University of Missouri–Columbia, is professor and chair of the counseling and personnel services department at the University of Maryland–College Park. He received his Ph.D. in counseling psychology from Virginia Commonwealth University in 1982. He is the editor-elect of *Group Dynamics,* the official journal of the Division of Group Psychology and Group Psychotherapy of the American Psychological Association. His research interests involve process and outcome relationships in group and individual counseling.

Rebecca A. Kraatz, M.A., L.P.C., is a Ph.D. student in counseling psychology at University of Missouri at Kansas City. She is a licensed professional counselor in Missouri. Her work experiences include teaching undergraduate adolescent development classes and assisting the operation of a community counseling center at UMKC. She has also worked as a behavioral health associate at a local hospital, as a social security disability advisor for individuals with chronic mental illness, and as a facilitator of psychoeducational groups on personal responsibility. She is a member of the Golden Key National Honor Society.

James A. Lani is a doctoral student in clinical psychology at Miami University in Oxford, Ohio. He is currently implementing a relapse prevention program for chronically mentally ill adults at Mercy-Franciscan Hospital and is conducting his dissertation research on the assimilation model of client change in psychotherapy.

Jim Mahalik earned his Ph.D. in counseling psychology from the University of Maryland in 1990. He is currently an associate professor in the Department of Counseling, Developmental and Educational Psychology at Boston College. His speciality interests include how men's conformity to masculinity norms affects developmental, psychological, and relational well-being, as well as men's utilization and experiences with psychotherapy.

Teresa Rose, Ph.D., is a counseling psychologist at the University of Missouri at Kansas City Counseling Health and Testing Center. Teresa also runs a private psychotherapy practice and engages in organizational consultation. Her research interest is in the area of empathy. She is also receiving advanced training in psychoanalytic psychology.

Alexander J. Schut, M.S., is completing his Ph.D. in clinical psychology at Pennsylvania State University. His principal research interests and publications are in the areas of psychotherapy process-outcome relationships, contemporary psychodynamic theory and practice, and personality assessment. He has served as student representative of the American Psychological Association's Division 29 Psychotherapy Research Committee and was the first-place winner of the Division 29 Student Paper Competition on Clinical Training and Education in 1999.

Marnie G. Shanbhag received her Ph.D. in counseling psychology from the University of Florida in 1998. She is a licensed psychologist and currently serves as the program director of Healthy Start in Gainesville, Florida. Her professional interests include reproductive health and multicultural counseling.

William B. Stiles is professor of psychology at Miami University in Oxford, Ohio. He taught previously at the University of North Carolina at Chapel Hill and held visiting positions at University of Sheffield and University of Leeds (UK), University of Joensuu (Finland), and Massey University (New Zealand). He is the author of *Describing Talk: A Taxonomy of Verbal Response Modes,* past president of the Society for Psychotherapy Research, and currently North American editor of the journal, *Psychotherapy Research.*

Terence J. G. Tracey is a professor in the Division of Psychology in Education and program director of the counseling and counseling psychology programs at Arizona State University. He received his Ph.D. from the University of Maryland, and worked as a counseling psychologist at the University Counseling Service at the State University of New York, Buffalo, and as a faculty member and training director of the counseling psychology program of the University of Illinois at Urbana–Champaign.

Georgiana Shick Tryon is a professor in the Ph.D. program in educational psychology at the City University of New York Graduate School and University Center. She received her Ph.D. from Kent State University, and was the director of the counseling center at Fordham University from 1973 to 1995.

Elizabeth Nutt Williams is an assistant professor of psychology at St. Mary's College of Maryland, a public liberal arts honors college. Dr. Williams received her B.A. in psychology from Stanford University in 1989 and her Ph.D. in counseling psychology in 1997 from the University of Maryland. Her primary research interests lie in the process of psychotherapy with particular emphasis on covert processes and the integration of feminist and multicultural issues in counseling. She also helped develop a research strategy called

Consensual Qualitative Research (CQR) and has conducted qualitative studies on therapist self-awareness, therapeutic impasses, and gift giving in therapy.

Susan S. Woodhouse, M.S., is currently a doctoral candidate in the counseling psychology program at the University of Maryland, College Park. She received her M.S. in counseling in 1996 from California State University, Hayward. Her research interests primarily focus on attachment phenomena in various relationships, including romantic, parent–child, and psychotherapy.

1

Engagement in Counseling

Georgiana Shick Tryon

City University of New York Graduate School and University Center

For successful counseling to occur, client and therapist must be engaged, or involved, in the counseling process. This engagement happens early—usually in the very first session. If engagement does not occur, clients leave counseling before it has really gotten started. Unfortunately, those clients who do not return for further sessions after the initial, or intake, session are often among the most troubled. This chapter addresses engagement research and provides suggestions for successful engagement of clients.

Chapter Questions

- What is engagement?
- How do various client and counselor characteristics relate to engagement?
- What takes place in an engagement interview?
- What issues relate to engagement with children and families?

In its simplest, most ideal form, counseling is a process whereby two people (a counselor and a client) meet on a regular basis to address the client's concerns. To these meetings, the counselor brings his or her counseling theoretical orientation and its associated counseling skills. The client brings life experiences and knowledge of his or her difficulties. Together they develop a working alliance that is characterized by a strong emotional bond and mutual agreement on the goals of counseling and the tasks necessary to achieve those goals (Bordin, 1979). They work together on the client's concerns. When both client and counselor mutually determine that the client's problems are ameliorated, they agree to terminate the meetings.

Most counselors will tell you, however, that many counseling relationships do not reach a desirable mutual termination. In fact, a substantial number of clients attend an intake, or first, session and then do not return for additional counseling sessions. Various studies (Betz & Shullman, 1979; Epperson, 1981; Epperson, Bushway, & Warman, 1983; Krauskopf, Baumgardner, & Mandracchia, 1981; Rodolfa, Rapaport, & Lee, 1983;

Wierzbicki & Pekarik, 1993) have found that 7% to 36% of clients do not return for the next scheduled counseling session after intake. Even higher percentages of clients at university counseling centers (40% to 60%) do not have a second counseling session either because they did not schedule one or because they did not show up for a scheduled appointment (Phillips, 1985; Tryon & Tryon, 1986).

For more than 20 years, I directed a university counseling center. The failure of clients to return to counseling after intake was a problem that concerned me greatly. Sometimes clients who had been seen only once at the center got into difficulties later on (i.e., suicide attempts or disciplinary problems) that may have been prevented had we counselors been able to hook these clients into the helping process. Generally, however, we did not hear about most of the clients who did not return for counseling after intake. Some of these clients may have received the help they sought in the one intake/counseling session they had, but others probably did not. We had numerous discussions in supervision and case conferences about this problem, but each year the percentage of clients at our center who came for only one visit remained about the same.

Finally, I decided to take a more systematic approach to the examination of client nonreturn for counseling after intake. What prompted this investigation was an interesting contrast. The counseling center served as a practicum training site for clinical and counseling psychology graduate students. One particular year, there was a practicum trainee who was rarely busy seeing clients. This trainee had initial interviews with lots of clients, but few of them returned for further counseling. There was another trainee who was almost always "booked" with clients. This trainee had seen relatively few clients for initial interviews, but the great majority of them had returned to her for continued counseling. This disparity in the experiences of these two trainees prompted me to examine the numbers of clients seen for various numbers of sessions by all counselors in the center.

A glance at the resulting big chart, which had each counselor's name and a frequency count of the number of clients he or she had seen for various numbers of sessions, revealed that the numbers of clients seen for 1 and for 10 or more sessions were the figures that discriminated most among counselors (Tryon, 1985). In other words, counselors who saw lots of clients for 1 session only, saw far fewer clients for 10 or more sessions. Counselors who saw fewer clients for 1 session only, however, saw more clients for 10 or more sessions. It appeared that those counselors who saw fewer clients for only 1 session were more adept at engaging their clients in the counseling process, which in our short-term counseling center lasted from 10 to 20 sessions. I calculated an engagement quotient (EQ) for each counselor. A counselor's EQ (see the example in the next section of this chapter) is the percentage of all the counselor's clients that the counselor has seen for more than 1 session.

The results of this examination (Tryon, 1985) appear in Table 1.1. As you can see, different counselors engaged clients at different rates. In other words, counselors' EQs differed. Counselor experience seemed to be a factor in engagement. The center's professional staff engaged clients at a rate of almost 70%. The mean EQs for practicum trainees and for first-year trainees were considerably lower than this. Table 1.1 also shows that counselor motivation may play a role in engagement. Two eager second-year trainees who requested and received supervised experience prior to their practicum year had EQs similar to those of experienced professionals.

This study help me to define engagement and oriented me to look at some factors associated with it (i.e., counselor characteristics). As a result, during the next several years, I

TABLE 1.1 *Engagement Quotients (EQs) by Counselors at Various Levels of Experience*

Level of Experience	Number of Sessions		Total Clients Seen	EQ[a]	Average for the Group
	1	*>1*			
Experienced					68%
Counselor A	8[b]	19	27	70%	
Counselor B	10	20	30	67	
Counselor C	3	6	9	67	
Practicum trainees					34%
Pr A	9	15	24	63%	
Pr B	24	20	44	45	
Pr C	26	13	39	33	
Pr D	31	13	44	30	
Pr E	36	13	49	27	
Pr F	35	9	44	20	
Prepracticum trainees					65%
PP A	2	6	8	75%	
PP B	6	9	15	60	
First experience trainees					17%
FE A	9	2	11	18%	
FE B	10	2	12	17	

[a]Engagement quotient is the percentage of clients seen for more than one session.

[b]Represents the number of clients.

Source: From "The Engagement Quotient: One Index of a Basic Counseling Task," by Georgiana Shick Tryon, 1985, *Journal of College Student Personnel, 26,* p. 353. Reprinted with permission of the American College Personnel Association (ACPA).

conducted a series of studies, which are reviewed in this chapter, to clarify engagement with the goal of ultimately helping counselors become better engagers. Studies conducted by others have also addressed engagement, and they will be reviewed as well.

The first sections of this chapter deal with the conceptualization of engagement as a unique phenomenon that either occurs or does not occur during the first session between counselor and client. Following this, factors associated with engagement are detailed. Next, the chapter examines what happens in an engagement interview. A separate section is devoted to engagement with children and families. Finally, implications for practice are discussed.

Review of Engagement Literature

Conceptualization of Engagement

Some authors (Epperson, 1981; Martin, McNair, & Hight, 1988; Mennicke, Lent, & Burgoyne, 1988) have conceptualized client nonreturn after intake as *early premature termination.* This implies that clients who do not return after intake have left an ongoing counseling relationship prematurely. In fact, in the initial interview, client and counselor are only beginning to know one another and to set the foundation to address client problems. It appears that rather than a termination, or ending, client nonreturn after intake represents a failure of the client and/or counselor to become involved, or engaged, in the counseling process.

Evidence for this conceptualization comes from the initial engagement study previously detailed (Tryon, 1985) that also found that third-year clinical psychology practicum trainees with higher supervisory ratings had greater percentages of their clients return for counseling after intake than did trainees with lower supervisory ratings. These higher-rated trainees also saw higher percentages of their clients for more than 10 sessions than did lower-rated trainees. These findings taken together appeared to indicate that trainees with higher supervisory ratings were engaging a higher percentage of their clients in an ongoing short-term counseling process than were trainees with lower supervisory ratings. In other words, higher-rated trainees seemed to be "hooking" their clients at intake into a process more successfully than lower-rated trainees.

The Engagement Quotient

To determine how successful an engager a particular counselor is, one may calculate an EQ for that counselor. To do this, consider *all* clients seen by the counselor as potentially engageable. Then divide the number of clients seen for more than one session by the total number of clients seen by that counselor. For example, counselor A has seen 54 clients this year, and 24 of them were seen by her for more than one session. The EQ for counselor A would be calculated as 24 divided by 54 or .44. Counselor A would have engaged 44% of the total clients she had seen, and so the EQ for counselor A would be 44.

Because some clients may receive the help they need at intake (Archer, 1984; Silverman & Beech, 1979; Stachowiak, 1994; Talmon, 1990), it is highly unlikely that any counselor would achieve an EQ of 1.00 (i.e., engage 100% of clients seen). Most problems, however, take longer than one session to solve; so EQs in the 60s and 70s would not be unexpected.

Other authors (Epperson, 1981; Epperson et al., 1983; Kokotovic & Tracey, 1987; Krauskopf et al., 1981; Zamostny, Corrigan, & Eggert, 1981) have only examined return rates for clients who scheduled an appointment after intake. This procedure results in higher counselor EQs and also gives a conservative picture of engagement (Pekarik, 1985). If clients do not schedule a second appointment, they are not considered in the engagement formulation. Thus, some clients who have problems that require further help are not counted as nonengaged simply because they did not schedule an additional appointment. Their data are eliminated from engagement consideration.

To gain a truer picture of engagement, it is advisable to consider all clients as potentially engageable in EQ calculations. A client who goes to counselor A and does not schedule a second appointment might have scheduled an additional appointment if he or she had seen counselor B instead. If all clients are considered as potentially engageable, this client would have been included as nonengaged had he or she seen counselor A and as engaged if he or she had seen and returned for a second appointment to counselor B. Thus, the EQs of counselors A and B would more accurately reflect engagement than if only data on clients with additional scheduled appointments were considered.

Figure 1.1 presents a distribution of counseling and clinical psychology practicum student EQs collected from a university counseling center during a 10-year period (Tryon,

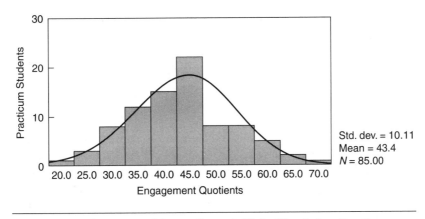

FIGURE 1.1 *Distribution of Counseling and Clinical Psychology Practicum Student EQs Collected From a University Counseling Center During a 10-year Period*

1999). The superimposed curve shows the distribution to be essentially normal. EQs ranged from 20 to 70. Comparable data for postdoctoral counselors and clinicians do not exist. In my engagement studies, doctoral-level counselors generally had EQs in the 60s (Tryon, 1985, 1989a, 1989b). In two studies, however, three professional counselors had EQs below 50. Because the average professional EQ was frequently in the 60s and the average trainee counselor EQ was in the 40s in the studies cited, it appeared that counselor ability to engage clients may improve with experience. It is discouraging for the counselor when a high percentage of clients at intake do not return for further counseling. So, it is possible that some doctoral-level professionals who are not good engagers may pursue other activities, such as administrative work or teaching, rather than direct counseling service.

Tryon and Tryon (1986) correlated EQs of 43 practicum trainees with the number of clients they had seen for varying numbers of sessions. Not surprisingly, we found that EQ was highly negatively related to number of clients seen for only one session. EQ was also highly negatively related to total number of clients seen. This latter finding yielded the troubling conclusion that the least engaging counselors will see more clients than the most engaging counselors.

There were no significant correlations between EQ and numbers of clients seen for intermediate numbers of sessions (2 to 10), but EQ correlated positively with number of clients seen for more than 10 sessions. These correlational data support the conceptualization of the intake as an engagement session where the client gets involved in the process of counseling. At the counseling center where data were collected, mutually terminated short-term counseling lasted from 15 to 20 sessions. The significant correlation of EQ with number of clients seen for more than 10 sessions and the lack of relationships of EQ to number of clients seen for 2 to 10 sessions indicates that higher engagers tended to lock their clients into the short-term counseling process in the very first session. How this engagement occurs and the factors associated with it are matters of continuing study, which are examined next.

Factors Associated With Engagement

Concern about the high percentage of clients leaving counseling after intake prompted investigators to look for correlates of this phenomenon. As Mennicke et al. (1988) expressed it, client nonengagement "poses a major obstacle to the delivery of counseling services" (p. 458). Some investigations focused on characteristics of the setting and service delivery system. Other investigations concentrated on client and counselor characteristics and the initial interview itself.

Unfortunately, procedures used in the various studies are not consistent, and the differential effects of these procedures on engagement have not been studied. For example, some studies (Betz & Shullman, 1979; Rodolfa et al., 1983) used a formalized intake followed by assignment of clients to either the intake or other counselors for the next session of counseling. In other studies (Tryon, 1985), clients were seen by the same counselor for both intake and continued counseling. Although most studies examined client return for a second appointment, some authors (Epperson, 1981; Epperson et al., 1983; Hoffman, 1985) examined client return for either or both the second and third appointments. Also, as mentioned previously, with the exception of my studies, most studies included only clients who had made additional appointments, thus providing a very conservative examination of engagement. A more accurate picture of engagement emerges when all clients, not only those who make additional appointments, are considered engageable.

Administrative Factors.

Counselors and clients have little influence over administrative factors, such as waiting lists, but these may contribute to nonengagement by making it difficult for clients to receive the help they need in a timely fashion. In some settings, clients who desire to continue counseling after intake must also wait to be assigned to a counselor and then wait for an appointment with that counselor. Rodolfa et al. (1983) found that the number of days between intake and counselor assignment was negatively associated with client engagement at a university counseling center. The longer clients had to wait to be assigned to a counselor, the more likely they were not to return after intake. Interestingly, the number of days clients were on a waiting list from intake to the next scheduled session was not related to client return for further counseling. Anderson, Hogg, and Magoon (1987) also found that length of time spent on a waiting list after intake was not related to college clients' return for second appointments. A study conducted at a community mental health center, however, found that waiting-list delays were associated with nonengagement (Folkins, Hersch, & Dahlen, 1980).

What happens to clients who do not return for further counseling after being placed on a postintake waiting list? Archer (1981; 1984) conducted two surveys of counseling center waiting-list clients who did not return for further counseling. Both surveys showed that more than 50% of these clients felt that they had received sufficient help at intake. Similar results were found in surveys by May (1990) and Silverman and Beech (1979). When Talmon (1990) surveyed 200 clients he has seen for only one session and found that 78% of them reported improvement, he developed single-session therapy techniques that involved strengthening client motivation to change and in-session practicing of problem solutions. His book presents successful single-session cases with clients who had a variety of problems.

Although a number of clients may receive the help they need in a single session, others do not. Pekarik (1983) found that only 15% of nonengaged clients reported symptom improvement at a three-month follow-up, and 31% reported feeling worse than they did at intake. Similar results were found when this study was replicated by Pekarik (1992) using both adult and child clients. Some clients are dissuaded from returning for further counseling by the length of the waiting list. Pulakos and Morris (1995) found that waiting-list clients who did not continue counseling "expressed moderate dissatisfaction with the [counseling] center" (p. 603). May (1990) found that 7% of nonreturning clients expressed dissatisfaction with the waiting list, another 7% sought help elsewhere, and 30% were no longer motivated to seek help for their concerns. In Archer's surveys (1981; 1984) 16% and 19% of clients said that the waiting list was a factor in their nonreturn for counseling after intake. Clients who were classified by counselors as being a threat to self or others were more likely to list waiting-list length as their reason for nonreturn. Fortunately, most agencies give priority for postintake counseling to more troubled clients.

Often the clients are assigned to a different counselor for the second session than the counselor who conducted the intake. One might assume that this may cause clients to feel rejected by the intake counselor and contribute to lower rates of engagement. Two studies (Reiher, Romans, Andersen, & Culha, 1992; Betz & Shullman, 1979), however, found that return rates for clients assigned to another counselor did not differ from those for clients who continued with the intake counselor. Surprisingly, Krauskopf et al. (1981) found that clients actually returned at higher rates after intake when they had been transferred to another counselor. Thus, the few studies conducted indicate that switching clients to another counselor after intake does not have a negative impact on engagement.

Finally, it appears that engagement may be affected by advertisement of services to potential clients. One study (Schiller, 1976) found that clients who had more positive attitudes toward counseling and a particular counseling center and those who had more information about the existence and effectiveness of the counseling center were more likely to continue in counseling after intake than were clients who felt less positively and had less information about the counseling center.

Results of studies in this section show that administrative procedures may influence client return for further sessions following intake (Rapaport, Rodolfa, & Lee, 1985). The effects of these procedures are not always consistent from one setting to another. Service demands may necessitate postintake waiting lists that serve as engagement deterrents for some clients. For the most part, procedures that make it more difficult for clients to receive services appear to contribute to nonengagement of certain clients.

Client Factors.   Perhaps there are particular types of clients who are more likely than others to become engaged. Some authors (Anderson & Myer, 1985; Tryon, 1989b) have examined demographic or personal history characteristics of engaged and nonengaged clients. Others (Richmond, 1992) have sought to identify personality characteristics of nonengaged clients in hopes that some kind of precounseling intervention or preparation can be done to increase the likelihood of these clients staying in counseling for more than one session.

Client Gender and Demographic Characteristics.   Several studies (Betz & Shullman, 1979; Hoffman, 1985; Krauskopf et al., 1981; Reiher et al., 1992; Rodolfa et al., 1983) examining client gender have found that it is not a factor in client engagement. Men and women clients become engaged at similar rates. Results of studies of other demographic variables and engagement are not so clear-cut. Hoffman (1985) found that client income, age, family size, and religion were not significantly related to engagement. Fiester, Mahrer, Giambra, and Ormiston (1974) also found that client socioeconomic status was not related to engagement. Richmond (1992), however, found that engagement rates were lower for clients who were less educated, younger, and members of minority groups. Trepka (1986) found that nonengaged clients at an out-patient clinic in Britain were more likely to be unemployed and from lower social classes than were engaged clients. Anderson and Myer (1985) found that international students engaged at lower rates than did U.S. students. Because counselors are often White, from higher socioeconomic classes, and not foreign born, these clients may not be engaged because counselors are not similar enough to them to relate to their problems in an engaging manner. Unfortunately, no studies to date have examined the effects of client–counselor ethnic/racial, socioeconomic, or cultural similarity and engagement.

History of Prior Counseling.   Having a history of prior counseling relates positively to engagement (Fiester et al., 1974; Hoffman, 1985). Client prior counseling experience seems particularly relevant when the counselor is a trainee. Tryon (1989a) found that clients who had received counseling before were more likely to be engaged by practicum trainees than clients with no previous counseling. Clients with and without previous counseling experience, however, were engaged at the same rate when they saw doctoral-level counselors. This finding, which was replicated twice (Tryon, 1989b, 1990), suggests that clients with past counseling experience may play a greater role in initiating engagement in the counseling process when their counselor is a novice than when the counselor holds a doctoral degree.

Symptoms and Personality Characteristics.   Severity of clients' symptoms has been found to relate both positively and negatively to engagement. Tryon (1986, 1990) found that counseling center clients rated as more disturbed by practicum trainees were more likely to become engaged that those rated as less disturbed. Similarly, Longo, Lent, and Brown (1992) found that engaged counseling center clients were more likely than nonengaged clients to have rated themselves preintake as having more severe problems and as more motivated to stay in counseling.

Studies at community mental health centers have yielded conflicting results. Hoffman (1985) found that clients diagnosed as psychotic were more likely to become engaged than were clients with less severe diagnoses. Richmond (1992) found, however, that clients who were more prone to unusual mannerisms, unusual thoughts, and hallucinations were less likely to become engaged. He also found that clients who had more suicidal intent were less likely to become engaged. Thus, in a setting, such as a counseling center, where client pathology tends to be more mild, more disturbed clients may engage more easily than other clients. In settings where client pathology tends to be more severe, this may not be the case. A study by Fiester and Rudestam (1975) indicates that the interaction of administrative factors with client disturbance may explain some of the differences in results.

They found that in one hospital-based community mental health center, clients who self-reported more disturbance were assigned to lower-status counselors, such as paraprofessionals and technicians. These clients were then engaged at lower rates than less disturbed clients who had been assigned to higher-status counselors.

Particular client diagnoses and associated personality characteristics may preclude engagement. Hilsenroth, Holdwick, Castlebury, and Blais (1998) found that clients meeting DSM-IV (American Psychiatric Association, 1994) criteria for antisocial personality disorder and narcissistic personality disorder were less likely to become engaged than clients with other types of personality disorders. These authors speculate that clients with these diagnostic characteristics are so egocentric and unconcerned about others that they are not able to form a therapeutic relationship. "It would seem that an individual requiring excessive admiration would become quickly disillusioned with many types of psychotherapy" (Hilsenroth et al., 1998, p. 172). Similarly, Richmond (1992) found that more hostile clients and clients with lower levels of guilt were less likely to become engaged. These clients were also more likely to have been referred by external sources than self-referred and were thus less motivated to seek help than clients who were self-referred. In contrast, Hilsenroth, Handler, Toman, and Padawer (1995) found that clients who had more cooperative and less hostile relationships outside the counseling situation were more likely not to return to counseling after the first session. Finally, not surprisingly, clients who scored higher on a measure of procrastination were less likely to return for counseling after intake (Pulakos & Morris, 1995).

Attractiveness as a Candidate for Counseling.   Counselors' judgments of the degree to which clients will be good counseling participants are also related to engagement. Tryon (1992) found that clients rated by their counselors as more attractive candidates for counseling were more likely to return for a second appointment than were clients rated as less attractive. In another study (Tryon, 1990), clients rated by their counselors as more motivated to change were more likely to become engaged than those rated as less motivated. Correspondingly, Phillips (1985) found that clients rated by their counselors as more likely to improve with counseling were engaged at a higher rate than were clients rated as less likely to improve. Clients who became engaged had also been rated more highly by counselors as someone with whom counselors would like to work. A similar finding was reported by Tryon (1986). Putting these results together, Phillips (1985) concluded

> Either something is going on at intake that is remarkably prescient or the ratings represent the beginning point of a self-fulfilling prophecy, namely, that therapists exert a remarkably subtle but somewhat far-reaching influence on clients at intake. (p. 84)

Even when a client is perceived by his or her counselor as a less attractive candidate for counseling, however, the client may still return for a second appointment if his or her counselor is a good engager. Table 1.2 presents engagement percentages for five higher-EQ counselors and five lower-EQ counselors and their 159 clients (Tryon, 1992). When a client who was perceived as a good candidate for counseling saw a counselor who was a high engager (i.e., had a higher EQ), engagement was almost a sure thing. When a counselor with a lower

TABLE 1.2   *Engagement Rates of Higher- and Lower-Engaging Counselors When Paired With More and Less Attractive Counseling Clients*

	Counselors	
Clients	*Higher Engager*	*Lower Engager*
More attractive	97%	85%
	(28 of 29 clients)	(41 of 48 clients)
Less attractive	90%	71%
	(36 of 40 clients)	(30 of 42 clients)

Note: χ^2 (3, $N = 159$) = 8.88, $p < .04$.

EQ was paired with a client rated as a less attractive counseling client, however, engagement took place less frequently. The table shows the influence of both counselor-rated client attractiveness and counselor skill in the engagement process.

Client Readiness.   Clients who have problems but are not ready to participate in the counseling process may also be viewed as unattractive candidates for counseling. Heilbrun (1972) found that clients who scored lower on the Counseling Readiness Scales (Heilbrun & Sullivan, 1962) were less likely to return for a second session than were higher-readiness clients. Longo et al. (1992) found that clients with greater counseling self-efficacy viewed themselves as better able to take the initiative in solving their problems, to talk about issues that were difficult for them, and to overcome obstacles to counseling attendance. These clients were more likely to become engaged than were clients who rated themselves lower on counseling self-efficacy. Client expectations about counseling may also contribute to engagement. Unfortunately, the only study to examine this found that precounseling expectations about counseling did not relate to engagement (Hardin, Subich, & Holvey, 1988). In this study, both engaged and nonengaged counseling center clients generally had high precounseling expectations and expected themselves to be positive contributors to the counseling experience.

A transtheoretical model of client change by Prochaska, DiClemente, and Norcross (1992) emphasizes the importance of client readiness. The model identifies five stages of client change: precontemplation, contemplation, preparation, action, and maintenance. During precontemplation, the client is unaware of problems and has no wish to change. In the contemplation stage, the client is aware of problems but has not decided to change. In the preparation stage, the client wants to act on his or her problems; and in the action stage, he or she begins to take effective action on problems. Finally, in the maintenance stage, the client makes significant behavioral changes and works to prevent relapse.

Smith, Subich, and Kalodner (1995) found that clients who entered counseling in the precontemplation stage of client change were less likely to become engaged than were clients entering counseling in the preparation and action stages. In other words, clients who had made attempts to address their problems *before* coming to counseling were more likely to become engaged than were clients who were unaware of problems or had no desire to change. Thus, clients who are already involved in the change process are easier to engage in the counseling process than those who are not. One can see how these clients might virtually engage themselves and would be perceived by their counselors as attractive clients. Clients who do not perceive themselves as having problems, however, such as those referred by external sources (Richmond, 1992), would be much harder to engage.

Pretraining has been seen as a way to increase client readiness for counseling and thereby increase engagement (Mennicke et al., 1988). Heilbrun (1972) found that engagement rates were higher for clients who had low scores on counseling readiness who were provided with a description of what to expect during the initial interview than for low-readiness clients who had no preparation for intake. In another study (Lawe, Horne, & Taylor, 1983), clients who listened to pretraining audiotapes were more likely to become engaged than clients with no pretraining. It appears that some type of precounseling outreach to clients facilitates engagement. As Mennicke et al. (1988) indicate, however, pretraining studies frequently do not operationalize their procedures in sufficient detail to allow application of findings.

Clients bring with them to counseling certain characteristics that may influence the engagement process. Some of these characteristics, such as hostility and procrastination, may make engagement more difficult. Others, such as a previous history of counseling, may make engagement easier. Frequently, when clients do not become engaged, counselors tend to view them as resistant to the counseling process (Pekarik & Finney-Owen, 1987). Although this perception may be accurate, it tends to place the burden of engagement on the client and relieves the counselor of responsibility for not engaging clients who are less attractive counseling candidates. No counselor can or should engage every client. But an exclusive concentration on client factors takes attention away from counselor characteristics and behaviors that influence engagement.

Counselor Factors.   Counselors vary in effectiveness of engaging clients (Tryon, 1999). What counselor factors are related to engagement? Investigators have explored the effects of gender (Betz & Shullman, 1979), experience (Epperson et al., 1983), social influence characteristics (Kokotovic & Tracey, 1987), and cognitive factors (Tryon & Tryon, 1986).

Counselor Gender.   Initially, investigators looked at counselor gender as it relates to engagement. Betz and Shullman (1979) found that clients who saw women counselors were more likely to return for an additional appointment than were clients with men intake counselors. This study has been replicated several times with differing results. Epperson and colleagues (Epperson, 1981; Epperson et al., 1983) found that clients were more likely to return for further counseling when they had been seen by a man counselor. Others (Krauskopf et al., 1981; Reiher et al., 1992; Rodolfa et al., 1983; Tryon, 1984) found no differences in engagement rates for male and female counselors. These results indicate that counselor gender may be a factor in engagement in some agencies, but findings achieved in one setting should not be generalized to other settings.

Counselor Experience.   Another variable thought to relate to engagement is experience. Studies in this area, however, generally have found no relationship between counselor experience and engagement of clients in the counseling process (Betz & Shullman, 1979; Epperson, 1981; Epperson et al., 1983; Fiester, 1977; Krauskopf et al., 1981; Longo et al.,

1992; Reiher et al., 1992; Rodolfa et al., 1983). These results led Krauskopf et al. (1981) to wonder, "If we expect our professional training and experience to make us more effective, then why is experience not related to return rates following intake interviews" (p. 520)? In contrast to these studies, Tryon's engagement studies generally found doctoral-level counselors to have EQs in the 60s and practicum trainees to have EQs in the 40s. Tryon's studies, however, employed relatively few doctoral-level counselors and were conducted at only one counseling center.

Counselor Social Influence Characteristics.   Strong (1968) conceptualized counseling as a social process whereby the counselor influences the client to change. He felt that counselors who were perceived by their clients as more attractive, experienced, and trustworthy would exert the most interpersonal influence over clients. It seems reasonable that higher-engaging counselors may be those perceived by clients as having higher levels of these interpersonal influence characteristics.

This has not been the case. Studies by Martin et al. (1988), Tryon (1989a), and Zamostny et al. (1981) found no significant relationship between client return for a second appointment and client-rated counselor attractiveness, experience, and trustworthiness. Kokotovic and Tracey (1987) found that "although trustworthiness and expertness significantly differed between [engaged and nonengaged clients], the discriminant analysis indicated that the significance of these variables was due to variance shared with satisfaction [with the intake interview] and not due to any unique relation with continuance" (p. 81). Although Strong's (1968) counselor interpersonal influence characteristics appear unrelated to engagement, they may relate to client unilateral termination later in counseling. Tryon (1989a) found that practicum trainees who were rated lower at intake by their clients on attractiveness, expertness, and trustworthiness were significantly more likely to have clients terminate unilaterally at some postengagement point (i.e., at sessions after the second session) than were trainees rated higher at intake on these characteristics.

Counselor variables such as empathy, warmth, and genuineness have also been posited to influence client change (Rogers, 1957) and may also be factors in client engagement. Tryon (1986) asked clients to rate their counselors on these characteristics at intake. None of these ratings related significantly to engagement. In another study (Tryon, 1989b) client-rated counselor understanding was not directly related to engagement; however, higher-EQ counselors were rated as more understanding than lower-EQ counselors by all of their clients (both engaged and nonengaged).

Counselor Cognitive Factors.   Tryon and Tryon (1986) investigated practicum trainee counselors' verbal and diagnostic skills using scores from the Graduate Record Examination (GRE), Millers Analogies Test (MAT), and grades in a clinical diagnostic course sequence. Verbal scores on the GRE, verbal-quantitative GRE discrepancy scores, MAT scores, grade in clinical diagnosis, and grade in advanced clinical diagnosis all correlated significantly and positively with counselor EQ. Counselor age also correlated highly and positively with EQ. Tryon and Tryon (1986) felt that higher-EQ counselors' greater diagnostic skills combined with their greater verbal facility enable them to identify client problems and communicate with clients about these problems in an engaging manner. They also believed that older counselors may be able to draw on their own life experiences to engage clients.

The studies investigating counselor characteristics relative to engagement have found few significant relationships. Counselors vary in engagement effectiveness, but this variability appears not to be related to counselor social influence variables, experience, or gender. Interpersonal influence characteristics (i.e., counselor attractiveness, expertness, and trustworthiness) may be related to client change, but they appear unrelated to getting clients initially involved in the counseling process. Engagement differences among counselors are more related to counselor verbal and diagnostic skills that may enable them to communicate more or less effectively with clients about their problems. To determine what counselors are communicating to clients to help them begin the counseling process the engagement interview itself needs to be studied.

The Engagement Interview.   What factors in the initial interview are related to engaging clients in the counseling process? Based on the preceding section, it appears that counselors may employ their verbal and diagnostic skills to communicate with clients in engaging ways. Studies in this area have examined client and counselor ratings of various aspects of the interview, such as satisfaction (Kokotovic & Tracey, 1987), interview length (Tryon, 1989a), and problem identification (Epperson, 1981). Only one study (Tryon, in press) has examined counselor intake verbal behavior relative to engagement. Client verbalizations may also relate to engagement, but these have not been studied.

Satisfaction With the Interview.   In his review of consumer satisfaction with mental health treatment, Lebow (1982) indicates that, "Consumer satisfaction is widely regarded by clients as an important goal of treatment. In part, treatments must be judged by whether consumers obtained what they wanted and were satisfied with their experience" (p. 255). If clients do not get what they want from the initial interview, they may be dissatisfied, and this dissatisfaction may lead to nonengagement.

Probably because they generally did not employ uniform measures of client satisfaction, earlier studies of satisfaction yielded differing results. Schiller (1976) and Heilbrun (1974) found no differences among clients who returned for a second session and those who did not in their satisfaction with the intake interview. In a community mental health setting, Fiester and Rudestam (1975) also found no differences in satisfaction with the initial interview among engaged and nonengaged clients; however, at a hospital-based counseling center, engaged clients were more satisfied with the initial interview than were nonengaged clients. Shueman, Gelso, Mindus, Hunt, and Stevenson (1980) found that engaged clients were more satisfied with their intake interviews and felt more helped and understood than did nonengaged clients.

Recently, studies have used either the three- or four-item version of the Client Satisfaction Questionnaire (CSQ; Larsen, Attkisson, Hargreaves, & Nguyen, 1979). The CSQ asks clients to rate on 4-point scales their level of general satisfaction with the interview, the degree to which their immediate concerns were addressed, and their likelihood of seeking further help at the agency. Higher scores on these items indicate more satisfaction with the interview. Studies using the CSQ (Greenfield,1983; Kokotovic and Tracey, 1987; Tryon, 1990) found that less satisfied clients were significantly less likely to return for further counseling following intake.

Client and counselor evaluations of the depth and smoothness of the initial, or intake, session are other indicators of satisfaction. The Session Evaluation Questionnaire (SEQ; Stiles, 1980) is a self-report instrument that contains depth and smoothness indexes composed of five bipolar adjectives each that are rated by clients and counselors on 7-point scales. Both clients and counselors rated engagement interviews as significantly deeper than nonengagement interviews (Tryon, 1990). Thus, both participants in engaged counseling dyads felt the intake was deeper, more full, more powerful, more valuable, and more special (the SEQ depth items) than did nonengaged participants. There were no differences in smoothness ratings for engagement and nonengagement interviews. It seems that intake interviews do not need to be relaxed, easy, pleasant, smooth, comfortable (the SEQ smoothness items) experiences for client and counselor to become engaged. In fact, Nash and Garske (1988) found that clients who rated intake interviews as smoother were more likely to discontinue counseling. They felt that smooth initial sessions might be indicative of client resistance that would mitigate against engagement in the counseling process.

Interview Length.   One might suspect that a deep, meaningful interview would consume more time than an interview rated as more shallow and worthless. Thus, an engagement interview may be longer than a nonengagement interview. Indeed, I (Tryon, 1989b) was prompted to examine the length of the intake interview by nonengaged client comments that their counselors spent too little time with them and my own observations that some interviews conducted at the center I directed seemed inordinately brief. In four studies, I (Tryon, 1989a, 1989b, 1990, 1992) found that engagement interviews were significantly longer than nonengagement interviews. The average length of an engagement interview from the four studies was 51.89 minutes (range = 50.33–53.61), and the average length of a nonengagement interview was 42.98 minutes (range = 39.35–46.53). The greater length of the engagement interview suggests that more is being said in an engagement interview than in a nonengagement interview. The greater expenditure of time indicates that the participants are probably more involved, or engaged, in the interview than they are in a nonengagement interview.

Only one other study attempted to examine length of intake interview and client return for more counseling. Unfortunately, Rodolfa et al. (1983) included the time it took intake counselors to write-up the interview along with length of the interview in their calculation of length of intake interview. They found that intake interviews plus write-ups with clients who returned after intake were significantly shorter than intakes plus write-ups with nonreturning clients. It is impossible to know the exact length of the interviews in their study. The longer times they recorded for nonengagement interviews could have been caused by several factors. For instance, in this study, nonengagement interviews, in fact, may have been longer than engagement interviews, or counselors could have taken longer to start writing or to complete notes from a nonengagement intake.

Identification of Client Problems.   It seems reasonable to assume that client and counselor agreement about the problem to be addressed would be important to engagement in the counseling process. If client and counselor are not focused on working on the same problem, why should the client want to return after intake for further counseling? Studies (Epperson, 1981; Epperson et al., 1983; Kokotovic & Tracey, 1987; Zamostny et al., 1981) of client–counselor problem agreement have used different assessment methods and, as a result, have achieved equivocal results. The initial interview is an active process, and simply asking client and counselor to complete a problem identification form that merely lists problems that clients may have, as most studies do, may not capture this process.

Clients frequently come to intake with vaguely defined problems. During the intake interview, the counselor may help them to clarify these problems and focus on how to work on them. Reflecting on my experiences and those of other counselors at intake, I (Tryon, 1986) conceptualized that this clarification process might even seem to clients as if counselors were identifying concerns for which they did not initially seek help. Clients who gave stronger endorsement of an item stating this were significantly more likely to return for a second appointment after intake than were clients who agreed less with this item.

I (Tryon, 1989b) hypothesized that this problem identification process involved teaching clients about their concerns. I developed three-item scales for both clients and counselors that included the item from the 1986 study and also asked the extent to which the counselor provided the client with new ways of understanding himself or herself and the extent to which the counselor taught the client about himself or herself. Items were rated on 5-point scales with higher ratings indicating more teaching about concerns. Higher ratings of these items by counselors related significantly to engagement (Tryon, 1989a, 1989b). Clients rated women counselors, who were higher engagers than men counselors, as teaching significantly more than men counselors (Tryon, 1989b). Thus, it appears that providing clients with new perspectives on their problems is positively related to engagement in the counseling process.

Counselor Verbalizations.   Examination of actual client and counselor verbal behavior would clarify what occurs in engagement and nonengagement interviews. Unfortunately, no one has studied client verbalizations and only one study (Tryon, in press) has recorded counselor verbalizations in engagement and nonengagement interviews. I used the Hill Counselor Verbal Response Category System (HCVRCS; Hill, 1978, 1993) to organize counselor verbalizations into 12 categories: minimal encourager, silence, approval, information, direct guidance, closed question, open question, paraphrase, interpretation, confrontation, self-disclosure, and other. The counselor was a Caucasian female clinical psychologist with a psychodynamic theoretical orientation and five years of post-PhD counseling experience. Her clients were 11 university students (8 women and 3 men) who sought help for personal concerns at a short-term (12-session limit) counseling service at a large, private, eastern university. Of the 11 clients, 7 returned for further counseling after intake.

Although the number of counselor verbal responses did not differ for engagement and nonengagement interviews, a significant effect was found for type of counselor verbal utterances in engagement versus nonengagement interviews. In engagement interviews, 40% of the counselor's verbalizations were information, and 29% were closed questions. In nonengagement interviews, 27% of verbalizations were information, 25% were closed questions, and 21% were minimal encouragers. Thus, engagement interviews had higher percentages of counselor information-providing and question verbalizations than did nonengagement interviews.

It should be noted that for all 11 intake interviews, closed questions, minimal encouragers, and information comprised the majority of counselor verbalizations (80.5%).

Similar to findings of other researchers (Friedlander, 1982; Lee, Uhlemann, & Haase, 1985; Lin, Kelly, & Nelson, 1996; Lonborg, Daniels, Hammond, Houghton-Wenger, & Brace, 1991), all the intake interviews in this study had higher percentages of therapist information, closed questions, and minimal encouragers and lower percentages of therapist interpretation, confrontation, and self-disclosure.

These percentages did not tell how engagement and nonengagement interviews progressed from beginning to end. To explore this, I examined patterns in the use of the most frequently employed verbal responses (i.e., numbers of minimal encouragers, closed questions, and information) for the first, second, and third parts of engagement and nonengagement interviews.

Figure 1.2 presents the graphs of the engagement status by thirds of interview interactions for closed questions, information, and minimal encouragers. In engagement interviews, the number of closed questions decreased during the course of the interviews. In nonengagement interviews, counselor use of closed questions increased from the first to the second third of the interviews and then fell in the final third. In nonengagement interviews, information verbalizations fell from the first to the second third of the interviews and increased again in the final third of the interviews. Counselor use of minimal encouragers followed a pattern similar to that of closed questions for engagement and nonengagement interviews. In engagement interviews, the number of counselor information verbalizations increased across the interviews.

Taken together, the graphs in Figure 1.2 suggest that in engagement interviews the counselor used questions and minimal encouragers to clarify client problems. The pattern of counselor questions, minimal encouragers, and information suggests that once problems had been made clear, the counselor provided information about them. The clients then returned for further counseling sessions. Although the specific content of the utterances was not coded, my review of the transcripts showed that problems were being clarified and communicated about in the manner suggested by the pattern of counselor verbal utterances previously described.

In nonengagement interviews, this pattern of decreasing questions and minimal encouragers and increasing information did not occur. The average number of counselor questions during the first third of nonengagement interviews were considerably less than the average number of questions during the first third of engagement interviews. Also, rather than increasing throughout the interview, the number of information verbalizations decreased. This suggests that in a nonengagement interview, there is less initial problem clarification, and, perhaps as a result of this, less information is given to the client later in the session. The clients then did not return to the counselor for further counseling. In nonengagement interviews, the counselor also used more minimal encouragers than in engagement interviews. Perhaps these were used in an attempt to encourage clients to continue talking so that the counselor could try to get a sense of client problems.

Discussions with the counselor in the study yielded anecdotal information that may prove useful in future engagement investigations. The counselor indicated that when clients presented with problems in areas in which she specializes, she felt confident in clarifying and teaching about these problems during the latter phases of the interviews. These clients subsequently returned to her for further counseling. When problems were outside her specialty areas or when she had difficulty discerning the exact problem, she did not

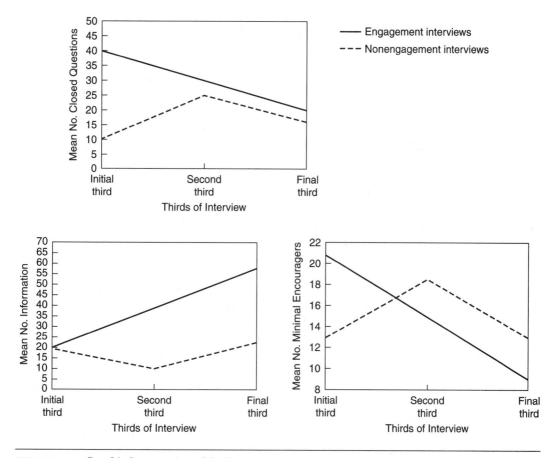

FIGURE 1.2   *Graphic Presentation of the Engagement Status X Third of Interview Interactions for Therapist Use of Closed Questions, Information, and Minimal Encouragers*

Source: From "A Therapist's Use of Verbal Response Categories in Engagement and Nonengagement Interviews," by Georgiana Shick Tryon, *Counseling Psychology Quarterly.* Reprinted with permission of Taylor and Francis.

have much information to give clients. These clients subsequently did not return to her for further counseling. Thus, an additional factor in engagement seems to be whether the counselor has experience dealing with the problem that the client presents.

Additional Verbal Behaviors That May Relate to Engagement.   Friedlander (1982) altered the HCVRCS in a way that may prove a useful tool in future studies of engagement. She classified eight of the HCVRCS categories into three levels according to the degree of structure that the counselor's verbal utterance would have on subsequent client verbalizations. Low-structure utterances, such as minimal encouragers or paraphrases, allow the client considerable response latitude. Closed questions and direct guidance (high-structure utterances) require more specific client responses.

Friedlander (1982) categorized segments of first and second interviews for 17 counseling dyads. Initial interviews were characterized by a high degree of structure with 38% of utterances associated with information seeking (i.e., questions). Moderate structure verbalizations (information and interpretation) comprised 23% of initial interviews. Low-structure utterances were used infrequently in first and second interviews. From the first to the second interview, high-structure (questioning) verbalizations fell slightly and moderate-structure (information-providing) verbalizations increased slightly. These categorical findings are similar to those in my study (Tryon, in press) of engagement interviews. This initial structuring through the use of questions and then the provision of information in engagement interviews may be a representation of Lennard and Bernstein's (1967) formulation that the counselor must initially teach the client how to be a client so that the counseling process may begin.

A related area of study is the degree to which engagement interviews demonstrate symmetrical or complementary client–counselor relationships. A symmetrical relationship is one in which one participant does not follow the topic of the other participant. Instead, he or she initiates a topic of his or her own. In a complementary interaction, one participant initiates a topic and the other participant follows the topic. Tracey, Heck, and Lichtenberg (1981) found that when client and counselor agreed on the roles they expected to play in counseling, they were more likely to display complementary relationships at intake. If role expectations were not matched, symmetrical relationships emerged with both client and counselor displaying similar topic initiation behaviors. Tracey et al. (1981) hypothesized that complementarity would lead to greater engagement, but they did not test this hypothesis. Tracey et al. indicated that it is the counselor's responsibility to ensure complementarity by altering his or her behavior so that this pattern of interaction occurs. In a later study, Tracey and Ray (1984) found that high complementarity in the first session was associated with successful time-limited counseling. Friedlander and Phillips (1984) found high complementarity in both first and second sessions. The most frequent participant response was topic following with either client or counselor making a "substantive contribution to the established topic" (Friedlander & Phillips, 1984, p. 146).

Several authors have developed ways of categorizing counselor or client interview behaviors that may shed light on the engagement interview. In addition to the HCVRCS, Hill (1992) has developed category systems for client verbal behaviors and reactions and for counselor intentions. Considering findings cited early in this chapter indicating that clients as well as counselors play a role in engagement, explorations of client verbalizations relative to engagement would seem a fruitful domain of study.

Counselor Theoretical Orientation.   Counselor verbalizations are related to counselor theoretical orientation (Brunink & Schroeder, 1979; Hill, Thames, & Rardin, 1979; Lee & Uhlemann, 1984; Stiles, 1979). Stiles (1979) found that client-centered counselors used reflection and acknowledgment; gestalt counselors used interpretations, questions, and advisement; and psychoanalytic counselors used interpretations and questions more than other verbal categories. Stiles indicated that, "much of the difference between schools [of counseling] is due to a preponderance of particular "favored" modes" (p. 60). Using another classification system, Brunink and Schroeder (1979) found similar differences in use of response modes between gestalt, psychoanalytic, and behavioral counselors. These investigators did not use initial interviews; so it is not possible to relate their results to engagement.

Studies by Hill et al. (1979) and Lee and Uhlemann (1984) categorized the verbalizations of leading psychologists who subscribed to differing theoretical orientations in interviews with the same client. The interviews were recorded to illustrate the different categories of verbal behavior associated with each counselor's theoretical orientation. Although they were initial interviews, they were not intended as examples of counselor engagement behavior.

Edwards, Boulet, Mahrer, Chagnon, and Mook (1982) compared the verbal responses of Carl Rogers during initial interviews with two clients. Even though the interviews were conducted more than 20 years apart, Rogers showed remarkable consistency in his use of verbal response categories. He used primarily minimal encouragers, restatements, and reflections. Elliot et al. (1987) reported response modes of initial sessions of three counselors with differing theoretical orientations. Similar to the verbalizations in engagement interviews in the Tryon (in press) study, the behavioral counselor and the gestalt-dynamic counselor used primarily information and questions. The dynamic-relationship counselor used interpretations, questions, and information.

These results indicate that the pattern of counselor verbalizations in my study of engagement interviews (Tryon, in press) may represent one of several possible verbal engagement patterns. Counselors with different theoretical orientations will probably differ in their use of verbal response modes during intake interviews. Obviously, this is an area for further study.

Engagement of Children and Families

Thus far, the engagement research reviewed has dealt exclusively with single adult clients. Counseling, however, is not confined to single adults. Adults seek counseling in couples and in groups. Children and adolescents also receive counseling for their problems. Engagement of children or adolescents in counseling is doubly difficult, because the counselor must engage both youths and their parents. Children and adolescents generally do not seek counseling on their own (Kazdin, 1995). Even when they do, parents or guardians must give permission for counseling and are generally involved with their children's treatment, and, therefore, a factor in whether children and adolescents return for postintake appointments. For adult clients, the intake generally is just one session long. For child clients, however, intake may consume several sessions of testing and information gathering by the counselor.

There have been fewer studies of engagement with children than with adult clients, and their results have been contradictory and inconclusive. Three studies (Levitt, 1957; Weisz, Weiss, & Langmeyer, 1987; Williams & Pollack, 1964) found no demographic, counselor, child, or parent differences between children who returned and those who did not return for counseling after intake. McAdoo and Roeske (1973) found no Minnesota Multiphasic Personality Inventory (MMPI) validity and clinical scale score differences between mothers and fathers in families who did not continue treatment after intake and parents in families who continued postintake treatment. In contrast, Gould, Shaffer, and Kaplan (1985) found that noncontinuers after a screening interview from a child clinic were likely to have more disturbed parents than were continuers.

Three studies indicate that school referrals may not facilitate engagement. Viale-Val, Rosenthal, Curtiss, and Marohn (1984) found that adolescents who did not return for postassessment counseling were more likely to have been referred by school staff than were adolescents who returned for counseling. Similarly, child clients who did not return to clinics after screening were more likely than those who returned to have been referred through the schools (Gould et al., 1985; Lake & Levinger, 1960). These results are similar to those of Richmond (1992) who found that adult clients referred by external sources were less likely to become engaged.

Ewalt, Cohen, and Harmatz (1972) found that postintake return for counseling was positively associated with younger child clients (under age 12) who had parent-perceived symptoms of stubbornness. Families with adoptive mothers or stepmothers who were worried about the effect of the problem on the child and wanted understanding of the child's problem and advice were more likely to become engaged in counseling. McAdoo and Roeske (1973) found that families who became engaged in counseling had rated the child's symptoms as being of longer duration at intake than did families who did not become engaged. Viale-Val et al. (1984) found that adolescents who did not become engaged in treatment after diagnostic intakes had initially reacted negatively to referral for treatment. Similar results were obtained by Szapocznik et al. (1988) who found that adolescent unwillingness to attend treatment was the primary reason for lack of engagement in 62% of the cases they surveyed. Findings of these studies have some similarity to engagement results from college studies that show clients who are more disturbed and motivated to seek help are more likely to become engaged (Longo et al., 1992; Phillips, 1985; Tryon, 1990).

Most studies focused on the characteristics of child and adolescent clients and their parents. This approach may indicate who is at risk for nonengagement, but it may not tell us how to engage them. For example, knowing that children and adolescents with fewer internalizing symptoms (Kendall & Sugarman, 1997) are at risk for nonreturn for therapy after intake does not inform us about what to do to enable these clients to become involved in the therapy process. Generally, we can do little about client characteristics per se, but we may be able to do something about the way we approach clients with particular characteristics to enable them to become involved in treatment.

Counselor characteristics that are important in adult engagement have not been studied nor have there been studies of the engagement interview. Recently, however, one group of investigators developed a strategic structural-systems approach to engage families with adolescent drug users (Szapocznik et al., 1988). To overcome family resistance to treatment, "the therapist joins with the family in a way that does not challenge the family structure and restructures only those interactions that prevent family members from getting into treatment" (p. 553). Compared to family therapy where the counselor did no restructuring of resistance and a group therapy condition, the strategic structural-systems approach resulted in an engagement rate of 81% compared to 62% for the other approaches (Santisteban et al., 1996). This approach seems promising and should be investigated using families with children who have other types of problems.

Another potentially promising approach for use in investigations of child and adolescent engagement in counseling is the barriers-to-treatment model (Kazdin, Holland, & Crowley, 1997). This model states that, in addition to demographic and client characteristics, child and adolescent therapy dropout is a result of several obstacles that families encounter during the course of treatment. These barriers relate to practical considerations (e.g., transportation difficulties) as well as treatment considerations (e.g., poor working alliance).

Kazdin et al. (1997) constructed a Barriers to Treatment Participation Scale (BTPS) composed of four scales: Stressors and Obstacles That Compete With Treatment, Treatment Demands, Perceived Relevance of Treatment, and Relationship With the Therapist. They administered it to parents and therapists at the termination of treatment and found that higher BTPS scores for both parent and therapist were significantly related to premature termination from child and adolescent therapy.

Although barriers to treatment may accumulate over time and thus contribute to premature termination, they may also present obstacles to initial engagement in therapy. BTPS scores may be used to predict client engagement. It is reasonable to assume that clients who have higher BTPS scores at intake, especially on the Stressors and Obstacles That Compete With Treatment and Perceived Relevance of Treatment scales, will be less likely than those who score lower to return for treatment after intake. Procedures and interventions to address these stressors instituted at intake may facilitate engagement.

Practical Application of Engagement Research

How do results of engagement studies inform counseling practice? Some conclusions are obvious. Long waiting lists can be avoided. They can contribute to the nonengagement of those clients who need help the most. Clients who have no history of prior counseling, are referred by someone other than themselves, have disturbances associated with interpersonal hostility, are from cultural backgrounds where counseling is less acceptable, and are not ready to change their behavior will be harder to engage. For these clients, some type of outreach or precounseling intervention may be necessary. Unfortunately, the literature is not specific about the content of this outreach, but it appears that a general education about counseling and what to expect helps to facilitate engagement. Research indicates that this outreach would probably be most effective if it facilitated client movement from the precontemplation stage where clients are unaware of problems and have no wish to change to the preparation stage where clients want to act on their problems.

Counselors can prepare themselves to be better engagers by honing their diagnostic and verbal communication skills through formal coursework and skills practice. Counselors who are better diagnosticians and better communicators are higher engagers. Thus, anything that counselors can do to increase these skills and abilities is advisable.

When clients come for help, they frequently do so after consulting others (i.e., friends, parents, or the clergy). Those whom they consult are generally empathic, warm, and understanding. Counselors should have these qualities too, but these characteristics alone do not appear to be responsible for engagement of clients in the counseling process. Counselors need to do something more than provide a sympathetic, understanding ear; otherwise, clients will not have reason to spend time and money getting professional help. To engage clients, counselors need to demonstrate their helpfulness at intake. Engagement occurs when counselors listen to clients' problems and reformulate them in a manner that makes them clearer to the client and sets the stage for addressing them in counseling. In short, it appears necessary for counselors to teach clients about their problems in order for clients to become engaged. If counselors do not do this, clients are not likely to return after intake.

Exactly how counselors provide clients with an engaging perspective on their problems needs further study. One approach appears to be for the counselor to question the client about the client's problems until these are clarified for the counselor. Then the counselor provides the client with information about the client's concerns and what might be done about them. Other approaches may also result in successful engagement. Counselors seem to employ different verbal categories depending on their theoretical orientation. For example, a counselor with a humanistic orientation may not be accustomed to providing clients with a great deal of information or asking numerous questions. Instead, a humanistically oriented counselor may employ paraphrases and minimal encouragers to direct clients to new perspectives on and greater understanding of their problems. Regardless of the type of counselor verbal behavior used, it seems important for clients to feel educated concerning their problems for engagement to occur.

To engage in the counseling process, clients must be motivated to change and believe that they are able to do what counseling requires for change. Many clients come to intake lacking such motivation and counseling self-efficacy. Despite this, some counselors are able to engage these clients in the counseling process. Is this simply because they teach their clients about their problems or are other factors involved? Longo et al. (1992) suggest "that counselors who regularly attain high client return rates do so, in part, by enhancing their clients' expectancies regarding self and counseling" (p. 452). Thus, it appears enhancing client counseling self-efficacy may be important to engagement.

Some clients are ready for counseling and easy to engage; others are not. They come to counseling in a hostile mood. They may have had a history of negative encounters with others and may not have chosen to seek counseling voluntarily. These clients are among the most difficult to engage, yet engagement can happen if they become educated about their concerns and the ways that they may be addressed. It is not that easy for a counselor to try to understand clients who direct hostile verbalizations at them, but understanding and reformulation of problems are what the clients need. The client does not want to be in counseling, and the counselor may not want to be in the situation either. Engagement could start from acknowledgment of this point of mutual agreement. After this, the counselor might say something similar to the following, "But because we are both here for the present, maybe we could talk about how we could try to get some of these people off your back." Starting where the client is (i.e., demonstrating interpersonal complementarity) rather than confronting or combating (i.e., displaying interpersonal symmetry) the client, as others in his or her environment probably do with some regularity, seems the best course to potential engagement.

Summary

As is true of most areas of research, the more we learn, the more questions we have. Engagement research is in its infancy. There are many issues that have not been addressed, and those that have been studied have frequently yielded equivocal results. What the client says in an engagement interview is undoubtedly as important as what a counselor says. Future studies need to be conducted on the verbalizations of both parties using counselors from a variety of theoretical perspectives.

A totally neglected area is client and counselor ethnic/racial background. We live in an increasingly multicultural world. Engagement in counseling must occur for all types of clients seeing all types of counselors. How does a client's ethnicity impact engagement? How does a counselor's ethnicity relate to engagement? How do client and counselor ethnicities interact in an engagement interview? No studies have addressed these questions, but the answers to them are of great importance to the twenty-first century practitioner.

In summary, results of engagement studies probably do not, and indeed should not, come as a surprise to the counseling practitioner. In some cases, these studies may clarify and illuminate what counselors know from experience. In other cases, they may offer new perspectives on and ideas about ways to engage clients in the process of counseling. Ultimately, the engagements studies raise more questions to be explored in both practice and research.

References

American Psychiatric Association. (1994). *Diagnostic and statistical manual of mental disorders* (4th ed.). Washington, DC: Author.

Anderson, T. R., Hogg, J. A., & Magoon, T. M. (1987). Length of time on a waiting list and attrition after intake. *Journal of Counseling Psychology, 34,* 93–95.

Anderson, T. R., & Myer, T. E. (1985). Presenting problems, counselor contacts, and "no shows": International and American college students. *Journal of College Student Personnel, 26,* 500–503.

Archer, J., Jr. (1981). Waiting list and client attitudes. *Journal of College Student Personnel, 22,* 370–371.

Archer, J., Jr. (1984). Waiting list dropouts in a university counseling center. *Professional Psychology: Research and Practice, 15,* 388–395.

Betz, N. E., & Shullman, S. L. (1979). Factors related to client return following intake. *Journal of Counseling Psychology, 26,* 542–545.

Bordin, E. S. (1979). The generalizability of the psychoanalytic concept of the working alliance. *Psychotherapy: Theory, Research and Practice, 16,* 252–260.

Brunink, S. A., & Schroeder, H. E. (1979). Verbal therapeutic behavior of expert psychoanalytically oriented, gestalt, and behavior therapists. *Journal of Consulting and Clinical Psychology, 47,* 567–574.

Edwards, H. P., Boulet, D. B., Mahrer, A. R., Chagnon, G. J., & Mook, B. (1982). Carl Rogers during initial interviews: A moderate and consistent therapist. *Journal of Counseling Psychology, 29,* 14–18.

Elliott, R., Hill, C. R., Stiles, W. B., Friedlander, M. L., Mahrer, S. R., & Margison, F. R. (1987). Primary therapist response modes: Comparison of six rating systems. *Journal of Consulting and Clinical Psychology, 55,* 218–223.

Epperson, D. L. (1981). Counselor gender and early premature terminations from counseling: A replication and extension. *Journal of Counseling Psychology, 28,* 349–356.

Epperson, D. L., Bushway, D. J., & Warman, R. E. (1983). Client self-terminations after one counseling session: Effects of problem recognition, counselor gender, and counselor experience. *Journal of Counseling Psychology, 30,* 307–315.

Ewalt, P. L., Cohen, M., & Harmatz, J. S. (1972). Prediction of treatment acceptance by child guidance clinic applicants: An easily applied instrument. *American Journal of Orthopsychiatry, 42,* 857–864.

Fiester, A. R. (1977). Clients' perceptions of the therapists with high attrition rates. *Journal of Consulting and Clinical Psychology, 45,* 954–955.

Fiester, A. R., Mahrer, A. R., Giambra, L. J., & Ormiston, D. W. (1974). Shaping a clinic population: The dropout problem reconsidered. *Community Mental Health Journal, 10,* 173–179.

Fiester, A. R., & Rudestam, K. E. (1975). A multivariate analysis of the early dropout process. *Journal of Consulting and Clinical Psychology, 43,* 528–535.

Folkins, C., Hersch, P., & Dahlen, D. (1980). Waiting time and no-show rate in a community mental health center. *American Journal of Community Psychology, 8,* 121–123.

Friedlander, M. L. (1982). Counseling discourse as a speech event: Revision and extension of the Hill Counselor Verbal Response Category System. *Journal of Counseling Psychology, 29,* 425–429.

Friedlander, M. L., & Phillips, S. D. (1984). Stochastic process analysis of interactive discourse in early counseling interviews. *Journal of Counseling Psychology, 31,* 139–148.

Gould, M. S., Shaffer, D., & Kaplan, D. (1985). The characteristics of dropouts from a child psychiatry clinic. *Journal of the American Academy of Child Psychiatry, 24,* 316–328.

Greenfield, T. K. (1983). The role of client satisfaction in evaluating university counseling services. *Evaluation and Program Planning, 6,* 315–325.

Hardin, S. I., Subich, L. M., & Holvey, J. M. (1988). Expectancies for counseling in relation to premature termination. *Journal of Counseling Psychology, 35,* 37–40.

Heilbrun, A. B., Jr. (1972). Effects of briefing upon client satisfaction with the initial counseling contact. *Journal of Consulting and Clinical Psychology, 38,* 50–66.

Heilbrun, A. B., Jr. (1974). Interviewer style, client satisfaction, and premature termination following the initial counseling contact. *Journal of Counseling Psychology, 21,* 346–350.

Heilbrun, A. B., Jr., & Sullivan, D. J. (1962). The prediction of counseling readiness. *Personnel and Guidance Journal, 41,* 112–117.

Hill, C. E. (1978). Development of a counselor verbal response category system. *Journal of Counseling Psychology, 25,* 461–468.

Hill, C. E. (1992). An overview of four tests developed to test the Hill process model: Therapist intentions, therapist response modes, client reactions, and client behaviors. *Journal of Counseling and Development, 70,* 728–739.

Hill, C. E. (1993). *Manual for Hill Counselor Verbal Response Category System* (Rev. ed.). Unpublished manuscript, University of Maryland, College Park.

Hill, C. E., Thames, T. B., & Rardin, D. K. (1979). Comparison of Rogers, Perls, and Ellis on the Hill Counselor Verbal Response Category System. *Journal of Counseling Psychology, 26,* 198–203.

Hilsenroth, M., Handler, L., Toman, K., & Padawer, J. (1995). Rorschach and MMPI-2 indices of early psychotherapy termination. *Journal of Consulting and Clinical Psychology, 63,* 956–965.

Hilsenroth, M. J., Holdwick, D. J., Jr., Castlebury, F. D., & Blais, M. A. (1998). The effects of DSM-IV cluster B personality disorder symptoms on the termination and continuation of psychotherapy. *Psychotherapy, 35,* 163–176.

Hoffman, J. J. (1985). Client factors related to premature termination of psychotherapy. *Psychotherapy, 22,* 83–85.

Kazdin, A. E. (1995). Bridging child, adolescent, and adult psychotherapy: Directions for research. *Psychotherapy Research, 5,* 258–277.

Kazdin, A. E., Holland, L., Crowley, M. (1997). Family experience of barriers to treatment and premature termination from child therapy. *Journal of Consulting and Clinical Psychology, 65,* 453–463.

Kendall, P. C., & Sugarman, A. (1997). Attrition in the treatment of childhood anxiety disorders. *Journal of Consulting and Clinical Psychology, 65,* 883–888.

Kokotovic, A. M., & Tracey, T. J. (1987). Premature termination at a university counseling center. *Journal of Counseling Psychology, 34,* 80–82.

Krauskopf, C. J., Baumgardner, A., & Mandracchia, S. (1981). Return rate following intake revisited. *Journal of Counseling Psychology, 28,* 519–521.

Lake, M., & Levinger, G. (1960). Continuance beyond application interview at a child guidance clinic. *Social Casework, 41,* 306–308.

Larsen, D. L., Attkisson, C. C., Hargreaves, W. A., & Nguyen, T. D. (1979). Assessment of client/patient satisfaction: Development of a general scale. *Evaluation and Program Planning, 2,* 197–207.

Lawe, C., Horne, A., & Taylor, S. (1983). Effects of pretraining procedures for clients in counseling. *Psychological Reports, 53,* 327–334.

Lebow, J. L. (1982). Consumer satisfaction with mental health treatment. *Psychological Bulletin, 91,* 244–259.

Lee, D. Y., & Uhlemann, M. R. (1984). Comparison of verbal responses of Rogers, Shostrom, and Lazarus. *Journal of Counseling Psychology, 31,* 91–94.

Lee, D. Y., Uhlemann, M. R., & Haase, R. F. (1985). Counselor verbal and nonverbal responses and perceived expertness, trustworthiness, and attractiveness. *Journal of Counseling Psychology, 32,* 181–187.

Lennard, H. L., & Bernstein, A. (1967). Role learning in psychotherapy. *Psychotherapy: Theory, Research and Practice, 4,* 1–6.

Levitt, E. E. (1957). A comparison of "remainers" and "defectors" among child clinic patients. *Journal of Consulting Psychology, 21,* 316.

Lin, M., Kelly, K. R., & Nelson, R. C. (1996). A comparative analysis of the interpersonal process in school-based counseling and consultation. *Journal of Counseling Psychology, 43,* 389–393.

Lonborg, S. D., Daniels, J. A., Hammond, S. G., Houghton-Wenger, B., & Brace, L. J. (1991). Counselor and client verbal response mode changes during initial counseling sessions. *Journal of Counseling Psychology, 38,* 394–400.

Longo, D. A., Lent, R. W., & Brown, S. D. (1992). Social cognitive variables in the prediction of client motivation and attrition. *Journal of Counseling Psychology, 39,* 447–452.

Martin, G. A., McNair, D., & Hight, W. (1988). Contributing factors to early premature termination at a college counseling center. *Journal of Counseling and Development, 66,* 233–236.

May, R. J. (1990). Are waiting lists really a problem? A follow-up survey of wait list dropouts. *Journal of College Student Development, 31,* 564–566.

McAdoo, W. G., & Roeske, N. A. (1973). A comparison of defectors and continuers in a child guidance clinic. *Journal of Consulting and Clinical Psychology, 40,* 328–334.

Mennicke, S. A., Lent, R. W., & Burgoyne, K. L. (1988). Premature termination from university counseling centers: A review. *Journal of Counseling and Development, 66,* 458–465.

Nash, J. M., & Garske, J. P. (1988, August). *Client and process variables as predictors of early counseling dropout.* Paper presented at the annual convention of the American Psychological Association, Atlanta.

Pekarik, G. (1983). Follow-up adjustment of outpatient drop-outs. *American Journal of Orthopsychiatry, 53,* 501–511.

Pekarik, G. (1985). The effects of employing different termination classification criteria in dropout research. *Psychotherapy, 22,* 86–91.

Pekarik, G. (1992). Posttreatment adjustment of clients who drop out early versus late in treatment. *Journal of Clinical Psychology, 48,* 379–387.

Pekarik, G., & Finney-Owen, K. (1987). Outpatient clinic therapist attitudes and beliefs relevant to client dropout. *Community Mental Health Journal, 23,* 120–130.

Phillips, E. L. (1985). *Psychotherapy revised: New frontiers in research and practice.* Hillsdale, NJ: Lawrence Erlbaum Associates.

Prochaska, J. O., DiClemente, C. C., & Norcross, J. C. (1992). In search of how people change: Applications to addictive behaviors. *American Psychologist, 47,* 1102–1114.

Pulakos, J., & Morris, J. D. (1995). Waiting list dropouts: An evaluation. *Journal of College Student Development, 36,* 603–604.

Rapaport, R. J., Rodolfa, E. R., & Lee, V. E. (1985). Variables related to premature termination in a university counseling service: A reply to Saltzman's (1984) comment. *Journal of Counseling Psychology, 32,* 469–471.

Reiher, T. C., Romans, J. S. C., Andersen, P., & Culha, M. (1992). Clients who don't return following intake: A replication and extension. *Journal of College Student Development, 33,* 473–474.

Richmond, R. (1992). Discriminating variables among psychotherapy dropouts from a psychological training clinic. *Professional Psychology: Research and Practice, 23,* 123–130.

Rodolfa, E. R., Rapaport, R., & Lee, V. E. (1983). Variables related to premature terminations in a university counseling service. *Journal of Counseling Psychology, 30,* 87–90.

Rogers, C. R. (1957). The necessary and sufficient conditions of therapeutic personality change. *Journal of Consulting Psychology, 21,* 95–103.

Santisteban, D. A., Szapocznik, J., Perez-Vidal, A., Kurtines, W. H., Murray, E. J., & LaPerriere, A. (1996). Efficacy of intervention for engaging youth and families into treatment and some variables that may contribute to differential effectiveness. *Journal of Family Psychology, 10,* 35–44.

Schiller, L. J. (1976). A comparative study of the differences between client continuers and dropouts at two university counseling centers. *Journal of Counseling Psychology, 23,* 99–102.

Shueman, S. A., Gelso, C. J., Mindus, L., Hunt, B., Stevenson, J. (1980). Client satisfaction with intake: Is the waiting list all that matters? *Journal of College Student Personnel, 21,* 114–121.

Silverman, W. H., & Beech, R. P. (1979). Are drop-outs, drop-outs? *Journal of Community Psychology, 7,* 236–242.

Smith, K. J., Subich, L. M., & Kalodner, C. (1995). The transtheoretical model's stages and processes of change and their relation to premature termination. *Journal of Counseling Psychology, 42,* 34–39.

Stachowiak, T. (1994). One-session counseling: A semester's end, waiting list alternative. *Journal of College Student Development, 35,* 144.

Stiles, W. B. (1979). Verbal response modes and psychotherapeutic technique. *Psychiatry, 42,* 49–62.

Stiles, W. B. (1980). Measurement of the impact of psychotherapy sessions. *Journal of Consulting and Clinical Psychology, 48,* 176–185.

Strong, S. R. (1968). Counseling: An interpersonal influence process. *Journal of Counseling Psychology, 15,* 215–224.

Szapocznik, J., Perez-Vidal, A., Brickman, A. L., Foote, F. H., Santisteban, D., & Hervis, O. (1988). Engaging adolescent drug abusers and their families in treatment: A strategic structural systems approach. *Journal of Consulting and Clinical Psychology, 56,* 552–557.

Talmon, M. (1990). *Single session therapy.* San Francisco: Jossey-Bass.

Tracey, T. J., Heck, E. J., & Lichtenberg, J. W. (1981). Role expectations and complementary/symmetrical therapeutic relationships. *Psychotherapy: Theory, Research and Practice, 18,* 338–344.

Tracey, T. J., & Ray, P. B. (1984). Stages of successful time-limited counseling: An interactional examination. *Journal of Counseling Psychology, 31,* 13–27.

Trepka, C. (1986). Attrition from an out-patient psychology clinic. *British Journal of Medical Psychology, 59,* 181–186.

Tryon, G. S. (1984). Effects of client and counselor sex on client attendance at counseling. *Sex Roles, 10,* 387–393.

Tryon, G. S. (1985). The engagement quotient: One index of a basic counseling task. *Journal of College Student Personnel, 26,* 351–354.

Tryon, G. S. (1986). Client and counselor characteristics and engagement in counseling. *Journal of Counseling Psychology, 33,* 471–474.

Tryon, G. S. (1989a). A study of engagement and premature termination in a university counseling center. *Counselling Psychology Quarterly, 2,* 419–429.

Tryon, G. S. (1989b). Study of variables related to client engagement using practicum trainees and experienced clinicians. *Psychotherapy, 26*, 54–61.

Tryon, G. S. (1990). Session depth and smoothness in relation to the concept of engagement in counseling. *Journal of Counseling Psychology, 37*, 248–253.

Tryon, G. S. (1992). Client attractiveness as related to the concept of engagement in therapy. *Counselling Psychology Quarterly, 5*, 307–314.

Tryon, G. S. (1999). [Engagement quotients for 85 practicum trainees]. Unpublished raw data.

Tryon, G. S. (in press). A therapist's use of verbal response categories in engagement and nonengagement interviews. *Counselling Psychology Quarterly.*

Tryon, G. S., & Tryon, W. W. (1986). Factors associated with clinical practicum trainees' engagement of clients in counseling. *Professional Psychology: Research and Practice, 17*, 586–589.

Viale-Val, G., Rosenthal, R. H., Curtiss, G., & Marohn, R. C. (1984). Dropout from adolescent psychotherapy: A preliminary study. *Journal of the American Academy of Child Psychiatry, 23*, 562–568.

Weisz, J. R., Weiss, B., & Langmeyer, D. B. (1987). Giving up on child psychotherapy: Who drops out? *Journal of Consulting and Clinical Psychology, 55*, 916–918.

Wierzbicki, M. & Pekarik, G. (1993). A meta-analysis of psychotherapy dropout. *Professional Psychology: Research and Practice, 24*, 190–195.

Williams, R., & Pollack, R. H. (1964). Some nonpsychological variables in therapy defection in a child guidance clinic. *Journal of Psychology, 58*, 145–155.

Zamostny, K. P., Corrigan, J. D., & Eggert, M. A. (1981). Replication and extension of social influence processes in counseling: A field study. *Journal of Counseling Psychology, 28*, 481–489.

2

Client Expectations About Counseling

Ann Westcot Barich

Lewis University

Regardless of the type of counseling or therapy used, client expectations about counseling may potentially impact treatment. If client expectations of counseling are not met, clients may refuse to cooperate in their treatment or leave counseling altogether. Although therapists sometimes inquire about the outcome clients expect, therapists usually do not ask clients during intake what their expectations are concerning the counseling process. The literature reviewed in this chapter strongly suggests that client expectations should be considered by therapists. Therapists may find that adjusting to these expectations or assisting clients to modify unrealistic expectations will result in more productive counseling. The chapter also highlights the need for study of the relationship of client expectations to therapy process and outcome.

Chapter Questions

- What are client expectations about counseling?
- How do client expectations relate to client characteristics?
- What therapist characteristics influence client expectations?
- How do client expectations relate to the counseling process?

Within the past 15 to 20 years, the construct of expectancy has gained popularity in psychological research. As early as 1909, Titchener conceptualized expectancies as cognitively mediated predispositions to behave in certain ways in a given situation. Rotter's (1954) social learning theory states that an expectancy is a subjectively held belief that a certain reinforcement will occur as the outcome of a specific behavior, such as a probability. In this chapter, I will examine the role of the expectancy in counseling process research, summarize the different areas of research pertaining to expectations about counseling, and suggest some applications for practice. Specifically, I will address the following questions:

1. How was the expectancy construct originally conceptualized?
2. How are expectations about counseling measured?
3. In what areas have expectations about counseling been researched?
4. How do expectations about counseling affect the counseling process?
5. How can client expectations about the counseling process be used to enhance the experience of counseling and increase the probability of counseling success?

Expectancies have been examined for years in alcohol research. An alcohol expectancy is defined as the subjectively interpreted consequences of alcohol use anticipated by an individual (Marlatt, Demming, & Reid, 1973). Research has shown that social learning factors determine a large part of interpersonal behavior when alcohol is being used (MacAndrew & Edgerton, 1969). In other words, what individuals have learned and believe about the effects of alcohol is an important predictor of how they behave while drinking. Using a research technique called the balanced placebo design, many researchers have demonstrated that the belief that one has consumed alcohol is often as powerful or more powerful than the actual pharmacological effects of alcohol in influencing behavior. The belief that one has consumed alcohol is enough to increase aggressive behavior and sexual arousal (Lang, Goeckner, Adesso, & Marlatt, 1975), reduce verbal aggression (Rohsenow, 1983), influence subjective pain reduction (Cutter, Maloof, Kurtz, & Jones, 1976), and influence social anxiety and tension (Abrams & Wilson, 1979).

Expectancies have also been used in vocational psychology to explain decision making. For example, Vroom (1964) used a mathematical model of expectancy to explain a person motivation to make a decision. The strength of a person's motivation is a function of the sum of the valence (attractiveness) of the outcome that might result from that course of action multiplied by the expectancy of the outcome occurring. Individuals tend to choose from among alternatives that have the strongest attractiveness and the highest likelihood of occurring.

Counseling and psychotherapy have been conceptualized by many theorists (e.g., Goldstein, 1966) as a type of social learning relationship to which clients bring expectancies regarding the therapy process and the roles that they and their counselors will assume. Strong (1968) expanded on this idea, stating that counseling is an interpersonal influence process in which a counselor attempts to influence or persuade the client to achieve the therapeutic goals. Strong stated that the success of counseling depends on the characteristics of the counselor as perceived by the client, the characteristics of the client, and the characteristics of the communication. He discussed three imperative characteristics of the counselor that affect the counseling process and its ultimate success. The first of these is expertness, which is evidenced in objective criteria, such as diplomas and titles, as well as confidence and reputation. The second is attractiveness, which indicates a compatibility or similarity between the counselor and the client. The third is trustworthiness, which is a function of honesty, social role, sincerity, openness, and lack of motivation for personal gain. From the client's perspective, Strong stated that involvement is a necessary characteristic for counseling success. Involvement is thought of as a function of intrinsic motivation or significance of counseling to the client. Other client characteristics that are essential for the success of counseling are clients' expectations about what will occur in the therapy encounter. Several early studies examined the notions of counselor and client characteristics, and counseling process variables, and laid the foundation for more recent research on client expectations about counseling.

Early Studies on Client Expectations

In an early study on expectations, Grosz (1968) examined the effects of client expectations on the counseling relationship. He noted that Rogers (1961) and Brammer and Shostrom (1960) maintained that clients' precounseling expectations can either help or hinder the development of a therapeutic relationship, which is an idea that has been researched extensively since that time. In this study, Grosz randomly assigned 30 male undergraduate students to three groups. In the first group, 10 students heard an audiotape that emphasized positive aspects of counseling and an example of an effective counseling session. In the second group, 10 students heard a similar tape that emphasized negative aspects of counseling; they heard an interview characterized as ineffective. The control group of 10 students did not hear a precounseling audiotape. As a measure of client expectations, all students completed a 30-item questionnaire designed for the study, asking for their reactions to the concept "counseling." A comparison between the groups indicated that there were differences in the precounseling expectations of the three treatment groups, with the control group and positive modification group having more positive attitudes toward counseling than the negative modification group.

All participants were then assigned to six counselors for a 30-minute counseling session in which they were instructed to discuss whatever problem they desired. The participants (both students and counselors) completed the Barrett-Lennard Relationship Inventory (Barrett-Lennard, 1962) following the session to determine the nature of the initial counseling interview. Two comparisons (one for clients and one for counselors) revealed that counselors did not view the therapeutic relationships with clients in each of the three treatment groups to be significantly different. Surprisingly, clients did not view the therapeutic relationships as being significantly different either, despite the modification of their precounseling expectations. Grosz (1968) concluded that positive client expectations do not need to be present prior to counseling in order for a therapeutic relationship to be established. He further concluded that even if a client has negative precounseling expectations, an effective counselor can adequately deal with these as part of the counseling process.

Another early study on expectations was conducted by Gladstein (1969), who investigated whether high school clients expect mainly vocational and academic help from counselors, whether experience in counseling changes one's expectations, and whether not meeting a client's expectations leads to dissatisfaction with counseling. In this study, a group of 181 students completed a Counseling Laboratory Registration Form (CLRF) prior to counseling, and a Counseling Reaction Form (CRF) following counseling. Precounseling client expectation was measured with one open-ended question on the CLRF that asked clients what they hoped to accomplish through the counseling experience. The CRF was designed for this study and included 28 items and four essay questions regarding the facilities of the center, the counselor's style, the counselor's use of materials and tests, the client's reasons for being in counseling, the level of satisfaction at the end of counseling, and suggestions for improving counseling services.

Client expectations fell into 17 categories, most pertaining to career/vocational issues (e.g., choose a vocation, pick a college), then academic issues (e.g., improve study habits), and finally personal issues (e.g., understand self better, improve personality). On the postcounseling measure, most clients indicated that their expectations had been met. However, the clients who indicated that their expectations had not been met did not differ in terms of satisfaction level from those whose expectations were met. A small number of clients (24) indicated that they had received no help at all; only this group reported significantly less satisfaction with counseling. In summarizing the results, the author stated that counseling experience does appear to modify client expectations in such a way that they are congruent with the counselor's expectations, supporting Strong's (1968) view of counseling as a social learning relationship. Also, it appears that clients come to counseling with a set of expectations, and they are generally satisfied with counseling even if only some of their expectations are met.

Tinsley and Harris (1976) conducted a study on client expectations for counseling which became a foundation study for the development of the most widely used measure of client expectancies, the Expectations About Counseling questionnaire (Tinsley, Workman, & Kass, 1980). Tinsley and Harris noted that previous research examining client expectations had narrowly focused on only one or two expectations (e.g., outcome or problem type). They set out to examine the relative strength of a variety of expectations that clients may have about counseling. A questionnaire was designed for this study in which 88 items were selected from a review of the literature (e.g., Lazarus; 1971, Truax & Carkhuff, 1967; Volsky, Magoon, Norman, & Hoyt, 1965). These items were grouped into nine clusters pertaining to counseling procedures; counseling outcome; counselor genuineness, expertise, acceptance, understanding, and directiveness; and client trust and responsibility. This preliminary questionnaire was given to 109 undergraduate students and submitted to item analysis. As a result, the responsibility scale was deleted, several items were reassigned to new scales, and six items were dropped, yielding an 82-item questionnaire with seven scales and nine items dealing with counseling procedures. The seven scales represented a variety of client expectations and were named Expertise, Genuineness, Trust, Acceptance, Understanding, Outcome, and Directiveness.

This questionnaire was then given to 287 undergraduate students. Mean scale values were highest for Expertise, Genuineness, Trust, and Acceptance and somewhat lower for Understanding, Outcome, and Directiveness. The authors interpreted this finding to mean that students believed that counseling can be helpful in general, but the students doubted whether it would be helpful to them personally. They raised the disturbing possibility that many potential clients may not seek counseling because they believe that they will not benefit from it. This pessimistic client perspective is reiterated often in the literature following this study.

A gender comparison for expectations indicated that females had higher expectations for acceptance, and males had higher expectations for directiveness. These gender differences seem consistent with previous findings (e.g., Apfelbaum, 1958), which suggest that females expect counselors to be warm, accepting, and supportive, whereas men expect counselors to be directive, logical, and critical. A significant difference was also found between college classes in which first-year students had higher expectations for counselors' expertise than juniors and seniors; sophomores' expectations for expertise did not differ from the expectations of other classes. However, sophomores had higher expectations for acceptance than seniors; the expectation for acceptance of first-year students and juniors did not differ from the other classes. In terms of counseling process, the students had the highest expectations regarding talking about their present concerns and seeing an experienced counselor. The authors interpreted this finding to mean that as students remain in college, they are less likely to expect a counselor to be an expert or to be accepting. The meaning of this is somewhat unclear, but it may be related to students' development of critical thinking.

Workman and Williams (1979) conducted an interesting early study examining the affect of counselor characteristics on clients' ratings of counseling effectiveness. A sample of 249 students were asked to rate several counselor behaviors and attributes as having a beneficial, detrimental, or neutral affect on their expectation of benefit from counseling. A 25-item list of counselor characteristics was designed for this study, which included personal behavior, professional knowledge, the counseling process, and counselor demographics. The characteristics that were found to have a positive affect on outcome included clear communication, accurate understanding, respect for confidentiality, and having a thorough knowledge of one's orientation. The characteristics that were found to have a negative affect on outcome included beginning sessions late, heavy drinking, disorganization, smoking during the session, and talking excessively during the session. The authors recommended that counselors should keep these characteristics in mind as they attempt to maximize client expectations for positive outcome.

In 1979, Sobel and O'Brien investigated expectations for positive results and long-term cure as a result of three different forms of counseling. The sample consisted of two groups of respondents—67 first-year undergraduate students (40 females and 27 males) and 52 adults (40 females and 12 males) from a community adult education evening program. All respondents reported either no prior experience or minimal counseling experience (less than three sessions). Three audiotaped educational lectures were developed by the researchers on analytic, behavioral, and gestalt counseling. All tapes addressed the same issues (e.g., orientation, philosophy) and used the second-person perspective to increase identification by the respondents. All respondents heard all three tapes, then completed a preference-expectation survey in which they rated each counseling modality for expectation of long-term cure for everyday adjustment problems and expectation of positive results at the conclusion of counseling. Respondents were also asked about their general preferences for each type of counseling. Data were analyzed using a series of repeated-measures analyses of variances (ANOVAs).

Results of several comparisons indicated no differences among the three counseling modalities in terms of positive counseling outcome, but adult females had higher expectations for a long-term cure using gestalt therapy over behavioral or analytic therapy. Following these initial analyses, the respondents were pooled across age groups to test for overall gender differences in expectations for positive results and overall general preference. Significant correlations were found between expectation for positive results and general preferences for each of the counseling types across both genders. Finally, the three counseling types were rank ordered using respondents' expectancy scores for long-term cure. Both age groups and both genders ranked behavioral counseling third after analytic and gestalt in terms of expectancy for long-term cure. It appears from these results that clients do not judge counseling type to be an important feature of the counseling process in terms of expectation for a positive result. However, there does seem to be a difference in terms of expectation for long-term cure, with behavioral therapy consistently ranking third.

The Expectations About Counseling Questionnaire

Following many preliminary studies on expectations about counseling conducted by various researchers, Tinsley et al. (1980) developed the Expectations About Counseling Questionnaire (EAC) in order to provide researchers with a reliable and valid measure of expectations. In this study, 203 items were written to measure 20 possible expectancies that were identified using a variety of past theoretical works. This formed the first version of the EAC, which was completed by 446 undergraduate students, none of whom reported previous counseling experience. The items were submitted to item analysis to assess convergent and discriminant validity. Also, internal consistency was evaluated; each scale was required to maintain internal consistency coefficients of between .70 and .85. Following the item analysis, two scales were dropped because of problems with internal consistency. Also, the Realism scale was deemed experimental because of differences in local practices and not included in the analysis. The resulting questionnaire consisted of 135 items, assigned to 17 scales. Internal consistency for each of the scales ranged from .77 to .89.

The 17 EAC scales were grouped by the researchers into five general categories representing various attitudes and behaviors. Each expectancy is measured using a 7-point Likert scale in which response options range from 1 (not true) to 7 (definitely true). Each item is prefaced with either "I expect to" or "I expect the counselor to." The first category, Client Attitudes and Behaviors, includes the following scales: Motivation (e.g., work with the counselor), Openness (e.g., speak frankly about my problems), and Responsibility (e.g., take responsibility for making my own decisions). The second category, Client Characteristics, encompasses 13 items represented by the Realism scale, which must be scored carefully to reflect the local situation in which the scale was completed. For example, in some counseling settings clients routinely take psychological tests, but in other settings they do not. It is important to determine which items are relevant to the immediate situation prior to using this scale. The third category, Counselor Attitudes and Behaviors, includes the Acceptance (e.g., expect the counselor to think I am worthwhile), Confrontation (e.g., expect the counselor to point out contradictions), Directiveness (e.g., expect the counselor to take initiative), Empathy (e.g., expect the counselor to know how I feel), Genuineness (e.g., expect the counselor to be sincere), Nurturance (e.g., expect the counselor to give me support), and Self-Disclosure (e.g., expect the counselor to relate his or her experiences to my problems) scales. The fourth category, Counselor Characteristics, includes the Attractiveness (e.g., expect to enjoy being with the counselor), Expertise (e.g., expect the counselor to know how to help me), Tolerance (e.g., expect the counselor to be patient), and Trustworthiness (e.g., expect the counselor to be someone I can count on) scales. Finally, the fifth category, Counseling Process and Outcome, includes the Immediacy (e.g., expect to talk about the relationship between myself and the counselor), Concreteness (e.g., expect the counselor to talk specifically about my current problems), and Outcome (e.g., expect to experience a significant change in my life) scales.

Tinsley et al. (1980) factor analyzed the scores on the 17 scales, which resulted in a four-factor solution accounting for 75% of the total variance. Factor 1 was named Personal Commitment and included the Responsibility, Openness, Motivation, Attractiveness, Concreteness, Immediacy, and Positive Outcome scales. Factor 2 was named Facilitative Conditions and included the Genuineness, Trustworthiness, Acceptance, Tolerance, Confrontation, and Concreteness scales. Factor 3 was named Counselor Expertise and included the Directiveness, Empathy, and Expertise scales. Finally, Factor 4 was named Nurturance and included the Acceptance, Self-Disclosure, Nurturance, and Attractiveness scales.

The authors gave possible interpretations of each of these factors, stating that for each, the most positive prognostic indicator for potential clients is a moderately high score. For example, clients who have moderately high expectations for their own personal commitment, the facilitative conditions of therapy, their counselors' expertise, and the nurturance that the counselor will exhibit will most likely benefit the most from counseling. However, extremely high or low scores on each of these factors are most likely detrimental to the counseling process. For example, extremely high scores may indicate a tendency for clients to be perfectionistic, to expect the counselor to meet some impractical ideal, or to expect the counseling process to be completely pain free, which is most likely not the case. Extremely low scores may indicate a tendency for clients to be unmotivated and looking for a magic cure; to be defensive, guarded, and unwilling to reveal any affect; or to have little belief that anyone can help them.

Much later, Tinsley, Bowman, and Barich (1993) conducted a study in which they directly examined the effects of these unrealistic expectations from the counselor's perspective. The sample consisted of 72 practicing counseling psychologists (43 men and 29 women), who were identified using the American Psychological Association Membership Register (Lazo, 1983). All respondents completed the Problem Survey, a questionnaire designed for the study. Each of the 17 EAC scales made up a section of the Problem Survey. Each section began with a definition of the expectation in question, followed by questions pertaining to how many of the respondent's clients had too little or too much of that expectation. Next, respondents were asked what they believed to be the effects of unrealistically high or low expectations (facilitative, neutral, detrimental, doesn't happen) at various stages of counseling (early, midway, late).

In terms of occurrence, the counseling psychologists perceived some, many, or most of their clients to have unrealistically low and unrealistically high expectations about counseling. Respondents reported that their clients had unrealistically low expectations about responsibility, openness, and motivation, for example, and unrealistically high expectations for counselor directiveness, nurturance, and outcome. When asked about the effects of these expectations, counseling psychologists reported that for the most part, unrealistic expectations are detrimental to the process of counseling. For example, unrealistically low expectations for motivation, openness, and responsibility were believed to have detrimental effects by a large majority of respondents. Also, unrealistically high expectations for counselor directiveness, attractiveness, empathy, and nurturance were believed to be detrimental to counseling. On a positive note, counseling psychologists reported that some unrealistic expectations may have facilitative effects, such as having a low expectation for directiveness and a high expectation for openness. Although this study was viewed as exploratory, the results raised several important issues to be examined in future research. The authors discussed several concerns, including the nature of detrimental effects, the influence of presenting problems on detrimental effects, and psychologists' modifications for unrealistic expectations.

An early study using the EAC was conducted by Parham and Tinsley (1980), who compared the expectations that respondents have for a counseling session with a friend versus a counseling session with a counselor. In this study, 167 undergraduate students completed the EAC, which was modified by replacing the word *counselor* with the word *friend* in order to measure expectations about the friendship encounter. Also, 441 undergraduates completed the unmodified EAC for comparison. Results indicated that respondents had stronger expectations for friends than for counselors to be genuine, self-disclosing, immediate, and attractive, and for themselves to be open. In comparison, respondents expected counselors to be more directive, expert, tolerant, and trustworthy than friends, and for themselves to be more responsible with a counselor than with a friend. The authors concluded that it is important for individuals to have friends to whom they can turn for help, but that a counseling psychologist serves as an important contact when the assistance of a friend is not adequate. They also noted that the expectancies that students held regarding counselors were primarily positive, indicating that this increases the likelihood that students will seek help from psychologists when they feel it is needed.

Two early related studies examined help-seeking behavior and expectations. In the first of these, Tinsley, de St. Aubin, and Brown (1982) had undergraduate students (60 males and 76 females) complete a 16-item questionnaire designed for this study, the Tendency to Seek Help questionnaire (TSH). The items represented 11 personal and 5 vocational problems that students often experience (e.g., relationships, finances, choosing a major, etc.). Each item was prefaced with a question asking respondents who they would talk to about that situation. A list of eight potential helpers then followed (close friend, close relative, self, professional counselor, a member of the clergy, academic advisor, paraprofessional counselor, and instructor), and respondents were instructed to rank order their choices.

Results of these relative rankings indicated that students experiencing personal problems would be more likely to seek help from a close friend but less likely to seek help from an instructor or advisor than from a professional counselor. For vocational problems, students stated that they would be more likely to seek help from an academic advisor, close friend, or instructor rather than a professional counselor. Beyond these relative rankings, students were asked whether they would actually seek help from each of the help-givers for each type of problem. For personal problems, about half of the students indicated that they would seek help from a professional counselor for emotional problems or suicidal thoughts, but a minority indicated that they would seek help from a professional counselor for financial problems or relationship issues. For career problems, academic advisors and instructors along with close friends and relatives would most likely be sought by the students. The authors concluded that professional counselors are not the first choice for students who are seeking help. In addition, the tendency to seek help varies with the type of presenting problem. In fact, 64% of the respondents would prefer to deal with a personal problem alone before seeking help from a professional counselor, and 74% would prefer to deal with a career problem alone. It appears that students prefer to access their own private support networks before resorting to professional counselors for personal or career issues.

A follow-up study was conducted by Tinsley, Brown, de St. Aubin, and Lucek (1984) that examined the relation between expectations for a helping relationship and the tendency to seek help from a campus help provider. In this study, 236 undergraduate students completed one of seven modified versions of the EAC and the TSH questionnaires. A control group only completed the TSH. In each form of the EAC, the instructions were modified to elicit expectations about seven potential campus help providers (advisor, career counselor, clinical psychologist, college counselor, counseling psychologist, peer counselor, and psychiatrist). Comparisons of EAC scale scores were made between the different types of help-givers.

Overall, it appears that students had similar expectations regarding achieving a beneficial counseling outcome with a counseling psychologist, psychiatrist, or clinical psychologist. Regarding their help-seeking behavior, respondents indicated tendencies to discuss career issues with a career counselor, college counselor, or advisor, rather than a clinical psychologist or psychiatrist. Further, when discussing a personal concern, they indicated a tendency to seek help from a counseling psychologist, psychiatrist, peer counselor, or clinical psychologist, rather than a career counselor. Group differences were found on seven EAC scales. The strongest differentiation occurred regarding career counselors, whom respondents expected to be less confrontive, directive, concrete, and immediate and less likely to bring about a positive outcome. In contrast, a counseling psychologist was expected by respondents to be more motivated, open, concrete, and immediate and more likely to bring about a positive outcome.

In 1982, Tinsley developed a brief version of the EAC (the EAC-Brief Form; EAC-B), which reduced the total number of items from 135 to 66. The brief form has internal consistencies that range from .69 to .82 for the 17 scales, with a median reliability of .76. Test–retest reliability during a 2-month interval ranged from .47 to .87 for the 17 scales. Tinsley (1982) stated that the EAC-B is preferable to the long form of the EAC, because it has acceptable internal consistency and test–retest reliability, correlates highly with the full scales, and is more economical in terms of respondent time.

One of the difficulties with early work on counseling expectations regarded the lack of differentiation among counseling preferences, perceptions, and expectations. This problem was discussed by Tinsley, Bowman, and Ray (1988) who defined "preference" as the extent to which a person desires an event, "perception" as a person's knowledge of an event and "expectation" as a person's understanding of the probability that an event will occur. Hayes and Tinsley (1989) investigated whether commonly used counseling process instruments are measuring the same construct or different constructs. They identified seven instruments that were frequently cited in the literature as measuring either perceptions or expectations about counseling. These instruments included 16 scales to measure counseling perceptions, and 17 scales to measure counseling expectations. The seven instruments include the following:

1. The Counselor Rating Form (CRF; Barak & LaCrosse, 1975), a 36-item measure of perceptions of counselor expertness, attractiveness, and trustworthiness.
2. The Counselor Effectiveness Rating Scale (CERS; Atkinson & Wampold, 1982), a 4-item scale that measures counselor expertness, attractiveness, trustworthiness, and utility.
3. The Counselor Effectiveness Scale (CES; Ivey, 1971), a 25-item measure of client attitudes toward the counselor.

4. The Personal Attributes Inventory (PAI; Parish, Bryant, & Shirazi, 1976), a 100-item adjective checklist used to describe the counselor.
5. The Counselor Evaluation Inventory (CEI; Linden, Stone, & Schertzer, 1965), a 21-item measure of counseling climate, client satisfaction, and counselor comfort.
6. The Barrett-Lennard Relationship Inventory (BLRI; Barrett-Lennard, 1962), an 85-item measure of level of regard, empathic understanding, congruence, unconditionality, and willingness to be known.
7. The EAC-B.

This battery of instruments was given to 253 undergraduate students after they viewed a 10-minute videotape in which one of three counseling styles was demonstrated (client-centered, gestalt, or rational-emotive). The videotapes were used as a point of reference for participants when they completed the perception instruments.

A factor analysis of all 33 scales was conducted, and 6 factors were extracted, accounting for almost 75% variance. Factor 1 was named Expectation of Facilitative Conditions and included 15 of the 17 EAC-B scales. Factor 2 was named Perception of Counselor Attributes and included 13 of the 16 scales from the perception instruments. Factor 3 was named Expectation of Counselor Expertise and included 10 EAC-B scales. Factor 4 was named Expectation of Personal Commitment and included 14 EAC-B scales. Factor 5 was named Perception of Facilitative Conditions and included 13 scales from perception instruments. Finally, Factor 6 was named Perception of Counselor Effectiveness and included 2 scales from the CEI. This factor analysis lends much support to the notion that perceptions of counseling are distinct from expectations about counseling. It also contributes to the construct validity of the EAC-B by providing evidence of discriminant validity.

Tinsley and Westcot (1990) completed an investigation of the construct validity of the EAC-B by determining whether it effectively measured expectations rather than perceptions or preferences. In this study, 16 male and 14 female undergraduate students completed the EAC-B individually. They were instructed to read each of the EAC-B statements out loud, think about what they expect counseling to be like, and say out loud all of their immediate thoughts. All responses were audiotaped for coding at a later time. Each item on the EAC-B was coded individually by a single judge. The majority of respondents (median 93%) made statements regarding expectations. In addition, the items were judged to have sufficient clarity and to be motivating to respondents. The authors concluded that each item on the EAC-B possesses at least a minimal level of validity, and they recommended the continued use of the EAC-B in counseling research.

Another construct validity study of the EAC-B was completed by Tinsley, Holt, Hinson, and Tinsley (1991). In this investigation, 100 female and 72 male undergraduate students completed the EAC-B, the Student Developmental Task Inventory (SDTI-2; Winston, Miller, & Prince, 1979), the Counseling Readiness Scale (CRS; Gough & Heilbrun, 1980), and the Career Counseling Diagnostic Inventory (CCDI; Arnold, 1985). The SDTI-2 is a measure of three developmental tasks of traditional-aged college students. These tasks include developing autonomy, purpose, and mature interpersonal relationships. Only the developing autonomy scale was used in the present study; it is a 48-item measure of a student's ability to make appropriate educational, career, and lifestyle plans.

The CRS is a measure of openness to change and potential to benefit from counseling. Separate scales exist for men (52 items) and women (37 items). The CCDI is a 42-item measure of cognitive, social, and emotional developmental problems, which may interfere with career counseling.

The data were factor analyzed, and a six-factor structure was extracted. Factor 1 included 12 of the 17 EAC-B scales, duplicating the personal commitment factor found in earlier studies (Tinsley et al., 1980; Hayes & Tinsley, 1989), thus it was named Expectation of Personal Commitment. Factor 2 included the three CCDI scales and was named Career Development Difficulties. Factor 3 consisted of the three SDTI-2 scales and was named Developing Purpose. Factor 4 consisted of 9 of the 17 EAC-B scales, which is a similar structure to the Facilitative Conditions factor that was found in earlier studies (Tinsley et al., 1980; Hayes & Tinsley, 1989), thus it was named Expectation for Facilitative Conditions. Factor 5 included 6 of the 17 EAC-B scales, which formed a similar structure to the Counselor Expertise factor that was found in earlier studies (Tinsley et al., 1980; Hayes & Tinsley, 1989), thus it was named Expectation of Counselor Expertise. Finally, Factor 6 included only the score on the Counseling Readiness scale, so it was named Counseling Readiness. This study contributed to the factorial validity of the EAC-B by demonstrating that separate components exist for the EAC-B and other measures of counseling readiness and development.

The development of the EAC was an important step in counseling expectations research. Previous to this measure's development, this area of research was plagued with methodological problems resulting from inconsistent measures. Hardin and Subich (1985) pointed out two concerns that tend to complicate the research on expectations about counseling. First, they pointed to the varied measures for expectations, but they concluded that the EAC is a remedy to this problem. The second concern is that the majority of research conducted on expectations about counseling uses nonclient samples (primarily undergraduate students). Do the expectations of these participants generalize to other groups? The authors examined this issue by comparing the responses to the EAC in client and nonclient samples. The nonclient, student sample consisted of 20 male and 20 female undergraduates; the client sample consisted of 20 male and 20 female former clients of the university clinic; finally, the nonstudent, client sample consisted of 18 males and 20 females from the community who had sought counseling at the university clinic. A comparison of EAC scores among these groups indicated no differences. This study lends support to the idea that research conducted on nonclient samples may be used to infer conclusions regarding actual clients' precounseling interviews. However, the authors made this recommendation cautiously.

In 1985, Subich and Coursol conducted a partial replication study to investigate the expectations of clients and nonclients for either group or individual treatment. The nonclient sample consisted of 40 male and 40 female undergraduate students; the client sample consisted of 20 males and 20 females who had sought individual counseling and 18 males and 27 females who had sought group counseling at a university counseling center. All participants completed the EAC-B; the participants in the client sample had completed the EAC-B as part of their intake packet. For the nonclient sample, the EAC-B was modified to manipulate whether the respondent was to imagine a session with a counselor in an individual setting or a group setting. Data were analyzed using a 2 (Respondent Sex) × 2 (Mode of Counseling) × 2 (Client/Nonclient Status) design, with EAC scores on the 17 scales as dependent variables.

Results indicated significant main effects for all three independent variables. None of the interaction terms were significant. First, a main effect was noted for mode of counseling, in which group respondents had lower expectations for responsibility, openness, and concreteness than individual respondents. The authors commented that this may have been caused by a sense of diffusion of responsibility on the part of group clients and a tendency to be less open in order to reduce their vulnerability. However, in terms of concreteness, when problem type (career versus personal) was accounted for in a follow-up multivariate analysis of covariance (MANCOVA), the significant effect did not hold up. A second main effect was found for sex of respondent, in which males expected more counselor self-disclosure than females. The authors interpreted this finding to mean that men expect the counselor to give advice in order to provide the client with a solution. It is interesting that there was only one gender difference in the present study. Gender differences in expectations are discussed in the next section. Finally, a main effect for client status was found, in which clients had higher expectations for responsibility, but lower expectations for acceptance, empathy, and nurturance than nonclients. The authors interpreted this finding to mean that clients may have a more realistic view of what to expect from counseling, whereas nonclients base their expectations on images portrayed in the media. Considering this finding, researchers need to consider generalizability carefully when using nonclient participants.

Expectations and Gender

One of the first areas to be examined in terms of differences in expectations about counseling is in regard to gender differences. The original EAC study by Tinsley et al. (1980) examined gender differences, finding that women had higher expectations for Personal Commitment (Responsibility, Openness, Motivation, Immediacy, Concreteness, Outcome, and Attractiveness) than men. Women also had higher expectations for Facilitative Conditions in the form of Acceptance, Confrontation, Genuineness, Trustworthiness, Tolerance, and Concreteness than the expectations of men for this factor. In contrast, men had higher expectations on the Counselor Expertise factor, as expressed by the EAC scales of Directiveness, Expertise, and Empathy. Finally, on the last factor of Nurturance (comprising the Acceptance, Self-Disclosure, Nurturance, and Attractiveness scales), there was not a significant gender difference.

Several studies have noted similar patterns of gender differences in the EAC scales (e.g., Parham & Tinsley, 1980; Craig & Hennessy, 1989; Hardin & Subich, 1985). However, one study examined the issue of gender differences by investigating not only the relation between respondent sex and expectations about counseling but also the relation between subject gender-role orientation and expectations. Sipps and Janeczek (1986) investigated this issue using a sample of 182 undergraduate students (85 males and 97 females). Each participant completed the EAC and the Extended Personal Attributes Questionnaire (EPAQ; Spence & Helmrich, 1979), which was used to assess gender traits. The EPAQ is a 40-item questionnaire with six scales measuring desirable and undesirable masculine and feminine traits. Only the desirable masculine and desirable feminine trait scales were used in this study.

The data were analyzed using stepwise multiple regression analysis. Of the 17 EAC scales, scores on 9 were significantly predicted by subject sex or gender traits (Responsibility, Openness, Motivation, Genuineness, Nurturance, Trustworthiness, Tolerance, Immediacy, and Outcome). What was most interesting regarding these results is that in six of the nine significant predictions, femininity accounted for the most variance. These six scales were Tolerance, Genuineness, Outcome, Nurturance, Trustworthiness, and Responsibility. Respondent sex (female) only entered the equation first in three predictions (for Immediacy, Openness, and Motivation). The authors concluded that it is the presence of feminine gender traits (particularly expressiveness and being communal) that accounts for many gender differences in expectations, rather than respondent sex or masculine gender traits.

In a follow-up study, Johnson and Knackstedt (1993) replicated Sipps and Janeczek's (1986) study but used the Bem Sex Role Inventory (BSRI; Bem, 1974) to measure femininity, masculinity, and social desirability. They found similar results, in that higher femininity scores were associated with higher expectations on 14 of the 17 EAC scales (Motivation, Openness, Responsibility, Acceptance, Confrontation, Genuineness, Nurturance, Self-Disclosure, Expertise, Tolerance, Trustworthiness, Concreteness, Immediacy, and Outcome). As in Sipps and Janeczek, gender showed little relation to expectations, with the exception of Immediacy, where men had higher expectations than women. Again, it appears that sex role orientation, rather than gender, determines counseling expectations. In a review of studies of the BSRI, Brems and Johnson (1991) concluded that the instrument measures two underlying factors: Interpersonal Sensitivity and Interpersonal Potency, rather than femininity and masculinity. Because counseling is an interpersonal situation that requires sensitivity and emotional expressiveness, it makes sense that these traits are related to more positive expectations about counseling.

Expectations and Racial/Cultural Differences

Beyond gender, the relation between expectations about counseling and racial/cultural differences has also been frequently researched. One of the earliest studies conducted on cultural differences in expectations was by Yuen and Tinsley (1981), who compared the EAC responses of a group of international students to a those of a group of U.S. students. Respondents included 40 U.S., 39 Chinese, 35 African, and 36 Iranian students, who were either first-year students or seniors. Students were contacted by telephone and completed the survey by mail, in class, or in orientation programs. EAC scores were compared for each of the cultural groups. Results indicated that the U.S. students tended to have lower expectations for Concreteness, Directiveness, Empathy, Nurturance, and Expertise than the international students. They also had higher expectations for Responsibility and Motivation. In contrast, the Chinese, Iranian, and African students had higher expectations for the counselor to be directive and expert (clearly an authority figure), whereas they viewed themselves as being less involved in the counseling process. Among the international students, there were no differences between the Iranian and African students on any scales. The Chinese students, however, had an expectancy set that included low Responsibility, Openness, and Motivation on their part, and low Concreteness, Confrontation, and Immediacy on the part of the counselor. The authors stated that this implied a desire for the counseling relationship to be courteous, respectful, and distant, which is typical of the behavior of Chinese in authority relationships. This is in marked contrast to the counseling style of many U.S. counselors. The authors made two important recommendations based on their findings. First, international students may need more information about the purpose and function of the counseling process, and second, counselors need to be sensitive to the relationship behavior of their clients who are from cultural groups different than their own.

In another study of cultural differences, Kenney (1994) investigated counseling expectations and preferences for counselor ethnicity and gender among Asian, African American, and European American students. The sample of 69 students (20 Asians, 27 African Americans, and 22 European Americans) completed a demographic questionnaire, and the EAC-B. Two modified versions of the EAC-B were used in which the respondents were instructed to imagine that they were seeing a counselor for either a career issue or a relationship issue. The data were analyzed using a 3 (Ethnicity) × 2 (Presenting Problem) MANCOVA with three EAC-B factor scores (Personal Commitment, Counselor Expertise, and Facilitative Conditions) as dependent variables, and gender and treatment history as covariates.

Results indicated a main effect for ethnicity with Asian and African American students reporting lower expectations for Personal Commitment than European American students. African American students had lower expectations for Facilitative Conditions than Asian students, and Asian students had higher expectations for Counselor Expertise than African American or European American students. No other main effect or interaction effect was detected. Chi-square results indicated that 70% of students preferred a counselor of the same ethnicity and 52% of students preferred a counselor of the same gender. Based on these results, the author concluded that students of different ethnicity bring a set of different expectations to counseling, so the counselor needs to be aware of and sensitive to the needs of clients from minority ethnic groups.

Several studies have examined the effect of acculturation on expectations about counseling. Leong, Wagner, and Kim (1995) investigated the expectations for group counseling among Asian American students. In this study, 134 Asian American participants completed a set of measures including the Loss of Face Scale (Zane, 1991), a 21-item measure of attitude toward losing face in public and one's behavioral attempts to maintain face, and the Acculturation Scale (Kim, 1988), a 56-item scale measuring assimilation, integration, separation, and marginalization toward a culture. Briefly, assimilation refers to gaining the attitudes and behaviors of the mainstream culture while giving up the heritage culture; integration refers to an individual being active in both cultures; separation refers to maintaining the heritage culture and rejecting the mainstream culture; and marginalization refers to a lack of connection with either culture. Finally, expectations for group counseling were measured using the Group Therapy Survey (Slocum, 1987), a 25-item measure of attitudinal and behavioral expectations for group psychotherapy, with three scales (Positive Attitudes, Self-Disclosure, and Misconceptions). In this study, only the 7-item Positive Attitudes scale was used, because of poor reliability of the other two scales. Data were analyzed using a hierarchical multiple regression in which gender, loss of face, the four acculturation scales, and interactions of gender with the other variables were used to predict positive attitudes toward group counseling.

Results indicated no significant main effects for gender or loss of face, but the integration scale of the acculturation measure significantly added to the model. None of the interaction terms were significant. The authors concluded that more highly acculturated Asian Americans have more positive expectations for group psychotherapy and that the integrationist perspective is associated with mental health. However, they note the surprising result that the assimilation scale was not associated with positive expectations for group therapy. Because assimilation represents identification with the mainstream culture, it was hypothesized to predict positive expectations. The authors discussed the fact that counselors need to be aware of within-group differences for Asian American clients and not to assume that all Asian American clients will have negative views of group therapy.

Kunkel, Hector, Coronado, and Vales (1989) conducted another study of acculturation and expectations about counseling with a sample from Yucatan, Mexico. In this study, 254 females and 233 males from a variety of settings (community, academic, and religious) completed a Spanish translation of the EAC-B. Ages ranged from 17 to 79, and 100 respondents indicated that they had previous counseling experience. A factor analysis of scores on the Spanish EAC-B was completed, which yielded a three-factor structure. Factor 1 was named Client Commitment and included the Personal Responsibility, Openness, Motivation, Immediacy, Concreteness, and Positive Outcome scales. Factor 2 was named Counselor Expertise and included the Acceptance, Directiveness, Empathy, Self-Disclosure, Nurturance, and Expertise scales. Factor 3 was named Counselor Warmth and included the Acceptance, Genuineness, Nurturance, Attractiveness, Trustworthiness, and Tolerance scales.

In examining gender differences in the factor structure, females had lower expectations for counselor expertise, and higher expectations for counselor warmth than males. In terms of scale scores, females had higher expectations for Motivation, Openness, Genuineness, Nurturance, Attractiveness, Tolerance, and Trustworthiness. Males had higher expectations for Self-Disclosure. Regarding age, no differences were found between factor scores, but older respondents had lower expectations on the Self-Disclosure and Acceptance scales than younger respondents. Finally, participants who had prior counseling experience had lower expectations for the counselor expertise factor than participants who had no counseling experience. On the individual scales, experienced respondents had higher expectations for Openness but lower expectations for Directiveness, Empathy, Self-Disclosure, and Tolerance. Results of this study suggest that the Spanish EAC-B is a useful measure of expectations about counseling for Spanish-speaking respondents. The underlying factor structure reflects similar constructs to those found in other studies (e.g., Tinsley et al., 1980; Hayes & Tinsley, 1989; Tinsley, Holt, Hinson, & Tinsley, 1991) further adding to the construct validity of the EAC-B.

In 1990, Kunkel investigated the relation between expectations about counseling and acculturation. A sample of 213 Mexican American students and 137 Anglo American students completed the EAC-B and the Acculturation Rating Scale for Mexican Americans (ARSMA; Cuellar, Harris, & Jasso, 1980), which consists of 20 items that differentiate levels of personal affiliation with Mexican or U.S. values and roles. Response options to the items on the ARSMA are very Mexican, Mexican-oriented bicultural, true bicultural, Anglo-oriented bicultural, and very Anglicized. All participants completed the two instruments in large groups. Following this, the participants were invited to participate in small group discussions facilitated by the investigators. The participants were encouraged to share their impressions of the study, their expectations of counseling, and the meaning of these expectations to them. The investigators recorded their impressions of emerging themes following these discussions.

Results indicated that the Anglo American students had more counseling experience than the Mexican American students. However, both groups of students had similar expectations about counseling. Both groups expected to be responsible in counseling with a genuine, accepting, nurturant, and trustworthy counselor. In addition, both groups expected a positive outcome from counseling. The effect of acculturation on expectations within groups was noteworthy. In particular, two EAC scales, Directiveness and Empathy, varied with acculturation. Anglo-oriented respondents expressed the lowest expectation for each of these, and Mexican-oriented respondents expressed the highest, possibly relating to each cultural group's views of authority. In summary, like other cross-cultural researchers, Kunkel (1990) recommended that Mexican American psychology must attend to both group and individual meanings in counseling.

Several studies have been conducted examining the expectations of African Americans, particularly in relation to therapy with White counselors. Watkins and Terrell (1988) investigated the relation between mistrust level and counseling expectations in Black client–White counselor relationships. In this analogue study, 95 male and 94 female Black students aged 18 to 23 years completed the Cultural Mistrust Inventory (CMI; Terrell & Terrell, 1981) and the EAC-B. The CMI is a 48-item questionnaire designed to measure the extent to which respondents mistrust Whites. A median split was used to divide the participants into low-mistrust and high-mistrust groups. The EAC-B was modified such that either the word *black* or *white* was placed before *counselor* in the instructions for the instrument. A 2 (Subject Sex) × 2 (Mistrust Level) × 2 (Counselor Race) design was used in which scores on the EAC-B scales were the dependent variables.

There was one significant interaction for subject mistrust level and counselor race on the following EAC-B scales: Genuineness, Self-Disclosure, Acceptance, Trustworthiness, Outcome, and Expertness. Highly mistrustful Black students viewed the White counselor less favorably on each of these variables. In addition, one significant main effect was found for subject mistrust level, in which highly mistrustful Black students viewed the counselor as less immediate and less attractive. This suggests that highly mistrustful Blacks expect less from counseling, regardless of counselor race. The authors suggested that Black client–White counselor dyads require sensitivity on the part of the counselor with regard to this mistrust issue.

This issue was furthered examined by Watkins, Terrell, Miller, and Terrell (1989) in a follow-up study. Specifically, the authors wished to examine the effects of cultural mistrust on respondents' expectations of counselor credibility, confidence in the counselor, and willingness to return for a second session. Although this study did not use the EAC, it examined counselor credibility, similar to the EAC Expertise scale. In this investigation, 60 Black male and 60 Black female students attending a predominantly Black college completed a set of questionnaires, which included the CMI (Terrell & Terrell, 1981), the CERS (Atkinson & Wampold, 1982), the Personal Problem Inventory (PPI; Schneider, 1985), and the Willingness to See the Counselor Scale (WSC; Andersen & Anderson, 1985). The CERS is a 10-item scale that is designed to measure counselor credibility. The PPI is a 20-item personal problems list that reflects many concerns that college students commonly experience. Finally, the WSC is a single-item measure of a respondent willingness to see the counselor.

All respondents read a description of a counselor who is a licensed psychologist with a degree in counseling psychology and experience working in a variety of settings with individuals, families, couples, and groups. Half of the respondents read that the counselor was Black, and half read that the counselor was White. A 2 (Respondent Sex) × 2 (Respondent Mistrust Level) × 2 (Counselor Race) design was used to analyze the data in which scores on the CERS, PPI, and WSC served as the dependent variables.

A significant interaction between subject mistrust level and counselor race was detected, such that highly mistrustful respondents viewed the White counselor as less credible. Regarding personal problems, there was a significant main effect for subject mistrust level in which highly mistrustful Blacks expected the counselor (either Black or White) to be less able to help them with sexual functioning difficulties. In addition, there was a significant interaction between subject mistrust and counselor race, such that highly mistrustful Blacks expected a White counselor to be less able to help them deal with general anxiety, shyness, difficulties in dating, and feelings of inferiority.

The findings of this study emphasized once again the need for counselors to be particularly sensitive to the mistrust level of Black clients, especially if the counselor is White. This study added to the results of Watkins and Terrell (1988) by detecting several specific problem areas where the mistrust issue may be very relevant, namely, shyness, anxiety, dating issues, and feelings of inferiority. With regard to sexual difficulties, counselor race did not seem to be an important factor in determining whether a mistrustful client would discuss this concern. The mistrust appears to outweigh consideration of the race of the counselor.

Kemp (1994) conducted an analogue study to investigate African American students' expectations about counseling from two university settings: one predominantly White and one predominantly Black in terms of enrollment. Eighty-seven male and 73 female African American students completed the EAC-B; 43% of the respondents were enrolled at a predominantly White university, and 57% were enrolled at a predominantly Black university. A 2 (Gender) × 2 (University) design was used to analyze the data. Main effects were found for both independent variables; no interaction effects were detected.

In terms of university type, African American students at predominantly Black universities had higher expectations on 14 of the 17 EAC-B scales; only Motivation, Empathy, and Attractiveness were the same for students at both universities. The author concluded that students at predominantly White universities may expect racial barriers to present difficulties in establishing a counseling relationship and benefiting from the counseling process. Only two EAC-B scales were significantly different for men and women. Men had higher expectations for Empathy and Directiveness, a trend noted in other studies.

Carter and Akinsulure-Smith (1996) investigated the relation between client expectations about counseling and White racial identity. The EAC-B and the White Racial Identity Attitude Scale (WRIAS; Helms & Carter, 1990) were administered to a sample of 221 White undergraduate students (97 females and 124 males). The WRIAS consists of five subscales that assess the attitudes of White individuals regarding their own and other racial groups (Contact—an awareness that other races exist; Disintegration—an acknowledgment that racism exists; Reintegration—a positive bias toward one's own racial group and prejudice toward others; Pseudoindependence—an intellectual acceptance of racial differences and similarities; and Autonomy—a true acceptance of racial differences and similarities).

Preliminary analyses indicated gender differences among EAC scores consistent with previous findings. In this study, women scored higher on Motivation, Openness, Responsibility, Acceptance, Confrontation, Genuineness, Nurturance, Trustworthiness, Concreteness, Immediacy, and Outcome. Men had higher expectations for Directiveness, Empathy, and Self-Disclosure. Gender differences were also found on the WRIAS, with men scoring higher on Disintegration and Reintegration, and women scoring higher on Contact, Pseudo-independence, and Autonomy. The authors speculated that this is because of differences in socialization for men and women in the United States. That is, Disintegration and Reintegration are typically associated with more negative emotions, which men are more socialized to express. Finally, a canonical correlation analysis was conducted to examine the relation between racial identity attitudes and expectations about counseling. No significant correlations were found. The authors suggested that race needs to be included in the measure of counseling expectations, but it is unclear how this would change the findings. Many other studies (Kenney, 1994; Yuen & Tinsley, 1981) have found differences on expectations between racial groups, so the lack of differences in this study is puzzling.

Finally, with regard to cultural differences, one study focused on the expectations of Native Americans. Johnson and Lashley (1989) investigated the influence of Native Americans' cultural commitment (level of acculturation) on preferences for counselor ethnicity and expectations about counseling. In this study, 55 female and 29 male Native American students representing 14 Native American tribes indicated their level of cultural commitment by choosing one of the following statements: (1) strong commitment to both Native American and Anglo American cultures, (2) strong commitment to Native American culture, weak commitment to Anglo American culture, (3) strong commitment to Anglo American culture, weak commitment to Native American culture, and (4) weak commitment to both cultures. Because small numbers of participants chose two of the levels, data were collapsed to form two categories: strong commitment to Native American culture, and weak commitment to Native American culture. Participants were also asked to indicate the degree to which they participated in tribal activities and their proficiency in the tribal language. Finally, they were asked to assess the importance of seeing a Native American counselor if they ever felt the need for counseling. Following these assessments, participants completed the EAC-B.

There were two significant findings, the first of which indicated that participants who have strong commitment prefer an ethnically similar counselor. The second finding indicated that those who have a stronger commitment to Native American culture had higher expectations for counseling on the Facilitative Conditions, Expertise, and Nurturance factors. There was no difference for the Personal Commitment factor. The authors interpreted the finding regarding expectations as those who have a strong commitment to Native American culture may possess a traditional respect for elders or those in authority (in this case, a counselor). Just as with gender in which sex-role orientation may be more important in explaining differences in expectations than gender itself (e.g., Sipps & Janeczek, 1986; Johnson & Knackstedt, 1993), it may be the degree of cultural commitment rather than ethnicity per se that influences preferences for counselor ethnicity and expectations about counseling.

Expectations and Age/Development

Only a few studies have investigated expectations about counseling and age or developmental differences. Kunkel and Williams (1991) conducted a study using two methodologies (quantitative and phenomenological) to investigate the effects of age on expectations about counseling. The authors noted that a large percentage (15% to 25%) of Americans over age 65 experience mental health problems, but few receive professional treatment. They speculated that this could be because of a reluctance on the part of counselors to work with the elderly, inaccessibility of services, or misunderstandings about counseling in general. To clarify this issue, two groups of participants completed the EAC-B. The first group was made up of 100 respondents (76 women and 24 men) aged 65 or older recruited from community centers, church groups, and retirement agencies. The group was predominantly White, with a mean age of 72 years. In addition to the EAC-B, the elderly group also completed a questionnaire that assessed who the elderly participants may talk to about their problems, their experiences with counseling, the problems that might cause them to seek counseling, and the accessibility of services. A sample of 100 undergraduate students (matched with the elderly group for gender and ethnicity) served as a comparison group. The data were analyzed using a 2 (Age) × 2 (Respondent Sex) MANOVA with the EAC-B scale scores as dependent variables.

Results indicated significant main effects for both independent variables, but no significant interaction effect was found. In terms of age, elderly participants only differed from student participants on the Self-Disclosure scale, such that they had lower expectations for self-disclosure from the counselor than did younger participants. In terms of sex, there were several differences with women once again expressing higher expectations for Motivation, Responsibility, Genuineness, Trustworthiness, and Confrontation, and men expressing higher expectations for Directiveness. Elderly participants indicated that they would seek help from several other sources (spouse, friend, son or daughter, clergy, doctor, or other relative) before contacting a counselor, and depression, death of a loved one, and substance abuse were the most common reasons for seeking treatment. Finally, in terms of accessibility of services, elderly participants responded that counseling was too expensive, that people should be able to help themselves, and that counselors cannot relate to the elderly as the primary obstacles to seeking treatment.

For the phenomenological section of the study, 200 additional elderly participants and 100 students were interviewed in large groups. The interviews were conducted by the authors and assistants using a semistructured format in which general content was introduced, but then the discussion was allowed to develop with minimal interference by the interviewers. These data were analyzed using Giorgi's (1985) phenomenological method in which transcripts of the interviews are read and reread to find themes or "meaning units." Three such meaning units were identified in the data. The first was named Guardedness versus Openness, and pertained to the elderly feeling much more threatened and acting more cautious in regard to the counseling process than the younger participants, who were much more eager, accepting, and curious about counseling. The second meaning unit was named Self-Reliance/God-Reliance versus Networking. This pertained to the elderly participants' belief that problems should be solved on one's own or with the help of God, compared to the younger participants' belief that problems happen to everyone and one should have a social support network on which to rely. The final meaning unit was named Extreme Problems/Extreme Remedies versus Normalcy. The elderly participants appeared to believe that counseling is a last resort, a painful and expensive solution to severe problems, whereas the younger participants appeared to believe that counseling can benefit anyone who wishes to gain self-understanding.

Although the EAC-B results indicated a similarity in expectations about counseling among the elderly and younger participants, the demographic and interview data suggest that the elderly have little confidence in the ability of counselors to help them cope with their problems. Their independence and guardedness serve as major obstacles to help-seeking. The authors suggested that counselors who have the opportunity to work with the elderly should be especially sensitive to their need for self-reliance by emphasizing their autonomy while providing supportive services.

D. J. Tinsley, Hinson, Holt, and H. E. A. Tinsley (1990) conducted a study that investigated the relation among several aspects of psychosocial development and expectations about counseling. They hypothesized that differences in expectations may be caused by differences in psychosocial development, perceived level of psychological difficulty, and counseling readiness. Undergraduate students (100 female and 72 male) completed a battery of instruments that included the EAC-B, the SDTI-2 (Winston, Miller, & Prince, 1979), the CRS (Gough & Heilbrun, 1980), and the CCDI (Arnold, 1985), previously discussed in this chapter.

Data were analyzed using a series of MANOVAs with the 17 EAC-B scale scores as dependent variables. Median splits were used to obtain high- and low-scoring groups for each of the three independent variables (SDTI-2, CRS, and CCDI). A significant difference was found between high- and low-scoring respondents for the SDTI-2, but not for the CRS or the CCDI. Follow-up univariate regressions were conducted in which each of the 17 EAC-B scales were regressed on gender, age, college-class level, and scores on the SDTI-2 subscales. Results indicated that students who had more well defined educational goals had higher-expectations scores on all EAC-B scales except Motivation. Students with more mature career plans had higher-expectations scores for seven EAC-B scales (Responsibility, Confrontation, Attractiveness, Tolerance, Trustworthiness, Concreteness, and Outcome). Finally, students with more mature lifestyle plans had higher-expectations scores for 11 EAC-B scales (Openness, Acceptance, Confrontation, Empathy, Nurturance, Self-Disclosure, Expertise, Trustworthiness, Concreteness, Immediacy, and Outcome). These results indicate that level of psychosocial development does, to some extent, relate to expectations about counseling. It appears that those students with more mature and future life plans have more positive expectations about counseling.

Expectations and Personality

A few studies have examined the relation between personality and expectations about counseling. One commonly researched personality variable is locus of control. Foon (1986) examined the relation between locus of control and expectations about counseling. Rotter (1966) emphasized that people with an internal locus of control assume responsibility for their situations, whereas externals tend to focus on feelings of lack of control or denial of responsibility. Foon hypothesized that matching the client's and counselor's locus of control may serve to explain a client's counseling expectations. A sample of 67 clients (31 males and 36 females) was chosen in which each client had a mild presenting problem, was participating in individual counseling, and had no previous counseling experience. Each client completed a questionnaire regarding locus of control and demographic variables (including age, social class, and sex). Clients then viewed eight 5-minute videotapes and estimated their success in therapy with each counselor portrayed in the scenarios. Each scenario showed a counselor interacting with a client who had a mild, neurotic presenting problem. Locus of control (internal or external) and social class (middle or lower class) of the counselor was manipulated in the scenarios; each combination was portrayed by a male and a female, yielding eight possible combinations.

Locus of control was measured using Rotter's (1966) internal–external scale. Social class of the client was measured by rating their own, their fathers', and their associates' occupations. Expectation of counseling success (similar to the EAC-B Outcome scale) was measured by a 2-item scale assessing comfort with and helpfulness of the counselor portrayed. Data were analyzed using hierarchical multiple regression in which the expectations measure was regressed against the characteristics of the client and the counselor. Only the interaction of the client and counselor locus of control contributed significantly to the explained variance. The author concluded that the matching of client and counselor locus of control leads to favorable expectations about the outcome of counseling, but she commented that it was surprising that clients with internal loci of control did not have different expectations about counseling than clients with external loci of control.

In another study of personality and expectations, Craig and Hennessy (1989) noted the continuing gender difference in expectations about counseling; however, they commented that a single, demographic process or context variable cannot possibly explain the structure of expectations across persons. They introduced conceptual system theory (CST; Harvey, Hunt, & Schroder, 1961) as a theoretical framework that may explain how personality affects expectations about counseling. CST resembles developmental models that emphasize either a change in identity and relationships, such as Erikson's theory, or a change in cognitive ability, such as Piaget's theory. In CST, four stages of conceptual functioning explain personality differences. Stage 1 is characterized by an intolerance of ambiguity and rigid obedience to rules and norms. Stage 2 is characterized by a reaction against the control inherent in Stage 1 and a rejection of authority. Stage 3 is characterized by a dependency on important individuals and a high value for interpersonal relationships. Stage 4 is characterized by interdependent, yet autonomous, behavior. Sixty clients completed the EAC-B and Harvey's (1969) This I Believe Test (TIB), a paragraph completion test designed to assess level of conceptual functioning. The instruments were completed prior to the first counseling session.

A discriminant function analysis revealed that differences in levels of conceptual functioning are related to expectations about counseling. Two discriminant functions were identified. The first concerned expectations related to counselor empathy, directiveness, and attractiveness. Stage 1 clients expected the counselor to be more empathic and directive than Stage 3 or 4 clients, and they had lowered expectations for counselor attractiveness. This makes sense, because Stage 1 individuals are less abstract and are more dependent on structure. In contrast, Stage 3 and 4 clients expected less empathy and directiveness, and more attractiveness. The second discriminant function concerned counselor self-disclosure, genuineness, and nurturance. In accordance with CST, Stage 2 and 4 clients expected more counselor self-disclosure and genuineness than Stage 3 clients who expected more nurturance. Stage 3 individuals tend to prefer more active, interpersonal exchanges, which may explain their higher expectation for a warm, supportive relationship. In summary, the authors found a relation between personality dimensions and expectations about counseling, which goes beyond simple gender or other demographic variable differences.

Expectations and Religiosity

One last demographic variable that has received research attention with regard to expectations is religiosity. Pecnik and Epperson (1985) conducted the initial inquiry, investigating expectations about counseling in Christian versus non-Christian participants with either a Christian or traditional counselor. In this analogue study, 238 undergraduate students (126 men and 112 women) completed the EAC, which was modified in two ways. First, the participants were asked to indicate their expectations for counseling with either a counselor described as a licensed psychologist who specialized in group and individual counseling or with a counselor described as a Christian counselor. The second modification was the addition of an expectancy scale for Religious Behavior; this scale had 11 items pertaining to the goals and processes of Christian counseling. Participants also completed the Shepherd Scale (Bassett et al., 1981), a 38-item measure of conservative/evangelical Christianity. Data were analyzed using a 2 (Sex) × 2 (Subject Religious Orientation) × 2 (Counselor Orientation) MANOVA with the EAC scale scores as the dependent variables.

Results indicated significant main effects for all three independent variables. In terms of subject's sex, females had higher expectations for Motivation, Openness, Acceptance, Responsibility, Confrontation, Genuineness, Attractiveness, Trustworthiness, Concreteness, Immediacy, and Outcome, and males had higher scores on Directiveness, Empathy, and Self-Disclosure. Again, these gender differences confirm those found in other studies. Regarding subject's religious orientation, Christians had higher expectations for counseling than non-Christians on 15 EAC scales (Openness, Responsibility, Acceptance, Empathy, Genuineness, Nurturance, Self-Disclosure, Attractiveness, Expertise, Tolerance, Trustworthiness, Concreteness, Immediacy, Outcome, and Religious Behavior). The authors comment that this finding may suggest a sense of social desirability in the Christian respondents, or it may be the result of a more tolerant and accepting attitudinal set that enabled them to view themselves and their counselors more favorably. Finally, in terms of counselor's orientation, participants who read the description of the traditional counselor had higher expectations for Motivation, Expertise, Concreteness, and Outcome. Participants who read the description of the Christian counselor had higher expectations for Religious Behavior. It is interesting to note that participants expected traditional counselors to be more effective than Christian counselors, despite descriptions of identical credentials. It is also notable that the interaction between subject and counselor religious orientation was not significant. The authors concluded that participants may have perceived the Christian counselor to be affiliated with clergy, which may have undermined their ideas of that counselor expertise and overall effectiveness.

In a replication study, Godwin and Crouch (1989) also examined expectations for Christian versus non-Christian counseling, but added the variables of counselor skill and social desirability. In this study, 204 students (96 males and 108 females) completed a modified version of the EAC-B in which there were four descriptions of the counselor: (1) a counselor with an unspecified orientation, (2) a Christian counselor, (3) a high-skill counselor with an unspecified orientation, and (4) a high-skill Christian counselor. In the high-skill descriptions, the counselor is described as having more than 20 years of experience in counseling and an outstanding professional reputation. The Religious Behavior scale, as described by Pecnik and Epperson (1985) was also included. Participants also completed the Shepherd Scale (Bassett et al., 1981), and the Marlow-Crowne Social Desirability Scale (Crowne & Marlowe, 1964), a 33-item measure of respondents' tendency to present themselves favorably.

Social desirability was not significantly correlated with subject's religious orientation or the majority of EAC-B scales. Because of this lack of findings, social desirability was excluded from further analysis. The data were analyzed using a 2 (Subject's Gender) × 2 (Subject's Religious Orientation) × 2 (Counselor's Religious Orientation) × 2 (Counselor's Skill) MANOVA. Main effects were found for all independent variables, and there were several significant interactions. In terms of gender, males had higher expectations for Directiveness, Empathy, Self-Disclosure, and Realism, and females had higher expectations for Motivation. Regarding subject's religious orientation, Christian respondents had higher expectations for counseling than non-Christian respondents on all EAC-B scales except for Motivation and Realism. This finding confirmed that of Pecnik and Epperson (1985). Christian counselors were rated higher on religious behavior, and as more accepting and attractive than non-Christian counselors. This was in contrast to Pecnik and Epperson who found that non-Christian counselors were expected to be more expert and effective than Christian counselors. One interesting finding was that the high-skill counselor was rated as less directive, empathic, and nurturant than the counselor of unspecified skill. Godwin and Crouch (1989) suggest that this could be because of feelings of dissimilarity on the part of the respondent; similarity between client and counselor may have a more positive effect on forming a therapeutic relationship. Finally, a significant interaction indicated that Christian respondents rated the high-skill counselor higher on Realism, Confrontation, Nurturance, Self-Disclosure, and Tolerance than did the non-Christian respondents.

Expectations and Counseling Process Variables

Many studies have focused on expectations and various aspects of the counseling process. Two studies examined the effects of precounseling orientations and intake procedures on expectations about counseling. Smith and Quinn (1985) based their study on the work of Truax and Carkhuff (1967), who suggested that counseling is a learning process that should be structured to some extent for clients to benefit the most. In this study, 47 prospective clients received a verbal precounseling orientation, and 50 received an audiovisual orientation. The presentations were equal in length, and both included information about the benefits of counseling, how to initiate counseling, and conditions under which counseling is provided. All prospective clients completed a pretest and posttest measure of counseling expectations. The 26-item measure of expectations was designed by one of the authors (Quinn, 1983) and contained two scales: the Affective Process Scale (relating to feelings, emotional support, and understanding) and the Directive Counselor Role Scale (relating to problem solving, information giving, and counselor responsibility). Results indicated that the audiovisual presentation increased expectations regarding affective processes, and the verbal presentation had no effect on these expectations. For expectations regarding counselor directiveness, neither presentation had an effect on client expectations. Although the findings are somewhat limited, it seems as though some type of precounseling orientation is important in helping clients to develop positive client role behaviors that can affect the outcome of counseling. In this study, an audiovisual orientation (which included a videotape segment of a client–counselor interaction) was most effective in promoting a positive change in client expectations.

A second study on precounseling procedures was conducted by Barron, Daniels, and O'Toole (1987), who investigated of the effects of computer-conducted versus counselor-conducted intake interviews on client expectations about counseling. They pointed out that the use of computers is greatly changing the manner in which counseling is conducted. For example, computers are used for test administration, interviewing, and some therapeutic interventions. In this study, 38 clients of a university counseling center were assigned to either the computer interview condition or counselor interview condition. For the computer interview condition, the Psychological/Social History Report (Rainwater & Coe, 1984) was used. This program contains 90 multiple-choice questions on a variety of issues and takes approximately 30 minutes to complete. The counselor interviewers used a printed form of the software program questions to ensure equivalent content coverage. Following either the computer or counselor intake, each client completed eight of the EAC-B scales (Motivation, Acceptance, Directiveness, Empathy, Genuineness, Nurturance, Self-Disclosure, and Confrontation). They also completed the Client Expectancy Inventory (CEI; Thro & Hollis, 1973), which is a 50-item measure of client overall expectancy, and expectancy related to cognitive and affective areas. Data were analyzed using a one-way ANOVA in which scores on the CEI, EAC-B, and intake reaction data were compared for computer-conducted versus counselor-conducted intakes. No significant differences were found between the groups on any of the scales. It appears that neither the computer interview nor counselor-conducted interview had positive or negative effects on client expectations. The authors recommend that agencies consider using computers to conduct intake interviews in order to standardize the information, reduce the demand on therapists, and increase the self-disclosure of sensitive information. With computers being used more frequently in mental health settings, this study gives information regarding the effects of their use on client expectations.

Subich and Hardin (1985) examined whether clients who pay for counseling have a different set of expectations than clients who do not pay for counseling services. In the first of two studies, 80 male and 80 female undergraduate students completed a telephone survey that included a set of items measuring probability of using the university counseling center, and three scales from the EAC (Responsibility, Motivation, and Outcome). Students were randomly assigned to one of four experimental conditions in which they received information about the fee schedule of some counseling centers (either no fee, a modest fee, a sliding scale, or a substantial fee). They were asked to respond to the items on the survey as if they were a student at a university that charged the fee for their given experimental condition. Data were analyzed using a 2 (Sex) × 4 (Fee Condition) MANOVA for the three EAC scales and four variables representing expected service use. Results indicated a significant main effect for sex but not for fee condition and no significant interaction. Female participants reported a higher likelihood of using services for general and study concerns, and higher expectations to take responsibility, be motivated, and experience a positive outcome than male participants.

In the second study (Subich & Hardin, 1985), 12 male and 31 female former clients of a psychology department clinic, none of whom paid for counseling services, and 7 male and 16 female students who had sought and paid for counseling services completed a questionnaire assessing three different variables. First, the level of satisfaction with the prior counseling experience was measured. Second, the likelihood of using a counseling service in the future if the fee structure differed from the prior experience was assessed. Participants responded to one of three situations, depending on their own prior experiences (free counseling is unavailable and minimal fee is required, free counseling is unavailable and a substantial fee is required, and a fee is not required and free counseling is available in a university setting). Third, the participants' expected satisfaction with counseling services as a function of the conditions described previously was assessed using the EAC Outcome scale. Data were analyzed using a one-way (Fee Condition) MANOVA with 11 dependent variables (satisfaction ratings, likelihood of use, and expected outcome).

No main effect was found, indicating that fee condition does not appear to affect willingness to seek counseling or expectations about counseling. The gender differences found in the first study were consistent with those found in other studies (e.g., Tinsley et al., 1980). Former clients reported no differences in satisfaction with counseling regardless of fee structure. The authors noted that this finding contradicts the assumption that clients who pay for counseling will be more motivated and have a more positive outcome than those clients who do not pay for services. They concluded that offering free services will not adversely affect client behavior in counseling and also that charging a minimal fee, if economically necessary, does not appear to have a negative effect on client use of services.

Two studies examined the relation between expectations about counseling and premature termination. Hardin, Subich, and Holvey (1988) noted that much of the research on expectations has not investigated the impact of negative expectations in a client population. Respondents in the study included 23 male and 57 female clients of a university counseling center of whom 10 men and 30 women returned to counseling after the initial interview. Their responses to the EAC-B were compared to those clients who did not return to counseling. All clients had completed the EAC-B as part of their intake packet before the first session. Also, on the intake form were questions regarding the respondent's age, sex, problem type (personal or career), and race. A 2 (Return Status) × 2 (Problem Type) design was used in which the 17 EAC scales were dependent variables. No significant main effects or interactions were detected. The authors concluded that clients who prematurely terminated did not have different precounseling expectations than those clients who continued until mutual termination with the counselor. Also, problem type did not affect expectations about counseling. Clients in both groups had high expectations about counseling, particularly for responsibility, openness, and motivation. This lack of finding is interesting, because other researchers have suggested that expectations can affect process and outcome of counseling by either confirming or disconfirming one's beliefs about the counseling process. The authors noted that one potential problem with the conclusion that expectations do not affect premature termination is the definition of "premature termination." In this study, clients were coded as premature terminators if they made a second appointment, but did not return. It is possible that these clients did not feel the need to return but made the appointment in order to please the counselor.

In another study of premature termination, Longo, Lent, and Brown (1992) applied Bandura's (1986) social cognitive theory to the process of counseling. According to Bandura, a person's self-efficacy beliefs affect outcome expectations and intention to pursue particular goals. In counseling, this can be interpreted to mean that clients' self-efficacy beliefs regarding their likelihood of successfully negotiating the counseling process may explain whether they will persist in therapy. Also, persistence may depend in large part on clients' expectations of positive outcomes. From this perspective, the authors set out to examine whether self-efficacy and outcome expectations predict motivation (persistence in therapy), whether these three variables predict actual return rate, and whether self-efficacy is related to self-esteem and state anxiety.

A sample of 139 clients of a university counseling center completed a battery of instruments following their intake interviews. Self-efficacy for client behaviors was measured using a 20-item scale designed for the study, which asked clients to rate their confidence in their ability to perform several tasks related to counseling (e.g., enact difficult in-session behaviors, manage barriers to therapy, take initiative in solving problems). The EAC-B Motivation scale was used to measure intention to remain in counseling, and the Outcome scale was used to measure expectations for a positive counseling outcome. The Client Problem Identification Questionnaire (CPIQ; Kokotovic & Tracey, 1987) was used to measure client's perceived distress level in four presenting problem areas (educational, vocational, personal, and interpersonal). The Rosenberg Self-Esteem Scales (SES; Rosenberg, 1965) is a 10-item scale that was used to measure global self-worth. State anxiety was measured with the State-Trait Anxiety Inventory–State Anxiety subscale (STAI-S; Spielberger, 1983). Preliminary analyses indicated that self-efficacy, outcome expectations, and motivation measures present distinct, related, latent dimensions. Also, correlations of self-efficacy to self-esteem and state anxiety were nonsignificant, indicating that feelings of self-worth and anxiety were unrelated to efficacy, so they were omitted from predictive analyses.

Data were analyzed using a hierarchical multiple regression to predict motivation from client gender, problem severity, counselor experience, self-efficacy, outcome expectations, and the interaction of self-efficacy and outcome expectations. Gender, problem severity, self-efficacy, and outcome expectations were significant predictors of motivation. A discriminant function analysis was conducted to determine the relation among client and counselor variables to client return status. Self-efficacy and motivation were most powerful in correctly classifying counseling persisters and dropouts. The authors concluded that both self-efficacy and outcome expectations contribute to motivation above and beyond client gender, problem severity, and therapist experience. Also, self-efficacy and motivation predicted client persistence in therapy.

Satterfield, Buelow, Lyddon, and Johnson (1995) conducted a more recent study of the effects of client stages of change on expectations about counseling. They present a theoretical model by Prochaska and DiClemente (1992) that describes four stages of change that are experienced by both clients and nonclients. The first stage, precontemplation, refers to clients not realizing that a problem exists. This is followed by the contemplation stage in which clients recognize that a problem exists and consider various options for addressing the problem. The action stage is characterized by efforts aimed toward change, and the maintenance stage focuses on preventing relapse and maintaining the changes that have been made.

In this study, 88 clients (66 women and 22 men) of a university counseling center completed the University of Rhode Island Change Assessment Scale (URICA; McConnaughy, Prochaska, & Velicer, 1983) and the EAC-B. The URICA is a 32-item measure containing four 8-item subscales, which assess the four stages of the change model. All clients completed the questionnaires at their intake interviews. Data were analyzed using a canonical correlation in which the two variable sets were scores on the four stages of change and the four composite EAC-B factors (Personal Commitment, Facilitative Conditions, Counselor Expertise, and Nurturance).

Two canonical roots were extracted; the first showed a significant relation between the four stages of change and two EAC-B factors (Personal Commitment and Facilitative Conditions). An interesting finding in this relationship is that the precontemplation stage was negatively related to these factors, whereas the contemplation, action and maintenance stages were positively related to these factors, indicating that individuals not yet engaged in the process of counseling have much lower expectations for their own commitment and the conditions supplied by the counselor. The second canonical root indicated a relationship between the two stages of contemplation and maintenance with the EAC-B factors of Facilitative Conditions, Counselor Expertise, and Nurturance, suggesting that clients who are in these stages have higher expectations for counselor attitudes and behaviors. The authors concluded that clients in different stages of change have different expectations about counseling, which gives counselors more information about how to address the individual needs of each client.

Tokar, Hardin, Adams, and Brandel (1996) investigated the relation between expectations about counseling the perceptions of the working alliance. The construct of a working alliance was originally proposed by Bordin (1979) as the relationship between the counselor and client that is based on agreement regarding the goals and tasks of treatment, and the development of a bond of trust. Tokar et al. introduced their study by reviewing an investigation by Al-Darmaki and Kivlighan (1993), which concluded that congruence in relationship expectations held by the client and the counselor is predictive of working alliance dimensions. In that study, however, a narrow range of expectations pertaining only to the counseling relationship was used, and expectations were measured after the third session of counseling. Tokar et al. chose to examine a wide range of expectations using the EAC-B, and they measured expectations prior to the beginning of the counseling relationship. The EAC-B was completed by 37 clients (25 females and 11 males) as part of the intake procedure, and working alliance was measured after the third session using the Working Alliance Inventory (WAI; Horvath & Greenberg, 1989). The WAI is a 36-item measure of the three working alliance dimensions (agreement on goals, agreement on tasks, and emotional bond).

Data were first analyzed for differences in WAI scores across sex, prior counseling experience, level of counselor training, and center in which counseling services were received. Finding none, data were collapsed across these categories for all further analyses. Three simultaneous multiple regression analyses were conducted to examine the prediction of each of the working alliance dimensions based on EAC scores. EAC-B factor scores (for Facilitative Conditions, Personal Commitment, Counselor Expertise, and Nurturance) were used in the analyses rather than individual scale scores. Results of the regression analyses indicated positive relationships between client scores on Personal Commitment and each of the WAI dimensions. That is, clients who expect to be responsible and motivated in counseling tend to experience the therapeutic relationship as cooperative and supportive. In addition, Counselor Expertise added to the prediction of WAI variables, but this relationship was negative. The authors interpreted this surprising finding to mean that those clients who expect the counselor to be directive, self-disclosing, and expert may tend to see themselves as taking a less active role in the therapeutic relationship. Finally, Facilitative Conditions and Nurturance did not add to the predication of WAI dimensions. The authors speculated that clients may believe that these conditions are always present in counseling relationships, so these do not add to working alliance dimensions.

Expectations and Career Counseling

Only a few studies have been conducted on the expectations of career clients or how expectations affect the career counseling process. Leong, Leong, and Hoffman (1987) examined the relation between decision-making style and expectations about counseling in a sample of 165 women and 82 men. All participants completed the EAC and the Assessment of Career Decision-Making Styles Scale (ACDMSS; Harren, 1980). The ACDMSS is a 94-item measure, which is divided into two sections, the Decision-Making Styles Scales and the Decision-Making Tasks Scales. The Decision-Making Styles section consists of three 10-item scales, which measure three decision-making styles: rational, dependent, and intuitive. Rational decision makers tend to gather and evaluate information systematically about a decision in a logical, analytic manner. Dependent decision makers tend to deny personal responsibility for decision making, looking to others for direction. Intuitive decision makers tend to use fantasy, immediate feelings and emotional self-awareness to make decisions (Buck & Daniels, 1985). The Decision-Making Tasks section consists of 64 items pertaining to a variety of academic and decision-making processes and was not used in this study. Participants were only included if they expressed a dominant style, which is defined as the style that received a raw score that was three or more points higher than the scores for each of the other two scales.

A comparison of the three styles on the EAC scales revealed that dependent decision makers had higher expectations than rational decision makers for Acceptance and Nurturance; intuitive decision makers had higher expectations than rationals and dependents for Attractiveness; and both intuitives and dependents had higher expectations than rationals on Expertise. No other differences were found. The authors commented that these results should be used to determine which type of career counseling interventions are most effective with certain types of clients. For example, a dependent decision maker may need a more structured approach to counseling, with an accepting and nurturant counselor. In contrast, an intuitive decision maker may desire a more unstructured approach to counseling.

Dorn (1989) examined the relation between client motivation and career certainty. Dorn cited earlier research (e.g., Heppner & Heesacker, 1982), which demonstrated that client motivation is related to Strong's (1968) counselor characteristics of expertness, attractiveness, and trustworthiness. The author noted, however, that there has been a lack of research addressing the motivation of career clients, and that these clients often perceive themselves as having less "need" for counseling, which reduces their motivation. In this study, 40 male and 40 female undergraduates seeking career counseling at a university counseling center completed the EAC Motivation scale, the CRF (Barak & LaCrosse,

1975), and the Career Decision Scale (CDS; Osipow, Carney, Winer, Yanico, & Koschir, 1976). As previously mentioned in this chapter, the CRF measures client perceptions of counselor expertness, attractiveness, and trustworthiness. The CDS is an 18-item scale that measures certainty and indecision about college major, lack of structure, external barriers, approach–approach, and personal conflict. Participants completed the instruments as part of a two-session structured workshop conducted by a male and female counselor on choosing a major. The CDS and EAC were completed prior to the first session, the CRF was completed after the first session, and the CDS was completed again after the conclusion of the second session. The workshop focused on barriers to choice of major, the career development process, and career information.

Results demonstrated that male and female participants perceived the male and female counselors as equal in social power (expertness, attractiveness, and trustworthiness). EAC scores were used to split clients into high-motivated and low-motivated groups. A two-way (motivation level, client sex) ANCOVA using the six CDS pretest scores as the covariate and CDS posttest scores as dependent variables revealed no sex motivation or differences. However, in analyzing the differences between pretest and posttest scores on the CDS, participants' scores on the certainty-of-college-major scale increased significantly, and their scores on lack of structure for a career decision decreased significantly. The lack of difference between high- and low-motivated clients is somewhat surprising, but the group climate of the workshop may have increased the motivation of the low-motivated clients.

Tinsley, Tokar, and Helwig (1994) investigated expectations about counseling and involvement in career counseling. They hypothesized that clients who have positive expectations about counseling would engage in a higher level of involvement during a career counseling intake interview than those who have negative expectations. Clients of a university career development center completed the EAC-B as part of their intake paperwork, and their initial interview was audiotaped. Once 20 tapes were collected, 5 were selected for further analysis; two pairs of clients, each pair being seen by one of two counselors, and a fifth client whose audiotape was selected to camouflage the nature of the hypothesis to the raters. Within each pair of clients, one had high-factor scores and one had low-factor scores on the EAC-B Personal Commitment and Facilitative Conditions factors. Client level of involvement was rated by judges using the Patient Experiencing Scale (EXP; Klein, Mathieu, Gendlin, & Kiesler, 1969), which is a 5-point scale used to assess client verbalizations to the counselor (e.g., external events, personal reactions, affective descriptions, explanation of feelings, connections between content). In addition, three items were written for this study assessing statements about oneself (self-reference), social undesirability, and uniqueness of behaviors and attitudes. Raters analyzed three 5-minute segments of audiotape, representing the first, middle, and last thirds of the session. Data were analyzed using a one-tailed sign test to compare the ratings of statements made by clients with positive versus negative expectations.

Results indicated that both clients who had positive expectations about counseling had significantly higher levels of involvement than clients with negative expectations. Clients with positive expectations were more likely to become emotionally and personally involved, whereas clients with negative expectations mainly described behavior and external events. Although this study was based on a very small sample, the results are notable for two reasons. First, very few studies have been conducted on the career counseling process, and second, the results indicate that expectations influence the counseling process by affecting levels of involvement.

More recently, Galassi, Crace, Martin, James, and Wallace (1992) proposed an instrument to measure precounseling expectations specifically in career clients. The authors used the term *anticipation* rather than *expectation* in order to clearly differentiate the construct from that of *preference*. They addressed several questions in this study, such as what clients prefer from career counseling, clients' perceptions of the career counseling process, what they dislike about career counseling, and whether their anticipations and preferences are congruent. Career counseling clients (22 men and 70 women) completed a 15-item, open-ended questionnaire designed for this study prior to the first session. The questions asked respondents to differentiate what they would like/hope to do during counseling sessions (preference) versus what they think they will do (anticipation). Responses were then coded into categories by independent raters.

Clients indicated that they would prefer and anticipated engaging in three sessions of counseling. In addition, clients indicated that they preferred and anticipated clarifying their career/major direction; however, preferences exceeded anticipations for this particular outcome. Within sessions, clients indicated a preference to discuss specific careers and decision making, but they anticipated that they would engage in self-exploration. Regarding counselor behavior, clients indicated a preference for counselors to provide advice, opinions, and answers, but they did not seem certain about what counselors actually do. They preferred career assignments related to researching and reading about careers, but they were unsure about what assignments they would actually be given. With regard to career testing, clients hoped to find a match between their personalities and careers, but again, they were unsure what they would actually learn from testing. Finally, regarding what they would dislike in career counseling, most clients did not know, indicating a lack of information about what occurs in career counseling. It seems that clients are fairly certain about their preferences for career counseling, but they are less certain about what actually occurs, and they are somewhat pessimistic about the process as evidenced by the mismatches between preferences and anticipations.

Expectations and Counselor Characteristics

Several studies have examined the relations between expectations and several specific counselor characteristics. In an early study of how counselor characteristics influence counseling process and outcome, Carter (1978) investigated impressions of counselors as a function of counselor physical attractiveness. She reviewed earlier research, which stated that client expectancy of a positive outcome is important in terms of actual symptom reduction and that one variable that may affect this expectancy is the physical attractiveness of the counselor. Sixty male and 60 female undergraduates listened to one of two audio recordings of either a male or female counselor, and viewed one of four photographs of a counselor (male/female, attractive/unattractive). Participants then completed two rating scales designed for this study. One assessed 12 impressions of the counselor (e.g., competent, friendly, trustworthy), and the other assessed confidence in the counselor effectiveness in dealing with 15 problems (e.g., shyness, depression, difficulties in dating). Taken together, these measured expectation for outcome.

A three-way ANOVA (Attractiveness, Sex of Counselor, Sex of Participant) was performed using the 12 impression ratings and a composite score as dependent variables. No main effect was found for attractiveness, but female counselors were rated more positively than male counselors on relaxation, warmth, friendliness, trustworthiness, and the composite score. Also, female participants rated the counselor more positively than male respondents on the characteristics of friendliness, trustworthiness, competence, sincerity, consideration, and the composite score. Two interactions were found, the first of which indicated that male participants rated male counselors the lowest of any group on impression ratings. The second interaction found that female participants rated attractive female counselors higher than male participants rated either attractive or unattractive male counselors.

A second three-way ANOVA was conducted using the ratings on counselor effectiveness in dealing with the 15 problems as dependent variables. A main effect was found for attractiveness in which attractive counselors were expected to be more able to help with sexual dysfunction, and unattractive counselors were expected to better help with test anxiety. Regarding sex of participant, females expected to be helped with career problems, and males expected help with alcohol difficulties. In terms of sex of counselor, female counselors were expected to help most with insomnia and had higher ratings on the composite score than male counselors. Overall, it appears that physical attractiveness is not as important to clients' outcome expectancies as anticipated. The author pointed out that the attractiveness ratings were not extreme, that is, the photographs represented the normal range of physical attractiveness, which did not produce the hypothesized effect. Significant sex differences, however, were noted such that female counselors were viewed more positively and more effectively than male counselors. Also, female participants had more positive expectations regarding the outcome of therapy. This is a gender difference that has been found in many others studies.

Counselor gender has been investigated from several perspectives. Subich (1983) examined the effects of counselor gender and respondent sex on expectations about counseling. In this study 120 male and 120 female undergraduates completed the EAC, which was modified to specify a male counseling psychologist for a third of the respondents, a female counseling psychologist for a second third of respondents, and a gender-unspecified counseling psychologist for the last third of respondents. There was one significant main effect for respondent sex, and one main effect that approached significance for counselor gender. Female respondents had higher expectations for Motivation, Responsibility, Acceptance, Confrontation, Genuineness, Nurturance, Tolerance, Immediacy, Outcome, and Trustworthiness, and lower expectations for Self-Disclosure than men. For the effect of counselor gender that approached significance, respondents had somewhat higher expectations for Acceptance, Confrontation, Nurturance, Self-Disclosure, and Expertness for the gender-unspecified counselor. The author commented that the gender specification on the instructions for the EAC, while detected by respondents, may not have been particularly salient. It is possible that viewing a videotape, or having in-person contact with the counselor may have produced a different result.

Hardin and Yanico (1983) examined the effects of counselor gender and type of presenting problem on expectations about counseling. They commented that preference for a male or female counselor may be related in part to the presenting problem, such that clients may prefer male counselors for vocational problems when they believe that they need more expertness and specific knowledge, and a female counselors for personal issues requiring more empathy and support. They investigated the interaction between counselor gender and problem type in a sample of 100 female and 100 male undergraduate students. All respondents completed one of four versions of the EAC, which was modified to reflect four experimental conditions: female counseling psychologist/vocational concern, male counseling psychologist/vocational concern, female counseling psychologist/personal concern, male counseling psychologist/personal concern. The data were analyzed using a 2 (Counselor Gender) × 2 (Problem Type) × 2 (Respondent Sex) design, with scores from the 17 EAC scales used as dependent variables.

There was a significant main effect for respondent sex only. No other main effects or interactions were detected. Women had higher expectations for Motivation, Openness, Responsibility, Acceptance, Confrontation, Genuineness, Attractiveness, Trustworthiness, Immediacy, and Outcome. Once again, men had higher expectations for Self-Disclosure and Directiveness. The lack of difference in expectations for a male versus a female counselor is somewhat surprising, but previous research on this issue has had mixed results. The authors pointed out that counselor gender could interact with professional title; "counseling psychologist" rather than "counselor" was used in the present study. The authors speculated that role may be more salient to potential clients than gender.

In a follow-up study, Yanico and Hardin (1985) examined the relation of specific problem type and expectations of counselor knowledge and understanding to gender preferences for counselors. In this study, 131 female and 57 male undergraduates completed a 19-page questionnaire in which the students reported their preferences for a male or female counseling psychologist, or indicated that they had no preference, for 35 different types of problems. Eleven problems were vocational or academic in nature, and 22 were personal concerns. Regarding the vocational problems, the results indicated that most of the students had no preference for gender of the psychologist. For those who did express a preference, male respondents preferred a male psychologist to some degree, but women responded with a preference for a male and female in equal numbers. Regarding personal concerns, however, preferences became much clearer. A female psychologist was preferred by both male and female respondents for rape, problem pregnancy, and harassment, and most women and half of the men preferred a same-sex psychologist when dealing with sexual problems. In general, for those women who did express a preference, most preferred a female psychologist. This did not hold true for men, who, when having a preference, preferred a male psychologist for only 10 of the 22 personal problems. Their preferences, however, were much weaker than those of the women. The authors concluded that specific problem type must be taken into account when examining counselor gender preferences.

Heppner and Heesacker (1982) investigated client expectations regarding counselor characteristics as they relate to counselor experience level. Counselors at three levels of experience (beginning practicum, advanced practicum, and doctoral intern) saw 31 clients over an average of eight sessions. All clients completed the EAC before they began counseling; specifically, the Motivation scale was of interest in this study. After the first session, clients completed the CRF (Barak & LaCrosse, 1975), a measure of counselor expertness, attractiveness, and trustworthiness, and counselors completed the Counselor Perceptions Questionnaire (CP) which was designed for this study. The CP is a 10-item scale that measures the counselor perception of the influence he or she had on the client. The clients completed the CRF and the counselors completed the CP again after the final session.

Results indicated that clients rated their counselors as more attractive following their last session in comparison to their first session. No differences were found over time on ratings of trustworthiness or expertness. When dependent *t* tests were conducted, however, it was discovered that 18 counselors were perceived by clients as increasing in expertness, attractiveness, and trustworthiness, but 12 counselors were perceived by clients as decreasing in these characteristics. When all counselors were considered together, the effect was negated. The clients of counselors whose ratings decreased reported more specific negative behaviors on the part of the counselor (unclear, confused), whereas clients of counselors whose ratings increased reported a more positive outcome. There was no main effect for counselor experience level on counselor characteristics. Also, motivation level, as measured by the EAC, did not affect client ratings of counselor characteristics. CP scores were used to assess perception of client need for a counselor (high versus moderate). In all analyses, client need did not influence client perceptions of counselor expertness, attractiveness, or trustworthiness. A final analysis examined the effects of the influence process within counseling. It appears that counselors perceived as highly attractive indicated that they had more impact on the client than counselors rated as less attractive.

Heppner and Heesacker (1983) examined expectations about counseling as related to perceived counselor characteristics, and client satisfaction with counseling. Respondents were 72 clients at a university counseling center (24 males and 48 females). The counselors were either beginning-level or advanced-level practicum students, predoctoral interns, or doctoral-level counseling psychologists. The respondents completed three measures: the EAC, the CRF (Barak & LaCrosse, 1975), and the CEI (Linden, Stone, & Schertzer, 1965). For this study, only 6 of the 17 EAC scales were used (Openness, Motivation, Acceptance, Expertness, Attractiveness, and Trustworthiness). The CEI is a 21-item instrument designed to assess client satisfaction with counseling and is comprised of three scales: counseling climate, counselor comfort, and client satisfaction. All clients completed the EAC prior to counseling and completed the CRF and the CEI during the final week of counseling.

Significant correlations were found between each of the CEI scales and each of the CRF scales. That is, as client perceptions of counselor expertness, attractiveness, and trustworthiness increased, so did their perceptions of climate, comfort, and satisfaction with the counseling experience. Expectations of openness and trustworthiness were correlated with counselor expertness, attractiveness, and trustworthiness and with counseling climate and the overall CEI score. In a multiple regression predicting CEI scores from EAC and CRF scores, CRF scores (particularly expertness) were the best predictors of CEI scores. The EAC scores did not significantly predict counselor characteristics (CRF scores) or counseling outcome (CEI scores).

The effects of experience level of the counselor on perceptions of counselor characteristics was examined using one-way ANOVAs. Counselor experience level did not affect perceived expertness, trustworthiness, or attractiveness. Also, counselor experience level did not affect perceptions of counseling climate, counselor comfort, client satisfaction, or the total CEI scores. The authors suggested that because of nonrandom assignment of clients to counselors, lower-functioning clients are assigned to more experienced counselors. This confound is difficult to examine, however, because random assignment of clients to counselors is often not possible.

Applications for Practice

It is apparent from this review of the literature that counseling expectations have many implications for counselors. Several themes emerge from the research. The first concerns client gender/sex-role orientation. It is obvious that men and women have different expectations about counseling, which appear to be a function of sex-role socialization. Counselors need to keep in mind that men may expect a more directive, advice-giving, rational approach to therapy, whereas women may expect a more nurturing, supportive, expressive environment. A second theme concerns racial differences and levels of acculturation. A common conclusion from these studies is that counselors need to be sensitive to the values and attitudes of ethnically diverse populations (as expressed in their expectations about counseling) and to be aware that within group differences are common because of various levels of commitment to U.S. culture.

A third theme concerns counselor characteristics, such as gender and perceived credibility. The research is less clear in this area, but it seems that clients have preferences for a male or female counselor partially depending on their presenting problems. As concerns the counseling process, it is imperative that counselors discuss during the early phase of counseling, perhaps even in the first session, what clients expect versus what can realistically be accomplished. Counseling expectations that are unrealistic need to be modified at the beginning of counseling before they can be detrimental to the process.

Psychotherapy has been called a pluralistic endeavor in which several hundred different theoretical approaches exist (Feltham, 1997). Much research attention has been directed toward the similarities and differences among theories. Because of the influence of managed care on the mental health profession, however, the effectiveness of psychotherapy seems to be influenced not only by theoretical approaches, but by nonspecific counseling process factors. Many therapists are using an eclectic approach in which they choose techniques that are appropriate for a certain client with a particular problem in a limited time frame. Managed care has caused the counseling process to become, more than ever, a business relationship that is outcome-directed.

The therapeutic relationship seems to be one factor that is extremely important for a successful outcome. The client's expectations about counseling obviously can have an effect, either positive or negative, on the process. To maximize the benefits a client can receive, therapists should openly discuss clients' expectations about gender, race, and even age and personality style when appropriate. In this way, therapists can attempt to modify negative client expectations and reinforce positive expectations in order to prevent premature termination and to fight resistance before it even occurs in the therapeutic relationship.

In the future, it appears likely that the use of time-limited, structured, problem-specific, and directive techniques will increase, whereas the use of historically oriented, unstructured, and passive procedures will decrease. Managed care will also likely call for an increase in the use of other cost-efficient procedures, such as more use of medication and more group therapy. Therapists will no longer have the option of using long-term forms of therapy, primarily because of economic considerations. If this is the case, then therapists need to continue to focus on what works most effectively and efficiently. For therapists, giving early attention to client expectations may be one way to approach this problem.

Summary

In an article commenting on research concerning expectations about counseling, Tinsley (1992) supported continued programmatic research and chapters such as this one to allow researchers to build on previous studies while eliminating shortcomings of earlier work. He stated that many studies on expectations about counseling built on previous research by making minor changes in design or altering a demographic variable. He concluded that research is needed in four areas: (1) identification and measurement of expectations about counseling; (2) examination of the relationships between expectations, preferences, and perceptions; (3) modification of client expectations; and (4) the relation of expectations to counseling process and outcome.

After completing this review of the literature, it is apparent that the goal of the vast majority of the studies that have been conducted was to alter or examine demographic variables in clients or counselors, and then observe how changes affect expectations about counseling. A few studies have proposed alternative measures of expectations, and several have distinguished between expectations, perceptions, and preferences. Research is sorely needed in the areas of modification of expectations, however, and more research is needed regarding how expectations affect outcome.

References

Abrams, D. B., & Wilson, G. T. (1979). Effects of alcohol on social anxiety in women: Cognitive versus physiological processes. *Journal of Abnormal Psychology, 88,* 161–173.

Al-Darmaki, F., & Kivlighan, D. M., Jr. (1993). Congruence in client–counselor expectations for relationship and the working alliance. *Journal of Counseling Psychology, 40,* 379–384.

Andersen, B., & Anderson, W. (1985). Client perceptions of counselors using positive and negative self-involving statements. *Journal of Counseling Psychology, 32,* 462–465.

Apfelbaum, D. (1958). *Dimensions of transference in psychotherapy.* Berkeley: University of California Press.

Arnold, R. A. (1985, March). Career decision-making difficulties as a result of cognitive, social and emotional deficits: A conceptual model. In H. E. A. Tinsley (Chair), *Assessment of Career Development Constructs.* Symposium presented at the meeting of the American College Personnel Association, Boston.

Atkinson, D. R., & Wampold, B. E. (1982). A comparison of the Counselor Rating Form and the Counselor Effectiveness Rating Scale. *Counselor Education and Supervision, 22,* 25–36.

Bandura, A. (1986). *Social foundations of thought and action: A social cognitive theory.* Englewood Cliffs, NJ: Prentice-Hall.

Barak, A., & LaCrosse, M. B. (1975). Multidimensional perception of counselor behavior. *Journal of Counseling Psychology, 22,* 471–476.

Barrett-Lennard, G. T. (1962). Dimensions of therapist response as causal factors in therapeutic change. *Psychological Monographs, 76* (43, Whole No. 562).

Barron, M. R., Daniels, J. L., & O'Toole, W. M. (1987). The effect of computer-conducted versus counselor-conducted initial intake interviews on client expectancy. *Computers in Human Behavior, 3,* 21–28.

Bassett, R. L., Sadler, R. D., Kobischen, E. E., Skiff, D. M., Merrill, I. J., Atwater, B. J., & Livermore, P. W. (1981). The Shepherd Scale: Separating the sheep from the goats. *Journal of Psychology and Theology, 9,* 335–351.

Bem, S. (1974). The measurement of psychological androgyny. *Journal of Consulting and Clinical Psychology, 12,* 155–162.

Bordin, E. S. (1979). The generalizability of the psychoanalytic concept of the working alliance. *Psychotherapy: Theory, Research and Practice, 16,* 252–268.

Brammer, L. M., & Shostrom, E. L. (1960). *Therapeutic psychology.* Englewood Cliffs, NJ: Prentice-Hall.

Brems, C., & Johnson, M. E. (1991). Re-examination of the Bem Sex Role Inventory: The Interpersonal BSRI. *Journal of Personality Assessment, 55,* 484–498.

Buck, J. N., & Daniels, M. H. (1985). *Assessment of career decision making (ACDM) manual.* Los Angeles: Western Psychological Services.

Carter, J. A. (1978). Impressions of counselors as a function of counselor physical attractiveness. *Journal of Counseling Psychology, 25,* 28–34.

Carter, R. T., & Akinsulure-Smith, A. M. (1996). White racial identity and expectations about counseling. *Journal of Multicultural Counseling and Development, 24,* 218–228.

Craig, S. S., & Hennessy, J. J. (1989). Personality differences and expectations about counseling. *Journal of Counseling Psychology, 36,* 401–407.

Crowne, D., & Marlowe, D. (1964). *The approval motive.* New York: Wiley.

Cuellar, I., Harris, L. C., & Jasso, R. (1980). An acculturation scale for Mexican American normal and clinical populations. *Hispanic Journal of Behavioral Sciences, 2,* 199–207.

Cutter, H. S., Maloof, B., Kurtz, N. R., & Jones, W. C. (1976). Feeling no pain: Differential responses to pain by alcoholics and non-alcoholics before and after drinking. *Journal of Studies on Alcohol, 37,* 273–277.

Dorn, F. J. (1989). An examination of client motivation and career certainty. *Journal of College Student Development, 30,* 237–241.

Feltham, C. (Ed.). (1997). *Which psychotherapy? Leading exponents explain their differences.* London: Sage.

Foon, A. E. (1986). Effect of locus of control on counseling expectations of clients. *Journal of Counseling Psychology, 33,* 462–464.

Galassi, J. P., Crace, R. K., Martin, G. A., James, R. M., & Wallace, R. L. (1992). Client preferences and anticipations in career counseling: A preliminary investigation. *Journal of Counseling Psychology, 39,* 46–55.

Giorgi, A. (1985). Sketch of a psychological phenomenological method. In A. Giorgi (Ed.), *Phenomenology and psychological research* (pp. 82–103). Pittsburgh, PA: Duquesne University.

Gladstein, G. A. (1969). Client expectations, counseling experience, and satisfaction. *Journal of Counseling Psychology, 16,* 476–481.

Godwin, T. C., & Crouch, J. G. (1989). Subjects' religious orientation, counselor orientation and skill, and expectations for counseling. *Journal of Psychology and Theology, 17,* 284–292.

Goldstein, A. P. (1966). Psychotherapy research by extrapolation from social psychology. *Journal of Counseling Psychology, 13,* 38–45.

Gough, H. G., & Heilbrun, A. B., Jr. (1980). *The Adjective Check List manual.* Palo Alto, CA: Consulting Psychologists Press.

Grosz, R. D. (1968). Effect of client expectations on the counseling relationship. *Personnel and Guidance Journal, 46,* 797–800.

Hardin, S. I., & Subich, L. M. (1985). A methodological note: Do students expect what clients do? *Journal of Counseling Psychology, 32,* 131–134.

Hardin, S. I., Subich, L. M., & Holvey, J. M. (1988). Expectancies for counseling in relation to premature termination. *Journal of Counseling Psychology, 35,* 37–40.

Hardin, S. I., & Yanico, B. (1983). Counselor gender, type of problem, and expectations about counseling. *Journal of Counseling Psychology, 30,* 37–40.

Harren, V. (1980). *Assessment of career decision making (ACDM): Preliminary manual.* Unpublished manuscript, Southern Illinois University.

Harvey, O. J. (1969). *Belief systems and education: Some implications for change.* Unpublished manuscript, University of Colorado, Boulder.

Harvey, O. J., Hunt, D. E., & Schroder, H. M. (1961). *Conceptual systems and personality organization.* New York: Wiley.

Hayes, T. J., & Tinsley, H. E. A. (1989). Identification of the latent dimensions of instruments that measure perception of and expectations about counseling. *Journal of Counseling Psychology, 36,* 492–500.

Helms, J. E., & Carter, R. T. (1990). Development of the White Racial Attitude Scale. In J. E. Helms (Ed.), *Black and White racial identity: Theory, research, and practice* (pp. 66–80). Westport, CT: Greenwood.

Heppner, P. P., & Heesacker, M. (1982). Interpersonal influence process in real-life counseling: Investigating client perceptions, counselor experience level and counselor power over time. *Journal of Counseling Psychology, 29,* 215–223.

Heppner, P. P., & Heesacker, M. (1983). Perceived counselor characteristics, client expectations, and client satisfaction with counseling. *Journal of Counseling Psychology, 30,* 31–39.

Horvath, A. O., & Greenberg, L. (1989). The development and validation of the Working Alliance Inventory. *Journal of Counseling Psychology, 36,* 223–232.

Ivey, A. E. (1971). *Microcounseling: Innovations in interview training.* Springfield, IL: Charles C Thomas.

Johnson, M. E., & Knackstedt, G. (1993). Sex role orientation and expectations about counseling. *The Journal of Psychology, 127,* 427–434.

Johnson, M. E., & Lashley, K. H. (1989). Influence of Native Americans' cultural commitment on preferences for counselor ethnicity and expectations about counseling. *Journal of Multicultural Counseling and Development, 17,* 115–122.

Kemp, A. D. (1994). African-American students' expectations about counseling: A comparative investigation. *Journal of Multicultural Counseling and Development, 22,* 257–264.

Kenney, G. E. (1994). Multicultural investigation of counseling expectations and preferences. *Journal of College Student Psychotherapy, 9,* 21–39.

Kim, U. (1988). *Acculturation of Korean immigrants to Canada: Psychological, demographic, and behavioral profiles of emigrating Koreans, non-emigrating Koreans, and Korean-Canadians.* Unpublished doctoral dissertation, Queens University, Kingston, Canada.

Klein, M. H., Mathieu, P. L., Gendlin, E. T., & Kiesler, D. J. (1969). *The Experiencing Scale: A research and training manual* (Vol. 1). Madison: University of Wisconsin Extension Bureau of Audiovisual Instruction.

Kokotovic, A. M., & Tracey, T. J. (1987). Premature termination at a university counseling center. *Journal of Counseling Psychology, 37,* 16–21.

Kunkel, M. A. (1990). Expectations about counseling in relation to acculturation in Mexican-American and Anglo-American student samples. *Journal of Counseling Psychology, 37,* 286–292.

Kunkel, M. A., Hector, M. A., Coronado, E. G., & Vales, V. C. (1989). Expectations about counseling in Yucatan, Mexico: Toward a "Mexican psychology." *Journal of Counseling Psychology, 36,* 322–330.

Kunkel, M. A., & Williams, C. (1991). Age and expectations about counseling: Two methodological perspectives. *Journal of Counseling and Development, 70,* 314–320.

Lang, A. R., Goeckner, D. J., Adesso, V. J., & Marlatt, G. A. (1975). Effects of alcohol on aggression in male social drinkers. *Journal of Abnormal Psychology, 84,* 508–518.

Lazarus, A. (1971). *Behavior therapy and beyond.* New York: McGraw-Hill.

Lazo, J. A. (1983). *1983 APA membership register.* Washington, DC: American Psychological Association.

Leong, F. T. L., Wagner, N. S., & Kim, H. H. (1995). Group counseling expectations among Asian American students: The role of culture-specific factors. *Journal of Counseling Psychology, 42,* 217–222.

Leong, S. L., Leong, F. T. L., & Hoffman, M. A. (1987). Counseling expectations of rational, intuitive, and dependent decision makers. *Journal of Counseling Psychology, 34,* 261–265.

Linden, J. D., Stone, S. C., & Schertzer, B. (1965). Development and evaluation of an inventory for rating counseling. *Personnel and Guidance Journal, 44,* 267–276.

Longo, D. A., Lent, R. W., & Brown, S. D. (1992). Social cognitive variables in the prediction of client motivation and attrition. *Journal of Counseling Psychology, 39,* 447–452.

MacAndrew, C., & Edgerton, R. B. (1969). *Drunken comportment.* Chicago: Aldine.

Marlatt, G. A., Demming, B., & Reid, J. B. (1973). Loss of control drinking in alcoholics: An experimental analogue. *Journal of Abnormal Psychology, 81,* 233–241.

McConnaughy, E. A., Prochaska, J. O., & Velicer, W. F. (1983). Stages of change in psychotherapy: Measurement and sample profiles. *Psychotherapy: Theory, Research and Practice, 20,* 368–375.

Osipow, S., Carney, C., Winer, J., Yanico, B., & Koschir, M. (1976). *The Career Decision Scale.* Columbus, OH: Marathon Consulting.

Parham, W. D., & Tinsley, H. E. A. (1980). What are friends for? Students' expectations of the friendship encounter. *Journal of Counseling Psychology, 27,* 524–527.

Parish, T. S., Bryant, W. T., & Shirazi, A. (1976). The Personal Attribute Inventory. *Perceptual and Motor Skills, 42,* 715–720.

Pecnik, J. A., & Epperson, D. L. (1985). Analogue study of expectations for Christian and traditional counseling. *Journal of Counseling Psychology, 32,* 127–130.

Prochaska, J. O., & DiClemente, C. C. (1992). Stages of change in the modification of problem behaviors. In M. Hersen, R. M. Eisler, & P. M. Miller (Eds.), *Progress in behavior modification* (pp. 163–200). New York: Brunner/Mazel.

Quinn, S. R. (1983). *The effects of a precounseling orientation program upon client expectations of counseling.* Unpublished master's thesis, California State University, Fresno.

Rainwater, G., & Coe, D. (1984). *Psychological/social history report* [Computer program]. Indian Harbour Beach, FL: Psychometric Software.

Rogers, C. R. (1961). *On becoming a person.* Boston: Houghton Mifflin.

Rohsenow, D. J. (1983). Drinking habits and expectancies about alcohol's effects for self versus others. *Journal of Consulting and Clinical Psychology, 51,* 752–756.

Rosenberg, M. (1965). *Society and the adolescent self-image.* Princeton, NJ: Princeton University Press.

Rotter, J. B. (1954). *Social learning and clinical psychology.* New York: Prentice-Hall.

Rotter, J. B. (1966). Generalized expectancies for internal versus external control of reinforcement. *Psychological Monographs, 80* (1, Whole No. 609).

Satterfield, W. A., Buelow, S. A., Lyddon, W. J., & Johnson, J. T. (1995). Client stages of change and expectations about counseling. *Journal of Counseling Psychology, 42,* 476–478.

Schneider, L. J. (1985). Feminist values in announcements of professional services. *Journal of Counseling Psychology, 32,* 637–640.

Sipps, G. J., & Janeczek, R. G. (1986). Expectancies for counselors in relation to subject gender traits. *Journal of Counseling Psychology, 33,* 214–216.

Slocum, Y. S. (1987). A survey of expectations about group therapy among clinical and nonclinical populations. *International Journal of Group Psychotherapy, 37,* 39–54.

Smith, H. D., & Quinn, S. R. (1985). The effects of two precounseling orientation presentations on client expectations of counseling. *Counselor Education and Supervision, 24,* 244–248.

Sobel, H. J., & O'Brien, B. A. (1979). Expectations for counseling success. *Journal of Counseling Psychology, 26,* 462–464.

Spence, J. T., & Helmrich, R. (1979). *Personal Attributes Questionnaire (PAQ).* Unpublished manuscript, University of Texas at Austin, Department of Psychology.

Spielberger, C. D. (1983). *Manual for the State-Trait Anxiety Inventory.* Palo Alto, CA: Consulting Psychologists Press.

Strong, S. R. (1968). Counseling: An interpersonal influence process. *Journal of Counseling Psychology, 15,* 215–224.

Subich, L. M. (1983). Expectancies for counselors as a function of counselor gender specification and subject sex. *Journal of Counseling Psychology, 30,* 421–424.

Subich, L. M., & Coursol, D. H. (1985). Counseling expectations of clients and nonclients for group and individual treatment modes. *Journal of Counseling Psychology, 32,* 245–251.

Subich, L. M., & Hardin, S. I. (1985). Counseling expectations as a function of fee for services. *Journal of Counseling Psychology, 32,* 323–328.

Terrell, F., & Terrell, S. L. (1981). An inventory to measure cultural mistrust among Blacks. *Western Journal of Black Studies, 5,* 180–184.

Thro, E. G., & Hollis, J. W. (1973). *Client expectancy inventory.* Muncie, IN: Accelerated Development.

Tinsley, D. J., Hinson, J. A., Holt, M. S., & Tinsley, H. E. A. (1990). Level of psychosocial development, perceived level of psychological difficulty, counseling readiness, and expectations about counseling: Examination of group differences. *Journal of Counseling Psychology, 37,* 143–148.

Tinsley, D. J., Holt, M. S., Hinson, J. A., & Tinsley, H. E. A. (1991). A construct validation study of the expectations about counseling—brief form: Factorial validity. *Measurement and Evaluation in Counseling and Development, 24,* 101–110.

Tinsley, H. E. A. (1982). *Expectations about counseling.* Unpublished test manual, Southern Illinois University, Department of Psychology, Carbondale.

Tinsley, H. E. A. (1992). Am I the fifth horseman of the apocalypse? Comment on Galassi, Crace, Martin, James, and Wallace (1992) and comments on research concerning expectations about counseling. *Journal of Counseling Psychology, 39,* 59–65.

Tinsley, H. E. A., Bowman, S. L., & Barich, A. W. (1993). Counseling psychologists' perceptions of the occurrence and effects of unrealistic expectations about counseling and psychotherapy among their clients. *Journal of Counseling Psychology, 40,* 46–52.

Tinsley, H. E. A., Bowman, S. L., & Ray, S. B. (1988). Manipulation of expectancies about counseling and psychotherapy: Review and analysis of expectancy manipulation strategies and results. *Journal of Counseling Psychology, 35,* 99–108.

Tinsley, H. E. A., Brown, M. T., de St. Aubin, T. M., & Lucek, J. (1984). Relation between expectancies for a helping relationship and tendency to seek help from a campus help provider. *Journal of Counseling Psychology, 31,* 149–160.

Tinsley, H. E. A., de St. Aubin, T. M., & Brown, M. T. (1982). College students' help-seeking preferences. *Journal of Counseling Psychology, 29,* 523–533.

Tinsley, H. E. A., & Harris, D. J. (1976). Client expectations for counseling. *Journal of Counseling Psychology, 23,* 173–177.

Tinsley, H. E. A., Tokar, D. M., & Helwig, S. E. (1994). Client expectations about counseling and involvement during career counseling. *The Career Development Quarterly, 42,* 326–336.

Tinsley, H. E. A., & Westcot, A. M. (1990). Analysis of cognitions stimulated by the items on the expectations about counseling—brief form: An analysis of construct validity. *Journal of Counseling Psychology, 37,* 223–226.

Tinsley, H. E. A., Workman, K. R., & Kass. R. A. (1980). Factor analysis of the domain of client expectancies about counseling. *Journal of Counseling Psychology, 27,* 561–570.

Titchener, E. B. (1909). *Lectures on the experimental psychology of the thought processes.* New York: Macmillan.

Tokar, D. M., Hardin, S. I., Adams, E. M., & Brandel, I. W. (1996). Clients' expectations about counseling and perceptions of the working alliance. *Journal of College Student Psychotherapy, 11,* 9–26.

Truax, C. B., & Carkhuff, R. R. (1967). *Toward effective counseling and psychotherapy.* Chicago: Aldine.

Volsky, T., Magoon, T. M., Norman, W. T., & Hoyt, D. P. (1965). *The outcome of counseling and psychotherapy.* Minneapolis: University of Minnesota Press.

Vroom, V. H. (1964). *Work and motivation.* New York: Wiley.

Watkins, C. E., & Terrell, F. (1988). Mistrust level and its effects on counseling expectations in Black client–White counselor relationships: An analogue study. *Journal of Counseling Psychology, 35,* 194–197.

Watkins, C. E., Terrell, F., Miller, F. S., & Terrell, S. L. (1989). Cultural mistrust and its effects on exceptional variables in Black client–White counselor relationships. *Journal of Counseling Psychology, 36,* 447–450.

Winston, R. B., Miller, T. K., & Prince, J. S. (1979). *Assessing student development: A preliminary manual for the Student Developmental Task Inventory* (Rev., 2nd ed.). Athens, GA: Student Development Associates.

Workman, E. A., & Williams, R. L. (1979). A brief method for determining the effect of selected counselor characteristics on clients' expectations of counseling success. *Journal of Behavior Therapy and Experimental Psychiatry, 10,* 41–45.

Yanico, B. J., & Hardin, S. I. (1985). Relation of type of problem and expectations of counselor knowledge and understanding to students' gender preferences for counselors. *Journal of Counseling Psychology, 32,* 197–205.

Yuen, R. K., & Tinsley, H. E. A. (1981). International and American students' expectations about counseling. *Journal of Counseling Psychology, 28,* 66–69.

Zane, N. (1991). *An empirical examination of loss of face among Asian Americans.* Unpublished manuscript, Graduate School of Education, University of California, Santa Barbara.

3

Understanding Client Resistance in Therapy

Implications From Research on the Counseling Process

James R. Mahalik
Boston College

Therapy represents a collaboration between client and therapist to ameliorate client problems. When this collaboration breaks down because the client does not cooperate by disclosing information or carrying out certain behaviors, therapy cannot be effective and the client may even leave treatment prematurely. This chapter discusses client resistance research from a psychodynamic-humanistic perspective. Resistance, however, is a pantheoretical concept. It occurs in all therapies regardless of therapeutic orientation. Thus, the research findings and suggestions are applicable to all types of therapies with all types of clients.

Chapter Questions

- How do clients express resistance?
- How does resistance affect clients' in-session behavior?
- How does resistance relate to therapeutic technique and therapist characteristics?
- How does resistance change over the course of successful therapy?

Resistance means opposition (Greenson, 1967). Descriptions of resistance in the psychotherapy literature focus on client resistance as an obstacle to therapeutic work in psychotherapy as in Greenson's (1967) observation that "resistance opposes the analytic procedure, the analyst, and the patient's reasonable ego. Resistance defends the neurosis, the old, the familiar, and the infantile from exposure and change" (p. 77). Patton and Meara (1992) describe resistance in these terms: "Resistance defends maladaptive solutions to problems and opposes the disclosure of these problems in counseling. Needless to say, resistance interferes with the client's capacity to understand and to change" (p. 204). Mahalik (1994) formulates resistance in the following way: "With its motivation being the avoidance of painful affect, resistance opposes the client's recollection of therapeutic material, as well as the therapist's efforts, change, and insight" (p. 58).

Because of this obstacle-like quality to client resistance, it is often described as something to be overcome or broken through in a way that suggests that resistance is strictly countertherapeutic in therapy. Basch (1982) captured this pejorative characterization of resistance when he wrote, "Resistance is a much more frustrating phenomenon if we believe on some level that the patient is willfully opposing us and could, if he were only a nicer person and less bent on making our life miserable, do something about it" (p. 4).

Although this obstacle-like quality reflected Freud's (1959) initial formulation of resistance, client resistance is also rich with opportunities to move the therapeutic work forward. Freud's later work (c.f., Freud, 1964) reflected this rethinking about resistance when he discussed resistances themselves as contributing important information about the patient, his or her symptomology, and feelings about the analysis and analyst.

Expanding on this notion that resistance is not all bad, Patton and Meara (1992) identified two important purposes that can be achieved through working with client resistances. First, by helping the clients talk directly about resistances they may be manifesting in session, therapists help the clients communicate more freely in the interview. For example, the therapist might ask the client what makes it difficult to talk about a certain topic or what might happen if the client were to act differently. This would be an example of the therapist working directly with the resistance rather than interpreting the meaning of the client's anxiety about that topic.

Patton and Meara (1992) also viewed such direct work with the client's resistance as fulfilling a second purpose, namely, promoting insight. "In other words, understanding of the resistances provides the client with deepened knowledge of how his or her mind works" (p. 222). For example, clients may start to develop an awareness of how they are self-protective in relationships. Thus, resistance is understood to be both an obstacle and an opportunity in therapy, as it is both a technical problem in the therapeutic work (i.e., opposition) and a signal that something very important is happening for the client.

Resistance is also a useful phenomenon in paradoxical interventions to bring about client change. Whereas dynamic approaches use client resistance as an opportunity for insight, paradoxical approaches use the opposition of the client to bring about client change. For example, the use of symptom prescription or restraining is seen as particularly effective with reactant (i.e., oppositional) clients (Dowd & Milne, 1986).

Because client resistance is a central concern in counseling and psychotherapy, client resistance is an important phenomenon in analytic (Greenson, 1967; Patton & Meara, 1992), cognitive-behavioral (Goldfried, 1982; Meichenbaum & Gilmore, 1982), gestalt (Breshgold, 1989), and rational-emotive psychotherapies (Ellis, 1985). Indeed, there is extensive clinical literature that discusses client resistance in terms of its structures (e.g., Blatt & Erlich, 1982), sources (e.g., Freud, 1959; Goldfried, 1982; Greenson, 1967), and manifestations in cases (e.g., Kohut, 1984). There is also no shortage of literature conceptualizing the phenomenon (Breshgold, 1989; Ellis, 1985; Goldfried, 1982; Horner, 1987;

Meichenbaum & Gilmore, 1982) or giving advice about how to work with resistance (e.g., Fenichel, 1941; Freud, 1958; Greenson, 1967; Langs, 1973; Lazarus & Fay, 1982; Madanes, 1981; Meichenbaum & Gilmore, 1982; Patton & Meara, 1992; Spinks & Birchler, 1982). Through reflections on their own clinical work, and that of their colleagues and students which they have observed, these persons have drawn our attention to the importance of resistance in psychotherapy and provided the field with a rich background for conceptualizing and working with resistance.

Given how extensive this clinical literature is about resistance, researchers who begin to study client resistance are often surprised at how little actual research evidence there is to either support or refute the ideas about resistance that have been put forward. Observations such as, "There has been relatively little data collected on client resistance, despite general agreement that client resistance is a critical phenomenon" (Stoolmiller, Duncan, Bank, & Patterson, 1993, p. 921) and "Although central in psychotherapy, client resistance has received little empirical attention concerning its relation to process and outcome in psychotherapy..." (Mahalik, 1994, p. 59), reflect the disparity between theoretical and empirical coverage of client resistance in the literature. The assessment by Patton, Kivlighan, and Multon (1997) is both most recent and fully descriptive of the current state of research on client resistance.

> Although a very large theoretical and clinical literature exists about resistance and how the counselor should address it, there are very few empirical studies that have investigated how it is recognized, what the effect of confronting resistance is on the client, what the relationship is between addressing resistance and client outcome, what the pattern of change is in client resistance across time, or how such a pattern of change relates to client outcome. (p. 191)

This is not to say that research on client resistance is nonexistent. Even as persons have noted the gap between the theoretical and empirical literatures (Luborsky, Barber, & Crits-Christoph, 1990), researchers have started to close this gap with their efforts to measure and examine client resistance empirically. Although some have focused on the phenomenon for more than one study (i.e., the Oregon Family Research Group and the Missouri Psychoanalytic Counseling Research Group), most efforts to examine client resistance have been unsustained. The result is that the literature on client resistance has little consistency regarding measurement, client or therapist samples from which to generalize findings, or types of treatments. Specifically, counseling process studies have used many different ways to operationalize resistance; they have studied very different client populations (e.g., families versus individual clients) with a variety of therapists (e.g., counselor trainees versus experienced therapists) and a wide variety of treatments (e.g., analytic-dynamic versus family).

In this chapter I examine what has been found in the psychotherapy process research literature and discuss some of the potential clinical implications of these findings. To do so, I have organized the chapter to focus on four aspects of the counseling process in relation to client resistance. In the first section, process research findings are reviewed that examine how clients manifest resistance and client characteristics that have been examined as affecting resistance. In the second section, process research findings are reported about how therapists and their characteristics affect client resistance. In the third section, process research examining the connection between therapeutic techniques and client resistance is examined. The last section of the review examines the relationship between client resistance and counseling outcome. Specifically, in this last section, I report on the findings of process studies that examine patterns of client resistance across the course of treatment and how those patterns of resistance relate to counseling outcome. Given the importance of client resistance to counseling and therapy as described previously, it is hoped that such an overview may provide guidance to practitioners in their work with clients.

Client Factors and Client Resistance

The three sets of studies reviewed in this section examine how clients manifest resistance in sessions, the effects of resistance on other clients verbal behavior, and what client characteristics are associated with resistance. The first set of studies focuses on how clients manifest resistance in sessions. This is a central concern for the counselor and therapist because "before we can analyze a resistance we have to be able to recognize it" (Greenson, 1967, p. 60). Thus, the first studies reviewed in this section focus on the different ways in which client resistance shows itself, verbally, in sessions. Specifically, these studies identified client verbalizations of resistance in sessions and differences in the ways in which clients are verbally resistant in sessions. Using the Client Resistance Scale, Mahalik (1994) examined the verbal structure of client resistance by measuring clients' opposition to expressing painful feelings, opposition to recalling therapeutic material, opposition to the directions of the therapist, opposition to change, and opposition to insight. By examining two clients (i.e., Gloria and Richard) in individual counseling with expert therapists (i.e., Rogers, Ellis, and Perls with Gloria; Meichenbaum, Beck, and Strupp with Richard), Mahalik (1994) found that clients differed in the manner in which they expressed resistance. Specifically, these two clients differed in terms of opposition to expressing painful feelings and opposition to insight.

In another study that reported client differences in resistance, Schuller, Crits-Cristoph, and Connolly (1991) used the Resistance Scale to evaluate the frequency and intensity of client resistance in 20 patients who differed on outcome. Their examination of client resistance through the subscales of Abrupt/Shifting, Oppositional, Flat/Halting, and Vague/Doubting found that individual differences among patients accounted for the majority of variability in the study. Finally, Patton et al. (1997) using the Resistance Scale reported substantial variation between clients in how much midtreatment resistance they displayed as well as the level of resistance decrease in individual clients.

These results indicated that, in general, clients exhibit resistance in different ways. The results also provide support for the notion that how resistance becomes evident in counseling sessions is as individual as the client him or herself. Greenson (1967) addresses this notion of the many forms of resistance when he writes "resistance may be conscious, preconscious, or unconscious, and may be expressed by means of emotions, attitudes, ideas, impulses, thoughts, fantasies, or actions" (p. 60). The individual studies discussed different issues regarding the purpose of these different manifestations of resistance. Mahalik's (1994) conclusion was that clients protected themselves from anxiety during sessions in different ways. Specifically, the male client Richard was more oppositional both in avoiding expressions of painful affect and insight in comparison to the female client Gloria. Speculatively, gender differences in how men and women are socialized to express emotion and be action oriented versus insight oriented may have contributed to these differences.

Schuller et al. (1991) concluded that these differences were indicative of characterological resistance. That is, the individual personality structures of clients contributed to the ways in which they managed anxiety in sessions. Although Patton et al. (1997) did not make specific conclusions about the individual differences in midtreatment resistance, one easily perceives that the individual client experiences of therapy at midtreatment would contribute to the individual manifestations of resistance in sessions.

I believe these results are of note for clinicians because they highlight the variability of how clients manifest resistance. Specifically, whether because of gender role socialization, reactance potential, or transference, how one client opposes the therapeutic work, the counselor, or change is different than how another client would do this. Because of this individual variability, it is of central importance that therapists recognize the idiosyncratic way that individuals may protect themselves in therapeutic work and the manner in which that may change during the course of treatment.

In the second set of studies, Hill et al. (1992) examined eight cases of short-term psychotherapy and found that lower client experiencing levels (Klein, Mathieu-Couglan, & Kiesler, 1986) were associated with client resistance. Another study examined client primary process and secondary process content in relation to resistant client sessions versus working ones (Reynes, Martindale, & Dahl, 1984). This study reported that clients demonstrated significantly more primary process content (i.e., dealing with drives, sensations, and regression) in working sessions as opposed to resistant sessions, whereas secondary process content (i.e., dealing with restraint, abstraction, social behavior, and moral imperatives) was significantly higher in resistant sessions compared to working ones.

The fact that these two studies showed client resistance to be related to less personal involvement and vulnerability in the way that clients talked in sessions is very important given the findings of the first set of studies. Namely, because client resistance is so idiosyncratic in the form it takes in sessions (Greenson, 1967, p. 60), the results of these studies suggest that, although the form of resistance may reflect the individual histories, dynamics, and contextual experiences of clients, the clinician can recognize that it is happening when the client becomes less involved and less open in the therapeutic process.

The third set of studies that focused on the client examined client pathology and negativity toward counseling to predict resistance. Examining client pathology, Horenstein (1973) focused on how client pathology in the initial phase of counseling was related to several phenomenon including resistance. Client pathology was measured using client self-ratings of severity in 10 areas (e.g, somatic complaints) and clinicians ratings of severity based on client written statements about problems in the 10 areas. Results indicated that although initial client disturbance was related to other variables in the study, for example, expectations of therapy, it was unrelated to resistance.

Two other studies found client negativity toward counseling to be associated with resistance. Exploring resistance in career counseling, Kerr, Olson, Claiborn, Bauers-Gruenler, and Paolo (1983) operationalized negative attitudes toward counseling as low scores on the Counselor Rating Form (Barak & LaCrosse, 1975) and the Counseling Semantic Differential (Grosz, 1968). Their results indicated that negative attitudes toward counseling predicted greater client resistance.

In a study examining families seeking treatment for child management problems, Chamberlain, Patterson, Reid, Kavanagh, and Forgatch (1984) examined resistance in relation to whether families were self-referred or agency-referred. Their results indicated that families who dropped out of treatment, as well as those who were agency-referred, demonstrated greater resistance than those who stayed in treatment and were self-referred.

Although the conclusion that clients with negative attitudes toward counseling are more resistant in counseling may not seem earth shattering to the reader, I believe the findings provide an important reminder of the priority of attending to the client's feelings and attitudes about coming to counseling and therapy. In an ideal therapeutic world, clients would be interested in counseling and therapy, willing and open to talk about the issues that contribute to their presenting problems, and follow through on the directions that the therapist suggests because they are open to change. Actual clients, however, vary considerably on all of these characteristics (Goldfried, 1982). The clinician would do well to anticipate negativity toward counseling and therapy, and pay special attention to the client who seems negative as they begin work. Working directly with the client's negativity may help reduce the client's fear of counseling (Patton & Meara, 1992), cover inaccurate notions about what happens in sessions, or realize the source of negative attitudes toward counseling (e.g., beliefs that "I should be able to solve my own problems").

Therapist Factors and Resistance

Studies reviewed in this section examined whether different therapists elicited different amounts of client resistance, what therapist characteristics were predictive of client resistance, and therapist in-session behavior that distinguished resistant from working sessions. Consistent with those who see resistance as a cooperative failure between client and therapist goals (Adler, 1956; Dreikers, 1967; Langs, 1981), Mahalik (1994) found that therapists affected the type and degree of resistance manifested by the two clients in sessions. Specifically, when Gloria was the client, Ellis elicited more opposition to expressing painful feelings than did Perls or Rogers, and Perls elicited more opposition to insight than did Rogers or Ellis. When Richard was the client, Beck and Strupp elicited more opposition to expressing painful feelings and more opposition to change than Meichenbaum.

I believe these findings help illustrate how client resistance can be a cooperative failure between the client's and therapist's goals. For example, it is interesting to note that, in comparison to Rogers, Ellis seems to have affected Gloria to protect herself from painful feelings and Perls seems to have affected her to protect herself from painful insights. It is probably true, as with many clients when they first sit down with a counselor, that Gloria's implicit expectations were that the counselor would listen to her and that she would have a chance to tell her full story. I believe it is likely that Ellis' push to teach Gloria rather than to listen, and Perls' push to provoke insight rather than allow her to experience herself were both therapist-derived goals that were not congruent with client goals. In this case, the evidence that Rogers focused on understanding the client and allowing her to experience herself was congruent with Gloria's goals, and, therefore, allowed for the greater feeling and insight in her session with him as compared to her sessions with Ellis and Perls, respectively.

In another set of studies examining counselor characteristics, two studies examined resistance from the perspective of the Interpersonal Influence Model of counseling (Strong

& Matross, 1973) and found that specific counselor characteristics predicted client resistance. In the first study, Ruppel and Kaul (1982) reported that counselors perceived as untrustworthy elicited greater resistance in clients than trustworthy counselors.

That clients should be more resistant with counselors they do not trust should not be a big surprise. Similar to how the findings about client's negative attitudes toward counseling predicted resistance, however, this finding helps provide a reminder of the importance of the client experiencing trust in the session with the therapist. As the therapist starts to notice the client becoming less involved or less open in the therapeutic work (i.e., the effects of resistance), the therapist will likely need to attend to the therapeutic relationship especially as concerns trust. In this case, the client's emerging resistance likely reflects a decreasing sense of safety in the therapeutic work, possibly as a result of emerging therapeutic material, especially as the material involves the therapist.

In the second study examining resistance and interpersonal influence, it was found that expert counselors, as measured by the Counselor Rating Form, elicited greater resistance than attractive counselors in a career counseling study (Kerr et al., 1983). In drawing clinical lessons from their findings, one need look not much further than how Kerr et al. operationalized attractive counselors. What we find is that counselors who used first-person pronouns when communicating with clients, asked open-ended as opposed to closed-ended questions, self-disclosed, and were less formal in speech and dress brought about less resistance. In effect, the attractive counselor was more personally available to the client in that he created less personal distance between himself and the client by being informal, interested in the experiences of the client, and transparent through his use of self-disclosure. In a nutshell, I believe he was less threatening than the expert therapist, and clients in the study felt less need to be self-protective (i.e., resistant) with him.

In a study that examined therapist talking in resistant sessions compared to working and neutral sessions, Reynes et al. (1984) found that therapists talked more (i.e., used more sentences and produced more words) during resistant sessions. This finding is interesting because there are useful clinical lessons to be learned from these results regardless of the causal direction of influence. For example, it may be that talkative therapists create client resistance because clients feel the therapist is not listening to them. This may lead to clients feeling misunderstood and having less trust for the therapist. Or, it may be that during sessions when clients are resistant that therapists tend to feel anxious and respond with talkativeness to fill client silences or other manifestations of resistance. Regardless of the causal direction of this finding, therapists need to be aware of the amount of talking they are doing in sessions and to understand its possible affect on the relationship with the client or how it may reflect therapist anxiety when the client is particularly resistant.

Therapy Techniques and Resistance

Studies in this section examine how resistance varies as a function of therapist technique. Specifically, the section reviews results from process studies that have examined psychoanalytic techniques, paradoxical techniques, and other general therapist techniques. Interpretation and paradox are highlighted because they are considered to be especially effective techniques in working with resistance from the analytic and behavioral models, respectively (Wachtel, 1987).

Psychoanalytic Techniques

In the analytic and dynamic frameworks, therapist interpretation is seen as the unparalleled technique for fostering affect, insight, transference material, and reducing client resistance (Schuller et al., 1991). Comparing segments of interpretations and noninterpretations in four analytic cases, Garduk and Haggard (1972) found that interpretations were associated with increases in resistance (as reflected in defensive and oppositional associations). Using a similar procedure, Schuller et al. (1991) examined segments of interpretations and noninterpretations in 20 cases of analytic therapy. However, their results found no differences between interpretation and noninterpretation segments. By contrast, Mahalik (1994) reported that clients were less resistant following interpretations compared to noninterpretations, but this was only for opposing insight.

From an interpersonal influence perspective, when the counselor makes interpretations that are discrepant from the client's prior beliefs about the problem, the client should become more resistant (Claiborn, Ward, & Strong, 1981). However, Claiborn et al. (1981) reported that clients receiving interpretations discrepant from their prior beliefs about the problem were less resistant compared to clients who received interpretations congruent with their beliefs.

Jones and Gelso (1988) compared how resistant clients' reactions to tentative and absolutistic interpretations differed from nonresistant clients. They found no effects connected to different interpretation styles and client resistance types.

These results from this set of studies examining client resistance show a very inconsistent set of findings when interpretation's effect on resistance is examined in isolation. An improvement in methodology that assessed interpretation's effect on resistance in the context of other analytic techniques was presented in a study by Kivlighan, Multon, and Patton (1996). In this study Kivlighan et al. (1996) found that interpretation alone was insufficient for the reduction of resistance. In their study of 256 therapy sessions conducted by six masters-level clinicians with 18 college student clients, they developed a process scale to assess how therapists address client resistance. This scale was based on Greenson's (1967) recommendations for addressing resistance and included steps such as (1) recognizing the resistance, (2) letting it build, (3) intervening to increase resistance to help it be noticed, (4) clarifying and interpreting the painful aspects of it, then (5) working through the resistance.

Their findings indicated that addressing client resistance did not occur frequently in sessions. Counselors were able to highlight and interpret resistance, however, when clients' express it. That is, "client resistance in one session may serve as a signal for the counselor to increase his or her efforts to highlight and interpret resistance the following session" (Greenspan, 1967, p. 303). It was notable that when counselors highlighted or interpreted resistance there was more client resistance as Greenson (1967) would suggest. When counselors were exploring and working through resistance, however, client resistance scores decreased. Their results showed that increases in the therapists' exploring and working through clients' resistance in one session led to less client resistance in the next two sessions.

Their results also suggested that Greenson's (1967) five-stage framework for working with resistance could be reconstructed. Specifically, Kivlighan et al., (1996) found that a two-factor structure of Highlighting/Interpreting and Exploring/Working Through was a simpler representation for how therapists in their study worked with client resistance than Greenson's (1967) structure. These two resistance-addressing techniques also seemed to be mutually exclusive in a given session, but they built on each other from one session to the next. That is, counselors either attempted to highlight/interpret resistance or explore/work through resistance. When counselors attempted to highlight or interpret client resistance in one session, however, they were more likely to explore and work through resistance in the following session. Kivlighan et al. (1996) concluded that "this finding may suggest that reductions in client resistance depend upon both sets of counselor interventions in sequence" (p. 304).

Supportive of these findings was Patton et al. (1997) study that examined resistance and other analytic constructs in their study of short-term psychoanalytic counseling with college student clients and trainee counselors. Results from their study indicated that confronting and exploring client resistance in one session led to lower levels of client resistance during two subsequent counseling sessions.

What should be of particular interest to clinicians was Kivlighan et al.'s (1996) reconstruction of the process of working with resistance and the role that interpretation played in that reconstruction. Specifically, they believed their data indicated that therapists highlighted and interpreted resistance when they observed client resistance. This led to exploring and working through the resistance that then reduced client resistance. In this reconstruction, Kivlighan et al. described the continued importance of interpretation, but they clarified both the role of highlighting/interpreting resistance and the process of reducing client resistance. As they write, "the clinical implications of our proposition suggest that therapists will have to pay more attention to the process of working through rather than relying solely on interpretive activity to achieve reduction in resistance" (p. 304).

Paradox

Allgood, Bischoff, Smith, and Salts (1992) examined therapist interventions affecting resistance in couples and families in therapy. Specifically, paradox was compared to all other interventions in couples and family therapy. Results were only significant for husbands' statements, and indicated that paradoxical interventions were associated with more resistance, and surprisingly, defusing-conflict interventions (i.e., to manage or diffuse angry or hostile interchanges between spouses) were associated with the highest resistance.

Kolko and Milan (1983) described a multiple baseline analysis across treatment for three youths considered resistant to treatment. The intervention combined the use of reframing as a means of enhancing opposition to therapeutic directives and paradoxical prescription of problematic behavior. Results indicated improvement on a number of dimensions (e.g., classes attended and grades).

The results from these two studies suggest that paradox increases resistance as it should because it capitalizes on clients' reactivity (Dowd & Milne, 1986). This reflects a great difference between analytic writers who view the positive effects of working with resistance as insight (e.g., Patton & Meara, 1992) as opposed to paradoxical strategies that rely on the client's opposition itself to bring about behavior change (Dowd & Milne, 1986).

Other Techniques

Several studies have examined the effects of other techniques on client resistance. Most of these have defined techniques as counselor response modes. Patterson and Forgatch (1985) examined the impact of therapist behavior on client noncompliance. Two studies examining six and seven families, respectively, in parent training procedures found that therapists' efforts to teach and confront in parent training produced significant increases in client's resistance with them becoming more noncompliant. Support and facilitation were accompanied by reduced likelihood of noncompliance.

Mahalik (1994) reported that, in addition to interpretation, the most effective therapist techniques in working with client resistance were open questions and minimal encouragers, whereas the least effective technique was closed question. Similarly, Bischoff and Tracey (1995) found that clients were resistant or cooperative as a function of whether the therapist was directive or nondirective. Specifically, therapists' directive behavior led to greater client resistance.

Beyond these studies examining therapist response modes, Bisese (1990) examined four therapist communication styles (unidirectional, collaborative, engaged, disengaged) covaried with three levels of loci of relationships (past relationship, current out of therapy, transference) with resonant versus resistant responses as the dependent variable. Results indicated that resistant responses were significantly more associated with disengaged rather than engaged counselor style, and a unidirectional rather than a collaborative counselor style. Also, within the collaborative and unidirectional analysis, transference locus produced the least resistance compared to past and current relationship locus.

What seems consistent in these findings across types of techniques is that techniques using the therapist's power to interpret or prescribe action (e.g., paradox, closed question, being unidirectional) led to increases in opposition from clients. Although this represented a good outcome for paradoxical interventions, it was when interpretation was coupled with working through, or the therapist was attentive to the client through minimal encouragers and open question, and collaborative with the client rather than unidirectional that resistance was less present in the therapeutic work. Bischoff and Tracey (1995) suggest that "listening, encouraging, and supportive behaviors may be called for when a client's resistance level is unduly interfering with the development of an alliance or movement toward treatment goals" (p. 492).

Course of Treatment and Resistance

In this section, I examine how levels of client resistance at different times in treatment relate to treatment outcome. One of the first studies to examine overall client resistance level and treatment outcome was Buckley, Conte, Plutchik, Wild, and Karasu (1984). They examined a number of dynamic and process variables in 21 medical students in therapy. Their results indicated that greater resistance as judged by the therapist was related to poorer outcome rated by both therapists and clients.

All other studies examining treatment outcome examine the levels of client resistance over treatment in relation to treatment outcome. For example, Graff and Luborsky (1977) examined the relationship of resistance and transference to outcome in four cases of long-term psychoanalysis. Results indicated that the two relatively successful analyses—as judged by the analyst and analysand—showed a trend toward lower levels of rated resistance together with higher levels of rated transference. More specifically, a noticeable drop in resistance marked both at the end of treatment. The two less successful treatments showed that transference and resistance curves tended to be closely associated and that resistance did not show a marked drop over time in these treatments. These results suggest that as clients are able to experience transference, but not become oppositional, especially near the end of treatment, that therapy is more successful.

Patton et al. (1997) examined resistance and other analytic constructs in their study of short-term psychoanalytic counseling with college student clients and trainee counselors and found that greater client resistance was related to a poorer working alliance and increasing transference in subsequent sessions. When they examined the patterns of resistance during the course of counseling in relation to counseling outcome, they noted several significant patterns. First, there was an overall decrease in client resistance during treatment. Second, clients who had a low–high–low pattern of resistance demonstrated better outcome.

Examining topic initiation and following patterns in successful and unsuccessful counseling dyads, Tracey and Ray (1984) found that successful counseling dyads had increases in resistance during the middle stage of therapy, however, unsuccessful dyads did not increase in resistance during the middle stage of therapy. Tracey (1986) found that low client resistance levels were associated with poor outcome.

Examining resistance using the Client Resistance Code in 27 families who were self- or agency-referred for family counseling, Chamberlain et al. (1984) found that resistance varied during the early, middle, and later stages of treatment. Similar to findings from the studies previously cited, resistance tended to begin low, increase at midtreatment, and decrease during the end of treatment with more successful cases having lower levels of resistance at the end of treatment. Also, significantly more high-resistance families dropped out of treatment than low-resistance families.

The finding that appears to be very consistent among these studies is that successful outcome seems to be associated with clients being resistant, especially when client resistance is high during the middle of treatment and low near the end of treatment. This finding lends support to the notion discussed at the beginning of the chapter that resistance is both an obstacle and opportunity for clinical work to progress.

These results most likely illustrate the fact that successful clients in talk-oriented therapies are engaged in the therapeutic process such that by the middle of treatment the painful material is the focus of the work. A higher level of resistance during this time is natural for the client to try to cope with the painful material of this middle-working phase of treatment and provides an opportunity for counselors to highlight that resistance and work through it during the next phase of counseling.

It should be noted that high resistance during the middle phase itself may be both an opportunity and indicator that the client is engaged in the therapeutic process, but it is also a time when the client is likely to drop out of treatment. This middle phase of treatment during which there are increased levels of resistance puts a premium on the counselor's response to the client. What seems important for the counselor to do during this middle stage of counseling is to highlight and work through the client's resistance during this stage of treatment. This seems to lead to less client resistance during the termination phase of treatment and with an accompanying better outcome.

Nature of Research Findings

In interpreting the research findings from these studies, it is important to keep in mind the difficulty of measuring the construct of resistance. The major issue regarding the validity of these findings is that client resistance varies in its accessibility to the observer. For example, many resistances are primitive or deeply repressed and, therefore, inaccessible to the observer. Others are closer to consciousness and are more accessible to awareness and observation. As such, there are many forms of resistance these studies do not measure.

The studies that I reviewed in this chapter measured episodic (i.e., a transient and limited interruption of the therapeutic process, Blatt & Erlich, 1982) and tactical resistance (i.e., immediate, objectively observable phenomena such as oppositional behavior, Stone, 1973) and found these phenomenon to be associated with client, therapist, technique, and outcome effects. Although episodic or tactical resistance does not reflect the deepest levels of client resistance, "successful handling of resistance at this level is important because it helps the patient feel that he or she is safe and understood by the therapist, and it provides the patient with a model for dealing with more difficult issues" (Schuller et al., 1991, p. 198). As such, these studies are useful to clinicians in that they examine observable dimensions of resistance that are often obstacles to therapeutic work with clients, but they may also serve as indicators that something important is happening with the client that the therapist should note and respond to in such a way that advances the therapeutic process.

Summary

Taken together, the results from these studies suggest that factors associated with clients, therapists, and techniques influence client resistance and that there are patterns of client resistance associated with successful outcome. Specifically, clients appear to differ regarding the ways in which they are resistant (e.g., one may oppose the therapist's directions, but another may not be able to remember important details of events). This puts a premium on the therapist's ability to recognize that client resistance may be happening when the client becomes less involved and open in the therapeutic process.

An important source of client resistance appears to be negative attitudes toward the counselor or counseling process. That client negativity relates to client resistance provides an important reminder of the priority of attending to the client's feelings and attitudes about coming to counseling and therapy.

The results from these process studies also suggest that client resistance is an interactional phenomena. Specifically, client perceptions of counselors and therapists being untrustworthy or interpersonally distant contribute to client resistance. This highlights the importance of the therapeutic relationship with the client both during the initial phase of counseling when the client may be negative and during the middle phase of treatment when client resistance should increase as he or she uncovers more painful therapeutic material.

That resistance is an interactional phenomena is also supported by studies examining therapist techniques. Simply said, directive techniques (e.g., paradox, closed question, being unidirectional) tended to increase client resistance. It appears that techniques that improved the relationship (i.e., listening and supportive behaviors) reduce resistance. When working from a dynamic perspective, it also appears that interpretation by itself is insufficient to reduce resistance. Instead, when interpretation was coupled with working through, resistance decreased in the therapeutic work.

Although an increase in resistance represented a good outcome for paradoxical interventions as presenting symptoms reduced when clients were oppositional to therapists directives, this was not true for other individual and family treatments. In these cases a low–high–low pattern of resistance was associated with good outcome in treatment. Putting the pieces together from the process research findings on client resistance, it appears that good outcome in talk oriented therapies has to do with having a positive attitude toward counseling and a belief that the counselor is trustworthy and interpersonally available. These preconditions allow the client to engage in the therapeutic process and uncover painful therapeutic material, which subsequently elicits greater client resistance. Highlighting and working through the resistance with a trustworthy and interpersonally available therapist during the middle phase of treatment appears to lead to reduced client resistance during the termination phase of treatment and better outcome.

References

Adler, A. (1956). *The individual psychology of Alfred Adler.* (H. Ansbacher & R. Ansbacher, Eds.). New York: Basic Books.

Allgood, S., Bischoff, R., Smith, T., & Salts, C. (1992). Therapist interventions: Do they really influence client resistance? *The American Journal of Family Therapy, 20,* 333–340.

Barak, A., & LaCrosse, M. B. (1975). Multidemensional perception of counselor behavior. *Journal of Counseling Psychology, 22,* 471–476.

Basch, M. F. (1982). Dynamic psychotherapy and its frustrations. In P. L. Wachtel (Ed.), *Resistance: Psychodynamic and behavioral approaches* (pp. 69–91). New York: Plenum Press.

Bischoff, M. M., & Tracey, T. J. G. (1995). Client resistance as predicted by therapist behavior: A study of sequential dependence. *Journal of Counseling Psychology, 42,* 487–495.

Bisese, V. (1990). Therapist specific communication styles and patient resistance: An analogue study. *Counseling Psychology Quarterly, 3,* 171–182.

Blatt, S., & Erlich, H. (1982). Levels of resistance in the psychotherapeutic process. In P. L. Wachtel (Ed.),

Resistance: Psychodynamic and behavioral approaches (pp. 69–91). New York: Plenum Press.

Breshgold, E. (1989). Resistance in gestalt therapy: An historical theoretical perspective. *The Gestalt Journal, 12,* 73–102.

Buckley, P., Conte, H., Plutchik, R., Wild, K., & Karasu, T. (1984). Psychodynamic variables as predictors of psychotherapy outcome. *American Journal of Psychiatry, 141,* 742–748.

Chamberlain, P., Patterson, G., Reid, J., Kavanagh, K., & Forgatch, M. (1984). Observation of client resistance. *Behavior Therapy, 15,* 144–155.

Claiborn, C., Ward, S., & Strong, S. (1981). Effects of congruence between counselor interpretations and client beliefs. *Journal of Counseling Psychology, 28,* 101–109.

Dowd, E. T., & Milne, C. R. (1986). Paradoxical interventions in counseling psychology. *The Counseling Psychologist, 14,* 237–282.

Dreikers, R. (1967). *Psychodynamics, psychotherapy, and counseling.* Chicago: Alfred Adler Institute.

Ellis, A. (1985). *Overcoming resistance.* New York: Springer.

Fenichel, O. (1941). *Problems of psychoanalystic technique.* Albany, NY: The Psychoanalytic Quarterly.

Freud, S. (1958). The dynamics of transference. In J. Strachey (Ed. and Trans.), *The standard edition of the complete psychological works of Sigmund Freud* (Vol. 12, pp. 98–110). London: Hogarth Press. (Original work published 1912)

Freud, S. (1959). Inhibitions, symptoms, and anxiety. In J. Strachey (Ed. and Trans.), *The standard edition of the complete psychological works of Sigmund Freud* (Vol. 20, pp. 77–179). London: Hogarth Press. (Original work published 1912)

Freud, S. (1964). Analysis terminable and interminable. In J. Strachey (Ed. and Trans.), *The standard edition of the complete psychological works of Sigmund Freud* (Vol. 23, pp. 211–256). London: Hogarth Press. (Original work published 1912)

Garduk, E. L., & Haggard, E. A. (1972). Immediate effects on patients of psychoanalytic interpretations. *Psychological Issues, 7,* 1–85.

Goldfried, M. R. (1982). Resistance and clinical behavior therapy. In P. L. Wachtel (Ed.), *Resistance: Psychodynamic and behavioral approaches* (pp. 95–114). New York: Plenum Press.

Graff, H., & Luborsky, L. (1977). Long-term trends in transference and resistance: A report on a quantitative-analytic method applied to four psychoanalyses. *Journal of the American Psychoanalytic Association, 25,* 471–490.

Greenson, R. R. (1967). *The technique and practice of psychoanalysis* (Vol. 1). New York: International Universities Press.

Grosz, H. J. (1968). The depression-prone and depression-resistant sibling: A follow-up note on marital state. *British Journal of Psychiatry, 114,* 1559–1560.

Hill, C., Corbett, M., Kanitz, B., Rios, P., Lightsey, R., & Gomez, M. (1992). Client behavior in counseling and therapy sessions: Development of a pantheoretical measure. *Journal of Counseling Psychology, 39,* 539–549.

Horenstein, D. (1973). Correlate of initial client disturbance: Expectations for therapy, dropout, resistance, and demographic description. *Journal of Clinical Psychology, 31,* 709–715.

Horner, A. J. (1987). Object relations and transference resistance. In D. S. Milman & G. D. Goldman, (Eds.), *Techniques of working with resistance* (pp. 227–247). Northvale, NJ: Aronson.

Jones, A. S., & Gelso, C. J. (1988). Differential effects of style of interpretation: Another look. *Journal of Counseling Psychology, 35,* 363–369.

Kerr, B., Olson, D., Claiborn, C., Bauers-Gruenler, S., & Paolo, A. (1983). Overcoming opposition and resistance: Differential functions of expertness and attractiveness in career counseling. *Journal of Counseling Psychology, 30,* 323–331.

Kivlighan, D. M., Jr., Multon, K. D., & Patton, M. J. (1996). Development of the Missouri Addressing Resistance Scale. *Psychotherapy Research, 6,* 291–308.

Klein, M. H., Mathieu-Coughlan, P., & Kiesler, D. J. (1986). The Experiencing Scales. In L. Greenberg & W. Pinsof (Eds.), *The psychotherapeutic process: A research handbook* (pp. 21–71). New York: Guilford Press.

Kohut, H. (1984). *How does analysis cure?* Chicago: University of Chicago Press.

Kolko, D., & Milan, M. (1983). Reframing and paradoxical instruction to overcome "resistance" in the treatment of delinquent youths: A multiple baseline analysis. *Journal of Consulting and Clinical Psychology, 51,* 655–660.

Langs, R. (1973). *The technique of psychoanalytic psychotherapy* (Vols. 1 and 2). New York: Aronson.

Langs, R. (1981). *Resistance and interventions.* Northvale, NJ: Jason Aronson.

Lazarus, A. A., & Fay, A. (1982). Resistance or rationalization? A cognitive-behavioral perspective. In P. L. Wachtel (Ed.), *Resistance: Psychodynamic and behavioral approaches* (pp. 115–132). New York: Plenum Press.

Luborsky, L., Barber, J., & Crits-Christoph, P. (1990). Theory-based research for understanding the process of dynamic psychotherapy. *Journal of Consulting and Clinical Psychology, 58,* 281–287.

Madanes, C. (1981). *Strategic family therapy.* San Francisco: Jossey-Bass.

Mahalik, J. R. (1994). Development of the client resistance scale. *Journal of Counseling Psychology, 41,* 58–68.

Meichenbaum, D., & Gilmore, J. (1982). Resistance from a cognitive-behavioral perspective. In P. L. Wachtel (Ed.), *Resistance: Psychodymanic and behavioral approaches* (pp. 133–156). New York: Plenum Press.

Patterson, G., & Forgatch, M. (1985). Therapist behavior as a determinant for client noncompliance: A paradox for the behavior modifier. *Journal of Consulting and Clinical Psychology, 53,* 846–851.

Patton, M. J., Kivlighan, D. M., & Multon, K. D. (1997). The Missouri psychoanalytic counseling research project: Relation of changes in counseling process to client outcomes. *Journal of Counseling Psychology, 44,* 189–208.

Patton, M. J., & Meara, N. (1992). *Psychoanalytic counseling.* New York: Wiley.

Reynes, R., Martindale, C., & Dahl, H. (1984). Lexical differences between working and resistance sessions in psychoanalysis. *Journal of Clinical Psychology, 40,* 733–737.

Ruppel, G., & Kaul, T. (1982). Investigation of social influence theory's conception of client resistance. *Journal of Counseling Psychology, 29,* 232–239.

Schuller, R., Crits-Christoph, P., & Connolly, M. (1991). The Resistance Scale: Background and psychometric properties. *Psychoanalytic Psychology, 8,* 195–211.

Spinks, S. H., & Birchler, G. (1982). Behavioral systems martial therapy: Dealing with resistance. *Family Process, 21,* 169–185.

Stoolmiller, M., Duncan, T., Bank, L., & Patterson, G. R. (1993). Some problems and solutions in the study of change: Significant patterns in client resistance. *Journal of Consulting and Clinical Psychology, 61,* 920–928.

Stone, L. (1973). On resistance to the psychoanalytic process. *Psychoanalysis and Contemporary Science, 2,* 42–73.

Strong, S., & Matross, R. (1973). Change processes in counseling and psychotherapy. *Journal of Counseling Psychology, 20,* 25–37.

Tracey, T. J. (1986). Interactional correlates of premature termination. *Journal of Consulting and Clinical Psychology, 54,* 784–788.

Tracey, T. J., & Ray, P. B. (1984). Stages of successful time-limited counseling: An interactional examination. *Journal of Counseling Psychology, 31,* 13–27.

Wachtel, P. L. (1987). *Action and insight.* New York: Guilford Press.

The Working Alliance

A Flagship for the "Scientist-Practitioner" Model in Psychotherapy

Michael J. Constantino, Louis G. Castonguay, and Alexander J. Schut

Pennsylvania State University

For counseling to be effective regardless of the treatment approach used, therapists and clients must develop a strong collaborative bond. If clients experience few emotional connections with therapists and do not agree with the methods therapists employ to address problems or the goals of treatment, they may be uncooperative or leave therapy before their troubles have been resolved. The working alliance is not static, and therapist–client relationship problems occur during the course of all treatments. This chapter reviews the extensive working alliance literature and supplies therapists with numerous helpful suggestions from this research.

Chapter Questions

- What is the working alliance?
- How do therapist and client contribute to the alliance?
- How does the working alliance relate to therapy outcome?
- What changes occur in the alliance during the course of treatment?
- How can therapists effectively deal with alliance problems?

A considerable amount of empirical findings have demonstrated the effectiveness of the psychotherapeutic endeavor (see Lambert & Bergin, 1994). After half a century of systematic research, it can be confidently asserted that psychotherapy leads to greater client improvement than the absence of treatment, the use of placebos, or the implementation of pseudotherapies. The current state of research also strongly suggests that with the exception of a number of specific problems, such as panic disorders or phobias, different therapeutic modalities harvest similar clinical effects (Luborsky, Singer, & Luborsky, 1975; Smith & Glass, 1977; Stiles, Shapiro, & Elliott, 1986). These overarching findings have led psychotherapy researchers to ask two important questions: (1) How is psychotherapy effective? and (2) What are the potential common elements of different forms of treatment that are responsible for client improvement? Both of these lines of inquiry have led to an increased focus on the therapeutic relationship as an important determinant of change that merits extensive theoretical and empirical attention (Horvath & Greenberg, 1994; Horvath & Luborsky, 1993).

For a long time, clinicians of diverse orientations have vouched for the curative properties of the therapeutic relationship (see Goldfried & Pawdawer, 1982). The nature and impact of the client–therapist relationship has also captured the interest of researchers, because the therapeutic alliance has become one of the most comprehensively studied treatment variables (Horvath & Greenberg, 1994). Reflecting its conceptual and clinical significance, the alliance has also been deemed the quintessential integrative variable spanning all forms of treatment modalities (Wolfe & Goldfried, 1988)—even behavior therapies where relationship factors were initially disregarded as important mechanisms of change (Castonguay, 1993; Goldfried & Castonguay, 1992; Raue & Goldfried, 1994).

The goals of this chapter are to (1) provide a brief historical review of the development of the alliance construct and its definitions, (2) present the major empirical findings related to general facets of the alliance, and (3) discuss potential applications of these research findings to the practice of psychotherapy. Our survey and discussion of the literature leads us to conclude that the alliance is not only the integrative variable "par excellence" but also a perfect example of the viability of the scientist–practitioner model. The attention it has received in the field, indeed, illustrates the synergetic impact that clinical reflection and empirical investigation can have on our understanding of the process of therapeutic change.

Historical and Conceptual Background

The Therapeutic Relationship in Historical Context

As a distinct construct, the therapeutic relationship has its roots in early psychodynamic and client-centered traditions. In his early writings on the construct of transference, Freud (1913/1958) emphasized the critical role of the relationship between analyst and analysand, and he discussed the possibility and importance of developing a reality-based attachment early in the therapy process that differs from, but can coexist with, the positive or negative distortions patients direct toward their therapists (i.e., positive or negative transference). According to Freud, the affectionate attachment to and identification with the analyst stemmed from the nonconflictual, positive aspects of the patient's relationships with primary caregivers.

Following Freud's seminal work was the emergence of several terms that seemingly captured Freud's proposition of different dimensions of the relationship between therapist and patient. For example, Sterba (1934) coined the term *ego alliance* to reflect the relationship between the reasonable aspects of the patient and therapist and the patient's capacity to both experience and observe the work of the analysis. According to Sterba, therapeutic success was at least partly a function of the patient's mature ego functioning and ability to work within the therapist's framework for treatment. This aspect of the therapist–patient interaction would later be termed the *working alliance* as discussed in a later section.

Zetzel (1956) was the first to use the term *therapeutic alliance,* which, similar to Freud, she viewed as the emergence of a positive, nonneurotic attachment to the therapist. Also in line with Freud's thinking, this bonding and identification with the therapist was argued to have emerged from the positive, trusting elements of the mother–child relationship. Greenson (1965), also working within a psychodynamic framework, elaborated on the distinction between alliance and transference. He introduced the term *working alliance* to capture the patient's ability to collaboratively work on personally relevant issues even in the context of distorted perceptions of the therapist. Greenson (1967) postulated that the alliance represented the only element of the therapeutic encounter that was not manifested in relations outside of treatment.

In the client-centered tradition, Rogers (1951, 1957) was the leading figure in conceptualizing the therapeutic relationship as a set of therapist-offered conditions, such as empathy, unconditional positive regard, and congruency. Within this school of thought, the therapist is assumed to play the key role in forging the alliance via displayed understanding and active involvement with the client. Although Rogers posited that the therapist-offered conditions were both necessary *and* sufficient for clinical change, it has become more widely accepted that these conditions represent only part of the complex system of relationship factors operating within successful treatment (Gelso & Carter, 1985; Horvath & Symonds, 1991; Mitchell, Bozart, & Krauft, 1977). For example, Rogers' initial propositions failed to adequately address the role of the client in the development of the alliance, for example, *receptivity* to the therapist-offered conditions, by assuming a uniform response to the therapist's empathic stance (Horvath & Luborsky, 1993). Subsequent research has demonstrated that client receptivity, or openness, to the therapy process, which inherently involves the therapist–client relationship, is a determinant of successful treatment outcome (Constantino & Castonguay, 1999; Orlinksy, Grawe, & Parks, 1994; Stiles, Agnew-Davies, Hardy, Barkham, & Shapiro, 1998).

In the midst of emerging conceptualizations of the alliance, some psychodynamic theorists have been less embracing of the notion of the alliance as a separate force within the treatment setting (e.g., Brenner, 1979; Curtis, 1979; Freebury, 1989) out of fear that the construct only dilutes or misdirects what should be the main foci in quality dynamic psychotherapy—that is, interpretation of the transference reactions. This "alliance-as-transference" stance posits that the therapeutic relationship is perpetually marked by misperceptions and directed by the client's past interpersonal experiences (Horvath & Luborsky, 1993). According to such critics, the idea of any aspect of a working relationship outside of the transference is inconsistent with the actual dynamics taking place in the therapeutic forum (e.g., Deserno, 1998).

Despite these critical voices, the alliance has developed into a core and distinct psychotherapeutic construct. Expanding on early psychodynamic and client-centered formulations, it is now assumed that a comprehensive definition of the alliance needs to account for both the influence of past important relational experiences *and* the current interpersonal process taking place between the client and the therapist (Gaston, 1990). With this expansion, however, controversy has developed regarding the validity of the concept, especially considering its numerous definitions and proposed underlying dimensions in the literature (Gaston & Marmar, 1994). There is also variability concerning the function of the alliance and its role in the change process. Several of the definitions and proposed roles of the alliance are briefly described in the next section.

Definitions of the Alliance

Working from a psychodynamic perspective, Luborsky (1976) described two elements of the alliance that operate at different points in the treatment process. In this now-classic paper (see Luborsky, 2000), he posited that the alliance early in treatment (i.e., "Type I") is comprised of the client's self-perception of receiving therapist-offered helpfulness and supportiveness (thus incorporating the importance of the therapist's relational capacity to foster a positive treatment environment) and believing that change will ultimately take place. Later in treatment (i.e., "Type II"), the alliance involves a bondedness component and the experience of collaboratively working toward agreed-on therapeutic goals aimed at ameliorating the client's presenting problems (on which the therapist and client have agreed in their origin). Frieswyk et al. (1986), however, focused on the client's participation in the tasks of treatment as representative of the alliance. Although Frieswyk et al. placed less emphasis on the therapist's contributions to the alliance, these authors still posited that the patient's contributions necessarily interacted with the therapist's behaviors. Thus, although these definitions may have slightly differed on the level of focus, they both took into account the therapist's *and* client's roles in the development of the alliance, thereby expanding on the client-centered view of the therapeutic relationship. Moreover, such differences in definition are not necessarily at odds with each other if they are viewed as representing different, but complementary, dimensions of the global construct of the alliance (Gaston & Marmar, 1994). Taking this complementary perspective, the *therapeutic* alliance refers more to the affective elements of the client's collaboration in treatment vis-à-vis the therapist's working style and personality characteristics. The *working* alliance refers more to the task-oriented aspects of the client's collaboration with the therapist (Gaston, 1990).

In a landmark contribution, Bordin (1979, 1994) attempted to generalize the construct of alliance beyond its early containment to psychodynamic and client-centered traditions. His pantheoretical model posits three main alliance components: (1) agreement on treatment *goals* (a cognitive component that focuses on the desired outcomes that are the targets of intervention), (2) agreement on *tasks* to achieve stated goals (a cognitive component that focuses on the in-session behaviors aimed at producing the desired outcomes), and (3) client–therapist *bond* (an affective component that focuses on the positive personal attachments between the client and the therapist, such as trust and acceptance). Bordin's integrative, tripartite model also offered an alternative to the traditional dichotomy between technical and relational variables in psychotherapy by emphasizing that the two are interdependent elements of change-producing therapy (Bordin, 1994). According to Bordin (1994)

A strong alliance refers to a condition in which a person seeking change has found that the change agent can participate in the effort to shed light and open new doors without reducing the partnership to the pairing of a leader-therapist with an assistant-patient. Its strength revolves around the experience of new possibilities in the patient's struggle rather than faith in a charismatic therapist-magician. (p. 15)

In another transtheoretical perspective of the alliance, Gaston (1990) argued against the need to view the differing definitions of the alliance as being mutually exclusive. Rather, she posited that the proposed definitions of the alliance that had emerged within the field reflected the multidimensionality of this construct. According to this perspective, four dimensions of the alliance are both compatible and complementary. The first dimension refers to the establishment of an affective bond between the client and the therapist. The second dimension reflects the client's capacity to garner the necessary ego strength to work purposefully in treatment. The third element of the alliance is the collaborative agreement between the client and the therapist on the tasks and goals of therapy. Finally, the fourth element represents the therapist's empathic attunement to the client's emotional needs and general involvement in the client's therapeutic plight.

Henry and Strupp (1994) have defined the alliance in terms of complex interpersonal actions and reactions, which are captured by two fundamental dimensions: degree of affiliation (love versus hate) and degree of interdependence (enmeshment versus differentiation). For these authors, a good alliance manifests itself by reciprocal transactions that are affiliative, autonomy granting, and devoid of hostile control. Reflecting their psychodynamic background, Henry and Strupp also posited that the alliance is fundamentally grounded in parent–child relational experiences. According to this perspective, the alliance serves as the context in which the client can engage in a corrective relational experience with the therapist in a manner that resembles the structure of the caregiver–child relationship but, ideally, involves the incorporation of more adaptive interpersonal processes of imitation (based on therapist modeling of adaptive processes) and identification.

Proposed Functions of the Alliance

Several theoretical differences have also emerged with respect to the function of the alliance as an ingredient of change. For example, some theorists have posited that the relationship is curative in and of itself (e.g., Balint, 1968; Rogers, 1957). According to this view, the therapist-offered relationship provides a relational involvement that has not been previously experienced by the client. In Rogerian terms, the conditions of worth that were imposed by the client's parents and that dictated the client's evaluation of self are replaced by conditions of change (empathy, unconditional regard, congruence) fostering self-acceptance and personal actualization. A more accepting view by another (i.e., the therapist) is thought to have a direct curative impact on the client by improving the quality of the client's relational patterns in session, which can, ideally, be generalized to otherwise maladaptive interpersonal relationships outside of session (Frieswyk et al., 1986).

Others theorists, however, have viewed the establishment of a quality alliance as a prerequisite for the successful implementation of theory-prescribed techniques (e.g., Freud, 1913/1958; Greenson, 1965). According to this perspective, a good alliance may encourage the client to remain in treatment and may provide a positive backdrop to the therapeutic endeavor thereby allowing technical interventions to better take hold (Horvath & Symonds, 1991). Without the establishment of a quality alliance as a mediator for effective therapist interventions, the client may not be receptive to techniques of change, and a countertherapeutic process may ensue. Still other theorists have conceptualized the alliance as constantly interacting with techniques to produce positive change (e.g., Bordin, 1994; Zetzel, 1956).

Henry and Strupp's (1994) interpersonal perspective seems to have captured all of the preceding therapeutic functions of the alliance. According to Henry and Strupp, the therapeutic relationship can be curative in and of itself with respect to several aspects of outcome, such as change in interpersonal functioning or self-esteem via alterations of cyclical maladaptive patterns, or it can serve to provide an affective climate that is conducive to symptomatic reduction or interpersonal change via interaction with effective psychotherapeutic techniques. As concerns the latter route to change, a good alliance may serve to soften the effect of therapist interpretations that the client may be initially unable to handle (Hanley, 1994; Henry & Strupp, 1994). According to Henry and Strupp, a good alliance should also ultimately allow the client to internalize the therapist's treatment with acceptance and less hostility, and begin treating him- or herself in that same manner, thereby creating a positive shift in the self-concept. This view reflects the interpersonal principle of "introjection," whereby individuals tend to treat themselves as they have been treated by important others (Sullivan, 1953). To the extent that the therapist becomes an important other, Henry and Strupp would argue that this relationship can wield a corrective interpersonal and intrapsychic influence.

Toward a Common View of the Alliance

Although there may not be across-the-board agreement on exactly *how* the alliance influences change, there is widespread agreement that the alliance plays *some* role in the healing process as a general, transtheoretical principle of change (Goldfried & Padawer, 1982). Furthermore, there has been an abundance of work aimed at clarifying the construct and separating it from other similar relational concepts such as transference and empathy (Bordin, 1979; Frieswyk et al., 1986; Gelso & Carter, 1985; Horvath & Symonds, 1991; Luborsky, 1976). There has also been an emergence and increased consensus on several common themes related to the alliance (Gaston, 1990). It is generally agreed that the alliance represents interactive, collaborative elements of the relationship (i.e., therapist and client abilities to engage in the tasks of therapy and to agree on the targets of therapy) in the context of an affective bond or positive attachment (Bordin, 1980; Gaston, 1990; Henry & Strupp, 1994; Horvath & Symonds, 1991; Luborsky, 1976; Marziali, 1984a). Although therapists from different theoretical orientations have placed greater emphasis on different aspects of the alliance (e.g., explicit goal formation may be more salient in cognitive-behavioral therapy than in dynamic therapy), and different studies have highlighted the differential impact of different dimensions (e.g., patient contributions versus therapist contributions; e.g., Krupnick et al., 1996), actual and perceived collaboration and therapeutic bond are considered by many to be crucial, transtheoretical components of the therapist–client relationship (Hatcher, 1999).

Westerman and Foote (1995) have also advanced an alliance construct that captures both the bond and collaboration aspects of the alliance: "patient coordination." According to these authors, patient coordination refers to how well a patient relates his or her contributions in the alliance vis-à-vis the therapist's as these contributions develop, worsen, and change over time. Low coordination reflects the maladaptive, defensive patterns manifested by the client that contribute to problems in the alliance, such as a patient's rejection of an accurate paraphrase by the therapist, whereas high coordination refers to the patient and therapist working in sync to address the patient's difficulties. This perspective of the alliance, although different from the focus of other perspectives, still underscores the bond and collaboration components of a general, overarching alliance definition.

Research Findings

As previously mentioned, the alliance has become one of the main concepts investigated by contemporary psychotherapy researchers. Several factors have led to this abundance of empirical attention since the mid-1970s (Horvath, 1994a). Briefly, such factors include the advancement of process research methodologies (Benjamin, 1974; Kiesler, 1973; Rice & Greenberg, 1984); the renewed interest in common factors (Grencavage & Norcross, 1990); the development of Bordin's (1979) eclectic model of the alliance, which expanded theory and research on the alliance outside of the more constrained realm of psychodynamic therapy; and the development of reliable instrumentation for specifically measuring the alliance construct and its proposed underlying dimensions (Horvath & Luborsky, 1993). This work has led the emergence of several trends that have greatly informed researchers and practitioners alike about the role of the alliance in effective psychosocial treatment. The most salient trend, which will be elaborated on soon, is that the working alliance has emerged as one of the strongest and most consistent predictors of positive treatment outcome (Horvath & Greenberg, 1994; Horvath & Symonds, 1991). Although there is certainly a need for continued empirical focus on this construct across different forms of treatment, for different presenting concerns, and with different constellations of therapeutic dyads, alliance research to date has provided us with invaluable information in several important areas.

The following sections briefly summarize the research findings on the measurement of the alliance, the relationship between alliance and outcome, the alliance across different treatment modalities, the alliance across time in therapy, and the client and therapist characteristics influencing the alliance. Following this, the development of the alliance, worsening of the alliance, resolution of alliance ruptures, and interaction between alliance and technique are discussed.

The Measurement of the Alliance

Instrumentation. As previously stated, one of the key determinants for the burgeoning work on the alliance was the development of reliable methods for measuring its theoretically proposed components (Horvath & Luborsky, 1993). Today, the most common instruments continue to parallel the theoretical state of the alliance. That is, the measures have significant overlap at a global level, which suggests growing agreement that the construct exists and that each measure is tapping the same general phenomenon (e.g., Bachelor, 1991). However, just as there continues to be theoretical divergences as to the components of the alliance and more fine-grained definitions, so too do the instruments diverge at the level of subscales (Horvath, 1994).

Horvath (1994) summarized the five principal clusters of related assessment instruments measuring the alliance: the California Psychotherapy Alliance scales (CALPAS/CALTARS; Gaston & Marmar, 1994; Marmar, Weiss, & Gaston, 1989; Marmar, Horowitz, Weiss, & Marziali, 1986); the Penn Helping Alliance scales (Penn/HAq/HAcs/HAr; Alexander & Luborsky, 1986; Luborsky, 1976); the Therapeutic Alliance Rating scale (TARS; Marziali, 1984b); the Vanderbilt Therapeutic Alliance scales (VPPS/VTAS; Gomez-Schwartz, 1978; Hartley & Strupp, 1983; O'Malley, Suh, & Strupp, 1983); and the Working Alliance Inventory (WAI; Horvath & Greenberg, 1989).

The *CALPAS/CALTARS scales* adhere to Gaston's (1990) conceptualization of the alliance and include four measurements: Patient Commitment, Patient Working Capacity, Therapist Understanding and Involvement, and Working Strategy Consensus. The *Penn scales* tap global measurements of helping behavior at different points in the therapy (e.g., Luborsky's 1976) "Type I" and "Type II" alliance dimensions previously described). The *TARS* yields measures of Patient's Positive Contribution, Therapist's Positive Contribution, Patient's Negative Contribution, and Therapist's Negative Contribution. The six alliance indexes produced by the *VPPS/VTAS scales* include Patient's Participation, Patient's Exploration, Patient's Motivation, Patient's Acceptance of Responsibilities, Therapist's Warmth and Friendliness, and Therapist's Negative Collaboration. Finally, the *WAI* taps the three dimensions of the therapeutic relationship articulated by Bordin (1979, 1994): agreement on goals, agreement on tasks, and the therapeutic bond.

Most of these measures are now available for assessing the alliance from different perspectives, such as client/therapist self-reports or observer-based coding, and have been shown to possess adequate psychometric properties (Horvath, 1994; Horvath & Luborsky, 1993). All assessment devices also seem to consider the two main elements of the alliance identified previously: the attachment between client and therapist and the collaborative investment in the process of treatment (Horvath & Luborsky, 1993).

Thus, researchers and clinicians are presented with several options when choosing a measure of the alliance, and most decisions are based on theoretical beliefs in the organization and focus of the subscales (Horvath, 1994). No one particular device has emerged as a better predictor of therapy process or outcome, and all measures have shown to be highly correlated among one another (Hatcher & Barends, 1996; Horvath, 1994; Luborsky, 1994; Tichenor & Hill, 1989). Although different outcomes have certainly been predicted differently by alternative measures (e.g., Tichenor & Hill, 1989), the main differences with respect to alliance-predicting outcomes have been at the level of rating source or perspective: therapist, client, or objective coder.

Rating Source.   Although all three perspectives are somewhat predictive of outcome (Luborsky, 1994), there are between-perspective differences with regard to both the judgment of the quality of the alliance and the link with therapy outcome. With respect to assessment of the alliance, Tichenor and Hill (1989) empirically demonstrated clear differences between client/therapist self-reports of the alliance and observer alliance judgments across several different measurement systems (e.g., the Haq, WAI, CALPAS, and VTAS). Bachelor (1991) found similar results when measuring therapist and client perspectives across several alliance instruments suggesting that different rating sources are not interchangeable (Horvath, 1994). Several studies have shown that therapist and client ratings of the alliance tend to be discrepant when measured early in treatment, but that this discrepancy may lessen as treatment progresses (e.g., Kivlighan & Shaughnessy, 1995; Mallinckrodt, 1993; Tichenor & Hill, 1989). Regardless of the time frame in treatment, Marmar, Horowitz, Weiss, and Marziali (1986) have argued that each rater's view of the alliance and its corresponding dimensions provides unique information about the client–therapist relationship.

In their meta-analysis of 24 studies on the relation between working alliance and outcome, Horvath and Symonds (1991) described several trends with respect to rating source effects. With respect to the *alliance ratings,* it was shown that client (mean effect size = .27) and observer (mean effect size = .23) evaluations are stronger predictors of outcome than are therapist judgments (mean effect size = −.03). These effect size values reflect the averages across all three rating sources of outcome (client, therapist, objective observer). With regard to the *outcome ratings,* it was revealed that client-rated outcome (mean effect size = .21) was moderately better predicted than therapist- (mean effect size = .17) or observer-rated outcome (mean effect size = .10) when averaged across all three alliance rating sources. Horvath and Symonds also reported on the relationships between the different combinations of alliance and outcome-rating sources. The strongest correlations were revealed between client-rated alliance and client-rated outcome and observer-rated alliance and therapist-rated outcome ($r = .31$ for both). Given that several heterogeneous ratings of alliance and outcome yielded relations that were as strong or almost as strong as when client's rated their own alliance and outcome, Horvath and Symonds argued against the possibility that the strong correlation between clients' self-rated alliance and outcome was biased by inflated and converging self-assessments (i.e., halo effect). Horvath and Symonds' meta-analysis also revealed that therapist-rated alliance scores were the least predictive of outcome as assessed from any perspective ($r = .13$ for client-rated outcome, −.04 for therapist-rated outcome, and −.17 for observer-rated outcome). The finding that therapist ratings of the alliance are the least predictive of outcome has also been demonstrated in recent studies (e.g., Barber et al., 1999).

Horvath (1994) offered several potential explanations regarding therapist ratings being poor predictors of outcome. First, he argued that the therapeutic relationship is not experienced in the same manner by client and therapist, despite this, at times, having been an underlying assumption of researchers. This argument that the alliance is not experienced in a symmetrical manner by client and therapist poses a measurement problem because therapist rating scales are often very similar in content and wording to the client scales. Although client's can directly report on their inner experience, therapists, on similar items tapping client's experience, often have to infer beliefs or feelings of the client. This inferential process may be related to perceptual inaccuracies and, possibly, to the poorer predictive validity of therapist ratings of the alliance. Second, Horvath argued that the therapist's assessment of the alliance is, to some extent, not as "pure" as that of the client's because it may be influenced by a more global and theory-driven perspective of the treatment process and is optimistic about expectations of change. Thus, in addition to potential problems related to inferring client's inner experience, theoretical knowledge of how the alliance should be developing or expectations of success in developing the alliance may alter the therapist's judgment of the relationship. Horvath also argued that the therapists' invest-ment in viewing themselves as empathic persons successfully engaged with clients may fa-cilitate misperceptions and distortions of the relationship based on the therapists' own relational dispositions. This self-view, which is consistent with role expectancies of a ther-apist, might be distorted in nature and could potentially mask problems in the alliance from the perspective of the rating therapist. Marmar et al. (1986) have also suggested that both therapists and clients have difficulty maintaining objectivity while they are involved in such an intensely subjective process. Consistent with this argument of subjective differ-ence on clients' and therapists' judgment of the alliance, Hatcher (1999) found that clients may experience more variation in their feelings of being cared for and respected by their therapists than therapists do in judging themselves on these dimensions.

Although not much research has been directly conducted to better understand the nature of the therapist's view of the alliance, a recent study by Hatcher (1999) has shown that from the therapist's point of view, "confident collaboration" (i.e., the therapist's per-ception that the client is confidently invested in the treatment and that it corresponds to ex-pectations of change) is the dimension of the alliance most related to the therapist's judgment of progress in therapy. Therapist rating of "confident collaboration" was also positively correlated with clients' assessment of the alliance and had the highest associa-tion with client-rated improvement (though this relationship was small) across several therapist-rated dimensions of the alliance. As noted by Hatcher and by Horvath (1994), future research should focus on the experiential differences between therapist and client so that measurement systems can be refined to consider these differences and alliance-out-come findings can be interpreted more meaningfully and confidently.

One potential shortcoming of the measures of the alliance previously described is that all of them are typically used to provide a global assessment of a substantial segment of therapeutic interaction, such as half a session, an entire session, or many sessions (Hor-vath, 1994). Such assessments may fail to capture the subtler, moment-to-moment pro-cesses taking place within the therapeutic dyad that can have a significant impact on the outcome of treatment. As argued by Henry and Strupp (1994), more fine-grained analyses of interpersonal transactions should be conducted to better understand the therapeutic in-fluence of the alliance. To this end, the assessment of the alliance has begun to grow beyond the initial five families of instrumentation to include measurement systems, meth-odologies, and data-analytic techniques that can capture the moment-to-moment processes taking place between the client and the therapist. Among these are the Structural Analysis of Social Behavior (SASB) (Benjamin, 1996; Constantino, 2000; Henry, 1996), case stud-ies (Alpher, 1991), task analysis (Rice & Greenberg, 1984), and Markov chain analysis (Benjamin, 1979; Lichtenberg & Heck, 1986; Tracey, 1985).

Working Alliance and Treatment Outcome

The link between the therapeutic alliance and clients' improvement has been convincingly documented in several reviews of the empirical literature (Gaston, 1990; Horvath & Lubor-sky, 1993; Horvath & Symonds, 1991; Luborsky, 1994; Saketopoulou, 1999). Horvath and Symonds' (1991) meta-analysis of 24 studies on the alliance-outcome association indi-cated a moderate to strong, statistically significant relationship between a positively rated alliance and client improvement (overall effect size = .26). These authors indicated that not only is this a substantial correlation for a variable being measured within the complex entity of psychotherapy but that the correlation is probably underestimated because of their use of an extremely conservative statistical approach in conducting their meta-analysis (see Horvath & Symonds, 1991, for a complete explanation of statistical procedures). Furthermore, the correlation between alliance and outcome was not significantly related to sample size, the length of the treatment provided, or whether the study was published. This latter finding suggested that there is no "file drawer" problem (Rosenthal, 1979) with respect to the alliance literature.

Empirical evidence has also consistently shown that a positive alliance accounts for significant amounts of outcome variance, even when initial levels of the outcome criteria are partialled out (Gaston, 1990). Moreover, several studies have demonstrated that the alliance's contribution to outcome is not simply a reflection of the client's in-treatment improvement (e.g., Gaston, Marmar, Thompson, & Gallagher, 1988; Marmar, Gaston, Gallagher, & Thompson, 1989). For example, Gaston et al. (1988) assessed initial symptomatology, symptomatic improvement through Session 5, and therapist- and client-rated alliance scores at Session 5 across diverse forms of therapy. These authors found that the alliance scores accounted for 19% to 57% of the outcome variance when controlling for pretreatment symptomatology and early improvement. Across diverse forms of treatment for depression, Marmar et al. (1989) analyzed the association between outcome and alliance at Session 5 controlling for pretreatment depression level and early treatment change in depression. These authors found a significant link between one alliance dimension (patient commitment) and client improvement.

Although these studies supported the conventionally held belief that the alliance wields a positive influence on outcome separate from the client's in-treatment improvement, other studies have failed to converge with this finding. For example, DeRubeis and Feeley (1990), in a treatment study of depression, found that a certain type of technical intervention ("abstract" cognitive techniques) and the therapeutic alliance were not predictive of client outcome. When measured later in treatment, moreover, the alliance was predicted by clients' prior improvement through the course of therapy. DeRubeis and Feeley argued that this latter finding suggested that symptomatic improvement led to a better alliance quality than vice verse. Feeley, DeRubeis, and Gelfand (1999), in an attempt to replicate DeRubeis and Feeley (1990), also found that "abstract" cognitive interventions and the alliance did not predict symptomatic change. Feeley at al. (1999), moreover, found that the alliance rated later in treatment was predicted by previous client improvement (although this finding only approached significance).

Although the DeRubeis and Feeley (1990) and Feeley, DeRubeis, and Gelfand (1999) findings did not converge with the impressive amount of studies that have demonstrated a positive link between alliance and outcome, other investigations have supported this positive association in an indirect manner. For example, Tryon and Kane (1990) found that the quality of the helping alliance as rated from the client perspective differentiated premature, unilateral treatment terminators from appropriate terminators such that the unilateral terminators were more likely to perceive a poor alliance as compared to their appropriately terminating counterparts. To the extent that premature, unilateral termination is considered a negative treatment outcome, the results of Tryon and Kane converge with the findings linking the quality of the alliance with posttreatment improvement. Similar to direct alliance-outcome investigations that have generally shown that therapist-rated alliance is a poor predictor of outcome, this study by Tryon and Kane also revealed an alliance-rating-perspective difference whereby therapist-rated helping alliance did not differentiate the two types of terminators. Tryon and Kane (1995), however, found that the unilateral termination was associated with weak alliance evaluations at Session 3 from the perspective of both therapist and client.

Global Measurement of the Alliance and Outcome.   The robust relationship between alliance and outcome has been demonstrated using different measurement systems and a wide variety of treatment populations. For example, using the CALPAS/CALTARS, Marmar et al., (1989) found a link between alliance and client improvement in various forms of treatment, such as dynamic, cognitive, and behavioral, for depression in older adults. Marmar et al., (1989) found that the Patient Working Capacity subscale of the CALTARS was positively associated with clients' symptomatic reduction and improved interpersonal functioning in dynamic psychotherapy for bereavement. In a study of an integrative form of cognitive therapy that emphasizes in-session communication about the therapeutic relationship (Safran & Segal, 1990), Safran and Wallner (1991) found that despite being grounded in a psychodynamic model, the CALPAS significantly predicted patient improvement (i.e., increased global ratings of success, decreased depression, and improvement on target complaints).

The Penn scales have also demonstrated a robust association between the alliance and outcome across several forms of treatment for different client samples. For example, Morgan, Luborsky, Crits-Christoph, Curtis, and Solomon (1982) found that observer-rated alliance scores predicted several objective measures of outcome in moderate-length dynamic psychotherapy. Additionally, Luborsky, McLellan, Woody, O'Brien, and Auerbach (1985) found that patient-rated alliance scores combined across three treatment groups (supportive-expressive, cognitive, and drug counseling) predicted improved social functioning across several indexes, including decreased drug use, increased employment, improved intrapsychic functioning, for clients being treated for drug addiction.

Using the TARS to assess the quality of the alliance in short-term psychodynamic therapy, Marziali, Marmar, and Krupnick (1981) reported a positive link between observer-rated alliance and client-rated outcome. Marziali (1984b) found that alliance scores predicted both patient-rated outcome (accounting for 9% of the outcome variance) and therapist-rated outcome (accounting for 35% of the outcome variance) when controlling for pretreatment levels of symptomatology. In attempting to replicate Marziali (1984b), Eaton, Abeles, and Gutfreund (1988) demonstrated that observer-rated TARS scores predicted symptomatic improvement in dynamic psychotherapy after partialling out pretreatment levels of symptomatology (TARS scores accounted for 19% to 35% of the outcome variance).

The VPPS/VTAS were created as part of Strupp and colleagues' large-scale research program at Vanderbilt University. The Vanderbilt I study (Strupp & Hadley, 1979) was designed to explore the relative contributions of specific (i.e., technical) and nonspecific (i.e., interpersonal) variables in psychotherapy. Several studies based on the Vanderbilt I data demonstrated that the presence of a positive therapeutic alliance by the end of the third session was generally associated with clients' improvement (e.g., Gomez-Schwartz, 1978; Hartley & Strupp, 1983; Moras & Strupp, 1982). Interestingly, the Patient Involvement scale of the VPPS emerged in these studies as the best predictor of outcome across all rating sources, even when Therapist-Offered Conditions (i.e., warmth and friendliness) were partialled out of the analyses (Henry & Strupp, 1994). The client's willingness and ability to become actively involved in treatment thus appears to be a particularly crucial factor in the process of change. Another illuminating finding from several of these studies (e.g., Gomez-Schwartz, 1978; O'Malley et al., 1983) was that the significant, positive relationship between Patient Involvement and outcome did not emerge until the third session, thus suggesting that Patient Involvement was not strictly a pretreatment patient disposition but rather a receptive stance that developed over the first several sessions probably at least partially because of the therapist's behaviors. This finding reveals the importance of the development of positive relational dynamics early in the treatment process.

In addition to these global findings, fine-grained analyses of therapist–client transactions revealed interesting differences between good and poor outcome cases selected from the Vanderbilt I study. High levels of conflictual interpersonal process, for example, were more frequent in poor outcome cases than in good outcome cases. Moreover, therapists tended to provide "blaming" or complex communications (seemingly "supportive" statements that also conveyed hostility or criticism) in poor outcome cases (Henry, Schacht, & Strupp, 1986).

Such findings led to the Vanderbilt II study, which was designed to study the effects of training in time-limited dynamic psychotherapy (with a specific focus on identifying and resolving the markers of negative interpersonal dynamics) on process and outcome. More fine-grained analyses of the Vanderbilt I and II data sets have provided the field with a better understanding of the effects of different types of interactional patterns between client and therapist, as well as client/therapist predispositional variables, on outcome. Some of these findings are further presented in following sections on fine-grained measurements of the alliance, and client and therapist predispositions that impact treatment.

Working within Bordin's (1979, 1980, 1994) pantheoretical framework of the alliance, several researchers have examined the predictive validity of the alliance as measured by the WAI. Based on eight studies conducted through 1991 (e.g., Safran & Wallner, 1991; Tichenor & Hill, 1989), Horvath (1994) reported an effect size of .33 for the relationship between client-based measures of the WAI and outcome. More recently, in a study of process and outcome in cognitive therapy for depression, Castonguay, Goldfried, Wiser, Raue, and Hayes (1996) found that early session alliance (as measured by the observer-based WAI) predicted improvement in depressive symptomatology and global functioning at midtreatment and depressive symptomatology at posttreatment. Also, Castonguay, Constantino, and Newman (1998) used the client and therapist versions of the WAI to assess the link between alliance and outcome in cognitive-behavioral treatment of generalized anxiety disorder. These authors found that client-rated alliance scores significantly predicted client improvement at posttreatment, 6-, and 12-month follow-ups. The therapist-rated alliance scores significantly predicted outcome at posttreatment and 12-month follow-up.

Momentary, Fine-Grained Measurement of the Alliance and Outcome.   Although many of the aforementioned measures of the alliance seem to overlap alliance dimensions, they mainly provide a global and rather inferential description of the therapy climate. Many of them also yield separate indexes for therapist and client contributions to the overall alliance (e.g., Patient Working Capacity and Therapist Understanding and Involvement of the CALPAS/CALTARS). Kiesler (1982) argued against considering patient and therapist factors separate from their momentary, reciprocal dyadic context. Echoing this argument, authors such as Henry and Strupp (1994) and Safran (1993) have conceptualized the therapeutic alliance as the ongoing interpersonal process within the therapist–patient dyad that should be investigated on a moment-to-moment basis. According to Henry and Strupp, the study of reciprocal client–therapist transactions can lead to greater behavioral specificity and reduce summary inferences in the examination of the therapeutic relationship. Several studies have used systems of measurement that allow for such "bottom-up" analysis of the working alliance.

Using the SASB, a circumplex system that can dissect complex transactional patterns taking place in any form of social behavior (including the therapeutic relationship), several studies have uncovered key findings related to the alliance-as-interpersonal process perspective. As previously mentioned, Henry, Strupp, and their colleagues on the Vanderbilt I and II studies have been the prominent figures in this line of research. Using data from Vanderbilt I, Henry, Schacht, and Strupp (1986) explored whether therapists, despite using similar technical interventions, were engaging in different interpersonal behaviors in their good and poor outcome cases. Based on the analyses of four good outcome and four poor outcome cases (one each per therapist), Henry et al. found several striking differences. These authors found that in their good outcome cases, therapists were engaging in significantly more interpersonal behaviors marked by affiliative control, such as helping and teaching behaviors, and affiliative autonomy-granting, such as affirming and understanding, than in their poor outcome cases. In these same good outcome cases, therapists engaged in significantly fewer behaviors marked by hostile control, such as blaming the client, than in their poor outcome cases. Also in this good outcome condition, the clients demonstrated greater friendly autonomy, such as open disclosure, and less hostile separation, such as walling off and avoidance, than clients in the poor outcome group.

In addition, Henry et al. (1986) found that good and poor outcome groups differed in terms of interpersonal complementarity. As predicted by these authors, the poor outcome cases were higher in frequencies of negative complementarity (i.e., disaffiliative interpersonal transactions such as reciprocal hostility) than the good outcome cases. Henry et al. also showed that therapists tended to engage in a greater degree of complex communications with the lower-change cases than with the high-change cases. An example of such complex communication involves the deliverance of a message indicating acceptance (for example, on the level of content) but in the context of a simultaneous message of dismissal (as on the level of process; e.g., a tone of voice suggesting a lack of genuine interest on the part of the therapist about what the client is talking).

In a subsequent study, Henry, Schacht, and Strupp (1990) assessed 14 cases from the first cohort of clients involved in the Vanderbilt II project. These authors used the SASB model to measure both process (momentary interpersonal transactions) and outcome (changes in patient self-concept). Inspired by the work of Sullivan (1953), the changes in self-concept measured by the SASB refer to the notion of "introject," which reflects the tendency for people to treat themselves in a manner consistent with how they have been treated by important others, for example self-blame consistent with a history of blaming communications on the part of the primary caregiver. In addition to predicting that differential interpersonal processes would affect the ability to alter a patient's negative introject, Henry et al. (1990) predicted that therapists' introject structure would be related to in-session interpersonal processes (i.e., therapists showing greater hostility toward themselves would treat their patient in a more hostile or controlling manner). Unlike any previous psychotherapy research, this study used a common descriptive language—based on the SASB—to measure the presenting problem (i.e., client's introject), therapist's personality (i.e., therapist's introject), treatment process (i.e., interpersonal transactions), and outcome (i.e., change in client's introject). Strupp, Schacht, and Henry (1988) have referred to this research approach as problem–treatment–outcome (PTO) congruence.

Henry at al. (1990) found that in the poor outcome group (i.e., clients who showed no change in negative introject) therapists exercised more disaffiliative interpersonal behaviors, such as belittling and blaming, ignoring and neglecting, than in the good outcome group. Within the good outcome condition, therapists displayed an almost complete absence of such negative interpersonal process. Similar to the findings of Henry, Schacht, and Strupp (1986) and consistent with Sullivan's (1953) interpersonal theory, these authors also found a significantly positive correlation between the frequency of therapist statements marked by disaffiliative control and hostility, and the frequency of patient utterances marked by self-criticism and self-blame. Also in line with the findings of Henry et al. (1986), both patients and therapists evidenced more complex communicative patterns in the poor outcome group than in the high-change group. With respect to therapist self-concept, Henry et al. (1990) found that compared to therapists with a self-affiliative introject, the therapists with a hostile introject structure engaged in three times as many disaffiliative communications with their patients; a pattern that had already been shown to relate to poorer outcome across different types of outcome measurement (Henry et al., 1986).

Svartberg and Stiles (1992), in a study of Sifneos's (1979) short-term, anxiety-provoking therapy, used the SASB to assess whether client improvement could be predicted from therapist competence in delivering the techniques prescribed in this approach and therapist–client complementarity. Although therapists' level of technical competence did not relate to positive client change, these authors found that, consistent with the findings of Henry et al. (1986), client–therapist positive complementarity, such as friendly and autonomy-enhancing interactions, in a selected early session was predictive of midtreatment client improvement. The general results of Henry et al. (1986, 1990) and Svartberg and Stiles have been replicated across different data sets (e.g., Coady & Marziali, 1994; Quintana & Meara, 1990) and in different countries (e.g., Coady, 1991a, 1991b; Harrist, Quintana, Strupp, & Henry, 1994; Hildenbrand, Hildenbrand, & Junkert-Tress, 1994).

These studies are examples of how the field of psychotherapy research has grown as researchers have applied innovative means to answering more and more specific questions about the process of psychotherapy. In concert with the initial sets of instrumentation that continue to provide valuable empirical information, a system such as SASB can help us to continue increasing our basic and applied knowledge base on the alliance construct.

The Alliance Across Different Treatment Modalities

As one can discern from the preceding report on the positive-alliance-outcome findings, different forms of treatment have *not* shown systematic differences with respect to the influence of the working alliance. Despite the origins of this construct being based in psychodynamic and client-centered orientations, reviews have demonstrated that the quality of the therapeutic bond has not proven to be a more important treatment factor in dynamic or humanistic therapy than in other modalities (e.g., Horvath & Luborsky, 1993; Horvath & Symonds, 1991; Orlinsky et al., 1994). Although a lot of the early studies on the alliance were conducted with dynamic therapies (e.g., Eaton et al., 1988; Luborsky, 1976; Luborsky & Auerbach, 1985; Piper, DeCarufel, & Szkrumelack, 1985; Saunders, Howard, & Orlinsky, 1989), more recent work has branched out into other types of treatment such as cognitive, behavioral, humanistic, gestalt, interpersonal, eclectic, supportive/self-directed, group, systemic couples and family, inpatient, 12-step, and pharmacotherapy (e.g., Barber et al., 1999; Carroll, Nich, & Rounsaville, 1997; Castonguay et al., 1998; Castonguay et al., 1996; Connors, Carroll, DiClemente, Longabaugh, & Donovan, 1997; Krupnick, et al., 1996; Lieberman, Von Rehn, Dickie, Elliott, & Egerter, 1992; Muran et al., 1995; Quinn, Dotson, & Jordan, 1997; Raue, Castonguay, & Goldfried, 1993; Raue, Goldfried, & Barkham, 1997; Rounsaville et al., 1987; Salvio, Beutler, Wood, & Engle, 1992; Sexton, 1993, 1996; Tuttman, 1997; Weiss, Gaston, Propst, Weisebord, & Zicherman, 1997; Wilson et al., 1999) and has continued to show that this relational construct is predictive of client improvement (Horvath & Luborsky, 1993; Luborsky, 1994).

In a direct assessment of the influence of the alliance on outcome across different treatment types, Horvath (1991) conducted a meta-analysis of 21 treatment studies (8 psychodynamic, 3 cognitive, and 10 eclectic) and found that the average alliance-outcome correlations were statistically significant in the positive direction for each treatment type (psychodynamic = .17; cognitive = .27; eclectic = .27). The differences among these correlations, however, were not significant, thus indicating parity across the different treatment forms with respect to the predictive power of the alliance. This same pattern of results was reported by Krupnick et al. (1996) who found significant relationships between alliance and outcome across four treatment conditions: cognitive-behavioral, interpersonal, and active and placebo pharmacotherapy with clinical management. The authors also found that there were "virtually no significant treatment group differences in the relationship between therapeutic alliance and outcome" (p. 536).

The Alliance Across Time in Therapy

As pointed out by Luborsky (1994), not enough empirical findings have been obtained to give us a completely adequate understanding of the relationship between the time course of the alliance and ultimate client outcome. There have been enough studies on this issue, however, to report on the general trends. The most parsimonious statement with respect to time-course findings is that, in general, alliance measures taken early in treatment are better predictors of client improvement than alliance measured later in the treatment or averaged across several time points (Horvath, 1994; Horvath & Symonds, 1991). In their meta-analysis, Horvath and Symonds found a greater effect size for early session assessment of the alliance (ES = .30) than for studies measuring alliance in either the middle phase of treatment or averaged across treatment (ES = .21). Several other investigations have supported the overarching trend that the alliance as measured early in treatment is a strong prognosticator of outcome (e.g., Castonguay et al., 1998; Kotovic & Tracey, 1990; Mallinckrodt, 1991; Marziali, Monroe-Blum, & McCleary, 1999; Piper, Azim, Joyce, & McCallum, 1991a; Randeau & Wampold, 1991) and client continuation in treatment (e.g., Tryon & Kane, 1990, 1995).

With respect to why such a trend has been obtained, Horvath and Greenberg (1994) have noted that the strong link between early alliance and outcome makes good therapeutic sense. According to these authors, the failure to engage early in the process of treatment or the failure to achieve a trusting bond will probably lead to disengagement from the curative tasks of treatment or lead to early termination. Several researchers (e.g., Kokotovic & Tracey, 1990; Mohl, Martinez, Ticknor, Huang, & Cordell, 1991) have empirically demonstrated that even very early alliance measures (e.g., first session) were predictors of client dropout, thus lending support to the argument that the early establishment of a trusting bond and the development of collaborative goals and tasks is crucial to the therapy trajectory. Such findings not only support the view that the alliance is critical in the early phase of treatment but also speak against the argument that the alliance is merely an epiphenomenon, or "by-product" of treatment gains (Horvath & Luborsky, 1993).

Another finding against the by-product argument is that of Safran, Crocker, McMain, and Murray (1990), who found that the alliance fluctuates over time, which would not be predicted if one agreed with the notion that a good alliance only results from incremental treatment improvements. The alliance-as-a-by-product argument would need to be supported by case analyses showing a linear progression of alliance measurement, which simply has not been the case. Safran et al. (1990) suggested that not only is the development of the alliance *not* a linear progression but that the ongoing emergence and repair of ruptures in the therapeutic relationship accounts for an extremely important part of the development of the alliance and the change process.

Although some studies have found that the alliance can be stable over time (see Brossard, Willson, Patton, Kivlighan, & Multon, 1998), others have demonstrated that the alliance frequently follows a curvilinear trajectory. These studies lend support to the assumption, held by many authors, that the alliance becomes most disrupted and incurs the most problems during the middle phase of treatment and is better during early and later treatment phases (Cashdan, 1973; Gelso & Carter, 1994; Mann, 1973; Tracey, 1993). Westerman (1998), for example, found that the patient's contribution to the alliance (described as "low coordination" as previously defined) evidenced the most difficulties during the middle phase of treatment whereas the early and late phases were marked by higher patient coordination (i.e., better alliance). As noted by Westerman, this finding was consistent with results of several other studies (e.g., Golden & Robbins, 1990; Horvath & Marx, 1990; Lansford, 1986) and provided important information as to the trajectory of the therapeutic relationship. With respect to the curvilinear model of the alliance and outcome, Tracey and Ray (1984) found that this quadratic trend differentiated good from poor outcome cases with the good ones showing the curvilinear trajectory. Patton, Kivlighan, and Multon (1997) have also found that a high–low–high pattern of alliance during the course of treatment was positively related to client improvement.

Tracey (1993) has argued that the positive link between the curvilinear model and outcome is the result of the central therapeutic process at work whereby in the middle phase of treatment the therapists are probably challenging existing maladaptive patterns in their patients' interpersonal functioning and, hopefully, providing a corrective experience (in the context of patients' initial defenses that may be contributing to poorer rated alliance at this middle phase of therapy). This model appears to agree with Henry and Strupp's (1994) notion that the alliance can be curative in and of itself to the extent that it disrupts cyclical, maladaptive patterns of interpersonal functioning and with Safran et al.'s (1990) perspective that alliance rupture and repair cycles are important elements of the change process.

Further strengthening the argument that the alliance is not simply a by-product of within-treatment improvement has been the findings that the alliance continues to predict posttreatment outcome even when early symptomatic gains are partialled out of the equation (e.g., Gaston et al., 1988; Marmar et al., 1989). As noted previously, however, DeRubeis and Feeley (1990) and Feeley et al. (1999) found that in their investigations the alliance as measured early in treatment was not predictive of subsequent change and that the alliance as measured later in treatment was predicted by client improvement. According to these authors, these results suggested that symptomatic improvement led to the development of positive alliances rather than the other way around.

Although it appears as though enough evidence has been gathered to suggest that the alliance is more than an epiphenomenon, or end result of successful steps in the treatment, there are still some inconsistencies being uncovered as evidenced by the DeRubeis and Feeley (1990) study and the Feeley et al. (1999) study. Further adding to the inconsistencies within this realm of alliance research is a recent finding by Stiles et al. (1998) who found that alliance measured later in treatment was more strongly correlated with outcome than alliance ratings taken in the middle phase of therapy. These authors argued that these results somewhat converge with the findings of Krupnick et al. (1996) that stronger alliance-outcome associations were evidenced for alliance ratings averaged across sessions than with the alliance measured only in the early treatment phase. Given the mixed findings related to the alliance and treatment time course, it is imperative that future research focus on how the alliance, as an important part of the treatment process, develops and fluctuates over time and the factors that impact its development, maintenance, and repair.

The Influence of Patient and Therapist Characteristics on the Alliance

As the link between alliance and outcome has become solidly established, attention has been devoted to potential client and therapist contributions to the quality of the therapeutic relationship. As described in the next sections, the client and therapist variables investigated so far have involved both pretreatment characteristics and in-session contributions.

Client Factors.   A number of investigations have explored the predictive value of several client demographic characteristics, such as gender, age, and education, with regard to the alliance (e.g., Gaston et al., 1988; Marmar, Weiss, & Gaston, 1989). With the potential exception of the level of education (Marmar, Weiss, & Gaston, 1989), these variables have not consistently predicted the quality of the alliance. In several studies using the CALPAS as the alliance measure, however, a moderate link was found between pretreatment symptom severity and the alliance. Specifically, greater severity was related to decreased engagement in the therapy process and a diminished sense of working with the therapist toward treatment goals (see Gaston and Marmar, 1994). Using the WAI, Raue et al. (1993) found that greater severity of client-rated symptoms was negatively correlated with the alliance in psychodynamic-interpersonal therapy. Assessing the level of patients' coordination (a measure of alliance that, as described previously, focuses on patients' patterns of defense during treatment) in insight-oriented therapy, Westerman and Foote (1995) found that hospitalized patients showed less coordinating interpersonal behavior than a group of better functioning outpatients. Luborsky (1975), using the Penn Helping Alliance scales, also found that the client's mental health was positively correlated with his or her capacity to form a therapeutic alliance.

It should be noted, however, that these particular "mental health" findings have not been consistently established because other studies have found that pretreatment severity, at least in and of itself, has not been a good prognosticator of the development of a quality alliance (see Horvath, 1994). Even clients diagnosed with borderline personality disorder, a condition characterized by severe relational deficits, have been shown in some studies to achieve alliances that are comparable to higher-functioning clients (Gunderson, Najavits, Leonhard, Sullivan, & Sabo, 1997). Although this finding certainly does not negate the unique challenge of successfully working with borderline clients, it suggests that level of pretreatment pathology does not necessarily doom or guarantee the development of a quality alliance.

Goren (1991) found no gender differences with respect to overall alliance scores and found no differences in alliance ratings across different patient–therapist gender combinations. This finding suggests that gender may not be a crucial factor as concerns the ability to forge a productive, working alliance. Other therapist–patient similarities, however, may play a greater role with respect to the alliance. For example, Luborsky, Crits-Christoph, Alexander, Margolis, and Cohen (1983) found that age match and similarity in religious activities were significantly correlated with helping alliance ratings. Much more work needs to be done to determine the extent to which client–therapist similarities may have a significant impact on the relationship in treatment. Clinical intuition has certainly driven decisions to work with clients or to refer them to providers that are seemingly more appropriate. It is now imperative that further research address these client–therapist "match" issues to provide direct guidance in determining the composition of client–therapist dyads.

Interestingly, with regard to a match between the client and the type of therapy, Elkin et al. (1999) found that the quality of the therapeutic relationship was predicted by what they called "patient-treatment fit," that is, the client's congruence between his or her assignment to the treatment condition and predilection for a particular form of therapy (as reflected by the client's view of the etiology of depression and expectations about helpful interventions). Using archival data from the National Institues of Mental Health (NIMH) Treatment of Depression Collaborative Research Program (Elkin et al., 1989), these authors demonstrated that such congruence was significantly related to the client's perception of the therapist's level of empathy, regard, and authenticity, as well as to the therapeutic alliance as measured from an observer perspective.

Empirical efforts have also been devoted to personal (intrapsychic and interpersonal) characteristics of clients and their relationship with the alliance. For example, Paivio and Bahr (1998) used the SASB to measure client introject in their study of the relationship among interpersonal problems, the alliance, and client outcome in a form of experiential therapy aimed at resolving "unfinished business" with a significant other. These authors found that high levels of distress related to interpersonal problems and low self-affiliation according to the introject measure were factors that hindered the initial development of a therapeutic alliance. Based on their findings, these authors argued that having clients rate their pretreatment self-concept may be a particularly useful marker for when clients may have problems in establishing an initial alliance with their therapist.

Based on the work of Sterba (1934), who conceptualized the alliance as stemming from the interaction between the patient's mature ego functioning and the therapist's use of techniques, Gaston and colleagues (1988) have investigated the link between the CALPAS and several patient variables and found some indirect support for the idea that the patient's ego functioning impacts the quality of the alliance. For example, Marmar, Weiss, and Gaston (1989) found that the therapeutic and working alliances were positively associated with the patient's degree of experiencing in session. They also found that the alliance was negatively related to patient's avoidant tendencies with respect to addressing and dealing with their stated problems (Gaston et al., 1988). The link between alliance and client's emotional involvement (experiencing) has been shown in subsequent studies (e.g., Randeau & Wampold, 1991; Sexton, Hembre, & Kvarme, 1996).

In a summary of 11 studies focusing on client variables (inter- and intrapersonal) and the alliance, Horvath (1991) reported that it is more difficult to forge a strong alliance with clients who have a general deficit in their ability to maintain social relationships (e.g., Moras & Strupp, 1982) or clients who have a history of poor familial relationships (e.g., Kokotovic & Tracey, 1990). Both of these interpersonal findings make intuitive sense to the extent that the therapeutic alliance is likely to involve core social skills, which in turn are likely to be dependent on how such skills are modeled and learned within the family of origin. As concerns intrapsychic factors, Horvath (1991) reported that there is also difficulty developing a strong, positive alliance with clients possessing poor object relations (e.g., Piper et al., 1991b), a defensive attitude (e.g., Gaston et al., 1988), or a hopeless stance (e.g., Ryan & Chicchetti, 1985). Horvath also found in these 11 studies that low psychological-mindedness on the part of the client was also linked to poor alliances.

As concerns familial interpersonal history, research has supported the hypothesis that the quality of early parental experience is positively correlated with a client's ability to form strong alliances in treatment (Mallinckrodt, 1991). As described in further detail in the next section, a recent study by Hilliard, Henry, and Strupp (2000) showed that client's early relations with their parents had a direct affect on both the alliance and the treatment outcome. These authors also found that the client's interpersonal history had an indirect impact on improvement, with the alliance serving the role of mediator.

The quality of object relations factor was further explored by Piper et al. (1991a) who also found that clients with poor early object relations have more difficulty productively engaging in a therapeutic alliance. As noted by Horvath and Luborsky (1993), however, the generalizability of Piper et al.'s results may be limited, as these authors used a unique and highly specific measure of alliance. Nevertheless, it seems intuitive that the degree to which one engaged in adaptive interpersonal processes with early important others will have an impact on the ability to engage in any form of affiliative relational interactions. In support of this clinical intuition, Hartley and Strupp (1983) found that the client's quality of object relations plays an especially important role in the early phase of treatment with its effect lessening as therapy progresses. According to these authors, the negative impact of poor quality of object relations is probably tempered as the client's maladaptive internal representations are modified via the therapeutic process. Considering the difficulties that individuals with poor object relations are likely to experience in psychotherapy, it is perhaps not surprising that strengthening the alliance during the course of treatment has been found to be more important for them than for individuals with a high quality of object relations (Piper, Boroto, Joyce, McCallum, & Azim, 1995).

As reported by Frieswyk et al. (1986) and by Horvath and Symonds (1991), clients who are overly resistant, negativistic, or hostile fail to form working alliances early in the treatment process. Muran, Segal, Samstag, and Crawford (1994) also found that cold and hostile scores as assessed by the Inventory of Interpersonal Problems (IIP; Horowitz, Rosenberg, Baer, Ureno, & Villasenor, 1988) were negatively related to the alliance in an integrative form of cognitive therapy.

Another intrapsychic variable that has been linked with the development of the alliance is client perfectionism. In a recent article, Zuroff et al. (2000) showed that depressed clients with high levels of perfectionism demonstrated difficulty developing strong alliances during the course of treatment, and this finding was consistent across cognitive-behavioral therapy, interpersonal therapy, pharmacotherapy, and a placebo condition. The results of this study also indicated that this difficulty in developing a robust alliance mediated the previously observed negative relationship between perfectionism and outcome across the same treatment conditions (Blatt, Quinlan, Pilkonis, & Shea, 1995). Blatt, Zuroff, Quinlan, and Pilkonis (1996) found that clients' positive perception of the therapeutic relationship, such as therapist's empathy, level of regard, and authenticity, mitigated the negative effect of moderate levels of perfectionism. Rector, Zuroff, and Segal (1999) also found that clients' pretreatment levels of depressogenic beliefs, which included perfectionistic attitudes, were negatively related to the alliance (i.e., therapeutic bond) in cognitive therapy.

It should be noted that many of these studies on client characteristics have yielded relatively moderate correlations with the alliance, which, according to Gaston and Marmar (1994), is a clinically encouraging result. As these authors note, moderate correlations suggest that the alliance is a malleable phenomenon that is influenced by client variables, but not solely driven by them. Although such variables are crucial, they do not guarantee nor preclude the development, progression, or maintenance of a quality therapeutic alliance. In fact, as some authors have argued (e.g., Henry & Strupp, 1994), it is through the process of the alliance, its establishment, tears, and resolution, that characterological change can come about via the alteration of cyclical maladaptive patterns of interpersonal functioning. Thus, not only would initial maladaptive client variables not preclude the development of an alliance, but they are also an integral part of the alliance when this construct is viewed as the ongoing interpersonal process taking place between client and therapist. Additionally, it is important to consider the contribution of therapist in-session and pretreatment characteristics as these may play an independent role in impacting the alliance or may interact with certain client characteristics for a qualitative effect on the therapeutic relationship.

Therapist Factors.   As cogently demonstrated by Luborsky (1994), empirical evidence suggests that the therapist is capable of having an impact on the alliance. Such evidence is very much in agreement with the writings of Rogers (1951, 1957), who highlighted the therapist's *responsibility* in establishing the alliance. Rogers emphasized the conditions that a therapist must offer, including empathy, unconditional positive regard, and congruency, in order to provide the safe forum in which patients can work through their difficulties and toward the self-actualizing process. As mentioned earlier, Rogers (1957) believed such conditions to be curative in their own right. Although empirical work has provided support for the therapeutic role of empathy, positive regard, and congruency (especially when measured from the client's perspective; e.g., Barrett-Lennard, 1985; Gurman, 1977), other findings have suggested that the relationship between therapist-offered conditions and outcome is not uniform across different treatment modalities and that it explains only a part of therapeutic success (Mitchell et al., 1977; Orlinksy & Howard, 1986).

Empirical work has begun to focus on other therapist in-session behaviors that contribute to the alliance. Clinicians, of course, want to know not only that the alliance is important but also specifically what they can do to establish and improve it, to avoid breaking it (at least when it is unnecessary for the client's change), and to repair it when it has suffered from significant tears. Answers to such questions clearly have important practice and training implications.

Development of the Alliance

As anybody involved in clinical supervision can assert, there are differences among therapists in their capacity to establish an alliance with their clients. Such differences, which have been empirically supported by Luborsky et al. (1985), are probably the result of various types of therapist activity. Theoretically, Freud (1913/1958) emphasized empathy as a necessary condition in establishing the alliance. Zetzel (1956) postulated that the development of an alliance could be enhanced if the therapist acknowledges the client's sorrow, pain, and suffering by means of supportive statements. This support and validation, it was argued, serves the role of moving closer to the client and helps to avoid the pitfall of the therapist being viewed as removed and unhelpful.

Watson and Greenberg (1994) reported that a consensus has emerged with respect to conditions that clients deem as essential aspects of a helpful, positive alliance. These authors noted that the literature has revealed that clients place a premium on feeling accepted, prized, understood, supported, and affirmed by their therapist. In a series of studies of helpful and detrimental processes occurring in client-centered/experiential therapy, Lietaer (1990, 1992) found that clients in the good outcome condition reported that therapist warmth, interest, involvement, empathy, acceptance, respect, and patience were helpful in developing a good working relationship. Also in the good outcome conditions, clients reported that their therapists demonstrated the valuing of their clients' personhood and were authentic in their interactions. These findings are consistent with a study by Luborsky, Crits-Christoph, Mintz, and Auerbach (1988) where an association was found between therapist-facilitating behaviors, such as warmth and support, and the alliance.

The work of Henry and his colleagues has also provided some insight with respect to the therapist's specific and concrete contributions to the development and improvement of the alliance. As mentioned previously, therapists' actions toward their clients in successful psychodynamic treatments were characterized by helping and teaching behavior as well as affirming and understanding communications (Henry et al., 1986).

Several studies have investigated the impact of therapists' interpretations on the working alliance, leading to rather mixed findings. Allen et al. (1996), for instance, found that the therapists' interpretation and focus on relationship (i.e., transference) issues were positively related to alliance, whereas noninterpretative (i.e., supportive) interventions and focus on nonrelationship issues were negatively related to the alliance. Other studies, however, have found that therapists' transference interpretations related negatively with the quality of alliance (Marmar, Weiss, & Gaston, 1989; Piper et al., 1991b). Furthermore, a number of studies have failed to find a link (positive or negative) between the frequency or accuracy of therapist interpretations and the alliance (Butler, Henry, & Strupp, 1995; Crits-Christoph, Cooper, & Luborsky, 1988; Gaston & Ring, 1992).

Crits-Christoph, Barber, and Kurcias (1993), however, found that the accuracy of a specific type of interpretation predicted change in the alliance (from early to late in the treatment), even after controlling for client improvement and pretreatment level of psychological health. The authors also demonstrated that the accuracy of the interpretation predicted alliance changes regardless of the initial level of alliance (high or low). Such accuracy (which many consider as a measure of skill or competence) seems, therefore, important to develop a good alliance or repair alliance ruptures.

Although some work has certainly been illuminating with respect to therapist activity that promotes and serves to maintain the alliance, this area of research is still in a relatively early stage. It is imperative that future research focuses on further clarifying links between particular therapist actions or skills and improvement in the alliance (Horvath, 1994). It is this type of research that will be of most benefit to practicing clinicians who will then be able to begin applying this knowledge to their own clinical work. As cogently argued by Horvath, "Research on the alliance will greatly diminish in practical importance if clinically viable methods of training therapists how to influence the development of the working alliance are not discovered" (p. 122).

Worsening of the Alliance

Research has also begun to provide information on how therapists can contribute to the emergence and maintenance of alliance problems in therapy. In a study investigating the process of change in cognitive therapy for depression, Castonguay et al. (1996) found that, although the working alliance was positively related to improvement, the therapist's focus on a central aspect of cognitive therapy rationale and technique (i.e., the cause and effect relationship between the client's intrapersonal issues, such as distorted thoughts, and negative emotions) was associated with the worst outcome. Content analyses conducted to better understand these findings suggested that the use of such rationale and techniques per se is not detrimental to the process of change. Rather, it is their use in an inappropriate interpersonal context that may interfere with outcome. Specifically, the content analyses revealed that when confronted with alliance ruptures, such as a client's reluctance to accept the therapist's view of depression or to engage in the techniques prescribed by the treatment protocol, therapists frequently increased their adherence to the rationale or techniques prescribed by the cognitive therapy manual. Rather than resolving problems in the relationship, however, such increased technical adherence seemed to worsen them. Therapists' attempts to convince the clients of the validity of the rationale or the effectiveness of the techniques frequently appeared to lead to an increased reluctance toward the rationale or techniques, which then led to further unsuccessful attempts by the therapist to persuade the client of the validity and effectiveness of the therapy rationale and techniques. At other times, signs of alliance ruptures, such as the client's lack of trust in or hostility toward the therapist, were treated as manifestations of distorted thoughts and became a focus of cognitive restructuring. Although prescribed by the cognitive therapy manual (Beck, Rush, Shaw, & Emery, 1979), this strategy did not appear to resolve relationship problems, but rather it seemed to have led to further unresponsiveness or opposition to the treatment on the part of the client.

Using the SASB, Critchfield, Henry, Castonguay, and Borkovec (1999) found that the nature of the therapeutic relationship discriminated between clients with good outcome (those showing a high level of functioning at the end of treatment and at 12-month follow-up), declining outcome (those showing a high level of functioning at posttreatment but a low level at follow-up), and poor outcome (those showing a low level of functioning at the end of therapy and at follow-up) in cognitive-behavioral therapy (CBT) for generalized anxiety disorder. Consistent with the directive or skill-training-oriented nature of CBT, high levels of therapist directiveness (or control) were found in the good outcome group. Higher levels of client directiveness (or control) toward the therapist were found in the two less desirable outcome groups. Furthermore, the manner in which the therapists' reacted to the clients' attempt to control them differentiated the clients in the declining group from those in the poor outcome group. Whereas in the former group the therapists "backed off" or granted interpersonal distance, therapists in the latter group pressed forward or attempted to control the session. Consistent with Castonguay et al. (1996), these findings suggest that the therapist's intervention (or level of directiveness) is not detrimental per se, but it is the continued use of such intervention in specific interpersonal contexts (i.e., when the client is reluctant to accept the therapist's effort or wants to direct the process of therapy) that may interfere with the process of change. As discussed in a later section, these results highlight the importance of achieving a balance between the therapists' challenge of the clients' problems and their need to be attentive to the clients' needs—or what Linehan (1993) eloquently describes as the dialectic process of challenge and acceptance.

A similar dynamic of increased adherence in reaction to client resistance or need for control may also take place in psychodynamic treatment. As mentioned previously, a number of studies have found that therapist focus on transference phenomena was related to poor alliances. For Allen et al. (1996), this may not indicate that such interventions are intrinsically unhelpful. For these authors, the negative effect of interpretation may in part reflect too much of a good thing. Consistent with the findings in CBT described previously, they argued that "interpretative strategies may be invoked more vigorously—and not necessarily successfully—to deal with resistance and impasses in the context of a poor alliance" (p. 260).

The potential harm associated with the therapist's strong or rigid adherence to prescribed techniques has also been demonstrated in the Vanderbilt II study that, as previously mentioned, was designed to explore the effect of training therapists in time-limited dynamic psychotherapy (Henry, Strupp, Butler, Schacht, & Binder, 1993). The very nature of this training was to improve therapists' ability to attend to negative interpersonal processes taking place within the therapy and to alter such a countertherapeutic course. Interestingly, these authors found that, although their training was successful in molding the therapists' technical interventions, there were also several negative effects. These effects included decreased approval, support, and optimism on the part of the therapists, in addition to the therapists, performing in an authoritarian and defensive manner. In other words, although the training was "successful" in terms of therapists doing as they were trained, the interpersonal process did not improve as was expected. In fact, the group of therapists exhibiting the highest technical adherence was also the group most vulnerable to negative interpersonal processes. Therapists doing more of what they were prescribed to do in order to successfully deal with the relationship problems were also the ones who showed the most disaffiliative transactions. This is particularly significant considering that these disaffiliative transactions, as described in the previous section, were related to the worst outcome (Henry et al., 1986, 1990).

As noted before, Henry et al. (1993) found that therapists' negative interpersonal styles were related to their relationships with themselves (i.e., introject): therapists hostile toward themselves also tended to be hostile with their clients, even when they were trained to quell such negative interpersonal processes. Thus, although the client's relational patterns may be re-created in session, these results suggest that the therapist's own interpersonal style—based on internal representations of past important relationships—has a significant impact on the development of the alliance. Interestingly, Henry and Strupp (1994) also reported on a study (Christianson, 1991) that demonstrated that therapists' negative perceptions of their relationship with their parents during childhood was linked to negative interpersonal processes observed in the session. As Henry and Strupp cogently argued, taken together, the Vanderbilt II findings "describe a theoretically coherent link between early actions by parents toward the therapist, the therapist's adult introject state, vulnerability to countertherapeutic interpersonal process with their patients, and differential outcome" (p. 66).

A recent study using the Vanderbilt II Psychotherapy Research Program (as well as different instruments based on the SASB) further confirmed and expanded this complex theoretical model (Hilliard et al., 2000). Consistent with Christianson's (1991) results, the findings showed a significant relationship between therapists' early parental relations and interpersonal process (or alliance). Hilliard et al. (2000) also showed that the client's early parental relations predicted the alliance. Furthermore, their findings indicated that the client's interpersonal history had both a direct impact on outcome, as well as an indirect effect on outcome through its impact on the alliance (which served as a mediator). Interestingly, Hilliard et al. (2000) also found that the alliance was significantly related to outcome, even when controlling for clients' and therapists' relationship histories. This latter finding, as the authors cogently argued, helps rule out the possibility that the link between alliance and outcome found in several studies is strictly because of the effect of a specific third variable (i.e., the interpersonal history of either participant).

In a landmark study, Jones and Pulos (1993) also found that negative interaction processes predicted worse outcome in cognitive and psychodynamic therapies. Although these processes were grouped under a factor called "patient resistance," several of them reflect interactional patterns between the client and therapist that are similar to the ones described previously. Similar to the Castonguay et al. (1996) and Critchfield et al. (1999) studies, some of these negative processes were related to the implementation of interventions (e.g., "patient rejects therapist's comments and observations"; "patient resists examining thoughts, reactions, or motivations related to problems"). Comparable to the studies of Henry and his colleagues (1986, 1990, 1993) other negative processes were related to the therapeutic relationship per se (e.g., "patient verbalizes negative feelings, such as criticism and hostility, toward therapist," "there is a competitive quality to the relationship").

As conveyed in a recent review of the literature by Binder and Strupp (1997), these negative interactional processes are by no means restricted to cognitive-behavioral and psychodynamic therapies. In fact, studies have demonstrated that such struggles for control or hostile interactions are present across a variety of treatments, including in orientations, such as humanistic, where the primary emphasis is on the establishment of a safe and nurturing relationship.

Resolution of Alliance Ruptures

Although therapists of all orientations can create obstacles in the therapeutic relationship, they can also help improve it. If this was not the case, most treatments would stop being beneficial at the first significant occurrence of alliance problems. And given that any demanding, complex, and personal relationship (such as the one between a client and therapist) frequently involves some degree of disappointment and frustration, most psychotherapy would end prematurely and without having facilitated client change.

As previously mentioned, a study by Crits-Christoph et al. (1993) has suggested that the accuracy of the therapist's interventions may facilitate the resolution of problematic relationships. This study, however, has not provided detailed information on how this could take place. Fortunately, a number of authors have begun to identify strategies that can be used by therapists of different orientations to repair alliance ruptures. David Burns (1989; Burns & Auerbach, 1996), a leader of the cognitive approach, has described several techniques to address clients' negative emotions regarding therapy and the therapeutic relationship. Burns emphasized listening skills, such as empathy or gentle inquiry of thoughts and feelings, to identify the client's negative emotions resulting from the therapist's previous failures to be empathic or attentive to the client's needs. Also crucial to Burns' contribution is a technique called "disarming," which refers to the therapist's explicit validation and exploration of the client's criticisms and hostility toward the therapist or the therapy. The therapist is encouraged to find some truth in the client's perception of the therapist and therapy (even when the client may seem "unreasonable" and "unfair") and to invite the client to express feelings of anger, disappointment, or frustration associated with this perception. According to Burns (1989), the therapist's acknowledgment and inquiry of client's negative emotions allows the client not only to feel validated and understood, but also to resume engagement in the therapeutic task prescribed in cognitive therapy.

Similar tools to resolve alliance ruptures have been developed by Jeremy Safran and his colleagues (Safran et al., 1990; Safran & Segal, 1990). To facilitate the detection of tears in the relationship, they encourage therapists to adopt the attitude of "participant–observer" described by Sullivan (1953). Therapists are also urged to use empathy in helping clients to identify and describe their experience related to difficulties in the therapeutic relationship. Although Safran and Segal (1990) argued that clients can contribute to alliance ruptures, they emphasized that therapists should first fully explore their own contributions to the relationship problems prior to exploring clients' cognitive-interpersonal patterns that may have elicited unhelpful behaviors from therapists (e.g., client's submissive behaviors pulling for therapist's controlling interventions) or that may have led to potential misconstruction of the therapist's intentions or behaviors. Such recognition and exploration of the therapist's contributions to relationship problems, for example, inadequate presentation the therapeutic rationale, misunderstanding the client's experience, or negative emotions toward the client, is clearly similar to Burns' (1989) procedure of disarming. For Safran and Segal, therapists' openness to their mistakes or empathic failures can facilitate clients' openness to their own roles in the alliance ruptures, which in turn can lead to the exploration of core schema that are at the root of maladaptive patterns of relationships with others.

Other well-known cognitive-behavioral therapists have described techniques to explore and repair alliance ruptures (e.g., Arnkoff, 1981; Goldfried, 1985; Linehan, 1993). Interestingly, like Burns (1989) and Safran (1993), their efforts are consistent with, if not based directly on, techniques from other orientations, such as the humanistic and interpersonal orientations. Linehan (1993), for example, has developed a treatment for borderline personality disorder (BPD) that "represents a balance between behavioral approaches, which are primarily technologies of change, and humanistic and client-centered approaches, which can be thought of as technologies of acceptance" (p. 110). Almost identical to the strategies previously described, the specific techniques of acceptance described by Linehan include the therapist's empathic reflection of the client's experience and their "direct validation" of clients' responses. Like Burns' (1989) disarming strategy, the direct validation technique is based on the assumption that there are always elements of wisdom, truth, and reasonableness in clients' behaviors, even when some characteristics of such behaviors are dysfunctional. Although Linehan recognized that clients' distorted thoughts and dysfunctional behaviors in the relationship can create alliance problems, she also emphasized that such alliance ruptures can be caused by therapist behaviors. When this is the case, she argued, the key to resolving alliance ruptures is the therapists' willingness to admit their mistakes (as well as their ability to accept clients' hostility). Like Burns and Safran, Linehan argued that alliance problems are frequent and that significant therapeutic benefit can be achieved by skillfully repairing relationship problems (including a generalization of the skills involved in resolving alliance ruptures to the difficulties experienced by clients in their relationships outside of the therapy sessions).

These strategies aimed at repairing alliance tears (and, ultimately, at improving the effectiveness of therapy) have begun to receive empirical attention. Safran and colleagues (Safran et al., 1990; Safran & Muran, 1996; Safran, Muran, & Samstag, 1994), for example, have provided preliminary evidence regarding the validity of a four-stage model that describes the characteristic processes through which ruptures in the therapeutic alliance are resolved. In Stage 1, the client presents some indication that there is a problem in the alliance, and the therapist focuses attention on the here and now of the therapeutic relationship. In Stage 2, the client begins to express concerns about the treatment or therapist, in a qualified or partial fashion. In Stage 3, the therapist helps the client explore interpersonal expectations or beliefs that block the direct expression of underlying concerns. In Stage 4, the client expresses underlying concerns, wishes, or needs in a direct, self-assertive fashion. Safran and colleagues have demonstrated both that the stages of the model occur more frequently in rupture–resolution than in nonresolution sessions, and that the theoretically predicted sequence of model stages is significantly more likely to take place in rupture–resolution sessions.

Foreman and Marmar (1985) found similar patterns of results in psychodynamic therapy by exploring the therapist activities for three cases in which the alliance improved from its initially poor status and three cases in which the alliance remained poor throughout treatment. Specifically, they found that the client's defenses and feelings in relation to the therapist were dealt with more frequently in the improved cases than in the no-change cases. In an investigation of cognitive therapy, Gaston, Marmar, and Ring (1989) similarly found that problems in alliance improved for those clients whose therapists were engaging in an examination of relationship problems rather than solely focusing on situational problem solving.

It should also be noted, however, that too much focus on the relationship has been found to relate negatively with the alliance (Marmar, Gaston et al., 1989; Piper et al., 1991b). Such focus on the therapeutic relationship, however, was taking place within the context of transference interpretations—which could suggest that problems in the therapeutic relationship are caused by clients' distortions of the therapist based on unresolved issues from the past. Rather than reflecting a recognition of reciprocal contribution to the alliance problem, such interventions may at times serve to blame clients (e.g., Wile, 1984) and, therefore, run the risk of creating obstacles in the therapeutic relationship.

Taken as a whole, these studies suggest that across different forms of therapy, the resolution of alliance ruptures is facilitated by what Binder and Strupp (1997) describe as the therapeutic metacommunication (a term they borrowed from Donald Kiesler, 1996), or the exploration of patient's and therapist's here-and-now experience of the therapeutic relationship. These strategies of metacommunication have also begun to be tested as part of treatment protocols in clinical trials. In a preliminary investigation conducted at Penn State University, 12 depressed individuals completed an integrative form of cognitive therapy (ICT; Castonguay et al., 2000). As implied by its name, ICT is a modification of cognitive therapy (CT) that involves the integration of procedures derived from other forms of therapy, for example, humanistic, interpersonal, and psychodynamic. The development of ICT was based on the process findings reported in Castonguay et al.'s (1996) study, which, as discussed previously, suggested that the strategies used in cognitive therapy to address the alliance may not only be ineffective but may at times exacerbate the very relationship problems they are attempting to resolve. Specifically, when therapists are conducting ICT, they are asked to follow the traditional cognitive therapy protocol as prescribed in Beck et al. (1979)—except when confronted with signs of alliance ruptures. Rather than increasing their adherence to the treatment rationale or methods in response to such ruptures (as was observed in cognitive therapy by Castonguay et al., 1996), therapists are instead instructed to use the strategies developed by Burns (1989) and Safran (1993): inquiring about the relationship problems, empathizing with the client's experience related to the alliance ruptures, and recognizing the therapist's contribution to these ruptures. Once the relationship problems have been explored and resolved, therapists then resume cognitive therapy—either by continuing to use the procedures they were using prior to the emergence of the alliance rupture or by shifting to other techniques prescribed by Beck et al.'s treatment manual.

Although systematic assessment of the therapeutic process has yet to be conducted, observations of a large number of therapy sessions (via video) revealed that alliance problems emerged relatively frequently during the application of cognitive techniques and that these problems seemed to be adequately addressed by the use of metacommunication strategies. With regard to outcome results, none of the 12 individuals who completed ICT met criteria for depression at the end of treatment. The findings also suggested that most of the therapeutic gains have been maintained at six-month follow up. The improvement of individuals who received ICT was also significantly higher than those who were assigned to a waiting group. Although this preliminary study did not involve a direct comparison of ICT and cognitive therapy, the results suggest that the graduate students who conducted ICT (and who had not been previously trained in cognitive therapy) did at least as well, if not better than experienced therapists who were involved in previous trials of cognitive therapy (e.g., Elkin et al., 1989).

The same strategies to repair alliance ruptures are also part of an integrative treatment for generalized anxiety disorder (GAD) that is also being investigated at Penn State University (Newman, Castonguay, & Borkovec, 1999). Preliminary evidence suggests that this new treatment may have a beneficial impact on GAD clients that have not fared well when given cognitive-behavioral therapy, which stands as the current golden standard treatment for this disorder (Borkovec & Whisman, 1996). A large-scale clinical trial is currently being conducted to directly compare the integrative therapy with cognitive-behavioral therapy.

Because current clinical trials involving new strategies to repair alliance ruptures are preliminary in nature, any of their findings should be considered tentative at best. These studies suggest, however, that such strategies can be integrated into a traditional form of therapy, such as cognitive-behavioral therapy, and that they show some promise with respect to improving its effectiveness.

Interaction Between Alliance and Technique

Although it has been argued that the therapeutic relationship by itself leads to change (see Goldfried & Pawdawer, 1982), it has long been postulated that the therapeutic value of the alliance is caused, at least in part, by its interaction with technical aspects of therapy. Freud (1913/1958), for example, viewed the development of a positive alliance as a prerequisite process in order to have subsequent techniques take effect. More recently, Bordin (1994) conceptualized the alliance not as a separate prerequisite, but as a treatment ingredient that allows the client to genuinely engage in the therapeutic journey and thus reap its benefits. According to Bordin, the process allows for advancement in the technical realm, and the technical realm can do the same for the process. Such theorizing has heightened the empirical focus on the interaction between the therapeutic relationship and therapeutic techniques.

Another factor that has turned the attention of psychotherapy researchers to a dual focus on technique and alliance has been the lack of consensus on studies exploring the isolated impact of technique use on client outcome. For example, although some investigators have found that greater adherence to prescribed techniques is significantly correlated with outcome (e.g., DeRubeis & Feeley, 1990; Feeley, DeRubeis, & Gelfand, 1999; Kerr, Goldfried, Hayes, Castonguay, & Goldsamt, 1992; Luborsky, McLellan, Woody, O'Brien, & Auerbach, 1985), others have failed to find a relationship between technical adherence or the frequency of use of techniques and improvement (Barber, Crits-Christoph, & Luborsky, 1996; Castonguay, Constantino, & Borkovec, 1998; DeRubeis, Evans, & Hollon,

1989; Henry et al., 1993). The lack of consistent findings linking technique adherence/use to outcome has pointed to the need for further exploration of the interaction between the use of prescribed techniques and other therapeutic factors, such as the therapeutic alliance, in facilitation of client change.

A number of studies have also begun to shed light on how alliance and technique interact with one another to impact on client change. Although such interaction failed to be related to outcome in some studies (e.g., Crits-Christoph, Cooper, & Luborsky, 1988; Svartberg & Stiles, 1992, 1994), it has predicted client improvement in others (e.g., Gaston, Piper, Debbane, Bienvenu, & Garant, 1994; Gaston & Ring, 1992; Gaston, Thompson, Gallagher, Cournoyer, & Gagnon, 1998; Rector, Zuroff, & Segal, 1999). In the context of psychodynamic therapy, the latter studies generally suggests that the use of exploratory interventions (e.g., interpretation) are beneficial when the alliance is strong, whereas supportive interventions (e.g., guidance) are helpful when the alliance is poor (at least in longer forms of psychodynamic therapy; see Gaston et al., 1998). Interestingly, Gaston et al. (1998) found that in cognitive-behavioral approaches (i.e., cognitive therapy and behavior therapy) exploratory interventions predicted outcome when used in the context of poor alliance. Insofar as these exploratory techniques might have involved the therapist addressing problematic reactions of the client (see Gaston et al. 1998 for the description of the exploratory techniques), these results could be consistent with another study by Gaston, Marmar, and Ring (1989), which, as described previously, found that the therapist's focus on the client's problematic reaction to the therapeutic relationship was associated with improvement of alliance.

In a recent study of patients with personality disorders, Bond, Banon, and Grenier (1998) found that a strong alliance interacts with technical interventions in dynamic psychotherapy. Specifically, these authors found that a strong alliance may serve to specifically mediate the effect of transference and defense interpretations. In another recent study, Rector, Zuroff, and Segal (1999) investigated the role of technical (i.e., cognitive change) and nontechnical (i.e., alliance) factors in cognitive therapy. They found that specific elements of the alliance (agreement on tasks and goals of therapy) predicted improvement in depressogenic cognitions. A significant interaction was also observed between another component of the alliance (therapeutic bond) and cognitive change, whereby clients who reported higher bond and greater reduction of depressogenic cognitions showed the most improvement. As argued by Rector et al. (1999), their results suggest that "certain aspects of the therapeutic alliance (i.e., goals and tasks) may facilitate the implementation of the technical factors of cognitive therapy, while other aspects of the alliance (i.e., bond) act in concert with technical factors to produce direct effects on depressed symptoms" (p. 320).

Despite these above findings on the interaction between specific (i.e., techniques) treatment factors and nonspecific (i.e., alliance/relationship) factors, Butler and Strupp (1986) have argued against the "specific/nonspecific" paradigm. (See Castonguay, 1993, for an argument against using the term *nonspecific* as it relates to psychotherapy variables.) Butler and Strupp have argued that separating technical and nontechnical aspects of treatment represents an inappropriate and fruitless approach to the study of therapeutic processes. According to this argument, psychotherapy techniques have no inherent meaning separate from their interpersonal context. According to this logic, it is conceptually impossible to isolate specific, active treatment ingredients from "nonspecific," interpersonal ones, and efforts aimed at doing so produce suspect results, regardless of their methodological or statistical sophistication. Butler and Strupp have adamantly postulated that the "purpose of psychotherapy research is to understand how one person (the therapist) influences or fails to influence another person (the patient) within a therapeutic context" (p. 37). These authors noted that this statement underscores the fundamentally interpersonal nature of any form of treatment and asserts that it is the therapist, working within this interpersonal context, that is the source of therapeutic influence (and not the therapy itself).

In line with this argument, Butler and Strupp (1986) argued that the traditional methods for isolating helping versus hindering technical interventions in group designs across multiple sessions need to be replaced by more context-sensitive designs. Similar to the design employed by Henry et al. (1986), Butler and Strupp argue that the systematic, multiple-case-study approach seems to represent the most appropriate and rigorous manner in which to uncover concrete helpful versus hindering techniques as they occur in a particular relational context. According to this perspective and a call for a paradigm shift, the greater focus on concrete, contextual therapeutic events should allow researchers and clinicians to work hand in hand to answer questions such as "what has happened here and why" (p. 38) and to use such fine-grained analyses to improve psychosocial treatments.

The argument of Butler and Strupp (1986) highlights the seeming consensus in the field that psychotherapy research needs to continue to move beyond its focus on demonstrating that psychotherapy works and more into the realm of isolating how it works or fails to work for particular clients, in particular forms of treatment, and in different relational contexts.

Clinical Implications

A tremendous amount of empirical research has been conducted on the alliance. As noted by Orlinsky et al. (1994), no facet of psychotherapy process has been as intensively studied in recent years as the therapeutic bond. Because the therapeutic relationship is a central component in virtually all forms of psychotherapy, it is not surprising that its empirical investigation has offered a number of clinical implications. Based on the preceding review, we now describe some of the major implications that can be derived from (1) the link between the alliance and outcome, (2) the client and therapist contributions to the quality of the alliance, (3) the fluctuating nature of the therapeutic relationship during the course of treatment, and (4) the measurement of the alliance in clinical practice.

Alliance and Outcome

The first implication related to the study of alliance and its link with outcome should be obvious. Based on the current state of our empirical knowledge, it seems reasonable to say that regardless of the treatment approach (psychodynamic, cognitive-behavioral, gestalt, interpersonal, eclectic, drug counseling, or management), the length of therapy, the type of problems presented by clients (depression, bereavement, anxiety, substance abuse, and so on), and the type of change aimed at (specific target complaints, symptom reduction, interpersonal functioning, general functioning, intrapsychic change and so on), therapists should make deliberate and systematic efforts to establish and maintain a good therapeutic alliance. Although very little consensus has emerged in psychotherapy research, it now appears that at least two things are clear: (1) psychotherapy works for a majority of clients; and (2) those who experience a positive attachment toward, and strong sense of collaboration with, their therapists tend to improve more than those who do not.

This implication may be especially important to emphasize as the field moves toward applying empirically supported treatments (EST), which typically put more explicit attention on techniques than on the establishment of the therapeutic relationship (Castonguay et al., 1999; Castonguay, Schut, Constantino, & Halperin, 1999; Henry, 1998). As mentioned previously, the negative consequences of mishandling the therapeutic relationship in the application of manualized and EST have been documented in a number of studies (e.g., Castonguay et al., 1996; Henry et al., 1990; Jones & Pulos, 1993).

Client Contribution to the Alliance

The empirical literature is revealing types of clients with whom it may be particularly difficult to establish or maintain a good alliance. Among the client characteristics that predict poor alliance are

- Low-education level
- Low-psychological mindedness
- No matching with therapist in terms of age and religion
- Lack of fit between client expectations and treatment rationale and goals
- High level of symptoms, distress, or hopelessness; low level of mental health or functioning (including ego functioning)
- Avoidance/resistance or defensiveness
- Lack of emotional involvement
- Low self-affiliation (i.e., negative introject)
- Difficulties or deficits with interpersonal relationships
- Poor object relations or negative (i.e., hostile) early relationship with parents
- Depressogenic cognitions, including perfectionism

The negative link between the alliance and some of these factors, such as low-education level and psychological mindedness, may in part indicate a discrepancy between the client and therapist in terms of their respective roles in treatment. This suggests, in turn, that some clients may particularly benefit from being prepared for what they should expect to do and to gain from therapy. As demonstrated by Orlinksy et al. (1994), patient role preparation appears to be beneficial for clients. The findings with regard to client and therapist lack of matching (i.e., age and religion), in particular, may well highlight the importance of the therapist's credibility in the eyes of the client. When working with clients of a different generation or religious background, it may be critical for the therapist to assess whether the clients believe that their perspective on life will be understood, their needs addressed, and their values respected.

When working with an individual who is not inclined to agree with the rationale and the tasks prescribed by the therapist's preferred orientation, however, it may be important to first acknowledge that different views exist and are likely to be valid (at least in part) with regard to the conceptualization and treatment plan of the client's problem. In addition to validating clients' perceptions of the sources of their difficulties and ways to resolve them, it may be beneficial for therapists to spend more time articulating the merits and limitation of their approachs and to draw some parallels, whenever possible, between the clients' and the therapists' views. If no common ground can be found and if the client is reluctant to give the benefit of the doubt to the therapist and engage (at least temporarily) in the proposed treatment protocol, the therapist may be forced to choose between one of two options: Use a method of intervention that is consistent with the client's view or refer the client to a therapist who practices a form of therapy more in line with the client's view.

Because they have mostly been obtained with psychodynamically oriented treatments, other findings, such as a high level of symptoms, resistance, or defensiveness, may suggest that therapists may wait before using exploratory methods of intervention until the client's distress and problems in impairment have been reduced. Related to the issue of defensiveness, therapists may find it helpful to use strategies developed to facilitate emotional deepening (e.g., Gendlin, 1978; Greenberg & Paivio, 1997; Greenberg, Rice, & Elliott, 1993), as the client's level of experiencing has been found to relate to the quality of alliance. Such a finding, of course, is consistent with the experience of many clinicians who have witnessed how the client's emotional disclosure and deepening foster, and are facilitated by, greater engagement in therapy and a closer relationship with the therapist.

As for the results pertaining to relational problems (interpersonal difficulties, poor object relations, early hostile relationships with parents), they suggest that therapists should expect the client to bring into the sessions, or pull for, ways of relating with others that can be problematic. The same suggestion could be made with respect to depressogenic (e.g., perfectionism) cognitions. As argued by Rector et al. (1999) such dysfunctional beliefs may "not only influence the processing of personally relevant information directed at self, but also serve as a 'blueprint' for how interpersonal interactions are processed and interpreted" (p. 326).

Above and beyond the particular implications that each of the aforementioned characteristics may suggest, the presence of all of them should inform therapists that they will likely be confronted with a number of signs of alliance ruptures. Whereas some of these signs are obvious and clearly indicate the deterioration of the therapeutic process, others are subtler. Safran and his colleagues (1990) have enumerated markers of alliance ruptures:

- Overt expression of negative sentiments
- Indirect communication of negative sentiments or hostility
- Disagreement about the goals or tasks of therapy
- Compliance (to avoid displeasing therapist)
- Avoidance maneuvers (e.g., ignoring therapist's comments, canceling sessions)
- Self-esteem-enhancing operations (e.g., self-aggrandizing comments)
- Nonresponsiveness to intervention (e.g., failure to use therapeutic intervention)

Of course, such instances of alliance ruptures can take place with any client, but the previously reviewed findings suggest that they are more probable with certain types of clients than others. It should also be mentioned that, if alliance ruptures can be expected, one should not assume that they have to be avoided at all cost. As argued by Safran and Segal

(1990), alliance ruptures can be opportunities for a corrective relational experience. And as is described in more detail later, the issue is to address alliance problems in a way that will resolve them and allow the therapy to provide an opportunity for the client to change.

Therapist Contribution to the Alliance

Although some client characteristics may predict more frequent alliance ruptures, this does not mean that problems in the relationship can be blamed solely on them. As argued by Safran et al. (1990), an alliance rupture should be considered as an interpersonal process and, therefore, in part created or maintained by the therapist.

The landmark study of Henry et al. (1993) has begun to provide us with some insight about therapists' personal contributions to alliance difficulties. As described previously, these authors found that therapists who show the greatest technical adherence and engage in more countertherapeutic interactional processes were also the therapists with a hostile introject.This suggests that therapists who tend to be harsh and severe toward themselves may have a tendency to treat clients in the same manner. They may, for instance, push the client excessively when therapy is not progressing fast enough. When attacked by the client, these therapists may also respond in a complementary hostile fashion rather than take a distance from the process.

Such empirical findings suggest that therapists who tend to be self-critical should make all possible efforts to maintain what Sullivan (1953) called a "participant–observer" attitude. Their engagement in therapy, in other words, should not only involved an application of therapeutic procedures but also an awareness of the process that is taking place between them and the client, including their own internal (feelings and thoughts) and interpersonal reactions to client behavior.

As shown by Henry et al. (1990), the disaffiliative interaction patterns found in the sessions of clients who failed to respond to therapy do not occur at a high rate. As these authors cogently argued, even a small amount of negative communication may have a powerful impact. Furthermore, because hostile interactions can be subtle and indirect (see Safran et al., 1990) it might be difficult at times, even for the most well-intentioned therapist, to detect and process them. Accordingly, supervision (including, when possible, audiovisual observations) may be particularly beneficial for therapists who are hostile toward themselves and, therefore, may be particularly at risk to display the same critical and non-accepting attitudes toward the people they are trying to help.

This, of course, by no means suggests that only therapists with certain personal characteristics would be wise to adopt a participant–observer attitude or to engage in supervision (or personal therapy). After all, no therapist can be constantly self-accepting or demonstrate at all times the type of interpersonal behaviors (affirming, understanding, helping, teaching) that seem to define a good alliance. Furthermore, Henry et al. (1986) demonstrated that the disaffiliative patterns of interaction that are taking place in less successful treatment can be complementary. This is consistent with the assumption, espoused by interpersonal therapists, that clients will tend to pull therapists into their maladaptive relationship patterns. As such, clients' actions and attitudes (e.g., hostile submission) may in part trigger therapists' unhelpful behaviors (e.g., hostile control). The main point here is that some therapists may have a tendency to engage in toxic relationships with themselves and should thus be especially attentive to the enactment of nonhelpful interpersonal processes on their part.

The empirical literature also suggests that some technical interventions, at least when applied in specific contexts, may play a role in maintaining and potentially increasing alliance ruptures. As described earlier, one study in cognitive therapy suggests that therapists may interfere with the process of change if they respond to the client's reluctance toward the rationale and techniques of this approach by attempting to persuade the client of the validity and effectiveness of such rationale and techniques (Castonguay et al., 1996). Therapists may also be well advised not to be too directive in reaction to their clients' attempts to control sessions (Critchfield et al., 1999). Although cognitive techniques and a directive style of intervention may be effective in a number of clinical situations, they may not be adequate as tools to address alliance ruptures or struggles for control.

So, what should one do when confronted with problems in the therapeutic relationship? Although only tentative answers can be provided to such a crucial question at this time, research evidence seems to suggest that when therapists become aware of hostility or control struggles in the relationship, they should stop what they are doing and reflect on their experience. Specifically, they should reflect on what is taking place in the session, in terms of the intervention they are using, the way they are using it, the client's behavior that may have led them to intervene in one way rather than another, and the impact that their actions have on the client. Stepping back from and processing their experience (emotional, cognitive, and behavioral) may be the first step in dealing with alliance ruptures. This will probably not resolve the situation, but it may prevent a spiraling cycle of hostile interactions or power struggles over the task and goals of therapy. This "stop and reflect" strategy, of course, is one of the components of Sullivan's (1953) participant–observer attitude.

Metacommunication (Kiesler, 1996) may be the best second step in addressing alliance ruptures. To metacommunicate is to direct the focus of therapy on the therapy per se. When we described the work of Burns (1989) and Safran (1983), we presented the crucial procedures involved in metacommunication: Inviting the client to talk about his or her experience of the relationship or reaction to the therapist's intervention, exploring and empathizing with the client's emotion as related to the alliance tears, sharing our own observation and reaction with the client including, above all, a recognition of our contribution to the relationship problem. Our clinical experience, as well as our preliminary research efforts (Castonguay, 1998; Castonguay et al., 2000), suggest that the recognition and exploration of the therapist's contribution (or what Burns [1989] eloquently described as "disarming") is particularly helpful. In fact, it is often followed by the client's acknowledgment of his or her role in the alliance rupture. This reciprocal recognition of responsibility is a powerful manifestation of a process eloquently captured several decades ago by Carl Rogers (1957): Openness to experience leads to openness to experience.

Metacommunicating, of course, is very difficult. It requires skills and courage to talk about negative feelings, to invite clients to criticize us, and to recognize how we may not have been empathic or helpful. Most therapists will be especially reluctant to invite emotional disclosure when a client is angry with them (Burns & Auerbach, 1996). They may believe that the use of such metacommunication strategies is like putting oil on the fire, whereby more direct and perhaps more intense anger will be triggered. While recognizing that seasoned clinicians from different theoretical backgrounds have openly acknowledged the difficulty of working with anger (Binder & Strupp, 1997; Burns & Auerbach, 1996; Newman, 1997; Strupp, 1980), it is crucial for the therapist to keep in mind that the best thing to do is to "avoid avoiding." If not addressed directly, negative feelings like anger are likely to remain present and interfere, in subtle or explicit ways, with the client's improvement. And although the therapist's fear of client hostility and anger is perfectly understandable, those who explore such reactions may well discover that the expression of negative affect during the course of a successful metacommunication frequently follows a pattern similar to the extinction curve of anxiety. First, the anger will increase, but with enough exposure (or sufficient recognition and acceptance), the affect will gradually decrease. As cogently expressed by Burns and Auerbach (1996), if part of the client's anger is based on the therapist's failure to be empathic, the therapist's validation of the client's anger will intrinsically remove the cause of the anger.

A phenomena that we again observed in our clinical and empirical work (Castonguay, 1998; Castonguay et al., 2000) is that when a therapist has integrated a participant–observer attitude and mastered metacommunication skills the therapist will be less inclined to avoid alliance ruptures in the first place. From both an interpersonal and technical perspective these ruptures are not only to be expected but also, to a certain extent, they should be desired. As we mentioned previously, interpersonal therapists argue that in order to fully understand and change the client's maladaptive interpersonal patterns, the therapist should be pulled into such patterns, for example, by becoming overcontrolling with a submissive client. Unlocking such patterns via the therapist's openness to an experience may lead the client to explore core interpersonal schema (Safran, 1993). Furthermore, the client's engagement in metacommucation with the therapist can provide the client with a direct and emotionally immediate experience with regard to dealing with interpersonal conflicts as they emerge in the client's daily life (Safran, 1993). As such, the resolution of the alliance ruptures can touch many of the principles of change that cut across different forms of intervention: reinforcement of the therapeutic relationship, acquisition of a new perspective of self and others, corrective experience, and generalization of the therapeutic learning to real life (Castonguay, 2000; Goldfried, 1980; Goldfried & Padawer, 1982; Goldfried & Castonguay, 1993).

From a technical point of view, alliance ruptures should also be expected. The process of change is frequently difficult; things have to get worse before they get better (Castonguay, Constantino, & Newman, 1998), and resistance can be viewed as an adaptive strategy in the course of improvement (Mahoney, 1991). Clients often have difficulty confronting their fears and rejecting their view of self (even when such a view is negative). As argued by Strupp (1977) the therapist's primary task is to influence and persuade the client to abandon old ways of being and behaving. Although these rigid ways of interacting with self and others have brought suffering, they are known ways to be and, therefore, are comfortable. Abandoning them is anxiety provoking and can be depressing. The therapist must thus convey to the client that the client can adopt new ways of living. The therapist must employ the right timing and method to make the client take risks. This difficult dance is beautifully captured by Linehan's (1993) metaphor of balance between change (or challenge) and acceptance. The therapist must be empathic with the client's fear but must also persuade the client that the client has the resources and courage to change. Interestingly, this dialectic of acceptance and change corresponds to Henry et al.'s (1986) notion of good interpersonal behavior: affirming, understanding, helping, and teaching. Not surprisingly, the level of balance achieved by the therapist was predictive of the client's improvement in dialectic-behavior therapy for borderline personality disorder (Shearin & Linehan, 1992).

Because it so eloquently captures a crucial aspect of therapeutic change, it is also not surprising that the dialectic process described by Linehan (1993) is consonant with views of change expressed by authors from different theoretical backgrounds. Working with borderline personality disorder, but from a psychodynamic perspective, Allen et al. (1996) emphasized the importance of balancing interventions. They write that "expressive and supportive strategies should not be polarized and pitted against one another. On the contrary, *expressive and supportive interventions should be blended optimally*" (p. 260, emphasis in original).

Time in Therapy

Research clearly indicates that the quality of the therapeutic alliance is particularly predictive of outcome when measured early in treatment. Empirical evidence also shows that a low-alliance score early in therapy is associated with premature termination (see Reis & Brown, 1999). The obvious implication is that one of the first concerns of therapists should be to provide the conditions for a bond and a collaborative involvement to develop as early as possible in therapy.

This might be especially important in settings where a considerable amount of time is spent with assessment. Therapists in settings (such as a training clinic associated with a doctoral program) that require clients to go through a systematic and comprehensive assessment battery may be well-advised to inform clients of the rationale and probable benefit of such a comprehensive assessment, as well as to monitor the client's expectations and reactions toward the assessment process.

Mixed findings with regard to the predictive validity of the alliance at midtreatment prevent definitive recommendations. It might be appropriate, however, to state that less-than-optimal alliance at midtreatment may not be detrimental to client improvement or indicative that further therapeutic efforts are doomed to failure. As mentioned previously, fluctuations in alliance should be expected and hoped for, as tears in the alliance can provide unique opportunities to explore maladaptive interpersonal schema and corresponding behavior.

Measurement

Clinicians have a number of reliable and valid instruments to measure the therapeutic alliance. The first obvious implication, from a scientist–practitioner perspective, is that therapists can and should use these psychometrically sound measures to monitor the quality of the therapeutic relationship during the course of treatment. As all clinicians ought to be concerned with how bound the client feels to the therapist and how willing and able the client is to work toward the treatment goals, the assessment of the alliance should be part of their day-to-day practice—it should not be restricted to research projects.

Because all measures of alliance depend on the same two major elements (attachment and collaborative involvement) and because all of them have strong psychometric qualities, it is difficult to suggest which measures clinicians should use. It may be appropriate, however, to recommend that clinicians use a scale that is theoretically consistent with the form of treatment they are performing with specific clients. It has been argued (Castonguay et al., 1996) that the use of psychodynamically based alliance measures in cognitive therapy may explain why a number studies have found no relationship between alliance and outcome in this form of treatment. Accordingly, if a therapist is conducting CT (or other nonpsychodynamic therapies), that therapist may want to use a transtheoretical measure such as the WAI. If a therapist is conducting psychodynamic treatment, that therapist will have a lot of choices and should base a decision on the dimension of the therapeutic relationship to be monitored. For instance, the VTAS could be used if one wanted to pay specific attention to things such as the patient's participation or acceptance of responsibilities and the therapist's warmth and friendliness, whereas the CALPAS could be used if one wanted to target aspects such as patient commitment and working capacity or therapist understanding.

Research clearly indicates that, where rating source is concerned, the alliance should first and foremost be measured from the perspective of the client. In general, the client versions of alliance measures have, indeed, been shown to have higher and broader predictive validity than observer and therapist versions. The use of client versions is not only dictated by empirical findings but, in fact, makes perfect sense. Because the client is the customer (the one with the problem, the one who decides to come back, and the one who pays for the services), the client's view about how well the treatment is progressing deserves attention. Nevertheless, other versions can be used, not only because they have been found to predict improvement but also because they provide a different lens through which to view the relationship and, therefore, may capture some subtle, but unhelpful, aspects of the therapeutic relationship that the client is not aware of or may not be yet willing to report.

An observer measure of the alliance would, of course, be onerous in clinical practice if one decided to use it in the same manner as in a process study (which involves the training and supervision of coders). A supervisor watching audio- or videotapes, however, might use observer versions of alliance measures. Moreover, without coding sessions with fine-grained instruments, such as the SASB, supervisors could systematize their feedback on the moment-to-moment process by taking into account the aspects of the therapeutic relationship revealed by such instruments (hostility or withdrawal of the therapist, complex communication between the participants).

The use of the therapist version of the alliance may be very helpful for the therapist, even if the predictive validity from this perspective has been less than optimal. Discrepancies between therapists' and clients' scores, which are expected considering the empirical findings, can help the therapist (1) to focus on client reluctance to express negative feelings toward the therapy/therapist (when the client scores are always higher than those of the therapist); (2) to become aware of the therapist's theoretical expectation or bias about the therapy process (see the second reason described by Horvath, 1994, for the discrepancy of scores between client and therapist, p. 89); and (3) to become aware of distorted views about the client or the relationship (i.e., countertransference; see the third reason described by Horvath). It is also important to consider the findings of Brossard et al. (1998), which indicate that the therapist's perception of the alliance has a significant impact on the client's perception of the alliance. As they cogently argued, the

Negative counselor perceptions of the working alliance, if accepted or left unnoticed may adversely affect the ability of the counselor and client to develop a healthy working alliance and ultimately damage the therapeutic endeavor. Some (e.g., Gelso & Carter, 1994; Patton & Meara, 1992) would argue that if counselors find themselves perceiving the working alliance as fragile, then steps should be taken immediately to repair or restore the working alliance. (p. 203)

Some therapists may be tempted to disregard the utility of systematically measuring the alliance using a standardized measure. They may think to themselves "I know when there is a problem in my relationship with a client, and I don't need a scale to confirm it." Because of their training, one would hope, indeed, that therapists are particularly sensitive to interpersonal cues. Therapists are also involved in a socially defined role, however, of an understanding and caring healer. We would venture to guess that it is as rare to meet a therapist proclaiming "I love therapy, but I'm not an empathic person" as it is to meet a person freely admitting to not being open-minded!

The fact is, however, that we are not always empathic with our clients. This should be obvious from the empirical results reviewed in the previous section, and it is also a fact of our day-to-day practice. It is simply not humanly possible to be constantly empathic and unconditionally accepting with every client with whom we work. Moreover, we are not always aware of our lack of empathy. The use of empathy and alliance scales in our own practice and supervision convinced us that our feelings and impressions at the end of a session ("Great, I nailed this one! I was totally with this person. It was as if I was in my client's shoes!" or "Gosh, what a terrible job I did! My client and I were working at cross-purposes and I was so directive and controlling that I did not give my client a chance to decide what he or she should do and how he or she feels!") are not always shared by our clients. Because the research shows that therapists' and clients' views of the alliance are typically discrepant, and because the same empirical literature demonstrates that the client's view has higher predictive value, all therapists should be encouraged to assign an alliance measure as part of their day-to-day practice—even (and perhaps especially) those who are convinced that they know how the client feels about them and the therapy that is being conducted.

Some therapists may also have concerns about imposing a time-consuming task on clients (and themselves) at the end of a session. This legitimate concern, however, can be circumvented with the use of a brief version of the WAI, which is composed of only 12 items and is highly correlated with the original 36-item version (Tracey & Kokotovic, 1989). Such a measure takes no more than a few minutes to complete.

Summary

The concept of the alliance has a long history. Perhaps more than ever before, and arguably more than any other construct in psychotherapy, it is still attracting a wealth of empirical, clinical, and theoretical attention (e.g., Gelso & Hayes, 1998; Horvath & Greenberg, 1994; Orlinsky et al., 1994; Safran & Muran, 1998, 2000). As one author of this chapter wrote elsewhere (Castonguay, 1997), we know of no psychotherapy book written in the past decade that has not referred to the alliance. It is fair to say that the alliance has reached the status of "leitmotiv" in psychotherapy. Although it emerged as a seminal contribution from the psychoanalytic tradition, it now stands as a necessary condition of change across all forms of psychotherapy. Not unlike most complex and crucial components of the process of change, the alliance has been defined in many ways. Despite the diversity of these definitions, however, the consensus in the field is that the alliance represents a positive attachment between therapist and client, as well as an active and collaborative engagement of these participants in therapeutic tasks designed to help the client. Reflecting the conceptual richness of the alliance, several instruments have been developed, initially reflecting psychodynamic and humanistic formulations of this construct, and more recently representing a transtheoretical view. Despite measuring different dimensions of the therapeutic relationship, each instrument directly addresses the two agreed-on components of the alliance: the bond and active collaboration. Furthermore, the major instruments that are currently available to researchers and clinicians provide both a global assessment of the quality of the therapeutic relationship and more fined-grained analyses of the complex and sequential transactional patterns between client and therapist. As a whole, current alliance measures have also shown more than adequate reliability and strong validity. Especially impressive is the level of predictive validity that these measures have demonstrated over a large number of studies. Regardless of the specific instrument used, assessment perspective (client, therapist, observer), form of therapy, length of treatment, and client problems, the data depict a rather clear and persuasive picture: The alliance is significantly related to client improvement. The empirical evidence also clearly points to the fact that both the client and therapist contribute substantially to the quality of the alliance. Consistent with definitions of the alliance as a phenomena that is intrinsically interactional (Henry & Strupp, 1994; Safran et al., 1990), the evidence suggests that client and therapist relationship histories have an impact on the therapeutic relationship. In addition, moment-to-moment analyses of therapy sessions also suggest that the quality of the alliance is probably determined by complementary transactions between client and therapist, rather than by the separate action of either one of these participants.

Not surprisingly, a number of important therapeutic implications can be derived from such clinically relevant findings. Put briefly, whatever form of therapy they are using, and whatever problems they are addressing, therapists should make explicit efforts to facilitate the creation of a positive and strong alliance in treatment. Because the alliance is such a robust predictor of outcome and because we now have psychometrically sound instruments to measure it, therapists should also systematically monitor the alliance with one of the available instruments, rather than relying only on clinical impression. Although the therapist's own use of alliance measures will provide good prognostic information about the treatment, it is important to keep in mind that the client's view of the alliance is currently the best-known predictor of outcome. Asking clients to fill out alliance measures, therefore, is particularly indicated. In addition, empirical evidence suggests that therapists should especially measure the bond and active collaboration early in therapy.

It may also be reassuring for therapists (and perhaps anxiety provoking at the same time) to know that problems in establishing or maintaining a strong alliance are predictable. Therapists are, indeed, able to benefit from paying close attention to specific personal and interpersonal difficulties of their clients (as well as their own) as early as possible in the course of therapy. This is because the interpersonal dynamics that are involved in the working alliance reflect, at least in part, the client's and therapist's interpersonal vulnerabilities. Moreover, strains in the client's collaboration, or resistance, should also be expected considering the emotional cost that is frequently involved in the modification of long-standing patterns of being and relating. In fact, interpersonal problems, such as client disappointment or hostility or therapist empathy failure or rigidity, and technical mishap or disengagement should not be surprising considering the goal of therapy, the complexity of the task, and the humanity of both participants. As such, alliance ruptures should be expected even in successful treatment and, although this is easier said than done, they should not be avoided. This means that therapists should be alert to markers of alliance ruptures and, when they emerge, should address them directly. They should do this by maintaining an attitude of participant–observer and by metacommunicating. Specifically, they should stop what they are doing, reflect on what is taking place inside of them and within the relationship, invite clients to talk about their experience in the relationship and the therapy, validate such experience, and recognized how they contribute to clients' negative experiences. Rather than being necessarily detrimental, alliance ruptures may actually provide a unique window of change. Their resolution may lead to a lasting change in clients' view of self and others, as well as their ability to deal with interpersonal difficulties in daily life. As beautifully captured by Linehan (1993), the key for dealing with healthy fluctuation of the alliance, and thus for creating the best condition of change, may well be to adopt a balance of challenge and acceptance toward those we try to help.

Despite the considerable research highlighting the therapeutic importance of developing, maintaining, attending to, and managing the alliance, there is still much more to discover about this relational construct and its impact on the process and outcome of therapy. Very few studies have investigated the potential relationship between the therapist's experience or training and the alliance. In addition, the results of the few studies available seem to be contradictory. Although Westerman and Foote (1995) found that clients working with experienced therapists demonstrated better alliances than clients of nonprofessional therapists, Henry et al. (1993) found that therapists demonstrated more hostile behavior toward their clients after receiving a systematic training regimen in psychodynamic intervention.

It is also important for researchers to pay more attention to the interaction between the technical aspects of therapy and the alliance. Although a small number of studies have investigated the interaction between the therapist's use of technique (or adherence) and alliance, there is an even greater paucity of studies addressing the interaction between the quality of intervention (or competence) and the therapeutic relationship.

Another area of strikingly scarce empirical attention relates to the alliance and minority groups. To our knowledge, there are currently no studies that systematically assess the alliance with ethnic minority clients or gay and lesbian clients. However, several studies have demonstrated that ethnicity is a strong predictor of premature, unilateral termination (UT; Greenspan & Kulish, 1985; Sue, 1977; Sue, McKinney, & Allen, 1976; Wierzbicki & Pekarik, 1993). Because the elevated incidences of UT with ethnic minority clients occur when they are being seen by White therapists, such incidences may be driven by therapists' inability to sensitively and effectively respond to the different needs, desires, expectations, and values of ethnic minority individuals (Reis & Brown, 1999; Sue, 1977). Specifically, ethnic minority clients prematurely terminate at a higher rate when they are being seen by White therapists.

Reis and Brown (1999) have argued, however, that the lack of an ethnic match with respect to the therapeutic dyad does not inherently impact the process of therapy in a negative manner, but rather it is the degree to which clients and therapists of different backgrounds evidence significant perspective differences that may lead to relational and treatment problems. Thus, although researchers have not directly assessed the alliance in the treatment of ethnic minorities (or other minority groups such as, gay and lesbian individuals), it could be the case that the early termination findings are mediated by difficulties in developing the alliance. Although not specifically investigating minority clients, several studies (e.g., Mohl et al., 1991; Tryon & Kane, 1990) have shown that a significant relationship exists between the alliance and UT, such that weaker alliances are associated with those clients who terminate treatment in a premature fashion. Future research should investigate whether the relationship between weak alliance and UT will hold for minority clients, with the alliance serving as the mediator of the already evidenced link between minority status and early termination.

The current call for more systematic investigation of the alliance construct as related to the treatment of minority groups should be guided by clinical observation, theory, and related research to date. For example, as reported by Reis and Brown (1999), the literature on UT intuitively suggests that in order to reduce UT rates, "clinicians need to acknowledge the divergent perspectives that so frequently estrange them from their clients, dooming to failure the enterprise that brings them together for a given period of time" (p. 132). This clinical suggestion seems to converge with alliance research that has pointed to the importance of the establishment of an early alliance (Horvath & Luborsky, 1993). It may be the case that to establish an early, quality alliance with minority clients, the therapist may need to become familiar with several core qualities that embody a given minority group or individual client. For example, research with Asian American clients has shown that these individuals, compared to Whites, tend to have a lower tolerance of ambiguity and prefer structured situations and practical problem-solving tactics (e.g., Sue, 1981; Sue & Kirk, 1972). To the extent that a given therapist attempts to employ a treatment approach that emphasizes ambiguity, an unstructured format, or insight over a problem-solving approach, it seems intuitive that a negative treatment process, such as disagreement with treatment tasks, might lead to premature termination.

Research with African Americans has also highlighted several aspects of this ethnic group that the therapist needs to be aware of prior to working with this population. As reviewed by Stevenson and Renard (1993), for instance, one particular African American attribute and strength lies in their tendency to have strong kinship bonds and a general family orientation. By way of example, if a therapist failed to recognize this aspect of an individual's personality, the therapist may remain wedded to an individual therapy approach despite the potential positive impact of incorporating family members in the treatment. And to the extent that the client may have wanted the family members to be involved, a failure on the part of the therapist to act on this desire may severely damage the alliance. Certainly, this is only one of many factors (e.g., experienced oppression leading to inherent mistrust) that needs to be taken into account when working with African American clients. The main point here is that therapists need to be sensitive to perspective divergences and assess whether clients feel as though their perspectives on life will be understood, their needs addressed, and their values respected.

It is our prediction that researchers will soon pay attention to these important issues. In fact, it is fair to say that research on alliance, by and large, has been anchored in clinical observations and theories. By investigating the importance of the relationship, researchers have tested and confirmed what has been clear to clinicians. Reciprocally, clinicians have and will continue to benefit from research knowledge. They will further contribute to empirical advances by continually defining new directions of research (as well as by becoming more involved in therapy studies; see Newman & Castonguay, 1999). As such, the alliance can not only be considered as the ultimate, integrative variable (Wolfe & Goldfried, 1988) but also as the "figure de proue" or ultimate exemplar of a scientific–practitioner approach to the advancement of psychotherapy.

References

Alexander, L. B., & Luborsky, L. (1986). The Penn Helping Alliance Scales. In L. S. Greenberg & W. M. Pinsof (Eds.), *The psychotherapeutic process: A research handbook* (pp. 325–366). New York: Guilford Press.

Allen, J. G., Coyne, L., Colson, D. B., Horowitz, L., Gabbard, G. O., Frieswyk, S. H., & Newson, G. (1996). Pattern of therapist interventions associated with patient collaboration. *Psychotherapy, 33,* 254–261.

Alpher, V. S. (1991). Interpersonal process in psychotherapy: Application to a case study of conflict in the therapeutic relationship. *Psychotherapy, 28,* 550–562.

Arnkoff, D. B. (1981). Flexibility in practicing cognitive therapy. In G. Emery, S. D. Hollon, & R. C. Bedrosian (Eds.), *New directions in cognitive therapy* (pp. 203–223). New York: Guilford Press.

Bachelor, A. (1991). Comparison and relationship to outcome of diverse dimensions of the helping alliance as seen by client and therapist. *Psychotherapy, 28,* 534–549.

Balint, M. (1968). *The basic fault.* London: Tavistock.

Barber, J. P., Crits-Christoph, P., & Luborsky, L. (1996). Effects of therapist adherence and competence on patient outcome in brief dynamic therapy. *Journal of Consulting and Clinical Psychology, 64,* 619–622.

Barber, J. P., Luborksy, L., Crits-Christoph, P., Thase, M. E., Weiss, R., Frank, A., Onken, L., & Gallop, R. (1999). Therapeutic alliance as a predictor of outcome in treatment of cocaine dependence. *Psychotherapy Research, 9,* 54–73.

Barrett-Lennard, G. T. (1985). The helping relationship: Crisis and advance in theory and research. *The Counseling Psychologist, 1,* 278–294.

Beck, A. T., Rush, A. J., Shaw, B. F., & Emery, G. (1979). *Cognitive therapy of depression.* New York: Guilford Press.

Benjamin, L. S. (1974). Structural analysis of social behavior. *Psychological Review, 81,* 392–425.

Benjamin, L. S. (1979). Use of structural analysis of social behavior (SASB) and Markov chains to study dyadic interactions. *Journal of Abnormal Psychology, 88,* 303–319.

Benjamin, L. S. (1996). Introduction to the special section on structural analysis of social behavior. *Journal of Consulting and Clinical Psychology, 64,* 1203–1212.

Binder, J. L., & Strupp, H. H. (1997). "Negative process": A recurrently discovered and underestimated facet of therapeutic process and outcome in the individual psychotherapy of adults. *Clinical Psychology: Science and Practice, 4,* 121–139.

Blatt, S. J., Quinlan, D. M., Pilkonis, P. A., & Shea, M. T. (1995). Impact of perfectionism and need for approval on the brief treatment of depression: The National Institute of Mental Health Treatment of Depression Collaborative Research Program revisited. *Journal of Consulting and Clinical Psychology, 63,* 125–132.

Blatt, S. J., Zuroff, D. C., Quinlan, D. M., & Pilkonis, P. A. (1996). Interpersonal factors in brief treatment of depression: Further analyses of the National Institute of Mental Health Treatment of Depression Collaborative Research Program. *Journal of Consulting and Clinical Psychology, 64,* 162–171.

Bond, M., Banon, E., & Grenier, M. (1998). Differential effects of interventions on the therapeutic alliance with patients with personality disorders. *Journal of Psychotherapy Practice and Research, 7,* 301–318.

Bordin, E. S. (1979). The generalizability of the psychoanalytic concept of the working alliance. *Psychotherapy, 16,* 252–260.

Bordin, E. S. (1980). *Of human bonds that bind or free.* Paper presented at the annual meeting of the Society for Psychotherapy Research, Washington, DC.

Bordin, E. S. (1994). Theory and research on the therapeutic working alliance: New directions. In A. O. Horvath & L. S. Greenberg (Eds.), *The working alliance: Theory, research and practice* (pp. 13–37). New York: Wiley.

Borkovec, T. D., & Whisman, M. A. (1996). Psychological treatment for generalized anxiety disorder. In M. R.

Mavissakalian & R. F. Prien (Eds.), *Long-term treatments of anxiety disorders* (pp. 171–199). Washington, DC: American Psychological Association.

Brenner, C. (1979). Working alliance, therapeutic alliance, and transference. *Journal of the American Psychoanalytic Association, 27,* 136–158.

Brossard, D. F., Willson, V. L., Patton, M. J., Kivlighan, D. M., Jr., & Multon, K. D. (1998). A time series model of the working alliance: A key process in short-term psychoanalytic counseling. *Psychotherapy, 35,* 197–205.

Burns, D. D. (1989). *The feeling good handbook.* New York: William Morrow.

Burns, D. D., & Auerbach, A. (1996). Therapeutic empathy in cognitive-behavioral therapy: Does it really make a difference. In P. M. Salkovskis (Ed.), *Frontiers of cognitive therapy* (pp. 135–164). New York: Guilford Press.

Butler, S. F., Henry, W. P., & Strupp, H. H. (1995). Measuring adherence in time-limited dynamic psychotherapy. *Psychotherapy, 32,* 629–638.

Butler, S. F., & Strupp, H. H. (1986). Specific and non-specific factors in psychotherapy: A problematic paradigm for psychotherapy research. *Psychotherapy, 23,* 30–39.

Carroll, K. M., Nich, C., & Rounsaville, B. J. (1997). Contribution of the therapeutic alliance to outcome in active versus control psychotherapies. *Journal of Consulting and Clinical Psychology, 65,* 510–514.

Cashdan, S. (1973). *Interactional psychotherapy.* New York: Grune & Stratton.

Castonguay, L. G. (1993). "Common factors" and "nonspecific variables": Clarification of the two concepts and recommendations for research. *Journal of Psychotherapy Integration, 3,* 267–286.

Castonguay, L. G. (1997). [Review of the book: *The working alliance: Theory, research and practice.* Edited by A. O Horvath & L. S. Greenberg (1994). New York: Wiley.] *Psychotherapy Research, 7,* 311–314.

Castonguay, L. G. (1998). *Integrating cognitive therapy.* Unpublished treatment manual. Pennsylvania State University.

Castonaguay, L. G. (2000). A common factors approach to psychotherapy training. *Journal of Psychotherapy Integration, 10,* 263–282

Castonguay, L. G., Arnow, B. A., Blatt, S. J., Jones, E. E., Pilkonis, P. A., & Segal, Z. V. (1999). Psychotherapy for depression: Current and future directions in research, theory, practice, and public policy. *Journal of Clinical Psychology/In Session, 55,* 1347–1370.

Castonguay, L. G., Constantino, M. J., & Borkovec, T. D. (1998, June). *Therapists' use of techniques in cognitive-behavioral therapy for generalized anxiety disorder: Is it related to outcome?* Poster session presented at the 29th annual meeting of the Society for Psychotherapy Research, Snowbird, UT.

Castonguay, L. G., Constantino, M. J., & Newman, M. G. (1998, November). *The working alliance and client improvement in cognitive-behavioral treatment for generalized anxiety disorder.* Poster session presented at the 32nd annual meeting of the Association for the Advancement of Behavior Therapy, Washington, DC.

Castonguay, L. G., Goldfried, M. R., Wiser, S., Raue, P. J., & Hayes, A. M. (1996). Predicting the effect of cognitive therapy for depression: A study of unique and common factors. *Journal of Consulting and Clinical Psychology, 64,* 497–504.

Castonguay, L. G., Schut, A. J., Aikins, D. E., Laurenceau, J-P., Bologh, L., & Burns, D. D. (2000, June). *Integrative cognitive therapy for depression: A first look at its efficacy.* Paper presented at the annual meeting of the Society for Psychotherapy Research, Chicago, IL.

Castonguay, L. G., Schut, A. J., Constantino, M. J., & Halperin, G. S. (1999). Assessing the role of treatment manuals: Have they become necessary but non-sufficient ingredients of change? *Clinical Psychology: Science and Practice, 6,* 449–455.

Christianson, J. (1991). *Understanding the patient–therapist interaction and therapeutic change in light of pre-therapy interpersonal relations.* Unpublished doctoral dissertation, Vanderbilt University, Nashville, TN.

Coady, N. F. (1991a). The association between client and therapist interpersonal process and outcomes in psychodynamic psychotherapy. *Research on Social Work Practice, 1,* 122–138.

Coady, N. F. (1991b). The association between complex types of therapist interventions and outcomes in psychodynamic psychotherapy. *Research on Social Work and Practice, 1,* 257–277.

Coady, N. F., & Marziali, E. (1994). The association between global and specific measures of the therapeutic relationship. *Psychotherapy, 31,* 17–27.

Connors, G. J., Carroll, K. M., DiClemente, C. C., Longabaugh, R., & Donovan, D. M. (1997). The therapeutic alliance and its relationship to alcoholism treatment participation and outcome. *Journal of Consulting and Clinical Psychology, 65,* 588–598.

Constantino, M. J. (2000). Interpersonal process in psychotherapy through the lens of the Structural Analysis of Social Behavior. *Applied and Preventive Psychology, 9,* 153–172.

Constantino, M. J., & Castonguay, L. G. (1999, November). *The effects of therapist competence and client receptivity in cognitive-behavioral treatment for generalized anxiety disorder.* Poster session presented at the 33rd annual meeting of the Association for the Advancement of Behavior Therapy, Toronto, Ontario.

Critchfield, K. L., Henry, W. P., Castonguay, L. G., & Borkovec, T. D. (1999). *Interpersonal process and outcome in variants of cognitive-behavioral psychotherapy.* Manuscript submitted for publication.

Crits-Christoph, P., Barber, J. P., & Kurcias, J. S. (1993). The accuracy of therapists' interpretations and the development of the therapeutic alliance. *Psychotherapy Research, 3,* 25–35.

Crits-Christoph, P., Cooper, A., & Luborsky, L. (1988). The accuracy of therapists' interpretations and the outcome of dynamic psychotherapy. *Journal of Consulting and Clinical Psychology, 56,* 490–495.

Curtis, H. C. (1979). The concept of the therapeutic alliance: Implications for the "widening scope," *Journal of the American Psychoanalytic Association, 27,* 159–192.

DeRubeis, R. J., Evans, M. D., & Hollon, S. D. (1989). Unpublished raw data [Variables of the therapeutic process].

DeRubeis, R. J., & Feeley, M. (1990). Determinants of change in cognitive therapy for depression. *Cognitive Therapy and Research, 14,* 469–482.

Deserno, H. (1998). *The analyst and the working alliance: The reemergence of convention in psychoanalysis.* Connecticut: International Universities Press.

Eaton, T. T., Abeles, N., & Gutfreund, M. J. (1988). Therapeutic alliance and outcome: Impact of treatment length and pretreatment symptomatology. *Psychotherapy, 25,* 536–542.

Elkin, I., Yamaguchi, J. L., Arnkoff, D. B., Glass, C. R., Sotsky, S. M., & Krupnick, J. L. (1999). "Patient-treatment fit" and early engagement in therapy. *Psychotherapy Research, 9,* 437–451.

Elkin, I., Shea, M. T., Watkins, J. T., Imber, S. D., Sotsky, S. M., Collins, J. F., Glass, D. R., Pilkonis, P. A., Leber, W. R., Docherty, J. P., Fiester, S. J., & Parloff, M. B. (1989). National Institutes of Mental Health Treatment of Depression Collaborative Research Program: General effectiveness of treatments. *Archives of General Psychiatry, 46,* 971–982.

Feeley, M., DeRubeis, R. J., & Gelfand, L. A. (1999). The temporal relation of adherence and alliance to symptom change in cognitive therapy for depression. *Journal of Consulting and Clinical Psychology, 67,* 578–582.

Foreman, S., & Marmar, C. R. (1985). Therapist actions that address initially poor therapeutic alliances in psychotherapy. *American Journal of Psychiatry, 142,* 922–926.

Freebury, D. R. (1989). The therapeutic alliance: A psychoanalytic perspective. *Canadian Journal of Psychiatry, 34,* 772–774.

Freud, S. (1958). On beginning treatment (Further recommendations on the technique of psychoanalysis). In J. Strachey (Ed. and Trans.), *The standard edition of the complete psychological works of Sigmund Freud* (Vol. 12, pp. 121–144). London: Hogarth Press. (Original work published 1913)

Frieswyk, S. H., Allen, J. G., Colson, D. B., Coyne, L., Gabbard, G. O., Horowitz, L. M., & Newsom, G. (1986). Therapeutic alliance: Its place as a process and outcome variable in dynamic psychotherapy research. *Journal of Consulting and Clinical Psychology, 54,* 32–38.

Gaston, L. (1990). The concept of the alliance and its role in psychotherapy: Theoretical and empirical considerations. *Psychotherapy, 27,* 143–153.

Gaston, L., & Marmar, C. R. (1994). The California Psychotherapy Alliance scales. In A. O. Horvath & L. S. Greenberg (Eds.), *The working alliance: Theory, research, and practice* (pp. 85–108). New York: John Wiley & Sons, Inc.

Gaston, L., Marmar, C., & Ring, J. (1989, June). *Engaging the difficult patient in cognitive therapy: Actions developing the therapeutic alliance.* Paper presented at the annual meeting of the Society for Psychotherapy Research, Toronto, Canada.

Gaston, L., Marmar, C. R., Thompson, L. W., & Gallagher, D. (1988). Relation of patient pretreatment characteristics to the therapeutic alliance in diverse psychotherapies. *Journal of Consulting and Clinical Psychology, 56,* 483–489.

Gaston, L., Piper, W. E., Debbane, E. G., Bienvenu, J. -P., & Garant, J. (1994). Alliance and technique for predicting outcome in short- and long-term analytic psychotherapy. *Psychotherapy Research, 4,* 121–135.

Gaston, L., & Ring, J. M. (1992). Preliminary results on the Inventory of Therapeutic Strategies (ITS). *Journal of Psychotherapy Research and Practice, 1,* 1–13.

Gaston, L., Thompson, L., Gallagher, D., Cournoyer, L. -G., Gagnon, R. (1998). Alliance, technique, and their interactions in predicting outcome of behavioral, cognitive, and brief dynamic therapy. *Psychotherapy Research, 8,* 190–209.

Gelso, C. J., & Carter, J. A. (1985). The relationship in counseling and psychotherapy: Components, consequences, and theoretical antecedents. *The Counseling Psychologist, 13,* 155–243.

Gelso, C. J., & Carter, J. A. (1994). Components of the psychotherapy relationship: Their interactional unfolding during treatment. *Journal of Counseling Psychology, 41,* 296–306.

Gelso, C. J., & Hayes, J. A. (1998). *The psychotherapy relationship: Theory, research, and practice.* New York: Wiley.

Gendlin, E. T. (1978). *Focusing.* New York: Everest House.

Golden, B. R., & Robbins, S. B. (1990). The working alliance within time-limited therapy: A case analysis. *Professional Psychology: Research and Practice, 21,* 476–481.

Goldfried, M. R. (1985). In vivo intervention or transference? In W. Dryden (Ed.), *Therapists' dilemmas.* London: Harper & Row.

Goldfried, M. R., & Castonguay, L. G. (1992). The future of psychotherapy integration. *Psychotherapy, 29,* 4–10.

Goldfried, M. R, & Castonguay, L. G. (1993). Behavior therapy: Redefining strengths and limitations. *Behavior Therapy, 24,* 505–526.

Goldfried, M. R., & Padawer, W. (1982). Current status and future directions in psychotherapy. In M. R. Goldfried (Ed.), *Converging themes in psychotherapy* (pp. 3–49). New York: Springer.

Gomez-Schwartz, B. (1978). Effective ingredients in psychotherapy: Prediction of outcome from process variables. *Journal of Consulting and Clinical Psychology, 46,* 1023–1035.

Goren, L. (1991). *The relationship of counselor androgyny to the working alliance.* Unpublished doctoral dissertation, University of Southern California.

Greenberg, L. S., & Paivio, S. C. (1997). *Working with emotions in psychotherapy.* New York: Guilford Press.

Greenberg, L. S., Rice, L. N., & Elliott, R. (1993). *Facilitating emotional change: The moment-by-moment process.* New York: Guilford Press.

Greenson, R. R. (1965). The working alliance and the transference neurosis. *Psychoanalysis Quarterly, 34,* 155–181.

Greenson, R. R. (1967). *The techniques and practice of psychoanalysis.* New York: International Universities Press.

Greenspan, M., & Kulish, N. M. (1985). Factors in premature termination in long-term psychotherapy. *Psychotherapy, 22,* 75–82.

Grencavage, L. M., & Norcross, J. C. (1990). Where are the commonalities among the therapeutic common factors? *Professional Psychology—Research and Practice, 21,* 372–378.

Gunderson, J. G., Najavits, L. M., Leonhard, C., Sullivan, C. N., & Sabo, A. N. (1997). Ontogeny of the therapeutic alliance in borderline patients. *Psychotherapy Research, 7,* 310–319.

Gurman, A. S. (1977). The patient's perception of the therapeutic relationship. In A. S. Gurman & A. M. Razim (Eds.), *Effective psychotherapy: A handbook of research* (pp. 503–543). Oxford: Pergamon Press.

Hanley, C. (1994). Reflections on the place of the therapeutic alliance in psychoanalysis. *International Journal of Psychoanalysis, 75,* 457–467.

Harrist, R. S., Quintana, S. M., Strupp, H. H., & Henry, W. P. (1994). Internalization of interpersonal process in time-limited dynamic psychotherapy. *Psychotherapy, 31,* 49–57.

Hartley, D. E., & Strupp, H. H. (1983). The therapeutic alliance: Its relationship to outcome in brief psychotherapy. In J. Masling (Ed.), *Empirical studies in analytic theories* (pp. 1–37). Hillside, NJ: Erlbaum.

Hatcher, R. L. (1999). Therapists' views of treatment alliance and collaboration in therapy. *Psychotherapy Research, 9,* 405–423.

Hatcher, R. L., & Barends, A. W. (1996). Patients' view of the alliance in psychotherapy: Exploratory factor analysis of three alliance measures. *Journal of Consulting and Clinical Psychology, 64,* 1326–1336.

Henry, W. P. (1996). Structural analysis of social behavior as a common metric for programmatic psychopathology and psychotherapy research. *Journal of Consulting and Clinical Psychology, 64,* 1263–1275.

Henry, W. P. (1998). Science, politics, and the politics of science: The use and misuse of empirically validated treatment research. *Psychotherapy Research, 8,* 126–140.

Henry, W. P., Schacht, T. E., & Strupp, H. H. (1986). Structural analysis of social behavior: Application to a study of interpersonal process in differential psychotherapeutic outcome. *Journal of Consulting and Clinical Psychology, 54,* 27–31.

Henry, W. P., Schacht, T. E., & Strupp, H. H. (1990). Patient and therapist introject, interpersonal process and differential psychotherapy outcome. *Journal of Consulting and Clinical Psychology, 58,* 768–774.

Henry, W. P., & Strupp, H. H. (1994). The therapeutic alliance as interpersonal process. In A. O. Horvath & L. S. Greenberg (Eds.), *The working alliance: Theory, research and practice* (pp. 51–84). New York: Wiley.

Henry, W. P., Strupp, H. H., Butler, S. F., Schacht, T. E., & Binder, J. L. (1993). The effects of training in time-limited dynamic psychotherapy: Changes in therapist behavior. *Journal of Consulting and Clinical Psychology, 61,* 434–440.

Hildenbrand, G., Hildenbrand, B., & Junkert-Tress, B. (1994, July). *Dropping out of therapy: Analysis of cyclic maladaptive pattern and interpersonal process in prematurely terminated dynamic psychotherapy.* Paper presented at the annual meeting of the Society for Psychotherapy Research, York, England.

Hilliard, R. B., Henry, W. P., & Strupp, H. H. (2000). An interpersonal model of psychotherapy: Linking patient and therapist developmental history, therapeutic process, and types of outcome. *Journal of Consulting and Clinical Psychology, 68,* 125–133.

Horowitz, L. M., Rosenberg, S. E., Baer, B. A., Ureno, G., & Villasenor, V. S. (1988). Inventory of interpersonal problems: Psychometric properties and clinical applications. *Journal of Consulting and Clinical Psychology, 56,* 885–892.

Horvath, A. O. (1991, June). *What do we know about the alliance and what do we still have to find out?* Paper presented at the annual meeting of the Society for Psychotherapy Research, Lyon, France.

Horvath, A. O. (1994). Research on the alliance. In A. O. Horvath & L. S. Greenberg (Eds.), *The working alliance: Theory, research, and practice* (pp. 259–286). New York: Wiley.

Horvath, A. O., & Greenberg, L. S. (1989). Development and validation of the Working Alliance Inventory. *Journal of Counseling Psychology, 36,* 223–233.

Horvath, A. O., & Greenberg, L. S. (1994). *The working alliance: Theory, research, and practice.* New York: Wiley.

Horvath, A. O., & Luborsky, L. (1993). The role of the therapeutic alliance in psychotherapy. *Journal of Consulting and Clinical Psychology, 61,* 561–573.

Horvath, A. O., & Marx, R. W. (1990). The development and decay of the working alliance during time-limited counseling. *Canadian Journal of Counseling, 24,* 240–260.

Horvath, A. O., & Symonds, D. B. (1991). Relationship between working alliance and outcome in psychotherapy: A meta-analysis. *Journal of Counseling Psychology, 38,* 139–149.

Jones, E. E., & Pulos, S. M. (1993). Comparing the process in psychodynamic and cognitive-behavioral therapies. *Journal of Consulting and Clinical Psychology, 61,* 306–316.

Kerr, S., Goldfried, M. R., Hayes, A. H., Castonguay, L. G., & Goldsamt, L. A. (1992). Interpersonal and intrapersonal focus in cognitive-behavioral and psychodynamic-interpersonal therapies: A preliminary analysis of the Sheffield Project. *Psychotherapy Research, 2,* 266–276.

Kiesler, D. J. (1973). *The process of psychotherapy: Empirical foundations and systems of analysis.* Hawthorne, NY: Aldine.

Kiesler, D. J. (1982). Interpersonal theory for personality and psychotherapy. In J. C. Anchin & D. J. Kiesler (Eds.), *Handbook of interpersonal psychotherapy* (pp. 3–24). New York: Pergamon Press.

Kiesler, D. J. (1996). *Contemporary interpersonal theory and research. Personality, psychopathology, and psychotherapy.* New York: Wiley.

Kivlighan, D. M., & Shaughnessy, P. (1995). Analysis of the development of the working alliance using hierarchical linear modeling. *Journal of Counseling Psychology, 42,* 338–349.

Kokotovic, A. M., & Tracey, T. J. (1990). Working alliance in early phase of counseling. *Journal of Counseling Psychology, 37,* 16–21.

Krupnick, J. L., Sotsky, S. M., Simmens, S., Moyer, J., Elkin, I., Watkins, J., & Pilkonis, P. A. (1996). The role of the therapeutic alliance in psychotherapy and pharmacotherapy outcome: Findings in the National Institute of Mental Health Treatment of Depression Collaborative Research Program. *Journal of Consulting and Clinical Psychology, 64,* 532–539.

Lambert, M. J., & Bergin, A. E. (1994). The effectiveness of psychotherapy. In A. E. Bergin & S. L. Garfield (Eds.), *Handbook of psychotherapy and behavior change* (4th ed., pp. 143–189). New York: Wiley.

Lansford, E. (1986). Weakenings and repairs of the working alliance in short-term psychotherapy. *Professional Psychology: Research and Practice, 17,* 364–366.

Lichtenberg, J. W., & Heck, E. J. (1986). Methodological approaches to the study of interpersonal influence in counseling interaction. In F. J. Dorn (Ed.), *The social influence process in counseling and psychotherapy.* Springfield: Charles C. Thomas.

Lieberman, P. B., Von Rehn, S., Dickie, E., Elliott, B., & Egerter, E. (1992). Therapeutic effects of brief hospitalization: The role of a therapeutic alliance. *Journal of Psychotherapy: Practice and Research, 1,* 56–63.

Lietaer, G. (1990). The client-centered approach after the Wisconsin Project: A personal view on its evolution. In G. Lietaer, J. Rombauts, & R. Van Balen (Eds.), *Client-centered and experiential psychotherapy in the nineties* (pp. 19–45). Leuven, Belgium: Leuven University Press.

Lietaer, G. (1992). Helping and hindering processes in client-centered/experiential psychotherapy: A content analysis of client and therapist post-session perceptions. In S. G. Toukmanian & D. L. Rennie (Eds.), *Psychotherapy process research: Theory-guided and phenomenological research strategies.* Beverly Hills, CA: Sage.

Linehan, M. M. (1993). *Cognitive-behavioral treatment of borderline personality disorder.* New York: Guilford Press.

Luborsky, L. (1975). Clinicians' judgements of mental health: Specimen case descriptions and forms for the Health-Sickness Rating Scale. *Bulletin of Menninger Clinic, 35,* 448–480.

Luborsky, L. (1976). Helping alliances in psychotherapy. In J. L. Cleghorn (Ed.), *Successful psychotherapy* (pp. 92–116). New York: Brunner/Mazel.

Luborsky, L. (1994). Therapeutic alliances as predictors of psychotherapy outcomes: Factors explaining the predictive success. In A. O. Horvath & L. S. Greenberg (Eds.), *The working alliance: Theory, research, and practice* (pp. 38–50). New York: Wiley.

Luborsky, L. (2000). A pattern-setting therapeutic alliance study revisited. *Psychotherapy Research, 10,* 17–29.

Luborsky, L., & Auerbach, A. (1985). The therapeutic relationship in psychodynamic psychotherapy: The research evidence and its meaning for practice. In R. Hales & A. Frances (Eds.), *Psychiatry update annual review* (pp. 550–561). Washington, DC: American Psychiatric Association.

Luborsky, L., Crits-Christoph, P., Alexander, L., Margolis, M., & Cohen, M. (1983). Two helping alliance methods for predicting outcomes of psychotherapy: A counting signs versus a global rating method. *Journal of Nervous and Mental Disease, 171,* 480–491.

Luborsky, L., Crits-Christoph, P., Mintz, J., & Auerbach, A. (1988). *Who will benefit from psychotherapy? Predicting therapeutic outcomes.* New York: Basic Books.

Luborsky, L., McLellan, A. T., Woody, G. E., O'Brien, C. P., & Auerbach, A. (1985). Therapist success and its determinants. *Archives of General Psychiatry, 42,* 602–611.

Luborsky, L., Singer, B., & Luborsky, L. (1975). Comparative studies of psychotherapies; "Is it true that everyone has won and all must have prizes?" *Archives of General Psychiatry, 32,* 995–1008.

Mahoney, M. J. (1991). *Human change processes: The scientific foundations of psychotherapy.* New York: Basic Books.

Mallinckrodt, B. (1991). Clients' representation of childhood emotional bonds with parents, social support, and formation of the working alliance. *Journal of Counseling Psychology, 38,* 401–409.

Mallinckrodt, B. (1993). Session impact, working alliance, and treatment outcome in brief counseling. *Journal of Counseling Psychology, 40,* 25–32.

Mann, J. (1973). *Time-limited psychotherapy.* Cambridge, MA: Harvard University Press.

Marmar, C. R., Gaston, L., Gallagher, D., & Thompson, L. W. (1989). Alliance and outcome in late-life depression. *The Journal of Nervous and Mental Disease, 177,* 464–472.

Marmar, C. R., Horowitz, M. J., Weiss, D. S., & Marziali, E. (1986). Development of the Therapeutic Rating System. In L. S. Greenberg and W. M. Pinsoff (Eds.), *The psychotherapeutic process: A research handbook* (pp. 367–390). New York: Guilford Press.

Marmar, C. R., Weiss, D. S., & Gaston, L. (1989). Towards the validation of the California Therapeutic Alliance Rating System. *Journal of Consulting and Clinical Psychology, 1,* 46–52.

Marziali, E. (1984a). Three viewpoints on the Therapeutic Alliance Scales similarities, differences, and associations with psychotherapy outcome. *Journal of Nervous and Mental Disease, 172,* 417–423.

Marziali, E. (1984b). Prediction of outcome of brief psychotherapy from therapist interpretive interventions. *Archives of General Psychiatry, 41,* 301–305.

Marziali, E., Marmar, C., & Krupnick, J. (1981). Therapeutic Alliance scales: Development and relationship to psychotherapy outcome. *American Journal of Psychiatry, 138,* 361–364.

Marziali, E., Monroe-Blum, H., McCleary, L. (1999). The effects of the therapeutic alliance on the outcomes of individual and group psychotherapy with borderline personality disorder. *Psychotherapy Research, 9,* 424–436.

Mitchell, K. M., Bozart, J. D., & Krauft, C. C. (1977). A reappraisal of the therapeutic effectiveness of accurate empathy, nonpossessive warmth, and genuineness. In A. S. Gurman and A. M. Razin (Eds.), *Effective psychotherapy: A handbook of research* (pp. 544–565). New York: Pergamon Press.

Mohl, P. C., Martinez, D., Ticknor, C., Huang, M., & Cordell, L. (1991). Early dropouts from psychotherapy. *Journal of Nervous and Mental Disease, 179,* 478–481.

Moras, K., & Strupp, H. H. (1982). Pretherapy interpersonal relations, patients' alliance, and outcome in brief therapy. *Archives of General Psychiatry, 39,* 405–409.

Morgan, R., Luborsky, L., Crits-Christoph, P., Curtis, H., & Solomon, J. (1982). Predicting the outcomes of psychotherapy by the Penn Helping Alliance Rating Method. *Archives of General Psychiatry, 39,* 397–402.

Muran, J. C., Gorman, B. S., Safran, J. D., Twining, L., Wallner Samstag, L., & Winston, A. (1995). Linking in-session change to overall outcome in short-term cognitive therapy. *Journal of Consulting and Clinical Psychology, 63,* 651–657.

Muran, J. C., Segal, Z. V., Samstag, L. W., & Crawford, C. E. (1994). Patient pretreatment interpersonal problems and therapeutic alliance in short-term cognitive therapy. *Journal of Consulting and Clinical Psychology, 62,* 185–190.

Newman, C. F. (1997). Maintaining professionalism in the face of emotional abuse from clients. *Cognitive and Behavioral Practice, 4,* 1–29.

Newman, M. G., & Castonguay, L. G. (1999). Reflecting on current challenges and future directions in psychotherapy: What can be learned from dialogues between clinicians, researchers, and policy makers *Journal of Clinical Psychology/In Session, 55,* 1407–1413.

Newman, M. G., Castonguay, L. G., & Borkovec, T. D. (1999, April). *New dimensions in the treatment of generalized anxiety disorder: Interpersonal focus and emotional deepening.* Paper presented at the 15th annual meeting of the Society for the Exploration of Psychotherapy Integration, Miami, FL.

O'Malley, S. S., Suh, C. S., & Strupp, H. H. (1983). The Vanderbilt Psychotherapy Process Scale: A report on the scale development and a process-outcome study. *Journal of Consulting and Clinical Psychology, 51,* 581–586.

Orlinsky, D. E., Grawe, K., & Parks, B. K. (1994). Process and outcome in psychotherapy—Noch einmal. In A. E. Bergin & S. L. Garfield (Eds.), *Handbook of psychotherapy and behavior change* (4th ed., pp. 270–376). New York: Wiley.

Orlinsky, D. E., & Howard, K. I. (1986). The psychological interior of psychotherapy: Explorations with the Therapy Session Report Questionnaires. In L. S. Greenberg & W. M. Pinsoff (Eds.), *The psychotherapeutic process: A research handbook.* New York: Guilford Press.

Paivio, S. C., & Bahr, L. M. (1998). Interpersonal problems, working alliance, and outcome in short-term experiential therapy. *Psychotherapy Research, 8,* 392–407.

Patton, M. J., Kivlighan, D. M., Jr., & Multon, K. D. (1997). The Missouri psychoanalytic counseling research project: Relation of changes in counseling process to client outcomes. *Journal of Counseling Psychology, 44,* 189–208.

Patton, M. J., & Meara, N. M. (1992). *Psychoanalytic counseling.* Chichester, England: John Wiley.

Piper, W. E., Azim, H. F. A., Joyce, A. S., & McCallum, M. (1991a). Transference interpretations, therapeutic alliance, and outcome in short-term individual therapy. *Archives of General Psychiatry, 48,* 946–953.

Piper, W. E., Azim, H. F. A., Joyce, A. S., McCallum, M., Nixon, G. W. H., & Segal, P. S. (1991b). Quality of object relations versus interpersonal functioning as predictor of therapeutic alliance and psychotherapy outcome. *Journal of Nervous and Mental Disease, 179,* 432–438.

Piper, W. E., Boroto, D. R., Joyce, A. S., McCallum, M., & Azim, H. F. A. (1995). Pattern of alliance and outcome in short-term individual psychotherapy. *Psychotherapy, 32,* 639–647.

Piper, W. E., DeCarufel, F. L., & Szkrumelack, N. (1985). Patient predictors of process and outcome in short-term individual psychotherapy. *Journal of Nervous and Mental Disease, 173,* 726–733.

Quinn, W. H., Dotson, D., & Jordan, K. (1997). Dimensions of the therapeutic alliance and their associations with outcome in family therapy. *Psychotherapy Research, 7,* 429–438.

Quintana, S. M., & Meara, N. M. (1990). Internalization of therapeutic relationships in short-term psychotherapy. *Journal of Counseling Psychology, 37,* 123–130.

Randeau, S. G., & Wampold, B. E. (1991). Relationship of power and involvement to working alliance: A multiple-case sequential analysis of brief therapy. *Journal of Counseling Psychology, 38,* 107–114.

Raue, P. J., Castonguay, L. G., & Goldfried, M. R. (1993). The working alliance: A comparison of two therapies. *Psychotherapy Research, 3,* 197–207.

Raue, P. J., & Goldfried, M. R. (1994). The therapeutic alliance in cognitive-behavior therapy. In A. O. Horvath & L. S. Greenberg (Eds.), *The working alliance: Theory, research, and practice* (pp. 131–152). New York: Wiley.

Raue, P. J., Goldfried, M. R., & Barkham, M. (1997). The therapeutic alliance in psychodynamic-interpersonal and cognitive-behavioral therapy. *Journal of Consulting and Clinical Psychology, 65,* 582–587.

Rector, N. A., Zuroff, D. C., & Segal, Z. V. (1999). Cognitive change and the therapeutic alliance: The role of technical and non-technical factors in cognitive therapy. *Psychotherapy, 36,* 320–328.

Reis, B. F., & Brown, L. G. (1999). Reducing psychotherapy dropouts: Maximizing perspective convergence in the psychotherapy dyad. *Psychotherapy, 36,* 123–136.

Rice, L. N., & Greenberg, L. S. (1984). *Patterns of change: Intensive analysis of psychotherapy process.* New York: Guilford Press.

Rogers, C. R. (1951). *Client-centered therapy.* Boston, MA: Houghton-Mifflin.

Rogers, C. R. (1957). The necessary and sufficient conditions of therapeutic personality change. *Journal of Consulting Psychology, 21,* 95–103.

Rosenthal, R. (1979). The file drawer problem and tolerance for null results. *Psychological Bulletin, 86,* 638–641.

Rounsaville, B. J., Chevron, E. S., Prusoff, B. A., Elkin, I., Imber, S., Sotsky, S., & Watkins, J. (1987). The relation between specific and general dimensions of the psychotherapy process in interpersonal psychotherapy of depression. *Journal of Consulting and Clinical Psychology, 55,* 379–384.

Ryan, E. R., & Chicchetti, D. B. (1985). Predicting quality of alliance in the initial psychotherapy interview. *Journal of Nervous and Mental Disease, 173,* 717–725.

Safran, J. D. (1993). Breaches in the therapeutic alliance: An area for negotiating authentic relatedness. *Psychotherapy, 30,* 11–24.

Safran, J. D., Crocker, P., McMain, S., & Murray, P. (1990). The therapeutic alliance rupture as a therapy event for empirical investigation. *Psychotherapy, 27,* 154–165.

Safran, J. D., & Muran, J. C. (1996). The resolution of ruptures in the therapeutic alliance. *Journal of Consulting and Clinical Psychology, 64,* 447–458.

Safran, J. D., & Muran, J. C. (1998). *The therapeutic alliance in brief psychotherapy.* Washington, DC: American Psychological Association.

Safran, J. D., & Muran, J. C. (2000). *Negotiating the therapeutic alliance.* New York: Guilford Press.

Safran, J. D., Muran, J. C., & Samstag, L. W. (1994). Resolving therapeutic alliance ruptures: A task analytic investigation. In A. O. Horvath & L. S. Greenberg

(Eds.), *The working alliance: Theory, research, and practice* (pp. 225–255). New York: Wiley.

Safran, J. D., & Segal, Z. V. (1990). *Interpersonal process in cognitive therapy.* New York: Basic Books.

Safran, J. D., & Wallner, L. K. (1991). The relative predictive validity of two therapeutic alliance measures in cognitive therapy. *Psychological Assessment: A Journal of Consulting and Clinical Psychology, 3,* 188–195.

Saketopoulou, A. (1999). The therapeutic alliance in psychodynamic psychotherapy: Theoretical conceptualizations and research findings. *Psychotherapy, 36,* 329–342.

Salvio, M. A., Beutler, L. E., Wood, J. M., & Engle, D. (1992). The strength of the therapeutic alliance in three treatments for depression. *Psychotherapy Research, 2,* 31–36.

Saunders, S. M., Howard, K. I., & Orlinsky, D. E. (1989). The therapeutic bond scales: Psychometric characteristics and relationship to treatment effectiveness. *Psychological Assessment: A Journal of Consulting and Clinical Psychology, 1,* 323–330.

Sexton, H. (1993). Exploring a psychotherapeutic change sequence: Relating process to intersessional and posttreatment outcome. *Journal of Consulting and Clinical Psychology, 61,* 128–136.

Sexton, H. (1996). Process, life events, and symptomatic change in brief eclectic psychotherapy. *Journal of Consulting and Clinical Psychology, 64,* 1358–1365.

Sexton, H. C., Hembre, K., & Kvarme, G. (1996). The interaction of the alliance and therapy microprocess: A sequential analysis. *Journal of Consulting and Clinical Psychology, 64,* 471–480.

Shearin, E. N., & Linehan, M. M. (1992). Patient–therapist ratings and relationship to progress in dialectical behavior therapy for borderline personality disorder. *Behavior Therapy, 23,* 730–742.

Sifneos, P. E. (1979). *Short-term dynamic psychotherapy: Evaluation and technique.* New York: Plenum Press.

Smith, M. L., & Glass, G. V. (1977). Meta-analysis of psychotherapy outcome studies. *American Psychologist, 32,* 752–760.

Sterba, R. (1934). The fate of the ego in analytic therapy. *International Journal of Psychoanalysis, 15,* 117–126.

Stevenson, H. C., & Renard, G. (1993). Trusting ole' wise owls: Therapeutic use of cultural strengths in African-American families. *Professional Psychology: Research and Practice, 24,* 433–442.

Stiles, W. B., Agnew-Davies, R., Hardy, G. E., Barkham, M., & Shapiro, D. A. (1998). Relations of the alliance with psychotherapy outcome: Findings in the second Sheffield psychotherapy project. *Journal of Consulting and Clinical Psychology, 66,* 791–802.

Stiles, W. B., Shapiro, D., & Elliott, R. (1986). Are all psychotherapies equivalent? *American Psychologist, 41,* 165–180.

Strupp, H. H. (1977). A reformulation of the dynamics of the therapist's contribution. In A. S. Gurman & A. M. Razin (Eds.), *Effective psychotherapy: A handbook of research* (pp. 1–22). Oxford: Pergamon Press.

Strupp, H. H. (1980). Success and failure in time-limited psychotherapy. Further evidence (Comparison 4). *Archives of General Psychiatry, 37,* 947–954.

Strupp, H. H., & Hadley, S. W. (1979). Specific versus nonspecific factors in psychotherapy. *Archives in General Psychiatry, 36,* 1125–1136.

Strupp, H. H., Schacht, T. E., & Henry, W. P. (1988). Problem–treatment–outcome congruence: A principle whose time has come. In H. Dahl & H. Kachele (Eds.), *Psychodynamic process research strategies.* New York: Springer.

Sue, D. W. (1981). *Counseling the culturally different: Theory and practice.* New York: Wiley.

Sue, D. W., & Kirk, B. A. (1972). Psychological characteristics of Chinese-American students. *Journal of Counseling Psychology, 19,* 471–478.

Sue, S. (1977). Community mental health services to minority groups: Some optimism, some pessimism. *American Psychologist, 32,* 616–624.

Sue, S., McKinney, H. L., & Allen, D. B. (1976). Predictors of the duration of therapy for clients in the community mental health system. *Community Mental Health Journal, 12,* 365–375.

Sullivan, H. S. (1953). *The interpersonal theory of psychiatry.* New York: Norton.

Svartberg, M., & Stiles, T. C. (1992). Predicting patient change from therapist competence and patient–therapist complementarity in short-term anxiety-provoking psychotherapy: A pilot study. *Journal of Consulting and Clinical Psychology, 60,* 304–307.

Svartberg, M., & Stiles, T. C. (1994). Therapeutic alliance, therapist competence, and client change in short-term anxiety-provoking psychotherapy. *Psychotherapy Research, 4,* 20–33.

Tichenor, V., & Hill, C. E. (1989). A comparison of six measures of working alliance. *Psychotherapy: Theory, Research and Practice, 26,* 195–199.

Tracey, T. J. (1985). The n of 1 Markov chain design as a means of studying the stages of psychotherapy. *Psychiatry, 48,* 196–204.

Tracey, T. J. (1993). An interpersonal stage model of the therapeutic process. *Journal of Counseling Psychology, 40,* 396–409.

Tracey, T. J., & Kokotovic, A. (1989). Factor structure of the Working Alliance Inventory. *Psychological Assessment: A Journal of Consulting and Clinical Psychology, 1,* 207–210.

Tracey, T. J., & Ray, P. B. (1984). The stages of successful time-limited counseling: An interactional examination. *Journal of Counseling Psychology, 31,* 13–27.

Tryon, G. S., & Kane, A. S. (1990). The helping alliance and premature termination. *Counseling Psychology Quarterly, 3,* 233–238.

Tryon, G. S., & Kane, A. S. (1995). Client involvement, working alliance, and type of therapy termination. *Psychotherapy Research, 5,* 189–198.

Tuttman, S. (1997). Protecting the therapeutic alliance in this time of changing health-care delivery systems. *International Journal of Group Psychotherapy, 47,* 3–16.

Watson, J. C., & Greenberg, L. S. (1994). The alliance in experiential therapy: Enacting the relationship conditions. In A. O. Horvath & L. S. Greenberg (Eds.), *The working alliance: Theory, research, and practice* (pp. 153–172). New York: Wiley.

Weiss, M., Gaston, L., Propst, A., Weisebord, S., & Zicherman, V. (1997). The role of the alliance in the pharmacological treatment of depression. *Journal of Clinical Psychiatry, 58,* 196–204.

Westerman, M. A. (1998). Curvilinear trajectory in patient coordination over the course of short-term psychotherapy. *Psychotherapy, 35,* 206–219.

Westerman, M. A., & Foote, J. P. (1995). Patient coordination: Contrasts with other conceptualizations of patients' contribution to the alliance and validity in insight-oriented psychotherapy. *Psychotherapy, 32,* 222–232.

Wierzbicki, M., & Pekarik, G. (1993). A meta-analysis of psychotherapy dropout. *Professional Psychology: Research and Practice, 24,* 190–195.

Wile, D. B. (1984). Kohut, Kernberg, and accusatory interpretations. *Psychotherapy. 21,* 353–364.

Wilson, G. T., Loeb, K. L., Walsh, B. T., Labouvie, E., Petkova, E., Liu, X., & Waternaux, C. (1999). Psychological versus pharmacological treatments of bulimia nervosa: Predictors and processes of change. *Journal of Consulting and Clinical Psychology, 67,* 451–459.

Wolfe, B. E., & Goldfried, M. R. (1988). Research on psychotherapy integration: Recommendations and conclusions from an NIMH workshop. *Journal of Consulting and Clinical Psychology, 56,448–451.*

Zetzel, E. (1956). Current concepts of transference. *International Journal of Psychoanalysis, 37,* 369–376.

Zuroff, D. C., Blatt, S. J., Sotsky, S. M., Krupnick, J. L., Martin, D. J., Sanislow, C. A., & Simmens, S. (2000). Relation of therapeutic alliance and perfectionism to outcome in brief outpatient treatment of depression. *Journal of Consulting and Clinical Psychology, 68,* 114–124.

5

The Learning Alliance of Supervision

Research to Practice

Elizabeth Holloway and Pilar González-Doupé

University of Wisconsin at Madison

All counselors learn how to do therapy under the supervision of a senior counselor. The process by which supervision is conducted is as complex as counseling itself. Although it is similar to counseling, supervision is a distinct procedure requiring different proficiencies and behaviors. This chapter reviews the research associated with the various aspects of the learning alliance between supervisor and supervisee using the pantheoretical Systems Approach to Supervision model.

Chapter Questions

- What is the Systems Approach to Supervision model?
- What are the components of the supervisory relationship?
- What role do supervisor, supervisee, client, and institutional factors play in the supervisory relationship?

In this chapter, we explore the dimensions of the supervisory relationship, emphasizing the supervisor's role in creating a learning context that will enhance their supervisees' abilities to devise effective strategies for their clients. Although our emphasis is on the empirically informed techniques and principles of supervision, we acknowledge that there still remains an undefined "artistry" to clinical supervision practice. Thus, supervisors play a critical role of encouraging their supervisees to apply research knowledge to practice yet without losing sight of the fact that therapy-in-practice is an artistic "exercise of intelligence"

(Schön, 1983b, p. 13). Schön's concept of the "reflective practitioner" reminds us of the importance of integrating empirical with intuitive knowledge in our therapy work.

The master–apprentice model has often been used to describe teaching/training models in several fields of professional education including music, medicine, architecture, and business. This analogy, however, falls short of capturing the elements of the supervisory/training relationship found in an applied clinical field, such as counseling and psychotherapy. During supervision, the professional therapist must be taught how to apply general theories to individual cases and how to selectively choose and adapt known intervention strategies to the particular needs of a given client. The professional therapist must be capable of adapting to the evolving needs of the client and of delivering interventions in a thoughtful fashion at an appropriate moment. The task of the supervisor is thus to help the therapist (1) to articulate the therapist's layers of thinking; (2) to conceptualize clinical issues, and (3) to apply interventions with intentionality. In essence, the supervisor helps the therapist translate theory and research into practice. Holloway and Wolleat (1994) have stated that

> because the goal of clinical supervision is to connect science and practice, supervision is among the most complex of all activities associated with the practice of psychology. The competent clinical supervisor must embrace not only the domain of psychological science, but also the domains of client service and trainee development. The competent supervisor must not only comprehend how these various knowledge bases are connected, but also apply them to the individual case. (p. 30)

The supervisory relationship contains the principal dynamic process of the supervisor teaching and the supervisee learning. The supervisory relationship essentially becomes the *process* by which the trainee acquires knowledge and skills, with *process* defined as the way teaching is conveyed and learning is absorbed. And communication, or the use of language, is the supervisor's key tool for helping therapists to learn and to translate theory into practice. This use of language in supervision creates a relational base from which to show understanding, build rapport, and challenge therapists in their work (Holloway & Poulin, 1995a). Thus, to truly understand the supervisory relationship, one must understand the supervisory *process* as

> a symbiotic relationship between communication and relational development. Communication influences relational development, and in turn (or simultaneously), relational development influences the nature of the communication between parties to the relationship. (Miller, 1976b, p. 15)

There has been considerable research done on the relationship and process of supervision (Ellis, Ladany, Krengel, & Schult, 1996; Holloway, 1992; Russell, Crimings, & Lent, 1984; Stoltenberg, McNeill, & Crethar, 1994). The purpose of this chapter is to refer to the relevant empirical literature and to identify the practical implications for supervision. Our specific focus is on the "learning alliance" between supervisor and supervisee as it emerges in the relationship of supervision. The Systems Approach to Supervision (SAS) model is used to frame our discussion, because the supervisory relationship forms the core of the SAS model.

Systems Approach to Supervision

Although the supervisory relationship is the core factor in the SAS model (see Figure 5.1), there are seven dimensions in the SAS model, each gleaned from the empirical, conceptual, and practical bases of knowledge in the field. In Figure 5.1, six factors are represented as wings connected to the one core dimension of the supervisory relationship, totaling the seven dimensions. The first two wings in the foreground represent the supervisory task and function with the four contextual influences of supervisor, trainee, client, and institution in the background. As a system, this heuristic model has been designed to suggest that each wing can be examined either independently or in combination with other factors. It is also understood that the components of the model are part of a dynamic process in which they are highly interrelated and can mutually influence one another.

The linchpin holding the whole SAS model together is the supervisory relationship with its multiple interwoven factors. The relationship core is best visualized rotating on its axis, spiralling, similar to a barbershop pole. This implied movement represents both the interrelatedness of the different contextual factors and their nonhierarchical nature.

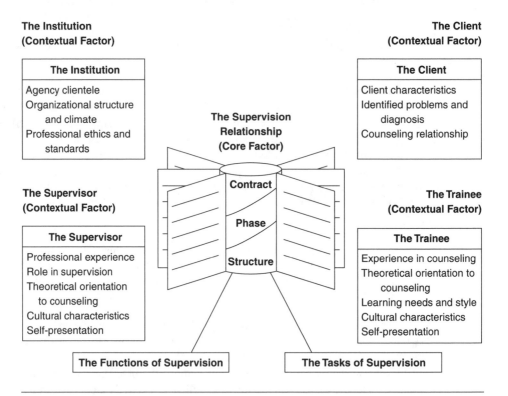

FIGURE 5.1 *The SAS Model: Relationship and Contextual Factors*

Source: From *Clinical Supervision: A Systems Approach* by E. Holloway, 1995, Thousand Oaks, CA: Sage Publications. Copyright © 1995 by Sage Publications. Reprinted with permission.

The Relationship: A Learning Alliance

Clinical supervision, as practiced today, is a very young field, dating back to the 1950s when Carl Rogers used case reports and audiotapes of counseling sessions to help trainees finesse their skills in employing the facilitative conditions of genuineness, empathy, and unconditional positive regard in counseling. Supervision has only been recognized as a unique profession, distinct from psychotherapy, however, since the 1980s (Holloway, 1995). Previously, it was thought that supervision was simply an extension of a given counseling theory and similar in practice. In more recent years, empirical research on supervision has played an important part in legitimizing supervision as a distinct field of practice from counseling. It appears that supervision has more in common with the process of teaching than the process of counseling. Research shows that supervisors spend more time providing information, opinions, and suggestions (being more task oriented) than they do giving emotional support or attending to the trainee's emotional life, as one might find in counseling interviews (Holloway & Wolleat, 1981; Lambert, 1974; Martin, Goodyear, & Newton, 1987; Rickards, 1984; Wedeking & Scott, 1976). In supervision, the supervisor and supervisee are both responsible for establishing a relational structure that is flexible enough to accommodate (1) the trainee's particular professional needs, (2) the client's presenting issues, (3) the supervisor's goals, and (4) any institutional requirements. The supervisor's role is particularly demanding because of the necessity to incorporate empirical knowledge from the *practice* of psychotherapy to the *teaching* of psychotherapy in supervision (Holloway & González-Doupé, 1999).

From the empirical literature and practice knowledge, Holloway (1995) has identified three essential elements that make up the supervision relationship core, as illustrated in Figure 5.1 of the SAS model: (1) the supervisory contract, (2) the phase of relationship, and (3) the interpersonal structure of the relationship. These are conceptual constructs that have been gleaned from empirical findings in supervision. By using this organizational framework, we hope to integrate the most current findings in the field on the supervision relationship and to summarize the practical implications for practice. Within each organizing dimension of contract, phase, and structure of the supervisory relationship, we explore the relative influence of the four contextual factors (supervisor, trainee, client, and institution) on the supervisory relationship. We have not included a discussion that is directly focused on the supervisory function/strategies or teaching objectives.

The Contract of Supervision

Inskipp and Proctor (1989) have identified the supervisory contract as critical to establishing a way of being together in the supervisory relationship. Not only do the supervisor and supervisee need to negotiate specific tasks but they also need to define the parameters of the relationship. The client's and the institution's felt presence in the supervisory relationship can vary and will, in part, determine the boundaries of the supervisory relationship. For instance, in certain training settings, the supervisor might sit in the therapy room in order to be in contact with the client and the therapist at the same time. Alternatively, live supervision of supervisors-in-training can occur in which a "metasupervisor" sits behind a one-way mirror, making the institutional requirement of regulating professional ethics and standards quite explicit. However, in standard supervision practice, client and institutional factors are often not as directly felt, although they are never altogether absent.

Contract: Supervisor Factors

Establishing the initial meeting with the supervisee is the first step in establishing a relevant and flexible contract process. The supervisor has a responsibility to ensure that the trainee is clearly informed of the evaluative structure of the relationship, especially because the supervisee is in a position of less power. Therefore, the supervisor must clearly state (1) the expectations and goals for supervision, (2) the criteria for evaluation, and (3) the limits of confidentiality in supervision. The negotiation of norms, rules, and commitments at the beginning of any relationship can reduce uncertainty and create a level of trust that will promote the degree of openness and vulnerability needed for a successful supervisory experience. It is also important, however, to keep in mind that each supervisor and supervisee will have idiosyncratic expectations of his or her role and function in supervision. Some expectations will be the result of past experiences in supervision, and others will be more directly related to the personal and cultural characteristics of each participant. The clarity of these expectations directly affects the quality of the working relationship and the specificity of the learning goals.

By being the one who initiates the contract, the supervisor is dealing directly with the inherent uncertainty that comes with beginning a new working relationship. During this stage of clarification, the supervisor can describe the content and relational characteristics expected from the trainee, and similarly, what the trainee can expect of the supervisor in terms of philosophical perspective, method of evaluation, and working style. This initial clarification also serves to outline the general trajectory for the supervisory relationship. By acting openly and purposefully, the supervisor can increase the probability that both participants will behave congruently with well-defined expectations (Miller, 1976). More importantly, the supervisee will receive an opportunity to participate in the construction of the relationship.

Research on the nature of relationship expectancies and supervisory needs is considerable. Much of this research has used self-report, paper-and-pencil instruments to assess participants' perceptions of the quality and purpose of the supervision. In practice settings, the Supervisory Styles Inventory (SSI; Friedlander & Ward, 1984), the Learning Alliance Inventory (Efstation, Patton, & Kardash, 1990), the Supervisor Reaction Personal Reaction Scale, and the Trainee Personal Reaction Scale (Holloway & Wampold, 1983) can help the supervisor determine the level of trainees' expectancies for personal self-disclosure, focus on task, degree of involvement, and level of trust in the supervisory relationship.

The supervisor, however, needs to have the necessary training to be alert and sensitive to the changing character of the relationship, with or without the use of self-report instruments. It is important for the supervisor to recognize the need for regular check-ins to reassess goals and relational expectations. Ongoing negotiation of content and process issues is built on the initial contract for teaching and learning established by the supervisor and supervisee, and on the quality of relationship that the participants build over time.

Poulin's (1992) dimensional analysis identified five primary dimensions that supervisors attend to in their supervision sessions (see Table 5.1). Poulin's dimensionalization of

TABLE 5.1 *Dimensions of the Supervision Interview*

- Framing a context for the discussion of the supervisory material
- Determining a focal point for the discussion
- Identifying a teaching–learning goal within this context
- Choosing a strategy appropriate for the teaching goal and the context in which supervisor and trainee are working
- Evaluating the appropriateness of the goal and the effectiveness of the teaching and learning

Source: From *Towards a Grounded Pedagogy of Practice: A Dimensional Analysis of Counseling Supervision,* by K. Poulin, 1992, Eugene, OR: University of Oregon.

reflected interviews of expert supervisors found that the supervisor thought of trainee characteristics in three categories: (1) as a person, (2) as a counselor, and (3) as a student. Within these categories the supervisor addressed the trainees' learning needs within the context of their learning style and their level of readiness to assimilate and make use of knowledge.

Contract: Trainee Factors

Ladany and Friedlander (1995) surveyed trainees' experience of role ambiguity and role conflict during a one-semester practicum. The authors hypothesized that if trainees and supervisors could form strong emotional bonds and could agree on goals and tasks for supervision, then trainees would be less likely to feel conflicted or confused about their role in supervision. Trainees, indeed, reported feeling less role ambiguity and role conflict when they felt they had a positive supervisory working alliance. Trainees who were surveyed were in masters practicums, doctoral practicums, and internship training, and yet no significant differences were found between experience level and potential for role ambiguity. These findings were confirmed later in another study on working alliance (Ladany, Brittan-Powell, & Pannu, 1997).

In a study three years earlier, however, Olk and Friedlander (1992) found different results: They found that there was a significant inverse relationship between trainees' level of experience and role ambiguity. Thus, more advanced trainees, those who had been previously supervised, appeared to have a clearer idea of their role in supervision and general expectations, as compared to beginning trainees. Olk and Friedlander's results might be explained by the fact that they surveyed beginning trainees with as little as four weeks' experience with supervision, thus indicating that entry-level trainees, with specifically little to no experience of supervision, are in greater need of role induction and clarity about supervision goals and expectations than those with more experience. In another study focused on beginning-level trainees (Holloway, 1998), a grounded dimensional analysis clearly found themes of role confusion and subsequent feelings of vulnerability emerging, thus corroborating the need for supervisors and supervisees to explicitly discuss their role expectations early in supervision.

It could be suggested that advanced supervisees, having a blueprint for the relationship of supervision from previous experiences, are able to truncate the discomfort of uncertainty and the need for reassurance by relying on known general expectancies for supervisory roles. Thus, they can move more quickly to establish specific expectancies for an interpersonal relationship. In contrast, beginning-level trainees are perhaps still learning their own role expectations and those of their supervisor, and, thus, are not as quick to enter into the interpersonal supervisory relationship. It is important to note, however, that no matter what level of experience a trainee might have, it seems that there is a natural relationship stage in which participants need to become familiar with the role expectations set up by the supervisor and the supervisory context. This initial stage of building familiarity serves to reduce ambiguity and uncertainty in the relationship overall. In an analogue study, Friedlander, Keller, Peca-Baker, and Olk (1986) investigated role demands in the supervisory relationship, that is, the relationship of supervisor–supervisee disagreement on intervention strategy to trainees' anxiety level, self-statements regarding experience of conflict, and their plans for a counseling interview. Trainees' self-efficacy expectations were used as a covariate. They found that planning performance of beginning-level counselors did not appear to be affected when conflict situations were present. However, there was a significant inverse relation between anxiety and performance, and anxiety and self-efficacy.

In another study (Gysbers & Johnston, 1965), the authors examined trainees' expectations of the supervisory relationship before and after their experience in supervision as measured by the BLRI (Barrett-Lennard Relationship Inventory). It was found that the trainees did not expect the degree of empathy, support, and congruency that they experienced from their supervisors because they had feared the evaluation component as having an overriding supervisory purpose. Trainees, particularly beginning trainees, can greatly benefit from making role expectations clear and detailing competency-based expectations at various intermediary stages of evaluation.

Contract: Client Factors

A supervisor's primary focus is on the professional development of the supervisee's skills within an organization and should ensure that the trainee is delivering effective service to the client (Holloway, 1995). Yet, ironically, there is little research that examines client change as an outcome of, or in relation to, the supervision process.

Contracting in the supervisory relationship occurs both on a grand scale at the beginning of the supervisory relationship, as well as on a minute scale, beginning in the first five minutes of each session when the supervisor asks, "What would you like to focus on today?" As such, the trainee is being asked to articulate, or contract for, the session's focus, whether it will be on the trainee's professional development or on client case issues.

The client is rarely present during supervisory sessions. The client is only indirectly present via the trainee's use of case reports or videotape recordings of actual case work. There is some evidence, however, that points to the influence of client progress on the supervisory relationship. For instance, Ward, Friedlander, Schoen, and Klein (1985) examined the influence of different self-presentational styles on supervisors' judgments of counselor competence. This was an analogue study in which the investigators created stimulus conditions where trainees either took a defensive or counterdefensive interpersonal style. Supervisors evaluated the defensive trainee as more self-confident, whereas the counterdefensive trainee was evaluated as more socially skilled. Interestingly, when the client was reported to have improved, trainees were judged to be altogether more competent, self-confident, expert, and attractive than when the client worsened, regardless of trainee style. It appears from this study that supervisors are influenced by client progress in judging trainee professional skills. The link between client outcome and supervisory methods has received little attention in the research, yet, this one study points to the important influence of one process on the other.

Contract: Institutional Factors

Whether supervision is a part of a training program or continuing professional development, it takes place in the context of institutional organizations, such as in-house departmental clinics, university counseling centers, hospitals, community mental health clinics, or other community service settings. The service demands of an organization often influence which goals are prioritized and how supervision is arranged. Yet, the influence of organizational variables on supervision has rarely been investigated or discussed in the professional literature. Institutional characteristics are defined in the SAS model as agency clientele, organizational structure and climate, and professional ethics and standards (see Figure 5.1). All of these factors might potentially have influence on the supervisory contract with the trainee.

In the past 10 years, training programs in psychology have became more focused on competency-based criteria in evaluating trainees' preparation for the counselor role. For their part, researchers have been studying the conditions that are thought to influence the acquisition of counselor behaviors deemed necessary for effective counseling. In particular, the use of empirically supported intervention programs are having a considerable influence on the training of therapists (Holloway & González-Doupé, 1999), and standards of competence are being linked to manual adherence. Clearly, if this training trend continues, supervisors will need to include such criteria in training contracts with their supervisees (Calhoun, Moras, Pilkonis, & Rehm, 1998).

The Phase of Relationship

In the SAS model, Holloway (1995) uses Mueller and Kell's conceptualization of the developing, mature, and terminating phases of the supervisory relationship (see Table 5.2). Relationships develop as they adjust to these new levels of personal knowledge. As the supervisory relationship develops, the participants will attempt to make predictions of each others' behavior, using more personally relevant, interpersonal, psychological, and differentiated information in an effort to reduce interpersonal uncertainty. Relationship crises might entail periods of nonmutuality as new information is incorporated and the relationship is redefined. If mutuality, or a shared definition of the relationship, cannot be attained, then the relationship is usually terminated (Morton, Alexander, & Altman, 1976, p. 105). In one grounded dimensional analysis study, professional counselors with 5 to 20 years of experience identified mutuality as a core dimension when asked what made for good supervision (Holloway, 1998). However, in the context of a training program, this option is often not available. How then does the presence, or absence, of mutuality impact the supervisory relationship?

TABLE 5.2 *Phases of the Supervisory Relationship*

Developing Phase

- Clarifying relationship with supervisor
- Establishment of supervision contract
- Supporting teaching interventions
- Developing competencies
- Developing treatment plans

Mature Phase

- Increasing individual nature of relationship, becoming less role bound
- Increasing social bonding and influence potential
- Developing skills of case conceptualization
- Increasing self-confidence and self-efficacy in counseling
- Confronting personal issues as they relate to professional performance

Terminating Phase

- Understanding connections between theory and practice in relation to particular clients
- Decreasing need for direction from supervisor

Phase: Supervisor Factors

Early researchers (Holloway, 1992) of supervision focused on determining the importance of supervisors' use of facilitative conditions in the supervisory relationship. More recently, supervisor gender, theoretical orientation, and experience level have been found to be related to trainee satisfaction with supervision, as have supervisor planning behaviors, in-session verbal behaviors, and interpersonal power style (Holloway, 1992; Russell, Crimmings, & Lent, 1984).

It has been suggested in the supervision literature that the supervisor engages in a developmental process of change that unfolds as the demands of the supervisory role change (Stoltenberg, McNeill, & Crethar, 1994). Empirically at least, it has been shown that the amount of experience a supervisor has in counseling and supervision seems related to the judgments the supervisor will make regarding self-disclosure, trainee performance, and choice of instructional approach to supervision. Other studies (Holloway & Poulin, 1995) have examined the changing patterns of communication across time in the supervision relationship. Wedeking and Scott (1976) found that supervisor messages changed from the beginning to the final stages of the relationship. Supervisors spent more time with informative verbal behaviors in the beginning session than in the final sessions. Supervisors used rapport-building strategies and structured the interview more in the initial part of beginning interviews, whereas these strategies were more prevalent in the middle of the interviews in final sessions of the relationship.

The association of relationship phase with supervisory behaviors has been investigated in case study designs using microanalytic techniques (Garb, 1989; Martin et al.,

1987; Strozier, Kivlighan, & Thoreson, 1993). Martin et al. used an intensive, longitudinal case study approach to examine participants' judgments of supervisory events and the characteristics of the supervisory discourse. The microanalytic data indicated that the supervisee decreased her proportional use of deferential messages across the span of the supervisory relationship.

Supervisor experience has been examined in relation to supervisor use of facilitative behaviors and judgments of trainee performance (Stone, 1980; Sundland & Feinberg, 1972; Worthington, 1984b). Sundland and Feinberg's study revealed that when given a positive view of the supervisee, supervisors with more experience provided the highest levels of facilitative conditions. When given a negative view of the trainee, however, the experienced supervisors provided the lowest level of facilitation. Thus, the influence of both interpersonal attraction to the trainee and experience as a supervisor influenced supervisors' use of their facilitative skills. Surprisingly, more experienced supervisors were more negatively influenced and thus less attracted to the negative-set trainees. The authors suggested an explanation: The more experienced supervisors in this study had not been trained in the experiential-didactic training model as had their less experienced counterparts (because of cohort group history), nor were they in as close proximity to the student role, and thus the more experienced supervisors were less tolerant of the negative-set supervisees.

In another study that examined supervisor experience with supervisor judgment of the trainee, Worthington (1984a) asked experienced and inexperienced counselors to assume a supervisor role, to read a 10-minute excerpt from a counseling session, and to rate counselors and clients on eight personality trait labels. Experience level of supervisor was defined by the amount of counseling experience they had had, ranging from no experience through postdoctoral experience. Half of the supervisors were led to believe that the counselor in the videotape vignette was at the beginning level, and the other half were told that the counselor was at the internship level. The results indicated that supervisors with more counseling experience made fewer trait attributions to the counselor than supervisors with little or no counseling experience. Theoretically, the argument was made that supervisors' experience in counseling promoted increased cognitive role-taking (i.e., empathy) and thus they were better able to attribute the supervisee's behaviors to situational variables rather than personal traits. The "set" of counselor's level of training had no significant effect on the supervisors' judgments of counselor traits. Furthermore, supervisors, regardless of counseling experience, did not differentially attribute trait labels to the client. These findings, in contrast to Sundland and Feinberg's (1972) findings, suggest that experience in supervision frees supervisors from making global personality judgments of the trainee and allows them to focus on the situational characteristics that might be influencing the trainee's performance. The supervisor's ability to recognize interpersonal and situational factors in counseling that may influence the counselor's behavior is critical to establishing an empathic relationship in supervision and to assisting the supervisee in devising different counseling strategies that respond to contextual factors.

Unfortunately, the definition of experience level in the Worthington (1984a) study limits the generalizability of the results. Because most supervisors have some counseling experience it is unlikely that counselors with no experience in counseling could realistically substitute for supervisors with no experience in supervision. However, given the situation that many training programs use doctoral students to supervise beginning-level counselors, the results of this study emphasize the importance of using more experienced counselors as supervisors and of teaching supervisors to focus on the situational influences that may be impinging on the supervisee's work.

Stone (1980) found that experienced supervisors, in contrast to inexperienced supervisors, focused more on counselor behavior in their before-session planning statements. Marikis, Russell, and Dell (1985) improved on Stone's study by including only participants with counseling experience and with at least one didactic course on supervision. Experience level of supervisors ranged from no supervisory experience to postdoctoral supervision experience. Additionally, they compared planning behavior to actual in-session behavior of the supervisors. Their findings indicated that there were no differences in planning behaviors among the different experience-level groups and that the most frequent planning behaviors were counselor-oriented statements, followed by client-oriented statements, subject-matter statements, and process statements. These results contrast with Stone's findings in which significant differences in planning behavior were found across the different experience groups. Marikis et al. also found that there was little relation between the planning process and in-session verbal behaviors. However, there were differences in verbal behaviors: Supervisors with some experience were more verbal in session, self-disclosed more, and provided more direct instruction of counseling skills.

Social role theories perceive the supervisor taking on several potential roles. The most frequently recognized roles are teacher, counselor, and consultant; however, the roles of evaluator, lecturer, and model of professional practice have also been used to describe supervisor behaviors and attitudes. Role theories of supervision outline the expectancies and behaviors that are considered to be a part of the supervisory relationship and, specifically, part of the supervisor role. A few research studies have investigated the types of roles typical of the supervisor (Ellis & Dell, 1986; Ellis, Dell, & Good, 1988; Gysbers & Johnston, 1965; Stenack & Dye, 1982). In an early study, Gysbers and Johnston asked supervisors and supervisees to respond to the Supervisor Role Analysis Form (SRAF). Supervisees' expectations for supervisor behaviors changed across the six-week practicum period from specific help, demonstration, and teaching behaviors to consultative and student-directed behaviors. Supervisors acknowledged their expectation to be responsible for structuring the learning experience, but they disagreed on the degree of specific direction or counseling support they should offer the students.

Similarly, Stenack and Dye (1982) had both faculty and graduate students with supervision experience indicate the correspondence of a list of 60 supervisor behaviors to the roles of teacher, counselor, and consultant. They found that the teacher and counselor roles were clearly distinguished, but the consultant role overlapped with the teacher role. It appeared that any differences between teacher and consultant were related to issues of supervisor control of the interaction rather than with specific supervisor behaviors. A more shared approach to control was indicative of the consultant role. They concluded that specific behaviors alone could not clearly define supervisor roles; other elements of the interaction such as goals, control, and focus were also believed to be determinants.

Ellis and associates conducted two related studies in which the role model theories of Bernard (1979) and Littrell, Lee-Borden, and Lorenz (1979) were examined using a multidimensional scaling methodology. In the first study (Ellis & Dell, 1986), supervisors' perceptions of the supervisor role were characterized by three dimensions: process versus conceptualization, consultant versus teacher/counselor, and cognitive versus emotional (or nonsupportive versus supportive). The findings in the subsequent study on counselor trainees' perceptions of supervisor roles (Ellis et al., 1988) corroborated the three-dimensional structure of supervision found in Ellis and Dell (1986). However, trainees differentiated between the teacher and counselor roles, whereas supervisors did not. The authors concluded that the results modestly supported Bernard's supervisor roles of teacher and counselor and supervisor functions of process, conceptualization, and personalization. There was little support, however, for the developmental dimension of supervision as posited by Littrell et al., because there were no differences across experience levels of trainees. The most apparent difference in the findings with the models was the emergence of an emotional-behavioral dimension.

Supervisors have the task of teaching trainees the application of theoretical principles of counseling as they are relevant to the individuals and the cases that trainees will encounter. Thus, supervisors rely explicitly and implicitly on their own knowledge base to determine what to teach as well as how to teach it. Trainees sometimes state a desire to learn a particular approach to counseling. Supervisors and trainees, however, are often assigned to one another without any consideration for the background of the supervisor or the expectations of the trainee. Alternatively, supervisors of a particular theoretical orientation may only choose to take on trainees who want to learn their specific approach.

The "counseling-bound" theories of supervision generally maintain that the supervisor's method is intrinsically linked to the counseling approach. Patterson (1983) maintains that this is the only way supervision can be considered. An example to consider is Albert Ellis' work in supervision reflecting his efforts to teach the supervisee the thinking of a rational-emotive therapist (Ellis & Dell, 1986).

The cross-theoretical approaches have tried to create theories unique to supervision that are not wholly dependent on theories of counseling. The SAS model could be classified in this latter group. This cross-theoretical approach does not imply that an individual supervisor's theoretical orientation to counseling or particular aspects of human behavior would be unimportant when analyzing a supervisor's behavior. Process research has indicated that theoretical orientation to counseling appears to be related to the structure of the supervisory relationship. When a supervisor refers to particular aspects of a personality or a counseling theory to explain client behavior, the supervisor's orientation is clearly manifesting itself in his or her decision making in supervision.

The influence of the supervisor's theoretical orientation on supervisory behavior has been the subject of several studies. Sundland and Garfield (cited in Sundland, 1977) and Beutler and McNabb (1981) found that students tend to adopt the theoretical orientation of supervisors or the director of clinical training. In an extensive study of clinical psychology graduates in a medical school practice setting, Guest and Beutler (1988) confirmed that orientations of prominent supervisors were particularly important in establishing trainees' viewpoints regardless of the correspondence between trainees' initial orientations and supervisors' orientations. Furthermore, trainee locus of control and other personality variables did not contribute to changes in orientation or values during the course of one training year or during the subsequent three to five years after training. Thus, supervision can be a powerful socialization factor in the profession. The supervisor's importance as a professional model is reflected in the trainees' adherence to the values of their teacher.

Although in this instance the researchers were only interested in the theoretical orientation of the supervisor as adopted by the trainee, we can easily extrapolate from these findings and consider what implication such findings might have for the transmittal of cultural values and professional attitudes. For instance, if the supervisor unwittingly or deliberately presents stereotypical, prejudicial attitudes toward other people or promotes disrespectful and exploitative behaviors toward clients, such attitudes could also be incorporated by the learning trainee.

Goodyear and Robyak (1982) found that regardless of theoretical orientation more experienced supervisors shared similar emphases in supervision, whereas less experienced supervisors were more divergent in ways consistent with their theoretical orientation. These results support similar studies in psychotherapy (Friedler, 1950) and an early study by Demos and Zuwaylif (1962) in supervision. In another study, Goodyear, Abadie, and Efros (1984) asked experienced supervisors to view supervision sessions of prominent supervision theorists working with the same supervisee. Findings indicated that supervisors of different theoretical orientations were rated differently in attractiveness (as measured by the Supervisor Rating Form; Heppner & Handley, 1982) and in their use of the critic role, the model role, and the nurturing role. They also were perceived as different in their use of the counselor and teacher roles and in their supervisory focus on such issues as case conceptualization, counseling skills, and transference.

Holloway, Freund, Gardner, Nelson, and Walker (1989) also studied the Goodyear (1982) videotape series and concluded that although there were prominent similarities in patterns of verbal behaviors, there were also predictable differences among the theorists. Thus, in these two studies of the same data set, theoretical orientation of the supervisor was related to perceived differences in supervisory behavior and actual differences in supervisory discourse. Goldberg (1985) believes that it is the supervisor's personality or character style and theoretical orientation that is the single most influential factor in the supervisor's behavior. Studies relating supervisor theoretical orientation and supervisor methods strongly support Goldberg's claim (Carroll, 1994; Putney, Worthington, & McCullough, 1992).

The theoretical orientation of the trainee has not received much attention in the research literature; however, most supervisors would concur that the views that a trainee holds about human behavior and change will certainly be a part of supervision. Perhaps, because much of the research in supervision has been about supervisees early in their professional training, there is not a clear theoretical designation expected of these individuals. Instead, the focus is on the development of a personal model of counseling that matches generally expected principles of personality and counseling theory.

The matching of supervisor and supervisee individual characteristics to trainee satisfaction and performance has been the approach of several investigators. Hester, Weitz, Anchor, and Roback (1976) looked at attitude similarity–dissimilarity, as measured by Byrne's Attitude Scale (Byrne, 1971) on trainees' attraction to the supervisor. Findings indicated that the skill level of the supervisor was a greater determinant of attraction than was attitude similarity. Lemons and Lanning (1979) found that similarity in value systems, as measured by Rokeach Value Survey (Rokeach, 1967), was not related to the quality of the relationship or satisfaction of the trainee; however, level of communication in supervision was related to these same variables. Kennard, Stewart, and Gluck (1987) found that theoretical similarities between supervisors and trainees enhanced trainees' perceptions of the quality of supervision. Again, referring to their extensive study of clinical psychology graduates in a medical school practice setting, Guest and Beutler (1988) found that trainees were often greatly influenced by the theoretical orientations of prominent supervisors, thus suggesting how powerful supervision can be as a socialization process.

Phase: Trainee Factors

The facilitative conditions of genuineness, empathy, and unconditional positive regard, so important in building the therapeutic relationship, are equally important in building the supervisory relationship, particularly at the beginning. Therapists-in-training, like clients, need to feel safe, supported, and trusting of their environment before they can feel comfortable enough to take risks and engage in self-reflexivity, practice new behaviors, and actively seek feedback. Rabinowitz, Heppner, and Roehlke (1986) found that advanced as well as beginning-level supervisees sought out the support and assurances of their supervisors at the beginning of the supervisory relationship. The difference was that advanced trainees, although still seeking initial support, more quickly desired experiences that included personal challenge and confrontation regarding their own interpersonal behaviors in counseling and supervision. Although these findings have been interpreted to reflect a developmental shift in the trainee, they might also be viewed as indicating a natural development in the supervisory relationship to attempt to reduce uncertainty before interactional patterns become established and familiar.

Zuniga (1987) developed a culturally focused supervision experience with Mexican American supervisees. The trainees' feelings of inadequacy and competence, not unusual for beginning-level counselors, were processed within a cultural context. The trainees developed insight into not only their own issues of working with Mexican American clients but also the relevance of their own experience of having developed strong survival skills in order to deal with a sometimes hostile and discriminatory environment.

The influence of same and mixed gender dyads has been the focus of two particular studies. Worthington and Stern (1985) examined a number of trainee variables including gender matching of supervisor and trainee. They found that male supervisors and trainees thought they had better relationships than did female supervisors and trainees, and that matching of gender was more important to trainees than to supervisors. Trainees believed that they had closer relationships with same-gender supervisors, and they attributed more influence to the same-gender supervisor than to other-gender supervisors. Goodyear (1990), using an analogue design, examined the extent to which gender of supervisor and supervisee was related to interpersonal influence strategies and global skill ratings of the supervisee. Both supervisors and supervisees perceived female supervisees to be more likely to employ a "person-dependent" influence style, that is, trainees were dependent on supervisor behaviors. There were no other significant main or interaction effects for gender on global skill ratings.

Trainee experience level has been a frequently studied factor in supervision research. Experience level of the trainee has been related to perceived supervisory needs and satisfaction with supervision (Stoltenberg et al., 1994). The predominant finding that distinguishes the expressed needs of very beginning level trainees from those of intern-level trainees centers on different relationship characteristics (Heppner & Roehlke 1984; Miars et al., 1983; Wiley & Ray, 1986; Worthington, 1984a; Worthington, 1984b). For example, initial-level trainees appear to require more support, encouragement, and structure in supervision, whereas interns demonstrate both increasing independence from the supervisor (Hill, Charles, & Reed, 1981; McNeil, Stoltenberg, & Pierce, 1985; Reising & Daniels, 1983; Wiley & Ray, 1986; Worthington, 1984a; Worthington & Stern, 1985) and more interest in exploring higher-level skills and personal issues affecting counseling (Heppner & Roehlke, l984; Hill et al., 1981; McNeil et al., 1985; Stoltenberg et al., 1994; Worthington & Stern, l985).

Since 1986, a few researchers have examined experience level of trainee and other personality factors to uncover the relation of trainee characteristics and supervisory needs. Developmental characteristics such as conceptual level (Harvey, Hunt, & Schroder, 1961) and ego development have been examined in light of the acquisition of counseling skills such as empathy and clinical hypothesis formation. Borders, Fong, and Neimeyer (1986) examined the relation between student counselors' experience level (practicum versus intern level) and ego development (Loevinger's scale) to perceptions of their clients. Their results indicated that ego development levels were more predictive of their descriptors than were experience levels. Lower-ego level students tended to use more simplistic, concrete descriptors, whereas those at higher-ego levels used more sophisticated, interactive descriptors.

Stoltenberg and Delworth (1987) prescribed matching conceptual level to the degree of structure in supervision. For example, the greater the tolerance for ambiguity and the more relativistic the thinking, the greater was the opportunity for the supervisor to offer a more unstructured approach to supervision (Stoltenberg et al., 1994). Unfortunately, there are few empirical findings to guide the supervisor in choosing those strategies that would reflect a structured versus an unstructured learning environment. At this point, qualitative interviews of supervisors and supervisees may offer the greatest insight into the relevance of such factors in the actual practice of supervision.

Holloway and Wampold (1986) conducted a meta-analysis on the interaction of conceptual level (CL), a construct that is related to social perceptual development, and learning environment. They found that low-CL students tend to prefer more structured learning environments, whereas higher-CL students tend to prefer more unstructured learning environments. These results support the work of Holloway and Wolleat (1980) in which the authors investigated the relation between CL, experience level, and clinical hypothesis formation. Although student experience level was not a significant factor, students with higher CL asked more divergent questions and had greater clarity in their clinical hypotheses than did low-CL students.

A series of investigations by Borders and associates have examined the relationship between trainees' ego development and (1) beginning- and advanced-level counseling skills (Borders, 1989), (2) perceptions of clients (Borders et al., 1986), and (3) in-session cognitions about actual counseling events (Borders, 1989; Borders & Fong, 1989; Borders & Fong, 1994). In each of these studies, with the exception of Borders et al. (1986), experience level of the participants was controlled by examining only one level of counseling experience. However, trainees at the same level of experience produced different types of cognitions relative to their level of ego development. Thus, preexisting personality constructs seem to mitigate the influences of experience level.

Several measures of counselor cognitive functioning have been of interest to researchers. In particular, conceptual systems theory (CST; Harvey, Hunt, & Schreder, 1961) has enjoyed considerable popularity since the early 1970s. The studies of conceptual level suggest that matching learning environment to the trainee's cognitive characteristics may be fruitful in creating facilitative supervisory environments.

Cognitive constructs related to CST such as ego development, dogmatism, and locus of control have also been investigated in relation to counseling skills and cognitions. Winter and Holloway (1991) completed an analogue study that examined the relation of supervisees' CL, experience level, and perception of supervisory approach to their choice of audiotaped passages presented for a simulated supervisory interview. Cognitively complex supervisees were more apt to choose passages with a focus on counseling skills than passages that focused on client conceptualization or personal growth. Descriptive data showed that nearly 75% of complex supervisees made explicit requests for supervisor feedback as compared to 50% of middle-CL group and 35% of low-CL group. Thus, cognitively complex counselors preferred to focus on passages that would encourage the supervisor to provide feedback on their counseling skills. Winter and Holloway interpreted this finding in light of the higher personal responsibility generally demonstrated by complex individuals in interpersonal situations. That is, high-CL participants selected segments that focused on their skills and actual behaviors in counseling sessions, thus, inviting the supervisor to provide direct feedback on their work and inviting the opportunity to improve on their skills.

Experience level had a significant effect on what counselors chose to focus on with their supervisors. Counselors with more experience requested less focus on client conceptualization and more focus on personal growth issues such as countertransference, self-efficacy, and self-awareness, and they showed a greater willingness to choose excerpts from their work that reflected less favorably on them as counselors. There were no interactive effects of CL and experience level nor did supervisor approach influence the choice of counseling passages. As discussed earlier, the results regarding experience level of trainees are consistent with numerous other studies that have examined supervisory needs at different levels of practical experience (Heppner & Roehlke, 1984; McNeil et al., 1985; Miars et al., 1983; Rabinowitz et al., 1986; Stoltenberg et al., 1994).

Tracey, Ellickson, and Sherry (1989) designed an analogue study to examine the relationship between supervisory structure and trainee learning. They were interested in finding out how counselor trainees' preferences for varying levels of supervision structure (high structure versus low structure) may be moderated by experience, content of supervision, and reactance potential. Reactance potential was described as a personality variable related to an individual's need to resist or comply with imposed structure or direction in interpersonal contexts. The content of supervision was described as either a noncrisis situation or a crisis situation that involved a suicidal client. The findings of this study revealed several interactive effects of the independent variables on trainees' preferences for supervisory structure. The authors concluded the following: (1) structure was important for beginning trainees and less so for more advanced trainees; (2) urgency of the client condition had a strong moderating effect on the experience-structure preference; and (3) in the noncrisis content condition, reactance potential accounted for structure preferences of advanced-level trainees. These findings partially support some of the previous work that has indicated that, as they progress through levels of experience, trainees need for supervisory structure diminishes (McNeil et al., 1985; Reising & Daniels, 1983; Stoltenberg et al., 1994; Wiley & Ray, 1986). However, the structure-experience relation is moderated by both personality variables of the trainees (in this case, reactance potential) and the situational determinants of the supervisory focus (crisis versus noncrisis client). This well-designed study presents a strong argument for researchers to include personality characteristics, experience level, and content conditions of supervision in studies of supervisory environments.

There is some research to indicate that the quality of the supervisory alliance is somewhat related to the quality of the counseling working alliance and to trainee adherence to a treatment model (Patton & Kivlighan, 1997). That is, trainee perception of the supervisory alliance was significantly related to the client's perception of the counseling alliance. The authors offer the explanation that trainees are presumably taking the knowledge that they gain from supervision about building and maintaining relationships and applying this knowledge to their working relationships with their clients. Thus, it is important for supervisors to be aware of their role in modeling certain relationship processes. Patton and Kivlighan, however, found no correlation between the supervisory working alliance and actual technical activity of the supervisor, therefore, no conclusions could be drawn between supervisory alliance and trainee skill. Nonetheless, the importance of the supervisor role is implied.

Worthen and McNeill (1996) conducted a phenomenological study of supervisees' impressions of "good" supervision events. One crucial component that defined a good supervision experience was the supervisor's ability to validate and appreciate abilities that the supervisee brought from past experiences. Therefore, taking the time to explore and delineate previous clinical experiences seems to be an important process for supervisees—in some ways, counterbalancing feelings of anxiety and fears of ineffectiveness, and serving to remind them of their innate abilities as people. Thus, supervisors play a critical role in helping trainees identify their natural and developed abilities, which is an important process in building one's professional identity.

In their study, Skovholt and Ronnestad (1992) found that among the 10 peer-nominated master therapists, six out of the nine qualities identified could be considered natural qualities that predated any formal clinical training:

1. They were voracious learners.
2. They drew heavily on accumulated experiences.
3. They were emotionally receptive.
4. They valued cognitive complexity and ambiguity.
5. They were mentally healthy and attended to their own emotional well-being.
6. They possessed strong relationship skills.

Therefore, supervisors need to be cognizant of the fact that trainees bring many attributes and natural skills, as well as formal and informal training experiences.

The counseling relationship is an important basis from which to understand the impact of different treatment strategies as well as the effectiveness of the trainee in creating a therapeutic relationship (Holloway & Neufeldt, 1995). Knox, Goldberg, Woodhouse, and Hill (1999) found that in the context of a good therapeutic relationship, clients developed internal representations of their therapist that included auditory, visual, and kinesthetic (felt presence) stimuli. Furthermore, the clients' frequency of, comfort with, and use of their internal representations increased during the course of therapy. The clients reported that they typically used these internal representations as a way to continue self-reflective processes initiated in a session. One wonders if this same phenomenon occurs in the supervisory relationship. Do therapists, at some point in the supervisory relationship, internalize their supervisor's voice or image, in the service of their clinical work? If so, it is vitally important to ask supervisees at the beginning of the supervisory relationship to describe previous supervisory experiences. They should not only talk about previous positive or negative supervision events (Worthen & McNeil, 1996) but they should also describe generally the characteristics of previous supervisors that they have internalized or have tried to emulate.

In the SAS model, cultural values, such as gender, ethnicity, race, sexual orientation, and religious beliefs, are seen as salient to trainees' attitudes and actions toward their clients and supervisors. Research in this supervision area is relatively limited, although there has been significantly more research on the relation of cultural variables to counseling relationship and counselor effectiveness (cf. Atkinson, Morten, & Sue, 1989; Pedersen, 1985; Sue & Sue, 1990; Tyler, Brome, & Williams, 1991). Bernard and Goodyear (1998) present an excellent chapter on the multicultural context of supervision and extrapolate findings from the counseling literature to issues of training. Tyler, Brome, and Williams address the issues of training in multicultural supervisory dyads and offer ways in which both supervisor and trainee can take responsibility for discussing issues of power and culture as they relate to their interactions with the trainee's clients.

Although the investigation of cultural and racial characteristics on the counseling relationship has generated considerable research in the past decades (Helms, 1984; Parham, 1989), only a few empirical studies were found in the supervision literature. Cook and Helms (1988) were interested in the predictability of satisfaction with cross-cultural supervision from relationship dimensions as measured by the Barrett-Lennard Relationship Inventory (BLRI; Barrett-Lennard, 1962), the Supervision Questionnaire (Worthington & Roehlke, 1979), and a personal data sheet. They asked four culturally diverse groups (Black, Hispanic/Latino, Asian American, and Native American) to respond to a survey regarding their supervision experiences. The results indicated that only supervisor-liking and conditional-liking relationship dimensions were related to satisfaction with supervision. Additionally, supervisees' perceptions of their supervision relationships varied according to their race or ethnicity:

1. Black, Hispanic/Latino, and Native American supervisees felt lower levels of liking from supervisors than did Asian American supervisees.
2. All groups except the Native American one felt that supervisors were emotionally comfortable with them.
3. Black and Native American supervisees perceived the highest mean levels of unconditional liking.
4. Black supervisees perceived significantly higher levels of unconditional liking than did Hispanic/Latino supervisees.
5. Native American supervisees perceived significantly higher levels of discomfort than any other group.

The limitations of this study warrant mention: The sample size for Native American supervisees was eight, only 51% of potential participants choose to respond, and the dependent measures reflected perceptions of the supervisor's attitudes rather than actual behaviors of the supervisor. It is important, given the paucity of research on this topic, however, to recognize the contribution of this research study and hope that it encourages future researchers to use diverse methods to understand the role of ethnicity and race on relationship dimensions in supervision.

Phase: Client Factors

Clients do not participate in supervision sessions (except for certain cases of live supervision), but their presence is, nonetheless, felt in supervision. The identification of the client's problem is often the first topic for discussion in supervision. This might include a formal *Diagnostic and Statistical Manual of Mental Disorders-Fourth Editon* (DSM-IV; American Psychiatric Association, 1994) assessment and diagnosis or a problem-solving description of the client's presenting concern. Supervisors in practice often screen clients for beginning-level trainees to ensure that they are only assigned cases that are appropriate to their level of competence. Supervisors may also choose cases for trainees based on the supervisors' areas of expertise. Pragmatically, the supervisor must frequently consider the client age, ethnicity, gender, and race in determining the appropriateness of a match between a counselor and a client. Supervisors should also consider problem-solving difficulties that may emerge in the counseling relationship. Characteristics and variables that have been studied include social class, personality traits, age, gender, education, race, and ethnicity. Some of these characteristics have real, practical value in determining the appropriateness of brief versus long-term therapy and premature termination (Garfield, 1994).

An important and frequently researched area has been the variety of client attributes as they relate to the process and outcome of psychotherapy. The relevance of these general client characteristics, as opposed to specific diagnostic attributes, has not been studied within the context of supervision or training. The literature on matching client gender or ethnic identity with that of therapists suggests that, although there appears to be a preference for ethnically similar counselors, this is not consistently evident in the empirical literature (Coleman, Wampold, & Casali, 1994). It behooves the supervisor to recognize that variables such as social desirability, attitudes, or values may play an important role in the counselor's potential effectiveness. Therapeutic ineffectiveness may be falsely attributed to the lack of similarity between client and therapist on general qualities when, in fact, a more in-depth analysis might reveal more implicit characteristics of the client or counselor to be inhibiting progress.

There are only a few studies that have examined client outcome measures in relation to supervision. Dodenhoff (1981) found that direct instructional methods were positively related to trainee effectiveness and supervisor ratings of client outcome. Steinhelber, Patterson, Cliffe, and LeGoullon (1984) evaluated the effects of supervision variables on client outcome. They found that there was no relationship between the amount of supervision and changes in ratings of clients on the Global Assessment Scale from pretherapy to posttherapy. There was a relationship, however, between those pre- to posttherapy changes and therapists' reports of congruence between their own theoretical orientation and that of their supervisor.

The complexity of using client outcome measures as a standard of supervision effectiveness is demonstrated by those studies that have compared ratings of client change from multiple sources. Similar to Dodenhoff's (1981) findings that supervisors' judgments of clients' change differed from other ratings, Najavits and Strupp (1994) also found that supervisors were not able to differentiate more effective from less effective therapists (based on outcome measures and length of stay), whereas therapists, independent observers, and clients were able to do so. Rounsaville, Chevron, and Weissman (1984), however, found that therapists' evaluations of their own work differed sharply from supervisors' evaluations of therapists' work based on reviewing videotapes of actual therapy sessions. Ratings of therapist competency is further complicated by client characteristics. Both Rounsaville, O'Malley, Foley, and Weissman (1988) and Strupp, Butler, and Rosser, (1988) found that evaluations of therapist competence at performing manualized treatments were confounded by patient difficulty: therapists with the most difficult clients were rated as less competent than therapists with less difficult clients.

In the psychotherapy literature, discrepancies among clients', therapists', and trained observers' perceptions of process and outcome variables are generally found (cf. Bloch & Reibstein, 1980; Caskey, Barker, & Elliot, 1994; Eugster & Wampold, 1996; Elliott, 1986; Wampold & Kim, 1989) It is disconcerting, however, to find that supervisors, who are responsible for ensuring that therapists are engaged in competent practice with clients, are perhaps more influenced by the trainee's interpersonal involvement in supervision than their effectiveness with the client.

Structure of the Relationship: Power and Involvement

Structure: Supervisor Factors

Power and involvement are helpful constructs in understanding the nature of the supervisory relationship. Supervision is a formal relationship in which the supervisor's task includes imparting expert knowledge, analyzing trainees' performance, and acting as a gatekeeper to the profession. Formal power, or power attributed to the position of supervisor, rests with the supervisor and thus the supervisory relationship is a hierarchical one.

The supervisor brings to the supervisory relationship an independent way of viewing human behavior, interpersonal relations, and social institutions, all of which are largely influenced by cultural socialization. Because cultural perspectives are relevant to the conceptualization of both professionalism and mental health, the SAS model considers cultural values to be salient to the supervisor's attitudes and actions. Cultural characteristics, which include gender, ethnicity, race, sexual orientation, religious beliefs, and personal values, strongly influence an individual's social and moral judgments. In the SAS model, the relationship of supervision is understood from a perspective of power and involvement—inherent qualities in cross-cultural and cross-gender interactions. Such nuances of the supervisory relationship are sometimes subtle, but they are always critical aspects of the supervisory work.

The relation of race and ethnicity to supervisory process has been researched in the context of the supervisor and trainee relationship. McRoy, Freeman, Logan, and Blackmon (1986) concluded, in a survey study of field supervision, that although there were numerous potential difficulties in cross-cultural supervisory relationships, only a few actual instances were reported. African American supervisors reported the following to be problematic at times: language differences; differences in communication styles; the role and authority of the supervisor; personality conflicts; and differences in opinions, backgrounds, and life experiences. The interaction between "power in role" and "power in society" was quite evident in that African American supervisors had to experience situations in which White students questioned their supervisory competency and were actually unwilling to accept supervision. White supervisors reported that lack of trust, poor communication, lack of knowledge of cultural differences, failure to clarify values, language barriers, prejudice or bigotry, differing expectations, and student defensiveness could all potentially cause problems in the supervisory relationship. Unfortunately, it is often difficult for students and supervisors to identify such sensitive situations and discuss them openly; however, research in this area would be of great practical use to the field.

The relation of gender to the perception of interpersonal power and interactional dynamics has been studied relatively frequently in supervision. In general, same-gender dyads have reported closer relationships. Women trainees were perceived to use more dependent styles to seek influence, but there were no differences found in males' and females' use of power strategies to influence client change. Interactional analysis of matched and mismatched gender dyads in supervision (Nelson & Holloway, 1990) showed that male and female supervisors used more powerful messages with female trainees and were less likely to support female trainees' attempts at high-power messages than those of male trainees. Nelson (1993), in a conceptual review, has examined the importance of gender in therapeutic and counseling relationships.

Specific training in didactic and experiential coursework is necessary to overcome cross-cultural barriers of communication. There are numerous writings on instructional approaches to sensitize students, educators, and supervisors to these issues in theory and practice (cf. Bernard & Goodyear, 1998). Pope-Davis, Reynolds, and Vasquez (1992) have specifically addressed cross-cultural events in practice, and have developed a training program which includes videotapes to facilitate counselor understanding and training. The SAS model is meant to encourage supervisors to recognize the importance of cultural factors in supervision, and to pay attention to how these issues interact with each of the other factors of the model.

Three preferred methods have been used in supervision research to describe the power of the supervisor: (1) French and Raven's (1960) sociological typology; (2) Strong, Hill, and Nelson's (1988) circumplex model; and (3) Penman's (1980) communication matrix. French and Raven conceptualize five types of power (see Table 5.3). Legitimate, expert, and referent power are the types of power most relevant to the process of supervision. The expert power base stems from specialized knowledge and skills. Referent power is derived from interpersonal attraction. Legitimate power is a consequence of perceived trustworthiness given that the professional is a socially sanctioned provider of services. French and Raven's model, however, in contrast to the other two schemes, does not fully operationalize the concept of involvement with power.

Leary's (1957), circumplex model, on which both the Strong et al. (1988) and Penman (1980) classification systems are based, provides a framework to place power in a relational system that includes a dimension of *involvement* or affiliation that, in his view,

TABLE 5.3 *Types of Power*

- **Reward power**—the perception that the other person has the ability and resources to mediate reward
- **Coercive power**—the perception that the other person has the ability and resources to mediate punishment
- **Legitimate power**—a person's perceived trustworthiness as a professional, socially sanctioned provider of services
- **Expert power**—attributed to a person because of mastery of knowledge and skills
- **Referent power**—derived from interpersonal attraction

Source: From "The Bases of Social Power," by J. R. P. French, Jr. and B. M. Raven, 1960, in D. Cartwright and A. Zander, *Group Dynamics: Research and Theory,* (p. 607–623). New York: Peterson.

every relationship has by definition. Involvement might also be referred to as intimacy that includes "attachments," the degree to which each person uses the other as a source of self-confirmation (Miller, 1976).

In the helping professions, power has often been viewed pejoratively, because the concept of control and dominance has appeared antithetical to the therapeutic tenets of mu-tuality and unconditional positive regard. This interpretation has limited our ability to con-ceptualize and define the nuances of the *mutually* empowering relationship. Dunlap and Goldman (1991) concluded, in a review of the historical roots of power in educational set-tings, that power has essentially been defined as "power over" or domination. However, early on, Follett (1941) introduced "power with," a concept that was both pluralistic and dy-namic, representing an ever-evolving process of human interaction. Follett's conception of power is based on the relationship of involvement and mutual influence. This basis of power is more consistent with the ideals of psychotherapy and supervision where the intent is not to control but rather to empower individuals to exercise choice and self-determination.

Leary's (1957) theory of interpersonal relations undergirds the SAS interpersonal structure of the supervision relationship (power through involvement). Although the super-visory relationship takes on a unique character that can be defined by power and involve-ment, the participants bring their own history of interpersonal interactions. These interpersonal histories influence how the supervisor and trainee ultimately present them-selves in forming their new relationship.

The introduction of the Penman (1980) classification scheme to supervision research heralded the use of a content analysis system that could be understood from the larger per-spective of relational qualities. The Penman scheme is based on the interpersonal theory of personality (Leary, 1957), and categories are arranged to provide information about the di-mensions of power and involvement in a relationship. Three studies in supervision have used this classification scheme (Holloway et al., 1989; Martin et al., 1987; and Nelson & Holloway, 1990). Martin et al. found that the process of supervision largely involved the su-pervisor's provision of advice, information, opinions, and suggestions, with few supportive or social-emotional statements. Holloway et al. used a sequential analysis technique in a multiple-case-study format. Their findings confirmed existing evidence that supervisors and trainees predominantly engage in a complementary teacher–learner interactional pattern: Specifically, the significant pattern of supervisors of different theoretical orientations is that the supervisor gives advice and the trainee agrees or encourages the supervisor in this activity. Although supervisors differed even with the same trainee in the type of involvement they sought in supervision, they consistently demonstrated use of high-power messages of varying types. The supervisor was again in the superordinate position and the trainee in the subordinate position.

Friedlander, Siegel, and Brenock's (1989) study of parallel process in supervision also revealed that there was little competitive symmetry or struggle for control in supervisory process, and the primary verbal patterns were complementary in that the supervisor tended to use one-up communications with the trainee more often than one-down. Strozier et al. (1993) found greater instances of support and affectively oriented material than did previous studies; however, the authors confirmed in their findings that the supervisor holds the "relational control" in the supervision interaction. In their field study, Nelson and Holloway (1990) examined the relation of gender and role to patterns of interaction between the supervisor and trainee, and also found the prevalent pattern to be expert, one-up responses from supervisors followed by one-down responses from trainees. However, gender of the student appears to have influenced the supervisor's interactional response (encouraging male trainees more often than female trainees to make expert statements). Supervisors need to be conscious of the way they respond to supervisees, given that supervision is also the context in which supervisees build a professional identity and professional confidence.

In a training setting, the supervisor is the one to guide the process of evaluation and support within the structure of a professional relationship, thus distinguishing the role of supervisor from that of supervisee. It appears that mutuality, or congruence of worldviews or philosophical orientation, might play a key role in evaluation. In their study, Kennard et al. (1987) were interested in what variables in the supervisory relationship might best predict congruence in the supervisors' and supervisees' perceptions of the quality of the relationship. The participants described their supervisory experiences from the first practicum through to the internship training levels. The findings suggest that trainees who reported positive supervisory experiences were evaluated more highly by supervisors than trainees who reported negative supervisory experience on two dimensions: (1) interest in the supervisor's feedback and (2) interest in the supervisor's suggestions for professional development. Trainees in this study also had the opportunity to rate their supervisors. Trainees who reported a positive experience rated their supervisors significantly higher on supportiveness and instructional and interpretative competence than did the negative experience group. Supervisors' self-perceptions of being confrontational and instructional in supervision were significant variables in the type of supervisory experience reported; likewise, the match in theoretical orientation between supervisor and trainee played a significant role in supervisory process.

Ladany, Inman, Constantine, and Holheinz (1997) studied the relationship of multicultural case-conceptualization ability in doctoral- and masters-level trainees. Despite the limitations of being an analogue study, there is a clear implication for the influence of supervision: Those trainees who received clear directions from the "supervisor" (written directions) to focus on multicultural issues were rated to have greater multicultural case-conceptualization ability than those trainees who did not receive direct instructions. The authors agree that this study should be replicated using real supervisors to see how developing a supervisory relationship would impact on these findings; supposedly, a real supervisor would not only direct the supervisee to focus on multicultural issues, but would also be available to show *how* to attend to such issues.

In sum, supervisors need to be aware of the fact that building an interpersonal relationship is part of every supervisory experience. In fact, whether intentional or not, supervisors become the models for their supervisees on how to use power and involvement in relationships. One study intimates just how aware supervisees are of their supervisors' actions: Ladany, Lehrman-Waterman, Molinaro, and Wolgast (1999) found that 51% of 151 beginning-to-intern level supervisees reported at least one ethical violation by their supervisors, ranging from not adhering to adequate performance evaluation to not being able to work with alternative perspectives. Furthermore, nonadherence to ethical guidelines was not only noticed by supervisees but was significantly related to impoverished supervisory alliance and decreased supervisee satisfaction. There is a paucity of empirical evidence on ethical dilemmas and decision making in supervision. Because of the hierarchical nature of the supervisory relationship, specific ethical principles may be easily overlooked: In particular, the supervisor may provide therapeutic treatment to the supervisee (dual relationship issues); supervisors may practice without sufficient training in supervision (competency principle); supervisee evaluation may establish a competency criteria (due process); there may be a lack of responsibility for the adequacy of client treatment, especially in the case of training supervision (vicarious liability); and there may be a lack of confidentiality of supervisory material (informed consent) (Campbell, 2000).

Structure: Trainee Factors

The structure of power and involvement in the supervisory relationship may be particularly complex in a cross-cultural context because of the added complexity of power in the general society between White and other racial or ethnic groups (Solomon, 1983). There has been limited research on the relation of gender and role (supervisor/supervisee) to such process characteristics as power and involvement (Nelson & Holloway, 1990). In this study, female trainees were less likely to be encouraged to use higher-power responses in their interactions. Because these responses included giving one's opinions and voicing one's ideas, the result was a decided disadvantage for female trainees to receive feedback. Although similar cross-cultural studies with trainees or supervisors with ethnic or racial identities other than White do not exist at this time, it is likely that the positional power of the supervisor or trainee might be in contradiction to that found in the larger society, and thus the supervisory interaction may conceivably become problematic.

McRoy et al. (1986) studied racial and power dynamics in supervisory relationships in an exploratory survey study. Although respondents identified few actual problems, they identified many potential areas of concern. There appeared to be few actual discussions about potential cultural conflicts in the supervisory relationship despite the fact that students perceived their supervisors to be sensitive to cultural differences. The unwillingness to discuss these issues as concerns the counseling relationship also has serious ramifications for culturally congruent treatment. It appears that participants were willing to identify potential cross-cultural problems in the abstract but were not able to discuss them openly. Gutierrez (1982) addressed the ways in which cross-cultural sensitivity and practice can be incorporated into the entire counseling curriculum. Building a program that enhances open communication and knowledge among White and non-White students and faculty is the necessary beginning to directly confronting these issues in the supervisory relationship.

Schlenker and Leary (1985) have studied the relation of social anxiety to self-presentational behaviors. *Self-presentation* is a term in social psychology that refers to the regulation of one's behaviors to create a particular impression on others (Jones & Pittman, 1982). In situations where individuals want to create a favorable impression, as certainly any trainee being evaluated will want to do, they will experience some level of social anxiety. This anxiety will be mitigated by their expectations for success, their degree of social uncertainty regarding expectations, and the importance they attribute to the person they are trying to impress. Schlenker and Leary concluded that under conditions of high social anxiety, where there is an overriding concern of evaluation, individuals will display changes in their communicative style; they will display greater cognitive withdrawal coupled with increased self-preoccupation, thus interfering with the effectiveness of information processing, sensitivity to ongoing events, self-monitoring, and self-control. For example, individuals may resort to approaches that are reticent or reserved or withdrawn, pleasing, compliant, and dependent, or aggressive, hostile, or defensive.

Ladany, Hill, Corbett, and Nutt (1996) surveyed 108 trainees concerning their non-disclosures to their supervisors. The principal issue that trainees chose not to disclose was "negative reactions" toward their supervisors. The most frequent reasons given for not disclosing this information was perceived unimportance, too personal, too negative, or a poor supervisory alliance. There was also the fear of political suicide, and therefore nondisclosures were a passive way of dealing with such interpersonal conflicts in the supervisory relationship. Thus, trainees' perceptions of their supervisors play an important role in the development of the supervisory relationship, yet, given their subordinate power position, trainees can have a difficult time dealing with such interpersonal conflict directly.

Occasionally, clients may be dealing with issues that are similar to a life circumstance that the trainee has not yet resolved, and the supervisor is forced to recommend client referral rather than risk the almost certain countertransference that would emerge in the therapeutic relationship, and perhaps even in the supervisory relationship. The reenactment of the relationship dynamics in the supervisory situation is a familiar phenomenon to supervisors and has been named the "parallel process" (Dodenhoff, 1981; Ekstein & Wallerstein, 1958). Parallel process occurs when the central dynamic process of the counseling relationship is unconsciously acted out by the trainee in the supervision relationship. The trainee may be experiencing difficulty with the client and feels powerless to change the situation therapeutically, so he or she takes on interpersonal strategies similar to those of the client. If the supervisor does not recognize the dynamic as a part of the counseling situation or the trainee's feelings of powerlessness, then the supervisor may collude with this reenactment by adopting a role similar to the trainee's in the counseling relationship. The obvious result is an impasse in supervision. A supervisor who recognizes the parallel process can intervene directly with the trainee, thus breaking the impasse in supervision while concurrently modeling effective interpersonal strategies for the trainee. Thus, with effective supervisory intervention, the trainee begins to understand, both experientially and conceptually, the meaning of the client's behavior and is able to resume a therapeutic approach to the problem.

Friedlander et al. (1989) used the ICRS, the Relational Communication Control Coding System (RCCCS; Ericson & Rogers, 1973), the Hill Counselor Verbal Response Category System–Revised (HCVRCS-R; Hill 1985), and a rating system developed for the study (Supervisory Feedback Rating System; SFRS) to study the parallel process in counseling and supervision as manifested in one case. Friedlander et al. (1989) argued that the relationships often mirrored each other by citing the parallel nature of the self-report data and verbal communication patterns across nine concurrent supervisory and counseling sessions. They concluded that supervision and counseling seem to be reciprocal and interlocking processes, but that trainees are in a highly vulnerable position as the linchpin between both relationships. This is one of a few studies (Doehrman, 1976; Wedeking & Scott, 1976) that has investigated the effects of the supervisory process on the counseling process.

Structure: Client Factors

The supervisor is responsible for ensuring that the client receives adequate treatment from the supervisee. In part, this assessment of the match between the supervisee's area and level of competence and the client's needs depends on the severity of the client's problem. Axis-IV of the DSM-IV (American Psychiatric Association, 1994) is reserved for rating the severity of the psychosocial stressors in an individual's life. The degree of stress is then examined in light of the client's mental condition, the nature of the problem, and the client's past adaptability in order to determine the course of treatment. If a client is severely depressed or aggressive and is experiencing a very high number of stressors, the supervisor and counselor may need to do a specific assessment for suicide or homicide potential.

In one study, Robyak, Goodyear, Prange, and Donham (1986) examined the relation of gender, supervised experience in counseling, and presenting client problem on students' preferences for using particular power bases to influence client change within an analogue study design. The findings indicate that the experience level of the trainee was related to preferences for legitimate and referent power bases, whereas gender and type of presenting problem had no significant effect. Students with less supervised counseling experience preferred to use legitimate and referent power bases with clients to a greater extent than did students with more supervised counseling experience. Robyak et al. explained their results from the perspective of social influence theory, stating that the legitimate power base allows beginning-level trainees to use the socially sanctioned role of counselor to structure the relationship and gain credibility. Additionally, the use of the referent power base mitigates the stiffness, or formality, of legitimate power by seeking to gain the client's confidence through personal qualities that can enhance interpersonal attractiveness. Although this research is limited by the analogue and survey approach to data collection, it does provide information regarding the role of counseling experience in the choice of power base within the formal working relationships of counseling and supervision. The trainee's use of different power bases across these two relationships may be an interesting area for future research.

Robyak, Goodyear, and Prange (1987), drawing from the interpersonal influence model of counseling (Strong, 1968; Strong & Matross, 1973), examined the influence of supervisor's gender, experience, and supervisory focus on the supervisor's preferences for expert, referent, and legitimate power bases (French & Raven, 1960). In this analogue study, male and female supervisors ranging in supervision experience from 1 month to 40 years, read a typescript of a female supervisee's comments and then selected from three possible supervisor responses. Each response reflected the use of one of the three power bases by the supervisor. The results indicated that both gender and amount of supervisory experience had significant main effects on the supervisor's preference for the referent power base but not on the expert or legitimate power bases. It appeared that males and in-experienced supervisors preferred the use of the referent power base. Supervisors who focused on self-awareness of the supervisee showed a greater preference for the expert power base than the supervisors who focused on client conceptualization; and the legitimate power base was not significantly related to any of the three independent variables.

Structure: Institutional Factors

There is virtually no empirical research on the influence of organizational factors on the structural aspects of the supervisory relationship. Although there is a large body of knowledge on power in institutional settings, critical factors in this area have not been connected to clinical supervision. However, as practitioners and supervisors are only too aware, organizational structure, climate, and leadership are often relevant to their decisions in supervision. The British literature on supervision has integrated the consideration of power and affiliation in organizations, looking at the role of workplace counselors and of workplace supervisors who oversee their work (Carroll, 1996; Carroll & Holloway, 1999; Holloway, 1998a; Holloway & Carroll, 1999).

Implications for Practice

It has been our intention in this chapter to consider the empirical and conceptual literature in the supervision field and to ascertain what might be some practical implications for supervision practice. By exploring the three larger organizing constructs of the SAS relationship model, there are several principles that we believe are particularly relevant to supervisory practice. These are (1) the importance of beginning well, (2) the relevance of a trainee's previous experience, (3) the relevance of power and involvement in the supervisory relationship, (4) the impact of the client issue, (5) the influence of evaluation.

The Importance of Beginning Well

The importance of beginning well cannot be overemphasized. Supervisors carry an important responsibility of providing the appropriate amount of support, structure, and technical guidance most suitable to their supervisees' learning. Beginning supervisees with little to no previous supervisory training are not only being taught what is expected of them as supervisees but also are learning what to expect from a supervisor. Guest and Beutler (1988) found that even after several years of training, early supervisory experiences still exerted an affect on clinicians' theoretical position. Thus, if early experiences in supervision can so deeply imprint on one's theoretical orientation, it is plausible to imagine that this same early supervision experience can influence what one comes to expect, or not expect, out of supervision.

The Relevance of a Trainee's Previous Experience

Each supervisor and supervisee brings to the relationship of supervision individual expectations of how the process will unfold. Some of these expectations will be the product of past experiences of supervision; others will develop from other formal and informal relational experiences; and still others will develop from knowledge of supervision gained through anecdotal materials and empirical literature. These past experiences will shape the process or the relationship structure that will, in turn, influence the participants' engagement in the process.

The Relevance of Power and Involvement in the Supervisory Relationship

The development of an interpersonal relationship promotes a focus on shared idiosyncratic rules created for that particular relationship. Supervision initially provides a general expectancy base for certain interactive behaviors; however, as the working relationship develops, it is individualized around the learning needs of the trainee and the teaching approaches of the supervisor. These idiosyncratic reciprocal rules are learned by the participants during the course of their interactive process (Miller & Rogers, 1976).

It is important for the supervisor from the very first meeting to provide the supervisee with a road map of what to expect from supervision and with the necessary information or tools to be an informed consumer of supervision. Thus, the supervisor can make explicit (1) the philosophical and theoretical orientation to supervision and psychotherapy, (2) work expectations, and (3) the conditions and timing of evaluation. Research indicates that supervisees benefit from being educated in how to *be* a supervisee, because it is a distinct role from that of counselor, client, or student, and each supervisory encounter is unique (Ladany & Friedlander, 1995). If the role and work expectations are not made clear, trainees can begin to feel role ambiguity or role conflict. Counselors are in a vulnerable position for role conflict because they are the linchpin, or the common factor, in the therapeutic and the supervisory relationships. The counselor-in-training in particular has to become versatile at alternating power roles between a superordinate power position (counselor) and the subordinate power position (student/trainee). Supervisors can encourage supervisees to discuss their experiences of power and influence in their roles as trainee, student, counselor, and supervisee. Such meta-analytic thinking can serve as a model for the supervisee on the importance of self-reflection and critical analysis in one's supervision work.

The Impact of the Client Issue

Regardless of training level, trainees benefit from having supportive and structured supervision at the beginning of their supervisory relationship (Rabinowitz et al., 1986). Therefore, if possible, it is important for the supervisor and trainee to set aside sufficient time to meet a couple of times at the beginning to discuss role expectations, previous counseling or related experiences, and working goals *before* the trainee begins to work with clients. As soon as clinical work has begun, the focus in supervision becomes naturally divided between client issues and trainee professional development issues. We also know that when clients are dealing with a crisis (suicidal gesture, trauma, emotional breakdown, and so on) trainees benefit from more consistent and structured supervision (Tracey et al., 1989). Thus, it is important for supervisors to be informed and current on clinical cases, and to arrange supervision in case of such crisis emergencies.

The Influence of Evaluation

Regardless of the trainees' level of experience, they will feel initial uncertainty about the role expectations and the conditions for evaluation; therefore, trainees require specific information, particularly at the beginning of the supervision relationship, about the criteria on which they will be evaluated, when they will be evaluated, and what options are available to them when their clinical work does not meet expectations. Formative evaluation, or evaluation done at critical points during the course of supervision, has several objectives: (1) It reassures trainees that they are developing clinical skills as expected; (2) it refocuses trainees on necessary skills that are underdeveloped; and (3) it points out progress and indicates new directions for skill development. Summative evaluation is the final point of evaluation, and it usually carries the gatekeeping responsibility of asserting who passes and who does not. This final feedback, however, should include comments that the trainee has already heard throughout supervision, because the trainee should have been given ample opportunity to address and correct any pertinent clinical skill.

Trainees will have different comfort levels with supervisory feedback; however, research seems to indicate that as trainees gain confidence in their clinical skill and trust in the supervisory relationship, they tend to actively seek out feedback on their clinical work and on personal issues that might be impacting on their clinical work.

Summary

The ideal supervisor has been described as a person who exhibits high levels of empathy, understanding, unconditional positive regard, flexibility, concern, attention, investment, curiosity, and openness (Carifio & Hess, 1987). Although such personal qualities are valuable in any relationship, these descriptors focus almost entirely on the intra- and interpersonal characteristics of an individual. They implicitly suggest that supervisors are born and not made. Certainly, supervisors have their own interpersonal characteristics, knowledge, abilities, and cultural values, which become the foundation on which the supervisory role is built. However, supervisors can also enhance their own interpersonal style, by the manner in which they choose to use their repertoire of interpersonal skills and clinical knowledge in each supervisory relationship.

References

American Psychiatric Association. (1994). *Diagnostic and statistical manual of mental disorders* (4th ed.). Washington, DC: Author.

Atkinson, D. R., Morten, G., & Sue, D. W. (1989). *Counseling American minorities: A cross-cultural perspective* (3rd ed.). Dubuque, IA: Brown.

Barrett-Lennard, G. T. (1962). Dimensions of therapists response as causal factors in therapeutic change. *Psychological Monographs, 76,* 1–33.

Bernard, J., & Goodyear, R. (1998). *Fundamentals of clinical supervision* (2nd ed.). Needham Heights, MA: Allyn and Bacon.

Bernard, J. M. (1979). Supervisor training: A discrimination model. *Counselor Education and Supervision, 19,* 60–68.

Beutler, L. E., & McNabb, C. E. (1981). Self-evaluation for the psychotherapist. In C. E. Walker (Ed.), *Clinical practice of psychology* (pp. 397–439). New York: Pergamon Press.

Bloch, S. Y., & Reibstein, J. (1980). Perceptions by patients and therapists of therapeutic factors in group psychotherapy. *British Journal of Psychiatry, 137,* 274–278.

Borders, L. D. (1989). Developmental cognitions of first practicum supervisees. *Journal of Counseling Psychology, 36,* 163–169.

Borders, L. D., & Fong, M. L. (1989). Ego development and counseling ability during training. *Counselor Education and Supervision, 29,* 71–83.

Borders, L. D., Fong, M. L., & Neimeyer, G. J. (1986). Counseling students level of ego development and perceptions of clients. *Counselor Education and Supervision, 26,* 37–49.

Byrne, D. (1971). *The attraction paradigm.* New York: Academic Press.

Calhoun, K. S., Moras, K., Pilkonis, P. A., & Rehm, L. P. (1998). Empirically supported treatments: Implications for training. *Journal of Consulting and Clinical Psychology, 66,* 151–162.

Campbell, J. M. (2000). *Becoming an effective supervisor.* Muncie, IN: Accelerated Development.

Carifio, M. S., & Hess, A. K. (1987). Who is the ideal supervisor? *Professional Psychology: Research and Practice, 3,* 244–250.

Carroll, C. (1994). *Building bridges: A study of employee counsellors in the private sector.* London: City University.

Carroll, M. (1996). *Workplace counselling.* London: Sage.

Carroll, M., & Holloway, E. (Eds.). (1999). *Supervision in context.* London: Sage.

Caskey, N. H., Barker, C., & Elliot, R. (1994). Dual perspectives: Clients' and therapists' perception of therapist responses. *British Journal of Clinical Psychology, 23,* 20–26.

Coleman H. L. K., Wampold, B. E., & Casali, S. L. (1994). Ethnic minorities' ratings of ethnically similar and European American counselors: A meta-analysis. *Journal of Counseling Psychology, 42,* 247–294.

Cook, D. A., & Helms, J. E. (1988). Visible racial/ethnic group supervisees' satisfaction with cross-cultural supervision as predicted by relationship characteristics. *Journal of Counseling Psychology, 35,* 268–274.

Demos, G. G., & Zuwaylif, F. (1962). Counselor attitudes in relation to the theoretical positions of their supervisors. *Counselor Education and Supervision, 2,* 280–285.

Dodenhoff, J. T. (1981). Interpersonal attraction and direct-indirect supervisor influence as predictors of counselor trainee effectiveness. *Journal of Counseling Psychology, 28,* 47–52.

Doehrman, M. J. (1976). Parallel processes in supervision and psychotherapy. *Bulletin of the Menninger Clinic, 40*(I), 1–104.

Dunlap, D., & Goldman, P. (1991). Rethinking power in schools. *Educational Administration Quarterly, 27,* 5–29.

Efstation, J. F., Patton, M. J., & Kardash, C. M. (1990). Measuring the working alliance in counselor supervision. *Journal of Counseling Psychology, 37,* 322–329.

Ekstein, R., & Wallerstein, R. S. (1958). *The teaching and learning of psychotherapy.* New York: Basic Books.

Elliott, R. (1986). Recall (IPR) as a psychotherapy process research method. In L. Greenberg & W. Pinsof (Eds.), *The psychotherapeutic process: A research handbook* (pp. 503–527). New York: Guilford Press.

Ellis, M. V., & Dell, D. M. (1986). Dimensionality of supervisor roles: Supervisors' perceptions of supervision. *Journal of Counseling Psychology, 33,* 282–291.

Ellis, M. V., Dell, D. M., & Good, G. E. (1988). Counselor trainees' perceptions of supervisor roles: Two studies testing the dimensionality of supervision. *Journal of Counseling Psychology, 35,* 315–324.

Ellis, M. V., Ladany, N., Krengel, M., & Schult, D. (1996). Clinical supervision research from 1981 to 1993: A methodological critique. *Journal of Counseling Psychology, 43*(1), 35–50.

Ericson, P. M., & Rogers, L. E. (1973). New procedures for analyzing relational communication. *Family Process, 12,* 245–267.

Eugster, S. L., & Wampold, B. E. (1996). Systematic effects of participant role on evaluation of the psychotherapy session. *Journal of Consulting and Clinical Psychology, 64,* 1020–1028.

Follett, M. P. (1941). The meaning of responsibility in business management. In H. C. Metcalf & L. Urwick (Eds.), *Dynamic administration: The collected papers of Mary Parker Follett* (pp. 141–166). London: Sir Issac Pitman and Sons.

French, J. R. P., Jr., & Raven, B. M. (1960). *The bases of social power.* In D. Cartwright & A. Zander (Eds.), *Group dynamics: Research and theory* (2nd ed., pp. 607–623). New York: Peterson.

Friedlander, M. L., Keller, K. E., Peca-Baker, T. A., & Olk, M. E. (1986). Effects of role conflict on counselor trainees' self-statements, anxiety level, and performance. *Journal of Counseling Psychology, 33,* 1–5.

Friedlander, M. L., Siegel, S. M., & Brenock, K. (1989). Parallel processes in counseling and supervision: A case study. *Journal of Counseling Psychology, 36,* 149–157.

Friedlander, M. L., & Ward, L. G. (1984). Development and validation of the Supervisory Styles Inventory. *Journal of Counseling Psychology, 4,* 541–557.

Friedler, F. (1950). A comparison of therapeutic relationships in psychoanalytic, nondirective, and Adlerian therapy. *Journal of Consulting Psychology, 14,* 436–445.

Garb, H. N. (1989). Clinical judgment, clinical training, and professional experience. *Psychological Bulletin, 105,* 387–396.

Garfield, S. L. (1994). Research on client variables in psychotherapy. In A. E. Bergin & S. L. Garfield (Eds.), *Handbook of psychotherapy and behavior change* (4th ed., pp. 190–228). New York: Wiley.

Goldberg, D. A. (1985). Process, notes, audio and videotape: Modes of presentation in psychotherapy. *The Clinical Supervisor, 3*(3), 3–13.

Goodyear, R. K. (1982). *Psychotherapy supervision by major theorists.* Manhattan, KS: Instructional Media Center, Kansas State University.

Goodyear, R. K. (1990). Gender configurations in supervisory dyads: Their relation to supervisee influence strategies and to skill evaluations of the supervisee. *The Clinical Supervisor, 8,* 67–69.

Goodyear, R. K., Abadie, P. D., & Efros, F. (1984). Supervisory theory into practice: Differential perception of supervision by Ekstein, Ellis, Polster, and Rogers. *Journal of Counseling Psychology, 31,* 228–237.

Goodyear, R. K., & Robyak, J. E. (1982). Supervisors' theory and experience in supervisory focus. *Psychological Reports, 51,* 978.

Guest, P. D., & Beutler, L. E. (1988). Impact of psychotherapy supervision on therapist orientation and values. *Journal of Consulting and Clinical Psychology, 56,* 653–658.

Gutierrez, F. J. (1982). Working with minority counselor education students. *Counselor Education and Supervision, 21,* 218–226.

Gysbers, N. C., & Johnston, J. A. (1965). Expectations of a practicum supervisor's role. *Counselor Education and Supervision, 2,* 68–75.

Harvey, O. J., Hunt, D. E., & Schroder, H. M. (1961). *Conceptual systems and personality organization.* New York: Wiley.

Helms, J. E. (1984). Toward a theoretical explanation of the effect of race on counseling: A Black and White model. *The Counseling Psychologist, 12*(4), 153–165.

Heppner, P. P., & Handley, P. G. (1982). The relationship between supervisory expertness, attractiveness, or trustworthiness. *Counselor Education and Supervision, 8,* 29–31.

Heppner, P. P., & Roehlke, H. J. (1984). Differences among supervisees at different levels of training: Implications for a developmental model of supervision. *Journal of Counseling Psychology, 31,* 76–90.

Hester, L. R., Weitz, L. H., Anchor, K. N., & Roback, H. B. (1976). Supervisor attraction as a function of level of supervisor skillfulness and supervisees' perceived similarity. *Journal of Counseling Psychology, 23,* 254–258.

Hill, C. E. (1985). *Manual for the Hill counselor verbal response modes category system* (Rev. ed.). Unpublished manuscript, University of Maryland at College Park.

Hill, C. E., Charles, D., & Reed, K. G. (1981). A longitudinal analysis of changes in counseling skills during doctoral training in counseling psychology. *Journal of Counseling Psychology, 28,* 428–436.

Holloway, E. L. (1995). *Clinical supervision: A systems approach.* Thousand Oaks, CA: Sage Publications.

Holloway, E. (1998, October 29). *The supervisee's view: An international sample.* Paper presented at the meeting of the Department of Educational and Counseling Psychology, University of Illinois, Urbana-Champaign.

Holloway, E., & Carroll, M. (Eds.). (1999). *Training counselling supervisors.* London: Sage.

Holloway, E. L. (1992). Supervision: A way of teaching and learning. In S. D. Brown & R. W. Lent (Eds.), *Handbook of counseling psychology* (pp. 177–214). New York: Wiley.

Holloway, E. L., Freund, R. D., Gardner, S. L., Nelson, M. L., & Walker, B. E. (1989). Relation of power and involvement to theoretical orientation in supervision: An analysis of discourse. *Journal of Counseling Psychology, 36,* 88–102.

Holloway, E. L., & González-Doupé, P. (1999, August). *Empirically supported intervention programs: Implications for supervision as a training modality.* The American Psychology Convention, Boston, MA.

Holloway, E. L., & Neufeldt, S. N. (1995). Supervision: Contributions to treatment efficacy. *Journal of Consulting and Clinical Psychology, 63,* 207–213.

Holloway, E. L., & Poulin, K. (1995). Discourse in supervision. In J. Siegfried (Ed.), *Therapeutic and everyday discourse as behavior change: Towards a micro-analysis in psychotherapy process research* (pp. 245–276). New York: Ablex.

Holloway, E. L., & Wampold, B. E. (1983). Patterns of verbal behavior and judgments of satisfaction in the supervision interview. *Journal of Counseling Psychology, 30,* 227–234.

Holloway, E. L., & Wampold, B. E. (1986). The relation of conceptual level and counseling-related tasks: A meta-analysis. *Journal of Counseling Psychology, 33,* 310–319.

Holloway, E. L., & Wolleat, P. L. (1980). Relationship of counselor conceptual level to clinical hypothesis formation. *Journal of Educational and Psychological Consultation, 5*(1), 23–43.

Holloway, E. L., & Wolleat, P. L. (1981). Style differences of beginning supervisors: An interactional analysis. *Journal of Counseling Psychology, 28,* 373–376.

Holloway, E. L., & Wolleat, P. L. (1994). Supervision: The pragmatics of empowerment. *Journal of Educational and Psychological Consultation, 5,* 23–43.

Inskipp, F., & Proctor, B. (1989). Skills for supervising and being supervised. (Principle of counselling audiotape series). East Sussex, UK: Alexia.

Jones, E. E., & Pittman, T. S. (1982). Toward a general theory of strategic self-presentation. In J. Suls (Ed.), *Psychological perspectives on the self.* Hillsdale, NJ: Erlbaum.

Kennard, B. D., Stewart, S. M., & Gluck, M. R. (1987). The supervision relationship: Variables contributing to positive versus negative experiences. *Professional Psychology: Research and Practice, 18,* 172–175.

Knox, S., Goldberg, J. L., Woodhourse, S. S., & Hill, C. E. (1999). Clients' internal representations of their therapists. *Journal of Counseling Psychology, 46,* 244–256.

Ladany, N., Brittan-Powell, C. S., & Pannu, R. K. (1997). The influence of supervisory racial identity interaction and racial matching on the supervisory working alliance and supervisee multicultural competence. *Counselor Education and Supervision, 36,* 284–304.

Ladany, N., & Friedlander, M. L. (1995). The relationship between the supervisory working alliance and trainees' experience of role conflict and role ambiguity. *Counselor Education and Supervision, 34,* 220–231.

Ladany, N., Hill, C. E., Corbett, M. M., & Nutt, E. A. (1996). Nature, extent, and importance of what psychotherapy trainees do not disclose to their supervisors. *Journal of Counseling Psychology, 43,* 10–24.

Ladany, N., Inman, A. G., Constantine, M. G., & Holheinz, E. W. (1997). Supervisee multicultural case conceptualization ability and self-reported multicultural competence as functions of supervisee racial identity and supervisor focus. *Journal of Counseling Psychology, 44,* 284–293.

Ladany, N., Lehrman-Waterman, D., Molinaro, M., & Wolgast, B. (1999). Psychotherapy supervisor ethical practices: Adherence to guidelines, the supervisory working alliance, and supervisee satisfaction. *The Counseling Psychologist, 44*(3), 284–293.

Lambert, M. J. (1974). Supervisory and counseling process: A comparative study. *Counselor Education and Supervision, 14,* 54–60.

Leary, T. (1957). *Interpersonal diagnosis of personality: A theory and a methodology for personal evaluation.* New York: Ronald Press.

Lemons, S., & Lanning, W. E. (1979). Value system similarity and the supervisory relationship. *Counselor Education and Supervision, 19,* 13–19.

Littrell, J. M., Lee-Borden, N., & Lorenz, J. (1979). A developmental framework for counseling supervision. *Counselor Education and Supervision, 19,* 129–136.

Loevinger, J. (1976). *Ego development: Conceptions and theories.* San Francisco: Jossey-Bass.

Marikis, D. A., Russell, R. K., & Dell, D. M. (1985). Effects of supervisor experience level on planning and in-session supervisor verbal behavior. *Journal of Counseling Psychology, 32,* 410–416.

Martin, J. S., Goodyear, R. K., & Newton, F. B. (1987). Clinical supervision: An intensive case study. *Professional Psychology: Research and Practice, 18,* 225–235.

McNeil, B. W., Stoltenberg, C. D., & Pierce, R. A. (1985). Supervisees' perceptions of their development: A test of the counselor complexity model. *Journal of Counseling Psychology, 32,* 630–633.

McRoy, R. G., Freeman, E. M., Logan, S. L., & Blackmon, B. (1986). Cross-cultural field supervision: Implications for social work education. *Journal of Social Work Education, 22,* 50–56.

Miars, R. D., Tracey, T. J., Ray, P. B., Cornfeld, J. L., O'Farrell, M., & Gelson, C. J. (1983). Variation in supervision process across trainee experience levels. *Journal of Counseling, Psychology, 30,* 403–412.

Miller, G. R. (1976). *Explorations in interpersonal communication.* Newbury Park, CA: Sage.

Miller, E. F., & Rogers, L. E. (1987). Relational dimensions of interpersonal dynamics. In M. E. Roloff & G. R. Miller (Eds.), *Interpersonal processes: New directions in communication research* (pp. 117–139). Newbury Park, CA: Sage.

Morton, T., Alexander, C., & Altman, I. (1976). Communication and relationship definition. In G. Miller (Ed.), *Explorations in interpersonal communication* (pp. 105–125). Beverly Hills, CA: Sage.

Mueller, W. J., & Kell, B. L. (1972). *Coping with conflict: Supervising counselors and psychotherapists.* Englewood Cliffs, NJ: Prentice-Hall.

Najavits, L. M., & Strupp, H. H. (1994). Differences in the effectiveness of psychodynamic therapists: A process-outcome study. *Psychotherapy, 32,* 114–123.

Nelson, M. L. (1993). A current perspective on gender differences: Implications for research in counseling. *Journal of Counseling Psychology, 40,* 200–209.

Nelson, M. L., & Holloway, E.,L. (1990). Relation of gender to power and involvement in supervision. *Journal of Counseling Psychology, 37,* 473–481.

Olk, M., & Friedlander, M. L. (1992). Trainees' experiences of role conflict and role ambiguity in supervisory relationships. *Journal of Counseling Psychology, 39,* 389–397.

Parham, T. A. (1989). Cycles of psychological nigrescence. *The Counseling Psychologist, 17,* 187–226.

Patterson, C. H. (1983). A client-centered approach to supervision. *The Counseling Psychologist, 11,* 21–26.

Patton, M. J., & Kivlighan, D. M., Jr. (1997). Relevance of the supervisory alliance to the counseling alliance and to treatment adherence in counselor training. *Journal of Counseling-Psychology, 44,* 108–115.

Pedersen, P. E. (1985). *Handbook of cross-cultural counseling and therapy.* Westport, CT: Greenwood.

Penman, R. (1980). *Communication processes and relationships.* London: Academic Press.

Pope-Davis, D. B., Reynolds, A. L., & Vasquez, L. A. (1992). *Multicultural counseling: Issues of ethnic diversity.* Iowa City, IA: AVC Marketing The University of Iowa.

Poulin, K. (1992). *Towards a grounded pedagogy of practice: A dimensional analysis of counseling supervision.* Eugene, OR: University of Oregon.

Putney, M. W., Worthington, E. L., Jr., & McCullough, M. E. (1992). Effects of supervisor and supervisee theoretical orientation and supervisor–supervisee matching on interns' perceptions of supervision. *Journal of Counseling Psychology, 39,* 258–265.

Rabinowitz, F. E., Heppner, P. P., & Roehlke, H. J. (1986). Descriptive study of process and outcome variables of supervision over time. *Journal of Counseling Psychology, 33,* 292–300.

Reising, G. N., & Daniels, M. H. (1983). A study of Hogan's model of counselor development and supervision. *Journal of Counseling Psychology, 30,* 235–244.

Rickards, L. D. (1984). Verbal interaction and supervisor perception in counselor supervision. *Journal of Counseling Psychology, 31,* 262–265.

Robyak, J. E., Goodyear, R. K., & Prange, M. (1987). Effects of supervisors' sex, focus, and experience on preferences for interpersonal power bases. *Counselor Education and Supervision, 26,* 299–309.

Robyak, J. E., Goodyear, R. K., Prange, M. E., & Donham G. (1986). Effects of gender, supervision, and presenting problems on practicum students' preference for interpersonal power bases. *Journal of Counseling Psychology, 33,* 159–163.

Rokeach, M. (1967). *Value Survey.* Sunnyvale, CA: Halgeen Tests.

Rounsaville, B. J., Chevron, E. S., & Weissman, M. M. (1984). Specification of techniques in interpersonal psychotherapy. In J. B. W. Williams & R. L. Spitzer (Eds.), *Psychotherapy research: Where are we and where should we go?* (pp. 160–172). New York: Guilford Press.

Rounsaville, B. J., O'Malley, S., Foley, S., & Weissman, M. M. (1988). Role of manual-guided training in the conduct and efficacy of interpersonal psychotherapy for depression. *Journal of Counseling and Clinical Psychology, 56,* 681–688.

Russell, R. K., Crimmings, A. M., & Lent, R. W. (1984). Counselor training and supervision: Theory and research. In S. Brown & R. Lent (Eds.), *The handbook of counseling psychology* (pp. 625–681). New York: Wiley.

Schlenker, B. R., & Leary, M. R. (1985). *Language and Social Psychology,* 4, iii–iv.

Schön, D. A. (1983). *Educating the reflective practitioner.* San Francisco: Jossey-Bass.

Skovholt, T. M. & Rønnestad, M. H. (1992). Themes in therapist and counselor development. *Journal of Counseling and Development, 70,* 505–515.

Solomon, B. (1983). Power: The troublesome factor in cross-cultural supervision. *Smith College School of Social Work Journal, 10,* 27–32.

Steinhelber, J., Patterson, V., Cliffe, K., & LaGoullon, M. (1984). An investigation of some relationships between psychotherapy supervision and patient change. *Journal of Clinical Psychology, 40,* 1346–1353.

Stenack, R. J., & Dye, H. A. (1982). Behavioral description of counseling supervision roles. *Counselor Education and Supervision, 21,* 295–304.

Stoltenberg, C. D., & Delworth, U. (1987). *Supervising counselors and therapists.* San Francisco: Jossey-Bass.

Stoltenberg, C. D., McNeill B., & Crethar, H. C. (1994). Changes in supervision as counselors and therapists gain experience: A review. *Professional Psychology: Research and Practice, 25,* 416–449.

Stone, G. L. (1980). Effects of experience on supervisor planning. *Journal of Counseling Psychology, 27,* 84–88.

Strong, S. R. (1968). Counseling: An interpersonal influence process. *Journal of Counseling, Psychology, 15,* 215–224.

Strong, S. R., Hill, H. I., & Nelson, B. N. (1988). *Interpersonal communication rating scale* (Rev. ed). Richmond: Department of Psychology, Virginia Commonwealth University.

Strong, S. R., & Matross, R. P. (1973). Change process in counseling and psychotherapy. *Journal of Counseling Psychology, 20,* 125–132.

Strozier, A. L., Kivlighan, D. M., & Thoreson, R. W. (1993). Supervisor intentions, supervisee reactions, and helpfulness: A case study of the process of supervision. *Psychotherapy: Theory, Research and Practice, 24,* 13–19.

Strupp, H. H., Butler, S. F., & Rosser, C. L. (1988). Training in psychodynamic therapy. *Journal of Consulting and Clinical Psychology, 56,* 689–695.

Sue, D. W., & Sue, D. (1990). *Counseling the culturally different: Theory and practice* (2nd ed.). New York: Wiley.

Sundland, D. M. (1977). Theoretical orientations of psychotherapists. In A. S. Gurman & A. M. Razin (Eds.), *Effective psychotherapy: A handbook of research* (pp. 189–222). New York: Pergamon.

Sundland, L. M., & Feinberg, L. B. (1972). The relationship of interpersonal attraction, experience, and supervisors' level of functioning in dyadic counseling supervision. *Counselor Education and Supervision, 12,* 187–193.

Tracey, T. J., Ellickson, J. L., & Sherry, P. (1989). Reactance in relation to different supervisory environments and counselor development. *Journal of Counseling Psychology, 36,* 336–344.

Tyler, F. B., Brome, D. R., & Williams, J. E. (1991). *Ethnic validity, ecology, and psychotherapy: A psychosocial competence model.* New York: Plenum Press.

Wampold, B. E., & Kim, K. H. (1989). Sequential analysis applied to counseling process and outcome: A case study revisited. *Journal of Counseling Psychology, 36,* 357–364.

Ward, L. G., Friedlander, M. L., Schoen, L. G., & Klein, J. C. (1985). Strategic self-presentation. *Journal of Counseling Psychology, 32,* 111–118.

Wedeking, D. F., & Scott, T. B. (1976). A study of the relationship between supervisor and trainee behaviors in counseling practicum. *Counselor Education and Supervision, 15,* 259–266.

Wiley, M. O., & Ray, P. B. (1986). Counseling supervision by developmental level. *Journal of Counseling Psychology, 33,* 439–445.

Winter, M., & Holloway, E. L. (1991). Effects of trainee experience, conceptual level and supervisor approach on selection of audiotaped counseling passages. *The Clinical Supervisor, 9*(2), 87–104.

Worthen, V., & McNeill, B. W. (1996). A phenomenological investigation of "good" supervision events. *Journal of Counseling Psychology, 43*(1), 25–34.

Worthington, E. L., Jr. (1984a). Empirical investigation of supervision of counselors as they gain experience. *Journal of Counseling Psychology, 31,* 63–75.

Worthington, E. L., Jr. (1984b). Use of trait labels in counseling supervision by experienced and inexperienced supervisors. *Professional Psychology: Research and Practice, 15,* 457–461.

Worthington, E. L., Jr. & Roehlke, H. J. (1979). Effective supervision as perceived by beginning counselors-in-training. *Journal of Counseling Psychology, 26,* 64–73.

Worthington, E. L., Jr., & Stern, A. (1985). The effects of supervisor and supervisee degree level and gender on the supervisory relationship. *Journal of Counseling Psychology, 32,* 252–262.

Zuniga, M.E. (1987). Mexican-American clinical training: A pilot project. *Journal of Social Work Education, 23*(3), 11–20.

6

Transference, Interpretation, and Insight

A Research-Practice Model

Dennis M. Kivlighan, Jr.

Department of Educational and Counseling Psychology
University of Missouri at Columbia

All clients respond to therapists as they have responded to others in the past. Some types of therapy are directed toward facilitating client understanding of these patterns of behavior. Other types of therapy address transference behaviors only when they interfere with the counseling process. This chapter examines transference from the former perspective and provides the reader with a thorough review of transference research and a model for practice based on this research. Particular emphasis is placed on the importance of assessment of transference, interpretation, and insight. Several brief assessment devices are presented for clinical use.

Chapter Questions

- What is transference and how is it assessed?
- What is the nature of the relationship between transference and alliance?
- What is interpretation and how does it relate to the counseling outcome?
- What is the nature of the relationship between therapist interpretation and working alliance?
- How is client insight assessed?

Luborsky and Crits-Christoph (1990) identified the description of transference as Freud's (1913/1958) most important clinical discovery. As pointed out by Gelso and Hayes (1998), however, the phenomenon of transference is complex and controversial. For example, some therapists believe that transference is simply an artifact, created and maintained by therapists' self-fulfilling prophecies (Gelso & Hayes, 1998). Partly because of the controversy surrounding transference, the past 50 years have witnessed more than 3,000 books and journal articles addressing various aspects of transference. Until the past 10 years, however, few of these articles represented an empirical examination of this important and controversial construct.

According to Gelso and Hayes (1998), there are three major ways that transference has been defined. From a strictly classical stance, transference is a client distortion that involves reexperiencing Oedipal issues in the therapeutic relationship. A modern constructivist position emphasizes intersubjective thought by defining transference as an unconscious organizing process to which both the therapist and the client contribute. Gelso and Hayes advocate a definition that incorporates both the notion of client distortion embedded in the classical definition and the phenomenon of intersubjectivity emphasized by the constructivists. Specifically, they define transference as *"the client's experience of the therapist that is shaped by the client's own psychological structures and past and involves displacement, onto the therapist, of feelings, attitudes and behaviors belonging rightfully in earlier significant relationships"* (p. 51, italics in original). Because we use Gelso and Hayes' definition of transference to organize our review of the empirical literature and make recommendations for practice, it is important to explore several implications of this definition.

As pointed out by Gelso and Hayes (1998), their definition of transference has several significant features. First, the definition incorporates the notion of templates or schema. Schema are psychological structures that the client (and therapist) use to encode, organize, and retrieve relational/interpersonal information. Schematic processing results in patterns of experiencing and relating. A second key component is the focus on repetition. The client's early experiences in relationships give rise to these organizing structures, which, in turn, determine how the client experiences and engages in current relationships. Third, the therapist cannot help but be a participant in the client's transference pattern. The client's experiences and reactions are, in part, in response to what the therapist does or does not do. Although transference is by definition a distortion, it is a complex process that simultaneously incorporates elements of distorted perception and realistic perception. Finally, distinguishing features of transference reactions are their rigidity and pervasiveness. Transference reactions are problematic for clients because the client tends to "hold onto" distorted perceptions despite evidence to the contrary. Additionally, transference reactions tend to occur across multiple relationships.

Closely linked to the concept of transference is the technique of therapist interpretation. In psychoanalytically oriented therapy, interpretations are seen as the only mutative aspect of the treatment. Book (1998) describes interpretation as "the real work of psychotherapy" (p. 12). He defines interpretations as "comments the therapist makes that tie together the patient's attitude and behavior toward significant others from the past with his or her attitudes and behavior toward people in the present, including the therapist" (p. 12). In other words, interpretations are the therapist's accurate identification and description of the client's displaced feelings, attitudes, and behaviors, coupled with an explanation of the origin of these displaced feelings, attitudes, and behaviors.

Book's (1998) definition emphasizes two separate aspects of interpretation: a description of the client's attitudes and behaviors, and an explanation of their origin. It is important to note, however, that every interpretation does not have to contain both elements.

As Book states "[o]ne interpretation does not a cure make" (p. 13). Through the use of many interpretations across time the client comes to understand personal transference patterns and their origins. This understanding of transference patterns and their origins is termed *insight*.

"Since Freud's time, insight has been perceived as the cornerstone of the psychoanalytic theory of structural change" (Crits-Christoph, Barber, Miller, & Beebe, 1993, p. 407). Specifically, insight should lead to an integrated, mature ego structure, which should, in turn, result in a reduction of the client's symptoms. As with transference, there are many definitions of insight. Integrating these many definitions, Gelso, Kivlighan, Wine, Jones, and Friedman (1997) defined insight as the "Extent to which the client displays accurate understanding of the material being explored. Understanding may be of the relationship, client's functioning outside of counseling, or aspects of the client's dynamics and behavior." (p. 212).

Theoretically, increases in client insight should be associated with symptom reduction. Wallerstein and Robbins (1956), however, suggested several other ways that client insight may operate in treatment. These are insights that may be (1) a precondition of symptom change, (2) a direct result of symptom change, (3) a cause of symptom change, or (4) a correlate of symptom change. Until recently, however, empirical research provided little information about the measurement or development of insight, or the relationship between insight and symptom change.

Often client transference, therapist interpretation, and client insight are discussed as if they were separate processes. Much of the research literature has perpetuated the view of client transference, therapist interpretation, and client insight as separate and unrelated processes by examining these constructs in isolation. The practitioner, however, realizes that client transference, therapist interpretation, and client insight are a part of a complex dynamic system of influences. Recent research supports this complex, dynamic view of the relationships among client transference, therapist interpretation, and client insight by showing the critical role of the interaction among these components (e.g., Gelso, Hill, & Kivlighan, 1991; Gelso et al., 1997). In this chapter I attempt to highlight the dynamic, interactive nature of client transference, therapist interpretation, and client insight.

In the first section of the chapter I review the empirical literature, examining client transference, therapist interpretation, and client insight, giving special emphasis to recent studies that examine the interactions among these components. In examining the research on transference, I first describe the various ways that researchers have attempted to operationalize transference and the construct validity of these measures. Next I review the studies that examine how transference develops over time. Finally, I describe studies that examine how transference interacts with other aspects of the therapeutic process.

Most of the empirical literature on therapist interpretation examines the frequency or type (e.g., here-and-now versus genetic) of interpretation. Initially, these studies are briefly reviewed. An exciting and heuristic area of research on therapist interpretation involves the accuracy of interpretation. My review highlights this important area of study by describing in detail some of the important recent studies of interpretive accuracy. Client insight has received far less empirical attention than either client transference or therapist interpretation. My review of this area concentrates on the various ways that researchers have attempted to operationalize client insight and the few recent studies that examined the development and consequences of client insight.

The second section of this chapter describes how the empirical findings from research on client transference, therapist interpretation, and client insight can be applied to the practice of therapy. Specifically, I use Pepinsky and Pepinsky's (1954) prescriptive model of the scientist–practitioner to form a bridge between the empirical findings from research on client transference, therapist interpretation, and client insight and the practice of therapy. Pepinsky and Pepinsky describe the therapist as an applied scientist. The therapist, as an applied scientist, engages in a reflective process of observation, hypotheses formation, hypotheses testing, and repeated observation. In relation to client transference, therapist interpretation, and client insight, the therapist (1) identifies the client's transference by observing the client's relationship patterns and forming hypotheses about the client's transference based on the observations, (2) tests these hypotheses by offering interpretations to the client, and (3) determines the accuracy and effectiveness of the interpretations (hypotheses) by observing expressions of client insight. Recently, Heppner, Kivlighan, and Wampold (1999) suggested that this process of observation, hypotheses formation, hypotheses testing, and repeated observation can be enhanced by formal data collection analysis during treatment. In the second section of the chapter I show how the measures developed by researchers examining client transference, therapist interpretation, and client insight can be used by practitioners to enhance their ability to recognize transference, make accurate interpretations, and assess client insight.

Research Findings

Measuring Transference

According to Gelso and Hayes (1998) there are three viable approaches to measuring transference. The three approaches correspond to three perspectives on the therapy relationship as seen by the client, the therapist, or outside experts. Clients can be interviewed about their reactions to and perceptions of their therapist, and about how these reactions and perceptions may be related to developmental experiences (e.g., Adelstein, Gelso, Haws, Reed, & Spiegel, 1971). Typically, client reports are analyzed unsystematically and there is little evidence for the reliability or validity of transference reactions assessed through these interview protocols.

Recently, Barber, Foltz, and Weinryb (1998) developed a more systematic, reliable, and valid approach for assessing transference from the client's perspective. Their Central Relationship Questionnaire (CRQ; Barber et al., 1998) is a self-report measure of people's characteristic manner of interacting with significant others. The CRQ is based on extensive research with Luborsky's (1977) Core Conflict Relationship Theme (CCRT; discussed later in the chapter), a clinician-rated method for identifying transference reactions from transcripts of therapy sessions. Like the CCRT, the CRQ assesses three aspects of a client's characteristic ways of relating to significant others: wishes, responses from others, and response of self. Wishes (Wish) refer to a person's desires or intentions. In classical terms wishes are expressions of drives. The responses from others (RO) involve the fantasized, anticipated, or actual ways that others respond to the client. The response of self (RS) is the client's thought, emotion, behavior, or symptom in response to the RO.

In its present form the CRQ has seven Wish subscales (49 items), seven RO subscales (39 items), and eight RS subscales (51 items). The seven Wish subscales are To Be

Supportive, To Be Independent, To Be in Conflict, To Be Recognized, To Be Trusted, To Be Sexual, and Not To Be Abandoned. The seven RO subscales are Hurts Me, Loves Me, Is Independent, Controls Me, Is Out of Control, Is Anxious, and Is Sexual. The eight RS subscales are Feel Valued, Care for Other, Feel Anxious, Feel Disliked, Avoid Conflict, Am Independent, Am Sexual, and Am Domineering. In the initial development sample all of the scales had good internal consistency, with alphas ranging from .71 for the Am Domineering subscale to .95 for the To Be Supportive, To Be Sexual, and Loves Me subscales. In addition, one-year test–retest reliability estimates were all statistically significant and moderate (e.g., $r = .44$ for Is Independent) to high (e.g., $r = .79$ for Loves Me).

Barber et al. (1998) established the validity of the CRQ by examining the correlations among the Wish, RO, and RS subscales and measures of interpersonal problems and symptomatology. Specifically, the Domineering, Vindictive, Cold, Socially Avoidant, Nonassertive, Exploitable, Overly Nurturant, and Intrusive scales from the Inventory of Interpersonal Problems (IIP; Horowitz, Rosenberg, Baer, Ureno, & Villasenor, 1988) defined interpersonal problems and the Beck Depression Inventory (BDI; Beck, Ward, Mendelson, Mock, & Erbaugh, 1961), Beck Anxiety Inventory (BAI; Beck, Epstein, Brown, & Steer, 1988), Symptom Checklist 90–Revised (SCL-90-R; Derogatis, 1977), and NEO-Five Factor Inventory (Costa & McCrae, 1991) were used to measure symptomatology. In general the correlations between the Wish, RO, and RS subscales and measures of interpersonal problems and symptomatology were as predicted by Barber et al. (1998). For example the Controls Me RO subscale was positively correlated with the Nonassertive and Exploitable scales from the IIP and with all of the measures of symptomatology.

As a final test of the validity of the CRQ, Barber et al. (1998) compared CRQ scores for student participants to those of participants who received at least one psychiatric diagnosis. As expected the diagnostic group scored higher on the CRQ subscales with negative themes (e.g., RO Hurts Me) and lower on the positively themed CRQ subscales (e.g., RO Loves Me). The results from the Barber et al. study suggest that the CRQ is a promising self-report measure for identifying clients' central relationship themes. As is discussed later in the chapter, the CRQ can be a valuable screening measure, alerting the therapist to the form of potential transference reactions and suggesting tentative interpretive themes.

A second approach to measuring transference is to have the therapist rate the amount of transference present in a therapy session. Typically, therapists are provided definitions of the constructs to be rated (e.g., positive transference and negative transference) and then make gross ratings on single-item scales. This approach has been used in several studies with interesting results (Graff & Luborsky, 1977; Gelso et al., 1991; Gelso et al., 1997). The problem with this approach is the lack of reliability for single-item scales. In addition, there is only limited evidence of validity for these single-item ratings.

Multon, Patton, and Kivlighan (1996) extended the use of therapist ratings of transference by developing a 43-item, therapist-rated measure of the amount of client transference. Their Missouri Identifying Transference Scale (MITS) consists of multiple adjectives designed to capture Greenson's (1967) five characteristics of client transference reactions. These characteristics are

1. Inappropriateness—reactions that are not justified by the therapist's objective behavior may be signals of transference.

2. Intensity or lack of emotion—strong feelings such as love or hate or complete lack of emotional involvement can indicate transference.
3. Hidden ambivalence—transference is often expressed by the client only seeing the positive or negative qualities of the therapist and repressing the opposite quality.
4. Capriciousness—rapidly changing or unstable feelings are often indicative of transference.
5. Tenacity—transference is indicated when the client has a rigid and narrow experience of the therapist.

A factor analysis of the MITS revealed two correlated factors that accounted for 52% of the item variance. Multon, Patton, and Kivlighan (1996) labeled these factors Negative (NTR) and Positive (PTR) Transference Reactions. Internal consistency estimates for the NTR and PTR scales were good, .96 and .88, respectively. The PTR scale was positively correlated with single-item ratings of amount of transference and amount of positive transference. The NTR scale was positively correlated with the single-item ratings of amount of negative transference and negatively correlated with the single-item rating of amount of positive transference.

As a further test of the validity of the MITS, Multon, Patton, and Kivlighan (1996) examined the relationship between NTR and PTR scores and the clients' perceptions of their parents on the Interpersonal Schema Questionnaire (ISQ; Safran & Hill, 1989). The ISQ scales described the amount of Control, Sociability, Affiliation, and Trust that each client experienced from each of his or her parents. The NTR scores changed quadratically across time, with more negative transference reactions during middle sessions and fewer negative transference reactions during initial and final sessions. In addition, the client's perception of his or her mother was related to midtreatment NTR. Specifically, when clients saw their mothers as controlling, untrustworthy, less social, and less affiliative, the therapist experienced more negative transference reactions during the middle sessions of treatment.

The MITS appears to be a promising therapist-rated measure of client transference. It is a quick, easy-to-use measure that therapists can fill out consistently or periodically during the course of treatment. Most important, this measure has greater reliability and validity than the single-item measures of transference that have predominated the research in this area. The MITS can provide the therapist with a useful way of examining transference reactions during the course of treatment.

Using outside experts to rate transference from therapy tapes or transcripts has had an explosive growth during the past two decades. Luborsky and Barber (1994) reviewed 15 of these approaches to measuring transference. There are also now several studies that compare across several of the systems by applying different approaches to the same transcribed therapy session. The most elaborate comparison of seven of these approaches was published in a special issue of *Psychotherapy Research* (Luborsky, Popp, Barber, & Shapiro, 1994). The authors used the Core Conflict Relationship Theme (L. Luborsky, Popp, E. Luborsky, & Mark, 1994), Configurational Analysis (Horowitz, 1994), Plan Formulation (Curtis, Silberschatz, Sampson, & Weiss, 1994), Structural Analysis of Social Behavior-Cyclic Maladaptive Pattern (SASB-CMP; Schacht & Henry, 1994), Consensual Response Psychodynamic Formulation (Rosenberg et al., 1994), Idiographic Conflict Formulation (Perry, 1994), and

Fundamental Repetitive and Maladaptive Emotion Structures (Dahl & Teller, 1994) methods to analyze a transcribed intake session. A comparison of these seven methods revealed striking similarities across measures (Luborsky, Popp, & Barber, 1994). This finding suggests that the measures are validly measuring a common transference pattern. In examining the individual measures, the CCRT and SASB-CMP methods were judged to be the most similar to the other methods. This suggests that these two methods share a number of common features with the other transference related measures.

Because the CCRT shares a number of features with other transference measures and because it has generated the most empirical research, this method will be the focus of this subsection. The CCRT had its origins in Luborsky's (1976) attempt to construct a measure of the therapeutic alliance. Specifically, he was attempting to determine how the helping alliance fit into the client's central relationship pattern (Luborsky, 1990a). In reviewing transcripts, Luborsky noticed that he could identify general relationship patterns by examining the stories that clients told about how they interacted with others and looking for what the client wanted from others, how these others were described as reacting to the client, and how the client reacted to these responses from others. From these observations it was a short step to developing the CCRT.

In using the CCRT, judges first examine transcripts of therapy sessions and locate narratives in which clients tell about their interactions with others. Luborsky (1990b), labels these narrative accounts relationship episodes (RE). Next, the judge reviews the REs and identifies the clients wishes, wants, and desires (Wish), how people respond (anticipated or real) to the client's wishes (RO, response from others), and how the client responds to others' responses (RS, response from self).

As defined by Luborsky (1990b), a RE is "a part of a session that occurs as a relatively discrete episode of explicit narration about relationships with others or with the self" (pp. 15–16). For each RE the judge identifies the main other person involved. REs are labeled as involving other people (RE Other People, family, friends, co-workers), the therapist (RE Therapist), or self (RE Self). To be scored, a RE must be complete. Judges rate completeness on a 1 (least detailed) to 5 (most detailed) scale, with a 2.5 rating used as a cutoff for scoring. The beginning and end of complete REs are marked on the transcript.

Once complete REs are identified, the CCRT can be scored. Scoring involves a four-step process: (1) identifying the types of CCRT components, (2) counting the components and formulating the CCRT, (3) reidentifying the types of CCRT components, and (4) recounting and reformulating the CCRT (Luborsky, 1990b). In identifying the types of CCRT components, the judge underlines parts of the transcript that contain a Wish, RO, or RS. ROs and RSs are identified as positive (PRO or PRS) or negative (NRO or NRS). For ROs judges also distinguish between those ROs that are expressed in action (RO-active) versus those ROs that represent the client's expectation of others responses (RO-expected). Once all of the Wishes, ROs, and RSs are identified, judges move to the second step, which involves first counting the various Wishes, ROs, and RSs, and then identifying the theme that applies to the most REs. The final steps in scoring the CCRT involve rechecking the identification of Wishes, ROs, and RSs and recounting and reformulating the CCRT.

Initially, CCRTs were "tailor-made" with idiosyncratic wording similar to the language used by the client. Quickly, Luborsky and his colleagues realized that a standard language for Wishes, ROs, and RSs would facilitate comparisons across cases. The standard categories for Wishes, ROs, and RSs were formulated to meet this need for cross-case comparisons (Barber, Crits-Christoph, & Luborsky, 1990). To develop standard categories, Barber et al. had judges rate the similarity of 35 wishes, 30 ROs, and 30 RSs from 16 clients. These similarity ratings were analyzed using cluster analysis. Barber et al. found eight clusters of Wishes: (1) To Assert Self and Be Independent, (2) To Oppose, Hurt, and Control Others, (3) To Be Controlled, Hurt, and Not Responsible, (4) To Be Distant and Avoid Conflicts, (5) To Be Close and Accepting, (6) To Be Loved and Understood, (7) To Feel Good and Comfortable, and (8) To Achieve and Help Others; eight clusters of ROs: (1) Strong, (2) Controlling, (3) Upset, (4) Bad, (5) Rejecting and Opposing, (6) Helpful, (7) Likes Me, and (8) Understanding; and eight clusters of RSs: (1) Helpful, (2) Unreceptive, (3) Respected and Accepted, (4) Oppose and Hurt Others, (5) Self-Controlled and Self-Confident, (6) Helpless, (7) Disappointed and Depressed, and (8) Anxious and Ashamed.

Studies addressing the reliability and construct validity of the CCRT offer promising results. There are two aspects to the reliability of the CCRT within a given sample. First, can judges reliably identify REs, and, second, can the standard categories be used reliably? Crits-Christoph, Luborsky, Popp, Mellon, and Mark (1990) address both types of reliability. In terms of completeness of the RE (rated on a 1 [least detailed] to 5 [most detailed] scale), Crits-Christoph et al. found an intraclass correlation of .68 for 111 episodes. In addition, two judges agreed 97% of the time on the identification of the other person referred to in the RE. Also the judges could reliably agree on the beginning (within 4.8 lines of transcribed text) and end (within 7.9 lines of transcribed text) of an RE. The category placement for Wishes, ROs, and RSs using standard categories was also accomplished reliably. The mean weighted kappa across seven samples of RE was .63, .66, and .69 for Wishes, ROs, and RSs, respectively (Luborsky, Popp, & Barber, 1994).

The validity of the CCRT can be established through a number of studies examining the operation of the CCRT in the therapy context. Across a number of clients, Luborsky, Barber, Schaffler, and Cacciola (1990) found that wishes to be separate and to be independent were the most frequently expressed. Separation and independence wishes set up a classic approach–avoidance conflict for the client. These conflicting wishes are in line with predictions from psychoanalytic theory (Luborsky, Barber, Schaffler et al.). In another study Crits-Christoph and Luborsky (1990a) examined the pervasiveness of the CCRT across sessions in therapy. Pervasiveness was defined as the ratio of the number of REs with the identified CCRT component to the total number of REs within a session. As predicted, pervasiveness of the CCRT decreased over time, indicating a decrease in the clients' transference reactions. Additionally, decreases in CCRT pervasiveness were correlated with changes in client symptoms.

Fried, Crits-Christoph, and Luborsky (1990) examined the parallel between the CCRT for the therapist and the CCRT for other people. REs for the therapist and REs for others were scored for the CCRT. CCRTs from the therapist were matched with CCRTs for others from the therapists' own client (correctly matched) and with CCRTs for others from clients of other therapists (mismatched). Correctly matched pairs of CCRTs were rated as statistically more similar than mismatched pairs of CCRTs. This result suggests that the client's transference pattern with the therapist parallels the transference pattern with significant others. Another study showed that the CCRT from therapy narratives agreed significantly with CCRTs scored from the client's dreams (Popp, Luborsky, & Crits-Christoph, 1990). Summarizing across the studies previously described and other studies using the CCRT, Luborsky, Popp, Luborsky, & Mark (1994) examined the validity of the CCRT by noting the correspondence between research on the CCRT and Freud's (1913/1958) writings about transference. Luborsky, Popp, Luborsky, & Mark (1994) identified 22 observations that Freud made about the origin, stimuli that elicit, and the consequences of transference. For 17 of Freud's 22 observations the CCRT corresponds to predictions from psychoanalytic theory (the other five observations have not been examined empirically). This analysis suggests that the CCRT is a valid measure of the transference template described by Freud.

As noted at the beginning of this section, Gelso and Hayes (1998) differentiate transference measures based on the source of the rating (client, therapist, outside expert). Although the transference measures were reviewed using Gelso and Hayes' classification scheme, there is a second fundamental difference among these measures. Measures like the CRQ and the CCRT attempt to operationalize the form or the content of the transference reactions. Using the CRQ or the CCRT researchers and practitioners can examine individual differences in clients' wishes, expected/experienced reactions of others, and self-reactions. In addition, by using measures such as the CRQ and CCRT researchers and practitioners can draw inferences about the valence of the transference. Measures such as the MITS address another aspect of the transference phenomenon. Using the MITS, for example, researchers and practitioners can examine individual differences in the valence and the amount (level) of the transference. A complete understanding of transference can only be obtained when the form/content, valence, and amount/level are taken into account. Therefore, researchers and practitioners should use multiple measures to describe the form/content, valence, and amount/level of transference. In the applications for practice section later in this chapter I discuss how the CRQ, CCRT, and MITS can be used to help the practicing therapist identify client transference reactions.

The Temporal Course of Transference

Psychodynamic treatment is fundamentally about changing the client's transference pattern. Freud (1913/1958) made the idea of change in transference patterns explicit when he posited that accurate interpretations would change the expression of the transference pattern (see Luborsky, Popp, Luborsky, & Mark, 1994). Building on Freud's (1913/1958) and other writers' ideas Gelso and Hayes (1998) proposed that "[t]he course of transference is predictable in psychoanalytic and nonanalytic therapy, and that the course will differ for successful and unsuccessful cases" (p. 72). Given the theoretical importance of change in transference patterns across treatment, it is not surprising that several authors have examined the temporal course of transference. It is important to note that neither Freud nor Gelso and Hayes were explicit about which aspects (form/content, valence, and amount/level) of the transference pattern would change over time. Three studies (Gelso et al., 1997; Graff & Luborsky, 1977; Patton, Kivlighan, & Multon, 1997) examined how the valence and amount of transference changes across treatment, whereas only one study (Crits-Christoph & Luborsky, 1990a) examined how the content of form of transference may change over time.

Graff and Luborsky (1977) examined changes in the amount of transference in long-term psychoanalytic therapy. Analysts rated the amount of transference in each session using a single-item scale. Contrary to their expectations, Graff and Luborsky found that in successful cases transference increased linearly across treatment. They had expected a lessening of transference near the end of treatment, indicating a resolution of the transference pattern. In the unsuccessful cases transference remained constant across time. Graff and Luborsky make sense of their counterintuitive finding with reference to client insight. The psychoanalysts in this study attempted to create conditions that would foster the expression of transference (Gelso & Hayes, 1998); therefore, it is not surprising that the successful clients would follow the prescribed tasks and increase their expressions of transference. With the unsuccessful clients the conditions for transference expression were apparently not accomplished. Graff and Luborsky also hypothesized that transference is not reduced in successful treatment; rather, the clients increasingly come to recognize and understand their transference reactions.

Patton, Kivlighan, and Multon (1997) examined the unfolding of transference in 20 sessions of psychodynamic counseling. Therapists used both the MITS and single items to rate the amount of transference in each counseling session. Patton et al. found a low–high–low pattern of transference expression across the 20 sessions of treatment. In addition, the successful clients showed an increasing pattern of transference expression across time. This result parallels the Graff and Luborsky (1977) result. In psychoanalytic treatments that seek to create conditions that allow for the expression of transference, increasing expressions of transference are related to successful outcome. Presumably, in these types of treatments therapists help clients to use and make sense of these transference expressions through the promotion of insight. The role of insight is discussed in more detail later in this chapter.

Gelso et al. (1997) followed a group of theoretically heterogeneous counselors doing brief time-limited treatment. As in the Graff and Luborsky (1977) study, counselors used single items to rate the amount of total, negative, and positive transference. Like Graff and Luborsky and Patton et al. (1997), successful and unsuccessful clients had different patterns of transference over time. The differential patterns were especially pronounced for the amount of negative transference. In the Gelso et al. study, however, it was the unsuccessful clients who had a linearly increasing pattern of transference over time. The successful clients had a low–high–low pattern of transference change over the four quarters of counseling.

Gelso and Hayes (1998) attempt to reconcile these divergent findings by hypothesizing a type of treatment by pattern of transference interaction. In treatments that seek to analyze transference, a linear increase in transference across time is related to treatment success. Success is probably a function of transference being increasingly available to therapists and clients for therapeutic work. In treatments that do not seek to analyze transference, examining transference is only important to the extent that transference (especially negative transference) may interfere with other therapeutic processes. In these nonanalytic treatments negative transference must be dealt with so that the therapist and client can concentrate on other therapeutic tasks. In these nonanalytic treatments linearly increasing transference may be a sign that the expression of transference is interfering with the other therapeutic tasks (Gelso & Hayes, 1998).

Crits-Christoph and Luborsky (1990a) examined how clients' CCRTs changed across treatment. Specifically, they examined the pervasiveness of the CCRT early and late in treatment. As described previously pervasiveness was defined as the ratio of the number of REs with the identified CCRT component to the total number of REs within a session. Crits-Christoph and Luborsky reasoned that (1) clients enter therapy with maladaptive relationship patterns that span a number of different relationships (i.e., that most REs from early in treatment will contain the same Wish, RO, and RS) and (2) therapy helps clients change these maladaptive relationship patterns, then (3) REs from late in treatment contain a wide range of Wishes, ROs, and RSs.

For 33 clients pervasiveness of Wishes, NROs, PROs, NRSs, and PRSs were calculated for sessions early and late in treatment. An analysis of early versus late pervasiveness scores showed that the pervasiveness of wishes remained unchanged across time. The pervasiveness of negative responses from others and negative responses of self decreased, and the pervasiveness of positive responses from others and positive responses of self increased from early to late sessions. Crits-Christoph and Luborsky (1990a) concluded that clients' wishes, needs, and intentions for relationships remain stable across time and treatment. Clients appear to have the same constellation of wishes at the end of treatment as they did at its inception. What does seem to change in therapy are the clients' expectations for others' responses and the clients' responses to self. Specifically, at the end of treatment clients expect others to respond to their wishes and experience others responding positively to their wishes, and their self-responses also become more positive.

Crits-Christoph and Luborsky (1990a) suggest that their results support Schlessinger and Robbins' (1975) view of change in psychodynamic therapy. That is, the form or content of the transference pattern remains unchanged with therapy. What changes is the client's reaction to and understanding of this pattern. What is clear from the Crits-Christoph and Luborsky (1990a), Gelso et al. (1997), Graff and Luborsky (1977), and Patton et al. (1997) studies is that some aspects of the form/content, valence, and amount/level of transference change across treatment. In addition, it is clear that the pattern of transference change is related to outcome. The results suggest that it is important for the therapist to keep track of how transference is unfolding across therapy. Keeping track of the client's unfolding transference is an important component of the practice model specified later in this chapter.

Transference and Counseling Process

Probably because the specification, measurement, and tracking of transference is so complex, few studies have examined how transference patterns interact with other aspects of the counseling process. How transference relates to variables such as the working alliance and resistance is of immense theoretical and practical significance. It is only in the most recent studies that researchers have begun to examine how transference may influence and be influenced by other process variables. The Gelso et al. (1991), Gelso et al. (1997) and Patton et al. (1997) studies examined how transference interacted with client insight, therapist techniques, working alliance, and client resistance.

Henry, Strupp, Schacht, and Gaston (1993) criticized researchers for not studying transference in context. For example, in 16 studies examining the effects of transference interpretations none of the researchers checked to see whether there were clear manifestations of transference when the transference interpretations were given. Addressing Henry et al.'s concern about the lack of context in the study of transference, Gelso et al. (1991) and Gelso et al. (1997) examined how transference and insight interacted to predict client outcome. Because these studies are described in more detail in the section addressing client insight, only a brief overview of their results is presented here. The difference between the two Gelso studies was the time frame examined. In Gelso et al. (1991) the relationship between transference and client insight in predicting the outcome of a single session was examined. Gelso et al. (1997) built on this initial study by examining how transference and client insight predicted outcome in short-term treatment. Both studies found a statistically significant interaction between transference and client insight in predicting client outcome. In both cases when transference was low there was no relation between client insight and outcome. When transference was high, however, client insight showed a positive linear relationship to outcome. This finding verifies Henry et al.'s suggestion that transference must be present for understanding to be useful.

Patton et al. (1997) examined the effects of transference within a network of other important process variables. Initially, Patton et al. collected numerous ratings of session process from the perspective of the clients, therapists, and trained judges. Potential measures of transference included the items on positive, negative, and amount of transference from Graff and Luborsky (1977) and the Positive and Negative Transference scales from the MITS. A P-technique factor analysis of this process data revealed four dimensions of counseling process: (1) Psychoanalytic Technique, (2) Client Resistance, (3) Working Alliance, and (4) Client Transference. The factor analysis results provide support for the construct validity of the transference measures. The transference measures had high loadings on the latent transference construct, and this transference construct was separate and distinguishable from other aspects of the counseling process.

Patton et al. (1997) used time-series analysis to examine the time-dependent relationships among the Psychoanalytic Technique, Client Resistance, Working Alliance, and Client Transference dimensions derived from the factor analysis. Analytic technique both influenced and was influenced by transference. Sessions where the therapist used more analytic techniques (e.g., exploration of resistances and interpretation) were followed by sessions with less client transference. Sessions with higher levels of client transference were followed by sessions with more exploration of resistance and interpretation. The working alliance influenced transference but was not influenced by it. When working alliance was high in a session, the following two sessions had high levels of client transference. Finally, client transference influenced client resistance but was not influenced by it. When client transference was high in a session the following three sessions had high levels of client resistance.

The process findings from Patton et al. (1997) corroborated several aspects of psychoanalytic theory. Greenson (1967), for example, details how transference is a type of resistance. If the client is experiencing (through transference) the therapist as punitive, it is likely that the client would be doubting or halting in the following sessions (types of resistance). Freud (1913/1958) in writing about the relationship between transference and resistance, recommended that the client be allowed to continue talking until transference becomes a resistance. Transference leading to higher levels of resistance is an expression of this phenomena. Higher levels of working alliance leading to greater expressions of transference is also congruent with theory. As described by Bordin (1979, 1994), the working alliance is the vehicle that allows the expression and examination of transference. Only if the alliance is strong can clients freely express and explore with the therapist the puzzling and frightening feelings involved in transference reactions. The complex relationship between analytical techniques, such as exploration of transference, and interpretation and client transference is also congruent with the theoretical literature. Client transference should serve as a signal to the therapist to explore and analyze the resistance through the use of analytical techniques. The use of these analytical techniques should in turn lead to a better understanding of the transference and to less in-session transference reactions.

The Gelso et al. (1991), Gelso et al. (1997) and Patton et al. (1997) studies attest to the complex interrelations among session process dimensions. Client transference both influences and is influenced by other aspects of counseling process. This suggests that it is not enough for the practicing therapist to simply track client transference reactions. Rather, the practitioner must also assess the state of the working alliance and client insight, as well as keep track of individual, personal use of techniques. This tracking task is complex. The research-based practice model presented in the final section of this chapter outlines a system for helping the therapist keep track of and respond to the dynamic processes surrounding transference.

Therapist Interpretation

"Therapist interpretation has been viewed as the central technique for producing self-knowledge and change." (Hill, Thompson, & Mahalik, 1989, p. 284). Despite the theoretical centrality of interpretation in the treatment process, there is little agreement about the definition of this therapeutic technique. At a general level Hill (1989) defines interpretation as

> Interpretation: Goes beyond what the client has overtly recognized. And provides reasons, alternative meanings, or new frameworks for feelings, behavior or personality. It may establish connections between seemingly isolated statements or events; interpret defenses, feelings, resistance, or transference; or indicate themes, patterns, or causal relationships in behavior or personality, related to present events to past events. (p. 15)

It is clear that Hill's definition of interpretation encompasses a broad array of therapist activity. In Hill's system an interpretation can be but does not have to be transference related. Piper, Azin, Joyce, and McCallum (1991) provide a narrower definition of interpretation. In addition, they distinguish between transference and nontransference interpretation. An interpretation is defined as an intervention that "contains a reference to one or more dynamic components. A dynamic component is one part of a patient's conflict that exerts an internal force on some other part of the patient, ego, wish, anxiety, or defense" (Piper et al., 1991, p. 947). The authors go on to define a transference interpretation as "an interpretation that includes a reference to the therapist" (Piper et al., 1991, p. 947).

Hopefully, it is clear from only these two brief definitions that studies on the surface examine therapist interpretation may in fact be examining very different phenomena. Given the problems with definitions, it is probably not surprising that studies examining therapist interpretation often come to contradictory conclusions about the effectiveness of this technique. The majority of studies examining therapist interpretation have correlated the number or relative frequency of interpretations to some indicator of outcome. The assumption in these studies is that more interpretations are better. Some studies show that the frequent use of interpretation is related to better outcome (e.g., Marziali, 1984) but other studies show that the frequent use of interpretation is related to poor outcome (e.g., Piper et al., 1991). Other studies examining the relative effectiveness of transference and nontransference interpretations have found null results (e.g., Silbershatz, Fretter, & Curtis, 1986). In general, neither the frequency of interpretation use nor the type of interpretation is consistently related to better outcome.

Recent studies have adopted a more sophisticated approach when examining the effects of therapist interpretations. Specifically, researchers have begun to examine the accuracy (e.g., Silberschatz et al., 1986) and the timing (e.g., Kivlighan, Thye, & Ji, in press) of interpretations as key elements in their effectiveness. The timing of interpretations is a key aspect in the clinical literature. For example, therapists are advised to only interpret transference that is just beyond the client's awareness (Fenichel, 1941). Additionally, a major category of therapists' mistakes are poorly timed interpretations.

Hill et al. (1989) examined the issue of timing by reviewing every interpretation made during a very successful short-term treatment. The researchers found that the therapist waited until the middle of treatment before beginning to interpret material about the client's past. A correlation of .83 between the number of interpretations and session number clearly illustrates the fact that the therapist waited for a good relationship to develop and gathered enough data to form adequate hypotheses before interpreting. Summarizing across the eight cases intensively examined, Hill (1989) concluded that the most helpful interpretations occurred late in therapy in the context of a good relationship. Hill et al. (1989) were also able to identify the sequence of therapist and client activity that resulted in client insight. This sequence began with the therapist focusing the client on an affective experience. Once the client experienced some catharsis, the therapist interpreted how present difficulties were linked to past difficulties. This interpretation was followed by suggestions about how the client might do things differently in the present.

Another way to examine the timing of interpretations is to determine the factors that must be in place for interpretation to be effective. This is the approach taken by Gaston, Thompson, Gallagher, Cournoyer, and Gagnon (1998) and Kivlighan, Thyer, and Ji (in press). Specifically, these researchers tested Gaston's (1990) hypothesis that the working alliance moderates the relationship between therapist techniques and outcome. In other words, the working alliance is a prerequisite for certain therapist interventions (e.g., interpretation) to be effective. Gaston distinguishes between two types of therapist techniques: supportive and exploratory. Examples of supportive techniques include empathy, support, and the mobilization of hope. Examples of exploratory techniques include interpretation, interpersonal feedback, and confrontation of resistance. Most studies show that supportive techniques are related to working alliance strength (e.g., Kivlighan & Schmitz, 1992; Multon, Kivlighan, & Gold, 1996). Once the alliance is formed, exploratory techniques are theorized to facilitate outcome.

Analytic writers (Freud, 1912/1966; Greenson, 1967) thought of the working alliance as a catalyst, or as a means to an end. For example, they contended that clients will be more likely to accept and work with their therapist's interpretations when the working alliance is strong. When the working alliance is weak, however, the client would likely reject the therapist's interpretations. Statistically, Freud's and Greenson's theories state that the working alliance moderates the relationship between therapist exploratory techniques and client outcome. Gelso and Carter (1985) also saw the working alliance as moderating the relationship between therapists' attempts to promote insight and client outcome. They hypothesized that it is the working alliance that allows the client eventually to accept therapist interpretation and eventually understand the transference reactions. Two studies (Gaston et al., 1998; Kivlighan, Thyer, & Ji, in press) found the predicted significant moderating effects of the working alliance on the relationship between therapist's use of exploratory techniques and client outcome. When the working alliance was high more interpretation was related to better client outcome. Conversely, when the working alliance was low more interpretation was related to worse client outcome. These results suggest that interpretations should only be given when the working alliance is strong. Therapists can monitor the state of the alliance to decide how supportive or interpretive they should be.

It seems like stating the obvious to suggest that interpretations must be accurate to be helpful. Clearly, no theorist would advocate inaccurate interpretations. "Despite the importance of giving accurate interpretations, few well-articulated guidelines are found in the literature" (Luborsky, Barber, & Crits-Christoph, 1990, p. 281). In addition, until recently there were no studies examining interpretive accuracy because there were no good means for operationalizing accuracy. French (1954) did provide guidelines for forming accurate interpretations. He said that the therapist should first identify the nuclear conflict, or as Luborsky, Popp, Luborsky, & Mark (1990) assert, the central relationship pattern. Once the pattern is identified, the therapist uses this understanding to select appropriate interpretations. Studies examining the accuracy of therapist interpretations have built on the guidelines provided by French.

As noted by French (1954), the first step in making accurate interpretations is to identify the transference. It was only after researchers designed systems to accurately and reliably identify transference that they were able to address the first step in French's model. The seminal research examining interpretive accuracy was performed by Silbershatz et al. (1986). Silbershatz et al. used the Plan Formulation Method to identify the transference pattern for three clients in psychodynamic therapy. The Plan Formulation Method (Curtis et al., 1994) is similar to CCRT in that clinical judges use initial session material to make a systematic formulation of the client. Unlike the CCRT, which uses the categories of Wish, Response from Others, and Response of Self, the Plan Formulation Method uses the following categories: (1) patient's problems, history, and goals for therapy; (2) central pathogenic belief that inhibits the attainment of the goals; (3) ways the client might test the therapist; and (4) insights that will disconfirm the pathogenic belief.

Silbershatz et al. (1986) used five sets of judges to make ratings for their analyses. The first set of judges reviewed intake material and initial session material, and used the Plan Formulation Method to write an individualized formulation for each of three clients. A second set of judges reviewed session transcripts and identified therapists' interpretations. A third set of judges classified these interpretations as transference or nontransference interpretations. The fourth set of judges reviewed the formulation for each client and then rated how compatible each therapist's interpretation was with the formulation. This compatibility rating was how Silbershatz et al. operationalized accuracy of interpretation. The final set of judges rated the client material immediately preceeding and immediately following each interpretation with the Experiencing Scale (Klein, Mathieu-Coughlan, & Kiesler, 1968). The Experiencing Scale measures the client's capacity to be experientially involved in the session coupled with the capacity to reflect on the experience.

Silbershatz et al. (1986) calculated change in client experiencing by comparing the level of client experiencing before and after every therapist interpretation. This analysis was done twice: first, by examining the interpretations as either transference or nontransference interpretations, and second, by using the compatibility rating of each interpretation. When classified as transference or nontransference, there was no relationship between the type of interpretation and change in the level of client experiencing. When the compatibility ratings were used, however, more compatible interpretations were followed by higher levels of client experiencing. These results were the first to empirically support the importance of interpretation accuracy.

Crits-Christoph, Cooper, and Luborsky (1988) used the methodology for defining therapist accuracy, developed by Silberschatz et al. (1986), to examine the relationship between therapist accuracy and treatment outcome. In this study outcome was assessed by examining pre- to posttherapy changes on a comprehensive battery of measures taken from the perspective of the clients, therapists, and independent judges. A team of three judges reviewed intake material and formulated a CCRT for each of the 43 clients in the study. A second set of judges used these CCRTs as the criterion for rating accuracy, defined as the convergence between the client's transference expectations in the CCRT and the therapists' interpretation. This accuracy rating was made for each interpretation in the third session of time-limited counseling. There was one accuracy score for Wish, one for Response from Others, and one for Response of Self.

Crits-Christoph et al. (1988) found that the accuracy scores for wishes and responses from others were highly correlated. They, therefore, created a composite rating for accuracy of combined wish and response from others. There was no relationship between the accuracy of response of self scores and overall outcome. However, the accuracy of wish and response from others was correlated .44 with the outcome composite. Crits-Christoph et al. suggested that it is most important for therapists to accurately interpret the interpersonal aspects of the client's difficulties. Taken together the results of the Silbershatz et al. (1986) and Crits-Christoph et al. studies show that the accuracy of therapists' interpretations has an effect on both the immediate and long-term counseling outcome.

Summarizing across all of the research on therapist interpretations, there seem to be several important conclusions. First, the amount of therapist interpretation is not a good indicator of client outcome. We need to know more than simply how much the therapist is using interpretations to judge their effectiveness. Second, the distinction between transference and nontransference interpretations has not proved to be a useful way to differentiate between effective and ineffective interpretations. Third, measuring the accuracy of an interpretation by comparing the content of the interpretation to the content of the client's formulation appears to be a very promising way to judge the effectiveness of interpretations. Finally, the helpfulness of an interpretation cannot be determined outside of the context of the therapy. In this regard, interpretations seem to be most helpful when delivered later in treatment and when given in the context of a strong working alliance. In the next section we examine client insight, the theoretical consequent of accurate well-timed therapist interpretation.

Client Insight

"Since Freud's time insight has been perceived as the cornerstone of the psychoanalytic theory of structural change" (Crits-Christoph et al., 1993, p. 407). Insight results in an integrated, mature ego structure, which should, in turn, result in symptom reduction. Although definitions of insight vary, most authors agree that insight involves a conscious awareness of the transference, which is usually defined in terms of the wishes, defenses, and compromises (Brenner, 1982; Wallerstein & Robbins, 1956) that interact to produce emotional conflict or deficits in psychological development. Gelso et al. (1997) defined insight as, "Extent to which the client displays accurate understanding of the material being explored. Understanding may be of the relationship, client's functioning outside of counseling, or aspects of the client's dynamics and behavior" (p. 212).

There is no clear consensus on how best to identify and construe insight, or how to operationalize it. Early researchers operationalized insight as the observed match or congruence between the client's descriptions of self and other's descriptions of the client following client-centered therapy (e.g., Dymond, 1948). The methodological problems associated with this approach, halo effects, inaccuracy of other-ratings, and rater bias have lead to a decline in its use. Other authors (e.g., Funder, 1980) attempted to develop self-report scales for measuring insight. More recent studies used client productions (i.e., client talk in counseling sessions) and observer ratings to assess insight (e.g., Grenyer & Luborsky, 1996; O'Connor, Edelstein, Berry, & Weiss, 1994). Typically transcripts and videotapes of counseling sessions have served as the client production to be rated. For example, insight is one of the eight nominal, mutually exclusive categories in Hill et al.'s (1992) Client Behavior System. A client utterance is classified as insight if "The client expresses an understanding of something about himself or herself and can articulate patterns or reasons for behaviors, thoughts, or feelings" (pp. 248–249). Unfortunately, statement by statement ratings are costly and time intensive to use. In addition, insight may develop over a longer time frame than a single client utterance.

A final method for measuring insight is to ask counselors to rate the extent of client insight in a counseling session. Gelso et al. (1997) asked counselors to complete postsession ratings of the amount of emotional and intellectual insight in a session. Although data from this rating method are easy to collect, there are several potential problems with the method. First, because data are obtained from one therapist, it is not possible to assess reliability by examining interjudge agreement. Second, the global nature of the method makes it impossible to determine which aspects of the client's in-session behavior are the focus of the counselor's ratings. Third, the counselor is not an unbiased observer of client insight (the level of client insight may reflect favorably or poorly on the counselor).

Few studies have examined the development of insight over the course of counseling. Changes in client insight over time are important to observe in order to examine the accuracy of the psychoanalytic proposition that insight is an ongoing and often recurrent phenomenon in psychological treatment (Greenson, 1967). If this were true in those therapeutic relationships that were successful, one would expect to see changes in the amount and kind of insight experienced by clients over the course of treatment. For example, Hohage and Kubler (1988) used the Emotional Insight Scale to rate patient statements at the beginning and at the end of psychoanalytic treatment. They found a significant increase in emotional insight from the beginning to the end of treatment. In a related study, Grenyer and Luborsky (1996) examined mastery of interpersonal conflicts early and late in therapy. These authors defined mastery as a type of insight as "the acquisition of emotional self-control and intellectual self-understanding in the context of interpersonal relationships" (p. 411). Using a paired sample t test, Grenyer and Luborsky found that insight ratings taken from late in therapy were significantly higher than the same ratings taken early in treatment.

The relationship between insight and counseling outcome has not been intensively studied. O'Connor et al. (1994) found that the higher the average level of insight across therapy the better the outcome. In another study, Luborsky, Crits-Christoph, Mintz, and

Auerbach (1988) operationalized insight as the client's awareness about core conflicts in different relationships. They found that some aspects of insight (self-understanding about the counselor and self-understanding about significant others) correlated with counseling outcome. Unfortunately, Luborsky et al. were unable to show that gaining insight across treatment was related to outcome. In the Grenyer and Luborsky (1996) study, changes in the level of mastery over the course of treatment were related to observer, counselor, and client ratings of outcome. In their study, change in mastery was determined by calculating a residual gain score for mastery, using mastery ratings taken from early and late in treatment.

The strongest data linking insight and outcome comes from a study by Kivlighan, Multon, and Patton (in press). In this study insight was rated from the Important Events Questionnaire (IEQ; Cummings, Martin, Hallberg, & Slemon, 1992), which asks clients to describe the most important session event and why this event was important. Trained judges used Morgan, Luborsky, Crits-Christoph, Curtis, and Solomon's (1982) Insight Rating Scale (IRS) to evaluate the weekly IEQs produced by the clients. In other words, client insight was made evidential by using the items from the IRS to make judgements about the "insightfulness" of the client's open-ended, written responses to the IEQ. Kivlighan, Multon, & Patton (in press) established the validity of using the IEQ and the IRS to operationalize insight by demonstrating a strong relationship between this method of measuring insight and Hill et al.'s (1992) and Gelso et al.'s (1997) methods of measuring client insight. In the study, outcome was assessed by having clients fill out a target complaints questionnaire after each counseling session. A time-series analysis showed that sessions with higher levels of client insight were followed by less target complaint distress during the subsequent week. This finding provides relatively strong evidence that changes in insight lead to changes in client symptoms.

Using the IEQ and the IRS to operationalize insight, as done by Kivlighan, Multon, & Patton (in press), has several potential advantages over the other methods for operationalizing insight. First, IEQs are a more convenient data source than videotapes or session transcripts. Second, because the IEQ asks general questions about the counseling session, there are no demand characteristics that clients must report insight events. Presumably, clients will only report insight if it is the most important thing that happened for them in a session. Third, judges can be used to rate insight. By using independent judges, potential counselor bias is eliminated, and interrater reliability can be assessed. The IEQ and the IRS provide a relatively easy method for counselors to track client insight.

The relationship between client insight and outcome may be more complex than suggested by the Kivlighan, Multon, & Patton (in press) study. Gelso et al. (1991) and Gelso et al. (1997) examined the relationship between insight and transference. Both studies supported Gelso and Hayes' (1998) proposition that "The effect of transference (both positive and negative) on process and outcome will depend on the amount of insight that accompanies the transference" (p. 77). In both Gelso et al. (1991) and Gelso et al. (1997), therapist's rated the amount of transference (items for total amount, positive, and negative) and amount of client insight (items for intellectual and emotional insight) after every session on a postsession checklist. To aide in these ratings Gelso et al. (1991) and Gelso et al. (1997) provided definitions for each item. In Gelso et al. (1991) outcome was assessed at the session level whereas in Gelso et al. (1997) it was assessed by client ratings one month after treatment termination.

Both studies found that there was an interaction between the amount of transference and the amount of client insight in predicting session and treatment outcome. When transference was low there was no relationship between client insight and outcome. When transference was high, however, there was a positive linear relationship between client insight and outcome. Specifically, low levels of client insight in the presence of high levels of transference was related to poor outcome, whereas high levels of client insight in the presence of high levels of client transference was related to good outcome. The results suggest that it is the complex interaction of insight with transference that results in favorable or unfavorable client outcomes.

Client insight has important links to treatment outcome. Similar to transference and therapist interpretation, however, client insight is not an isolated event. Client transference, therapist interpretation, and client insight all interact in a complex manner to produce treatment outcome. The preceding sections provide a summary of the research in each of these domains and a compilation of the major conclusions that can be drawn from this research. The next section provides an integrative model based on these conclusions.

Transference, Interpretation and Insight: A Research-Based Model

Figure 6.1 is a schematic of a counseling model based on the research previously summarized. As seen in the figure the model has two phases. This model depicts the process of individual sessions as well as the process of treatment across sessions. Just as ontogeny reflects phylogeny I believe that the structure of treatments reflect the structure of individual sessions. The solid arrows in the figure represent direct relationships between constructs that have support in the research literature. The dashed lines represent interactive relationships. For example, working alliance and therapist interpretation interact to produce a working alliance by therapist interpretation construct. The relationship depicts that therapist interpretation by itself is not related to other aspects of the model. It is only in conjunction with the working alliance that therapist interpretation has effects.

The initial phase of the model is labeled Building the Working Alliance and Promoting and Identifying the Transference. There are two major goals of this phase of treatment. The first goal is to establish a strong working alliance. As suggested by the model, this is done using therapist supportive techniques. A strong working alliance is important because the research suggests that therapist interpretations are most effective when the working alliance is strong. The second goal is to promote the expression of transference. Concrete, in-session expressions of transference are important because client insight is most effective when transference is present. The model suggests that the strong working alliance will promote expressions of client transference.

When the working alliance is strong and there are concrete, in-session expressions of transference, the therapy moves to the second phase. During the second phase the therapist begins to offer accurate interpretations to the client (and encourage the client to make his or her own interpretations). These accurate interpretations are based on the therapist's accurate understanding of the client's transference that was identified during Phase 1. In the

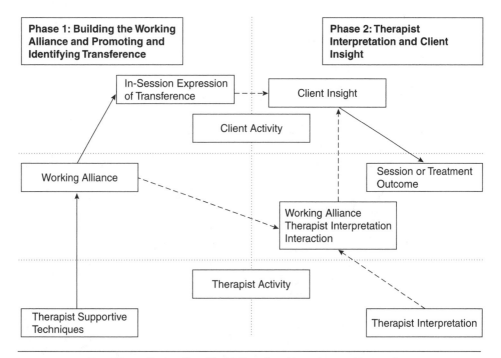

FIGURE 6.1 *Two-Phase Counseling Model Based on Transference Research*

context of a strong working alliance, insights interact with the ongoing experience of transference to produce a positive session or treatment outcome.

Applications for Practice

The recommendations for practice developed in this section are based on (1) the Transference, Interpretation, and Insight Research-Based Model described previously; (2) Pepinsky and Pepinsky's (1954) descriptions of the scientist practitioner; (3) writing and research concerning the use of assessments as an adjunct in counseling; and (4) Book's (1998) book, *How to Practice Brief Psychodynamic Psychotherapy: The Core Conflictual Relationship Theme Method.*

Applied psychologists have repeatedly confirmed their commitment to the scientist–practitioner model of training (e.g., Meara et al., 1988). This model defines training in applied psychology as incorporating activities from scientific and practitioner domains. The scientist–practitioner model has two implications for the day-to-day activity of practicing psychologists. First, psychologists are expected in varying degrees to engage in both scientific and practice activities (e.g., Gelso, 1979; Heppner et al., 1999). Second, practicing psychologists should bring a scientific attitude to and use the scientific method in their therapy interactions (Claiborn, 1987; Heppner et al., 1999; Pepinsky & Pepinsky, 1954).

The second implication of the scientist–practitioner model has received little empirical attention. As early as 1954, Pepinsky and Pepinsky (1954) articulated a prescriptive model for counseling practice, based on the idea of the counselor as an applied scientist. This model consists of a reflective process of observations, inferences, hypothesis formation, and hypotheses testing through new observations. More recently, Heppner et al. (1999) suggested that the scientist–practitioner model of counseling practice be formalized by having therapists engage in formal data collection (the observation aspect of Pepinsky and Pepinsky's model) and formal data analyses (the hypothesis testing aspect of the model) as a part of their ongoing clinical work. They hypothesized that the counseling process would be enhanced when counselors engaged in systematic data collection and data analysis as a part of their clinical work.

Although counselors have informally collected data as a part of their ongoing clinical assessment and treatment, several authors have implored counselors to formalize this practice (Dies, 1980; Hayes, Nelson, & Jarret, 1987; Marsh & Hunsley, 1993). In addition, Hayes et al. (1987) said that "In practical terms, the sine qua non of the modes, methods, devices, strategies, and theories of clinical assessment is their contribution to treatment outcome" (p. 963). Hayes et al. defined "the treatment utility of assessment" as the degree to which assessment contributes to enhanced treatment process or treatment outcome (Hayes et al.). According to Hayes et al., "Apparently no studies have yet been conducted that are designed to measure directly the treatment utility of given devices" (p. 965).

Since Hayes et al. (1987) several studies have examined the treatment utility of assessments. In a quasi-experimental study, Flowers, Booraem, and Schwartz (1993) examined the relationship between the amount of formal assessment that group counselors used in their clinical work and group client outcome. Three conditions were constructed that made it increasingly easy for counselors to use clinical assessment instruments. The researchers found that counselors used more assessment instruments with their group clients when these assessment instruments were computer administrated and scored. In addition, when counselors used more assessment instruments their clients had fewer DSMIII-R symptoms when compared to clients of counselors who used fewer assessment instruments. Brown (1989) replicated and extended Flowers et al.'s findings by showing that the formal session-by-session assessment of the counseling process resulted in enhanced treatment outcome. Based on these writings and research, the practice model that I present incorporates the use of formal pretreatment and process assessments. The specific assessments that can be used with this model are displayed in Table 6.1. In addition to the name of the assessment, the table indicates from whose perspective the assessment is accomplished and the purpose of the assessment.

Book (1998) uses the CCRT method as the basis for a short-term treatment approach. His approach has three phases of treatment that he labels as (1) Demonstrating the Ubiquity of the CCRT, (2) Identifying and Working Through the RO (response from others), and (3) Termination. At the core of Book's treatment model is the identification of the client's CCRT. To identify the CCRT, Book recommends that the therapist listen for and elicit relationship episodes (REs). He believes that it is particularly useful for the therapist to record, word for word if possible, these REs.

According to Book (1998), an RE is a vignette or story that describes a client's interaction with a significant other. To be complete the RE has to have three parts: (1) what the

TABLE 6.1   *Assesment Measures Use in the Transference, Interpretation, and Insight: A Research-Based Model*

Assessment Device	Rating Perspective	Purpose
Pre-Assessments		
1. Central Relationship Questionnaire	Client self-report	Initial assement of transference pattern by focusing on relationship themes
2. Adult Attachment Scale or Adult Attachment Interview	Client self-report or therapist generated and scored	Attachment style: indication of the client's capacity to form a working alliance
Process Assessments		
1. Working Alliance Inventory—Short Form	Client self-report	Monitoring the strength of and fluctuations in the working alliance
2. Missouri Identifying Transference Scale	Therapist perspective on client in-session behavior	Identify amount of fluctuations in negative and positive transference
3. Important Event Questionnaire and Insight Rating Scale	Client self-report and therapist rating	Capture client expressions of insight and rate amount of client insight

client wanted to happen, (2) how the other person responded to the client, and (3) how the client felt about or reacted to the response received. The therapist's job is to help the client tell complete REs. Often client's do not narrate complete REs. For example, what the client wants from others is often implicit. Book gives a number of examples of how the therapist can make the client's Wish, RO, or RS explicit. As an example, a Wish can be made explicit by asking the client "What were you hoping for?" or "What did you want to happen?" in relation to a specific RE.

For every RE that the therapist records the Wishes, ROs, and RSs are identified that are associated with that particular RE. Once a number of REs have been collected, and the Wishes, ROs, and RSs have been identified for each RE, the therapist is in a position to identify the client's CCRT. This is done by summarizing the Wishes, ROs, and RSs across the various REs into a composite formulation. According to Book (1998), this formulation should take the form of a sentence that describes the client's main wishes, how he or she expects others to respond to these wishes, and how the client in turn responds to others' responses. An example from Book illustrates a CCRT. "Mr. Black has a wish (Wish) to speak up forcefully when wronged or overlooked. However, he experiences others as responding to him vindictively (RO) should he do so. So he bites his tongue, remains silent, and ends up feeling resentful and down on himself (RS)" (p. 22). These ideas presented by Book are also incorporated into our practice model.

Phase l: Building the Working Alliance and Promoting and Identifying the Transference

The goal of Phase 1 is twofold: Build a strong working alliance, and identify the transference. Although the working alliance is covered in depth in Chapter 4, I present some research-associated practical applications in this chapter as they relate to this model. The tasks of building a strong working alliance and identifying the transference can begin with the help of good initial assessments. For this model two assessment areas seem particularly relevant. First, it is important for the therapist to understand the client's capacity to form a working alliance. Research by Mallinckrodt and his colleagues (Mallinckrodt, 1991; Mallinckrodt, Gantt, & Coble, 1995) suggest that the client's attachment style or pattern is an excellent predictor of the client's capacity to form a working alliance with the therapist.

Given these findings, it is important for the therapist to assess attachment prior to treatment. A simple self-report device that measures adult attachment is the Adult Attachment Scale (AAS; Collins & Read, 1990). The AAS is brief, easily administered, and easily scored. A more in-depth assessment of the client's attachment style can be gained with the Adult Attachment Interview (George, Kaplan, & Main, 1996). Once the capacity to form a working alliance is known, the therapist can begin to determine the most appropriate strategies for building the working alliance with the client.

When the client has a good capacity to form a working alliance (as determined in part by pretreatment assessments), research suggests that the working alliance is built using supportive techniques (e.g., Multon, Patton, & Kivlighan, 1996). Supportive techniques include empathy, reassurance, support, advice, and reinforcement (Gelso & Hayes, 1998). The therapist should avoid giving too much information or asking for too much information during the initial phase of therapy (Kivlighan, 1990). These informational types of intentions tend to put the client in a more passive-reactive stance and discourage the type of active-collaborative stance that defines a strong working alliance.

When the client's capacity to form a working alliance is low, the therapist must take a different stance during the initial phase of treatment. Foreman and Marmar (1985) and Kivlighan and Schmitz (1992) examined the therapist techniques associated with helping clients who initially had poor working alliances establish strong working alliances. In the Foreman and Marmar study the therapist actions associated with improved alliances were (1) addressing the client's defenses, (2) addressing the client's guilt and expectation of punishment, (3) addressing the client's problematic feelings in relation to the therapist, and (4) linking the problematic feelings in relation to the therapist with the client's defenses. In the Kivlighan and Schmitz study therapists were relatively more challenging, thematically focused, and here-and-now oriented in dyads with improving working alliances.

Theoretically and empirically the working alliance is not a static construct. Bordin (1979), Safran, Crocker, McMain, and Murray (1990), and Gelso and Carter (1985) theorize that it is the therapist's ability to repair the inevitable tears or breaches in the alliance that is related to effective counseling. Therefore, the therapist must be able to detect and repair ruptures in the working alliance. Bordin (1979, 1994) emphasized the "central importance of the events surrounding strain [rupture] in the therapeutic alliance and to the understanding of how and why change [rupture and repair] occurs" (Bordin, 1994, p. 17). According to Bordin (1994), these ruptures can come from one of two sources: (1) the client's characteristic patterns of self-sabotage or (2) counselor mistakes (failures in empathy or countertransference behaviors). Theoretically, the source of the working alliance rupture is expected to affect the repair process that will be most appropriate.

Little research has addressed the rupture–repair process that Bordin (1994) depicts. In terms of alliance repair, Lansford (1986) found that rated (unspecified rating scale) effectiveness in addressing ruptures was related to better counseling outcome. In addition, Lansford found that client factors were most salient in alliance repair. The only therapist intervention that was related to alliance repair was the therapist pointing out similarities between extratherapy and in-therapy relationships.

Through a series of studies Safran and his colleagues (Safran et al., 1990; Safran, Muran, & Samstag, 1994) have articulated a model of working alliance repair. Research with this model suggests that working alliance repair is related to (1) attending to the rupture marker, (2) exploration of the rupture experience, (3) exploration of avoidance, and (4) exploration of the client's interpersonal schema. Bordin (1994) points out the limitations in this research effort as only concentrating on therapist-initiated ruptures at the expense of examining client-initiated ruptures.

Binder and Strupp (1997) offer an alternative view of the rupture/tear process. They contend that tears, rather than being exclusively client or counselor initiated, are an interactive phenomena. Specifically, tears occur when counselors do not appropriately respond to instances of client negativity. Kivlighan and Goetz (1998) tested Strupp's speculations. They found that clients were relatively more distressed and the therapists were relatively more distant in sessions where a tear occurred. In sessions where the working alliance was repaired, therapists were more involved and more interpretive.

Clearly, assessing clients' ability to form working alliances, building these alliances, and maintaining the working alliances through possible tears is a complex therapeutic task. As suggested, assessing the client's capacity to form a working alliance can be aided through psychometric assessments. Likewise, the monitoring of the ongoing state of the working alliance is an important therapist activity that can be aided through systematic assessment. Specifically, the therapist can have the client fill out the short form of the Working Alliance Inventory (Horvath & Greenberg, 1989; Tracey & Kokotovic, 1989) after each counseling session. The Working Alliance Inventory gives the counselor information not only about the relative strength of the working alliance but also session-to-session fluctuations in the working alliance that can be indicative of working alliance tears. The strength of the working alliance is one of the two key indicators that the therapist can initiate in Phase 2 of the model.

The second goal of Phase 1 is to promote and identify the transference. The therapist can begin to identify the client's transference reactions by having the client complete the CRQ prior to initiating therapy. As described previously, this instrument is a self-report of the client's predominant wishes, ROs, and RSs. The CRQ can give the therapist initial information about the form that the transference reaction may take. There is evidence that there is a significant relationship between the wishes, ROs, and RSs, identified through self-report and these same dimensions derived from judges' ratings of REs obtained from treatment (Crits-Christoph & Luborsky, 1990b). In addition to giving the therapist an initial perspective on the client's relationship themes, the CRQ can also be used to judge the client's initial level of awareness or self-insight. This judgment is made by comparing the relationship themes identified by the CRQ to relationship themes identified by the therapist from REs obtained in the sessions.

Once Phase 1 has commenced, the therapist can start a more comprehensive assessment of the form of the client's transference by using the method detailed by Book (1998). This involves (1) listening for and eliciting the client's description of REs; (2) ensuring that REs are complete by making unspoken wishes, ROs, and RSs complete; (3) recording the REs and analyzing them for wishes, ROs, and RSs; and (4) formulating a CCRT by synthesizing wishes, ROs, and RSs across the collected REs. A critical question for this model of therapy is the extent to which therapists can accurately identify the client's CCRT from the collected REs.

Accurately identifying the CCRT is not a simple task. In their research Luborsky and Crits-Christoph (1990) use experienced and highly trained judges to make CCRT ratings. In their studies the reliability for combined (aggregated) judgments is good but the reliability of a single judge is always substantially less than the reliability of aggregate judgments. This suggests that accurately identifying a CCRT is a difficult task for a single judge. Recent research by Hamilton (1999) shows one of the reasons why it is difficult for a single judge or therapist to accurately identify the CCRT from the client's REs. Hamilton had therapists examine a series of REs (taken from different patients in Luborsky & Crits-Christoph, 1990) and identify the wishes, ROs, and RSs. He also had the same therapists participate in Relationship Anecdotes Paradigm (Luborsky, 1990b) interviews to elicit therapists' REs. These therapist REs were scored for wishes, ROs, and RSs by trained judges. Hamilton then correlated the therapists' own wishes, ROs, and RSs with the pattern of wishes, ROs, and RSs they identified in the REs that they had judged. There were no significant relationships between the therapists' own ROs and RSs and the ROs and RSs in the REs that they judged. There was, however, a strong relationship between the therapists own pattern of wishes and the wishes he or she saw in others' REs. This finding suggests that therapists are likely to have a hard time identifying the wish component of their clients' CCRT because they cannot always separate their own wishes from those of their clients.

Hamilton (1999) also tried to determine which therapist characteristics were related to the therapists' tendency to see their own wishes in the REs of others. Because of their significance in the theoretical and clinical literature, Hamilton examined the relationship between a therapist's experience either giving or receiving therapy and their tendency to see their wishes in others' REs. Neither the therapist's experience as a therapist nor the hours of personal therapy was related to the tendency to see wishes in others' REs. There was a significant interaction between therapist's experience giving and receiving therapy and the tendency to see wishes in others' REs. When experience doing therapy was low, there was no relationship between the amount of personal therapy received and the tendency to see wishes in others' REs. When experience doing therapy was high, however, there was a strong, positive relationship between the amount of personal therapy received and a reduced tendency to see wishes in others' REs. Significant experience as a therapist and receiving therapy are necessary for the therapist to be able to separate personal wishes from those of the client.

In sum, using the CCRT method to identify the form of the client's transference during Phase 1 of treatment is a complex task. Even with the help of information from the CRQ and written REs, this task is still difficult. Because it is particularly difficult for therapists to separate their own wishes from those of their clients, it is important for therapists (especially those who are inexperienced clinically and who have not examined their own relationship patterns through personal therapy) to seek some type of outside consultation (e.g., supervisor or peer group supervision) when trying to use the CCRT method to identify the form of the client's transference pattern. It is the correct identification of the form of the transference pattern during Phase 1 that allows the therapist to make accurate interpretations during Phase 2.

In addition to correctly identifying the form of the transference pattern, the therapist must also track the amount of transference that is occurring in sessions. The MITS can aide the therapist in tracking the amount of transference present in a session. Because single-item ratings of transference (amount, positive, negative) are only moderately correlated with the MITS (Multon, Kivlighan, & Gold, 1996), this suggests that therapists may not be able to accurately determine the amount of transference present in a session by simply reflecting on the amount of positive or negative transference experienced. The multiitem format of the MITS is important, because it ensures that the therapist pay attention to a wide variety of indicators of transference expression and not simply rate the amount of positive and negative transference present in a session. Despite the multiitem format, the MITS is still very easy to complete quickly (usually, in less than two minutes).

To summarize, the tasks of Phase 1 are to (1) build, monitor, and maintain the working alliance (2) identify the form of the transference, and (3) track the amount of transference present in the sessions. These tasks are aided by the following pretreatment and process assessments: (1) the CRQ, (2) the AAS or AAI, (3) the short form of the WAI, and (4) the MITS. Indicators that the therapist can move to Phase 2 of treatment are (1) the establishment and maintainance of a strong working alliance and (2) significant in-session expressions of transference.

Phase 2: Interpreting the Transference and Promoting Client Insight

The major therapeutic task during Phase 2 of treatment is to provide accurate interpretations to clients and to encourage clients to begin to make these interpretations for themselves. This interpretive process should result in an increased level of client awareness and insight. It is important to remember, however, that interpretations seem to be most effective when delivered in the context of a strong working alliance and that client insight is most effective when obtained in conjunction with relatively high levels of expression of transference. Therefore, it is critical that the therapist continue to monitor the strength of the working alliance and the amount of transference expressed throughout Phase 2.

Logically, a well-formulated CCRT should help the therapist make accurate interpretations. Unfortunately, research has not addressed this simple proposition. We do know that accuracy ratings for therapist interpretations are generally low to moderate in the studies that have examined interpretation accuracy. For example, in the Crits-Christoph et al. study (1990) accuracy scores, made on a four-point scale (1 = no congruence between interpretation and CCRT formulation; 4 = high congruence between interpretation and CCRT formulation), were 1.81, 1.44, and 1.69, respectively, for Wish, RO, and RS. The rating level for all three components indicates only some congruence between the interpretations that the therapists were making and the judge-derived CCRTs. The therapists in the accuracy studies did not formally formulate CCRTs for their clients. So we do not know if having therapists formally formulate CCRTs for their clients, by following the steps outlined for Phase 1, would improve their interpretive accuracy.

There are at least two explanations for the relatively low level of accuracy found in the studies examining therapist interpretations. First, the therapist could be incorrectly identifying the client's transference and thereby making "incorrect" interpretations. The Hamilton (1999) study suggests that the therapist's own characteristic pattern of wishes could cause an incorrect identification of the client's transference pattern. Second, the therapist may not be following an interpretive theme. Sometimes the therapist may be accurately interpreting the client's main transference, and other times the therapist may be accurately interpreting a minor or unrelated relationship pattern that the client displays.

Whether therapists follow an interpretive theme is an interesting and important question. Unfortunately, there is little systematic research addressing this question. Kivlighan and Schmitz (1992) found that following an interpretive theme was related to increasing client-rated working alliance. Summarizing across her eight intensively studied cases, Hill (1989) suggested, "It was helpful when therapists used an interpretive theme" (p. 314). Barlow, Burlingame, Harding, and Behrman (1997) attempted to determine the degree to which treatment outcome was related to therapeutic focusing. For expert, professional, group therapists the degree of therapeutic focusing independently predicted client improvement. The results of these studies suggest that it is important for the therapist to maintain a focused line of interpretation centered around the main relationship conflict described in the CCRT.

During Phase 2 the therapist must attempt to maintain a focused line of interpretation centered on the client's CCRT. One way to assess the degree of therapeutic focusing is for the therapist to record the interpretations made in sessions. Hopefully, the number of therapist interpretations will be limited, so the task of recording them will not become too tedious and laborious. Research by Hill (1989) suggests that interpretations, while rated as very helpful by clients, are only used about 8% of the time in treatment. Hill also suggests that interpretations probably should not be used extensively in treatment.

In addition to maintaining an interpretive focus, therapists should also track the level of client insight. Kivlighan, Multon, and Patton (in press) showed that a simple and cost-effective way of assessing client insight is to have clients fill out the Important Events Questionnaire (IEQ) after each session. In its most basic form the IEQ simply asks clients to identify the most important event in a session and to explain why they thought this event was important. Therapists can use the Insight Rating Scale (IRS) to determine the amount of insight in the client's IEQ. The IEQ can also be used to track whether the insights that the client is reporting are congruent with the interpretations that the therapist is making. This can provide important clues about how the client is experiencing and using (or not using) the therapist's interpretations.

To summarize, the tasks of Phase 2 are to (1) continue to monitor the working alliance and the amount of transference expressed, (2) make accurate interpretations of the transference, and (3) monitor the amount and type of insight the client experiences in the sessions. These tasks are aided by the following process assessments: (1) the short form of the WAI and the MITS as in Phase 1 and (2) the IEQ with ratings using the IRS. The major indicator that the tasks of Phase 2 have been accomplished is the clients' consistent report of insight on the IEQ that matches the formulation provided in the CCRT.

The two-phase model I present is based on the research examining transference, interpretation, and insight. There is at least some empirical support for each aspect of this model. Nevertheless, there are important questions that need considerably more empirical investigation. In particular, we need additional research on how to apply the proposed model. In terms of the model itself, the link between the working alliance by therapist interpretation interaction construct and client insight has the least empirical support. We need research to examine whether client insight mediates the relationship between interpretations delivered in the context of a strong working alliance and client outcome. In terms of applying the model, research is needed on (1) the therapist's ability to correctly identify the CCRT from REs produced in treatment and recorded by the therapist, (2) how to help the therapist maintain an interpretive theme, and (3) the congruence between the therapist's interpretation and the client's insight. The research to date allowed me to specify a fairly elaborate model of how transference, interpretation, and insight operate in therapy. Hopefully, future research will enable us to refine and elaborate this initial attempt at model building.

References

Adelstein, D. M., Gelso, C. J., Haws, R., Jr., Reed, K. G., & Spiegel, S. B. (1971). The change process following time-limited therapy. In C. J. Gelso & D. H. Johnson (Eds.), *Explorations in time-limited counseling and psychotherapy* (pp. 63–81). New York: Teachers College Press.

Barber, J. P., Crits-Christoph, P., & Luborsky, L. (1990). A guide to the CCRT standard categories and their classification. In L. Luborsky & P. Crits-Christoph (Eds.), *Understanding transference: The CCRT method* (pp. 1–11). New York: Basic Books.

Barber, J. P., Foltz, C., & Weinryb, R. M. (1998). The Central Relationship Questionnaire: Initial report. *Journal of Counseling Psychology, 45,* 131–142.

Barlow, S. H., Burlingame, G. M., Harding, J. A., & Behrman, J. (1997). Therapeutic focusing in time-limited group psychotherapy. *Group Dynamics, 1,* 254–266.

Beck, A. T., Epstein, N., Brown G., & Steer, R. A. (1988). An inventory for measuring clinical anxiety: Psychometric properties. *Journal of Consulting and Clinical Psychology, 56,* 893–897.

Beck, A. T., Ward, C., Mendelson, M., Mock, J., & Erbaugh, J. (1961). An inventory to measure depression. *Archives of General Psychiatry, 4,* 561–571.

Binder, J. L., & Strupp, H. H. (1997). "Negative process:" A recurrently discovered and underestimated facet of therapeutic process and outcome in the individual psychotherapy of adults. *Clinical Psychology: Science and Practice, 4,* 121–139.

Book, H. E. (1998). *How to practice brief psychodynamic psychotherapy: The Core Conflictual Relationship Theme method.* Washington, DC: American Psychological Association.

Bordin, E. S. (1979). The generalizability of the psychoanalytic concept of the working alliance. *Psychotherapy: Theory, research, and practice, 16,* 252–260.

Bordin, E. S. (1994). Theory and research on the therapeutic working alliance: New directions. In A. O. Horvath & L. S. Greenberg (Eds.), *The working alliance: Theory, research, and practice* (pp. 13–37). New York: Wiley.

Brenner, C. (1982). *The mind in conflict.* New York: International Universities Press.

Brown, P. J. (1989). *Development of the things not said questionaire.* Unpublished master thesis, University of Missouri, Columbia, MO.

Claiborn, C. D. (1987). Science and practice: Reconsidering the Pepinskys. *Journal of Counseling and Development, 65,* 286–288.

Collins, N. L., & Read, S. J. (1990). Adult attachment, working models, and relationship quality in dating couples. *Journal of Personality and Social Psychology, 58,* 644–663.

Costa, P. T., & McCrae, R. R. (1991). *NEO-FFI* (Form S). Odessa, FL: Psychological Assessment Resources.

Crits-Christoph, P., Barber, J. P., Miller, N. E., & Beebe, K. (1993). Evaluating insight. In N. E. Miller, L. Luborsky, J. P. Barber, & J. P. Docherty (Eds.), *Psychodynamic treatment research: A handbook for clinical practice* (pp. 407–422). New York: Basic Books.

Crits-Christoph, P., Cooper, A., & Luborsky, L. (1988). The accuracy of therapists' interpretations and the outcome of dynamic psychotherapy. *Journal of Consulting and Clinical Psychology, 56,* 490–495.

Crits-Christoph, P., & Luborsky, L. (1990a). Changes in CCRT pervasiveness during psychotherapy. In L. Luborsky & P. Crits-Christoph (Eds.), *Understanding transference: The CCRT method,* (pp. 133–146). New York: Basic Books.

Crits-Christoph, P., & Luborsky, L. (1990b). The perspective of patients versus clinicians in the assessment of central relationship themes. In L. Luborsky & P. Crits-Christoph (Eds.), *Understanding transference: The CCRT method* (pp. 197–208). New York: Basic Books.

Crits-Christoph, P., Luborsky, L., Popp, C., Mellon, J., & Mark, D. (1990). Reliability of choice of narratives and of the CCRT measure. In L. Luborsky & P. Crits-Christoph (Eds.), *Understanding transference: The CCRT method* (pp. 93–101). New York: Basic Books.

Cummings, A. L., Martin, J., Hallberg, E. T., Slemon, A. G. (1992). Memory for therapeutic events, session effectiveness, and working alliance in short-term counseling. *Journal of Counseling Psychology, 39,* 306–312.

Curtis, J. T., Silberschatz, G., Sampson, H., & Weiss, J. (1994). The plan formulation method. *Psychotherapy Research, 4,* 197–207.

Dahl, H., & Teller, V. (1994). The characteristics, identification, and application of FRAMES. *Psychotherapy Research, 4,* 253–276.

Derogatis, L. R. (1977). *The S. L.-90: Administration, scoring and procedures manual: I for the revised version.* Baltimore, MD: Johns Hopkins Hospital.

Dies, R. R. (1980). Group psychotherapy: Training and supervision. In A. K. Hess (Ed.), *Psychotherapy supervision: Theory, research, and practice.* New York: Wiley.

Dymond, R. (1948). A preliminary investigation of the relation of insight and empathy. *Journal of Consulting Psychology, 12,* 228–233.

Fenichel, O. (1941). *The psychoanalytic theory of neurosis.* New York: Norton.

Flowers, J. V., Booraem, C. D., Schwartz, B. (1993). Group therapy client outcome and satisfaction as a function of the therapists' use of rapid assessment instruments. *Small Group Research, 24,* 116–126.

Foreman, S. A., & Marmar, C. R. (1985). Therapist actions that address initially poor therapeutic alliances in psychotherapy. *American Journal of Psychiatry, 142,* 922–926.

French, T. M. (1954). *The integration of behavior.* (Vol. 2). Chicago, IL: University of Chicago Press.

Freud, S. (1966). Recommendations for physicians on the psycho-analytic method of treatment. In Riviere (Ed. and Trans.), *Collected papers* (Vol. 2, pp. 323–333). New York: Basic Books. (Original work published 1912)

Freud, S. (1958). On beginning the treatment: Further recommendations on the technique of psychoanalysis. In J. Strachey (Ed. and Trans.), *The standard edition of the complete psychological works of Sigmund Freud* (Vol. 12, pp. 145–156). London: Hogarth Press. (Original work published 1913)

Fried, D., Crits-Christoph, P., & Luborsky, L. (1990). The parallel of the CCRT for the therapist with the CCRT for other people. In L. Luborsky & P. Crits-Christoph (Eds.), *Understanding transference: The CCRT method* (pp. 147–157). New York: Basic Books.

Funder, D. C. (1980). On seeing ourselves as others see us: Self-agreement and discrepancy in personality ratings. *Journal of Personality, 48,* 473–493.

Gaston, L. (1990). The concept of the alliance and its role in psychotherapy: Theoretical and empirical considerations. *Psychotherapy: Theory, research and practice, 27,* 143–153.

Gaston, L., Thompson, L., Gallagher, D., Cournoyer, L., & Gagnon, R. (1998). Alliance, technique and their interactions in predicting outcome of behavioral, cognitive and brief dynamic therapy. *Psychotherapy Research, 8,* 190–209.

Gelso, C. J. (1979). Research in counseling: Methodological and professional issues. *The Counseling Psychologist, 8* (3), 7–35.

Gelso, C. J., & Carter, J. A. (1985). The relationship in counseling and psychotherapy: Components, consequences, and theoretical antecedents. *The Counseling Psychologist, 13,* 155–243.

Gelso, C. J., & Hayes, J. A. (1998). *The psychotherapy relationship: Theory, research, and practice.* New York: Wiley.

Gelso, C. J., Hill, C. E., & Kivlighan, D. M., Jr. (1991). Transference, insight, and the counselors intentions during a counseling hour. *Journal of Counseling and Development, 69,* 428–433.

Gelso, C. J., & Kivlighan, D. M., Wine, B., Jones, A., & Friedman, S. C. (1997). Transference, insight and the course of time-limited therapy. *Journal of Counseling Psychology, 44,* 209–217.

George, C., Kaplan, N., & Main, M. (1996). *Adult Attachment Interview.* Unpublished protocol, Department of Psychology, University of California, Berkley.

Graff, H., & Luborsky, L. (1977). Long-term trends in transference and resistance: A quantitative analytic method applied to four psychoanalyses. *Journal of the American Psychoanalytic Association, 25,* 471–490.

Greenson, R. R. (1967). *The technique and practice of psychoanalysis* (Vol. 1). New York: International Universities Press.

Grenyer, B. F. S., & Luborsky, L. (1996). Dynamic change in psychotherapy: Mastery of interpersonal conflicts. *Journal of Consulting and Clinical Psychology, 64,* 411–416.

Hamilton, J. (1999). *Effect of therapists' countertransference on formulation of client transference.* Unpublished doctoral dissertation, University of Missouri, Columbia.

Hayes, S. C., Nelson, R. O., & Jarret, R. B. (1987). The treatment utility of assessment: A functional approach to evaluating assessment quality. *American Psychologist, 42,* 963–974.

Henry, W. P., Strupp, H. H., Schacht, T. E., & Gaston, L. (1993). Psychodynamic approaches. In S. L. Garfield & A. E. Bergin (Eds.), *Handbook of psychotherapy and behavior change* (4th ed., pp. 467–508). New York: Wiley.

Heppner, P. P., Kivlighan, D. M., Jr., & Wampold, B. E. (1999). *Research design in counseling* (2nd ed.). Pacific Grove, CA: Brooks/Cole.

Hill, C. E. (1989). *Therapist techniques and client outcomes: Eight cases of brief psychotherapy.* Newbury Park, CA: Sage.

Hill, C. E., Corbett, M. M., Kanitz, B., Rios, P., Lightsey, R., & Gomez, M. (1992). Client behavior in counseling and therapy sessions: Development of a pantheoretical measure. *Journal of Counseling Psychology, 39,* 539–549.

Hill, C. E., Thompson, B. J., & Mahalik, J. R. (1989). Therapist interpretation. In C. E. Hill, *Therapist techniques and client outcomes: Eight cases of brief psychotherapy* (pp. 284–310). Newbury Park, CA: Sage.

Hohage, R. Kubler, J. C. (1988). The Emotional Insight Rating Scale. In H. Dahl, H. Kachele, & H. Thoma (Eds.), *Psychoanalytic process research strategies* (pp. 243–265). Heidelberg: Springer.

Horowitz, L. M., Rosenberg, S. E., Baer, B. A., Ureno, G., & Villasenor, V. S. (1988). Inventory of Interpersonal Problems: Psychometric properties and clinical applications. *Journal of Consulting and Clinical Psychology, 56,* 885–892.

Horowitz, M. J. (1994). Configural analysis and the use of role-relationship models to understand transference. *Psychotherapy Research, 4,* 184–196.

Horvath, A. O., & Greenberg, L. (1989). Development and validation of the Working Alliance Inventory. *Journal of Counseling Psychology, 36,* 223–232.

Kivlighan, D. M., Jr., (1990). Relation between counselors' use of intentions and clients' perception of working alliance. *Journal of Counseling Psychology, 37,* 27–32.

Kivlighan, D. M., Jr., & Goetz, J. W. (1998). A quantitative analysis of breaches in the working alliance. Part of a symposium presented at the annual convention of the american psychological association, Toronto, Canada.

Kivlighan D. M., Jr., Multon, K. D., & Patton, M. J. (in press). Insight and symptom reduction in time-limited psychoanalytic counseling. *Journal of Counseling Psychology.*

Kivlighan, D. M., Jr., & Schmitz, P. (1992). Counselor technical activity in cases with improving and continuing poor alliances. *Journal of Counseling Psychology, 39,* 32–38.

Kivlighan, D. M., Jr., Thye, R. A., & Ji, P. Y. (in press). Mediating and moderating effects of the working alliance on client outcome. *Psychotherapy Research.*

Klein, M. H., Mathieu-Coughlan, P., & Kiesler, D. (1968). The Experiencing Scale. In S. L. Greenberg and W. M. Pinsof (Eds.), *The psychotherapeutic process: A research handbook* (pp. 21–71). New York: Guilford Press.

Lansford, E. (1986). Weakening and repairs of the working alliance in short-term psychotherapy. *Professional Psychology: Research and Practice, 17,* 364–366.

Luborsky, L. (1976). Helping alliances in psychotherapy: The groundwork for a study of their relationship to its outcome. In J. Claghorn (Ed.), *Successful psychotherapy* (pp. 92–116). New York: Brunner/Mazel.

Luborsky, L. (1977). Measuring a pervasive psychic structure in psychotherapy: Core Conflict Relationship Theme. In N. Freedman & S. Grand (Eds.), *Communicative structures and psychic structures* (pp. 367–395). New York: Plenum Press.

Luborsky, L. (1990a). Early development of the Core Conflictual Relationship Theme idea. In L. Luborsky & P. Crits-Christoph (Eds.), *Understanding transference: The CCRT method* (pp. 1–11). New York: Basic Books.

Luborsky, L. (1990b). A guide to the CCRT method. In L. Luborsky & P. Crits-Christoph (Eds.), *Understanding transference: The CCRT method* (pp. 15–36). New York: Basic Books.

Luborsky, L., & Barber, J.P. (1994). Perspectives on seven transference related measures applied to the interview with Ms. Smithfield. *Psychotherapy Research, 4,* 152–154.

Luborsky, L. Barber, J. P., & Crits-Christoph, P. (1990). Theory-based research for understanding the process of dynamic psychotherapy. *Journal of Consulting and Clinical Psychology, 58,* 281–287.

Luborsky, L. Barber, J. P., Schaffler, P., & Cacciola, J. (1990). The narratives told during psychotherapy and the types of CCRTs within them. In L. Luborsky & P. Crits-Christoph (Eds.), *Understanding transference:*

The CCRT method (pp. 117–132). New York: Basic Books.

Luborsky, L., & Crits-Christoph, P. (1990). *Understanding transference: The CCRT method.* New York: Basic Books.

Luborsky, L., Crits-Christoph, P., Mintz, J., & Auerbach, A. (1988). *Who will benefit from psychotherapy? Predicting therapeutic outcome.* New York: Basic Books.

Luborsky, L., Popp, C., & Barber, J. P. (1994). Common and special factors in different transference-related measures. *Psychotherapy Research, 4,* 277–286.

Luborsky, L., Popp, C., Barber, J. P., & Shapiro, D. A. (1994). Editor's introduction. *Psychotherapy Research, 4,* 151.

Luborsky, L., Popp, C., Luborsky, E., & Mark, D. (1994). The Core Conflict Relationship Theme. *Psychotherapy Research, 4,* 172–183.

Mallinckrodt, B. (1991). Clients' representations of childhood emotional bonds with parents, social support, and formation of the working alliance. *Journal of Counseling Psychology, 38,* 401–409.

Mallinckrodt, B., Gantt, D. K., & Coble, H. M. (1995). Working alliance, attachment memories, and social competencies of women in brief therapy. *Journal of Counseling Psychology, 42,* 79–84.

Marsh, E. J., & Hunsley, J. (1993). Assessment considerations in the identification of failing psychotherapy: Bringing the negatives out of the darkroom. *Psychological Assessment, 5,* 292–301.

Marziali, E. (1984). Three viewpoints on the therapeutic alliance: Similarities, differences, and associations with psychotherapy outcome. *Journal of Nervous and Mental Disease, 172,* 417–423.

Meara, N. M., Schmidt, L. D., Carrington, C. H., Davis, K. L., Dixon, D. N., Fretz, B. R., Myers, R. A., Ridley, C. R., & Suinn, R. M. (1988). Training and accreditation in counseling psychology. *The Counseling Psychologist, 16,* 366–384.

Morgan, R. W., Luborsky, L., Crits-Christoph, P., Curtis, H., & Solomon, J. (1982). Predicting the outcomes of therapy using the Penn Helping Alliance rating method. *Archives of General Psychiatry, 39,* 397–402.

Multon, K. M., Kivlighan, D. M., & Gold, P. B. (1996). Changes in counselor treatment adherence across time. *Journal of Counseling Psychology, 43,* 356–363.

Multon, K. M., Patton, M. J., & Kivlighan, D. M., (1996). Development of the Missouri Identifying Transference Scale. *Journal of Counseling Psychology, 43,* 259–260.

O'Connor, L. E., Edelstein, S., Berry, J. W., & Weiss, J. (1994). Changes in the patient's level of insight in brief psychotherapy: Two pilot studies. *Psychotherapy, 31,* 533–544.

Patton, M. J., Kivlighan, D. M., Jr., & Multon, K. D. (1997). The Missouri psychoanalytic counseling research project: Relation of changes in counseling process to client outcomes. *Journal of Counseling Psychology, 44,* 189–208.

Pepinsky, H. B., & Pepinsky, P. N. (1954). *Counseling theory and practice.* New York: Ronald Press.

Perry, J. C. (1994). Assessing psychodynamic patterns using the idiographic conflict formulation method. *Psychotherapy Research, 4,* 239–252.

Piper, W. E., Azin, H. F. A., Joyce, A. S., & McCallum, M. (1991). Transference interpretations, therapeutic alliance, and outcome in short-term individual psychotherapy. *Archives of General Psychiatry, 48,* 946–953.

Popp, C., Luborsky, L., & Crits-Christoph, P. (1990). The parallel of the CCRT from therapy narratives with the CCRT from dreams. In L. Luborsky & P. Crits-Christoph. *Understanding transference: The CCRT method* (pp. 159–172). New York: Basic Books.

Rosenberg, S. E., Horowitz, L. M., Hanks, S., Hartley, D., Levenson, H., Schulman, T. G., & Skuja, A. (1994). The consensual response psychodynamic formulation: Part 2. Application to the case of Mrs. Smithfield. *Psychotherapy Research, 4,* 234–238.

Safran, J., Crocker, P., McMain, S., & Murray, P. (1990). Therapeutic alliance rupture as therapy event for empirical investigation. *Psychotherapy, 27,* 65.

Safran, J. D., & Hill, C. (1989). *Interpersonal Schema Questionnaire.* Unpublished manuscript, University of Toronto, Toronto, Ontario, Canada.

Safran, J., Muran, J. C., Samstag, L. W. (1994). Resolving therapeutic alliance ruptures: A task analytic investigation. In A. O. Horvath & L. S. Greenberg (Eds.), *The working alliance: Theory, research, and practice* (pp. 225–255). New York: Wiley.

Schacht, T. E., & Henry, W. P. (1994). Modeling recurrent patterns of interpersonal relationship with the Structural Analysis of Social Behavior: SASB-CMP. *Psychotherapy Research, 4,* 208–221.

Schlessinger, N., & Robbins, F. (1975). The psychoanalytic process: Recurrent patterns of conflict and change in ego. *Journal of the American Psychoanalytic Association, 23,* 761–782.

Silberschatz, G., Fretter, P., & Curtis, J. (1986). How do interpretations influence the process of psychotherapy? *Journal of Consulting and Clinical Psychology, 54,* 646–652.

Tracey, T. J., & Kokotovic, A. M. (1989). Factor structure of the Working Alliance Inventory. *Psychological Assessment: A Journal of Consulting and Clinical Psychology, 1,* 207–210.

Wallerstein, R. S., & Robbins, L. L. (1956). Concepts: The psychotherapy research project of the Menninger Foundation. *Bulletin of the Menninger Clinic, 20,* 239–262.

7

Empathy

Changming Duan, Teresa B. Rose, and Rebecca A. Kraatz

University of Missouri at Kansas City

Most therapists would consider themselves empathic, but therapists from some theoretical orientations (e.g., humanistic) place considerable importance on empathy as a necessary ingredient of therapeutic change. Regardless of their theoretical orientation, however, all therapists need to understand their clients in order to discern client problems and build working relationships with them. Because most investigators of therapeutic empathy subscribe to a psychodynamic viewpoint, this chapter explores the concept of empathy from this perspective. As with all chapters in this volume, however, research findings and suggestions for clinical application are useful to therapists of all theoretical orientations.

Chapter Questions

- What is therapeutic empathy?
- How does empathy relate to therapy outcome?
- What therapist characteristics are associated with therapist empathy?
- How can empathy be taught to beginning clinicians and counselors?

In the history of professional psychotherapy and counseling, empathy as a clinical phenomenon as well as a psychological concept has held a salient and irreplaceable position. Researchers and practitioners both cherish this important, yet intriguing, concept. Voluminous research findings and writings have accumulated, and a large array of perspectives on this concept have been presented. Although the research findings concerning the therapeutic role of empathy have not been consistent (see Gladstein, 1987; Duan & Hill, 1996) and theoretical conceptions of empathy have not been unified (e.g., Moore, 1990; Sexton & Whiston, 1994), the general understanding of empathy has been enriched and improved by the research during the past few decades.

In this chapter, we present a review of the literature on the concept of empathy and its functions and predictors, summarize what we know or do not know about the nature and therapeutic role of empathy, and discuss ways in which we can apply what we know in clinical practice and training. The chapter is organized to address the following questions: What is empathy? What do we know about empathy and its functions and predictors? How can we apply what we know in clinical practice? And how can we learn or teach empathy?

Literature Review

Definitions of Empathy

Empathy is not a foreign term to those who are working or studying in the field of psychology or to those who are interested in understanding interpersonal relationships. Few would disagree, probably, that empathy is a pervasive human phenomenon that is ever-present in many aspects and levels of human interactions. Psychotherapy/counseling, as a special form of interpersonal interaction, is not exempt from empathy's influence. In fact, theories and empirical evidence have highlighted the necessity of empathy in positive therapeutic outcomes. Interestingly, however, the answer to the question "what is empathy?" has been debatable.

Historically, the term *empathy* and many of its descriptions derive from aesthetics (Post, 1980). Late in the nineteenth century, the Hegelians and the Herbartian objective philosophies of art and metaphysics faced a crisis in German aesthetics (Gilbert & Kuhn, 1939), and the artist had to turn to the working of the mind to account for the essential feature of human aesthetic contemplation of the world. The psychology of aesthetic appreciation was seen as involving a projection of the self into the beauty of the object (Wispe, 1987). Early in the twentieth century, the term *empathy* was coined to mean a feeling, or projection, of one's self into an object with social implications (Titchener, 1915).

Later theorists elaborated on the meaning of empathy. Kohler (1929) specified an empathic response as solely an observer's understanding of an individual's affect, whereas Mead (1934) moved empathy from the pure reactive–projective perspectives of the aesthetic scholars to a conscious, deliberate, role-taking action. He referred to empathy as "putting yourself in his place" (p. 366), which recognized the self–other differentiation as the heart of the empathic process. In contemporary psychology, where empathy found new life soon after the concept was introduced, various definitions emerged to describe empathy. For instance, Downey (1929) viewed empathy as a process of "feeling-in," (p. 76) Murphy (1947) called it "direct apprehension of the state of mind of another person...feeling as that other person does" (p. 985), and Allport (1961) defined it as "imaginative transposing of oneself into the thinking, feeling, and acting of another." (p. 536)

Despite the extensive history of development of the empathy construct in mainstream psychology, the concept of empathy seems to have developed independently in counseling and psychotherapy research. Psychotherapy and counseling theories "came onto empathy from their own practical, clinical experience" (Gladstein, 1984, p. 49). For example, relying primarily on his clinical experience, Freud (1921/1923) treated empathy as a therapeutic process in his identification–imitation–empathy formulation. Likewise, Rogers (1951, 1957, 1959) described empathy as one of several crucial conditions of therapy, focusing on the role-taking quality. In this chapter, we use "therapeutic empathy" or "therapist empathy" when discussing empathy in the context of psychotherapy or counseling.

As diverse as the therapeutic experiences of the theorists are, their views on therapeutic empathy are also diverse. To organize similarities as well as differences among various views of empathy, we briefly review them along two dimensions: *the stability* and *the nature* of empathy. Rather than focusing on discriminating and excluding theories from each other, we hope to promote an inclusive approach and delineate all relevant elements across theory lines that need to be considered in understanding the phenomenon of therapeutic empathy.

The Stability of Therapeutic Empathy: A Trait, an Experience, or a Process.

Generally, empathy has been viewed as a personality trait or general ability (e.g., Davis, 1983; Feshbach, 1975; Hoffman, 1982, 1984; Iannotti, 1975), as a situation-specific experience (e.g., Batson & Coke, 1981; Katz, 1963; Stotland, 1969), or as a process involving communication (e.g., Bohart & Greenberg, 1997; Hackney, 1978). In the context of psychotherapy/counseling, therapist empathy has also been studied and discussed as the therapist's ability to empathize (e.g., Hogan, 1969; Kerr, 1947; Rogers, 1949), as therapist experience of clients' feelings and thoughts (e.g., Kohut, 1959; Rogers, 1957; Truax & Carkhuff, 1967), and as the therapist's experiencing–communicating process consisting of different elements (e.g., Barrett-Lennard, 1981, 1993; Rogers, 1975). It is probably fair to say, based on the literature, that all of these types of empathy exist and each has its independent identity and plays its unique function in therapeutic relationships.

In the writing of those who are mainly concerned with individual differences, empathy refers to one's ability to take another's perspective or to feel another's emotions. Unsurprisingly, developmental psychologists find such a view appealing, because they are interested in how empathic ability is developed in individuals and why some individuals are more empathic than others. Drawn by the interest in knowing who are suited to be counselors and who are not, psychotherapy theorists see this perception as useful and functional too. For instance, Hogan (1969), who was interested in understanding "empathic disposition," "role-taking ability," and "social sensitivity" of therapists, viewed empathy as embodying "a dimension which includes social competence, intellectual promises and sense of self-worth" (p. 309). Rogers (1957), who probably deserves the most credit in bringing empathy to the psychological literature and counseling practices, once perceived empathy as a "basic ability" or an interpersonal orientation. For him, empathy as a relatively invariable trait may distinguish high- or low-facilitative counselors. Similarly, Buie (1981) defined empathy, from a psychoanalytic viewpoint, as a "human capacity to know another person's inner experience" (p. 282).

Because they are interested in understanding what may elicit empathy and how empathy feels to empathizers, many theorists believe empathy is a situation-specific experience. In other words, empathy refers to a specific experience, an experience elicited by observing another person's situation or experience. From this perspective, empathy is commonly defined as responding "vicariously" to a stimulus or a stimulus person (Batson & Coke, 1981; Katz, 1963; Stotland, 1969). Therapist empathic experience is viewed as sensing the client's private world "as if" it were one's own (Rogers, 1959; Truax & Carkhuff, 1967). Operationally, a match between the observer's and the stimulus person's affect or cognition (e.g. Feshbach & Roe, 1968; Stotland, 1969) or the degree to which a therapist understands and feels client experiences (e.g. Carkhuff, 1969; Truax & Carkhuff, 1967) has been used as a criterion to label empathy.

Empathy has also been viewed as an "emotional knowing," involving understanding or experiencing another person's feelings (Greenson, 1960), or "experience-near" attempts to understand the client's world (Bohart & Greenburg, 1997). To empathize indicates that one temporarily shares or experiences the feelings and views of the other person. In the early work of Rogers (1949, 1951, 1957, 1959), empathy was treated as a state of knowing "the internal frame of reference of another with accuracy and with the emotional components and meanings which pertain thereto as if one were the person, but without ever losing the 'as if' condition" (1959, pp. 210–211). By definition, Rogers indicated that empathy was voluntary and elicited by another's feeling state. Following Rogers, Truax and Carkhuff (1967) employed the psychoanalytic conception of accurate empathy defined as "trial identification." They believed that this "trial identification" allowed the counselor to "step into the patient's shoes and view the world from his emotional and perceptual vantage point" (p. 285) and "allows him for the moment to experience the world, events and significant people *as if* he were the client himself" (p. 285).

Instead of being perceived as an end product of an interpersonal interaction, therapeutic empathy is often defined in process terms that focus on the important moment-to-moment therapist empathic experiences. Freud (1921/1923) indicated that empathy could result from identification by way of imitation and involve attempts to fully apprehend the inner experiences of another and then to compare the experience with one's self. Similarly, Fliess (1942) discussed empathy as the process of transient introjection and projection to access "first-hand" (p. 212) another's experiences, and Fenichel (1945) defined empathy as an identification with another person, followed by an awareness of one's own feelings after the identification, and thus an awareness of the object's feelings. Stewart (1956) further expanded empathy into a multistage interpersonal process, including raw identification, deliberate identification, resistance, and deliberate reidentification.

In a stage theory form, Reik's (1948) described the four stages of empathy: identification, incorporation, reverberation, and detachment. He believed that the first three stages provided the observer with an extended opportunity to "try on" the target person's ongoing emotional experience, whereas the detachment stage allowed the observer to gain distance from the other to engage in cognitive analysis. The earlier stages reflected more affective elements, whereas the last stage specified a cognitive process. Similar to this stage model, Emery (1987) viewed empathy as "a multistage process involving the therapist's affective attunements and their subsequent transformations into a series of inferences, judgements, and provisional working models of the patient's psychic reality" (p. 514).

In more recent literature, Rogers (1975) offered his description of the empathic process as involving "being sensitive, moment to moment, to the changing felt meanings which flow in this other person...to whatever he/she is experiencing" (p. 4). According to him, empathy "means temporarily living in" (p. 4) this other person's life and "includes communicating your sensing of his/her world as you look with fresh and unfrightened eyes" (p. 4). This definition implied two stages: (1) temporarily living in the client's life and (2) communicating the sensing of that life to the client. Similarly, Barrett-Lennard (1981, 1993) postulated and elaborated a cyclical model, which treated empathy as a complex and multisided phenomenon. The model delineates a cycle of processes through which empathy is experienced and expressed: therapist empathy set, therapist experiences empathic resonation, communicating empathy to client, client receives empathy, and client feedback. This model not only considers the empathizer's inner process of empathic reaction to others but also includes the empathizer's communicational act and the receiver's reactions to empathy as distinct stages in empathic interactions.

The Nature of Empathy: Cognitive, Affective, or Multicomponent.

Theories of empathy also vary on the view of the nature of empathy, whether it is seen as a trait or an experience. Some see it as primarily affective (e.g., Allport, 1961; Mehrabian & Epstein, 1972; Stotland, 1969) and others as mainly cognitive (e.g., Barrett-Lennard, 1981; Borke, 1971; Kalliopuska, 1986; Katz, 1963; Rogers, 1959, 1986; Woodall & Kogler-Hill, 1982). A third view holds that empathy contains both cognitive and affective elements (e.g., Hoffman, 1977; Shantz, 1975) or that it can be either cognitive or affective depending on the situation (e.g., Gladstein, 1983). As pointed out by Duan and Hill (1996), all of these observations are valid and both cognitive and affective elements are identifiable in empathy.

Empathy is probably most commonly understood as one person's experience of another person's emotions. Expressions such as "the sharing of another's emotion," an "emotional reaction," or a "vicarious emotion" are often discernable in writings about empathy. For example, the psychologists, who are interested in the role of empathy in social behaviors, explicitly called empathy "an observer's reacting emotionally because he perceives that another is experiencing or is about to experience an emotion" (Stotland, 1969, p. 272) or "an emotional response elicited by and congruent with the perceived welfare of someone else" (Batson & Coke, 1981, p. 169). In the eyes of some psychoanalysts, empathy has been traditionally viewed as identification with affective connotations (Fenichel, 1945; Freud, 1921/1923; Stewart, 1956) such as an emotion linkage (Sullivan, 1940) or "taking in the other's ego" as "for the time being, a part of your ego" (Reik, 1949, p. 112).

In therapeutic empathy research, more attention has been paid to the cognitive aspect than the affective aspect of empathy. Following Mead's (1934) view of empathy as a human "capacity to take the role of the other person" and as "putting yourself in his place" (p. 366), the "role-taking" and "transposing oneself into the thinking, feeling and acting of another" (Dymond, 1950, p. 344) became the central focus of therapeutic empathy theories. An example would be Rogers' (1949) theory that made the distinction clear between "empathic identification" and "emotional identification," indicating that empathy did not necessarily imply an emotional tie with the other. For him, empathic identification occurred when "the counselor is perceiving the hopes and fears of the client through immersion in an empathic process" (p. 86). Later he defined empathy as perceiving "the internal frame of reference of another with accuracy" (1959, p. 210). Similarly, Truax and Carkhuff's (1967) theory of accurate empathy also focused on the degree to which therapists successfully assumed the internal frame of reference of clients.

Although the views of empathy as a cognitive or an affective phenomenon may seem incompatible, the difference between the extreme theories may not be as great as it appears. One argument is that the difference may be attributable to whether empathy is considered in *product* or *process* terms (Feshbach, 1975; Strayer, 1987). For example, empathy as a product could be defined as an affective (or cognitive) state, whereas the process that leads to the state could be cognitive (or affective). Feshbach (1975) asserted that affective processes and cognitive responses could potentially mediate each other, and it could be "an almost arbitrary decision to specify the sequence of affect and cognition" in empathy (p. 25). Thus, it makes good sense to talk about "components" of empathy (Strayer, 1987).

Although they may still differ in the viewed dominance of each component, most authors agree that both affective and cognitive components are involved in empathy. Some would view the involvement in "product" as well as in "process" terms, however, and others would focus on this involvement as a "process" that precedes the product of empathy only. Katz (1963), for instance, postulates the presence of both affective and cognitive elements in the whole experience of empathy in that "we see, we feel, we respond and we understand as if we were, in fact, the other person" (p. 3). Kohut (1984) described empathy as both an information-collecting activity and as an emotional reaction necessary for being successfully supportive and therapeutic.

Greenson (1960) also described a dual process of empathy—intuition, in which one needs intuition to get ideas and empathy to reach feelings. He did not think empathy and intuition always go hand-in-hand, but he did believe that the best therapists had both. This description of intuition and empathy resembles the description of affective and cognitive components of empathy by others. Schafer (1959) used the term *generative empathy* to describe a comprehensive phenomenon involving both affective and cognitive activities in therapy. On the one hand, he considered experiencing the client's feelings to have a dual role in therapeutic treatment: the re-creation of affect through recall of how it felt to be in a similar past situation and a countertransferential affective reaction. On the other hand, he considered cognitive analytic functions to be necessary to provide distance and perspective from the object, thereby enhancing its reality. For Schafer, the cognitive component of empathy allowed for perceptual attention to cues and inferences about the affective precursors of the situation, and the affective component involved affective reactions.

To minimize the confusion caused by different conceptions of empathy, Gladstein (1983) formally introduced the terms *affective empathy* and *cognitive empathy*. Cognitive empathy was defined as "intellectually taking the role or perspective of another person" and affective empathy as "responding with the same emotion to another person's emotion" (p. 468). Although this differentiation provided a useful framework for empathy research, Duan and Hill (1996) noted that the terms used were not precise or descriptive enough and could represent a false dichotomy when the arguments about the inseparability of cognitive and affective elements of empathy were considered. Believing that the two types of empathy are identifiable and coexist, they proposed that *intellectual empathy* and *empathic emotion* be used instead. These terms will be used in the remaining portion of this chapter.

As a relatively new trend, researchers have become interested in integrating different views into a multidimensional construct of therapeutic empathy. These investigators (Barrett-Lennard, 1981; Greenberg & Elliott, 1997; Rogers, 1975) believe that empathy involves not only sensitively comprehending and experiencing a client's affective and cognitive world but also accurately and adequately communicating the understanding to the client, namely, communicating the sensing. Barrett-Lennard (1981) included communication as a major component of his empathy model, believing that the communication of empathic reactions is a distinct phase directly involved in the process of rational empathy. In his review article, Hackney (1978) noticed an increase in the stress put on empathy as a communication skill.

Although *empathy* has been used as an umbrella term and appears an elusive construct, some identifiable and common elements of empathy can be extrapolated from various theories. It is probably unarguable at this point that empathy may involve a cognitive aspect (intellectual empathy) and an affective aspect (empathic emotion). Particularly in the context of psychotherapy, empathy communication process is also involved, and how the client perceives the empathy should be considered. As Bohart and Greenberg (1997) summarized, empathy involves understanding, experiencing, and communicating. These elements can be examined and discussed together or separately.

Empirical Findings of Empathy Research

Therapist Empathy and Therapeutic Outcome. As a part of the modernist tradition in Western psychology, researchers examined the role of empathy in psychotherapy/counseling through empirical observations, following Carl Roger's (1957) discussion of empathy as one of the "necessary and sufficient conditions of therapeutic personality change" (p. 95). Significant efforts were devoted to proving the facilitative functions of empathy in achieving positive therapeutic outcomes. The typical research paradigm used in such outcome studies was measuring and correlating counselor/therapist empathy and client outcome. Empathy was usually measured by therapist/counselor self-report, client perception, or observer's ratings, and outcome was determined by client self-reported feelings, client perceived quality of therapist–client relationship, client or counselor evaluation of the helpfulness of the treatment, or by symptom reduction as measured by objective standard tests (e.g., Minnesota Multiphasic Personality Inventory [MMPI]) after the interview or treatment. Research findings, by and large, have confirmed that empathy plays important roles in positive client changes (e.g., Cabush & Edwards, 1976; Gomez-Schwartz, 1978; Jones, Wynne, & Watson, 1986; Lafferty, Beutler, & Crago, 1989; Luborsky, Chandler, Auerbach, Cohen, & Bachrach, 1971; Miller, Taylor, & West, 1980; Truax & Carkhuff, 1967).

This conclusion, however, has not gone without being challenged. Inconsistent research results have been cited (e.g., Parloff, Waskow, & Wolfe, 1978). After reviewing a large amount of empirical findings, Bergin and Lambert (1978) pointed out that the relationship between empathy and outcome "was more ambiguous than was once believed" (p. 167). Bergin and Suinn (1975) concluded that empathy (and other facilitative conditions) were not sufficient for bringing out positive outcome "except in highly specific, client-centered type conditions" (p. 462). Similarly, Lambert and Bergin (1992) believed these conditions were more relevant for milder disorders than for more severe disturbances.

The fact that research findings are neither sufficient nor consistent in addressing the issue about whether empathy is a necessary and sufficient condition for positive client change can be partially explained by the limitations of the available methodology and research tools. Because a therapeutic relationship, where empathy plays a crucial role, is always present in psychotherapy/counseling, it is methodologically difficult, if not impossible, to examine whether empathy is necessary. In addressing the sufficiency of empathy in therapy, research has not been able to provide convincing cause–effect evidence (Duan & Hill, 1996). Nevertheless, the available evidence and theoretical reasoning do seem to support the conclusion that empathy is necessary for any form of psychotherapy where a therapeutic relationship is required (Patterson, 1984). Even in extreme situations, such as behavioral therapy or cognitive retraining, empathy is theoretically necessary. Without empathy there will be no accurate understanding of what the client needs or what can serve as a reinforcer or incentive to encourage changes. The sufficiency of empathy, however, may be more situation specific. It may be sufficient in some forms of therapy but not in others.

Predictors of Therapist Empathy.   As mentioned earlier, empathy both as a human ability and as a situation-specific experience has elicited researchers' interest. The examination of predictors of either type of empathy implies that some individuals are more empathic than others. Assuming that the understanding of individual characteristics that are associated with high empathy may be helpful in empathy training, empirical research has examined, in relation to empathic ability and experience, a number of personal characteristic variables, including gender and sex-role orientation, cognitive complexity, personality types, communication style, cognitive antecedents of empathic emotion, and cultural values.

Gender and Sex-Role Orientation.   Although the research findings are not consistent, many researchers believe that women are more empathic than men when empathy is defined in affective terms (Eisenberg & Lennon, 1983; Feshbach & Roe, 1968; Hoffman, 1977). There is no consistent evidence showing gender differences when empathy is assessed as taking another's perspective. Some studies showed that female counselors were more empathic than their male counterparts (e.g., Kimberlin and Friesen, 1977) and some found no gender differences (e.g., Carlozzi & Hurlburt, 1982; Petro & Hansen, 1977). Recently, research attention has been turned to the sex-role orientation defined as a self-endorsement of masculine or feminine behaviors (Bem, 1974) as a predictor of counselor empathy. Carlozzi and Hurlburt (1982) discovered that endorsement of feminine traits was positively related to empathic emotion, whereas endorsement of masculine traits was not related to empathy. Fong and Borders (1985) found that the masculine sex-role oriented trainees were rated less effective than the undifferentiated sex-role oriented trainees on empathy and other counseling skills.

Cognitive Complexity.   In counseling settings, researchers have demonstrated a positive correlation between counselors' cognitive complexity level and counselors' ability to empathize with their clients. For example, evidence has been presented that high-conceptual-level counselors expressed significantly higher levels of empathy toward clients than did low-conceptual-level counselors (Alcorn and Torney, 1982; Lutwak and Hennessy, 1982). In addition, Blaas and Heck (1978) discovered that low-conceptual-level counselors were significantly more empathic with a personal/emotional client than with a vocational client. Much of this research was analogue and empathy was assessed as more of a cognitive phenomenon. Thus, the generalizability of the conclusions to real counseling practice remains to be demonstrated.

Personality Types.   Research has shown that empathy is related to some personality variables, such as level of self-esteem, personality type (Type A versus Type B), ego development, and self-monitoring. When empathy was defined and measured in affective terms, Nemoto (1973) discovered that it was positively associated with high self-esteem when the perceived status of others was low and with low self-esteem when the perceived status of others was high. Davis (1983) found that both perspective-taking and personal distress aspects of empathy were modestly related to self-esteem. Individuals with higher self-esteem were more able to take another's perspective and experienced less personal distress than those with lower self-esteem.

Participants in the study by Kulberg and Franco (1975) rated their partners as more empathic when they were both either Type A or Type B than when they were of different personality types, and those with Type B personality were rated by their partners as more empathic than Type A individuals. Gillam and McGinley's (1983) study also found that B-type participants elicited higher levels of empathy when they interacted with other B-type participants whereas any dyad that contained an A-type resulted in a lower level of empathy when compared to the empathy found in B–B dyads.

Ego development was also found to be a predictor of empathic ability (Pecukonis, 1990). The level of ego development was found to be positively related to empathic emotion. Moreover, Mill (1984) discovered that high self-monitoring individuals were less empathic than low self-monitoring individuals. Mill speculated that "an accurate empathic response requires a responsive and genuine interplay with another" (p. 381). Compared with high self-monitoring individuals, the low self-monitors had communication styles that were more genuine and responsive, which may enhance their ability to express empathy.

Communication Style.   When clients' perceived empathy was considered, both verbal and nonverbal communication variables became significant predictors. For instance, the therapist's linguistic style, such as use of sophisticated polysyllabic language (Barrington, 1961) and concreteness of wording (Schauble & Pierce, 1974), was found to be positively related to clients' ratings of counselors' empathic understanding. Suit and Paradise (1985) noted that the use of narrative analogy increased the level of empathy perceived by the client. In Barkham and Shapiro's (1986) clinical research, counselors' use of fewer general advisements was perceived as more empathic. Hermansson, Webster, and McFarland (1988), through an analogue study, demonstrated that communication of empathy was facilitated by counselors' nonverbal behavior—deliberate posture shift to leaning forward.

Cognitive Antecedents of Empathic Emotion.   Differing from most of the other studies, Stotland (1969) and his colleagues examined perspective-taking, perceived similarity, and other cognitive antecedents of affective empathy. By manipulating the degree of perspective-taking, they demonstrated that perspective-taking increased empathic emotion (measured by palmar sweating). This finding led to Stotland's conclusion that "any interpersonal process, symbolic or overt, which causes an individual to imagine himself in another's position would lead him to empathize (affectively) with the other person" (p. 297). Consistently, participants reacted more strongly to a person under stress, who was doing a similar task, than to a stressed person who was working on a dissimilar task in a study by Stotland & Dunn (1963). Similarly, Houston (1990) demonstrated that similarity in cognitive representations of the self could lead to empathy. When exposed to a target displaying either dejection or agitation because of certain cognitive representations of the self, participants who shared the similar representation experienced more intellectual empathy and empathic emotion.

Cultural Values.   The understanding of the affect of cultural values or cultural value differences between the person who empathizes and the person to be empathized with is at a preembryonic stage. Some preliminary research findings, however, seem to support Duan and Hill's (1996) hypothesis that individuals, including counselors, holding different cultural values may be differentially ready to empathize with others endorsing different values. Duan, Geen, Wei, and Wang (2000) reported that collectivism was positively correlated with dispositional intellectual empathy and empathic emotion, but individualism was not. In addition, collectivism predicted experienced empathic emotion and individualism predicted experienced intellectual empathy. In examining empathic experiences in cultural contexts, Rose and Duan (1999) found that when the "client" had difficulty saying "no" to her mother concerning her career choice, empathic emotion was found to be related to observers' individualistic values. Further, the evidence that empathic emotion can be induced through "cultural sensitivity training" (Wade & Bernstein, 1991) or "cultural role taking" (Scott & Borodovsky, 1990) also supports the assumption that cultural values have a role in empathy. Being able to appreciate another's cultural values and customs may enable the individual to empathize with that person.

There is support for the central position of therapeutic empathy in psychotherapy and counseling and for the claim that some individuals tend to be more empathic than others and that situational factors such as individuals' cultural values and communication methods may affect experienced empathy. Such information can be used to inform clinical practice of counseling in that therapists should make conscious efforts to empathize with the client, emotionally as well as intellectually, and that our training programs should teach trainees empathy skills.

What We Know About Therapeutic Empathy and Its Functions

Although the outcomes of empathy research have not been conclusive or sufficient because of the complexity of the construct and various theoretical disagreements among researchers (Duan & Hill, 1996; Gladstein, 1983), a certain level of understanding of therapeutic empathy has been achieved through both empirical and clinical observations. These observations, by and large, have confirmed the belief that empathy is important or necessary in bringing about positive therapy outcomes (e.g., Rogers, 1949, 1951, 1975; Gladstein, 1987). We summarize what we understand about therapeutic empathy in this section, hoping that the knowledge can be applied in the counseling and psychotherapy practice.

Empathy as a Necessary Therapeutic Condition.   Many theorists see empathy as a necessary condition (Bohart & Greenberg, 1997), a prerequisite (Freud, 1921/1923), an "enabling factor" (Hamilton, 1995), or an "enabler" (Schlien, 1997) in psychotherapy and therapeutic relationships. In both the theoretical and empirical literature, the therapeutic relationship between the client and the therapist has been viewed and proven to contribute to the success of the therapeutic process and outcome (e.g., Gelso & Carter, 1994; Luborsky et al., 1971; Orlinsky & Howard, 1986). In this relationship, empathy, regardless of how it is defined, holds an unarguably important position. For Rogers (1959), empathy allows the therapist to understand the client's world; for Kohut (1959), empathy is the basis for forming an analyst–patient emotional bond; for Mahrer (1996), empathy determines the therapist–client alignment; and for O'Hara and Jordan (1997), there is no therapeutic relationship without an empathic therapist. Barrett-Lennard (1981) views empathy as having the power of dissolving client fear and denial; Jenkins (1997) believes empathy is necessary in providing safety for the client and leading to client self-disclosure; and Bohart and Greenberg (1997) highlight empathy as the process "by which therapist and client dialogue, share, codiscover, and cocreate new meaning" (p. 440).

Although the necessity of empathy for psychotherapy has not been sufficiently addressed by empirical research, the belief of it has been unchallenged and widely endorsed by theorists, researchers, and practitioners. Knowing the nature of therapist–client interactions in psychotherapy, it is not hard to be convinced that empathy is the basis for a helpful therapeutic relationship. Even in therapies that were traditionally viewed as not being interested in the concept of empathy, such as cognitive, or behavioral therapies, empathy has recently been recognized as necessary (Franks, 1994). From the perspective of a dialectical behavior therapy, Linehan (1993, 1997) described empathy as necessary for clinical validation of the client and his or her behavior, a key element of the therapy. Beck, Rush, Shaw, and Emery (1979) also recognized the importance of therapist empathy in therapeutic relationship building.

Empathy as the Basis for Understanding.   No one would argue that the therapist's understanding of the client is important in psychotherapy. Understanding a client fully and accurately is probably not possible without therapist empathy, which serves roles as fundamental as gathering information and providing observations for understanding. Carl Rogers (1951), the creator of person-centered therapy, first noted the crucial role of therapist empathy in reaching a deep, nonjudgmental understanding of the client. For him, therapist understanding of the client was through "entering the private perceptual world of the other...being sensitive, moment by moment, to the changing felt meanings which flow in this other person" (Rogers, 1980, p. 142). As observed by Bozarth (1990), empathy's role is so central in Rogerian therapy that the therapist would not have goals for the client, and would simply go with the client, in the client's ways of thinking, feeling, and processing, and at the client's pace.

The essential role of empathy in therapeutic understanding is also a center piece in Kohut's psychoanalytical theory. He promoted empathy and believed that "to think and feel oneself into the inner life of another person" (Kohut, 1984, p. 82) was the crucial process leading to understanding. He believed that psychological data were understood by introspection and empathy as physical phenomena were grasped by our senses. Through clinical observations and demonstrations, Kohut drew attention to the experience-near mode of observing as the methodology by which analysts accessed and observed a patient's inner, psychological life. From this perspective, it is impossible to completely understand a patient's experience, which may encompass a complex blend of inner responses without empathy, and this understanding is one of the two steps that constitutes psychoanalysis process. It should be noted, however, Kohut's self-psychology does not view empathy as experience-near observation to mean being "nice" or "kind," but rather, to be the key to in-depth understanding of the inner life of patients (MacIsaac, 1997).

Other theories, such as phenomenological and existential counseling theories, also recognize empathy as the basis for understanding the client. For instance, in Adlerian therapy, the therapist's understanding of the client's lifestyle is achieved through empathy, which involves attention to feelings as well as beliefs of the client (Scharf, 1996). Similarly, Vanaerschot (1997) views empathy as a specific way of knowing. Through empathy the therapist's inner experience may come to resemble as closely as possible the client's. Without this process, the therapist will not be able truly to understand the client. Viewing empathy as a temporary merger of the counselor and client ego and psychic state, May (1989) believes that the art of counseling lies in therapist empathy. From an existential perspective, without internally experiencing what the client experiences (feelings, thoughts), the desirable and therapeutic therapist understanding can not be obtained (Havens, 1986).

Empathy as a Therapeutic Curative Agent.   Although some may find the statement that empathy is a sufficient condition for positive therapeutic change provocative, empathy has been viewed as a therapeutic curative agent. In the view of Rogers' (1975) person-centered therapy, the client's perception of the therapist's experiencing of acceptant, empathic understanding is one of the primary growth-facilitating ingredients in psychotherapy sufficient for therapeutic change. With the recognition of the individual's universal, developmental need for empathy and need to self-actualize, Rogers believed that when therapist empathy was received, therapeutic outcome would occur in which

> (1) The non-evaluative and acceptant quality of the empathic climate enables the client, as we have seen, to take a prizing, caring attitude toward himself. (2) Being listened to by an understanding person makes it possible for him to listen more accurately to himself, with greater empathy towards his own visceral experiencing, his own vague felt meanings. But (3) his greater understanding of, and prizing of, himself opens up part of a more accurately based self. His self is now more congruent with his experiencing. Thus, he has become, in his attitudes toward himself, more caring and acceptant, more empathic and understanding, more real and congruent. (pp. 7–9)

According to Rogers (1980), therapist empathy "dissolves alienation" and leads the client to feel "valued, cared for, accepted" as the person that he or she is.

Kohut seems to share with Rogers the linkage between the idea of a developmental need for empathy and the nature of therapeutic "cure" (see Eagle & Wolitzky, 1997). He saw empathic understanding as the essential therapeutic ingredient and as a curative agent. He described the cure as "the opening of a path of empathy between self and self object, specifically, the establishment of empathic in-tuneness between self and self object on more mature adult levels" (Kohut, 1984, p. 66). As noted by Eagle and Wolitzky, in Kohut's account of the therapeutic process, "positive change is as much due to the therapist's failures (albeit optimal failures) in empathy, as to the therapist's provision of empathy" (p. 241). The patient's working through reactions to therapist empathy failures may ultimately lead to the increasing acquisition of psychic structure.

Outside of the person-centered therapy and self-psychology traditions, there are other views of empathy as having curative functions. For example, from an experiential perspective, Warner (1997) noted that empathy can be curative because "it generates a particular sense of experiential recognition within the receiver—both the sense of being recognized in one's experience of the moment by another human being and the sense of recognizing one's own experience in the moment" (p. 130), and allows clients who have experienced empathic failure in childhood "to reconnect with previously thwarted developmental processes" (p. 139).

Therapeutic Empathy as a Clinical Intervention.   "Empathic responses" have been seen as important and effective interventions. Empathy can provide the therapist connections with the client and a means of communicating to the client that "I understand you" or "I am with you." From the humanistic and existential perspectives, feeling understood is probably the most helpful and most fundamental outcome that a client can get out of psychotherapy or counseling. Rogerian therapies would rely on empathic responses to communicate genuineness and unconditional acceptance, and Adlerians would use empathic responses to "reflect the acknowledgment of the lifestyle" (Scharf, 1996, p. 137).

Empathy is a major component of the second major clinical step of psychoanalysis "explaining" for Kohut, who believed that explaining "must include the experience-near ingredient for it to encompass the fullness of the patient's experience" (MacIsaac, 1997, p. 252). Whether an explanation captures the fullness of the patient's experience is contingent on whether the explanation is given with sensitivity to the patient's vulnerabilities as well as the patient's psychological readiness to hear a higher-level empathic intervention (MacIsaac, 1997). In Kohut's view, only empathic explanations can help the client work through "empathic failures" or "frustrations" stemming from "faulty empathy," which is the key in building a healthy psychological structure.

Because empathy is the basis for understanding, one can conclude that there is no effective intervention without empathy and all effective interventions have to be empathic. This conclusion is also true for therapies that view building healthy therapeutic relationships as the most important therapeutic intervention. Without empathy, there will be no meaningful therapeutic relationships, and thus, no useful therapeutic interventions. Empathy in these therapies is indeed a single factor that forms the basis for therapy and determines the effectiveness of clinical interventions.

What Else We Need to Know About Empathy

Although the significant role of empathy in psychotherapy and counseling has been widely recognized, there are still important questions that are yet to be answered before we can clearly understand how empathy develops and operates in therapy. In the following sections, we identify areas in which research and further understanding are necessary.

The Relationship Between Intellectual Empathy and Empathic Emotion.   Many empathy theories recognize that intellectual empathy and empathic emotion are identifiable and separate elements of empathic experience, and they refer to different psychological processes (Duan & Hill, 1996; Gladstein, 1983; Smither, 1977). However, little research has been done to understand the interaction between the two. It is not clear how a therapist's feeling of the client's emotions affects the therapist's intellectual understanding of the client's concerns, or vice versa, or how this interaction (or lack of interaction) affects the therapist's observation and understanding of the client. One could argue that taking a person's perspective and feeling his or her emotions should be related because they both involve reactions to the same situation. Thus, the better one understands another, the more likely he or she will experience the other's emotions or vice versa. For instance, perceiving a client as being angry is probably not sufficient to lead to the therapist's feeling anger without understanding why the client is angry, but knowing the exact anger-provoking circumstances may cause empathic anger even if the angry person is not present. Equally likely, someone who has never felt suicidal probably cannot understand a suicidal person's perspective accurately, and experiencing someone's depression may increase the understanding of the situation from that person's perspective. Understanding the relationship between the two types of empathy can help us understand the limits of, as well as the different mechanisms involved in, each type of empathy.

Indirect research evidence has suggested that cognitive processes can influence emotional processes. For instance, changing depressive patients' cognitions may lead to alleviation of the entire depressive complex, including mood and vegetative signs (Beck, 1967). The perception of a victim's innocence may increase empathic response in the observer (Hoffman, 1984). In an analogue study, Krulewitz (1982) showed that participants reacted to a rape victim more empathically when the rape was committed by a stranger than by a date. It seems that the different knowledge of the situation leads to different attributions of responsibility, which in turn leads to different empathic responses to the victim's emotions.

Research has also shown that affective state can influence cognitive activities. A happy mood was facilitative of learning and memorizing positive information and of making positive judgments about the stimuli, whereas a negative mood had the opposite effect (Bower, 1983; Forgas & Bower, 1987; Snyder & White, 1982). In a study of the effect of mood on person-perception, Forgas and Bower discovered that happy subjects formed more favorable impressions and made more positive judgments of a stimulus person than did subjects in a bad mood. People in a happy mood were found to be charitable, loving, and positive in interpreting information about others (Bower), and happy judges made more lenient judgments and more situational attributions of a transgression when the transgressor had a good excuse to violate a law than did depressed judges (Duan, 1988). In psychotherapy, clients' positive presession mood was positively related to their judgments of therapist helpfulness and depth of the session (Hill, Thompson, Cogar, & Denman, 1993).

Studying both intellectual empathy and empathic emotion as separate but related phenomena seems reasonable. We speculate that intellectual empathy and empathic emotion may be related sometimes and under some circumstances. It is important to understand the conditions under which these two types of empathy are related or not related in psychotherapy, so that therapists can recognize and use their experience of intellectual empathy and empathic emotion effectively.

Roles of Client Emotions in Therapeutic Empathy.   Some emotions may be easier to empathize with than others, intellectually or emotionally. One can speculate that positive emotions may be more likely to elicit empathic emotion than negative ones, because feeling positive emotions is rewarding. Some preliminary research findings support this speculation. Participants of an analogue study reported more empathic emotions when the "client" was experiencing positive emotions than when the "client" was experiencing negative emotions (Duan, 1992). There are circumstances, however, where observers feel more empathic toward someone with negative emotions than someone with positive emotions. For instance, many people feel more empathic when watching or reading tragedies than comedies. There may be egoistic needs in humans other than hedonic needs. In many cultures, the norm exists that one should show empathy to people who suffer. Consequently, individuals are socialized to feel good about themselves for empathizing with others who are suffering.

Based on this reasoning and evidence, we speculate that therapist intellectual empathy and empathic emotion are subject to the affect of the client emotions. The nature of emotions, pleasant or unpleasant, probably influences the likelihood and amount of intellectual empathy and empathic emotion. Assuming that humans are generally pleasure seeking, pleasant target emotions may be more likely to elicit empathic emotion than unpleasant ones, whereas negative emotions may be more likely to elicit intellectual empathy than positive ones, because intellectually taking the perspective of someone who is suffering is probably not as aversive as feeling the negative emotions. Besides, being intellectually empathic with others may make one feel good about oneself. In terms of empathic emotion, feeling an aversive emotion is more difficult than feeling a nonaversive emotion. The former may not only require recalling one's unpleasant past experience of the emotion, but may also affect one's current mood. If the negative emotion is not too aversive or difficult to feel (e.g., sadness), however, people would be likely to feel empathic emotion.

Obviously, emotions differ in aspects other than pleasantness. Some emotions may develop earlier in life and be more readily felt than others (Oatley & Johnson-Laird, 1987), and some emotions cost more to experience than others (Smith & Ellsworth, 1985). Thus, emotions vary in their ability and strength to elicit intellectual empathy and empathic emotion, and individuals are more susceptible to some emotions than to others when empathizing with another person. Therapeutic empathy is probably no exception. Therapists may be more prone to feel certain client emotions than others and more able to understand some client emotions than others. A good understanding of the role of client emotion in therapist empathy is necessary for therapists to use their felt emotions therapeutically and watch for the "weak spots" in their empathic experience.

The Role of Motivation to Empathize.   To answer questions such as whether people empathize with others spontaneously, or when and why and under what situations they do or do not empathize, we need to understand the role of motivation in empathic experiences. The fact that the induction of empathy, intellectually or emotionally or both, has been achieved through "empathy instructions" in experimental studies (e.g., Stotland, 1969) seems to imply that motivation may facilitate empathy. But whether motivation is necessary and how important its role is in determining the amount of experienced empathy is not clear.

In discussing the functional relations between cognition, motivation, and emotion, Lazarus (1991) argues that "without a goal and personal stake in a transaction, an encounter will not generate an emotion" (p. 824). He believed that a motivational element, an appraisal of personal stake, is both necessary and sufficient in any felt emotion in an interpersonal encounter. This argument can be borrowed to support the assumption that empathic emotion may, to an extent, be regulated by the person's motivation, which is based on the appraisal of what is happening for personal well-being in a given situation.

Lazarus' (1991) argument emphasized the necessity of cognitive activities and motivation in emotion and failed to make any clear point concerning possible influence of appraisal on cognitive activities, such as intellectual empathy. Because intellectual empathy is other-centered, it is reasonable to argue for a positive influence of motivation. To empathize intellectually with someone may also involve personal implications. As shown by the exploratory findings of Duan (2000), motivation to empathize increased participants' intellectual empathy toward someone experiencing a negative emotion but not toward the one experiencing a positive emotion. The social expectation exists that we should empathize with those who suffer. Again, empirical findings are necessary to address the issue concerning the role of motivation, which may help therapists identify possible reasons why they feel too much or too little empathy in a given relationship and may also help with empathy training programs.

Cultural Differences in Experience of Empathy. Cultural considerations regarding how one evaluates a situation and determines the gain or cost of a transaction to personal well-being is relevant in understanding intellectual empathy and empathic emotion. Unfortunately, little attention has been given to this area of research in the literature. If the assumption about the presence of the effect of motivation is accepted, researchers need to examine individual and cultural differences in values, commitment, and appraisal standards, which are always present in situational evaluations. For instance, observing someone willing to take personal pain to please a group leader may result in more positive appraisal and stronger motivation to empathize for someone from a collectivistic culture than for someone from an individualistic culture. Certain reactive emotions, such as shame and guilt, may be perceived as more or less understandable or reasonable in some cultures than in others (Markus & Kitayama, 1991).

Theoretically, the role of individuals' cultural values in their decision to empathize and ability to empathize is apparent. The human value system may affect individuals' perception, situation evaluation, and judgment as well as their ability to experience and express emotions. For instance, having family conflicts may be perceived as more disturbing in some cultures than in others, as is the expression of certain emotions. If an observer cannot appreciate another's plight or fortune, or does not see the other's emotions as acceptable for the given situation, it is unrealistic to expect the person to experience empathy. Although counselors are always expected to empathize with their clients regardless of their values, their ability and readiness to empathize with clients who subscribe to different cultural values can be expected to vary. As the demand for multicultural counseling increases, the need to understand cultural differences in empathy increases. When working with culturally different clients, counselors' appraisal of clients' situation, attitudes toward the counselor–client relationship, and motivation to empathize become particularly important. Thus, both counseling practice and clinical empathy training will have to be enriched by a good understanding of the role of culture in empathy.

Empathic Readiness and Empathic Experience. Do empathic dispositions predict counselors' experienced empathy toward clients? Theoretically, the answer should be positive. That is, high intellectual empathic responsiveness should lead to high intellectual empathy, and high emotional empathic readiness should predict high empathic emotion.

Some limited evidence exists that emotional predispositions influence emotional reactions to targets in areas such as personal distress (Archer, Diaz-Loving, Gollwitzer, Davis, & Foushee, 1981) and feelings of sympathy (Davis, 1983). But the extent to which these emotional reactions reflect clinical empathic emotion and the role of intellectual empathic responsiveness in therapist empathy is not clear.

Empathic dispositions may predict the frequency of felt empathy (Iannotti, 1975), but in given situations or under certain circumstances empathic readiness may not always lead to empathic experience. Those who are high in empathic readiness may also be more sensitive to the cost and gain of empathizing in a given situation than those who are low in empathic readiness. According to the principle of social exchange (e.g., Blau, 1964), when the cost is perceived to be too high, one may not involve him- or herself in empathic experience in certain situations. It can also be inferred that those sensitive individuals may be more sensitive to the influence of other factors, such as the nature and intensity of the target's emotion, value conflicts, moral standards, and external expectations of them being empathic. In counseling and psychotherapy, it is reasonable to believe that the relationship between empathic disposition and empathic experience may also be influenced by therapist professional judgment.

Helpful Empathy Versus Unhelpful Empathy.   Therapist empathy has not been viewed as always being helpful (e.g., Gladstein, 1983). Duan and Hill (1996) speculated that perhaps some kinds of empathy are helpful but others are not, or that empathy may be helpful in some situations but not in others. They also speculated that there may be an optimal level of empathy and that too much or too little is unhelpful. It is clinically valuable that we understand (1) What types of empathy are helpful and what are not? (2) What are the situations in which a certain type of empathy is helpful or not? (3) What is the client's role in determining the effectiveness of any type of empathy? and (4) How much empathy is optimal?

In studying client-perceived therapist empathy, Bachelor (1988) discovered that different clients perceive therapist empathy as different types. Some found the therapist's accurate recognition of the client's ongoing innermost experience, state, and motivation as empathy; some perceived the therapist's participation in the client's ongoing feeling as being empathic; some saw the therapist's self-disclosing as empathy; and some viewed the therapist's being supportive, totally attentive, and present in the relationship as being empathic. Clients in each of these groups expressed different levels of desirable effects of the empathy they perceived. These findings support the inference that different clients have different psychological needs for empathy from the therapist. The therapist's empathy will not be helpful if it does not fit the client's needs.

The timing and context of empathy and empathy communication are important factors to consider (Duan & Hill, 1996). The research on the accuracy of therapists in perceiving clients' reactions by Hill and her colleagues (e.g., Hill et al., 1993; Thompson & Hill, 1991) supports the argument that empathy may be helpful sometimes but not always. They measured the accuracy of therapists' perceptions of clients' reactions (intellectual empathy) and found that when clients had negative reactions to therapists' interventions, accurate therapists will be rated low in helpfulness. If clients' reactions are positive, however, accurate therapists were perceived as helpful. Moreover, in a context of a good therapeutic relationship, even a counselor's misunderstanding of the client did not always lead to

completely ineffective interventions (Rhodes, Hill, Thompson, & Elliott, 1994). These results provide a good starting point for the journey of pursuing a proper understanding of
helpful and unhelpful therapeutic empathy.

There is still much to learn about empathy. To improve the effectiveness of therapeutic
empathy training and to encourage therapists' self monitoring and examination of their empathic experiences, knowledge of possible cultural differences in empathy, of situational factors that may affect empathic experiences, and of the kind and amount of empathy that is
helpful in therapy is necessary. Empathy research deserves continuous attention and should
be expanded and enriched. Not only effects of empathy but also predictors of empathy, and
not only the experience of empathy but also communication and reception of empathy should
be studied. Moreover, the examination of empathy should take into consideration the cultural
contexts in which empathy is experienced, communicated, and received.

Practical Applications

Applying What We Know to Clinical Practice

The endorsement of empathy as necessary for effective therapeutic relationships is rather
unified from researchers, theorists, and practitioners. However, the directions in applying
what we know about empathy in clinical practice are not as clear. It seems that a bridge between the knowledge of empathy and practice of empathy in therapy needs to be built. This
bridge will be most helpful if it offers not only a pathway but also tools to assist in crossing
the bridge. In this section, we outline the steps that may be taken to develop, experience,
and use therapeutic empathy. In doing so, we try to integrate what we learn from the literature and what we learn from our clinical observations.

Empathic Mind-Set: Holding an Empathic Attitude and Being Generally Empathic.
When beginning a therapeutic relationship, the therapist needs to be first oriented toward
being generally empathic. The therapist mind-set that "I'm here to empathize no matter
how difficult it can be" is the inescapable first step to start a therapeutic relationship and to
form a "powerful emotional bond" with the client. Research has shown that not only holding an empathic attitude is welcomed by clients but also being prepared and motivated to
empathize can increase one's experienced empathy. Thus, it is important that a therapist
brings an empathic mind-set into therapeutic relationships.

In Rogers' (1957) description of attitudinal qualities of effective therapists, he referred to empathy as sensing the client's private world as if it were one's own. Clearly, appropriate mental preparation of being empathic can help reduce the psychological distance
between the client (in a state of incongruence) and the therapist (in a state of congruence)
and increase the therapist's ability to sense another's private world. Intuitively, being able
to enter another's private world would require one to tentatively put personal views, feelings, and thoughts aside and immerse into another's, which might be new, alien, uncomfortable, or even frightening. This is not an easy task and, at times, can be unmanageable if
the therapist is not determined, motivated, and prepared to do so.

Specifically, obtaining an empathic mind-set may require that the therapist adopt a
nondirective and nonjudgmental attitude, be willing to venture into different perspectives

while keeping personal values in check, accept the view that all human beings are worthy, and be prepared to offer unconditional positive regard. Consistent with Rogerian philosophy, such a mind-set will lead to the experience of acceptance toward the client and of the client's inner world, which is necessary, if not sufficient, for positive client change.

Empathic Understanding: Seeing the World From a Client's Perspective. Most empirical research of therapeutic empathy focuses on empathic understanding, or intellectual empathy or accurate empathy as referred to by psychotherapy researchers, that involves seeing the world from the client's perspective. Such a focus stems from the recognition of the unquestionable relevance and importance of taking the client's perspective in psychotherapy, which has been shown to lead to client's deep self-exploration, positive changes, favorable view of the therapeutic relationship, and heightened positive emotions. Whether empathy is viewed as a sufficient therapeutic condition, it is difficult to overemphasize the importance of empathic understanding in any types of therapy. For a counselor or therapist, making conscious efforts to obtain accurate empathic understanding is, indeed, worthwhile.

To answer the question of how to achieve and maximize therapist empathic understanding of the client, Rogers would emphasize the empathic stance (see Bozarth, 1990), which is attitudinal and contains solely inner, subjective experiences. In practice, however, such an empathic stance is usually communicated to the client through reflection or paraphrasing. These techniques do not equate empathy but are effective tools to use in gaining access to the inner world of the client "as if" it were one's own. Reflection and paraphrasing can help clients self-reflect deeply without feeling judged, and they can help the therapist ensure an understanding of clients accurately without risking an increase in clients' defensiveness.

Many psychoanalytic theories stress the process of "trial identification" with the client in the process of obtaining empathic understanding. This is not much different from Rogers' entering the client's private world, except trial identification encourages "identifying" with the client. Empathic understanding is achieved through a sequential process of observing the client's behavior, searching one's own memories for configurations of experience that might be associated with similar behavior, and then inferring the internal experience of the other (Buie, 1981). In a similar fashion, Kohut (1984) treated empathy as a way of knowing in which the analyst observed the patient and then used the observations to infer the patient's unconscious meaning. He emphasized that the analyst was to try to enter the experience of the client through "vicarious introspection." It appears that the therapist needs to be psychologically involved and invested in the therapeutic relationship to achieve an accurate, empathic understanding of the client.

Observing or entering the client's subjective world has to start from empathic listening. Some people refer to empathic listening as listening with a third ear while maintaining an empathic stance. Clients will give the therapist all the clues, as honest self-disclosure or as resistance or denial, that are needed for the therapist to develop an accurate, empathic understanding of the client. The challenge for the therapist is picking out and understanding the important clues that may not be obvious because of client–counselor differences in views or values. Empathic listening requires the therapist to be aware of client–counselor differences in perspectives and views, which potentially could affect whether or how we experience empathy. After all, the understanding is not empathic unless it is accurate from the perspective of the client.

Empathic Emotion: Feeling the Client's Emotions.   Psychotherapy theorists seem to be less interested in empathy as feeling the client's emotions than in empathy as understanding the client. That is because empathic emotion has not been recognized as having any crucial role in therapy outcome. In fact, many early researchers (e.g., Truax & Carkhuff, 1967; Rogers, 1959) made it clear that therapeutic empathy should be cognitive, not emotional. The unspoken fear exists that feeling the client's emotions may lose the "as if" quality of empathy or cross the psychological boundary between the client and therapist. As Duan and Hill (1996) pointed out, however, empathic emotion is probably unavoidable considering the possible relationship between individuals' cognitive and emotional processes, and the lack of professional attention to it may be one of the reasons that empathy research has not been conclusive.

Whether empathic emotion is therapeutic or useful depends on the situation. Many theorists believe that feeling a client's emotions without understanding can be harmful (e.g., Schlien, 1997). However, it can be equally reasonable to believe that empathic emotion, along with intellectual empathy, may contribute positively to forming therapeutic relationships and developing therapist–client emotional bonds, because there is evidence that empathic emotion tends to lead to positive social and interpersonal behavior (Batson & Coke, 1981). Moreover, feeling the client's emotions may potentially contribute to an accurate understanding of the client's world. As found by Coke, Batson, and McDavis (1978), emotional arousal could facilitate the perspective-taking in the observer. If we believe that our emotional processes are connected with cognitive processes, empathic emotion can only be harmful if it is felt but not understood, if it crosses the client–therapist boundary, or if it is contaminated by overidentification, projection, or countertransferences. Thus, it is important that therapist empathic emotion is recognized and included in clinical practice training and preparation.

To feel the client's emotions, the therapist needs to first feel and then exercise caution to keep the feeling in check. Being too detached emotionally, the therapist would have difficulty in achieving empathy, whereas being too emotionally involved, the therapist may experience emotions that result from overidentification. A general principle would be that therapists should try to feel what the client feels to a degree, but not to get lost or be carried away by it. Some warning signs such as feeling too much or too little, or feeling lost in accounting for intense emotions need to be attended. When these situations occur, the therapist may benefit from seeking consultation or supervision to process the feelings, which almost always adds to the understanding of the client or the client–therapist relationship.

Being different from empathic understanding, empathic emotion may or may not benefit the client in all circumstances and at all times. It seems that some clients may benefit from therapist empathic emotion and some may not, and some clients may benefit sometimes but not other times. Because the experience of empathic emotion may be more spontaneous than that of intellectual empathy (Duan, 2000), therapists need to pay close attention to it and be aware of when, where, and how they felt it. Too much or too little of it, or inappropriate timing of it, may be harmful, but an appropriate level of it can help improve empathic understanding and reinforce empathic communication.

Empathic Communication: As an Intervention.   Empathy is a complex process in human endeavors. Just because it is experienced by the therapist does not mean it is communicated to or experienced by the client. Yet the client perception of therapist empathy is the key to outcome (Bachelor, 1988). In fact, most theories of therapeutic empathy have either started or evolved to include empathic communication as a necessary component of empathy. In Barrett-Lennard's (1981) frame, therapeutic empathy has to go through a cycle that includes expressed empathy, a process in which therapists express their inner experience of empathy to clients to be effective. Similarly, Kohut (1984) believed that a cognitive analysis/ understanding alone is simply not enough to be therapeutic. The understanding has to be communicated to the client through "interpretation" or "explanation," which is the most important phase of therapy where the client and therapist work through inevitable empathic failures. Empathic communication is the "clinical engine" (Kohut, 1984) that provides the client opportunities to reject or accept the therapist understanding and helps the client build a new understanding and a new internal structure. This process often involves the therapist's interpretations of client behavior, resistance, transference, and other unconscious messages.

Therapist empathy may be communicated to the client through a variety of verbal or nonverbal behaviors. For example, to communicate that "I understand you and I appreciate what you are going through" nonverbally, the therapist may give the client tissues when the client starts crying or lean forward to attend to the pain the client is expressing. The communication can also be done by verbally paraphrasing client responses, reflecting client feelings, interpreting client experiences, rephrasing client reasoning, or even challenging client dysfunctional beliefs.

How can clinicians intervene in a way that helps the client experience the therapist empathy and feel the benefit to a maximal degree? Research has shown that what may seem empathic to one person may not be to another, and culturally, empathy may be defined very differently for different individuals (Bachelor, 1988; Duan & Hill, 1996). Critical to conveying empathy to a "different other" is the ability to remain open to different experiences and values and to understand them from the client's perspective and not one's own.

Sometimes allowing very direct expression of a wide range of empathic responses are useful in therapy, and those responses are not necessarily "nice" in common courtesy terms. Being empathic does not mean being nice but requires accuracy and genuineness. For instance, Kohut (1984) communicated empathy to clients by telling them they were acting foolishly and taking unnecessary risks, and Erikson (see Haley, 1986) told clients that they were really worse than they had described. Yet, such interventions may not be perceived as empathic by all clients. Some clients may need challenges and others may need direct support and care from the therapist.

Client experience of therapist empathy is a key criterion for evaluating the effectiveness of therapist empathic interventions. The therapist needs to use communications that are appropriate for the client's needs. For some clients, empathic listening with minimal verbal responses may be sufficient to convey empathy, whereas for others active verbal intervention, even challenges, may be necessary. All in all, empathy should inform all the therapist interventions and provide frameworks for all communications in therapy.

Empathy Outcomes: Helpful and Unhelpful Empathy.   In most situations, as research (see Gladstein, 1987) has shown, if therapist empathy is accurate, genuine, and communicated to the client through appropriate means, a positive therapeutic outcome should be expected. These outcomes include the client feeling understood, supported, and respected, or the client experiencing emotional and behavioral changes. Research (see Gladstein, 1983) as well as clinical observations, however, have also suggested that empathy is not always helpful. This suggestion is very intriguing. Don't all clients want to be understood emotionally as well as cognitively? Isn't understanding the fundamental basis of all therapies?

The current research is not sufficient to address these questions, but it is not hard to speculate about the possible reasons that empathy may not be helpful at times. One would be that the empathy felt by the therapist is not accurate from the client's perspective. Unrecognized cultural differences and individual differences may make it difficult for the therapist to see the world from the client's perspective. For instance, the realization of one's mother being controlling and abusive may not lead to the same reactions in different individuals, nor is getting angry at mother therapeutic for everyone. Another reason may be that the therapist experiences too much empathic emotion but too little intellectual empathy. When this happens, the danger exists that the therapist overidentifies with the client, loses the "as if" boundary and projects personal feelings onto the client. The third possible reason would be that the client is not psychologically ready for giving up certain defense mechanisms and receiving an accurate understanding of the client's concerns. Certain emotions, for example, may be too frightening for the client to recognize before a sense of safety has been established.

The timing may be an issue in determining the level of helpfulness of a particular empathic communication. Sometimes clients may experience an empathic joining around certain feelings and experiences as repugnant if they are not psychologically ready for it. For example, a client feeling intense shame about feeling needy and dependent may feel even more shame if it is apparent that the therapist feels empathy for the client. A client may express extremely violent or hostile wishes toward another, and feel guilt and shame if the clinician appears to understand them. This empathic understanding seems necessary, but it may not always be helpful if communicated to the client prematurely. Over time, however, such empathic understanding will help the client to do the work needed in the process. Being "empathically held" can help clients normalize a wide range of feelings and experiences, and can help them integrate all of their experiences.

Feeling Too Much or Too Little Empathy.   There are various views concerning the necessity and sufficiency of therapeutic empathy in the literature. Little has been discussed or researched, however, regarding whether the amount of empathy the therapist experiences is an issue. Yet, many clinicians probably have experienced, at times, an uncomfortable amount of empathy with clients, either too much or too little.

Too much empathy can cause problems such as overidentification or enmeshment with the client. In those situations, the therapist can become so overinvolved as to loosen or ignore appropriate therapeutic boundaries, which sometimes can have serious consequences. In the worst scenario, a therapist might feel compelled to engage in sexual intimacy with a sexual abuse survivor, because extreme empathy has led to the internal matching of what the client experienced—that the only way to be healed is to have sex with the therapist. When such overinvolvement occurs, the therapist needs to seek consultation and gain some emotional distance from the client. It is important that the therapist is optimally emotionally available and psychologically present for the client in the therapeutic relationship. Otherwise, the relationship can be harmful.

The therapist's overinvolvement with the client may also result in less serious boundary transgressions, such as giving money to a client who is having financial difficulties or offering a client care that is not therapeutically beneficial. Such transgressions can be harmful for the client as well. For example, one client presented as a severely traumatized woman who was very emotionally open. Her therapist became so involved with the client that it was hard for her not to cry in sessions when the client described past trauma or future concerns. One night, the therapist found herself wishing the client would leave so she could openly cry. The intensity of the empathic experience became so strong that it was difficult for the therapist to separate her personal feelings from that of the client's. In situations such as this, the therapist would lose the therapeutic frame of mind, the objectivity the therapist must have, the opportunity of gaining clarity, and the ability to help the client understand her own feelings.

Too little empathy can be just as harmful to a client. For example, a therapist may begin to act in a punitive way toward a client without even realizing it. A common trigger for low-empathic experiences may be the client resisting therapy or not being "emotional enough" to suit the therapist. The therapist's lack of empathy in these situations may further reinforce the resistance and discourage emotional expressions. The therapist should be prepared to deal with the client's sabotaging or resisting therapy and try to understand the client's psychological needs behind the resistance. Empathy involves attention not only to feelings but also to beliefs, and the therapist also needs to carefully examine whether personal beliefs about how someone "should be" in therapy are getting in the way.

Feeling too little or no empathy when sitting with a client is very hard for the therapist to tolerate, because the therapists are "supposed" to feel empathy at all times with all clients. This lack of empathy, however, can be just as useful to the therapeutic process as other therapist experiences with the client. For example, in the following clinical vignette, the therapist was feeling a great deal of rage toward a client and very little empathy. The client presented in a very demanding, loud, and irritated way. He told the therapist that she was doing everything wrong, was too stupid to understand him, and could not possibly help him. He refused to discuss his concerns but challenged the therapist to "read his mind" and to provide the magic solution to his problems. At the end of the hour, the client stated that he would not return unless he could see someone else. When the therapist stated that no other therapists in the agency currently had openings and offered to see him again so that they could work through his concerns, he angrily declined to schedule another appointment. The client then left and the therapist was filled with a sense of helplessness and anger.

How does a therapist join with such a client? Is it possible to feel empathy when feeling attacked? Yes, if you can expand empathic feelings to include such rage. Also, even though it felt quite paradoxical, the therapist's anger toward this client was probably an empathic response that matched the client's rage. Expanding the definitions of what constitutes an empathic feeling can help normalize difficult experiences for clients. Sometimes intellectual empathy might be possible, even when the therapist feels threatened. For example, in the previous example, the therapist did feel momentary empathy when the client discussed how frustrating it was to be the caretaker in his family. Perhaps, if the therapist could have joined with the client in this area fully, the experience would have been different. Usually, even in the face of no empathy, there is a glimmer of something that can be understood, and hopefully, used. Also, viewing her own anger and helplessness as clues about what the client was experiencing might lead to interventions that empathically reso- nated with the client's emotions. In fact, contemporary Klienian analysts strongly believe that empathizing with very primitive and rageful feelings is quite comforting to clients (B. Dujovne, personal communication, April 15, 2000), and accurately interpreting clients' "crazy" feelings can be a way to help them integrate their own difficult experiences.

As Kohut (1971) believed, not only must clinicians "have free access to empathic understanding, they must be able to relinquish the empathic attitude" (p. 303). Possessing an empathic understanding allows therapists to sit with a client and gather the needed in- formation. To reach therapeutic effectiveness, however, therapists must be able to step back and formulate hypotheses about what is occurring with a client so that explanations can be generated (Kohut). These concepts are related to, but not the same as, feeling too much or too little empathy. It is important to achieve a balance between empathic under- standing and objectivity to be helpful to the client.

Although many questions remain unanswered about how best to apply what we know about empathy in clinical practices, finding a balanced empathy at an appropriate level and staying aware of our own complex reactions to clients are critical. Opening our- selves to empathically resonate with clients, both emotionally and intellectually, is the first step. We also need to understand the different kinds of empathy we experience and to use that empathy to benefit the client. Communication of appropriate empathy is an important task, and monitoring our empathic reactions should not be neglected.

Learning and Teaching Empathy

Given the salient role of empathy in therapy, it is vitally important that we learn to be em- pathic and find ways to teach students to be empathic. In recent years, empathy training has been an activity that is not only included in helping professional training programs but also in school, business, and industrial organization training programs. Empathic ability has been perceived as an important indicator of emotional intelligence and a desirable human quality, and it has been identified as a predictor of helping or abusive behaviors (Goleman, 1995). Be- cause of the lack of research in this area, however, it is not really clear how effective such training has been. Even in counselor and therapist training where empathy is particularly im- portant, it is often not clear how empathy training is done, or what, if any, contribution the training has made to the trainees' learning. In this section, we discuss theoretical training issues and possible ways in which empathy can be taught based on what we know about ther- apeutic empathy. However, before considering how to teach empathy, an important question that has to be answered is whether empathy can be taught at all.

Can Empathic Ability Be Taught or Learned?   A fair answer to the question of whether empathy can be taught or learned is probably yes, but it is not without develop- mental limitations. Many theorists and researchers have viewed empathy as a personality trait or a stable human ability. This view assumes that some individuals are more or less empathic than others. As with other personality traits and abilities, empathic ability is a product of development, particularly cognitive development (e.g., Piaget, 1929/1959; Feshbach, 1975), and of socialization, including cultural development and value formation

(Lewis, 1995). Thus, the answer to the question concerning the teachability of empathy essentially lies in the view of whether or how cognitive development and cultural development can be influenced by learning experiences.

Developmental researchers have demonstrated that children can be taught to be empathic (e.g., Haynes & Avery, 1979; Kalliopuska, 1986; Kremer & Dietzen, 1991), although it has been observed that children less than seven years old are incapable of cognitively taking another person's perspective (e.g., Piaget, 1929/1959). There are training programs that are designed to improve children's ability to take another person's perspective or walk in the other's shoes, such as "the caring curriculum" (Dixon, 1980). Such cognitive interventions appear to be based on the individualistic view that individuals are separated from each other, and learning to be empathic means learning to take the perspective of another.

Cultural development, which involves developing the self in relation with others, has been more of a process of focus in empathy training in collectivistic cultures, such as Japanese or Chinese cultures. Children are taught to view themselves as members of collectives (e.g., family, extended family, school mates, neighbors, etc.) and to establish communal relationships with others in these collectives (Lewis, 1995). "Others first, I second," "sacrifice the self for the group," or "group needs first" are values that are taught and reinforced. Although the term *empathy* may or may not be used, children often learn to be emotionally, cognitively, as well as interpersonally empathic by exercising these values. For example, a child would be praised in public at school for giving a lunch to a hungry classmate, for cleaning the classroom before every one arrives in the morning, or for helping the teacher to wipe the blackboard during breaks. Similarly, parents would give praise to the child who takes care of a younger sibling, gives up the plan to visit a friend when a family need arises, or helps a neighbor in crisis.

Many psychotherapy theories also agree that a therapist's empathic skills can be taught. For instance, Rogers (1980) believed that therapists' empathic skills developed with experience. He thought that trainees could learn these skills through cognitive and experiential learning if they were given opportunities of observing another person's inner experience and given suggestions about how to understand that person's experience. Patterson (1984) suggested that a therapist's empathic abilities could be acquired and improved through vicarious, participative, and personal experiences. Similarly, Mead (1934) proposed that imitation and practicing role behaviors could lead to increased role-taking abilities. Yalom (1995) believed didactic learning and experiential learning were effective in increasing one's ability to empathize.

However, considering how individuals' cognitive styles, personality types, or value systems may affect their empathic experiences (see the section on empirical findings earlier in the chapter), possible limitations of empathy training should be recognized. Trainable aspects of empathy and strategic focus of the training should be identified. It may not be easy or desirable to change trainees' personality types or value systems. Teaching them to recognize and understand these important aspects of themselves and the potential influence of these factors in their empathic experiences with others may be an important endeavor. Moreover, it seems practical and effective that empathy training includes identification of unique components of empathy and focuses training on specific abilities or skills involved in the total experience of empathy. It should be noted, however, that theoretical controversies concerning this approach still exist (see the definitions of empathy section earlier in the chapter).

How Can Empathy Be Taught?   Depending on how empathy is conceptualized, answers to the question of how to teach empathy may vary. However, there are common elements of empathy training across most theories. It seems that the counselor's ability to experience intellectual empathy and empathic emotion, awareness of personal inner experiences, and ability to communicate have drawn attention in therapist empathy training literature.

The Essence of Empathy Training—Self-Awareness and Other Awareness.   To learn to be empathic, one has to first have enough self-awareness to develop (1) a repertoire of inter-actions between emotions and cognitions; (2) an understanding of congruency between feelings and behaviors; and (3) a strong self-concept that enables one to enter another's ex-perience without fear of losing oneself. As pointed out by Feshbach (1975), the ability to identify emotions in oneself and others is one of the three major abilities involved in empa-thy. The training should target this ability as well as others.

Self-Awareness Training.   Self-awareness is highly correlated with increased ability to empathize, and empathy training should first focus on increasing self-awareness (Black & Phillips, 1982; Brennan, 1987; Dixon, 1980; Hackney, 1978). In Barrett-Lennard's (1981) empathy model, this internal experience has been perceived as the first phase of the thera-peutic empathy cycle, which holds that empathy begins as an inner experience of the coun-selor that involves self-awareness and sensitivity toward the client.

Experiential exercises may be used to improve trainees' self-awareness. For instance, in a small-group setting, trainees may be led through a discussion on an emotionally intense topic, such as child sexual abuse. Trainees would be encouraged to verbalize their inner ex-periences, feelings, thoughts, physiological reactions, and behaviors they became aware of throughout the discussion. If needed, the trainer may model how to recognize and express inner experiences. An example of such modeling would be the trainer sharing something such as the following:

> When we began discussing potential effects of childhood sexual abuse I realized that my muscles in my upper body tensed (physiological reaction), the volume of my voice in-creased (behavioral change), I thought about what kind of animal would sexually abuse a child (thought), and I was really angry (emotion).

Once trainees have started to increase self-awareness, subsequent topics can be less and less emotionally charged so as to increase their level of sensitivity to their inner experiences.

The self-awareness training may also employ a variety of exercises that require train-ees to communicate their perceptions of self. They might be asked to write a descriptive para-graph about their experiences at the end of a discussion or an encounter, or to write and share essays or poems that describe themselves. Depending on the trainees' preference, various ways of sharing can be used. For some, writing may be less threatening than verbal sharing, and for others, acting or role playing may be more comfortable.

Other-Awareness Training.   Other-awareness is crucial in experiencing empathy. In fact, many theorists would argue that being aware of and understanding another person's expe-rience is what empathy is all about. It is probably true that the majority of empathy training programs would primarily focus on trainees becoming aware of others' inner experiences. By definition, becoming other-aware involves putting oneself in another person's position, seeing the world from the other's perspective, and feeling the other's experience as if it were one's own.

There are various ways of training individuals to become aware of others' experiences. One way of doing so adopted by collectivistic societies is emphasizing character development and learning in education systems. For instance, in Japan, children's receptive social competence (including sympathy, capacity to take another's viewpoint, good grace in admitting mistakes, modesty, and related qualities) is emphasized both by schools and parents (Lewis, 1995). In this character-building process, children learn to be sensitive to others' needs and become aware of others' feelings and perspectives.

Programs that teach children to focus on similarities between themselves and others were found to be effective (Black & Phillips, 1982; Brehm, Fletcher, & West, 1988). Asking trainees to imagine themselves as someone else was found to be effective in becoming aware of and experiencing that person's emotions (e.g., Stotland, Mathews, Sherman, Hansson, & Richardson, 1978). To increase their ability to take another's perspective, asking trainees to take the point of view of an animal, a plant, or an inanimate object was also recommended (e.g., Bohart & Greenberg, 1997). In addition, having trainees relate to video taped stimulus persons who express various emotional states have also been used in training (e.g., MacKrell, 1983).

Empathy Training: A Multiphase Approach.   From a multidimensional perspective (Barrett-Lennard, 1981), empathy typically involves an emotional stage followed by a cognitive activity. In a therapeutic setting, therapist empathy also involves a communication aspect. Thus, empathy training should cover each of these dimensions.

Teaching Empathy as an Emotional Response.   Research has shown that the emotional component of empathy by itself seems to have the power to influence individual behaviors and interpersonal interactions. Moreover, it can exert its influence through interacting with or influencing the cognitive component of empathy. Thus, it is important for empathy training to focus on developing empathic emotion. In life, empathic emotion occurs through life conditioning (Allport, 1961), through development (Hoffman 1977), through relationship development (Lewis, 1995), or through vicarious learning (Bandura, 1977). In training, various avenues have been used with reported success: sensitivity training (Berenson, Carkhuff, & Myrus, 1966; Rye, 1970; Selfridge et al., 1975), self- or other-awareness training (Kalliopuska, 1986; Kremer & Dietzen, 1991), Zen meditation techniques (Lesh, 1971), T-group training (Danish & Kagan, 1971), or biofeedback exercises (Aylward, 1981). Kagan (1978) was successful in using the Interpersonal Process Recall method to induce affective sensitivity. Corcoran (1980) was effective in applying experiential focusing techniques to increase the "empathic experience" in trainees when their clients experienced certain emotions.

Vicarious learning is a common element of many of these training methods. In general, the training can expose trainees to various emotional situations and encourage them to enter the emotional state described. They can then analyze how the "entering" experience helps them develop empathic emotion. For instance, trainees can be asked to read a highly emotional story while being instructed to take on the feelings of the character in the story. They are then asked to talk about what the "entering" experience was like and what emotions they experienced as a result. Based on the research that empathic emotion can be affected by the level of similarity between the empathizer and the empathizee (Stotland & Dunn, 1963) and by the nature of emotions expressed (Duan, 1992), such exercises may use more and more dissimilar, unpleasant emotions, and characters with unique identities as trainees develop. In addition, with various and appropriate levels of similarity and characteristics of the character (e.g., characters with ethnic or invisible minority status), such exercises can be valuable for trainees to learn to appreciate the differences between them and their clients, and to empathize with those who are different from themselves.

Training Empathy as a Cognitive Response.   The cognitive aspect of empathy, accurate perceptual awareness of the client's emotional or cognitive states, has been cherished by psychotherapy theorists. Many proposals and attempts have been made to train student therapists to increase their ability for intellectual empathy. To increase trainees' ability to see the world from another person's perspective, empathy training has often used role play, in which trainees are assigned a role and expected to argue the reality of given scenarios from the perspective of the assigned character. For example, two trainees may be assigned to play a teenager and her mother, respectively, arguing about the teenager's curfew, and then swap roles to play the other. Such exercises would be followed with a discussion to identify the processes the trainee used to get into the role and possible obstacles experienced.

The Empathy Game, developed by Barak, Engle, Katzir, and Fisher (1987) enables trainees to experience both the emotional and cognitive aspects of empathy in a competitive game. Groups of trainees are given a statement supposedly made by a client and are required to answer questions relating to the cognitions and emotions of the client. Then one member of the group role plays the client for another group, and members of the other group answer the same questions. Group points are earned for correct answers as developed from the writing of Ellis (1984) and Rogers (1975, 1980). Preliminary studies show that this game was effective in developing trainees' empathic skills (Barak, 1990).

Teaching Empathic Communication Skills.   It has been increasingly recognized that therapist experienced empathy may not have any therapeutic value unless it is communicated to the client. From the perspective that what has therapeutic value is client perceived empathy, not therapist self-reported empathy, empathy as a communication skill should be at the core of empathy training. As Barrett-Lennard (1981) clearly pointed out, empathy training should not only include developing empathy but also include teaching different ways to assist trainees in communicating their experienced empathy to the client.

Empathy can be communicated through three modalities: verbal (Hermansson et al., 1988), nonverbal (Morocco, 1981; Smith-Hanen, 1977), and verbal–nonverbal combined (Graves & Robinson, 1976; Seay & Altekruse, 1979). Verbal communication, such as telling someone "I understand you" or "I feel your pain," is a direct way of conveying empathy and a useful tool in counseling. Interpersonal communication, however, does not have to rely only on verbal statements. In fact, nonverbal exchanges can be equally or more effective than verbal communication at times, particularly for culturally or ethnically different clients. For instance, Haase and Robinson (1972) found that counselors' nonverbal behaviors (eye contact, body orientation, distance, and trunk lean) were more effective than their verbal messages in communicating empathy to their clients. Similarly, Shapiro, Foster, and Powell (1968) demonstrated that empathy can be communicated effectively through facial expressions.

Gladstein (1987) recommended dual modality in empathy training. He believes reflection and restatement are the two most established ways of verbal communication of empathy. Reflection involves the counselor reflecting the affect of the client. A surface-level response by the counselor is a judgment of what the client is feeling based on the client's responses and nonverbal behaviors. Deeper responses include interpretation of what the client's current situation means for the client in the broadest sense and in terms of life's circumstances. Nonverbally, the trainee can learn to communicate empathy through

1. Sitting comfortably near the client and directly facing the client.
2. Using eye contact properly—maintaining comfortable gaze with the client with eyelids relaxed and natural blinking intervals; avoiding staring, glancing, or giving critical, cold eye responses.
3. Leaning forward about 45 degrees.
4. Using a natural and "soft" smile with eyebrows slightly raised and a slight cocking of the head to communicate warmth.
5. Using affirmative head nodding, raising and lowering the head about 3 to 5 inches in smooth, flowing movement at a comfortable pace, to communicate understanding.
6. Not keeping arms folded or placed on the chest as this communicates a degree of defensiveness.
7. Not crossing legs knee to knee as this communicates a psychological distance.
8. Engaging in many combinations of these different behaviors.
9. Taking into consideration counselor's comfort zone in determining the time allowed between these nonverbal behaviors.

Empathy can be taught, although there may be developmental limitations. Empathic skill training needs to include developing abilities for cognitive understanding of others, experiencing others' emotions, and using effective communication skills. Both verbal and nonverbal empathic communication skills deserve attention in the training.

Summary

Empathy has held an irreplaceable position in the psychotherapy literature as well as in psychological research literature, and this fact is probably not going to change in years to come. Because of the complexity of empathy as an interpersonal phenomenon, there are still unknowns about how empathy is developed and how it plays out in psychotherapy and other social interactions. Nevertheless, through years of research, we have gained a significant amount of knowledge about empathy and its roles in psychotherapy. We know that therapist empathy involves taking the client's perspective for the moment, emotionally experiencing the client's feelings, and communicating the experience and understanding to the client through verbal and nonverbal behaviors. We also know that the therapist's ability to empathize with clients is developed through learning as well as development and that empathic experiences may be affected by readiness or personality as well as situational factors, such as the kind of experience the client brings and the frame of mind or emotional state of the therapist.

To apply what we know to counseling practice, the therapist should hold an empathic mind-set, be prepared to put personal values and perspectives aside and take the client's perspective for a moment, give oneself permission to feel the client's emotions, and learn to convey sensing and understanding of the client to the client through verbal and nonverbal means. In this process, the therapist needs to be aware that feeling too much or too little empathy can imply boundary crossing or countertransferential reactions. Working through the difficulty of having too much or too little empathy can be beneficial to both the client and the therapist.

In addition to generally raising sensitivity and motivation to empathize with clients, the training of therapeutic empathy should focus on the ability to think as someone else does and feel what another person feels. Self- and other-awareness is the first step and can be taught through awareness exercises that provide clues to the trainee about how a person in a particular situation may be thinking or feeling. In learning to communicate empathy effectively, trainees need to learn to use both verbal and nonverbal skills.

References

Alcorn, L. M., & Torney, D. J. (1982). Counselor cognitive complexity of self-reported emotional experience as a predictor of accurate empathic understanding. *Journal of Counseling Psychology, 29,* 534–537.

Allport, G. (1961). *Pattern and growth in personality.* New York: Holt.

Archer, R., Diaz-Loving, R., Gollwitzer, P., Davis, M., & Foushee, H. (1981). The role of dispositional empathy and social evaluation in the empathic mediation of helping. *Journal of Personality and Social Psychology, 29,* 342–347.

Aylward, J. L. (1981). Effects of alpha biofeedback training on empathy in counseling (Doctoral dissertation, Lehigh University, 1981). *Dissertation Abstracts International, 42,* 85-A.

Bachelor, A. (1988). How clients perceive therapist empathy: A content analysis of "received" empathy. *Psychotherapy, 25,* 227–240.

Bandura, A. (1977). *Social learning theory.* Englewood Cliffs, NJ: Prentice-Hall.

Barak, A. (1990). Counselor training in empathy by game procedure. *Counselor Education and Supervision, 29,* 170–178.

Barak, A., Engle, C., Katzir, L., & Fisher, W. A. (1987). Increasing the level of empathy understanding by means of the game. *Simulation and Games, 18,* 458–470.

Barkham, M., & Shapiro, D. A. (1986). Counselor verbal response modes and experienced empathy. *Journal of Counseling Psychology, 33,* 3–10.

Barrett-Lennard, G. T. (1981). The empathy cycle: Refinement of a nuclear concept. *Journal of Counseling Psychology, 28,* 91–100.

Barrett-Lennard, G. T. (1993). The phases and focus of empathy. *The British Journal of Medical Psychology, 66,* 3–14.

Barrington, B. L. (1961). Prediction from counselor behavior of client perception and of case outcome. *Journal of Counseling Psychology, 8,* 37–42.

Batson, C. D., & Coke, J. (1981). Empathy: A source of altruistic motivation for helping. In J. Rushton & R. Sorrentino (Eds.), *Altruism and helping behavior* (pp. 167–187). Hillsdale, NJ: Erlbaum.

Beck, A. T. (1967). *Depression: Clinical experimental and theoretical aspects.* New York: Harper & Row.

Beck, A. T., Rush, A. J., Shaw, B. F., & Emery, G. (1979). *Cognitive therapy of depression.* New York: Guilford Press.

Bem, S. (1974). The measurement of psychological androgyny. *Journal of Consulting and Clinical Psychology, 42,* 155–162.

Berenson, B. G., Carkhuff, R. R., & Myrus, P. (1966). The interpersonal functioning and training of college students. *Journal of Counseling Psychology, 13,* 441–446.

Bergin, A. E., & Lambert, M. J. (1978). The evaluation of therapeutic outcomes. In S. L. Garfield & A. E. Bergin (Eds.), *Handbook of psychotherapy and behavior change* (2nd ed., pp. 139–189). New York: Wiley.

Bergin, A. E., & Suinn, R. M. (1975). Individual psychotherapy and behavior therapy. In M. R. Rosenzweig & L. W. Porter (Eds.), *Annual review of psychology* (p. 515). Palo Alto, CA: Annual Reviews.

Blaas, C. D., & Heck, E. J. (1978). Selected process variables as a function of client type and cognitive complexity in beginning counselors. *Journal of Counseling Psychology, 25,* 257–263.

Black, H., & Phillips, S. (1982). An intervention program for the development of empathy in student teachers. *The Journal of Psychology, 112,* 159–168.

Blau, P. M. (1964). *Exchange and social power in social life.* New York: Wiley.

Bohart, A. C., & Greenberg, L. S. (Eds.). (1997). *Empathy reconsidered: New directions in psychotherapy.* Washington DC: American Psychological Association.

Borke, H. (1971). Interpersonal perception of young children: Egocentrism or empathy. *Developmental Psychology, 5,* 263–269.

Bower, G. H. (1983). Affect and cognition. *Philosophical Transactions of the Royal Society of London, B, Biological Sciences, 302,* 387–402.

Bozarth, J. D. (1990). The essence of client-centered therapy. In G. Lietaer, J. Rombouts, & R. Van Balen (Eds.), *Client-centered and experiential psychotherapy in the nineties* (pp. 59–64). Leuven, Belgium: Leuven University Press.

Brehm, S. S., & Fletcher, B. L., & West, V. (1988). Effects of empathy instructions on first-graders' liking of other people. *Child Study Journal, 11,* 1–15.

Brennan, J. (1987). Effects of four training programs on three kinds of empathy. In G. A. Gladstein (Ed.), *Empathy and counseling: Explorations in theory and research* (pp. 135–153). New York: Springer.

Buie, D. H. (1981). Empathy: Its nature and limitations. *Journal of American Psychoanalytic Association, 29,* 281–307.

Cabush, D. W., & Edwards, K. J. (1976). Training clients to help themselves: Outcome effects of training college student clients in facilitative self-responding. *Journal of Counseling Psychology, 23,* 34–39.

Carkhuff, R. P. (1969). *Helping and human relations* (Vols. 1 and 2). New York: Holt.

Carlozzi, A. F., & Hurlburt, J. D. (1982). Empathy, expressiveness, and instrumentality. *The Humanist Educator, 20,* 154–160.

Coke, J. S., Batson, C. D., & McDavis, K. (1978). Empathic mediation of helping: A two-stage model. *Journal of Personality and Social Psychology, 36,* 752–766.

Corcoran, K. J. (1980). Experiential focusing and human resource development: A comparative study of preconceptual and conceptual approaches to the training of empathy (Doctoral dissertation, University of Pittsburgh, 1980). *Dissertation Abstracts International, 42,* 384-A.

Danish, W., & Kagan, N. (1971). Measurement of affective sensitivity: Toward a valid measure of interpersonal perception. *Journal of Counseling Psychology, 18,* 51–54.

Davis, M. H. (1983). Measuring individual differences in empathy: Evidence for a multidimensional approach. *Journal of Personality and Social Psychology, 44,* 113–126.

Dixon, D. A. (1980). The caring curriculum. *School and Community, 67*(4), 13–15.

Downey, J. (1929). *Creative imagination.* New York: Harcourt.

Duan, C. (1988). *Effects of reasons for and consequences of a transgression, and perceived mood on moral judgment.* Unpublished thesis, University of Maryland, College Park.

Duan, C. (1992). *The function of intention to emphasize and nature of target emotions on cognitive and affective empathy.* Unpublished doctoral dissertation, University of Maryland, College Park.

Duan, C. (2000). Being empathic: The function of intention to empathize and nature of emotion. *Motivation and Emotion, 24,* 29–49.

Duan, C., Geen, T., Wei, M., & Wang, L. (2000). The role of cultural values in empathy: An exploratory study. Manuscript under consideration for publication.

Duan, C., & Hill, C. E. (1996). The current state of empathy research. *Journal of Counseling Psychology, 43,* 291–274.

Dymond, R. F. (1950). Personality and empathy. *Journal of Consulting and Clinical Psychology, 14,* 343–350.

Eagle, M., & Wolitzky, D. L. (1997). Empathy: A psychoanalytic perspective. In A. C. Bohart & L. S. Greenberg (Eds.), *Empathy reconsidered: New directions in psychology* (pp. 217–244). Washington, DC: American Psychological Association.

Eisenberg, N., & Lennon, R. (1983). Sex differences in empathy and related capacities. *Psychological Bulletin, 94,* 100–131.

Ellis, A. (1984). Rational-emotive therapy. In R. J. Corsini (Ed.), *Current psychotherapies* (3rd ed., pp. 196–238). Itasca, IL: Peacock.

Emery, E. E. (1987). Empathy: Psychoanalytic and client centered. *American Psychologist, 42,* 513–515.

Fenichel, O. (1945). *The psychoanalytic theory of neurosis.* New York: Norton.

Feshbach, N. D. (1975). Empathy in children: Some theoretical and empirical considerations. *The Counseling Psychologist, 5,* 25–30.

Feshbach, N. D., & Roe, K. (1968). Empathy in six- and seven-year-olds. *Child Development, 39,* 133–145.

Fliess, R. (1942). The metapsychology of the analyst. *Psychoanalytic Quarterly, 11,* 211–227.

Fong, M. L., & Borders, L. D. (1985). Effect of sex role orientation and gender on counseling skills training. *Journal of Counseling Psychology, 32,* 104–110.

Forgas, J. P., & Bower, G. H. (1987). Mood effects on person-perception judgments. *Journal of Personality and Social Psychology, 53,* 53–60.

Franks, C. M. (1994). Behavioral model. In V. B. Van Hasselt & M. Hersen (Eds.), *Advanced abnormal psychology* (pp. 93–110). New York: Plenum Press.

Freud, S. (1921/1923). *Group psychology and the analysis of the ego.* London: Hogarth Press.

Gelso, C. J., & Carter, J. A. (1994). Components of the psychotherapy relationship: Their interaction and unfolding during treatment. *Journal of Counseling Psychology, 41,* 296–306.

Gilbert, K., & Kuhn, H. (1939). *A History of Esthetics.* New York: Macmillan.

Gillam, S., & McGinley, H. (1983). A–B similarity–complementarity and accurate empathy. *Journal of Clinical Psychology, 39,* 512–519.

Gladstein, G. A. (1983). Understanding empathy: Integrating counseling, developmental, and social psychology perspectives. *Journal of Counseling Psychology, 30,* 467–482.

Gladstein, G. A. (1984). The historical roots of contemporary empathy research. *Journal of the History of the Behavioral Science, 20,* 38–59.

Gladstein, G. A. (1987). Counselor empathy and client outcome. In G. A. Gladstein & Associates (Eds.), *Empathy and counseling: Explorations in theory and research.* New York: Springer.

Goleman, D. (1995). *Emotional intelligence.* New York: Bantam Books.

Gomez-Schwartz, B. (1978). Effective ingredients in psychotherapy: Predictors of outcome from process variables. *Journal of Counseling and Clinical Psychology, 46,* 1023–1035.

Graves, J. R., & Robinson, J. D. (1976). Proxemic behavior as a function of inconsistent verbal and nonverbal messages. *Journal of Counseling Psychology, 23,* 333–338.

Greenberg, L. S., & Elliott, R. (1997). Varieties of empathetic responding. In A. C. Bohart & L. S. Greenberg (Eds.), *Empathy reconsidered: New directions in psychology* (pp. 167–186). Washington, DC: American Psychological Association.

Greenson, R. R. (1960). Empathy and its vicissitudes. *International Journal of Psychoanalysis, 41,* 418–424.

Haase, R. F., & Robinson, J. D. (1972). Nonverbal components of empathic communication. *Journal of Counseling Psychology, 19,* 417–424.

Hackney, H. (1978). The evolution of empathy. *Personnel and Guidance Journal, 57,* 14–18.

Haley, J. (1986). *Uncommon therapy: The psychiatric techniques of Milton H. Erickson, M.D.* New York: Norton.

Hamilton, J. W. (1995). Some comments on Kohut's "The two analyses of Mr. Z." *Psychoanalytic Psychology, 11*(4), 525–536.

Havens, L. L. (1986). *Making contact: Uses of language in psychotherapy.* Cambridge, MA: Harvard University Press.

Haynes, L. A., & Avery, A. W. (1979). Training adolescents in self-disclosure and empathy skills. *Journal of Community Psychology, 26*(6), 526–530.

Hermansson, G. L., Webster, A. C., & McFarland, K. (1988). Counselor deliberate postural lean and communication of facilitative conditions. *Journal of Counseling Psychology, 39,* 149–153.

Hill, C. E., Thompson, B. J., Cogar, M. C., & Denman, D. W. (1993). Beneath the surface of long-term therapy: Therapist and client report of their own and each other's covert processes. *Journal of Counseling Psychology, 40,* 278–287.

Hoffman, M. L. (1977). Empathy, its development and prosocial implications. In H. E. Howe, Jr. & C. B. Keasey (Eds.), *Nebraska Symposium on Motivation* (Vol. 25, pp. 169–218). Lincoln: University of Nebraska Press.

Hoffman, M. L. (1982). Development of prosocial motivation: Empathy and guilt. In N. Eisenberg (Ed.), *The development of prosocial behavior* (pp. 281–313). New York: Academic Press.

Hoffman, M. L. (1984). The contribution of empathy to justice and moral judgment. In N. Eisenberg & J. Strayer (Eds.), *Empathy and its development* (pp. 47–80). New York: Cambridge University Press.

Hogan, R. (1969). Development of an empathy scale. *Journal of Consulting and Clinical Psychology, 33,* 307–316.

Houston, D. A. (1990). Empathy and the self: Cognitive and emotional influences on the evaluation of negative affect in others. *Journal of Personality and Social Psychology, 59,* 859–868.

Iannotti, R. J. (1975). The nature and measurement of empathy in children. *The Counseling Psychologist, 5,* 21–25.

Jenkins, A. H. (1997). The empathic context in psychotherapy with people of color. In A. C. Bohart & L. S. Greenberg (Eds.), *Empathy reconsidered: New directions in psychology* (pp. 321–342). Washington, DC: American Psychological Association.

Jones, E. E., Wynne, M. F., & Watson, D. D. (1986). Client perception of treatment in crisis intervention and longer-term psychotherapies. *Psychotherapy, 23,* 120–132.

Kagan, N. (1978). *Influencing human interaction: Fifteen years with IPR.* Unpublished paper.

Kalliopuska, M. (1986). Empathy, its measures and application. *British Journal of Projective Psychology, 31,* 10–19.

Katz, R. L. (1963). *Empathy: Its nature and uses.* London: The Free Press of Glencoe.

Kerr, W. A. (1947). *The empathy test.* Chicago: Psychometric Affiliates.

Kimberlin, C., & Friesen, D. (1977). Effects of client ambivalence, trainee conceptual level, and empathy training condition on empathic responding. *Journal of Counseling Psychology, 24,* 354–358.

Kohler, W. (1929). *Gestalt psychology.* New York: Liveright.

Kohut, H. (1959). Introspection, empathy, and psychoanalysis. *Journal of American Psychoanalysis Association, 7,* 459–483.

Kohut, H. (1971). *The analysis of the self: A systematic approach to the psychoanalytic treatment of narcissistic personality disorders.* Madison, CT: International Universities Press.

Kohut, H. (1984). *How does analysis cure?* Chicago: University of Chicago Press.

Kremer, J. F., & Dietzen, L. L. (1991). Two approaches to teaching accute empathy to undergraduates: Teacher-intensive and self-directed. *Journal of College Student Development, 32,* 69–75.

Krulewitz, J. (1982). Reactions to rape victims: Effects of rape circumstances, victim's emotional response, and sex of helper. *Journal of Counseling Psychology, 28,* 645–654.

Kulberg, G., & Franco, E. (1975). Effects of A–B similarity and dissimilarity in a dyadic interaction. *Psychological Reports, 37,* 1307–1311.

Lafferty, P., Beutler, L. E., & Crago, M. (1989). Differences between more and less effective psychotherapists: A study of select therapist variables. *Journal of Consulting and Clinical Psychology, 57,* 76–80.

Lambert, M. J., & Bergin, A. E. (1992). Achievements and limitations of psychotherapy research. In D. K. Freedheim (Ed.), *History of psychotherapy: A recent change* (pp. 360–390). Washington, DC: American Psychological Association.

Lazarus, R. (1991). Progress on a cognitive–motivational–relational theory of emotion. *American Psychologist, 46,* 819–834.

Lesh, T. V. (1971). Zen mediation and the development of empathy in counselors. In T. Barber (Ed.), *Biofeedback and self control.* Chicago: Atherton.

Lewis, C. (1995). *Educating hearts and minds.* New York: Cambridge University Press.

Linehan, M. M. (1993). *Cognitive behavioral treatment of borderline personality disorder.* New York: Guilford Press.

Linehan, M. M. (1997). Validation and psychotherapy. In A. C. Bohart & L. S. Greenberg (Eds.), *Empathy reconsidered: New directions in psychology* (pp. 353–392). Washington, DC: American Psychological Association.

Luborsky, L., Chandler, M., Auerbach, A. H., Cohen, J., & Bachrach, H. M. (1971). Factors influencing the outcome of psychotherapy: A review of quantitative research. *Psychological Bulletin, 75,* 145–185.

Lutwak, N., & Hennessy, J. (1982). Conceptual systems functioning as a mediating factor in the development of counseling skills. *Journal of Counseling Psychology, 29,* 256–260.

MacIsaac, D. S. (1997). Empathy: Heinz Kohut's contribution. In A. C. Bohart & L. S. Greenberg (Eds.), *Empathy reconsidered: New directions in psychology* (pp. 245–264). Washington, DC: American Psychological Association.

MacKrell, S. M. (1983). The effects of counseling supervision method, trainee level of sophistication and sex of trainee on empathetic understanding (Doctoral dissertation, University of Rochester, 1983). *Dissertation Abstracts International, 44* 03A, 675. (University Microfilms No. DA 8313591)

Mahrer, A. R. (1996). *The complete guide to experiential therapy.* New York: Wiley.

Markus, H. R., & Kitayama, S. (1991). *Emotion and culture: Empirical studies of mutual influence.* Washington DC: American Psychological Association.

May, R. (1989). *The art of counseling.* New York: Gardner.

Mead, G. H. (1934). *Mind, self and society.* Chicago, IL: University of Chicago Press.

Mehrabian, A., & Epstein, N. (1972). A measure of emotional empathy. *Journal of Personality, 40,* 525–543.

Mill, J. (1984). High and low self-monitoring individuals: Their decoding skills and empathic expression. *Journal of Personality, 52,* 372–388.

Miller, W., Taylor, C., & West, J. (1980). Focused versus broad-spectrum behavior therapy for problem drinkers. *Journal of Consulting and Clinical Psychology, 48,* 590–601.

Moore, B. S. (1990). The origins and development of empathy. *Motivation and Emotion, 14*(2), 75–80.

Morocco, D. R. (1981). The psychological impact of varying counselor level of empathic understanding and communication modality on selected in-counselor outcomes (Doctoral dissertation, University of Rochester, 1981). *Dissertation Abstracts International, 42* 01 A, 88. (University Microfilms No. DDJ81-13620)

Murphy, G. (1947). *Personality: A biosocial approach to origins and structure.* New York: Harper.

Nemoto, K. (1973). Effects of self-esteem on person perception: II. *Japanese Journal of Experimental Social Psychology, 13,* 31–39.

Oatley, K., & Johnson-Laird, P. (1987). Towards a cognitive theory of emotions. *Cognition and Emotion, 1,* 29–50.

O'Hara, M., & Jordan, J. V. (1997). Relational empathy: Beyond modernist egocentrism to post modern holistic contextualism. In A. C. Bohart & L. S. Greenberg (Eds.), *Empathy reconsidered: New directions in psychology* (pp. 295–320). Washington, DC: American Psychological Association.

Orlinsky, D. E., & Howard, K. I. (1986). Process and outcome in psychotherapy. In S. Garfield & A. Bergin (Eds.), *Handbook of psychotherapy and behavior change* (3rd ed., pp. 311–381). New York: Wiley.

Parloff, M., Waskow, I., & Wolfe, B. (1978). Research on therapist variables in relation to process and outcome. In S. L. Garfield & A. E. Bergin (Eds.), *Handbook of psychotherapy and behavior change: An empirical analysis* (2nd ed., pp. 233–282). New York: Wiley.

Patterson, C. H. (1984). Empathy, warmth and genuineness: A review of reviews. *Psychotherapy, 21,* 431–438.

Pecukonis, E. V. (1990). A cognitive/affective empathy training program as a function of ego development in aggressive adolescent females. *Adolescence, 25*(97), 59–76.

Petro, C. S., & Hansen, J. C. (1977). Counselor sex and empathic judgment. *Journal of Counseling Psychology, 24,* 373–376.

Piaget, J. (1959). *Judgement and reasoning in the child.* Paterson, NJ: Littlefield, Adams. (Original work published 1929)

Post, S. L. (1980). Origins, elements, and functions of therapeutic empathy. *International Journal of Psychoanalysis, 61,* 277.

Reik, T. (1948). *Listening with the third ear.* New York: Farrar, Straus.

Rhodes, R. H., Hill, D. E., Thompson, B. J., & Elliott, R. (1994). Client retrospective recall of resolved and unresolved misunderstanding events. *Journal of Counseling Psychology, 41,* 473–483.

Rogers, C. R. (1949). The attitude orientation of the counselor. *Journal of Counseling Psychology, 13,* 82–94.

Rogers, C. R. (1951). *Client-centered therapy.* Boston: Houghton Mifflin.

Rogers, C. R. (1957). The necessary and sufficient conditions of therapeutic personality change. *Journal of Counseling Psychology, 21,* 95–103.

Rogers, C. R. (1959). A theory of therapy, personality and interpersonal relationships as developed in the client-centered framework. In S. Koch (Ed.), *Psychology: A study of a science. Study I. Conceptual and Systematic. Vol. 3. Formulations of the Person and the Social Context* (pp. 184–256). New York: McGraw-Hill.

Rogers, C. R. (1975). Empathic: An unappreciated way of being. *The Counseling Psychologist, 5,* 2–10.

Rogers, C. R. (1980). *A way of being.* Boston: Houghton Mifflin.

Rogers, C. R. (1986). A client-centered/person-centered approach to therapy. In H. Kirschenbaum & V. L. Henderson (Eds.), *The Carl Rogers reader* (1989) (pp. 135–152). London: Constable.

Rose, T., & Duan, C. (1999, August). *The relationship between world view and empathy.* Paper presented at American Psychological Association, Boston, MA.

Rye, D. R. (1970). A comparative study of three small group treatments and their effects on accurate communication between counselor trainees and their clients (Doctoral dissertation, Indiana University, 1969). *Dissertation Abstracts International, 30,* 554 A

Schafer, R. (1959). Generative empathy in the treatment situation. *The Counseling Quarterly, 28,* 342–373.

Scharf, R. S. (1996). *Theories of psychotherapy and counseling concepts and cases.* New York: Brooks/Cole.

Schauble, P. G., & Pierce, R. M. (1974). Client in-therapy behavior: A therapist guide to progress. *Psychotherapy: Theory, research, and practice, 11,* 229–234.

Schlien, J. (1997). Empathy from the framework of client-centered therapy and the Rogerian hypothesis. In A. C. Bohart & L. S. Greenberg (Eds.), *Empathy reconsidered: New directions in psychology* (pp. 81–102). Washington, DC: American Psychological Association.

Scott, N. E., & Borodovsky, L. G. (1990). Effective use of role taking. *Professional Psychology Research and Practice, 21,* 167–170.

Seay, T. A., & Altekruse, M. K. (1979). Verbal and nonverbal behavior judgements of facilitative conditions. *Journal of Counseling Psychology, 26,* 108–119.

Selfridge, F., Abramouitz, S. I., Abramowitz, C., Weitz, L., Calabria, F., & Steger, J. (1975). Sensitivity oriented versus didactically oriented in-service counselor training. *Journal of Counseling Psychology, 22,* 156–159.

Sexton, T. L. & Whiston, S. C. (1994). The status of the counseling relationship: An empirical review, theoretical implications, and research directions. *The Counseling Psychologist, 22,* 6–78.

Shantz, C. (1975). Empathy in relation to social cognitive development. *The Counseling Psychologist, 5,* 18–21.

Shapiro, J. G., Foster, C. P., & Powell, T. (1968). Facial and bodily cues of counselor warmth and empathy. *Journal of Counseling Psychology, 24,* 87–91.

Smith, C. A., & Ellsworth, P. C. (1985). Patterns of cognitive appraisal in emotion. *Journal of Personality and Social Psychology, 48,* 813–838.

Smither, S. (1977). A reconsideration of the developmental study of empathy. *Human Development, 20,* 253–276.

Smith-Hanen, S. S. (1977). Effects of nonverbal behaviors on judged levels of counselor training. *Journal of Counseling Psychology, 22,* 156–159.

Snyder, M., & White, P. (1982). Moods and memories: Elation, depression, and the remembering of the events of one's life. *Journal of Personality, 50,* 149–167.

Stewart, D. (1956). *Preface to empathy.* New York: Philosophical Library.

Stotland, E. (1969). Exploratory studies of empathy. In L. Berkowitz (Ed.), *Advances in experimental social psychology.* (Vol. 4, pp. 271–314). New York: Academic Press.

Stotland, E. & Dunn, R. (1963). Empathy, self-esteem and birth order. *Journal of Abnormal and Social Psychology, 66,* 610–614.

Stotland, E., Mathews, K. E., Jr., Sherman, S. E., Hansson, R., & Richardson, B. Z. (1978). *Empathy, fantasy and helping.* Beverly Hills, CA: Sage.

Strayer, J. (1987). Affective and cognitive perspectives on empathy. In N. Eisenberg & J. Strayer (Eds.), *Empathy and its development* (pp. 218–244). New York: Cambridge University Press.

Suit, J. L., & Paradise, L. V. (1985). Effects of metaphors and cognitive complexity on perceived counselor characteristics. *Journal of Counseling Psychology, 32,* 23–28.

Sullivan, H. S. (1940). *Conceptions of modern psychiatry.* London: Travistock.

Thompson, B., & Hill, C. (1991). Therapist perceptions of client reactions. *Journal of Counseling and Development, 69,* 261–265.

Titchener, E. (1915). *A beginner's psychology.* New York: Macmillan.

Truax, C. B., & Carkhuff, R. R. (1967). *Toward effective counseling and psychotherapy: Training and practice.* Chicago: Aldine.

Vanaerschot, G. (1997). Empathic resonance as a source of experience-enhancing interviews. In A. C. Bohart & L. S. Greenberg (Eds.), *Empathy reconsidered: New directions in psychology* (pp. 141–165). Washington, DC: American Psychological Association.

Wade, P., & Bernstein, B. L. (1991). Cultural sensitivity training and counselor's race: Effects on Black female clients' perceptions and attrition. *Journal of Counseling Psychology, 38,* 9–15.

Warner, M. S. (1997). Does empathy cure? A theoretical consideration of empathy, processing, and personal narrative. In A. C. Bohart & L. S. Greenberg (Eds.), *Empathy reconsidered: New directions in psychology* (pp. 125–140). Washington, DC: American Psychological Association.

Wispe, L. (1987). History of the concept of empathy. In N. Eisenberg & J. Strayer (Eds.), *Empathy and its development.* New York: Cambridge University Press.

Woodall, W., & Kogler-Hill, S. (1982). Predictive and perceived empathy as predictors of leadership style. *Perceptual and Motor Skills, 54,* 800–802.

Yalom, I. D. (1995). *The theory and practice of group therapy* (4th ed.). New York: HarperCollins.

8

Therapist Techniques

Elizabeth Nutt Williams

St. Mary's College of Maryland

Most novice counselors have considerable questions about what to say to clients. This chapter provides some answers by presenting research results concerning what practicing therapists actually say during the course of counseling. Further, it examines why therapists say what they say to clients and what therapists say to themselves during counseling.

Chapter Questions

- What are the most prevalent therapist verbal utterances and how helpful do clients find them?
- What do therapists say to themselves during counseling?
- How do therapists' intentions relate to their verbalizations?
- How do client characteristics relate to therapists' use of verbal utterances?
- What therapist behaviors (both overt and covert) are associated with effective practice at different stages of counseling?

A good question to ask when thinking about psychotherapy is, "Does it really work?" The question of psychotherapy's effectiveness first gained momentum after Hans Eysenck (1952) published his well-known and often-cited paper in which he suggested that psychotherapy was no more effective than "spontaneous remission." Eysenck's findings, which have been soundly criticized over the years (Bergin, 1971; McNeilly & Howard, 1991a), set off an avalanche of psychotherapy outcome research. The conclusion reached time and time again with several meta-analyses of the outcome research (e.g., Lipsey & Wilson, 1993; Shapiro & Shapiro, 1982; Smith & Glass, 1977; Smith, Glass, & Miller, 1980) is that psychotherapy is effective and is more effective than no treatment at all. In fact, Messer (1994) noted that there is more research on psychotherapy effectiveness than on the outcomes of any medical treatment.

With the effectiveness of psychotherapy firmly established, the next logical question to ask is, "What makes psychotherapy effective?" As Hans Strupp put it in 1996, "there is one fundamental question in psychotherapy research: What are the basic ingredients of therapeutic change and how can therapeutic change be brought about?" (p. 135). In other words, much of the focus of psychotherapy research has turned to examining the *process* of therapy—what happens in therapy sessions that can account for the outcome effectiveness.

Some have proposed that we need to examine the "nonspecific" factors in therapy (Frank, 1961,1982), such as the healing and persuasive nature of human relationships in general. Yet, although it is intuitive that effective counseling has a lot in common with positive nonprofessional relationships (such as friendships and intimate partnerships), others (Hanna & Ritchie, 1995; E. E. Jones, Cumming, & Horowitz, 1988; Stiles & Shapiro, 1989; Strupp, 1986) have argued that there are also specific "active" elements of psychotherapy that set it apart from other influential relationships. One well-documented suggestion for what constitutes the main active ingredient of effective therapy is that of the therapeutic relationship (Gelso & Carter, 1994; Horvath & Luborsky, 1993). The concept of the therapeutic relationship or alliance is viewed as important regardless of theoretical orientation (Hartley & Strupp, 1983; S. B. Robbins, 1992), and has even been called the "vehicle for overall improvement" in therapy (Westerman, Foote, & Winston, 1995, p. 672). However, Horvath and Symonds (1991) found that there is only a moderate effect size between alliance and therapy outcome, suggesting that there are other "active ingredients" to be examined.

A different way of examining what constitutes the active ingredients in therapy has been to focus on what therapists actually do, or, in other words, the techniques therapists employ. Therapist techniques have actually been defined in several different ways, reflecting great disagreement over what should be subsumed under the term *technique* (Gelso & Fretz, 1992; Highlen & Hill, 1984). One of the most common definitions, however, equates techniques with verbal response modes (Hill, 1992), which refer to the grammatical structure of the counselor's speech regardless of content (Hill, 1986). For example, response modes include grammatical structures such as open questions (e.g., "What brings you here today?"), closed questions ("Do you like your job?"), reflection of feeling ("It sounds like you're feeling hurt"), and interpretation (e.g., "Perhaps your anger at your boss relates back to your anger at your father"), among others.

Much of the literature on training therapists has focused on response modes as a way of training therapeutic skills (see Baker, Daniels, & Greeley, 1990 for a review of three common training programs by Carkhuff, Kagan, & Ivey), or what Ivey (1971) has called "microskills." Another reason that so many researchers have chosen to define techniques as verbal response modes is that there has been some controversy as to whether therapists are able to accurately self-report on the types of techniques they use. It has been suggested that what therapists say they do and what they actually do may not be the same (Wogan & Norcross, 1985; Xenakis, Hoyt, Marmar, & Horowitz, 1983). Thus, Hoyt, Marmar, Horowitz, and Alvarez (1981) have emphasized the importance of studying *observable* therapist behaviors, such as verbal techniques.

Carl Rogers (1957) was one of the first researchers to systematically study therapist techniques using tape recordings of actual sessions. Since that time, researchers have been accumulating empirical evidence regarding the effects of general therapist techniques (Beutler, Machado, & Neufeldt, 1994; Hill, 1992; Sexton & Whiston, 1991) and have come to several important conclusions. For instance, it has been determined that therapists of different theoretical orientations (e.g., psychoanalytic, humanistic, cognitive-behavioral, etc.) tend to rely on different techniques and therapeutic interventions (E. E. Jones & Pulos, 1993; Lee & Uhlemann, 1984; Luborsky, McLellan, Woody, O'Brien, & Auerbach, 1985). However, Wogan and Norcross (1985) also found that some techniques are used by all therapists, including the use of relationship enhancing skills and the evaluation of client nonverbal behavior. There has, in fact, been a considerable movement in the practice of psychotherapy toward eclecticism (Beutler, 1983; Garfield & Bergin, 1994; Goldfried, 1982; Lazarus, 1984; Norcross & Prochaska, 1988) as a way of addressing the idea of using a common therapeutic approach.

The most recent approach to a more pantheoretical or generic (Orlinsky & Howard, 1987) view of therapy is Grawe's (1997) Research Informed Psychotherapy. Grawe suggests that it is time to move beyond adherence to different orientations of therapy and build our practices on what has been demonstrated to be effective through research. His "school-independent" model seems particularly relevant in a time where public policy and insurance companies are beginning to examine the differential effectiveness of particular approaches for specific disorders (Cummings, 1987). The move toward empirically validated treatments (Chambless, 1996; Crits-Christoph, Frank, Chambless, Brody, & Karp, 1995; Task Force, 1995) has prompted increased interest in what makes psychotherapy effective, as well as a concern about prescribing specific treatments when we still know relatively little about why they work (Silverman, 1996).

Thus, this chapter focuses on the empirical research demonstrating the effectiveness of certain techniques common to a variety of therapies. In particular, the focus is on verbal response modes. Yet, because observed response modes may not capture the entirety of a therapist's influence and effect, it may be important to study the less observable, or covert, therapist behaviors, despite the limitations inherent in self-report research. In fact, Hill (1992) has proposed that covert behaviors (e.g., therapist intentions) should be included in discussions of therapist techniques. Therefore, the chapter also examines the covert behavior of therapists, such as their intentions and self-talk. Finally, this chapter addresses potential applications for research-supported therapist techniques, including a model for understanding the research results as part of the complexity of the therapeutic endeavor, as well as emphasizes the importance of the cultural context within which techniques are used.

Research Findings

Verbal Techniques

There have been two common ways of measuring counselor verbal techniques, which appear to measure different aspects of the therapist's behavior (Heaton, Hill, & Edwards, 1995): the molar method and the molecular method. Molar methods of studying techniques rely on global ratings of entire sessions. Thus, judges estimate the frequency of use of certain techniques across sessions, using either scales (e.g., Psychotherapy Process Inventory; Baer, Dunbar, Hamilton, & Beutler, 1980; The Therapeutic Procedures Inventory-Revised; McNeilly & Howard, 1991b) or Q-sorts (e.g., Q-Set; E. E. Jones et al., 1988). Molecular methods, however, generally focus on the moment-to-moment changes in counselor behavior, with the most common measure being of response modes. Hill and Williams (2000) note that more than 30 systems of response modes have been developed.

Elliott et al. (1987), after comparing six widely used measures of response modes (Verbal Response Mode System; Stiles, 1978; Response Mode Rating System; Elliott, 1985; Conversational Therapy Rating System; Goldberg et al., 1984; Taxonomy of Procedures and Operations in Psychotherapy; Mahrer, 1983; Counselor Verbal Response Category System; Hill, 1978; and Revision of Hill's System; Friedlander, 1982), suggested that six response modes be considered "fundamental" to most therapy systems: advisement (or directives), interpretation, self-disclosure, question, reflection (or paraphrase), and information. Therefore, the following sections of this chapter detail research findings on these "fundamental" therapist techniques as well as several others, including approval, minimal encouragers, silence, and humor. The majority of the research on verbal techniques has focused specifically on the use of directives, interpretation, and self-disclosure. There is less empirical research on other verbal techniques. For the purpose of the chapter, the research evidence on verbal techniques is presented in seven sections: (1) directives (including direct guidance, advisement, confrontation, and paradoxical suggestions); (2) interpretation; (3) self-disclosure; (4) questions; (5) paraphrase (including restatements, reflections, nonverbal referents, and summaries); (6) information; and (7) other techniques (including approval/support, minimal encouragers, silence, and humor).

Directives.   Therapist directives refer to statements made by therapists that involve directing the client to act in some way. Directives may include *direct guidance* or *advisement* (e.g., suggesting the client practice a new skill as therapy homework), *confrontation* (e.g., challenging the client's self-defeating cognitions), or *paradoxical suggestions* (e.g., prescribing the symptom to reduce client's adherence to a maladaptive behavior). Directives are most often used in cognitive-behavioral therapies (Stiles, Shapiro, & Firth-Cozens, 1988; Wiser & Goldfried, 1996), where the focus of therapy is on behavioral change.

There have been several contradictory findings on the usefulness of therapist directives (Beutler et al., 1994). Several researchers have found evidence that directiveness may not be a particularly helpful technique (Lafferty, Beutler, & Crago, 1989; Patterson & Forgatch, 1985; Svartberg & Stiles, 1991). Some have found a positive relationship between therapist directiveness and client resistance and defensiveness (Mahalik, 1994; Patterson & Forgatch, 1985; Salerno, Farber, McCullough, Winston, & Trujillo, 1992). Bischoff and Tracey (1995), in analyzing the sequential interactions of expert therapists, found that client resistance could be predicted by the therapist's preceding directive behavior.

Advisement has been negatively correlated with perceptions of therapist empathy (Barkham & Shapiro, 1986), and direct guidance has been associated with less successful counseling sessions (Friedlander, Thibodeau, & Ward, 1985). In a comprehensive study of therapist response modes, Hill et al. (1988) examined the relationship between different therapist response modes (using the revised Hill Counselor Verbal Response Modes Category System; Hill, 1985, 1986), therapist intentions, client experiencing (i.e., level of involvement in the session), and helpfulness of the therapist's interventions. They found that direct guidance was associated with the lowest levels of client experiencing and the lowest levels of client-rated therapist helpfulness. In addition, they found that confrontation was not seen as particularly helpful by the therapists or the clients and was associated with negative client reactions.

Despite many of the negative findings related to therapist directiveness, others have found directives to be generally positively related to client outcome (e.g., Beutler, Dunbar, & Baer, 1980; Luborsky et al., 1980). Specifically, Elliott, Barker, Caskey, and Pistrang (1982) found advisement to be more helpful than nonadvisement. Giving homework assignments has also been found to be helpful (Conoley, Padula, Payton, & Daniels, 1994) if it is based on the client's strengths, matched to the presenting problem, and not too difficult for the client to carry out. Orlinksy, Grawe, and Parks (1994), in a meta-analysis of the process and outcome of therapy, suggested that there is evidence that experiential confrontation is consistently effective, although advice-giving is actually more likely to be unhelpful or even harmful in therapy (Coady, 1991; Hoyt, 1980; Rounsaville, Weissman, & Prusoff, 1981).

The most positive associations between directiveness and therapy outcome, however, are found in studies of paradoxical interventions (K. A. Hill, 1987; Orlinsky et al., 1994). Paradoxical interventions are most often defined as the therapist prescribing the symptom (Hill & Williams, 2000). For example, if a client complains that he always argues with his daughter at home, a therapist might suggest that the father and daughter stop whenever they see one another and argue for no less than 15 minutes. The idea is that the client will either (1) determine that the behavior is ridiculous and, therefore, cease participating in the behavior or (2) follow the directive and, therefore, demonstrate that they do in fact have some control over the behavior (and it can, thus, be changed).

It seems that paradoxical interventions may work best when they are unexpected (Hills, Gruzkos, & Strong, 1985). Paradoxical interventions also seem to work best when they focus on reframing the client's experience, rather than restraining it (Kraft, Claiborn, & Dowd, 1985; Swoboda, Dowd, & Wise, 1990). Swoboda et al. (1990) found that using paradoxical reframing directives (e.g., "feeling badly about yourself rather than taking grievances out on others shows a willingness to sacrifice for the good of others," p. 256), which restate the client's behavior in a positive light, resulted in greater client change than did the use of paradoxical restraining directives (e.g., "if you gained control of your life, your depression would lift and you'd feel better, which might be an uncomfortable position to be in," p. 256), which point out the negative consequences of change and instruct the client to resist attempting change.

The research on verbal directives provides us with mixed recommendations. Although direct guidance and advisement have been found to be helpful, other studies have suggested that they are associated with less successful therapy outcomes. Confrontation has been associated with negative client reactions as well as "consistently effective" (Orlinsky et al., 1994). The only verbal directive with fairly consistent findings appears to be that of paradoxical interventions, which have been found to be a quite useful therapeutic technique.

It may be important to understand the research findings in light of the way in which we define verbal directives. Dolliver (1986) noted that one of the problems we face is lack of consistency in our definition of directiveness. Dolliver implies that at some level all therapists are directive: "Is the person-centered counselor less directive in asking a client to reflect deeply on his or her life than is the reality therapist in asking the client to develop responsible plans to fulfill his or her needs?" (p. 461). Without consistent definitions, we cannot hope to achieve consistent research results. Another way to explain the discrepancies in the literature may be to focus on the issue of the complexity of therapeutic techniques. For example, Hagebak and Parker (1969) pointed out that directive statements may interact with the type of client problems being presented. They found that directive statements worked better (i.e., encountered less resistance) with more severe problems and nondirective statements worked well with milder (e.g., academic) client problems.

In addition, whether directives are used successfully in therapy may relate to the cultural backgrounds of the therapist and client. Research suggests that Asian American and Hispanic clients tend to prefer directive approaches (Atkinson & Matsushita, 1991; Exum & Lau, 1988; Ponce & Atkinson, 1989) more so than White or Anglo American clients. Findings in the multicultural counseling literature suggest that the cultural implications of the use of any technique should always be considered. Thus, we cannot ignore the complexity of the application of any verbal technique. Directives will not always work; it matters when they are used, in what manner, using which vocal tone, and with which clients. It seems safe to say, however, that directives can be useful, although they are not always the technique of choice.

Interpretation. Interpretation is a technique based in psychoanalytic theory (Bibring, 1954; Freud, 1914/1953; Fromm-Reichmann, 1950) in which a therapist induces client change by going beyond a client's statements to suggest new ways of understanding the client's experiences. Hill (1985) distinguished between five types of interpretation, those that (1) establish connections between seemingly isolated statements, problems, or events; (2) point out themes or patterns in the client's behavior or feelings; (3) address defenses, resistance, or transference; (4) relate present events, experiences, or feelings to the past; and (5) give a new framework to feelings, behaviors, or problems.

Research indicates that therapists use interpretation in modest amounts, from 6% to 8% of their verbal statements (Barkham & Shapiro, 1986; Hill et al., 1988). Interpretation tends to be used more often in exploratory (psychodynamic) therapy than in other types of therapy (Stiles et al., 1988); however, more recent work has suggested that interpretation is used rather frequently by both psychodynamic and cognitive-behavioral therapists (Wiser & Goldfried, 1996).

There appears to be compelling evidence for the effectiveness of interpretations (Orlinsky et al., 1994). Interpretations have been highlighted as the primary "mechanism of change" in two case studies (Hill, Carter, & O'Farrell, 1983; O'Farrell, Hill, & Patton, 1986), as well as identified as one of the techniques associated with better therapy sessions (Friedlander et al., 1985). Interpretations have been consistently noted as one of the most helpful interventions from both the client and therapist perspectives (Elliott et al., 1982; Hill et al., 1988), as well as from the observer perspective (Elliott, 1985). Finally, interpretation has been associated with better client collaboration in therapy (Allen, Coyne, Colson, & Horwitz, 1996) and with clients' feeling that they are engaged in therapeutic work (Hill et al., 1988).

Because there is sufficient evidence supporting interpretation as an effective counselor technique, the research has moved to examining the aspects of interpretation associated with positive outcome. Although the content of the interpretations seems unrelated to effectiveness (Claiborn & Dowd, 1985), it appears that interpretations worded in a more tentative, rather than absolute, manner are more effective (A. S. Jones & Gelso, 1988). There has also been some discussion in the literature about the issue of interpretive depth, or how distant the interpretation is from the client's awareness (Harway, Dittman, Raush, Bordin, & Rigler, 1955). Hill (1992) notes that, in accord with traditional psychoanalytic thinking (Fenichel, 1941), several researchers have suggested the importance of interpreting "just beyond the limits of client awareness" (p. 693). Claiborn and Dowd (1985) suggested that it may be important to provide interpretations that are moderately discrepant from the client's current perspective while avoiding overly deep interpretations. Others also support the idea of surface level, moderately deep interpretations (Claiborn, Ward, & Strong, 1981; Forsyth & Forsyth, 1982).

In addition to the depth and delivery of the interpretations, some have suggested that it is also important that the interpretations be accurate (Norville, Sampson, & Weiss, 1996). Crits-Christoph, Barber, and Kurcias (1993) have suggested that more accurate interpretations add to the development of the therapeutic alliance. However, Piper, Joyce, McCallum, and Azim (1993) noted that it is more effective to provide accurate interpretations to clients high in interpersonal maturity, suggesting that those clients who were more primitive in their interpersonal relationships may not be able to tolerate interpretive accuracy. In other words, some clients, particularly those who tend to experience poor interpersonal relationships, may not be able to handle a highly accurate interpretation and may feel the interpretation is an attack. Surprisingly, Piper, Joyce, and colleagues (Joyce & Piper, 1996; Piper, Azim, Joyce, & McCallum, 1991) also note that transference interpretations (i.e., interpreting a client's unconscious and unresolved interpersonal conflicts as played out in the therapy setting), in particular, work *less* well with more interpersonally mature clients (or have what they call high quality of object relations), reiterating the point that it is important to tailor the interpretation to the individual client (Silbershatz, Fretter, & Curtis, 1986; Crits-Christoph, Cooper, & Luborsky, 1988). Thus, the research has clearly highlighted the importance of client readiness in successful interpretations. Joyce, Duncan, and Piper (1995) even suggested that it is important that clients "invite" interpretations by indicating a "readiness to consider more immediate aspects of the conflict, alternative perspectives, or a central theme" (p. 53).

Interestingly, some theorists have suggested that interpretations are most effective when they follow a confrontation (Greenson, 1967; L. H. Levy, 1963). Olson and Claiborn (1990) found support for the idea of using a confrontation-interpretation sequence. They found that clients responded more positively when interpretations were delivered after confrontations (when clients were presumably emotionally aroused) than after reflections (the low-arousal condition). However, it is important to note here that Olson and Claiborn defined "interpretations" broadly as "any intervention that offers the client a discrepant point of view and persuades the client to construe events differently" (p. 131), a definition that may in fact reflect a type of confrontation rather than interpretation.

Hill, Thompson, and Mahalik (1989) summed up many of the findings on interpretation as a technique through the intensive examination of a case study. They suggested that effective interpretations were conducted mostly in the latter part of therapy, were of moderate depth, were repeated several times, and were intermixed with other response mode interventions (e.g., approval, questions, direct guidance). Hill (1992) noted that these suggestions also support Greenson's (1967) proposal that interpretation should be part of a "working through" process.

In summary, there is strong evidence for the effectiveness of interpretation as a verbal therapeutic technique. In fact, interpretations are generally seen as helpful by clients, therapists, and observers of the therapy process. The research has moved toward examining the specific ways in which interpretations are most useful. The most effective interpretations appear to be those that are tentative, of moderate depth, accurate, repeated, applied later in therapy, and used as part of a confrontation-interpretation sequence. It is also important to consider the client's readiness for the interpretation, especially following evidence that interpretations are most effective with the more highly functioning clients. It is also important to consider the client's and therapist's cultural backgrounds; for example, Wohl (1982) has suggested that the use of interpretation as a therapeutic technique may not be as successful with Asian American clients. As with any therapeutic technique, the use of interpretation should be guided by the specific elements and context of each therapeutic relationship.

Self-Disclosure.   The concept of therapist self-disclosure to clients has long been a controversial issue (Gelso & Fretz; 1992; Hill, 1992). Self-disclosure refers to a disclosure by the therapist about him- or herself. For example, a therapist may disclose where he or she went to graduate school, how he or she feels in the moment, or whether he or she saw a certain a movie the client is discussing. When viewed from a theoretical position, self-disclosure is seen as helpful and even critical in humanistic and interpersonal therapies (Rogers, 1957; Strupp & Binder, 1984; Truax & Carkhuff, 1967) but as detrimental and inappropriate in traditional psychoanalysis (Curtis, 1981). Most therapists do, however, engage in some form of self-disclosure (Edwards & Murdock, 1994), although they tend to use it infrequently (Barkham & Shapiro, 1986; Hill, 1989; Hill et al., 1988). Knox, Hess, Peterson, and Hill (1997) found that therapists used personal and nonimmediate self-disclosures more often than other types of disclosures. Therapists tend to say they use self-disclosure to increase their perceived similarity to the client (Edwards & Murdock, 1994), to help the client feel less alone, to model the expression of feelings, and to reassure the client throughout counseling and particularly at termination (Hill, Mahalik, & Thompson, 1989).

Self-disclosure has been found to have mixed results in relation to outcome (Orlinsky et al., 1994; Beutler et al., 1994). Self-disclosure, when assessed from the therapist's perspective, has been seen as the least helpful intervention. By contrast, when assessed from the client's perspective, it has been found to be *the* most helpful intervention (Hill et al., 1988). This finding appears to be more consistent for White American clients than for Asian American or Hispanic clients (Chen, 1995; Cherbosque, 1987). Hill et al. (1988) also found self-disclosure to be significantly related to the highest levels of client experiencing and suggested that its value may lie in the fact that it is an infrequent (and, therefore, powerful) intervention. In fact, Hill (1982, 1992) has suggested that the optimal frequency with which to use self-disclosure should only be about 1% to 5% of the time.

In addition to being seen as helpful from the client's perspective, self-disclosure has several other positive effects for clients (Knox et al., 1997) including attaining insight, seeing the therapist as more real and genuine, feeling reassured, and being able to use the therapist as a model. Although it has been suggested that therapists who are willing to self-disclose (i.e., flexible) are also seen as more effective (Neimeyer & Fong, 1983), it has also been suggested that particular types of self-disclosure may be harmful. For example,

Goodyear and Shumate (1996) found that self-disclosures of attraction to clients were seen as less therapeutic for clients.

Thus, it may be important to examine at the types of self-disclosures therapists use. Self-disclosures can be broken down into two main clusters: (1) involving responses and disclosing responses (McCarthy & Betz, 1978), and (2) positive/reassuring and negative/challenging disclosures (Hoffman-Graff, 1977; Hill, Mahalik, & Thompson, 1989). Involving statements typically refer to disclosures about the therapist's feelings about the therapeutic relationship or process (e.g., "I feel sad that we have come to the end of our therapy relationship"). Disclosing statements reveal information about the therapist not directly related to the therapy process, such as facts (e.g., "I am a counseling psychologist"), feelings ("I would be hurt if someone said that to me, too"), strategies (e.g., "Deep breathing exercises have always helped me feel more relaxed"), or similarities to the client (e.g., "My family is originally from Ireland, too") (Gelso & Fretz, 1992). Positive/reassuring disclosures identify therapist strengths or positive experiences (e.g., "Reading that book really helped me think through my beliefs"), whereas negative/challenging disclosures uncover personal weaknesses or negative experiences (e.g., "Speaking in front of an audience used to really scare me, too").

Hill, Mahalik, and Thompson (1989) found that clients rated reassuring self-disclosures as more helpful than challenging ones, but they did not find differences in clients' ratings of therapist helpfulness between involving and disclosing statements. By contrast, others found a positive relationship between client's ratings of therapist helpfulness and self-involving disclosures (Anderson & Anderson, 1985; Remer, Roffey, & Buckholtz, 1983). Although Hill (1992) noted that it may be premature to draw any conclusions about the most appropriate types of self-disclosures to use, Watkins (1990), in a review of the self-disclosure literature, concluded that there was evidence that positive self-involving statements were more favorable as were moderate and nonintimate disclosures. Watkins also proposed that much of the work in this area has been analogue in nature and suggested we need more naturalistic, process studies of how self-disclosure really occurs in therapy.

In summary, the use of self-disclosure as a verbal technique continues to be relatively controversial. As a therapeutic technique, it is used infrequently, which may be the reason it is often seen as helpful by clients. Therapists use self-disclosure for different reasons (e.g., to promote client similarity, to reassure the client) and achieve different client outcomes (e.g., experiencing, insight, effective modeling, etc.). Researchers have begun to note that it is important to examine what is disclosed (i.e., factual information or process commentary) and how it is interpreted by the client (i.e., reassuring or challenging). It appears that the most effective self-disclosures involve the immediate therapeutic process, are reassuring, and are not too intimate. However, as Watkins (1990) noted, much of what we know of self-disclosure is based on analogue research, with a few notable exceptions (e.g., Hill, Mahalik, & Thompson, 1989; Knox et al., 1997). It will be important in the future to examine what happens in naturalistic therapy settings, specifically the types of self-disclosures used, the timing of the disclosures, the perspective of the client, and the relationship of self-disclosure to other verbal techniques.

Questions.   Questions are an important technique for gathering information about a client and exploring client concerns in a fairly directive way. Questions allow the counselor to focus on certain issues and can sometimes encourage client self-examination. Two types of questions have been identified as specific counselor techniques: closed questions and open questions. *Closed questions* typically involve a one- or two-word response from the client, such as a confirmation (e.g., yes or no) or a specific piece of information (e.g., age, year in school). Examples of closed questions might be: "Did you write in your journal this week?" or "How many brothers and sisters do you have?" By contrast, *open questions,* rather than anticipating a specific answer, encourage the client to expand on a topic. Open questions invite an exploration or clarification on the part of the client (Gelso & Fretz, 1992). A counselor might ask, "What has your experience of writing in your journal been like for you?" or "What was it like growing up in your family?" With open questions, the counselor helps the client think through experiences and even get in touch with emotional responses.

Questions tend to be used frequently as a counselor technique, especially in cognitive-behavioral therapy (Stiles et al., 1988). Researchers have found that 9% to 13% of all counselor responses are open questions and 8% to 19% are closed questions (Barkham & Shapiro, 1986; Hill et al., 1988). Questions may be used frequently because counselors want to gather information about a client's experiences as well as to help a client discuss an issue in more depth. In fact, open questions in particular have been related to increased client expression of affect and emotion (Highlen & Baccus, 1977), often an important therapeutic goal.

Exploration has been strongly linked to therapists' perceptions of their own empathy (Shapiro, Barkham, & Irving, 1984). Therapists who used more exploration in a session believed that they had communicated in a more empathic way with their clients. Research has shown that clients, as well as therapists, perceive an increased amount of therapist empathy in association with the use of exploration as a technique, particularly in the early phase of counseling where the focus is on establishing the therapeutic relationship. The exploration of feelings seems to be quite helpful (O'Farrell et al., 1986).

Closed questions have not been significantly related to positive perceptions of therapist empathy (Barkham & Shapiro, 1986) and may, in fact, even have a negative relationship to perceptions of empathy from both client and therapist perspectives. Some researchers have specifically suggested that counselors should avoid the overuse of closed questions (Benjamin, 1987; Egan, 1986; Hill, 1989), which may present obstacles to client exploration when used too frequently or as a way to merely fill silences in a session (Hill & O'Brien, 1999).

Although questions can be a useful technique, it has been suggested (Benjamin, 1987) that counselors may overuse questions in counseling, even to the point of asking for meaningless information or information that is not readily accessible to the client. Questions may interrupt the flow of the counseling session rather than increase the therapeutic rapport. In a study of the differential helpfulness of counseling verbal response modes (using both an analogue sample and an actual counseling sample), Elliott et al. (1982) examined the relationship between client and therapist ratings of helpfulness of several response modes, including questions. They found that questions were rated by both clients and therapists as a less helpful intervention than other interventions, although they noted that questions were seen as a "somewhat helpful" rather than a hindering technique. Friedlander et al. (1985) also found that more information-seeking behaviors were not associated with better counseling sessions.

Although therapists may have believed they were being at least moderately helpful, clients tended to think that questions were not very helpful at all (Hill et al., 1988). In fact, Hill et al. found that the use of questions is associated with either no client reaction at all or the client feeling challenged by the therapist. They suggested that open questions in particular may be "a very powerful intervention that made clients feel uncomfortable" (p. 230). An alternate explanation for the finding that questions may not be the most helpful response might be that using questions may feel more like an interview for the client rather than an emotionally involving therapeutic relationship (Gelso & Fretz, 1992).

In summary, some have noted that both closed and open questions are frequently used verbal techniques in counseling but that there are mixed results in terms of the helpfulness of the technique. Clients tend not to like questions much (they may feel vulnerable or exposed beyond their comfort level when the therapist probes for more information), but they do seem to express greater levels of affect after being asked a question (a potentially positive immediate therapeutic outcome). Therapists, however, tend to believe that they are *more* empathic when using exploration. Thus, questions may be helpful to some extent and necessary at times to gather information and assist the client in exploring a topic in greater depth; however, it is important not to overuse questions as a therapeutic technique. The power of the question may lie, as with self-disclosure, in its sparing and accurate use.

Paraphrase.   The concept of paraphrase contains four related ideas (Hill, 1985): restatements, reflections, nonverbal referents, and summaries. *Restatements* are a simple rephrasing or repeating of what a client has said. A therapist might respond to a client's statement (e.g., "After the fight with my roommate, everyone has stopped talking to me") with a simple restatement: "It's as if everyone is ignoring you." One can use restatements to convey to the client that one understands his or her perspective and to help clarify the client's thoughts in a concrete manner. *Reflections of feeling* are similar to restatements but explicitly include a reference to the client's feelings and emotions. A therapist may mirror back to the client how the client feels by applying a label to a feeling (e.g., "It sounds like you feel hurt by your friends"). The therapist attempts to clarify the feeling, whether it was overtly stated by the client (e.g., "I'm so upset about this") or was indirectly inferred by the therapist as a response to the client's behavior (e.g., the client's eyes welled up with tears). Reflections help to clarify clients' feelings and may help them express a variety of related feelings (Teyber, 1997), especially when the therapist is able to use a wide range of feeling words (Hill & O'Brien, 1999), such as synonyms for sadness, for example (blue, gloomy, miserable, unhappy, and so on.).

Nonverbal referents specifically address an aspect of the client's nonverbal behavior. A counselor might point out the client's body posture, voice tone, facial expression, or gestures (e.g., "You smiled when you mentioned your grandmother"). The idea is to examine the client's nonverbal behavior for clues about how the client is feeling. *Summaries* help tie together different ideas and themes. Summaries are often used at the end of a session, but they may also be used to recap parts of sessions or even the entire treatment (i.e., at termination). For example, a counselor might state "So, all in all, part of what makes your adjustment to college so difficult is that you really miss your family."

Researchers have found that paraphrase (i.e., restatements, reflections, nonverbal referents, and summaries) account for about 10% to 31% of all therapist interventions

(Barkham & Shapiro, 1986; Hill et al., 1988) and may be the most frequently used technique by counselors (Hill, 1989). Others have shown that paraphrase is used more often in exploratory therapy (e.g., psychodynamic therapy) (Stiles et al., 1988; Wiser & Goldfried, 1996) than in other types of therapy.

Paraphrase seems to be positively related to other aspects of the counseling process. Allen et al. (1996) found that more clarification (i.e., restatement, summary) has been associated with better client collaboration in treatment. Wiser and Goldfried (1998) found the use of reflections to be associated with higher client experiencing levels. Paraphrase has also been seen as a helpful intervention from both client and therapist perspectives (Hill et al., 1988). Hill et al. also found paraphrase to be related to the client's level of emotional experiencing in-session and increased feelings of being supported. Similarly, Highlen and Baccus (1977) reported the reflection of feeling was significantly related to increased expression of client affect.

Although the process of using paraphrase seems to be quite positive, there does not seem to be any relation between the use of reflection and clarification with therapeutic outcome (Orlinsky et al., 1994); however, there is no reason to believe that the use of paraphrase is harmful in any way. Before concluding that the lack of relationship to outcome suggests that paraphrase is inert or unhelpful, it may be important to recognize the possible role of paraphrase as a moderator variable in outcome. Although the relationship may not be direct, it is possible that using paraphrase, and thus increasing client collaboration and expression of emotion, may help establish and build a strong therapeutic alliance, which has itself been strongly correlated with outcome (Horvath & Symonds, 1991). Uhlemann, Lee, and Martin (1994) have suggested that the success of paraphrase, as with other techniques, may depend on the skill of its delivery, rather than on the number of times the technique is used in a session.

In summary, paraphrases (including reflection of feeling, restatements, nonverbal referents, and summaries) are probably the most frequently used verbal techniques in counseling. There is compelling evidence that paraphrase is associated with other positive aspects of the counseling process, such as increased collaboration and client emotional experiencing. Both clients and therapists have tended to believe this technique is helpful. There is little evidence linking paraphrase and reflection of feeling directly to therapeutic outcome. The power of the technique may lie in its ability to enhance collaboration, rapport, and a strong therapeutic alliance between the client and the counselor. It is also important, as with other techniques, to recognize the skill in delivering the technique; a well-timed and clearly worded reflection of feeling will be much more effective than a continuous parroting of the client's own words. Reflections and paraphrase have the potential to be very potent verbal techniques, and, at the very least, are unlikely to be harmful to clients.

Information.   Information refers to providing the client with some form of direct knowledge or facts. Information is used frequently in career counseling (Nagel, Hoffman, & Hill, 1995), where providing knowledge about the world of work is a crucial element of successful counseling. Radio talk show psychologists tend to use information more than any other technique (D. A. Levy, 1989). Research suggests that the use of information is fairly common across all types of therapy, and it is used from 11% to 24% of the time (Barkham & Shapiro, 1986; Hill et al., 1988).

The research on information is actually quite sparse, however. What there is, though, seems positive. Friedlander et al. (1985) found that giving information was associated with better therapy sessions. Most other studies on information, however, have focused on test interpretations. Much more research is needed to investigate the use of different kinds of information given and the most appropriate ways in which to provide information in a counseling session.

Other Techniques.   Like information, there is less empirical research on other techniques, such as approval, minimal encouragers, silence, and humor. However, given the frequency with which therapists use these techniques in practice, a review of what we do know is warranted. First, *approval* refers to encouraging the continuance of client behavior (e.g., support for expressing emotions in the therapy session). Hill et al. (1988) found that approval was used 6% of the time and was associated with clients feeling supported. According to a study by Barkham and Shapiro (1986), however, therapists tended to use reassurance as much as 46% of the time!

There is some evidence for the efficacy of approval as a directive technique. Greater levels of encouragement, approval, and reassurance have been associated with more successful therapy (Friedlander et al., 1985), and clients generally rate approval as moderately helpful (Hill et al., 1988). However, there are other studies that suggest that increased levels of praise may be associated with poorer client collaboration in treatment (Allen et al., 1996). In addition, and contrary to intuition, Barkham and Shapiro (1986) found using reassurance to be negatively related to therapists' perceptions of their own empathy. Therapists believed they conveyed less empathy when they expressed more reassurance, a finding not substantiated by the clients' perspectives. Orlinsky et al. (1994) suggested that therapist support and encouragement is not a terribly effective intervention (although they also note there is no evidence that it can be harmful).

Second, *minimal encouragers* are short phrases that indicate acknowledgment, agreement, or understanding (Hill, 1985). Minimal encouragers have also been referred to as "acknowledgments" (Stiles, 1978). A minimal encourager might be when the counselor says "Um-hum," "yeah," "sure," or "I see." Minimal encouragers urge the client to continue talking but are in and of themselves neutral responses (i.e., they do not communicate approval or disapproval) in terms of grammatical structure if not effect. Some have disagreed about whether minimal encouragers are in fact a verbal response mode (Elliott et al., 1987). The purpose of using a minimal encourager is to communicate to the client that the therapist is following what the client is saying but not to interrupt the flow of the client's speech.

Some researchers have found minimal encouragers to be the most common response mode for both dynamic and cognitive-behavioral therapists (Stiles et al., 1988), as well as the most common mode used by therapists in training (Lonborg, Daniels, Hammond, Houghton-Wenger, & Brace, 1991). Others have noted that minimal encouragers are used less often in both dynamic and cognitive-behavioral therapies than interpretation (Wiser & Goldfried, 1996). Minimal encouragers have been recommended as an important technique for communicating that one is attending to the client (Hill & O'Brien, 1999) and are common in high-rapport segments of interviews with therapists in training (Sharpley & Guiddara, 1993). Minimal encouragers appear to be helpful at least in terms of building an alliance with the client. Although not the focus of this chapter, it is important to note that minimal encouragers serve many of the same purposes as other less verbal or nonverbal techniques (e.g., eye contact, facial expression, body movement or position, etc.) in communicating attention and respect to the client (Fretz, Corn, Tuemmler, & Bellet, 1979; E. S. Robbins & Haase, 1985; Sharpley & Sagris, 1995).

Third, *silence* was defined by Ladany, Hill, Thompson, and O'Brien (1999) as a purposeful pause in the dialogue where neither the client nor therapist are speaking. Pausing before responding verbally to a client can be a very powerful technique. Through silence one can communicate caring, patience, and a respect for the client's emotions. It is sometimes a good idea to allow the client time to reflect on what has just happened in a session without interruption.

Gelso and Fretz (1992) have noted that novice counselors tend to "undervalue silence" (p. 166). Novice therapists may believe that they need to intervene in some way, without recognizing that silence itself can be an intervention. There is, of course, a balance to be reached in determining how much silence is "enough." Benjamin (1987) notes that extensive silences (e.g., longer than a minute) should be avoided by therapists in training. However, more and longer silence has been associated with higher client-rated rapport with therapists in training (Sharpley, 1997). Overall, silence is an important part of therapeutic communication (Leira, 1995), but it needs to be used with care.

One final technique that has been growing as a focus of research and clinical interest is that of the use of *humor* in counseling (Fry & Salameh, 1987; Warner & Studwell, 1991). Humor as a therapeutic technique has a long and controversial history. Some have asserted that humor in therapy can be destructive and damaging (Kubie, 1970), but others have called it "indispensable" to therapy (Rosenheim, 1974). Most have suggested that humor be used sparingly, if used at all (Schwarz, 1974), and that sarcasm should be avoided (Cade, 1986; Schnarch, 1990).

As a therapeutic technique, humor has been used explicitly in Adlerian counseling (McBrien, 1993), with disabled clients (Marini, 1992), in alcoholism counseling (von Wormer, 1986), and in career counseling (Nevo, 1986). However, there has been very little empirical research on the actual process of counseling in relation to the use of humor (Shaughnessy & Wadsworth, 1992). Much more research is needed before clear recommendations can be drawn.

Only two studies have specifically examined at the role of client laughter in the helping process, a concept related to humor. Gervaize, Mahrer, and Markow (1985) found strong client laughter to be associated with the therapist directing the client to engage in interpersonally risky behaviors. Falk and Hill (1992) found that most client laughter is mild or moderate. They identified six categories of therapist humor: revelation of truth, exaggeration/simplification, disparagement, release of tension, other humor (e.g., surprise, incongruity, word play, nonverbal, anecdotes, etc.), and nonhumor. Falk and Hill found that ridiculous descriptions of the client (which was coded as a risk intervention rather than strictly as humor) led to the most client laughter; release of tension as a humor approach was also related to strong client laughter. Falk and Hill did not replicate the findings of Gervaize et al. (1985). They did find that humorous interventions were associated with client laughter (mostly in relation to release of tension), but that humorous interventions were not necessarily related to increased therapeutic work. Much more research is needed to explore the relationship between the use of humor and successful therapeutic outcome and the relationship of humor to other process variables (e.g., the working alliance, client collaboration, therapist helpfulness, client emotional experiencing, etc.).

In summary, although there is less cumulative empirical work on approval, minimal encouragers, silence, and humor, we have learned a few valuable points. Giving the client direct approval may not be the most effective intervention despite the fact that it may be used quite frequently. It has been associated with positive experiences in therapy from the client perspective, and there is no evidence that it is a harmful technique. Both minimal encouragers and silence can be helpful counselor techniques. Minimal encouragers are frequently used and may help build and sustain the therapeutic alliance. Silence can be used to communicate a shared connection with the client; a moment of quiet in therapy may be more intimate than several astute interpretations. Silence can be used to provide time for the client (and therapist) to self-reflect or gain insight. Humor has not been discussed as much in the counseling literature as some of the other techniques. Yet, many have suggested that it can be a quite effective therapeutic skill. As controversial as self-disclosure, humor may also be as powerful. At this time, however, there is very little empirical work to guide the use of humor in counseling. Anecdotally, many therapists do use humor at times in their work, and some studies have suggested the need to examine client laughter as part of the therapeutic process (Falk & Hill, 1992; Gervaize et al., 1985). Yet we know very little about the actual use of humor in therapy. When is it used and with which clients? When is it helpful and when is it harmful? Much more research is needed.

For all the verbal techniques, we have accumulated a good deal of research, though more work is clearly needed. We have some solid evidence of the effectiveness of some techniques (e.g., paradoxical interventions, reflections, etc.), but we also have an accumulation of complex and contradictory findings. It may be ineffective to search for the "best techniques" in such a general sense. As Paul put it in 1967, "*What* treatment, by *whom*, is most effective for *this* individual with *that* specific problem, and under *which* set of circumstances?" (p. 111, italics in original). One must consider the skill with which the therapist applies the technique, the timing, the readiness of the client, the cultural backgrounds of the therapist and client, the strength of the therapeutic alliance, and the sequencing of the other techniques used. We need to look beyond the mere surface of the therapy process to study the covert experiences of the counseling participants.

Covert Behaviors

In addition to observable counselor techniques, there lies under the surface another layer of activity. Beneath the verbal and nonverbal techniques of counselors and the responses of their clients exist covert variables, such as counselor intentions, self-talk, and clients' internal reactions. Not only must counselors be aware of what they are saying and doing in a counseling session (and the verbal and physical behaviors of their clients), but they must also attend to their own thoughts and feelings and even guess at the reactions of their clients. Two primary cognitive-mediational models have been proposed that consider the importance of covert processes (e.g., counselor self-talk and client reactions) in counseling sessions (e.g., Hill & O'Grady, 1985; Martin, 1984). Both note that the complexity of the counseling situation is significantly increased when one addresses the covert as well as the overt therapy process. Martin, Martin, Meyer, and Slemon (1986) have suggested that it is easier to achieve consistency between one's own internal reactions and external behaviors than it is to "read another's mind" (p. 120) and act on one's beliefs accordingly. For example, if a counselor thinks to herself, "I'd like to help the client explore that feeling in more depth," she may react overtly by asking an open-ended question. If, however, she misinterprets the ensuing silence as evidence that the client has reacted negatively (i.e., attempting to "read" the client's mind), she may err by jumping in with another question before the client has a chance to respond.

Research has determined that therapists are not very adept at guessing their clients' reactions (Hill, Thompson, Cogar, & Denman, 1993; Regan & Hill, 1992; Thompson & Hill, 1991), especially negative reactions (Hill, Thompson, & Corbett, 1992), which clients often try to hide from their counselors (Hill et al., 1993; Rennie, 1992, 1994). In addition, there are some intriguing findings about whether the ability to accurately perceive client reactions is even helpful. Thompson and Hill (1991) found that when therapists accurately identified their clients' hidden reactions as relating to the therapeutic work, their subsequent interventions were seen as more helpful; however, Hill et al. (1992) pointed out that when therapists accurately identified their clients' hidden reactions as negative, their subsequent interventions were *less* helpful. Being aware of positive client reactions seems to be helpful for therapists, but being aware of negative client reactions seems to negatively affect the counselor's subsequent performance.

Although it may not be clear yet whether it is helpful to be aware of one's clients' covert reactions, there seems to be some agreement that awareness of one's own covert reactions may be quite important in a counseling situation (Kelly, Hall, & Miller, 1989; Martin, 1984; Nutt-Williams & Hill, 1996; Singer & Luborsky, 1977). In fact, Hill et al. (1983) introduced the idea that therapist cognitions are an important part of counseling and should be studied in their own right. Although there are still relatively few studies on counselor covert behavior, some specific variables have been examined in the research literature, specifically: therapist intentions, self-talk, cognitive awareness, and cognitive management strategies.

Therapist Intentions.   Counselors do not randomly use techniques. The use of techniques usually involves having a plan, goal, or intention. For example, a counselor does not ask an open-ended question every five minutes, give an interpretation every 10, and employ minimal encouragers every 30 seconds, regardless of what the client has said. This may seem ridiculous, but it highlights the idea that *what* the therapist wants to accomplish is at least as important, if not more, to study to increase our understanding of therapist techniques. Hill (1992) asserted that any description of therapist techniques should include a discussion of intentions, and Stiles et al. (1996) stated that therapist intentions are important to include in "any multiperspective account of how therapy works" (p. 411). Research has also shown that therapist intentions have accounted for more of the variance in outcome than verbal response modes (Hill et al., 1988), highlighting the important impact intentions can have on the process and outcome of therapy.

Therapist intentions have been defined in several ways (Gaston & Ring, 1992; Hill & O'Grady, 1985; Stiles et al., 1996). One of the most commonly used measures of therapist intentions is the Therapist Intentions List (Hill & O'Grady, 1985), which provides a list of 19 intentions. The 19 intentions include the following:

1. Set limits (i.e., structure the session, goals, objectives, or parameters of the relationship, such as fees, time limit, etc.).
2. Get information (i.e., find out specific facts).
3. Give information (i.e., educate, give reasons, etc.).
4. Support (i.e., provide a supportive environment, build rapport, etc.).
5. Focus (i.e., refocus direction of session, change subject, etc.).
6. Clarify (i.e., solicit elaboration or specification from the client).
7. Hope (i.e., build morale, convey confidence in the client's ability to change, etc.).
8. Cathart (i.e., help the client express feelings, relieve tension).
9. Cognitions (i.e., identify problematic or maladaptive thoughts or attitudes).
10. Behaviors (i.e., identify client's problematic behaviors and their consequences).
11. Self-control (i.e., encourage client mastery, help client assume personal responsibility for thoughts and feelings, etc.).
12. Feelings (i.e., encourage awareness and acceptance of hidden or unexpressed emotions).
13. Insight (i.e., help client understand reactions, underlying dynamics, assumptions, etc.).
14. Change (i.e., help client develop new skills, cognitions, assumptions, etc.).
15. Reinforce change (i.e., to give feedback about changes, encourage maintenance of new ways of behaving, etc.).
16. Resistance (i.e., overcome obstacles to progress, etc.).
17. Challenge (i.e., confront client behavior, point out contradictions, help client question old ways of behaving, etc.).
18. Relationship (i.e., enhance the working alliance, uncover transference issues, address impasses in the therapeutic relationship, etc.).
19. Therapist needs (i.e., protect self, relieve anxiety, attempt to feel good even at the expense of the client).

Hill et al. (1988) proposed that seven clusters of intentions should be the focus of future research: set limits; provide assessment (e.g., get information, focus, and clarify); give support (e.g., support, hope, and reinforce change); educate (e.g., give information); explore (e.g., cognitions, behaviors, and feelings); restructure (e.g., insight, challenge, and resistance); and change.

Using a revised, session-level version of the Therapist Intentions List, Stiles et al. (1996) examined the intentions of cognitive-behavioral and psychodynamic-interpersonal therapists. They found that therapists of different orientations have predominantly different intentions. Dynamic therapists tend to focus more intentions on feelings-awareness and insight, whereas cognitive-behavioral therapists tend to rely on intentions of setting limits, changing, and reinforcing change. Stiles et al. (1996) also factor analyzed the various intentions and arrived at seven primary clusters of intentions representing the focus of each intention: treatment context, session structure, affect, obstacles, encouraging change, behavior, and cognition-insight. They found, after examining the patterns of the focus on intentions across sessions, that there remained general differences between the two forms of treatment. Specifically, dynamic therapists focused more on affect and obstacles, and cognitive-behavioral therapists focused more on treatment context, encouraging change, and behavior.

Horvath, Marx, and Kamann (1988) proposed that researchers ought to distinguish reason (i.e., why the therapist chooses an intervention) from plan (i.e., what the therapist has in mind for the client). Horvath et al. suggested that previous research had only examined the reasons for interventions but not the plans. In other words, Horvath et al. pointed out that it is just as important to know what the counselor intended with an intervention as the actual impact the intervention had on the client, a suggestion shared with Stiles (1987). It seems that therapists use a variety of interventions to accomplish the same intentions (Stiles, Shapiro, & Firth-Cozens, 1989). For example, a therapist might intend to merely acknowledge what a client had said; to accomplish this end, the therapist might say "right" or "ok," which might be coded as approval at the grammatical level, or the therapist might say "umhumm," which might be coded as a minimal encourager. Thus, it does seem quite important how the client receives the therapist intervention (i.e., feels supported versus interrupted).

The impact of "intentions" and interventions on clients has been examined through the use of helpfulness ratings. Elliott (1985) found that therapists rated the intentions of inform, advise, and reassure as helpful, and clients rated the intentions of advise, reassure, and share self as helpful. In contrast, clients rated gather information as less helpful, which corresponds to research showing that clients don't find questions to be a particularly helpful intervention (Elliott et al., 1982; Hill et al., 1988). Both Hill and O'Grady (1985) and Hill et al. (1988) found that therapist intentions were consistently connected to specific helping skills, although there was some variability. In order to encourage clients to explore feelings, therapists used open questions, reflections, and interpretations, but to give the client information, therapists used direct guidance and self-disclosure. Martin, Martin, and Slemon (1989) found evidence of distinct patterns of interventions following specific intentions. For example, when therapists intended to get information, they used open questions. When they intended to challenge the client, they used confrontation. When they intended to support the client, they used approval and reflection. And when they intended to promote insight, they used interpretation and reflection.

Kivlighan (1989) found that, after a semester of training, graduate student counselors decreased their intentions of assessment and increased intentions to explore, suggesting that training not only affects the kinds of interventions counselors choose but also how they think about the counseling process. Kelly et al. (1989) also found that more experienced therapists-in-training were better at articulating their intentions, and more anxious therapists had a more difficult time clearly stating their intentions, again supporting the idea that training helps therapists with their therapeutic cognitions as well as their behaviors.

Kivlighan and Angelone (1989) found a relationship between the intentions novice counselors use and the types of clients they see. When working with introverted clients, novice counselors expressed more intentions to challenge clients and fewer intentions to support clients. Client-rated smoothness of the sessions was also significantly related to the intentions of support and challenge, with greater use of support and less use of challenge associated with smoother sessions. The findings suggest that the counselor's perception of the client (i.e., introverted) may be related to their intentions, which in turn may be related to the session smoothness (one indicator of outcome). In addition, Kivlighan (1990) found a relationship between client-rated working alliance (another indicator of outcome) and counselor intentions, such that when therapists intended to assess, explore, and support, clients rated the working alliance lower. Because these findings seem counterintuitive, it is important to remember that it was only the frequency of the intentions that was examined, not their appropriateness or timing.

Although there appears to be some relationship between counselor intentions and client ratings of session outcome, it is important to note that clients often misperceive their therapists' intentions (Fuller & Hill, 1985). Fuller and Hill suggested that it may not be necessary or desirable for clients to know what the therapists intend as a condition of successful therapy. In fact, clients who are concentrating on "decoding" their therapists' behaviors may not be focused on their own therapeutic work (Hill, 1990). In support of this idea, Martin, Martin, and Slemon (1987) found a negative correlation between transparency (i.e., clients' accurate perception of therapist intentions) and the participants' ratings of therapeutic effectiveness.

In summary, therapist intentions appear to be quite important as well as complex. Although different therapists rely on different intentions, it may also be true that therapists may use different verbal techniques to accomplish the same intention (Stiles et al., 1989). Although it may be important to know what the counselor actually intended to do in the session, it may be equally important to understand how the client perceived the intervention. It may be important to know that Counselor X intended to gather information from her client (and so asked an open-ended question), but it may be even more important to know that the client perceived the counselor's intention as a challenge.

It is also interesting that the clarity of intentions seems to increase with experience and that choice of intentions seems to vary with the type of client one is seeing. Although there appears to be consensus that intentions are important to the counseling process, more research needs to be done to help us understand the actual relationship between intentions, techniques, and outcome.

Therapist Self-Talk and Internal Reactions.   Therapist intentions represent one way of thinking about what is happening in a counseling session. A broader view of the kinds of things therapists think about has been captured by the term *self-talk.* Self-talk has long been regarded as an important part of *client* behavior, especially in cognitive-behavioral therapies (Bandura, 1986; Beck, 1976; Ellis, 1973; Meichenbaum, 1977); however, recently there has been a more distinct focus on *therapist* self-talk. Although therapist covert activity has been an important aspect of many well-established counselor training programs (e.g., Ivey, 1971; Kagan, 1975), research on counselor self-talk has only been gaining interest since the 1980s.

Morran (1986) examined two specific types of counselor self-talk: task-facilitative and task-distractive. Task-facilitative self-talk represents how much a counselor focuses on understanding the client and planning productive interventions. Task-distractive self-talk refers to how often counselors are focused on themselves and concerns about their performance. Morran did not, however, find any relationship between either form of self-talk and therapeutic performance (measured by client satisfaction). Morran used global measures, both of self-talk and performance outcome, which may account for the inconclusive findings. The self-talk scale Morran used was developed by Fuqua, Newman, Anderson, and Johnson (1986) to assess different aspects of internal dialogue. The measure is a 23-item scale, with items rated on a Likert format, assessing overall self-talk (e.g., "I hope the supervisor thinks I'm as good as the other students"). Fuqua et al. (1986) identified six scales (Social Comparison, Anxiety, Task Management, Stimulus Discrimination, Personal Adequacy, and Anticipation of Outcome) corresponding with two global dimensions (task-facilitative and task-distractive self-talk). It may be more accurate, however, to assess self-talk using the actual cognitions of the therapists, such as by using a thought-listing procedure (Cacioppo & Petty, 1981).

Using a thought-listing procedure where therapists write down their thoughts free-form after a counseling session, Morran, Kurpius, and Brack (1989) examined the self-talk of 40 beginning counselors in an analogue counseling situation. Morran et al. identified 14 categories of self-talk, including

1. Behavioral observations (e.g., thoughts focused on client behavior).
2. Client-focused questions (e.g., questions about the client or therapy session).
3. Summarizations (e.g., review of what the client has said).
4. Associations (e.g., thoughts relating client experience to others, including self).
5. Inferences or hypotheses (e.g., forming tentative hypotheses about the client).
6. Relationship assessment (e.g., thoughts focusing on the therapeutic relationship).
7. Self-instruction (e.g., self-coaching thoughts).
8. Anxiety or self-doubt (e.g., negative thoughts about performance).
9. Corrective self-feedback (e.g., evaluative thoughts that may serve to change therapist behavior).
10. Positive self-feedback (e.g., self-reinforcing thoughts).
11. Reaction to client (e.g., thoughts expressing an emotional response to the client).
12. Self-questions (e.g., self-directed questions about how to react in the session).
13. External (e.g., thoughts focused on issues outside of the immediate therapy setting).
14. Self-monitoring (e.g., awareness of self and one's reactions).

Morran et al. found the categories could be subsumed under two overarching dimensions (Information Seeking-Attending/Assessing and Integrative Understanding-Intervention Planning), using multidimensional scaling, and suggested that future research examine the sequence and timing of thoughts, as well as the content.

Using a different coding scheme, Borders, Fong-Beyette, and Cron (1988) explored the self-talk of one counselor in training. Borders et al. used Dole et al.'s (1982) Counselor Retrospective Coding System, which measures six dimensions of self-talk: Time (past, present, or future), Place (in-session or out-of-session events and feelings), Focus (client, counselor, client–counselor interaction relationship, or supervisor), Locus (external or internal), Orientation (professional or personal), and Mode (cognitive or affective). Borders et al. found there was a preponderance of self-scrutinizing and self-doubting thoughts but relatively few intentional thoughts, suggesting that, at least for novice counselors, planning interventions are only one small piece of the complex cognitions occurring during counseling sessions. Borders et al. found more negative thoughts about the self but an equal distribution of cognitively and affectively focused thoughts. By contrast, Uhlemann, Lee, and Hiebert (1988) found that novice counselors experienced predominantly positive self-talk.

Nutt-Williams and Hill (1996) examined the naturally occurring self-talk of novice therapists in real counseling situations (i.e., not analogue) to address the idea that what had been previously missing from the research literature was the association of self-talk to any other process variables. They examined counselor self-talk using a thought-listing procedure and then coded all the thoughts into two dimensions: Focus (self versus other) and Affect (negative to positive valence). Nutt-Williams and Hill found that trainees' cognitions were significantly related to their perceptions of their own helpfulness and of their clients' reactions. After partialling out the effect of the working alliance, they found that negative and self-focused self-talk was related to lower estimations of the therapists' helpfulness and a higher proportion of perceived negative client reactions. They noted that more research was needed to assess the impact of negative, self-focused self-talk on the actual performance of the therapists (and the actual reactions of the clients). In fact, Hiebert, Uhlemann, Marshall, and Lee (1998) found a relationship between anxiety, self-talk, and performance, suggesting that the more anxious counselors experienced more negative self-talk, less positive self-talk, and impaired performance.

A great deal of the work in the area of therapist self-talk has focused on how best to train novice counselors. Kline (1983) reviewed the literature on novice counselor anxiety and found that anxiety has a cognitive component (i.e., self-talk) that may be related to increases in counselor trainees' self-evaluative thinking. Kline proposed a cognitive behavior modification method intended to reduce trainee anxiety (and thus, self-evaluative self-talk). Morran, Kurpius, Brack, and Brack (1995) have also proposed a cognitive-skills training model that could be useful in helping novice therapists learn to use their covert processes (e.g., hypothesis formation, intervention planning, self-instruction) to facilitate their work. There is some evidence (e.g., Kurpius, Benjamin, & Morran, 1985) that training may reduce the amount of task-distractive self-talk trainees experience. Fuqua, Johnson, Anderson, and Newman (1984) summarized their review of cognitive training methods by suggesting that all the models share one goal: to increase trainee confidence and decrease performance anxiety.

Much of the work on therapist and counselor self-talk has focused on categorizing different forms of self-talk (e.g., task-distractive, cognitive versus affective, negative self-focused) and on relating self-talk to effective ways to train novice counselors. There has been less focus on examining the relationship of self-talk to the process of therapy or the outcome. It does appear, however, that self-talk is important and may be related to other aspects of the therapeutic process (e.g., Nutt-Williams & Hill, 1996) as well as to novice counselor anxiety (e.g., Hiebert et al., 1998). Williams, Polster, Grizzard, and Rockenbaugh (1999) have begun to examine the changes in self-talk from novice counselors to experienced counselors. There is a great deal to be learned about the effect of what counselors say to themselves during sessions. It will be interesting to learn more about how intentions interact with self-critical thoughts and with distracting thoughts as well as with choice of techniques and interventions.

Therapist Self-Awareness and Cognitive Strategies.   Another area of covert therapist activity to examine is that of the counselor's awareness of internal reactions during sessions as well as the ability to manage those reactions. Although Morran (1986) suggested that "it is not how much one self-talks, but the quality of the self-talk that counts" (p. 399), it may be more accurate to say that it is the awareness of one's self-talk and the person's ability to control self-talk that counts. What happens if a therapist is unaware of intentions or self-critical self-talk? What is the effect on the process? In what ways do therapists attempt to control or manage their internal reactions (i.e., feelings, self-talk)?

Williams, Judge, Hill, and Hoffman (1997) examined the experiences of novice therapists in a prepracticum setting. They examined the perceptions of novice therapists, clients, and supervisors of the therapists' reactions and management strategies. Using both a quantitative and qualitative methodology, they found that trainees experienced both positive and negative reactions (e.g., empathy and anxiety) and that their concerns focused on their performance, conflicts in the therapeutic relationship, and interpersonal stressors. Some trainees had difficulty managing their feelings and reactions, which were displayed as negative or incongruent behaviors in session, avoiding affect, or losing objectivity. In order to manage their reactions (e.g., frustration, anxiety, inadequacy), the therapists reported three main strategies: focusing on the client, using their self-awareness, and suppressing their feelings and reactions. Williams et al. found that novice therapists were aware of a variety of internal reactions during counseling and attempted to manage those reactions by focusing on what the client was saying, ignoring their own feelings, or attempting to understand and then use their feelings to help in the process (i.e., choice of interventions, understanding of the client).

One interesting question is whether therapists' self-awareness and management strategies change over time. Williams et al. (1999) conducted a follow-up study to examine the differences in both self-awareness and management strategies used by novice and experienced therapists. They found that for all therapists, self-awareness had, at one time or another, the effect of being hindering in some way (e.g., as a distraction) but that more experienced therapists reported that self-awareness had also been beneficial to them (e.g., by helping them keep focused or planning certain interventions). They also found that the novice therapists reported using self-coaching and self-disclosure as techniques to manage their feelings and reactions in sessions, whereas the experienced therapists reported that they would refocus on the client. As Van Wagoner, Gelso, Hayes, and Diemer (1991) have suggested, it may be crucial to understand how therapists, especially beginning therapists, manage their anxiety and other reactions (including countertransference reactions) during counseling sessions. Unfortunately, we still do not know enough about how therapists manage their reactions (Williams et al., 1997) and how aware therapists are of their reactions. It will be important to examine how aware therapists *should* be (i.e., very self-aware or moderately self-aware) and which are the most effective strategies for managing their reactions and self-talk.

Much more work is needed to understand the covert level of activity in counseling sessions. As several studies have pointed out (e.g., Hill, 1992; Martin, 1984; Stiles et al., 1996), the covert activity of both therapists and clients may be at least as important as the more overt layer of counseling process. Although some work has been done in investigating therapist intentions, more is needed to examine other covert variables, such as therapist self-talk, self-awareness, and cognitive management strategies. It is intuitive to suppose that all of that covert activity has an effect on the observable aspect of the counseling process, but without more empirical work, we have little to guide our understanding of the impact of covert variables.

Applications for Practice

The research on therapist techniques, specifically verbal response modes, can be useful in guiding therapeutic practice. Particularly in a time when there is a growing trend toward eclecticism (Norcross & Goldfried, 1992), practitioners are adhering less to rigid theoretical models and more to pantheoretical approaches that rely on common factors or techniques. As Grawe (1997) suggested, it will continue to be important to apply "research-informed" psychotherapy techniques to what counselors do in practice.

The array of research results discussed in this chapter may seem, at times, confusing and disconnected. Therefore, I suggest an overarching model, proposed by Hill and O'Brien (1999), to cluster the research results into an understandable gestalt for applying the research to actual clinical practice (see Table 8.1). Hill and O'Brien suggested a three-part approach to counseling and the training of basic helping skills: exploration, insight, and action. The exploration stage is based on humanistic and person-centered theories (e.g., Rogers, 1957) and is the stage in which therapists and clients establish rapport, develop the therapeutic relationship, and begin to explore the client's thoughts and feelings. The insight stage is derived mainly from psychoanalytic and dynamic theories (e.g., Freud, 1914/1953; Greenson, 1967) and is the stage of counseling in which the therapist helps the client achieve insight, better understands the presenting problems, and arrives at new perspectives. The action stage is informed by cognitive-behavioral theories (e.g., Bandura, 1986; Ellis, 1973) and is focused on helping clients make decisions and implement changes in their lives and behaviors.

The research on therapist techniques may be best understood by grouping them under Hill and O'Brien's (1999) model. For example, under exploration, Hill and O'Brien include such techniques as attending behaviors (i.e., minimal encouragers, silence, and other nonverbal behaviors), paraphrase and reflection of feeling, and open questions. All of these techniques have been found to be used quite frequently by counselors, but they are generally not strongly related to therapeutic outcome. As was noted earlier, the importance of these techniques may be as moderators of outcome through the building and strengthening of the therapeutic alliance. Thus, despite weak direct links to outcome, one could consider these vital skills in rapport-building and emotional exploration with clients.

In the insight stage, a counselor is likely to rely on the use of interpretation and, at times, even self-disclosure (Hill & O'Brien, 1999). By using the confrontation-interpretation cycle suggested by Olson and Claiborn (1990), therapists can help move their clients to

TABLE 8.1   *Cumulative Model of the Six Fundamental Therapist Techniques Discussed Using Hill and O'Brien (1999)*

Stage 1: Exploration	Stage 2: Insight	Stage 3: Action
Questions	Interpretation	Information
Paraphrase	Self-disclosure	Directives

greater self-understanding. Both interpretation and self-disclosure have been linked to immediate outcomes (i.e., helpfulness ratings), particularly from the client's perspective. By contrast to the techniques used in the exploration stage, insight-oriented techniques tend to be used more sparingly. In the action stage, the techniques one might rely on include giving information and direct guidance, the more directive techniques often used in cognitive-behavioral therapies (Stiles et al., 1988; Wiser & Goldfried, 1996). Although there are some contradictory findings in how helpful the more directive techniques are, at least one directive technique (paradoxical interventions) is believed to be effective.

The reverse-order relationship of the techniques to therapeutic outcome (with exploration techniques being rarely linked directly to outcome and action techniques being often linked directly to outcome) may be a function of the cumulative effect of all the techniques used across the three stages. The most conclusive process-outcome results are evident with the more directive techniques; perhaps this is because those techniques often occur once the therapeutic relationship has been established and the client has gained some degree of insight into concerns. The techniques used more in the "working" stages of therapy carry with them the effects of the early rapport-building and insight-focused techniques. Honing one's skills with regard to each of the verbal techniques addressed in this chapter may be a useful approach, despite the different relationships of the techniques to outcome.

Although the microskills approach has been a popular way of training therapists (Baker et al., 1990), the focus has been on communication techniques, rather than how counselors reach an understanding of the client's problems (Robinson & Halliday, 1987). It is also important to assess the ways in which therapists think about their clients and themselves, or their covert behavior. We need to attend to the impact of therapists' intentions, self-talk, and cognitive management strategies on in-session behavior. The things counselors say to themselves internally may impact the kinds of interventions they choose and the skill with which they deliver the techniques. It might be hard to provide an accurate reflection of feeling if one is distracted by negative self-talk and, therefore, has not really heard the client. Although we have focused on what the therapist actually does in session, there is some evidence that therapists are not always in control of their own actions. There is evidence that suggests that the techniques a therapist uses can be shaped by client reinforcement (Lee, Hallberg, Hassard, & Haase, 1979). This reminds us that not only is therapy highly complex, with both overt and covert levels, but also that it is inherently an interpersonal process (Claiborn & Lichtenberg, 1989; Kiesler, 1986; Strong, 1968).

Although several verbal response modes and covert experiences of therapists have been covered in detail in this chapter, it is important to note that there are other process factors that may be important to positive therapeutic outcomes. For example, the facilitative conditions put forth by Rogers (1957) (e.g., accurate empathy, unconditional positive regard, and therapeutic genuineness), the therapeutic alliance, level of experience, psychological well-being, and social influence variables (Strong, 1968), such as expertness, attractiveness, and trustworthiness, have all been connected to successful therapeutic outcome (Greenberg, Elliott, & Lietaer, 1994; Horvath & Symonds, 1991; Lambert & Bergin, 1994). Another crucial consideration is the role of cultural factors in the therapeutic process. Multicultural counseling theory (Sue, Ivey, & Pedersen, 1996) states that it is crucial to understand the "worldviews" of both clients and therapists. Our perceptions of the world, our attitudes, our values, and our decisions are influenced by the cultural context in which we were raised. Clients of various cultural backgrounds often have different expectations of counseling (Atkinson & Lowe, 1995) and may respond quite differently to the same therapeutic techniques (Sue & Sue, 1999). Asian American clients often prefer a more active style from their counselors (Leong, 1986); thus, the more directive techniques may be more effective than the more reflective ones. Techniques cannot be assumed to be equally effective across cultures, genders, or individual clients; rather we must discover how techniques are most effectively used in different multicultural contexts.

The growing emphasis on technical eclecticism (Lazarus, 1984), theoretical integration in psychotherapy (Norcross & Goldfried, 1992), and multicultural counseling approaches (Ponterotto, Casas, Suzuki, & Alexander, 1995) remind us that we must consider the research on therapist techniques in a broad context. The verbal response modes approach to studying therapist techniques promotes the pantheoretical perspective on what therapists actually do in sessions. The research findings are both important and useful. We can learn a great deal from psychotherapy process research. Yet, as we apply the findings, we must also recognize the complex, interpersonal, and multicultural context in which therapy actually occurs.

Summary

This chapter describes the research on therapist techniques and suggests ways in which the individual practitioner can apply the research information to practice. Although some practicing clinicians do not use or value psychotherapy research (Cohen, Sargent, & Sechrest, 1986; Suinn, 1993), with the advent of new research approaches (e.g., interpersonal process research, sequential analysis, etc.), the perceived usefulness of psychotherapy process research may be increasing (Elliott, 1983; Stiles & Shapiro, 1989). To the extent that research can help answer the question, "How can I be a more effective counselor?" it will be useful to practitioners.

The research on therapist techniques has helped answer some questions. We have some information about more and less useful techniques as well as specific types of techniques (e.g., reassuring versus challenging self-disclosures), when the techniques may be most appropriate (e.g., the use of interpretation later in the therapy process), and with which clients (e.g., using challenging techniques with more highly functioning clients). We can draw some clinical insights from the research, which may help us apply our techniques more astutely.

Although the research results are helpful, one major concern with psychotherapy research is that it tends to oversimplify the complexity of the therapeutic process (Morrow-Bradley & Elliott, 1986). We need to examine and apply the research results with the understanding that particular techniques may have been singled out for study from the interactive complexity of the therapy relationship. Strupp (1986) has suggested that it may not be possible to separate interpersonal therapeutic factors (i.e., the alliance) from the procedures used (i.e., techniques), adding that "it may not be possible to tease them apart without destroying the process" (p. 124). The use of techniques in counseling may be highly intuitive, intricately woven into the fabric of the therapy. If we try to pull out one strand to examine, we may end up unraveling the cloth. Practitioners and researchers should be cautioned not to make sweeping statements about the efficacy of independent techniques (e.g., "it is always best to use paradoxical interventions, interpretations and infrequent self-disclosures"). We still need to take into account the other "strands" of the cloth: the client, the other techniques used, the therapist's intentions, the timing, the cultural context, and, probably, most importantly, the skill with which the techniques are applied.

Along with the acknowledgment of the importance of the therapist's skills (Sachs, 1983; Strupp, 1996), there has been growing interest in examining the individual therapist as a whole (Lambert, 1989; Luborsky et al., 1985) rather than studying the therapist's specific contributions to the process (e.g., verbal response modes), as had traditionally been done. Research has shown that therapist techniques account for only a small proportion of the variance in immediate therapeutic outcome (Elliott, 1985; Hill, 1989; Hill et al, 1988). A focus on the whole therapist, as it were, reminds us that all the techniques covered in this chapter are both potentially useful and potentially harmful. All that the therapist does, and perhaps is, can have an affect on the client and the therapy process.

Being a skilled therapist involves understanding when certain techniques are most appropriate and having the proficiency needed to employ those techniques with accuracy. But it involves much more than the ability to apply certain techniques and interventions. Skilled therapists attend to the subtle issues of relationship, cultural differences, and empowerment of the client. As Kottler (1991) pointed out, "there is a distinctively passionate, human quality to the performance of a virtuoso in any field" (p. 174) that characterizes the expert therapist. Therapists must study the research to learn about the effectiveness of specific techniques and then infuse the use of those techniques with personal style and empathic understanding of the client.

References

Allen, J. G., Coyne, L., Colson, D. B., & Horwitz, L. (1996). Pattern of therapist interventions associated with patient collaboration. *Psychotherapy, 33,* 254–261.

Anderson, B., & Anderson, W. (1985). Client perceptions of counselors using positive and negative self-involving statements. *Journal of Counseling Psychology, 32,* 462–465.

Atkinson, D. R., & Lowe, S. M. (1995). The role of ethnicity, cultural knowledge, and conventional techniques in counseling and psychotherapy. In J. G. Ponterotto, J. M. Casas, L. A. Suzuki, & C. M. Alexander (Eds.), *Handbook of multicultural counseling* (pp. 387–414). Thousand Oaks, CA: Sage.

Atkinson, D. R., & Matsushita, Y. J. (1991). Japanese-American acculturation, counseling style, counselor ethnicity, and perceived counselor credibility. *Journal of Counseling Psychology, 38,* 473–478.

Baer, P. E., Dunbar, P. W., Hamilton, J. E., & Beutler, L. E. (1980). Therapists' perceptions of the psychotherapeutic process: Development of a psychotherapy process inventory. *Psychological Reports, 46,* 563–570.

Baker, S. B., Daniels, T. G., & Greeley, A. T. (1990). Systematic training of graduate-level counselors: Narrative and meta-analytic reviews of three major programs. *The Counseling Psychologist, 18,* 355–421.

Bandura, A. (1986). *Social foundations of thought and action: A social cognitive theory.* Englewood Cliffs, NJ: Prentice-Hall.

Barkham, M., & Shapiro, D. A. (1986). Counselor verbal response modes and experienced empathy. *Journal of Counseling Psychology, 33,* 3–10.

Beck, A. T. (1976). *Cognitive therapy and emotional disorders.* New York: International Universities Press.

Benjamin, A. (1987). *The helping interview.* Boston: Houghton Mifflin.

Bergin, A. E. (1971). The evaluation of therapeutic outcomes. In A. E. Bergin & S. L. Garfield (Eds.), *Handbook of psychotherapy and behavior change* (pp. 217–270). New York: Wiley.

Beutler, L. E. (1983). *Eclectic psychotherapy: A systematic approach.* New York: Pergamon Press.

Beutler, L. E., Dunbar, P. W., & Baer, P. E. (1980). Individual variation among therapists' perceptions of patients, therapy process and outcome. *Psychiatry, 43,* 205–210.

Beutler, L. E., Machado, P. P., & Neufeldt, S. A. (1994). Therapist variables. In A. E. Bergin & S. L. Garfield (Eds.), *Handbook of psychotherapy and behavior change* (4th ed., pp. 229–269).

Bibring, E. (1954). Psychoanalysis and the dynamic psychotherapies. *Journal of the American Psychoanalytic Association, 2,* 745–770.

Bischoff, M. M., & Tracey, T. J. G. (1995). Client resistance as predicted by therapist behavior: A study of sequential dependence. *Journal of Counseling Psychology, 42,* 487–495.

Borders, L. D., Fong-Beyette, M. L., & Cron, E. A. (1988). In-session cognitions of a counseling student: A case study. *Counselor Education and Supervision, 28,* 59–70.

Cacioppo, J. T., & Petty, R. E. (1981). Social psychological procedures for cognitive response assessment: The thought-listing technique. In T. V. Merluzzi, C. R. Glass, & M. Genest (Eds.), *Cognitive assessment* (pp. 309–342). New York: Guilford Press.

Cade, B. (1986). The uses of humour in therapy. *Family Therapy Collections, 19,* 64–76.

Chambless, D. (1996). In defense of dissemination of empirically supported psychological interventions. *Clinical Psychology: Science and Practice, 3,* 230–235.

Chen, G. (1995). Differences in self-disclosure patterns among Americans versus Chinese: A comparative study. *Journal of Cross-Cultural Psychology, 26,* 84–91.

Cherbosque, J. (1987). Differential effects of counselor self-disclosure statements on perception of the counselor and willingness to disclose: A cross-cultural study. *Psychotherapy, 24,* 434–437.

Claiborn, C. D., & Dowd, E. D. (1985). Attributional interpretations in counseling: Content versus discrepancy. *Journal of Counseling Psychology, 32,* 186–196.

Claiborn, C. D., & Lichtenberg, J. W. (1989). Interactional counseling. *The Counseling Psychologist, 17,* 355–443.

Claiborn, C. D., Ward, S. R., & Strong, S. (1981). Effect of congruence between counselor interpretations and client beliefs. *Journal of Counseling Psychology, 28,* 101–109.

Coady, N. F. (1991). The association between complex types of therapist interventions and outcomes in psychodynamic psychotherapy. *Research on Social Work Practice, 1,* 122–138.

Cohen, L. H., Sargent, M. M., & Sechrest, L. B. (1986). Use of psychotherapy research by professional psychologists. *American Psychologist, 41,* 198–206.

Conoley, C. W., Padula, M. A., Payton, D. S., & Daniels, J. A. (1994). Predictors of client implementation of counselor recommendations: Match with problem,

difficulty level, and building on client strengths. *Journal of Counseling Psychology, 41,* 3–7.

Crits-Christoph, P., Barber, J. P., & Kurcias, J. S. (1993). The accuracy of therapists' interpretations and the development of the therapeutic alliance. *Psychotherapy Research, 3,* 25–35.

Crits-Christoph, P., Cooper, A., & Luborsky, L. (1988). The accuracy of therapists' interpretations and the outcome of dynamic psychotherapy. *Journal of Consulting and Clinical Psychology, 56,* 490–495.

Crits-Christoph, P., Frank, E., Chambless, D. L., Brody, C., & Karp, J. F. (1995). Training in empirically validated treatments: What are clinical psychology students learning? *Professional Psychology: Research and Practice, 26,* 514–522.

Cummings, N. A. (1987). The future of psychotherapy: One psychologist's perspective. *American Journal of Psychotherapy, 41,* 349–360.

Curtis, J. M. (1981). Indications and contraindications in the use of therapist's self-disclosure. *Psychological Reports, 49,* 499–507.

Dole, A. A., Burton, L., Gold, J., Lerner, J., Nissenfeld, M., & Weis, D. (1982). *Six dimensions of retrospections by therapists and counselors—A manual for research.* JSAS: Catalog of Selected Documents in Psychology, 12(2), 23, (MS2454).

Dolliver, R. H. (1986). Counselor directiveness and client task-readiness reviewed. *The Counseling Psychologist, 14,* 461–464.

Edwards, C. E., & Murdock, N. L. (1994). Characteristics of therapist self-disclosure in the counseling process. *Journal of Counseling and Development, 72,* 384–389.

Egan, G. (1986). *The skilled helper* (3rd ed.). Monterey, CA: Brooks/Cole.

Elliott, R. (1983). Fitting process research to the practicing psychologist. *Psychotherapy, 20,* 47–55.

Elliott, R. (1985). Helpful and nonhelpful events in brief counseling interviews: An empirical taxonomy. *Journal of Counseling Psychology, 32,* 307–322.

Elliott, R., Barker, C. B., Caskey, N., & Pistrang, N. (1982). Differential helpfulness of counselor verbal response modes. *Journal of Counseling Psychology, 29,* 354–361.

Elliott, R., Hill, C. E., Stiles, W. B., Friedlander, M. L., Mahrer, A. R., & Margison, F. R. (1987). Primary therapist response modes: A comparison of six rating systems. *Journal of Consulting and Clinical Psychology, 55,* 218–223.

Ellis, A. (1973). *Humanistic psychotherapy: The rational-emotive approach.* New York: McGraw-Hill.

Exum, H. A., & Lau, E. Y. (1988). Counseling style preference of Chinese college students. *Journal of Multicultural Counseling and Development, 16,* 84–92.

Eysenck, H. (1952). The effects of psychotherapy: An evaluation. *Journal of Consulting Psychology, 16,* 319–324.

Falk, D. R., & Hill, C. E. (1992). Counselor interventions preceding client laughter in brief therapy. *Journal of Counseling Psychology, 39,* 39–45.

Fenichel, O. (1941). *The psychoanalytic theory of neurosis.* New York: Norton.

Forsyth, N. L., & Forsyth, D. R. (1982). Internality, controllability, and the effectiveness of attributional interpretations in counseling. *Journal of Counseling Psychology, 29,* 140–150.

Frank, J. D. (1961). *Persuasion and healing.* Baltimore, MD: Johns Hopkins University Press.

Frank, J. D. (1982). Therapeutic components shared by all psychotherapies. In J. H. Harvey & M. M. Parks (Eds.), *Psychotherapy research and behavior change.* Washington, DC: American Psychological Association.

Fretz, B. R., Corn, R., Tuemmler, J. M., & Bellet, W. (1979). Counselor nonverbal behaviors and client evaluations. *Journal of Counseling Psychology, 26,* 304–311.

Freud, S. (1953). Remembering, repeating, and working through. *Complete psychological work* (standard ed., Vol. 12). London: Hogarth. (Original work published 1914)

Friedlander, M. L. (1982). Counseling discourse as a speech event: Revision and extension of the Hill Counselor Verbal Response Category System. *Journal of Counseling Psychology, 29,* 425–429.

Friedlander, M. L., Thibodeau, J. R., & Ward, L. G. (1985). Discriminating the "good" from the "bad" therapy hour: A study of dyadic interaction. *Psychotherapy, 22,* 631–642.

Fromm-Reichmann, F. (1950). *Principles of intensive psychotherapy.* Chicago: University of Chicago Press.

Fry, W. F., & Salameh, W. A. (Eds.). (1987). *Handbook of humor and psychotherapy: Advances in the clinical use of humor.* Sarasota, FL: Professional Resource Exchange, Inc.

Fuller, F., & Hill, C. E. (1985). Counselor and helpee perceptions of counselor intentions in relationship to outcome in a single counseling session. *Journal of Counseling Psychology, 32,* 329–338.

Fuqua, D. R., Johnson, A. W., Anderson, M. W., & Newman, J. L. (1984). Cognitive methods in counselor training. *Counselor Education and Supervision, 24,* 85–95.

Fuqua, D. R., Newman, J. L., Anderson, M. W., & Johnson, A. W. (1986). Preliminary study of internal dialogue in a training setting. *Psychological Reports, 58,* 163–172.

Garfield, S. L., & Bergin, A. E. (1994). Introduction and historical overview. In A. E. Bergin & S. L. Garfield (Eds.), *Handbook of psychotherapy and behavior change* (pp. 3–18). New York: Wiley.

Gaston, L., & Ring, J. M. (1992). Preliminary results on the Inventory of Therapeutic Strategies. *Journal of Psychotherapy Research and Practice, 1,* 1–13.

Gelso, C. J., & Carter, J. (1994). The relationship in counseling and psychotherapy: Components, consequences, and theoretical antecedents. *The Counseling Psychologist, 13,* 155–244.

Gelso, C. J., & Fretz, B. R. (1992). *Counseling psychology* (pp. 157–189). New York: Harcourt.

Gervaize, P. A., Mahrer, A. R., & Markow, R. (1985). What therapists do to promote strong laughter in patients. *Psychotherapy in Private Practice, 3,* 65–74.

Goldberg, D. P., Hobson, R. F., Maguire, G. P., Margison, F. R., O'Dowd, T., Osborn, M., & Moss, S. (1984). The clarification and assessment of a method of psychotherapy. *British Journal of Psychiatry, 144,* 567–580.

Goldfried, M. R. (Ed.). (1982). *Converging themes in psychotherapy.* New York: Springer.

Goodyear, R. K., & Shumate, J. L. (1996). Perceived effects of therapist self-disclosure of attraction to clients. *Professional Psychology: Research and Practice, 27,* 613–616.

Grawe, K. (1997). Research-informed psychotherapy. *Psychotherapy Research, 7,* 1–19.

Greenberg, L., Elliott, R., & Lietaer, G. (1994). Research on experiential psychotherapies. In A. E. Bergin & S. L. Garfield (Eds.), *Handbook of psychotherapy and behavior change* (4th ed., pp. 509–539). New York: Wiley.

Greenson, R. R. (1967). *The technique and practice of psychoanalysis* (Vol. 1). Madison, CT: International Universities Press.

Hagebak, R. W., & Parker, G. V. (1969). Therapist directiveness, client dominance, and therapy resistance. *Journal of Consulting and Clinical Psychology, 33,* 536–540.

Hanna, F. J., & Ritchie, M. H. (1995). Seeking the active ingredients of psychotherapeutic change: Within and outside the context of therapy. *Professional Psychology: Research and Practice, 26,* 176–183.

Hartley, D. E., & Strupp, H. H. (1983). The therapeutic alliance: Its relationship to outcome in brief psychotherapy. In J. Masling (Ed.), *Empirical studies in analytic theories* (pp. 1–37). Hillside, NJ: Erlbaum.

Harway, N., Dittman, A., Raush, H., Bordin, E., & Rigler, D. (1955). The measurement of depth of interpretation. *Journal of Consulting Psychology, 19,* 247–253.

Heaton, K. J., Hill, C. E., & Edwards, L. A. (1995). Comparing molecular and molar methods of judging therapist techniques. *Psychotherapy Research, 5,* 141–153.

Hiebert, B., Uhlemann, M. R., Marshall, A., & Lee, D. Y. (1998). The relationship between self-talk, anxiety, and counselling skill. *Canadian Journal of Counselling, 32,* 163–171.

Highlen, P. S., & Baccus, G. K. (1977). Effect of reflection of feeling and probe on client self-referenced affect. *Journal of Counseling Psychology, 24,* 440–443.

Highlen, P. S., & Hill, C. E. (1984). Factors affecting client change in counseling. In S. Brown & R. Lent (Eds.), *Handbook of counseling psychology* (pp. 334–396). New York: Wiley.

Hill, C. E. (1978). The development of a system for classifying counselor responses. *Journal of Counseling Psychology, 25,* 461–468.

Hill, C. E. (1982). Counseling process research: Philosophical and methodological dilemmas. *The Counseling Psychologist, 10,* 7–19.

Hill, C. E. (1985). *Manual for Counselor Verbal Response Modes Category System* (Rev. ed.). Unpublished manuscript, University of Maryland, College Park.

Hill, C. E. (1986). An overview of the Hill counselor and client verbal response modes category systems. In L. Greenberg & W. Pinsoff (Eds.), *The psychotherapeutic process: A research handbook* (pp. 131–160). New York: Guilford Press.

Hill, C. E. (1989). *Therapist techniques and client outcome: Eight cases of brief psychotherapy.* Newbury Park, CA: Sage.

Hill, C. E. (1990). A review of exploratory in-session process research. *Journal of Consulting and Clinical Psychology, 58,* 288–294.

Hill, C. E. (1992). Research on therapist techniques in brief individual therapy: Implications for practitioners. *The Counseling Psychologist, 20,* 689–711.

Hill, C. E., Carter, J. A., & O'Farrell, M. K. (1983). A case study of the process and outcome of time-limited counseling. *Journal of Counseling Psychology, 30,* 3–18.

Hill, C. E., Helms, J. E., Tichenor, V., Spiegel, S. B., O'Grady, K. E., & Perry, E. S. (1988). The effects of therapist response modes in brief psychotherapy. *Journal of Counseling Psychology, 35,* 222–233.

Hill, C. E., Mahalik, J. R., & Thompson, B. J. (1989). Therapist self-disclosure. *Psychotherapy, 26,* 290–295.

Hill, C. E., & O'Brien, K. M. (1999). *Helping skills: Facilitating exploration, insight and action.* Washington, DC: American Psychological Association.

Hill, C. E., & O'Grady, K. E. (1985). List of therapist intentions illustrated in a case study and with therapists of varying theoretical orientations. *Journal of Counseling Psychology, 32,* 3–22.

Hill, C. E., Thompson, B. J., Cogar, M. M., & Denman, D. W., III. (1993). Beneath the surface of long-term therapy: Client and therapist report of their own and each other's covert processes. *Journal of Counseling Psychology, 40,* 278–288.

Hill, C. E., Thompson, B. J., & Corbett, M. M. (1992). The impact of therapist ability to perceive displayed and hidden client reactions on immediate outcome in first sessions of brief therapy. *Psychotherapy Research, 2,* 143–155.

Hill, C. E., Thompson, B. J., & Mahalik, J. R. (1989). Therapist interpretation. In C. E. Hill, *Therapist techniques and client outcome: Eight cases of brief psychotherapy.* Newbury Park, CA: Sage.

Hill, C. E., & Williams, E. N. (2000). The process of individual psychotherapy. In R. Lent & S. Brown (Eds.), *Handbook of counseling psychology* (3rd ed., pp. 670–710). New York: Wiley.

Hill, K. A. (1987). Meta-analysis of paradoxical interventions. *Psychotherapy, 24,* 266–270.

Hills, H. I., Gruzkos, J. R., & Strong, S. R. (1985). Attribution and the double bind in paradoxical interventions. *Psychotherapy, 22,* 779–785.

Hoffman-Graff, M. A. (1977). Interviewer use of positive and negative self-disclosure and interviewer-subject sex pairing. *Journal of Counseling Psychology, 24,* 184–190.

Horvath, A. O., & Luborsky, L. (1993). The role of the therapeutic alliance in psychotherapy. *Journal of Consulting and Clinical Psychology, 61,* 561–573.

Horvath, A. O., Marx, R. W., & Kamann, A. M. (1988). Thinking about thinking in therapy: An examination of clients' understanding of their therapists' intentions. *Journal of Consulting and Clinical Psychology, 58,* 614–621.

Horvath, A. O., & Symonds, B. D. (1991). Relation between working alliance and outcome in psychotherapy: A meta-analysis. *Journal of Counseling Psychology, 38,* 139–149.

Hoyt, M. F. (1980). Therapist and patient actions in "good" psychotherapy sessions. *Archives of General Psychiatry, 37,* 159–161.

Hoyt, M. F., Marmar, C. R., Horowitz, M. J., & Alvarez, W. F. (1981). The Therapist Action Scale: Instruments for the assessment of activities during dynamic psychotherapy. *Psychotherapy, 18,* 109–116.

Ivey, A. E. (1971). *Microcounseling: Innovations in interviewing training.* Springfield, IL: Charles C Thomas.

Jones, A. S., & Gelso, C. J. (1988). Differential effects of style of interpretation: Another look. *Journal of Counseling Psychology, 35,* 363–369.

Jones, E. E., Cumming, J. D., & Horowitz, M. J. (1988). Another look at the nonspecific hypothesis of therapeutic effectiveness. *Journal of Consulting and Clinical Psychology, 56,* 48–55.

Jones, E. E., & Pulos, S. M. (1993). Comparing the process in psychodynamic and cognitive-behavioral therapies. *Journal of Consulting and Clinical Psychology, 61,* 306–316.

Joyce, A. S., Duncan, S. C., & Piper, W. E. (1995). Task analysis of "working" responses to dynamic interpretation in short-term individual psychotherapy. *Psychotherapy Research, 5,* 49–62.

Joyce, A. S., & Piper, W. E. (1996). Interpretive work in short-term individual psychotherapy: An analysis using hierarchical linear modeling. *Journal of Consulting and Clinical Psychology, 64,* 505–512.

Kagan, N. (1975). Influencing human interaction: Eleven years with IPR. *Canadian Counselor, 9,* 44–51.

Kelly, K. R., Hall, A. S., & Miller, K. L. (1989). Relation of counselor intention and anxiety to brief counseling outcome. *Journal of Counseling Psychology, 36,* 158–162.

Kiesler, D. J. (1986). Interpersonal methods of diagnosis and treatment. In J. Cavenar (Ed.), *Psychiatry* (Vol. 1, pp. 1–24). Philadelphia: Lippincott.

Kivlighan, D. M. (1989). Changes in counselor intentions and response modes and in client reactions and session evaluation after training. *Journal of Counseling Psychology, 36,* 471–476.

Kivlighan, D. M. (1990). Relation between counselors' use of intentions and clients' perception of working alliance. *Journal of Counseling Psychology, 37,* 27–32.

Kivlighan, D. M., & Angelone, E. O. (1989). Helpee introversion, novice counselor intention use, and helpee-rated session impact. *Journal of Counseling Psychology, 38,* 25–29.

Kline, W. B. (1983). Training counselor trainees to talk to themselves: A method of focusing attention. *Counselor Education and Supervision, 22,* 296–302.

Knox, S., Hess, S., Peterson, D., & Hill, C. E. (1997). A qualitative analysis of client perceptions of the effects of helpful therapist self-disclosure in long-term therapy. *Journal of Counseling Psychology, 44,* 274–283.

Kottler, J. A. (1991). The compleat therapist. San Francisco: Jossey-Bass.

Kraft, R. G., Claiborn, C. D., & Dowd, E. T. (1985). Effects of positive reframing and paradoxical directives in counseling for negative emotions. *Journal of Counseling Psychology, 32,* 617–621.

Kubie, L. S. (1970). The destructive potential of humor in psychotherapy. *American Journal of Psychiatry, 127,* 861–866.

Kurpius, D. J., Benjamin, D., & Morran, D. K. (1985). Effects of teaching a cognitive strategy on counselor trainee internal dialogue and clinical hypothesis formulation. *Journal of Counseling Psychology, 32,* 263–271.

Ladany, N., Hill, C. E., Thompson, B. J., & O'Brien, K. M. (1999, June). *An examination of therapist use of silence.* Paper presented at the annual meeting of the International Society for Psychotherapy Research, Braga, Portugal.

Lafferty, P., Beutler, L. E., & Crago, M. (1989). Differences between more and less effective psychotherapists: A study of select therapist variables. *Journal of Consulting and Clinical Psychology, 57,* 76–80.

Lambert, M. J. (1989). The individual therapist's contribution to psychotherapy process and outcome. *Clinical Psychology Review, 9,* 469–485.

Lambert, M. J., & Bergin, A. E. (1994). The effectiveness of psychotherapy. In A. E. Bergin & S. L. Garfield (Eds.), *Handbook of psychotherapy and behavior change* (4th ed., pp. 143–189). New York: Wiley.

Lazarus, A. A. (1984). Multimodal therapy. In R. J. Corsini (Ed.), *Current psychotherapies.* Itasca, IL: Peacock.

Lee, D. Y., Hallberg, E. T., Hassard, J. H., & Haase, R. F. (1979). Client verbal and nonverbal reinforcement of counselor behavior: Its impact on interviewing behavior and postinterview evaluation. *Journal of Counseling Psychology, 26,* 204–219.

Lee, D. Y., & Uhlemann, M. R. (1984). Comparison of verbal responses of Rogers, Shostrom, and Lazarus. *Journal of Counseling Psychology, 31,* 91–94.

Leira, T. (1995). Silence and communication: Nonverbal dialogue and therapeutic action. *Scandinavian Psychoanalytic Review, 18,* 41–65.

Leong, F. T. (1986). Counseling and psychotherapy with Asian-Americans: Review of the literature. *Journal of Counseling Psychology, 33,* 196–206.

Levy, D. A. (1989). Social support and the media: Analysis of responses by radio psychology talk show hosts. *Professional Psychology: Research and Practice, 20,* 73–78.

Levy, L. H. (1963). *Psychological interpretation.* New York: Holt.

Lipsey, M., & Wilson, D. (1993). The efficacy of psychological, educational, and behavioral treatment. *American Psychologist, 48,* 1181–1209.

Lonborg, S. D., Daniels, J. A., Hammond, S. G., Houghton-Wenger, B., & Brace, L. J. (1991). Client and counselor verbal response mode changes during initial counseling sessions. *Journal of Counseling Psychology, 38,* 394–400.

Luborsky, L., McLellan, A. T., Woody, G. E., O'Brien, C. P., & Auerbach, A. (1985). Therapists success and its determinants. *Archives of General Psychiatry, 42,* 602–611.

Luborsky, L., Mintz, J., Auerbach, A., Crits-Christoph, P., Bachrach, H., Todd, T., Johnson, M., Cohen, M., & O'Brien, C. P. (1980). Predicting the outcome of psychotherapy: Findings of the Penn Psychotherapy Project. *Archives of General Psychiatry, 37,* 471–481.

Mahalik, J. R. (1994). Development of the Client Resistance Scale. *Journal of Counseling Psychology, 41,* 58–68.

Mahrer, A. R. (1983). *Taxonomy of procedures and operations in psychotherapy.* Unpublished manuscript, University of Ottawa, Canada.

Marini, I. (1992). The use of humor in counseling as a social skill for clients who are disabled. *Journal of Applied Rehabilitation Counseling, 23,* 30–36.

Martin, J. (1984). The cognitive mediational paradigm for research on counseling. *Journal of Counseling Psychology, 31,* 558–571.

Martin, J., Martin, W., Meyer, M., & Slemon, A. (1986). Empirical investigation of the cognitive mediational paradigm for research on counseling. *Journal of Counseling Psychology, 33,* 115–123.

Martin, J., Martin, W., & Slemon, A. (1987). Cognitive mediation in person-centered and rational-emotive therapy. *Journal of Counseling Psychology, 24,* 251–260.

Martin, J., Martin, W., & Slemon, A. G. (1989). Cognitive-mediational models of action-act sequences in counseling. *Journal of Counseling Psychology, 36,* 8–16.

McBrien, R. J. (1993). Laughing together: Humor as encouragement in couples counseling. *Individual Psychology: Journal of Adlerian Theory, Research, and Practice, 49,* 419–427.

McCarthy, P. R., & Betz, N. E. (1978). Differential effects of self-disclosing versus self-involving therapist statements. *Journal of Counseling Psychology, 25,* 251–256.

McNeilly, D. L., & Howard, K. I. (1991a). The effects of psychotherapy: A reevaluation based on dosage. *Psychotherapy Research, 1,* 74–78.

McNeilly, D. L., & Howard, K. I. (1991b). The Therapeutic Procedures Inventory: Psychometric properties and relationship to phase of treatment. *Journal of Personality Integration, 1,* 223–235.

Meichenbaum, D. (1977). *Cognitive-behavior modification: An integrative approach.* New York: Plenum Press.

Messer, S. B. (1994). Adapting psychotherapy outcome research to clinical reality: A response to Wolfe. *Journal of Psychotherapy Integration (Newsletter Section), 4,* 280–282.

Morran, D. K. (1986). Relationship of counselor self-talk and hypothesis formulation to performance level. *Journal of Counseling Psychology, 33,* 395–400.

Morran, D. K., Kurpius, D. J., & Brack, G. (1989). Empirical investigation of counselor self-talk categories. *Journal of Counseling Psychology, 36,* 505–510.

Morran, D. K., Kurpius, D. J., Brack, C. J., & Brack, G. (1995). A cognitive-skills model for counselor training and supervision. *Journal of Counseling and Development, 73,* 384–389.

Morrow-Bradley, C., & Elliott, R. (1986). Utilization of psychotherapy research by practicing psychotherapists. *American Psychologist, 41,* 188–197.

Nagel, D. P., Hoffman, M. A., & Hill, C. E. (1995). A comparison of verbal response modes used by master's level career counselors and other helpers. *Journal of Counseling and Development, 74,* 101–104.

Neimeyer, G. J., & Fong, M. L. (1983). Self-disclosure flexibility and counselor effectiveness. *Journal of Counseling Psychology, 30,* 258–261.

Nevo, O. (1986). The uses of humor in career counseling. *Vocational Guidance Quarterly, 34,* 188–196.

Norcross, J. C., & Goldfried, M. R. (Eds.). (1992). *Handbook of psychotherapy integration.* New York: Basic Books.

Norcross, J. C., & Prochaska, J. O. (1988). A study of eclectic (and integrative) views revisited. *Professional Psychology: Research and Practice, 19,* 170–174.

Norville, R., Sampson, H., & Weiss, J. (1996). Accurate interpretations and brief psychotherapy outcome. *Psychotherapy Research, 6,* 16–29.

Nutt-Williams, E., & Hill, C. E. (1996). The relationship between therapist self-talk and counseling process variables for novice therapists. *Journal of Counseling Psychology, 43,* 170–177.

O'Farrell, M. K., Hill, C. E., & Patton, S. (1986). Comparison of two cases of counseling with the same counselor. *Journal of Counseling and Development, 65,* 141–145.

Olson, D. H., & Claiborn, C. D. (1990). Interpretation and arousal in the counseling process. *Journal of Counseling Psychology, 37,* 131–137.

Orlinsky, D. E., Grawe, K., & Parks, B. K. (1994). Process and outcome in psychotherapy—Noch einmal. In A. E. Bergin & S. L. Garfield (Eds.), *Handbook of psychotherapy and behavior change* (4th ed., pp. 270–376). New York: Wiley.

Orlinsky, D. E., & Howard, K. I. (1987). A generic model of psychotherapy. *Journal of Integrative and Eclectic Psychotherapy, 6,* 6–28.

Patterson, G. R., & Forgatch, M. S. (1985). Therapist behavior as a determinant for client noncompliance: A paradox for the behavior modifier. *Journal of Consulting and Clinical Psychology, 53,* 846–851.

Paul, G. L. (1967). Strategy of outcome research in psychotherapy. *Journal of Consulting Psychology, 31,* 109–118.

Piper, W. E., Azim, H. F. A., Joyce, A. S., & McCallum, M. (1991). Transference interpretations, therapeutic alliance and outcome in short-term individual psychotherapy. *Archives of General Psychiatry, 48,* 946–953.

Piper, W., Joyce, A. S., McCallum, M., & Azim, H. F. A. (1993). Concentration and correspondence of transference interpretations in short-term psychotherapy. *Journal of Consulting and Clinical Psychology, 61,* 586–595.

Ponce, F. Q., & Atkinson, D. R. (1989). Mexican-American acculturation, counselor ethnicity, counseling style, and perceived counselor credibility. *Journal of Counseling Psychology, 36,* 203–208.

Ponterotto, J. G., Casas, J. M., Suzuki, L. A., & Alexander, C. M. (Eds.). (1995). *Handbook of multicultural counseling.* Thousand Oaks, CA: Sage.

Regan, A. M., & Hill, C. E. (1992). Investigation of what clients and counselors do not say in brief therapy. *Journal of Counseling Psychology, 39,* 168–174.

Remer, P., Roffey, B. H., & Buckholtz, A. (1983). Differential effects of positive versus negative self-involving counseling responses. *Journal of Counseling Psychology, 30* 121–125.

Rennie, D. L. (1992). Qualitative analysis of the client's experience of psychotherapy: The unfolding of reflexivity. In S. G. Toukmanian & D. L. Rennie (Eds.), *Psychotherapy process research: Paradigmatic and narrative approaches* (pp. 211–233). London: Sage.

Rennie, D. L. (1994). Clients' deference in psychotherapy. *Journal of Counseling Psychology, 41,* 427–437.

Robbins, E. S., & Haase, R. F. (1985). Power of nonverbal cues in counseling interactions: Availability, vividness, or salience? *Journal of Counseling Psychology, 32,* 502–513.

Robbins, S. B. (1992). The working alliance. In M. Patton & N. Meara (Eds.), *Psychoanalytic counseling* (pp. 97–121). Chichester, England: Wiley.

Robinson, V., & Halliday, J. (1987). A critique of the microcounseling approach to problem understanding. *British Journal of Guidance and Counseling, 15,* 113–124.

Rogers, C. R. (1957). The necessary and sufficient conditions of therapeutic personality change. *Journal of Consulting Psychology, 21,* 95–103.

Rosenheim, E. (1974). Humor in psychotherapy: An interactive experience. *American Journal of Psychotherapy, 28,* 584–591.

Rounsaville, B. J., Weissman, M. M., & Prusoff, B. A. (1981). Psychotherapy with depressed outpatients: Patient and process variables as predictors of outcome. *British Journal of Psychiatry, 138,* 67–74.

Sachs, J. S. (1983). Negative factors in brief psychotherapy: An empirical assessment. *Journal of Consulting and Clinical Psychology, 51,* 557–564.

Salerno, M., Farber, B. A., McCullough, L., Winston, A., & Trujillo, M. (1992). The effects of confrontation and clarification on patient affective and defensive bonding. *Psychotherapy Research, 2,* 181–192.

Schnarch, D. M. (1990). Therapeutic uses of humor in psychotherapy. *Journal of Family Psychotherapy, 1,* 75–86.

Schwarz, B. E. (1974). Telepathic humoresque. *Psychoanalytic Review, 61,* 591–606.

Sexton, T. L., & Whiston, S. C. (1991). A review of the empirical basis for counseling: Implications for practice and training. *Counselor Education and Supervision, 30,* 330–354.

Shapiro, D. A., Barkham, M., & Irving, D. L. (1984). The reliability of a modified Helper Behavior Rating System. *British Journal of Medical Psychology, 57,* 45–48.

Shapiro, D. A., & Shapiro, D. (1982). Meta-analysis of comparative therapy outcome studies: A replication and refinement. *Psychological bulletin, 92,* 581–604.

Sharpley, C. F. (1997). The influence of silence upon client-perceived rapport. *Counselling Psychology Quarterly, 10,* 237–246.

Sharpley, C. F., & Guiddara, D. A. (1993). Counsellor verbal response mode usage and client-perceived rapport. *Counselling Psychology Quarterly, 6,* 131–142.

Sharpley, C. F., & Sagris, A. (1995). Does eye contact increase counsellor-client rapport? *Counselling Psychology Quarterly, 8,* 145–155.

Shaughnessy, M. F., & Wadsworth, T. M. (1992). Humor in counseling and psychotherapy: A 20-year retrospective. *Psychological Reports, 70,* 755–762.

Silbershatz, G., Fretter, P. B., & Curtis, J. T. (1986). How do interpretations influence the process of therapy. *Journal of Consulting and Clinical Psychology, 54,* 646–652.

Silverman, W. (1996). Cookbooks, manuals, and paint-by-numbers: Psychotherapy in the 90's. *Psychotherapy, 33,* 207–215.

Singer, B. A., & Luborsky, L. (1977). Countertransference: The status of clinical versus quantitative research. In A. S. Gurman & A. M. Razdin (Eds.), *Effective psychotherapy: Handbook of research* (pp. 433–451). New York: Pergamon Press.

Smith, M. L., & Glass, G. V. (1977). Meta-analysis of psychotherapy outcome studies. *American Psychologist, 32,* 752–760.

Smith, M. L., Glass, G. V., & Miller, T. I. (1980). *The benefits of psychotherapy.* Baltimore, MD: Johns Hopkins University Press.

Stiles, W. B. (1978). Verbal response modes and dimensions of interpersonal roles: A method of discourse analysis. *Journal of Personality and Social Psychology, 36,* 693–703.

Stiles, W. B. (1987). Some intentions are observable. *Journal of Counseling Psychology, 34,* 236–239.

Stiles, W. B., & Shapiro, D. A. (1989). Abuse of the drug metaphor in psychotherapy process-outcome research. *Clinical Psychology Review, 9,* 521–543.

Stiles, W. B., Shapiro, D. A., & Firth-Cozens, J. (1988). Verbal response mode use in contrasting psychotherapies: A within-subjects comparison. *Journal of Consulting and Clinical Psychology, 56,* 727–733.

Stiles, W. B., Shapiro, D. A., & Firth-Cozens, J. (1989). Therapist differences in the use of verbal response mode forms and intents. *Psychotherapy, 26,* 314–322.

Stiles, W. B., Startup, M., Hardy, G. E., Barkham, M., Rees, A., Shapiro, D. A., & Reynolds, S. (1996). Therapist session intentions in cognitive-behavioral and psychodynamic-interpersonal psychotherapy. *Journal of Counseling Psychology, 43,* 402–414.

Strong, S. R. (1968). Counseling: A social influence process. *Journal of Counseling Psychology, 15,* 215–224.

Strupp, H. H. (1986). Psychotherapy: Research, practice, and public policy (how to avoid dead ends). *American Psychologist, 41,* 120–130.

Strupp, H. H. (1996). Some salient lessons from research and practice. *Psychotherapy, 33,* 135–138.

Strupp, H. H., & Binder, J. L. (1984). *Psychotherapy in a new key: A guide to time-limited dynamic psychotherapy.* New York: Basic Books.

Sue, D. W., Ivey, A. E., & Pedersen, P. B. (1996). *A theory of multicultural counseling and therapy.* New York: Brooks/Cole.

Sue, D. W., & Sue, D. (1999). *Counseling the culturally different: Theory and practice* (3rd ed.). New York: Wiley.

Suinn, R. M. (1993, February). Psychotherapy: Can the practitioner learn from the researcher? *Behavior Therapist,* 47–49.

Svartberg, M., & Stiles, T. C. (1991). Comparative effects of short-term psychodynamic psychotherapy: A meta-analysis. *Journal of Consulting and Clinical Psychology, 59,* 704–714.

Swoboda, J. S., Dowd, E. T., & Wise, S. L. (1990). Reframing and restraining directives in the treatment of clinical depression. *Journal of Counseling Psychology, 37,* 254–260.

Task Force on Promotion and Dissemination of Psychological Procedures. (1995). Training in and dissemination of empirically-validated psychological procedures: Report and recommendations. *Clinical Psychologist, 48,* 3–23.

Teyber, E. (1997). *Interpersonal process in psychotherapy: A relational approach.* Pacific Grove, CA: Brooks/Cole.

Thompson, B. J., & Hill, C. E. (1991). Therapist perceptions of client reactions. *Journal of Counseling and Development, 69,* 261–265.

Truax, C. B., & Carkhuff, R. R. (1967). *Toward effective counseling and psychotherapy.* Chicago: Aldine.

Uhlemann, M. R., Lee, D. Y., & Hiebert, B. (1988). Self-talk of counsellor trainees: A preliminary report. *Canadian Journal of Counselling, 22,* 73–79.

Uhlemann, M. R., Lee, D. Y., & Martin, J. (1994). Client cognitive responses as a function of quality of counselor verbal responses. *Journal of Counseling and Development, 73,* 198–203.

Van Wagoner, S. L., Gelso, C. J., Hayes, J. A., & Diemer, R. A. (1991). Countertransference and the reputedly excellent therapist. *Psychotherapy, 28,* 411–421.

von Wormer, K. (1986). Aspects of humor in alcoholism counseling. *Alcoholism Treatment Quarterly, 3,* 25–32.

Warner, M. J., & Studwell, R. W. (1991). Humor: A powerful counseling tool. *Journal of College Student Psychotherapy, 5,* 59–69.

Watkins, C. E. (1990). The effects of counselor self-disclosure: A research review. *The Counseling Psychologist, 18,* 477–500.

Westerman, M. A., Foote, J. P., & Winston, A. (1995). Change in coordination across phases of psychotherapy and outcome: Two mechanisms for the role played by patients' contribution to the alliance. *Journal of Consulting and Clinical Psychology, 63,* 672–675.

Williams, E. N., Judge, A. J., Hill, C. E., & Hoffman, M. A. (1997). Experiences of novice therapists in prepracticum: Trainees', clients', and supervisors' perceptions of therapists' personal reactions and management strategies. *Journal of Counseling Psychology, 44,* 390–399.

Williams, E. N., Polster, D., Grizzard, B., & Rockenbaugh, J. (1999, August). *Cognitive strategies of novice and experienced therapists: Changes over time.* Poster presented at the annual meeting of the American Psychological Association, Boston.

Wiser, S., & Goldfried, M. R. (1996). Verbal interventions in significant psychodynamic-interpersonal and cognitive-behavioral therapy sessions. *Psychotherapy Research, 6,* 309–319.

Wiser, S., & Goldfried, M. R. (1998). Therapist interventions and client emotional experiencing in expert psychodynamic-interpersonal and cognitive-behavioral therapies. *Journal of Consulting and Clinical Psychology, 66,* 634–640.

Wogan, M., & Norcross, J. C. (1985). Dimensions of therapeutic skills and techniques: Empirical identification, therapist correlates, and predictive utility. *Psychotherapy, 22,* 63–74.

Wohl, J. (1982). Eclecticism and Asian counseling: Critique and application. *International Journal for the Advancement of Counselling, 5,* 215–222.

Xenakis, S. N., Hoyt, M. F., Marmar, C. R., & Horowitz, M. J. (1983). Reliability of self-reports by therapists using the Therapist Action Scale. *Psychotherapy: Theory, Research, and Practice, 20,* 314–320.

9

Stages of Counseling and Therapy

An Examination of Complementarity and the Working Alliance

Terence J. G. Tracey
Arizona State University

Regardless of therapist orientation, all therapy has a beginning, middle, and end. Different tasks are important at different times. For instance, in the beginning it is important for the therapist and the client to determine what will be addressed in therapy and to establish some basic rules for working on the problem. This chapter focuses on the stages of therapy and how they relate to client change. The stages are explained according to an interpersonal model of therapy, but the author indicates and illustrates that the stages may be described according to behavioral, information-processing, or psychodynamic models as well. All types of therapies have stages, and it appears that similar therapist–client interchanges occur at different stages in the change process regardless of the type of therapy employed.

Chapter Questions _____

- What is client–therapist complementarity?
- Why is the operationalization of complementarity important?
- How does complementarity change during the course of therapy?
- How does complementarity relate to counseling outcome?
- How do complementarity and working alliance vary during the course of successful therapy?

As anyone familiar with the literature on counseling and psychotherapy knows, there is a myriad of research studies that examine aspects of the therapy process, or what occurs in therapy. There are fewer that relate the in-session behavior to outcome. There are fewer still that examine changes during treatment and relate this to outcome. Such absence of studies examining how in-session behaviors of the client and therapist vary over time and are related to outcome is perhaps the biggest hole in the literature, because they have the most potential to inform clinical practice. Therapy is not a static process but one that manifests certain ebbs and flows. As many clinicians know, it is the knowledge of these variations in the process over time and their management that is related to successful treatment. The focus of this chapter is on reviewing some of the literature on fluctuations in the therapy process over time and their relation to outcome. Specifically, I will focus on the research on the three-stage model of therapy proposed by interactional theorists (e.g., Kiesler, 1996; Claiborn & Lichtenberg, 1989; Strong & Claiborn, 1982; Tracey, 1986a, 1993)

Stage conceptions of the therapy process are not unknown in the theoretical literature of therapy (e.g., Bugental & Kleiner, 1993; Prochaska, DiClemente, & Norcross, 1992; Rogers, 1957); however, they have rarely been examined empirically. Certainly, much of the reason for the relative dearth of research is that it is very difficult to conduct, requiring data from the entire course of treatment. But focusing on clients and how they change during the course of treatment is exactly what clinicians do. For research to have clinical utility, it should approximate the actual process of therapy in its entirety. Examination of stage models requires an examination of the entire course of treatment, not a session or two. It is common for researchers to assess a key behavior in one session and then relate this to outcome. Such a design, however, implicitly assumes that the process of therapy is static, that the key variable has always been at that level and will continue to stay at that level throughout the course of treatment. Although the static nature of many of the therapeutic behaviors may be true, I have found that far more of what transpires in therapy varies during the course of treatment. Account needs to be taken of how important behaviors of both the client and therapist change during the course of treatment and how this pattern of change is related to outcome. This focus on the pattern of change and its relation to outcome is the basis of most stage models.

Besides accounting for time, research on stage models also needs to account for individual variation in the process. Therapists adapt their interventions to their clients. Although a therapist may hold a conceptual model for how clients change, there is variation in the pacing and specifics of each therapy. Some clients may be able to move quickly into certain areas with ease, whereas others take longer. For some clients rapport is a central issue to the therapy, and for others rapport is so easily accomplished that it is almost immaterial. Any good model of the therapy process should also take account of individual variation among clients. Stage models focus on the pattern changes in certain behaviors during the course of treatment. These patterns need to follow a certain predictable path for stages to be present. But the pacing of these patterns over time can vary greatly from dyad to dyad. Evaluations of stage models thus need to examine therapy behavior during the course of treatment, looking for clear patterns in the behaviors, and there needs to be account taken of individual differences in the movement through the pattern. For example, if one hypothesized that successful treatment is associated with a low–high–low pattern of resistance over time (e.g., Patton, Kivlighan, & Multon, 1997), then it is imperative to measure resistance over the whole course of treatment and to look for individual variation in timing. One dyad may manifest a quick peaking of resistance in the second or third session and then a gradual decrease over the remaining 10 sessions. Another dyad may nicely fit the pattern with low initial resistance, increasing resistance until a peak in the middle session and then a decrease until termination. A third dyad may evidence an increasing pattern until three-quarters of way through treatment and then a sudden decrease toward termination. All three dyads fit the same general stage pattern but not with the same pacing. Aggregating these dyads together would cloud any evidence of the stage model. Only by accounting for individual differences in stage adherence, which reflects actual clinical practice, can the research provide an accurate test of the validity of stages.

Obviously, many of the constructs that have been examined in the therapeutic literature have some relation to a stage model. For example, several chapters in this volume relate to specific time-defined aspects of the therapy process. Chapter 1 on engagement focuses on crucial components of the early sessions of treatment. Chapter 6 on transference and chapter 3 on resistance focus on the middle sessions of therapy. And chapter 12 on termination focuses on issues relevant in the final sessions. So many conceptions of the therapy process implicitly assume a stage structure in that there are different issues or behaviors that are relevant at different time periods. Steenbarger (1992) has nicely summarized much of the existing research on the three-stage model of time-limited therapy.

This chapter focuses solely on an interactional conception of the therapy process. Interactional and interpersonal theorists (e.g., Kiesler, 1996; Claiborn & Lichtenberg, 1989; Strong & Claiborn, 1982; Tracey, 1986a, 1993) have conceptualized the successful therapeutic process as having three stages, and these stages can be represented by the relative amounts of complementarity exhibited. I will provide a description of the three-stage model of complementarity and then review the research literature pertaining to this model. Part of the presentation of the research focuses on the issues involved in operationalizing complementarity. Not all definitions of complementarity are isomorphic, and interpretation of any results rests on what exactly is being measured. I also review the stage research on the working alliance, because several of the theoretical assumptions involved in the stage model of complementarity also relate to the working alliance. Finally, I apply the research and the model to practice.

Defining Complementarity

Complementarity is a general construct that refers to the extent to which the behaviors of interactants in a dyad "fit" together. It has been viewed as an indicator of the general interactional harmony in any relationship (e.g., Tracey, 1986a). The more the behaviors of the two interactants "fit" together, or complement each other, the higher the harmony. This construct has been applied to the therapy process and a variety of conflicting conclusions have been yielded. Some of the equivocal nature of the research, however, can be tied to the specific definitions of complementarity used. There are several models of operationalizing complementarity used in the literature and their differences need to be recognized in interpreting study results as well as generalizing to practice.

Bateson (1936/1958) first proposed the construct of complementarity in his anthropological studies of interaction patterns across several cultures. He proposed status (also called power, control, and dominance) as a primary construct involved in all human communication and relationships. Every behavior (which includes verbal and nonverbal aspects) carries information about how the actor perceives him- or herself relative to the other with respect to status. The extent to which the behavior of the two actors in a dyad behave in manners that agree with each other defines the type of interaction. Bateson postulated two basic types of interactions: complementary (where there is an unequal amount of status) and symmetrical (where there is equal status). In a complementary interaction, each person is agreeing on the relative status positions (i.e., who determines what is to occur and who is to follow along). If the behaviors of the actors complement each other, there is a smooth interaction that is productive as the dyad agrees on what is to be done. In essence, one actor initiates and the other follows. However, if the behaviors of the two actors indicate equal status, resulting in a symmetrical interaction, there is more tension in the interaction and less is accomplished. Each actor is defining the interaction in a manner that is not agreed to by the other actor. An example of a symmetrical interaction is where both actors are initiating behaviors for the dyad to follow, but neither is following the initiations of the other. Bateson argued that a fairly high proportion of complementary interactions are required for orderly interaction and for any relationship to continue over time. Symmetrical interactions are viewed as indicative of relationship tension and, if continued over time, bode ill for relationship continuation.

It is important to note that complementary and symmetrical interactions refer only to behavioral interchanges and not larger aggregates, such as a relationship. How behaviors of the interactants complement in any single interchange (i.e., one behavior of one participant followed by a behavior of the other participant) is the focus. The interchange is either complementary or symmetrical. Most of the interchanges need to be complementary for the relationship to continue. However this high level of complementarity does not mean that one individual is always the one with the higher status (i.e., the initiator) and the other always has low status (i.e., follows along). The specific person doing the initiating at any time can vary, but the key is that when one individual initiates, the other complements by following. It is possible that both individuals initiate equally over time; when each initiates the other follows, so there is an equal status over time. In any one interchange, however, there can be unequal status and smooth interaction. Aggregating the number of complementary and symmetrical interactions over time yields an index of the relative proportion of complementarity in the relationship. This proportion of complementarity can then be examined with respect to relationship continuance.

A key aspect of the construct of complementarity is its inherent interactional nature. The examination of status, power, control, or dominance (these terms are used interchangeably in this chapter as they are often so used in the literature and there is little empirical work differentiating them) in therapy is far from new (e.g., Snyder, 1945), but typically this research has focused on the relative presence of high-control behaviors in the client's or the therapist's behavior. The question involved in this research is, "Is there a relationship between the relative presence of therapist (or client) controlling behavior and outcome?" Or "Is the therapist acting in a leading or controlling manner good?" These questions implicitly assume that the context of the behavior is irrelevant: It does not matter where the controlling behavior occurs, just that it occurs. Complementarity focuses not on the relative merits of controlling behaviors but on their placement in the interaction, that is, their interactional nature. If the therapist acts in an ascendant manner every time the client tries to initiate something is a very different interaction than if the therapist acts ascendantly only in other contexts.

In a simple example, suppose a therapist is convinced that a client needs to talk about her (the client's) issues with her mother. We could examine the number of times the therapist initiates and leads the discussion to issues of the mother. We could then see if these initiations were related to outcome. At an extreme, however, two very different interactional processes could result with the exact same number of therapist initiations. In one case, every time the therapist raised the issue of the mother, the client could shift away or argue (both expressing status and resulting in a symmetrical interaction with both the therapist and the client initiating). In this symmetrical case, there would be little discussion of the mother by the client. Another case could have each initiation of the content of the client's relationship to the mother followed by the client's discussion of the mother (complementary interactions). In this complementary interaction case, there would be a good deal of discussion about the mother.

Complementarity takes account of the sequence or context of behaviors and is thus an interactional variable. Such a construct fits better with the inherent interactional nature of human relationships and also with the process of psychotherapy. Therapists do not behave independently of the client. Therapists select their behavior in reaction to what clients do. We alter our behavior with the behavior of the client. One appeal of the construct of complementarity is that it is one of the few constructs that implicitly takes this interactional basis of behavior into account and is thus a good means of examining how the client and therapist actually behave with each other and how this interaction process unfolds over time.

General Stage Model of Complementarity

I (Tracey, 1986a, 1987, 1993; Tracey & Ray, 1984) have proposed a general three-stage model of complementarity that occurs in successful therapy and will summarize it here. Specifically, dyads with successful therapeutic outcome should demonstrate a curvilinear, high–low–high pattern of complementarity over the course of treatment and less successful dyads should not demonstrate this pattern. The relative levels of complementarity and the concomitant therapist tasks involved define the three stages (see Table 9.1).

Initial Rapport Building Stage

The first stage is one of rapport building. To successfully navigate this stage, the client needs to feel understood and that both participants are working well together. Such understanding is demonstrated in the level of complementarity attained in the relationship. High levels of complementarity indicate that each person is implicitly agreeing with how things are progressing and the role each is playing. Whenever one of the participants initiates, the other will probably follow, indicating agreement with the initiation and acceptance of and agreement with how things are going. Complementarity is, thus, indicating relationship agreement at the overt, behavioral level.

The attainment of initial high levels of complementarity result largely from the therapist adhering to the client's definition of the relationship. A major premise of interpersonal theory (e.g., Carson, 1969, Kiesler, 1983, Tracey, 1993) is that all individuals need other people to validate their image of themselves. Individuals strive to have others act toward them in a manner that validates their view of themselves. Thus, people try to evoke

TABLE 9.1   *Three-stage Model of Successful Therapy*

Name	Stage		
	Rapport	*Conflict*	*Termination*
Sequence	Early	Middle	Late
Complementarity	High	Moderate/low	High
Affective tone	Positive	Negative	Positive
Relational definition	Client	Neither or therapist	Mutual
Therapist task	Adhere to client relationship definition	Know client evoking behavior Alter response	Act as real person
Successful indicators	Client–therapist match	Therapist awareness of behavior sequence	Therapist allowing shift to mutuality
	Therapist flexibility	Therapist flexibility	Therapist flexibility
Failure	Premature termination	Premature termination	Inability to separate
		No initiation of change	Inability to establish real relationship

certain self-validating behaviors from others. Clients are assumed to have habitual ways or patterns of interacting with others, and these patterns are a key component of their difficulties in that they tend to be fairly rigid and inflexible. As such, clients will manifest these rigid and inflexible patterns of interacting with others in therapy with the therapist. Clients will attempt to get the therapist to behave in manners that fit with their conceptions of themselves (Andrews, 1990, 1991; Baldwin, 1992; Swann, 1992). They will act in an attempt to *evoke* complementarity behavior from the therapist. For example, if a client views problems as resulting from the behavior of others, the client will try to get the therapist to confirm this view. The client will act in ways to evoke a similar view from the therapist. If the therapist initiates discussion focusing on the client's contribution to the problem, the client will not feel understood and will attempt to redirect the conversation away from such a view. At the behavioral level, a noncomplementary interaction would have occurred as the therapist initiated discussion regarding the client's contribution to the problems and the client challenged such a view. Had the therapist endorsed the client's view that the problems were attributable to others, then a complementary interaction would have resulted. By the therapist adhering, to some extent, to the client's definition of the relationship, the client will feel understood and complementary interaction will result.

In general, this initial rapport building is not difficult to accomplish. Therapists are trained in many of the skills to help them attend to client issues and respond in appropriate manners. But in addition, therapists self-select into the profession because they have good social skills. Typically, individuals who become therapists have an interest in people and view themselves as being able to work with a variety of people. They are skilled at making a variety of individuals feel comfortable. In a sense, therapists are social chameleons (Beier & Young, 1984), able to adapt to the different evoking behaviors of others.

The initial rapport is difficult to obtain with some clients. Some clients may be trying to evoke behaviors that are not in the therapist's repertoire, either because of the constraints of therapy itself, or the individual characteristics of the therapist. Some clients may be so rigid in their presentation that there is little room for the therapist to act. For example, a client may be so rigid in a belief to always be right that the client will listen to nothing the therapist offers. In extreme cases of rigidity, there is little the therapist can do and therapy cannot start, because a realistic relationship between the therapist and client cannot be defined. Another example would be the client who rigidly will take no responsibility for problems. At least at minimum levels, clients need to give therapists some input and to view at least some of the problem as within their control for therapy even to start.

Another reason for failure of rapport attainment is that the client requests something that is not in the therapist's repertoire because of either the therapist's choice or behavioral rigidity. If the client is seeking the therapist to take charge and structure the interaction, and the therapist does not like to engage in this type of behavior (for theoretical or personal reasons), the client's attempts to get the therapist to take charge will not be complemented by the therapist. The therapist will try to get the client to take charge instead. Both participants will be trying to define what the other is to do, while not agreeing as to what this is. If this lack of complementarity continues with neither participant capitulating, premature termination is hypothesized to result. The client and the therapist will not have engaged each other, because no agreement occurred regarding how they were to interact. Given that clients are the ones with the problems and these relate to rigid styles of self-presentation and that the therapists' role is to help clients, and generally have more flexible self-presentation styles, it is the therapists that accommodate client styles. The consequence of therapist failure to complement client self-presentation and evoking styles is premature termination.

The process of rapport attainment is an evolving one. Initially, clients present themselves in socially appropriate and overt manners and only with time will the more subtle requests be made. As the therapists adhere to initial overt client evoking behaviors, the clients will feel more understood and will slowly begin revealing more subtle evoking behaviors. Rapport attainment is the process of complementing both the overt behavioral requests of the client and also the increasing, and more covert, behavioral requests. For example, it is not uncommon for clients to present a superficial problem and see if the therapist deals with it in a complementary manner. If such a problem is dealt with in a complementary manner, then more central, and, perhaps, poorly defined and articulated problems will come to the fore. The client will look for these to be complemented also. However, these less overt problems may require a very different style of complementarity than that provided for the overt problems. For example, a client may desire the therapist to structure interaction around an initial issue of inability to study and as this goes well (as indicated by continued complementarity), the client may slowly start to request not a structuring, solution-focused response but a more accepting response from the therapist. The client may start shifting to an area about which he or she is much less comfortable. Another example would be the initially agreeable client who requests therapist suggestions and adheres to them, but, over time, starts to ignore the suggestions that are given. The therapist needs to be attentive to the changing nature of the requests made by the client for complementary behavior. These requests take both an overt, and more importantly, a covert form. When complementarity is high, the therapist knows that he or she is fitting with the client's self-presentation. When complementarity is low, the therapist knows that in some way, he or she is not acting in the manner evoked by the client. So initial rapport attainment is a function of the therapist being able to complement both the initial overt and increasing covert aspects of the client's behavior.

Client–therapist matching and therapist flexibility enhance the attainment of initial rapport and complementarity. If the specific behavior desired by the client is the preferred behavior of the therapist, then rapport and complementarity are all but guaranteed. Lennard and Bernstein (1960) proposed that if the roles that the client prefers mesh with the roles that the therapist prefers, then initial rapport is easily accomplished. Some clients and therapists naturally fit well together and this results in high initial complementarity. However, much initial rapport is related to the therapist's ability to adapt to a variety of client presentation styles to achieve complementarity.

The pattern of complementarity during the course of treatment is depicted in Figure 9.1. To navigate the first stage successfully, the therapist needs to adhere to the client's definition of the relationship and this results in high levels of complementarity. Lines A, B, and D in Figure 9.1 represent successful negotiation of the rapport building stage as demonstrated by the attainment of relatively high levels of complementarity. Line C represents a failure of this stage. The dyad never obtained high levels of complementarity and thus resulted in premature termination.

Middle Conflict Stage

After high levels of complementarity have been obtained, the interaction may enter the second stage of therapy, that of conflict. The progression into the conflict stage is because of the natural progression of events and skillful therapist behavior. First, the therapist has been

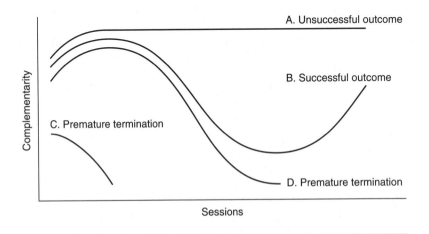

FIGURE 9.1   *Pattern of Complementarity During the Course of Therapy*

adhering to the client's definition of the relationship for quite a time. This becomes taxing in the long haul. As social chameleons, we can adapt to a wide variety of individuals for a short amount of time. But as time goes on, everyone would like some self-confirmation. Therapists also validate themselves through interaction, and extended periods of interaction where preferred styles are not allowed become frustrating for the therapist. For example, if the therapist views herself as very loving and the client prefers to engage in more distant, argumentative exchanges, the therapist can accommodate this behavior for a while. But increasingly the therapist will grow dissatisfied with the relationship because she is not able to engage in roles she prefers. The more rigid the client is in self-definition, the less the therapist may be able to act in ways not fitting the client's presentation style. Over time, the therapist will naturally feel a growing dissatisfaction with the constraints of acting in a certain manner and will try new behaviors. With the argumentative client, the therapist will feel growing dissatisfaction with the interaction as any attempts to engage in the preferred close, friendly interaction are thwarted by the client. The choice presented to the therapist is to act according to the client's preferred pattern of interaction or not have a relationship. Therapists will naturally feel the increased urge to act in their preferred mode of interaction. Therapists acting according to their preferences instead of the client's will result in more noncomplementary interactions. An increasing argumentative act by the client will follow the friendly close response by the therapist. So therapists' natural dissatisfaction with having little input into the relationship definition over time will increase conflict and lower complementarity.

A key proposition of interpersonal models of therapy (e.g., Kiesler, 1996) is that it is this point of complementarity struggle that characterizes the client's major problem. The client has constructed a relationship with the therapist similar to relationships with other significant individuals in the client's life. The client desperately needs validation of his or her view of self, and getting the therapist to act in a complementary manner is the means of doing so. The choice given the therapist is to obey or threaten the relationship. If the therapist deviates from the client's preferences, stress is introduced into the relationship and the client. The client increases efforts to get the therapist to act in a complementary way. Each therapist deviation from complementarity is met with increased client constraining behaviors. The client is communicating that it is so important to the client that the therapist act in a certain manner that any deviations threaten the continuation of the relationship. This is the choice given to other people in the client's life: adhere or leave. Adherence can take many forms. For some clients, adherence could be that everything that the client says is right, or for other clients, it could be that the client is so dependent that he or she cannot do anything without the therapist's guidance and approval. With this latter client, any attempt on the therapist's part to instill autonomy will be met with increased dependence and neediness. The task for the therapist is to skillfully redefine the relationship away from the client's definition of "either my way or no way."

Redefining the relationship is a difficult endeavor, because the relationship has already progressed for awhile with the client doing the defining. It is difficult for the therapist to start deviating from the initial basis of the relationship. Doubts will arise because it seemed to be going so well in the initial stage. The middle stage is thus one where the relationship becomes less defined by the client. The therapist attempts to deviate from client control. As a result, neither participant is defining what is to occur. Each is trying to influence the other participant while not adhering to the influence attempts of the other. This deviation away from the initial relationship definition by the client is what results in change. The therapist is attempting to get the client to engage in new, more realistic behaviors that are responsive to the other participant in the relationship.

The key is to find the optimal level of complementarity. Too much complementarity indicates that the therapist is still adhering to the original client definition of the relationship. No change is being introduced. As a result, the interaction may be very pleasant to both parties but nothing new is occurring. This type of middle stage often occurs with clients and therapists that naturally fit in the first stage. The way the client and therapist wish to interact is so comfortable to both that there is little urge for the therapist to deviate. Conversely, the therapist may sense a need to deviate from what the client desires but is too afraid to introduce any deviation because of the more extreme influence attempts by the client, and as such, the therapist continues engaging in the role defined by the client. This pattern of continued acceptance of client relationship definition in the middle stage is represented by line A in Figure 9.1.

If the therapist deviates too much from complementarity, there is too much stress introduced into the relationship. Too much deviation from complementarity means that there is little validation of the client's self-perception by the therapist. Without a modicum of complementarity and hence validation, the relationship cannot continue. In this case of too little complementarity being introduced by the therapist, premature termination can result. Assuming, as is done in interpersonal models (e.g., Kiesler, 1996), that the therapeutic relationship is a recapitulation of significant relationships in the client's life, such a premature termination would be similar in character to these other relationship endings. The therapist would engage in a relationship defined by the client and then attempt to deviate from the client's definition more than the client desires and the relationship would end poorly. The optimal degree of complementarity in this middle stage is thus somewhere between the high level associated with the therapist's acceptance of the client's relationship definition and the low level associated with too much deviation by the therapist that results in ending the relationship.

The degree of change introduced by the therapist in this middle stage is obviously a function of the degree of client maladjustment. In interpersonal theory (e.g., Kiesler, 1996; Tracey, 1993), adjustment is associated with interpersonal flexibility. Better adjusted individuals are able to adapt their behavior to fit a wide variety of situations and individuals. Less adjusted individuals are less flexible. The self-view of these less adjusted individuals is more restricted and tenuous, and they strive harder to obtain validation from others. Because they have a greater need for validation, less adjusted individuals are less likely to leave this validation to chance. Maladjusted individuals are more likely to engage in extreme or rigid behavior because these are more constraining on others' behavior. Less adjusted individuals would thus be less willing to engage in relationships where the other individual does not engage in highly complimentary behavior. Hence less adjusted clients will be less tolerant of deviations from the previous high levels of complementarity obtained in the beginning, rapport-building stage. The introduction of less complementary responding by the therapist in the middle, conflict stage needs to be more gradual with less adjusted clients. Better adjusted clients can tolerate greater deviation from complementarity. So with less adjusted clients there needs to be a more gradual deviation from complementarity than with better adjusted clients, and greater deviation can be introduced by the therapist.

For the therapist to optimally deviate from complementarity in the middle stage, he or she must know the client's evoking pattern, that is, how the client is constraining the therapist to behavior. Often such constraints are fairly subtle and require close examination to identify. One of the best cues to how the client is constraining the therapist is the therapist's feelings (Beier & Young, 1984). In this view, much of the therapist's affective experience is in reaction to client elicitation. If the therapist can be aware of his or her affect, this could be used to understand how the client is self-viewing and what is being validated. For example, if the therapist feels critical toward a client, this could have been elicited by the client. The therapist could then look for other relationships in the client's life that manifest this critical quality for confirmation. The therapist would need to become aware of when and how the client elicits such critical behavior from the therapist. These are the times it is most important to start deviating from the complementary pattern. The emotions of the therapist can be used to identify and locate the key aspects of complementary interaction defined by the client.

Another cue to the client's evoking style is the extremity of behavior. Clients engage in extreme behavior in order to reestablish the relationship according to their definition. If extreme behavior is evident, there was a previous deviation from complementarity on the therapist's part. If the therapist can notice when extreme behavior occurs and then look at what was done immediately prior to the occurance, the therapist can find the behavior that is threatening to the client. The therapist could then test the hypothesis that this behavior was threatening to the client by engaging in the behavior again to see if the client again engages in extreme behavior. If the hypothesis were supported, then the therapist would know the areas to focus on in the deviation from complementarity.

A final cue of the client's evoking style is the presence of shifts in topic and flow by the client. If the client abruptly deviates from a situation, something just previously occurred that stimulated the shift. Examination of the therapist behavior preceding the shift can provide clues as to issues or behaviors that the client finds threatening.

It is not always clear what behavior the therapist should engage in to deviate from complementarity. The behavior that the therapist needs to engage in varies greatly from client to client and depends on what each finds comforting and threatening. So the therapist needs to understand how the client evokes or constrains the therapist's behavior in order to know what to do. However, Beier and Young (1984) have proposed the two techniques of paraphrase and metacommunication that are useful in most contexts, because they are not complementary to many behaviors. Paraphrasing is certainly an old stand-by of clinical practice. It is useful in that it does not really confirm or validate the client's evoking behavior, it merely restates. Paraphrasing can sometimes be used to see clients engage in extreme behavior and attempt to get the therapist to validate their view of themselves.

Also metacommunication, or the communication about how the client and therapist are communicating, is useful. It neither complements nor does not complement the client's evoking behaviors, but it involves the therapist describing how the client is evoking behavior from the therapist. In the preceding example with the therapist realizing that the client was evoking critical feeling from her, a metacommunication would involve the therapist presenting this pattern of interaction to the client.

By way of summary, the three possible patterns in the middle stage are depicted in Figure 9.1. Successful negotiation of the middle conflict stage is represented by Line B, which depicts the optimal amount of complementarity to effect change. Lines A and D represent suboptimal levels of complementarity. Line A represents the failure on the therapist's part to introduce noncomplementary responses. Hence, no change was introduced. Line D represents too little complementary responding on the therapist's part and as such too little validation of the client, resulting in a premature end to the relationship.

Thus, the pattern of successful therapy is one of an initial high level of complementarity, followed by a lower level of complementarity, and finally a rise in level of complementarity toward the end of treatment. This pattern is assumed to hold in short-term therapy models as well as long-term therapy. The only thing that would vary is the relative slope and abruptness of changes in complementarity over time. Most briefer models of therapy are focused on specific problems and administered to less severely disturbed clients (e.g., Mann, 1973; Sifneos, 1987). Figure 9.2 represents the pattern of complementarity for three successful therapies of different lengths. The therapy of the longer duration has much more gradual changes in complementarity. Presumably the focus is much broader within this therapy and the client is less adjusted. More abrupt shifts in therapist behavior could be more difficult for this client to handle. With better-adjusted clients, the briefer and less gradual pattern would characterize successful work. The relative slope of the drop in complementarity relates to the optimal level concept. If the client is better adjusted, he or she is more able to withstand abrupt shifts in the process and the therapist's behavior. Less well-adjusted individuals would presumably find such shifts more disturbing and be prone to leave therapy prematurely. So more gradual levels of the therapist altering his or her behavior is called for. There does not currently appear to be a means of more specifically defining the optimal level of complementarity or the amount of noncomplementarity to introduce. In general, the introduction of change should be more gradual with less adjusted clients. Better-adjusted clients can withstand much more extreme shifts in therapist behavior. In this model, it is crucial that the therapist introduce change via noncomplementary responding and the relative degree of this type of responding should be tailored to the specific client, taking into account his or her ability to withstand such change.

End Termination Stage

The deviation from complementarity in the middle stage by the therapist only partially validates the self-presentation of the client. As the client starts to realize that an evoking style is not working well, the client will slowly start to engage in new behaviors. These new behaviors will be more tentative and exploratory than the extreme behaviors of the other stages because they are new behaviors. Therapists need to pay careful attention to the demonstration of these new, more tentative behaviors on the part of the client and to complement them as they occur.

Complementing these new behaviors, however, is not always obvious given their subtlety. For example, a particular client may have been acting especially helpless and evoking the therapist to take care of the client. After the therapist used optimal deviations from this complementarity pattern in the middle stage, the client may make tentative overtures at initiation, perhaps by taking more active control of the topic of conversation in the session. The therapist may be tempted to laud the client's improvement but this would not be complementing the client's new behavior. Instead of letting the client lead the conversation by

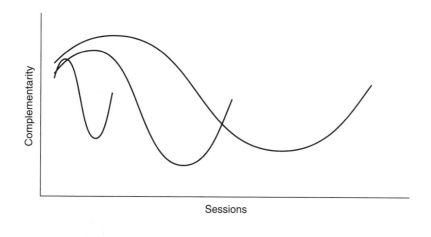

FIGURE 9.2 *Pattern of Complementarity for Successful Dyads of Varying Lengths*

having the therapist follow along and thus complement, the therapist would be acting in a noncomplementary manner by telling the client that the therapist is really the one in control, not the client. Although this intervention is well intended on the therapist's part, it serves to keep the client in the needy position of looking to the therapist for guidance and support.

The final stage thus involves the identification of new behaviors on the client's part and the complementing of these new behaviors, thus reinforcing these behaviors. As the client starts to engage in the new behaviors and sees that they are complemented, the client is able to get validation for different aspects of him or herself. These newer aspects can then be incorporated into the client's self-presentation. The client will be able to offer a more varied and flexible repertoire of behaviors in interacting with the therapist and others.

The relationship becomes more mutually defined. The client is offering a wider range of behavior and the behavior is at a less extreme level. Hence, the therapist can respond in a wide variety of manners, and the client is not so heavily invested in having the therapist respond in one specific manner. The relationship takes on a more mutual give and take quality. The therapist is demonstrating to the client how relationships can be negotiated so as to meet the needs of the individuals. Strong and Claiborn (1982) noted that during the end of successful therapy, therapists often feel urges to share more of themselves. In the earlier stages, the client is more concerned with getting certain behavior from the therapist and not in knowing the therapist, per se. As clients ease off their unilateral definition of the relationship in the end stage, therapists often sense this and are tempted to share more of themselves because it will be heard by the client. The task of the therapist in this end stage is to act more as a real person and not simply in the role of the therapist and to interact with the client at a mutual level.

As the client becomes able to engage the therapist in a mutually defined relationship, it is assumed that the client will expand the self-view to incorporate these new behaviors and then to try out these behaviors with others outside of therapy. The therapy relationship is viewed as the vehicle of change. Because it is initially shaped by the client's definition, the therapy relationship takes the same form as the relationships in the client's life. As the therapist shows the client other ways of engaging in relationships that are more mutual, the client should try these new behaviors with individuals outside therapy. Therapy moves from a unilateral relationship definition provided by the client through a conflict stage where there is less client definition, and finally to a mutual relationship definition between the therapist and client at the end. This process of successful therapy is represented by the varying levels of complementarity over time.

I have taken an interpersonal representation of the process of change. This model assumes the primacy of the therapeutic relationship and the importance of complementarity as an indicator of the relationship. However, the same stage process of change could be explained using behavioral, information-processing, systems, or psychodynamic models. In a behavioral explanation of this process, clients have been intermittently reinforced for their evoking behaviors; their behaviors work somewhat. But the intermittent reinforcement makes it very difficult to extinguish evoking behaviors and to get new behaviors that can be reinforced. The process of optimal deviation from complementarity in the middle stage is one of extinction. As the problematic behaviors are extinguished, newer ones are tried and these can be reinforced. Complementarity is the means of reinforcement. In an information-processing model (e.g., Anderson, 1983; Carver & Scheier, 1982) the client's procedural knowledge (i.e., automatic processing of how relationships work) would be found lacking in the middle stage because of its inability to account for what occurred in the therapeutic relationship. The therapist is neither adhering to the client script nor ending the relationship, but creating a new pattern between the two. The lack of complementarity in the middle stage would not fit with the typical interaction procedural knowledge script and thus how people interact and one's view of self would be examined as declarative knowledge (i.e., deliberate rational processing). In a systems perspective, the initial relationship equilibrium, which was defined largely by the client, was challenged with positive feedback (i.e., noncomplementary responding) by the therapist, wherein the relationship enters a period of flux in the middle, to be followed by a new, more mutual relationship equilibrium at the end. Finally, adopting a psychodynamic view, the therapist engaging in noncomplementary behavior in the middle stage is similar to therapist failure to gratify clients. With increasing frustration through lack of gratification, material is more likely to come to conscious awareness and thus become alterable. So the process of change proposed is not unique, but the centrality put on the relationship and complementarity is what is different.

Empirical Examinations of the Three-Stage Model

Many aspects of the stage model have been examined empirically in the literature. In general, the support varies depending on the specific methods of operationalizing the construct of complementarity. There are several different methods of operationalizing the construct of complementarity. The differences in the definitions of complementarity must be clearly understood in order to interpret the research. The major methods of operationalization vary on (1) the number of dimensions used in defining complementarity, specifically one, two, or three dimensions; (2) the overt versus covert basis of the behaviors examined; and (3) the level of aggregation. The one dimensional model, often called the interactional view, is most similar to the construct defined by Bateson (1936/1958) in that it focuses only on the relative status or control demonstrated in interaction. The two- and three-dimensional methods, both referred to as interpersonal views, add the dimensions of affiliation (two-dimensional representation) or affiliation and interdependence-independence (three-dimensional representation).

The overt versus covert basis of the behaviors examined focus on the relative obviousness of the behaviors examined. In overt operationalizations, control is defined in terms of the form the behavior takes. Behaviors stereotypically associated with leadership, such as giving orders and issuing commands, are viewed as controlling, and behaviors associated with followers and underlings such as asking for directions and submitting are viewed as ceding control. However, other, less overt, definitions of control focus on the introduction of new material regardless of the form. The process of initiating anything new is viewed as stating one has the control to initiate. As such, it is possible in these covert definitions of control for "more submissive" behaviors, such as asking for guidance, to be controlling as it structures what is to follow. Tracey (1991) examined the agreement of overt, form definitions of control with the covert, initiation-based definitions of control in therapy interactions and found minimal overlap. So it would not be expected that examination of complementarity using the two different approaches would yield similar results.

The final basis on which the methods of complementarity operationalization vary is the level of aggregation. Some methods focus on the behavioral interchange (i.e., what each person does immediately after the behavior of the other). This method of looking at complementarity fits best with the interactional basis of the construct of complementarity (see Tracey, 1994) but is often the most demanding to conduct given the complexity of the rating of each individual behavior unit involved. Other approaches involve more aggregate approaches. One method (e.g., Kielser's CLOPT rating system; Kiesler, 1984) involves rating the behaviors exhibited in an entire interaction (such as a session). The behaviors exhibited by the client and therapist are rated and then the complementarity is examined. This is much easier to conduct but harder to make links to the actual sequential interactions that occurred. For example, it is possible for the aggregate behaviors of the therapist and client to appear complementary but in no single interchange did one complement the other.

Dimensions of Control Operationalization

There are two major ways of operationalizing control using the unidimensional, interactional definition of complementarity: topic determination (Tracey, Heck, & Lichtenberg, 1981; Tracey & Ray, 1984) and relational control (Ericson & Rogers, 1973; Heatherington, 1988; Lichtenberg & Barke, 1981). Topic determination focuses on each speaking turn as being either a topic initiation (introduction of new content) or a topic following response. Each initiation is viewed as an attempt to control the topic and flow of the conversation, thus having high status. A following response is viewed as an acceptance of the status quo, current topic and flow. A complementary interaction occurs when a topic initiation is followed by a topic-following response. A symmetrical interaction (or noncomplementary response) occurs when a topic initiation is followed by another topic-initiating response (i.e., equal status). Topic determination is the ratio of the number of topic initiations made that were subsequently followed over the number of total topic initiations and is, thus, indicative of overall complementarity.

Relational control focuses on the form of each speaking turn; whether the speaking turn is "one-up," "one-down," or "one-across." One-up refers to behavior that appears controlling in nature, and one-down refers to behavior that appears submissive where the control is granted to the other. One-across is viewed as neutral with respect to control or status. The proportion of one-up behaviors followed by one-down behaviors and the proportion of one-down behaviors followed by one-up behaviors provides an index of complementarity. Symmetrical interactions are those that have similar statuses (i.e., one-down followed by one-down and one-up followed by one-up).

Although relational control and topic determination both focus on the relative status of the behaviors of the interactants, there are differences in what is in focus. As demonstrated by Tracey (1991) and Tracey and Miars (1986), the two do not measure the same process. Relational control definitions focus on the form of the behavior (i.e., is the behavior controlling, as in giving orders), whereas topic determination whereas is subtler and does not necessarily involve acting in a controlling manner. Topic determination focuses only on what is discussed. There are many ways of initiating topics that are not overtly controlling (e.g., offering a new topic deferentially). Topic control focuses more on the context of the behavior (is the topic new or not?) rather than on the form of the behavior (is it controlling or submissive?). The two definitions yield different conclusions (Tracey, 1991; Tracey & Miars, 1986), because they focus on different aspects of status. A discussion of the relative merits of these two definitions is beyond the scope of this chapter and the reader is referred to Tracey (1991, 1993), Claiborn and Lichtenberg (1989), and Friedlander (1993) for a more complete discussion of the issues. The relational control approach to the study of complementarity has been applied to therapy dyads (e.g., Lichtenberg, & Barke, 1981), but it has not been examined as it varies during the course of treatment. There is no literature on the three-stage model using this system. There have been several studies (Tracey, 1985, 1987; Tracey & Ray, 1984) using the variable of topic determination as it varies over time and its relation to outcome.

Interactional Measures

The importance of complementarity, as indicated by topic determination, in the initial stage of therapy has received some support. Tracey, Heck, and Lichtenberg (1981) measured the roles that both clients and therapists expected the therapists to fill in the first session (therapist as nurturer, therapist as critic, or therapist as model). They found that topic determination was higher in those dyads where both the client and therapist expected the same role for the therapist. Presumably, the matching roles indicated that there was agreement on how the participants were to interact and the higher levels of topic determination reflected this. Those dyads with nonmatching role expectations, did not agree as to how they would interact and, thus, had lower levels of topic determination. So topic determination appears indicative of agreement among the interactants regarding the roles each is to fill.

Two studies on premature termination (Tracey, 1986b) found that those dyads that terminated prematurely (i.e., the client did not return for a scheduled appointment within the first five sessions) had lower levels of topic determination than those dyads that continued past five sessions. This result provides some support for differentiating Line C from Lines A, B, and D in Figure 9.1. Premature termination dyads had lower complementarity, as indicated by topic determination. They did not establish the rapport necessary to engage.

Tracey and Ray (1984) supported the general curvilinear pattern of topic determination. The best three and worst three outcome dyads from a pool of 18 time-limited therapy dyads containing professional therapists were examined for the complementarity pattern. They found that the three most successful dyads all manifested the high–low–high pattern of complementarity over time and that none of the three least successful dyads demonstrated the pattern. The interaction in the least successful dyads was fairly static during the course of treatment (mirroring Line A of Figure 9.1). The key distinguishing feature among the three most successful and three least successful dyads was the pattern over time. With respect to mean levels of topic determination, there were no differences between the three most successful and three least successful dyads. So mean complementarity did not differ across outcome groups but only for the pattern over time. To examine whether therapists in the middle stage of successful therapy deviated more from the predictable pattern of interaction, I (Tracey, 1985) examined the relative predictability of topic-following and topic-initiating behavior. As expected, the behavior of more successful therapists was found to be less predictable in the middle stage than was the behavior of less successful therapists. The more successful therapists deviated more from the established pattern of interaction than did the less successful therapists.

To rule out any potential therapist effects, Tracey (1987) examined the early, middle, and late interaction from a successful and less successful case for each of eight different therapists (advanced doctoral students, interns, and professional therapists). The similar high–low–high pattern of topic determination over time was found in the successful cases and not in the less successful cases. So even for the same therapist, the high–low–high pattern of topic determination was associated with more successful outcome and a flat profile over time was associated with less successful outcome. In addition, an examination of the predictability of behavior across stages revealed that there was more mutuality in the final stage for the most successful dyads but not for the less successful dyads. So for this sample, it appears that the most successful dyads progressed from a more unilateral client definition of interaction to a more mutual definition toward the end. The less successful dyads did not demonstrate this mutuality at the end.

Strong and Claiborn (1982) proposed a somewhat different version of the three-stage model, one where the relationship moves from incongruent relationship definitions through change, to a final congruent relationship definition between the therapist and client. Each participant enters therapy with ideas about how the relationship should be and each tries to influence the other to adhere to his or her definition. It is assumed that clients' definitions are less adaptive than are those of the therapists and further the clients' definitions are related to their symptomology and problems. So initially, the relationship definitions of the client and therapist do not match (i.e., they are incongruent), then the therapist uses influence to get the client to slowly alter the client's relationship definition, and at the end of treatment, the client's relationship definition matches that of the therapist (i.e., they are congruent).

Lichtenberg et al. (1998) examined this hypothesized congruence process in a sample of seven dyads using the predictability of directness versus acquiescence of the responses of each participant during the course of treatment. They proposed that this congruence of relationship definition is indicated by the relative predictability of relational control. In this sense, their predictability is somewhat similar to complementarity. The directness versus acquiescence variable seems similar to the relational control coding system mentioned previously in that it focuses on the relative overt nature of the behavior demonstrated (i.e., form). Using this definition of control, Lichtenberg et al. found no support that the stage model was related to outcome.

Using topic determination as the indicator of complementarity, there is some support across several studies for the presence of the three-stage model of complementarity, its relation to outcome (low initial levels of topic determination are associated with premature termination, and unchanging levels of topic determination are associated with poorer outcome). Also, the pattern of moving from client to mutual relationship definition received some support. However, one study using a more form-based definition of complementarity (Lichtenberg et al., 1998) found no support for the relation of stage pattern to outcome. It appears that how complementarity is defined and examined may be related to the presence of the stage pattern. The stage model is supported when control is examined in the subtler ways of initiating topics rather than the more overt indicators of acting in an ascendant manner or not.

Interpersonal Circumplex Measures

The interpersonal methods of operationalizing complementarity (both the two- and three-dimensional models) view behavior as characterized by interpersonal circles or circumplexes. The two-dimensional model adds the bipolar dimension of affiliation (friendly–hostile) to the dimension of control (dominant–submissive) and can be traced to the original work of Leary and his colleagues (Freedman, Leary, Ossario, & Coffey, 1951; LaForge, Leary, Naboisek, Coffey, & Freedman, 1954; LaForge & Suczek, 1955; Leary, 1957). Behaviors can be characterized as a combination of control and affiliation and can be depicted as a point on a circle defined by these two dimensions. This two-dimensional model is typically referred to as the interpersonal circle or interpersonal circumplex and has received extensive examination with respect to individual differences at the trait level (Gifford & O'Connor, 1987; Gurtman, 1992; Horowitz, Dryer, & Krasnoporova, 1997; Wiggins, 1979, 1982; Wiggins & Broughton, 1985; Wiggins, Phillips, & Trapnell, 1989).

Carson (1969) proposed that complementarity using this model is defined by similar behavior on the affiliation dimension (friendly is a complement to friendly, and hostile is a complement to hostile) and reciprocal behavior on the control dimension (dominance is a complement to submission and vice-versa). So the control dimension is similarly used in defining complementary interactions in both the unidimensional model of Bateson (1936/1958) and the interpersonal circle model, but affiliation is added. Each behavior is viewed as not only carrying control information but also affective closeness information. If one person acts in a friendly manner, that person is proposing that the other person respond in the same manner (the same is true of hostile behavior). Complementarity is the extent to which each behavior is responded to opposite on the control dimension and similar to on the affiliation dimension. The inclusion of affective tone makes the definition of complementarity very different. To differentiate complementarity based on the interpersonal circumplex from that based only on control, I will refer to circumplex-based complementarity as interpersonal complementarity.

There are a variety of ways of portraying behaviors using the interpersonal circumplex varying mostly on how many slices are used in representing the circle. Most coding systems use quadrants, octants, or sixteenths. The definition of complementary behaviors for the quadrant and octant representations is presented in Figure 9.3. The dashed lines indicate behaviors that are defined as complementary.

In a pioneering study on the stages of therapy, Dietzel and Abeles (1975) examined the pattern of interpersonal complementarity in a sample of successful ($n = 10$) and unsuccessful (n = 10) therapy dyads using early, middle, and late sessions. They rated each speaking turn in the selected sessions as one of the four quadrants of the interpersonal circle (friendly–dominant, friendly–submissive, hostile–dominant, and hostile–submissive); then they looked at the complementarity of therapist responses given the immediately preceding client behavior. Three possible levels of complementarity resulted: complementary (both control and affiliation are complemented), acomplementary (partial complementarity where either control or affiliation are complemented but not both) or anticomplementarity (neither control nor affiliation are complemented). They found that there were few differences in complementarity across stage and outcome group except that the successful outcome group had lower complementarity in the middle stage. The successful outcome group had a high–low–high pattern of interpersonal complementarity during the course of treatment, whereas the unsuccessful outcome group had a constant high level of complementarity over time, supporting the three-stage model of complementarity using a different definition of complementarity.

Thompson, Hill, and Mahalik (1991) examined the interpersonal complementarity during the course of treatment in eight cases. Instead of using ratings of specific behavioral interchanges, they used aggregate ratings of behaviors demonstrated over the whole session (i.e., the CLOPT; Kiesler, 1984). Although complementarity can be calculated at this level (see Kiesler, 1996, and Tracey & Schneider, 1995), interpersonal complementarity exists at the interchange level, and, as such, aggregate ratings can only serve as a distal

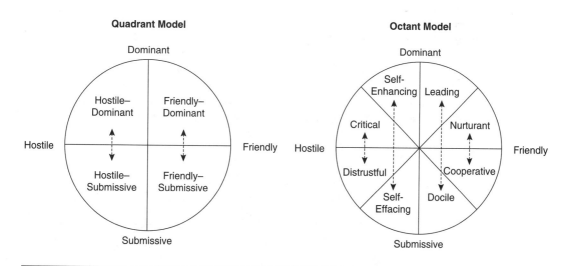

FIGURE 9.3   *Quadrant and Octant Representations of the Interpersonal Circumplex (complementary behaviors are indicated by dashed lines). (Octant model uses octants defined by Strong, Hills, and Nelson, 1988.)*

proxy for the interaction process. Thompson et al. did not find any systematic patterns in complementarity over time. The three-stage complementarity model, however, posits a pattern that differentiates successful and less successful dyads. Thompson et al. did not relate the pattern over time to differential outcome so little can be said about the relative support for the proposed stage model.

Although she did not focus on the entire process of therapy, Weinstock-Savoy (1986) did study the relation between initial session interpersonal complementarity and outcome. She used the same aggregate session rating method (i.e., Kiesler's [1984] CLOPT) used by Thompson et al. (1991), and the complementarity ratings in the first sessions were related to eventual outcome. High initial complementarity was positively related to outcome supporting the initial high stage of complementarity as related to outcome.

Another examination of the relationship of early interaction was conducted by Reandeau and Wampold (1991). They examined the interpersonal behavior of the client and therapist in the first three sessions from two high- and two low-alliance dyads. Although they did not assess outcome, they focused on the working alliance, which has been found to strongly relate to outcome (e.g., Horvath & Symonds, 1991). They used a coding system by Penman (1980) that is not purported to be an interpersonal circumplex model, but it does share many similar properties in that it places behaviors in the two-dimensional space defined by power and involvement rather than control and affiliation. High involvement is somewhat analogous to friendly behavior and low involvement is akin to hostile behavior. They found that high-alliance dyads had a greater proportion of therapist power behavior followed by client low power and high involvement, which resembles a friendly complementarity interaction. Low-alliance dyads had a greater number of therapist high power behaviors followed by client avoidance (low complementarity).

In a review of the literature on interpersonal complementarity, Orford (1986) noted several problems with the operationalization and construct validity of interpersonal complementarity. Perhaps one of the most striking problems is the lack of similarity in complementarity between behaviors on the hostile half of the circumplex and those on the friendly half. He noted that complementarity rates were low for previous hostile behaviors, whereas they were high for previous friendly behaviors. Tracey and Hayes (1989) supported this difference between therapist complementary responding to friendly and hostile client behaviors. These results of differences between friendly and hostile complementarity call into question the validity of the circumplex structure in its use in defining complementarity.

Hays (1991) examined the different patterns of friendly and hostile complementarity in early, middle, and late sessions in six dyads (a successful and less successful case from each of three therapists). Building on the three-stage complementarity model, she hypothesized a high–low–high pattern for friendly complementarity as related to outcome but a low–moderate–low pattern for hostile complementarity. She rated each of the clients and therapists responses using the Interpersonal Communication Rating Scale-Revised (ICRS-R; Strong, Hills, & Nelson, 1988), which rates each behavior as falling into one of the interpersonal octants. Although she did not find support for her three-stage model, she did find support for the different paths of friendly and hostile complementarity over time. Successful dyads had overall higher levels of friendly complementarity and lower levels of hostile complementarity than less successful dyads.

To examine the relative difference between friendly and hostile complementarity, Hoyt, Strong, Corcoran, and Robbins (1993) examined the interaction in one fairly successful case that involved Mann's (1973) psychodynamic time-limited therapy. All therapist and client responses during the 14 sessions of treatment were categorized using the ICRS-R. They defined two separate indexes: one, standard complementarity as conceived by Carson (1969), and the other, engagement. Engagement was similar to complementarity except that it posited different relations for friendly and hostile complementarity. If a response followed a friendly behavior, it was rated for engagement using the complementarity rules as previously described (similar on affiliation and opposite on control); however, if a response followed a hostile behavior, it was rated for engagement as opposite on both affiliation and control. Unlike complementarity, the engagement variable coded hostile–hostile interchanges as not complementary. So, although Hoyt et al. did not examine friendly and hostile complementarity separately, they did incorporate these differences in their variables of complementarity and engagement. Hoyt et al. found that engagement, not interpersonal complementarity, manifested the curvilinear pattern associated with the proposed three-stage model. Although this result is based on only one dyad, it does present some interesting possibilities and warrants further investigation.

I have argued (Tracey, 1993) that perhaps complementarity needs to be examined separately in response to hostile or friendly behaviors because of the very different meaning ascribed to friendly and hostile behaviors. I proposed that the pattern of friendly and hostile interpersonal complementarity over time are different from each other in successful therapy. Friendly interpersonal complementarity was hypothesized to follow a high–low–high pattern but hostile complementarity was hypothesized to follow a similar curvilinear pattern but to be behind that for friendly complementarity in phase (i.e., it would move to initial high levels slower, then move down slower and finally rise a bit slower than the pattern of friendly complementarity).

The differential pattern of friendly and hostile interpersonal complementarity was examined by Tracey, Sherry, and Albright (1999) in a study of 20 clients seen by 4 professional therapists (5 clients each) using a similar cognitive-behavioral, six-session, time-limited intervention. The responses of each participant during the course of treatment were rated using the ICRS-R. An examination of both friendly and hostile complementarity during the course of treatment found that outcome was related to the high–low–high pattern of both types of complementarity. There was little evidence of a differential pattern of interpersonal friendly and hostile complementarity that was related to outcome. The only difference in the pattern of friendly and hostile complementarity was that in the middle stage of more successful therapy, the therapists, but not the clients, were found to continue in a relative high level of hostile complementarity. The therapists in successful dyads manifested the curvilinear pattern for friendly complementarity but not for hostile complementarity. Successful clients manifested a similar curvilinear pattern for both friendly and hostile complementarity. This study supported the general high–low–high pattern of complementarity in all cases except therapist hostile complementarity, where no pattern over time existed.

The Tracey et al. (1999) study was informative in that the pattern of interpersonal complementarity was related to outcome in a structured cognitive-behavioral intervention providing support for the presence of the three-stage model in pantheoretical contexts. The three-stage complementarity model was related to differential outcome even in a nonrelationship-based intervention. The three-stage interpersonal model focuses on the process of therapy, rather than the content, that is, what gets discussed. Cognitive-behavioral models focus heavily on the content of the intervention. It may be that the relationship aspects of therapy pervade all types of therapeutic intervention. With respect to cognitive-behavioral models, Safran (1990) claimed that such attention to the relationship is necessary prior to many cognitive-behavior techniques becoming effective. Regardless, it appears important to pay attention to the pattern of complementarity even in interventions that focus little on such relationship aspects.

Overall, findings on the stage model of complementarity using interpersonal complementarity as the means of operationalization are equivocal. The support for the stage model is less than was true when using topic determination. Adding affiliation to control in defining complementarity does not result in a similar pattern of results. It appears that friendly and hostile behaviors are responded to differently and perhaps the degree of complementarity involved needs to be examined separately for each. Complementing with respect to hostile behavior is not the same as complementing with respect to friendly behavior. More examination is needed to understand the relative patterns and their relation to outcome.

Structural Analysis of Social Behavior (SASB)

The structural analysis of social behavior (SASB) model (Benjamin, 1974, 1982, 1993) is another interpersonal circumplex model. Instead of two dimensions, it uses three dimensions to define complementarity. The SASB model retains the affiliation dimension of the interpersonal circumplex (friendly–hostile), but control is divided into two dimensions: autonomy versus dominance and autonomy versus submission. When one is focusing on the other participant, behavior can vary from autonomous to dominant, when one is focusing on one's self, behavior can vary from autonomous to submissive. This coding system is more complex than the models previously discussed and has received increasing attention in the therapy research literature. The SASB system can be used in rating behavioral interchanges as well as more aggregate levels. In addition it also has self-report forms.

Quintana and Meara (1990) used the SASB system in their examination of the experience of 48 clients. The clients completed a self- and therapist-perception questionnaire after the first session and after termination. The complementarity of the self and other questionnaires was examined. They found that overall perceived complementarity was high early in treatment and that it remained at similar high levels at the end. This is an important application of the SASB system; however, it has little bearing on the complementarity stage model. It uses only client perceptions of complementarity, which may or may not be accurate, it does not examine differential relations to outcome, nor does it look for stage differences.

Perhaps one of the first studies to examine the differences between hostile and friendly complementarity was conducted by Henry, Schacht, and Strupp (1986). They labeled friendly complementarity as positive complementarity and hostile complementarity as negative complementarity, but to remain consistent here, I will use the terms *friendly* and *hostile complementarity*. Henry et al. found that friendly and hostile complementarity measured in the third session using the SASB model (rating actual behavioral interchanges) were differentially related to outcome. Hostile complementarity was related to eventual poor outcome. Although there was no examination of the two complementarity measures over the course of treatment, such results partially support Orford's (1986) argument for separating out friendly and hostile complementarity. Given that complementarity is defined fairly differently in the interpersonal circumplex and the SASB models, such conclusions should be made tentatively.

However Tasca and McMullen (1992), did examine the stage model of friendly and hostile complementarity using the SASB. They rated the responses for the client and therapist from eight dyads (one successful and one unsuccessful case from four therapists) and examined the pattern as it covaried with outcome. They found that in the early and late sessions unsuccessful cases engaged in more hostile complementarity than successful cases, whereas there were no differences between successful and unsuccessful cases in the middle sessions. So they found a low–high–low curvilinear pattern for unsuccessful cases with respect to hostile complementarity. With respect to friendly complementarity, Tasca and McMullen found that successful dyads had higher levels than unsuccessful dyads in the early and late sessions but that there were no differences in the middle sessions, supporting the high–low–high curvilinear pattern for friendly complementarity.

Although the SASB defines complementarity differently than the interpersonal circle does, similar results were yielded. There is some support for the three-stage pattern of complementarity with respect to friendly complementarity but there is less support for the curvilinear pattern for hostile complementarity. The drop of friendly complementarity in the middle stage clearly indicates that there is conflict regarding how the participants are to act. However the failure of the high–low–high curvilinear pattern for hostile complementarity indicates that, across the two different models, hostility is dealt with differently than friendly behavior in therapy. As argued by Tracey (1993), friendly and hostile behaviors have very different meanings and probabilities of being demonstrated. Successful therapists manifested a consistent pattern of low to moderate levels of hostile complementarity. In unsuccessful dyads, the therapists had higher levels of hostile complementarity. So relative to practice, therapists should attend to the different levels of friendly and hostile complementarity. It appears best to engage in lower levels of hostile complementarity and not to vary this during the course of treatment. The key seems to be that in successful therapy the therapist and client do not engage in hostile exchanges, regardless of the control involved. It does appear beneficial to look for the curvilinear pattern with respect to friendly complementarity.

For the various methods of defining and examining complementarity, there is much support for the three-stage model of complementarity and its relation to outcome. Using the more subtle indicators of topic determination, there is fairly strong support for the model. Across a wide variety of interpersonal circumplex models, there also is support for the stage model with respect to friendly complementarity. Perhaps what matters most is the complementarity on the control dimension. If the differences in complementarity across friendly and hostile behaviors were only examined with respect to the degree of complementarity on the control dimension, it is probable that the differences in the two indexes would decrease. Hoyt et al. (1993) reconceptualized complementarity into engagement to take account of these differences and found support for the curvilinear model. So the key aspect of defining complementarity, at least as it relates to successful therapy, is to focus on the relative control implied in each behavior. This is the level at which complementarity should occur and the level at which the three-stage model of complementarity appears valid.

Working Alliance

Complementarity is an indicator of how well the client and therapist are getting along and of how well they agree on what each is doing in their relationship. Given this view of complementarity, it has some conceptual overlap with the construct of the working alliance. In addition, Kiesler and Watkins (1989) yielded some empirical support for the covariance of complementarity and the working alliance. Bordin (1979) defined the working alliance as the extent to which the therapist and client (1) experience an emotional bond, (2) agree on the goals of therapy, and (3) agree on the tasks used to get to those goals. (See chapter 4 for a review of the literature on the working alliance.) Complementarity seems to relate most to the agreement on tasks: what exactly each is to do in therapy. If the client and therapist agree on what is to be done and how it is to be done in therapy, complementarity should be high. Low levels of complementarity would be expected in cases where there is less agreement on who is to do what because each participant would be trying to get the other to adhere to their definition. Given this conceptual overlap, it might be expected that the alliance would manifest the high–low–high curvilinear pattern also.

There are some differences, however, between the constructs of complementarity and the working alliance. Gelso and Carter (1994) specify that there are two separate aspects of the therapeutic relationship: the real relationship and the transferential relationship. The real relationship refers to the realistic adult-to-adult interaction and bond between the participants, whereas the transferential relationship refers to the stylized pattern of interacting that clients and therapists bring to the relationship (e.g., expecting to be criticized in all relationships). The working alliance is posited to exist at the real relationship level where the two participants negotiate in an adult manner the specifics of how therapy will progress. As discussed earlier, complementarity is proposed to exist at the behavioral exchange level and thus would incorporate both the real and transferential relationship. The logic behind the complementarity stage model almost focuses more on the transferential relationship than the relationship where the transferential or stylistic patterns of the client are the focus. Although there are similarities between the constructs of the working alliance and complementarity, there are clear differences in scope.

Notwithstanding these differences, Gelso and Carter (1994) hypothesized the presence of the curvilinear stage pattern over time in successful dyads for the working alliance. They posited that the drop in the working alliance in the middle stage is an important component in the determination of outcome. Conversely, Bordin (1979) views the working alliance as a necessary component of therapy. He does not discuss any fluctuations over time but implies that strong working alliances enable therapeutic interventions to be successful. In this view, the working alliance provides the necessary bedrock for the process. There are data concerning the variability of the working alliance over time (e.g., Hartley & Strupp, 1982), but it is not clear that there is a pattern to this variability and whether this variability is related to outcome. If Gelso and Carter are correct, the working alliance should manifest the three-stage curvilinear pattern over time in successful outcomes. If Bordin is correct, the working alliance should not manifest a curvilinear pattern but should evidence a constant high level that is associated with outcome. The question is one of which model better fits the data, the curvilinear high–low–high alliance stage model or the constant alliance model.

There is a wealth of literature relating the working alliance to outcome, but most of it focuses on assessing the alliance once, typically relatively early in therapy (usually in the third session) and then correlating it with outcome (e.g., Horvath & Symonds, 1991). The positive correlation between the working alliance and outcome has repeatedly been supported but there is relatively little research on the pattern of the alliance during the course of treatment and its relation to outcome. Only such an examination over time can help determine if the stage model of the alliance is appropriate. For example, in a sample of two therapy dyads, Golden and Robbins (1990) found that the working alliance (when examined from the clients' perspective) demonstrated a drop in the middle sessions. Such an examination over time demonstrates the curvilinear pattern, but because there was no evaluation of the pattern relative to outcome, little about the relative merit of the curvilinear pattern versus the constant pattern model of the working alliance can be yielded.

As in the case of complementarity, there are a variety of indicators of the working alliance and they are not isomorphic. Hatcher and Berends (1996) demonstrated that the many measures of the working alliance assess varying aspects of the broad construct of the working alliance. Hence, any research needs to be examined relative to the specific measure used. Perhaps the most common indicator of the working alliance is the Working Alliance Inventory (WAI; Horvath & Greenberg, 1986, 1989, and its shorter version, WAI-S; Tracey & Kokotovic, 1989). Although the WAI assesses the three separate specific components of the working alliance proposed by Bordin, (1979) (i.e., task, bond, and goals), it also measures the more global, shared, general alliance factor.

Sexton, Hembre, and Kvarme (1996) examined the working alliance using the WAI-S during the course of brief therapy in 32 dyads (which included 10 professional therapists). They examined the course of the alliance and were interested in the general pattern of development. They found that the working alliance was essentially set in the first session and then stayed at a fairly constant level during treatment. They did not assess the alliance relative to outcome, so there was no information provided about the relative merits of the curvilinear or constant pattern of the alliance with respect to outcome. However, the finding of the establishment of the general level of the alliance in the first session has important implications relative to attending to the alliance in this initial work.

Kivlighan and Shaughnessy (1995) also used the WAI-S in the third, middle, and final sessions and related these to outcome in a sample of 21 therapy dyads (with beginning and advanced graduate student therapists). They found support for a linear pattern of growth in WAI-S scores over the three sessions as related to outcome. Better outcome was associated with increasing alliance scores over time. This result is important in relating the pattern of alliance over time, but the use of only three data points does not allow for an adequate test of the curvilinear pattern, nor does it allow individual variation in the pattern over time.

Using WAI measures from every therapy session, Patton et al. (1997) examined the covariation of the pattern of the alliance with outcome in 16 dyads, containing six advanced graduate student therapists conducting psychodynamic short-term therapy. They found support for the curvilinear high–low–high relationship between the alliance, using the client-rated form of the WAI, and outcome.

Kivlighan and Shaughnessy (in press) conducted two studies where they examined the client-rated WAI scores for all sessions during the course of a four-session treatment. Their sample consisted of novice therapists-in-training meeting with recruited participants from an undergraduate class, so the results may not be generalizable, but they had a fairly good size sample and examined variation over time. In the first study on 31 dyads, they found three clear patterns of WAI scores over treatment: a stable, a linear (increasing over time) growth, and a quadratic (high–low–high) growth pattern. In a second replication study with 41 dyads, they found the same three patterns and further found that the quadratic pattern was associated with the highest outcome scores.

Although they did not examine the covariation of the alliance pattern over time with outcome, Brossard, Willson, Patton, Kivlighan, and Multon (1998) did examine the pattern of client and therapist ratings over the course of treatment using 6 advanced graduate student counselors conducting psychodynamic short-term therapy with 11 clients. They found that therapist ratings of the alliance had an affect on client ratings of the alliance. Therapist perceptions of how well the sessions were going affected future client perceptions. Given this result, the high–low–high pattern of the alliance should follow a slightly different phase between the therapist and the client, with the therapist demonstrating the middle drop and final rise slightly before the client.

Although not explicitly focusing on the working alliance, Tracey (1989) examined the pattern in-session evaluation (i.e., general favorableness) during the course of treatment conducted by 11 therapists with 33 clients. He found that there was a high–low–high curvilinear pattern associated with those dyads with the highest outcome for both client and therapist satisfaction ratings. Less successful dyads did not manifest this curvilinear pattern at all. There was also a linear growth pattern in therapist ratings associated with outcome similar to the results of Kivlighan and Shaughnessy (1995).

Westerman (1998) has used client coordination as a proxy for the working alliance. Client behavior is rated for the extent to which it relates to current therapist and previous client behavior. Westerman and Foote (1995) have argued that the extent to which a client coordinates behavior is an indicator of the client's contribution to the alliance. Westerman, Foote, and Winston (1995) examined client coordination over the course of therapy in two types of therapy: Short-Term Dynamic Psychotherapy (STDP; Davanloo, 1980) and Brief Adaptive Psychotherapy (BAP). Twelve professional therapists (six in each therapy condition) participated. Three early, three early middle, three late middle, and three late sessions of the 40-session treatment were sampled. Outcome was related to a constant high level of client coordination in the BAP and in a slightly increasing pattern in STDP. These results are interesting because they indicate that the pattern of coordination may vary with the type of therapy. STDP would put more focus on the examination of the therapeutic relationship than would BAP, and, as such, it might be expected that this type of therapy would evidence more pattern variability in client coordination than would BAP. The results of Westerman et al. (1995), however, have little bearing on the curvilinear versus constant alliance question as there was no assessment of curvilinear trend. To correct this, Westerman specifically examined the validity of the curvilinear versus constant alliance trend. In one study, using 16 clients meeting with 8 professional and 8 novice therapists, there was support for a high–low–high pattern of coordination during the course of therapy. However, there was no assessment of outcome in this study. To determine whether this pattern was related to outcome, Westerman examined the same data used in Westerman et al. for curvilinearity. He found support for a general curvilinear trend but that it was not related to outcome. He proposed that the curvilinear trend is a general aspect of the therapy process and not related to outcome. These results are interesting, but they agree little with the rest of the literature cited. The discrepancy could be a function of the different measure used, observer-rated client coordination not therapist- and client-rated alliance. The overlap among these measures needs examination. And it could relate to the limited sample of sessions. Using only 12 sessions of the total 40 could leave a good deal of variance undiscovered, especially individual variation.

With respect to the literature on the pattern of the working alliance over time, there does appear to be several conflicting results. However if focus is placed on those studies examining the participants' perceptions of the alliance using the WAI, there is some support for the superiority of the high–low–high curvilinear pattern over the constant alliance pattern being related to outcome. Further with the results of Brossard et al. (1998) it appears that it is the therapist that sets the alliance tone. The therapist's assessments of the alliance affects subsequent assessments by the client.

Summary

I have conducted a selective review of the literature on the stages of therapy specifically focusing on aspects of complementarity and the working alliance when examined over time in covariance with outcome. Clearly, there are a variety of other constructs that have been hypothesized to be related to outcome in a time-based way, but it is less common that they have been examined empirically as they vary over time and outcome. Complementarity and the working alliance are associated with theories that hypothesize certain specific changes during the course of therapy that is related to outcome, and, hence, there has been more research examining the stage process on these constructs.

The body of research on the stages of complementarity and the working alliance is noteworthy in its external validity. All of the studies involve real clients receiving therapy from therapists in typical mental health agencies, rather than constrained clinical trials. Most of the therapists in the research are professionals working their trade as they typically do. Further, much of the research incorporates individual variation in the process by examining the pattern over all sessions in replicated single-case designs or growth curve analyses that enable examination of each dyad separately. So there are few assumptions made that all dyads will manifest the same pattern in the same sessions. Some dyads may move through the first stage quickly, whereas others take more time in the first stage but move through the second stage quickly. Such individual variation in how dyads fit the general pattern of the stage model also fits better with actual practice. I have argued elsewhere (Tracey & Glidden-Tracey, 1999) that quality research is highly consistent across theory, design, measurement, and analysis. One of the aspects of much of the research cited is the premium placed on representing what actually transpires in psychotherapy. Many of the decisions made by the researchers in the individual studies demonstrate this consistency across measurement and design relative to external validity. Hence, the results can be said to characterize current therapy practice.

A point made repeatedly throughout this chapter has been that any conclusions apply only to the specific methods of construct operationalization used. There were many different means of representing complementarity and the working alliance applied in the literature. When examined as a whole, however, there was a wealth of equivocal findings. When the research was examined with an eye to method of operationalization, however, a clearer picture emerged. Within most methods of operationalization, there was greater consensus. Equivocal results occurred across variables. Such comparison of results across methods of construct operationalization helps provide greater understanding of the limits of the larger constructs.

With regard to complementarity, the curvilinear stage model was supported when complementarity was indicated using the topic negotiation sequence. The ability to control the topic of conversation was shown to follow the curvilinear pattern over time in successful dyads. When complementarity was examined using the two- or three-dimension interpersonal circle, however, there were less supportive results for the curvilinear complementarity pattern. The main problems revolved around the different complementarity patterns for friendly and hostile behaviors. Behaviors exhibited following friendly behavior adhered to the high–low–high curvilinear model for successful outcome dyads, but those behaviors following hostile behaviors did not follow the pattern, calling into question the basic premise of applying the interpersonal circle in such contexts.

Looking across all the different complementarity stage studies, it appears that where there is support for the pattern of complementarity, it involves focus mostly on the control dimension. When complementarity was defined using the control dimension, the curvilinear pattern of complementarity was supported. When account was also taken of affiliation, the results decreased. So complementarity, as originally conceived by Bateson (1936/ 1958), appears to have gotten the most support in the literature. It is true that there are a variety of methods used to examine the control dimension and that these all do not agree (see Tracey, 1991), but focus on the dimension of control appears to be key in applying the construct of complementarity to psychotherapy. More focus is needed in applying the various measures of control to determine which ones are the best indicators of the process and which can be easily tracked by therapists to provide information about the process.

Using control negotiation as an indicator of the process can facilitate therapist intervention. The therapist can easily monitor the relative topical exchanges of the client and therapist to get a relative idea of where in the stage process the dyad is. If both the client and therapist have continued in an easy topic exchange pattern for several sessions, the therapist needs to start introducing change. The therapist will know that important issues are being addressed when the client repeatedly changes the topic from that desired by the therapist. It is hoped that therapists can use the model presented in this chapter to think about the progress of interaction with clients during the course of therapy.

The literature on the pattern of the working alliance during the course of therapy also appears to have equivocal results. Indeed, the literature has been called equivocal by Brossard et al. (1998) and Westerman (1998). However when account is taken of the specific variable used to indicate the working alliance, there is less difference than initially thought. When the perspective of the client or therapist is used as the indicator of the alliance and it is related to outcome with a sufficient sampling of therapy sessions, the curvilinear pattern has been supported (Patton et al., 1997). When the alliance has been assessed using observer ratings of client behavior (e.g., Westerman), however, there is no support for the curvilinear pattern with respect to outcome. Overt behaviors on the client's part do not appear to manifest the curvilinear pattern relative to outcome. Given that the working alliance is typically referred to as something perceived by the participants (e.g., Bordin, 1979), it makes most sense to assess it using the perspectives of the participants. It is not always easy for an external observer to pick up the emotional cues that may be central to the alliance.

The issue of attending to methods of construct operationalization also relates to how outcome is defined. Howard, Moras, Brill, Martinovich, and Lutz (1996) proposed a three-phase model of therapy that focuses on the types of outcomes of therapy. They label the first phase remoralization, and it consists of increasing client hope. They view this being accomplished in only a few sessions. They view this remoralization as focusing on the subjective well-being of the client. The second phase is one of remediation where the focus is on symptom improvement. This is typically more gradual than remoralization. The final phase is one of rehabilitation, which focuses on general life functioning involving unlearning troublesome, maladaptive, habitual behaviors to establish new ways of coping with life's issues. Howard et al. believe these three phases of therapy represent different goals and are far from isomorphic. Although psychotherapy clearly has been used to address all three phases of change, I am most concerned with the third, rehabilitation, phase, because it is the typical focus of psychotherapy. When one is reviewing research relative to therapeutic outcome, however, it is helpful to understand the exact type of outcome being assessed. It could easily occur that different phases of outcome are being represented in different studies. It is plausible that the process of change in increasing hope or subjective well-being is different from that of decreasing symptomology, which in turn is different from the process associated with rehabilitation.

It would be desirable to say unequivocally that the curvilinear high–low–high pattern of complementarity or the working alliance characterizes successful psychotherapy, because it would simplify things. Hopefully, this review demonstrates that no such conclusion can be drawn. However, some conclusions can be drawn when the specifics of the research are examined. Some may bemoan the lack of apparent uniformity in the research results and turn away from the literature because it is viewed as unrelated to practice (e.g., Elliot, 1983; Hayes & Nelson, 1981). I wish to argue that the skilled clinician pays attention to the specifics of the research. The skilled clinician would realize that there are a variety of ways of doing things in therapy. For example, there are a number of ways of thinking about the establishment of rapport. The therapist may monitor the general affective tone of the client, or the expressions of progress. Each of these has been viewed as a sign of strong rapport. However, each of these signs is flawed. Expressions of negative affect may indicate that the client feels enough rapport to risk bringing up unpleasant material. Similarly, client expressions of progress could be masking defensiveness or dependence. The point is that for any theory to be good, it needs to provide *specific* behaviors or cues that the therapist can use. These specifics occur at the very particular level of the operationalizations of the constructs. Although at a general level, much of the therapeutic literature may be equivocal, it is not always so when the specifics of the research are examined.

Two conclusions that may be gleaned from the research reviewed here are that the curvilinear pattern of complementarity and the working alliance are related to outcome when it is measured using control and the participants' perceptions, respectively. Using other definitions of complementarity and the alliance do not yield support. Not all measures are equivalent. The research has provided some important cues that the clinician can apply to a practice. These variables are specific and fairly clear. The research results exist at a specific level and not a general level. It is this specific level that actually fits better with clinical practice, because it indicates how the constructs should be viewed and assessed by the clinician. Clinicians can use the topical exchange to assess complementarity and their own and their clients' perceptions to assess the alliance.

References

Anderson, J. R. (1983). *The architecture of cognition.* Cambridge, MA: Harvard University Press.

Andrews, J. D. W. (1990). Interpersonal self-confirmation and challenge in psychotherapy. *Psychotherapy, 27,* 485–504.

Andrews, J. D. W. (1991). Integrative psychotherapy of depression: A self-confirmation approach. *Psychotherapy, 28,* 232–250.

Baldwin, M. W. (1992). Relational schemas in the processing of social information. *Psychological Bulletin, 112,* 461–484.

Bateson, G. (1958). *Naven.* London: Cambridge University Press. (Original work published 1936)

Beier, E. G., & Young, D. M. (1984). *The silent language of psychotherapy.* Chicago: Aldine.

Benjamin, L. S. (1974). Structural analysis of social behavior. *Psychological Review, 81,* 392–425.

Benjamin, L. S. (1982). Use of structural analysis of social behavior (SASB) to guide intervention in psychotherapy. In J. C. Anchin and D. J. Kiesler (Eds.), *Handbook of interpersonal psychotherapy* (pp. 190–212). New York: Pergamon Press.

Benjamin, L. S. (1993). *Interpersonal diagnosis and treatment of personality disorders.* New York: Guilford Press.

Bordin, E. S. (1979). The generalizability of the psychoanalytic concept of the working alliance. *Psychotherapy: Theory, Research and Practice, 16,* 252–259.

Brossard, D. F., Willson, V. L., Patton, M. J., Kivlighan, D. M., Jr., & Multon, K. D. (1998). A time series model of the working alliance: A key process in short-term psychoanalytic counseling. *Psychotherapy, 35,* 197–205.

Bugental, J. F. T., & Kleiner, R. I. (1993). Existential psychotherapies. In G. Stricker & J. R. Gold (Eds.), *Comprehensive handbook of psychotherapy integration* (pp. 113–142). New York: Plenum Press.

Carson, R. C. (1969). *Interactional concepts of personality.* Chicago: Aldine.

Carver, C. S., & Scheier, M. F. (1982). Control theory: A useful conceptual framework for personality, social, clinical and health psychology. *Psychological Bulletin, 92,* 111–135.

Claiborn, C. D., & Lichtenberg, J. W. (1989). Interactional counseling. *The Counseling Psychologist, 17,* 355–453.

Davanloo, H. (1980). *Short-Term Dynamic Psychotherapy.* New York: Aaronson

Dietzel, C. S., & Abeles, N. (1975). Client–therapist complementarity and therapeutic outcome. *Journal of Counseling Psychology, 22,* 264–272.

Elliot, R., (1983). Fitting process research to the practicing psychotherapist. *Psychotherapy: Theory, Research and Practice, 29,* 47–55.

Ericson, P. M., & Rogers, L. E. (1973). New procedures for analyzing relational communication. *Family Process, 12,* 245–267.

Freedman, M. B., Leary, T., Ossario, A. G., & Coffey, H. S. (1951). The interpersonal dimension of personality. *Journal of Personality, 20,* 143–161.

Friedlander, M. L. (1993). Does complementarity promote or hinder client change in brief therapy: A review of the evidence from two theoretical perspectives. *The Counseling Psychologist, 21,* 457–486.

Gelso, C. J., & Carter, J. A. (1994). Components of the psychotherapy relationship: Their interaction and unfolding during treatment. *Journal of Counseling Psychology, 41,* 296–306.

Gifford, R., & O'Connor, B. (1987). The interpersonal circumplex as a behavior map. *Journal of Personality and Social Psychology, 52,* 1019–1026.

Golden, B. R., & Robbins, S. B. (1990). The working alliance within time-limited therapy: A case analysis. *Professional Psychology: Research and Practice, 21,* 476–481.

Gurtman, M. B. (1992). Trust, distrust, and interpersonal problems: A circumplex analysis. *Journal of Personality and Social Psychology, 62,* 989–1002.

Hartley, D. E., & Strupp, H. H. (1982). The therapeutic alliance: Its relationship to outcome in brief psychotherapy. In J. Masling (Ed.), *Empirical studies of psychoanalytic theories* (Vol. 1, pp. 1–37). Hillsdale, NJ: Erlbaum.

Hatcher, R. L., & Berends, A. W. (1996). Patients' view of the alliance in psychotherapy: Exploratory factor analysis of three alliance measures. *Journal of Consulting and Clinical Psychology, 64,* 1326–1336.

Hayes, S. C., & Nelson, R. O. (1981) Clinically relevant research: Requirements, problems, and solutions. *Behavioral Assessment, 3,* 209–215.

Hays, K. (1991). *An examination of positive and negative complementarity across the stages of successful counseling.* Unpublished doctoral dissertation, University of Illinois, Urbana-Champaign.

Heatherington, L. (1988). Coding relational communication control in counseling: Criterion validity. *Journal of Counseling Psychology, 35,* 41–46.

Henry, W. P., Schacht, T. E., & Strupp, H. H. (1986). Structural analysis of social behavior: Application to a study of interpersonal process in differential psychotherapeutic outcome. *Journal of Consulting and Clinical Psychology, 54,* 27–31.

Horowitz, L. M., Dryer, D. C., & Krasnoporova, E. N. (1997). The circumplex structure of interpersonal problems. In R. Plutchik, & H. R. Conte, (Eds.), *Circumplex models of personality and emotions* (pp. 347–384). Washington, DC: American Psychological Association.

Horvath, A. O., & Greenberg, L. S. (1986). The development of the Working Alliance Inventory. In L. S. Greenberg and W. M. Pinsof (Eds.), *The psychotherapy process: A research handbook* (pp. 529–556). New York: Guilford Press.

Horvath, A. O., & Greenberg, L. (1989). Development and validation of the working alliance inventory. *Journal of Counseling Psychology, 36,* 223–233.

Horvath, A. O., & Symonds, B. D. (1991). Relation between working alliance and outcome in psychotherapy: A meta-analysis. *Journal of Counseling Psychology, 38,* 139–149.

Howard, K. I., Moras, K., Brill, P. I., Martinovich, Z., & Lutz, W. (1996). Evaluation of psychotherapy: Efficacy, effectiveness, and patient progress. *American Psychologist, 51,* 1059–1064.

Hoyt, W. T., Strong, S. R., Corcoran, J. L., & Robbins, S. B. (1993). Interpersonal influence in a single case of brief counseling: An analytic strategy and a comparison of two indexes of influence. *Journal of Counseling Psychology, 40,* 166–181.

Kiesler, D. J. (1983). The 1982 interpersonal circle: A taxonomy for complementarity in human transactions. *Psychological Review, 90,* 185–214.

Kiesler, D. J. (1984). Check list of psychotherapy transactions (CLOPT) and check list of interpersonal transactions (CLOIT). Richmond: Virginia Commonwealth University.

Kiesler, D. J. (1996). *Contemporary interpersonal theory and research: Personality, psychopathology, and psychotherapy.* New York: Wiley.

Kiesler, D. J., & Watkins, L. M. (1989). Interpersonal complementarity and the therapeutic alliance: A study of the relationship in psychotherapy. *Psychotherapy, 26,* 183–194.

Kivlighan, D. M., Jr., & Shaughnessy, P. (1995). Analysis of the development of the working alliance using hierarchical linear modeling. *Journal of Counseling Psychology, 42,* 338–349.

Kivlighan, D. M., Jr., & Shaughnessy, P. (in press). Patterns of working alliance development: A typology of working alliance ratings. *Journal of Counseling Psychology.*

LaForge, R., Leary, T., Naboisek, H., Coffey, H. S., & Freedman, M. P. (1954). The interpersonal dimension of personality: 2. An objective study of repression. *Journal of Personality, 23,* 129–153.

LaForge, R., & Suczek, R. F. (1955). The interpersonal dimensions of personality: III. An interpersonal checklist. *Journal of Personality, 24,* 94–112.

Leary, T. (1957). *The interpersonal diagnosis of personality.* New York: Ronald Press.

Lennard, H. L., & Bernstein, A. (1960). *The anatomy of psychotherapy: Systems of communication and expectation.* New York: Columbia University Press.

Lichtenberg, J. W., & Barke, K. H. (1981). Investigation of transactional communication relationship patterns in counseling. *Journal of Counseling Psychology, 28,* 471–480.

Lichtenberg, J. W., Wettersten, K. B., Mull, H., Moberly, R. L., Merkley, K. B., Corey, A. T. (1998). Relationship formation and relational control as correlates of psychotherapy quality and outcome. *Journal of Counseling Psychology, 45,* 322–337.

Mann, J. (1973). *Time-limited psychotherapy.* Cambridge, MA: Harvard University Press.

Orford, J. (1986). The rules of interpersonal complementarity: Does hostility beget hostility and dominance, submission? *Psychological Review, 93,* 365–377.

Patton, M. J., Kivlighan, D. M., Jr., & Multon, K. D. (1997). The Missouri psychoanalytic counseling research project: Relation of changes in counseling process to client outcomes.. *Journal of Counseling Psychology, 44,* 189–208.

Penman, R. (1980). *Communication processes and relationships.* London: Academic Press.

Prochaska, J. O., DiClemente, C. C., & Norcross, J. C. (1992). In search of how people change: Applications to addictive behaviors. *American Psychologist, 47,* 1102–1114.

Quintana, S. M., & Meara, N. M. (1990). Internalization of therapeutic relationships in short-term psychotherapy. *Journal of Counseling Psychology, 37,* 123–130.

Reandeau, S. G., & Wampold, B. E. (1991). Relationship of power and involvement to working alliance: A multiple-case sequential analysis of brief therapy. *Journal of Counseling Psychology, 38,* 107–114.

Rogers, C. R. (1957). The necessary and sufficient conditions for therapeutic personality change. *Journal of Consulting Psychology, 21,* 95–103.

Safran, J. D. (1990). Towards a refinement of cognitive therapy in light of interpersonal theory: I. Theory. *Clinical Psychology Review, 10,* 87–105.

Sexton, H. C., Hembre, K., Kvarme, G. (1996). The interaction of the alliance and therapy microprocess: A sequential analysis. *Journal of Consulting and Clinical Psychology, 64,* 471–480.

Sifneos, P. E. (1987). *Short-term dynamic psychotherapy.* New York: Plenum Press.

Snyder, W. U. (1945). An investigation of the nature of non-directive psychotherapy. *Journal of General Psychology, 33,* 193–224.

Steenbarger, D. N. (1992). Towards science-practice integration in brief counseling and therapy. *The Counseling Psychologist, 20,* 403–450.

Strong, S. R., & Claiborn, C. D. (1982). *Change through interaction.* New York: Wiley.

Strong, S. R., Hills, H. I., Kilmartin, C. T., DeVries, H., Lanier, K., Nelson, B. N., Strickland, D., & Meyer, C. W., III. (1988). The dynamic relations among interpersonal behaviors: A test of complementarity and anticomplementarity. *Journal of Personality and Social Psychology, 54,* 789–810.

Strong, S. R., Hills, H., & Nelson, B. (1988). *Interpersonal Communication Rating Scale* (Rev. ed.). Richmond: Virginia Commonwealth University.

Swann, W. B., Jr. (1992). Seeking "truth," finding despair: Some unhappy consequences of a negative self-concept. *Current Directions in Psychological Science, 1,* 15–18.

Tasca, G. A., & McMullen, L. M. (1992). Interpersonal complementarity and antithesis within a stage model of psychotherapy. *Psychotherapy, 29,* 515–523.

Thompson, B. J., Hill, C. E., & Mahalik, J. (1991). A test of the complementarity hypothesis in the interpersonal theory of psychotherapy: Multiple case comparisons. *Psychotherapy, 28,* 572–579.

Tracey, T. J. (1985). Dominance and outcome: A sequential examination. *Journal of Counseling Psychology, 32,* 119–122.

Tracey, T. J. (1986a). The stages of influence in counseling and psychotherapy. In F. J. Dorn (Ed.), *Social influence processes in counseling and psychotherapy* (pp. 107–116). Springfield, IL: Charles C Thomas.

Tracey, T. J. (1986b). Interactional correlates of premature termination. *Journal of Consulting and Clinical Psychology, 54,* 784–788.

Tracey, T. J. (1987). Stage differences in the dependencies of topic initiation and topic following behavior. *Journal of Counseling Psychology, 34,* 123–131.

Tracey, T. J. (1988). Topic following/not following as a measure of complementary/symmetrical communication. *Journal of Communication Therapy, 4,* 37–57.

Tracey, T. J. (1989). Client and therapist session satisfaction over the course of psychotherapy. *Psychotherapy, 26,* 177–182.

Tracey, T. J. (1991). The structure of control and influence in counseling and psychotherapy: A comparison of several definitions and measures. *Journal of Counseling Psychology, 38,* 265–278.

Tracey, T. J. (1993). An interpersonal stage model of the therapeutic process. *Journal of Counseling Psychology, 40,* 396–409.

Tracey, T. J. (1994). An examination of the complementarity of interpersonal behavior. *Journal of Personality and Social Psychology, 67,* 864–878.

Tracey, T. J. G., & Glidden-Tracey, C. E. (1999). Integration of theory, research design, measurement, and analysis: Toward a reasoned argument. *The Counseling Psychologist, 27,* 299–324.

Tracey, T. J., & Hays, K. (1989). Therapist complementarity as a function of experience and client stimuli. *Psychotherapy, 26,* 462–468.

Tracey, T. J., Heck, E., & Lichtenberg, J. W. (1981). Role expectations and symmetrical/complementary therapeutic relationships. *Psychotherapy, 18,* 338–344.

Tracey, T. J., & Kokotovic, A. M. (1989). Factor structure of the Working Alliance Inventory. *Psychological Assessment: A Journal of Consulting and Clinical Psychology, 1,* 207–210.

Tracey, T. J., & Miars, R. D. (1986). Interpersonal control in psychotherapy: A comparison of two definitions. *Journal of Clinical Psychology, 42,* 585–592.

Tracey, T. J., & Ray, P. B. (1984). Stages of successful time-limited counseling: An interactional examination. *Journal of Counseling Psychology, 31,* 13–27.

Tracey, T. J. G., & Schneider, P. L. (1995). An evaluation of the circular structure of the checklist of Interpersonal Transactions and the Checklist of Psychotherapy Transactions. *Journal of Counseling Psychology, 42,* 496–507.

Tracey, T. J. G., Sherry, P., & Albright, J. M. (1999). The interpersonal process of cognitive-behavioral therapy: An examination of complementarity over the course of treatment. *Journal of Counseling Psychology, 46,* 80–91.

Weinstock-Savoy, D. E. (1986). *The relationship of therapist and patient interpersonal styles to outcome in brief dynamic psychotherapy.* Unpublished doctoral dissertation, Boston University, Boston.

Westerman, M. A. (1998). Curvilinear trajectory in patient coordination over the course of short-term psychotherapy. *Psychotherapy, 35,* 206–219.

Westerman, M. A., & Foote, J. P. (1995). Patient coordination: Contrasts with other conceptualizations of patients' contributions to the alliance and validity in insight-oriented psychotherapy. *Psychotherapy, 32,* 222–232.

Westerman, M. A., Foote, J. P., & Winston, A. (1995). Change in coordination across phases of psychotherapy and outcome: Two mechanisms for the role played by patients' contribution to the alliance. *Journal of Consulting and Clinical Psychology, 63,* 672–675.

Wiggins, J. S. (1979). A psychological taxonomy of trait-descriptive terms: The interpersonal domain. *Journal of Personality and Social Psychology, 37,* 395–412.

Wiggins, J. S. (1982). Circumplex models of interpersonal behavior in clinical psychology. In P. C. Kendall and J. N. Butcher (Eds.), *Handbook of research methods in clinical psychology* (pp. 183–221). New York: Wiley.

Wiggins, J. S., & Broughton, R. (1985). The interpersonal circle: A structural model for the integration of personality research. In R. Hogan and W. H. Jones (Eds.), *Perspectives in personality: Theory, measurement, and interpersonal dynamics* (Vol. 1, pp. 1–47). Greenwich, CT: JAI Press.

Wiggins, J. S., Phillips, N., & Trapnell, P. (1989). Circular reasoning about interpersonal behavior: Evidence concerning some untested assumptions underlying diagnostic classification. *Journal of Personality and Social Psychology, 56,* 296–305.

Social Influence in Counseling

Application of the Elaboration Likelihood Model to Counseling

Martin Heesacker and Marnie G. Shanbhag

University of Florida

All counseling or therapy involves influencing clients to behave in ways that therapists be-lieve will be helpful to the clients. Some clients come to counseling with an understanding of and a willingness to perform the therapeutic exercises associated with the particular type of counseling offered. Other clients need to be educated and persuaded regarding the usefulness and importance of various interventions. This chapter presents a model and as-sociated methods to enhance the effectiveness of all types of therapeutic procedures by al-tering clients' attitudes toward them.

Chapter Questions

- How can mental health professionals influence the attitudes of their clients in productive ways?
- Are there practically useful theories of how to improve the dysfunctional attitudes of clients?
- What does the current research suggest about attitude change in counseling?
- When are clients' attitudes most likely to really influence their behavior?
- Are there different kinds of attitudes, with different importance for counseling?
- What practical steps make a counselor influential with clients?

James, a 34-year-old, white, male, undergraduate student, sought counseling at his univer-sity's counseling center at the request of his wife of three years. James reported that his wife thought he had problems with anger and that he needed to figure out a better way to handle his occasional outbursts of aggressive behavior. James made it clear in the first session that he did not believe he had a problem but did want his marriage to continue. During the next several sessions, the counselor worked with James to establish a therapeutic relationship and to help him change his attitudes toward his aggressive behavior. Once this attitude change had been achieved, James and his counselor were able to understand the roots of his aggression, which were based on his sense of entitlement as a man in American society, coupled with his feelings of inadequacy and frustration, and his lack of effective communication strategies. With continued work by both counselor and client, much of which focused on changing James attitude's and beliefs, James (1) came to accept the negative impact of his aggressive behavior; (2) took responsibility for his behavior and its consequences; (3) rethought the appropriateness and utility of believing that men are entitled to special status and privileges; (4) responded to his feelings of inadequacy and frustration with alternate, nonaggressive behaviors; and (5) adopted and implemented new skills for communicating with his wife. After 16 sessions, he, his counselor, and his wife believed he was ready to terminate counseling.

Definitions

Building on Strong's (1968) seminal article "Counseling: An Interpersonal Influence Process," a large body of research defines counseling as a process in which counselors and clients engage in attempts to influence one another. Although social influence research in counseling includes some other kinds of influence, for example what Claiborn (1986) called influence at the "relationship level" (p. 31), most social influence research has focused on enhancing therapeutic behavior change via changes in people's attitudes (see reviews by Corrigan, Dell, Lewis, & Schmidt, 1980; Heesacker, Conner, & Prichard, 1995; P. P. Heppner & Claiborn, 1989; P. P. Heppner & Frazier, 1992). An attitude can be defined as an enduring evaluation of a person, object, or situation along a positive–negative continuum. Although in the past 15 years studies in this area have more clearly reflected recognition of the complexity of counselor–client interactions, attitude change research in counseling has traditionally focused primarily on the relationship between a client's perceptions of the counselor and the client's attitude change.

Definitions of attitudes, which emphasize evaluation, are commonly used in attitude research; however, definitions emphasizing cognitive, affective, and behavioral aspects are also common, and generally are compatible with the way the term is used here. The evaluation definition includes affective and cognitive components but not a behavioral component. In the attitude change model employed here, a distinction is made between a type of attitude change that is likely to influence behavior and one that is less likely to influence behavior; therefore, the behavioral component is not ignored. In fact, its relationship to the affective and cognitive components is more explicit than in most other models of attitude change.

Building on the cognitive revolution occurring throughout psychology in the 1970s and 1980s, and using a depth of cognitive processing approach that led to important advances in the psychology of memory, Petty and Cacioppo (1981, 1986) developed their elaboration likelihood model (ELM). The ELM can be defined as a general model of the cognitive processes that lie at the heart of attitude change. More recent theoretical and conceptual work has highlighted and clarified how this general model of attitude change can be applicable to counseling practice. The ELM takes into account clients' use of cues, such as clients' perceptions of counselor credibility, just as Strong's (1968) model does, but the ELM goes further than Strong's model to focus on clients' elaborated thought processes as a second and more effective avenue by which attitudes can be changed.

Purpose

This chapter (1) describes these two routes (clients' use of cues and clients' elaborated thought processes) to attitude change in counseling; (2) reviews some of the basic and applied, counseling-relevant research on this two-route approach; and (3) provides guidelines for effective implementation of the model in counseling practice. Counseling interactions can involve a variety of forms of attitude change. A counselor may attempt to influence a client to believe that the client has a particular problem, that counseling is useful, or that a particular treatment would be helpful. For example, a counselor may attempt to persuade an alcoholic client to examine the drinking behavior in order to see that a substance abuse problem exists and work toward its resolution as needed. A counselor may need to convince another client, for example, a recently divorced client who is unsure if counseling is an appropriate place to deal with divorce issues, not that there is a problem, but of the usefulness of counseling for dealing with that problem and the importance of the client's commitment to counseling in solving the problem.

A counselor may need to convince another client, not that there is a problem, not that counseling is worth committing to, but rather that a specific treatment direction is worth pursuing. For example, a couple may know that they have a marital problem and be committed to counseling, but they may not think that a communication exercise can help them solve their problem. In one form or another, effective counseling often involves some type of attitude change. There is growing evidence that the counseling process and its successful outcome may be more fully understood when the cognitive processes associated with attitude change are considered in addition to a more traditional focus on client perceptions of counselors (see reviews by Cacioppo, Claiborn, Petty, & Heesacker, 1991; Cacioppo, Petty, & Stoltenberg, 1985; Heesacker, 1986a; Heesacker & Mejia-Millan, 1996, McNeill & Stoltenberg, 1989; Stoltenberg, 1986).

Several theoretical approaches to attitude change are cognitive in nature and recognize the important role of cognitive activity in attitude change processes (see Eagly & Chaiken, 1993; Petty & Wegener, 1999). These cognitive approaches view a person's own thoughts and cognitive elaboration (based on amount and depth of thought) as essential to attitude change. According to this general view, a person is most persuaded by personal thoughts, rather than by the argumentation of others. Cognitive approaches to attitude change include Janis' (1968) role-playing research, Tesser's mere thought research (Tesser & Leone, 1977), and Petty, Ostrom, and Brock's (1981) cognitive response approach. Arguably the most thoroughly developed and tested of these approaches, and the only one for which there is a substantial body of research applied to counseling, is Petty and Cacioppo's (1986) ELM, which is described in the next section (see Eagly & Chaiken, 1993, for a review of cognitive theories of attitude change; and Heesacker et al., 1995, for a review of the ELM counseling literature).

Review of the Literature

From the perspective of the ELM (Petty & Cacioppo, 1986), attitude change can be viewed along a continuum anchored by the central route at one end and the peripheral route at the other. Elaboration likelihood refers to the likelihood that the recipient of a persuasive message will cognitively elaborate on (or think about) the topic being discussed or the points being made about that topic. The motivation and ability of a person to think about a message determine which route of attitude change is most likely to be taken in the attitude change process. The route that is taken influences the relative impact of various features of the context. For example, message variables, such as how convincing the client believes the counselor's comments to be, assume greater importance for central route attitude change processing, whereas cue variables, such as counselor expertness, attractiveness, and trustworthiness, assume greater importance for peripheral route processing (see Figure 10.1).

What is the role of the ELM-based approaches in counseling? Such approaches are intended both to describe an aspect of the counseling process as it naturally occurs and to enhance the efficacy of existing treatments, such as systematic desensitization, working through, or cognitive reframing.

Effective persuasive communication by counselors can be no more helpful to clients than the accuracy of assessment and the appropriateness of a specific treatment. The strength of persuasive communication approaches lies in their ability to improve understanding of attitude change processes and to enhance acquisition and retention of therapeutically relevant attitudes and behaviors. One important implication of this role for the ELM in counseling is that it is not inherently limited in the kinds of client concerns for which it can be useful, nor is it inherently limited in the kinds of treatment approaches with which it is compatible.

Foundation of the ELM

Seven postulates serve as the intellectual foundation of the ELM (see Petty & Cacioppo, 1986, Chapter 1 for details). First, the ELM posits that people's motive in attitude formation or change is to hold a correct attitude. That is, people are motivated to be accurate in their evaluations of persons, objects, or situations. Second, tempering this motive to hold a correct attitude is the notion that people limit the amount and depth of cognitive processing, or thinking, in which they are willing to engage. For many people and in many situations, this cognitive processing limit is powerful enough that people are only willing to cognitively process relevant information at a minimal level, despite their desire to hold a correct attitude. For other people and in other situations, people are willing to expend greater cognitive effort. Third, a variable may affect attitude change in one of three ways: (1) by serving as an argument for a position, (2) by serving as a cue associated with an attitude position, or (3) by influencing how much or little effortful thinking people do. Fourth, some variables increase or decrease unbiased processing, which is processing in which people are open to both topic favorable and topic unfavorable thoughts. Fifth, some variables increase or decrease biased processing, which is processing in which people are open to either topic favorable or topic unfavorable thoughts, but not both. Sixth, as people's motivation and ability to engage in

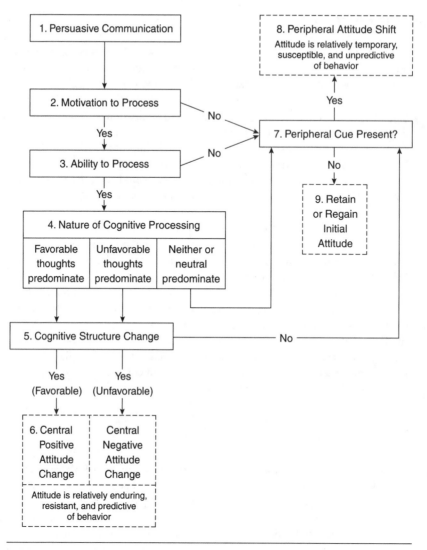

FIGURE 10.1   *Schematic Depiction of the Elaboration Likelihood Model of Attitude Change*

Source: Adapted from Petty & Cacioppo (1981).

topic relevant, effortful, cognitive processing increase, so does the importance of persuasive message arguments or content. Conversely, as motivation and ability decrease, the importance of cues in determining attitudes increases. Seventh, attitudes developed or changed in cognitively effortful and elaborated ways will be more enduring, influential, and resilient than attitudes developed or changed in less effortful and elaborated ways.

Two other important foundation issues deserve mention. First, in the ELM the person determines the values of important model components, including the following: (1) whether something is motivating, (2) whether the person is able to think effortfully about the attitude topic, (3) what elicits thought and in what ways, and (4) whether a stimulus serves as a cue. Second, from an ELM-based perspective, the person constructs meaning out of experience, rather than the person having access to an objective meaning that resides in, for example, the persuasive argument or the cue. This concept is manifested in the ELM notion that there is no objective standard for which persuasive message arguments or cues will elicit favorable or unfavorable responses. What will elicit favorable thoughts or associations differs for different people.

Two Routes to Attitude Change

As described earlier, the ELM distinguishes two routes to attitude change: a central or thoughtful route, one with high elaboration likelihood; and a peripheral or economical route, one with relatively low elaboration likelihood, in which thought is employed sparingly or economically. This section describes these routes in detail. Moderate elaboration likelihood, in which a client is initially neither high nor low in elaboration likelihood is also discussed.

One of the most important distinctions that the ELM holds for counselors is that the two attitude change routes, central and peripheral, hold quite different potential for resulting attitude and behavior change. The central route has the potential for eliciting attitude changes that last over time, are resistant to counterpersuasion, and result in greater attitude–behavior consistency than the peripheral route. For counselors, the clear implication of this is that the factors associated with increasing central route attitudes should be emphasized much more strongly in work with clients than peripheral route factors, because even if a counselor is successful in producing peripheral route change, the result is unlikely to produce the kind of enduring changes that clients seek. From an ELM-based perspective, one avenue for maintaining treatment gains is to establish central route attitudes that support therapeutic goals.

It is also important to distinguish between conformity and attitude change as two ways to influence people's behavior. In conformity, people engage in behavior because they feel coerced or pressured to do so from outside sources, for example, joining a treatment program because the counselor expects it. In attitude (Milgram, 1974) change, people engage in the behavior because they feel the desire to do so from within. Research suggests that people will persist in conformity behavior only as long as they feel external pressure. In general, we believe that effective social influence in counseling must be based on attitude change, not conformity, because the changes desired in counseling typically need to generalize beyond the counseling sessions and beyond the times when the counselor can be present. Sometimes counselor expertness, attractiveness, and trustworthiness may serve to increase conformity rather than attitude change. Counselors need to be careful not to mistake conformity for attitude change.

Central Route Attitude Change

The central route (corresponding to the left side of Figure 10.1, that is, items 1–6) involves cognitive processing of the topic, and typically the content, of a persuasive communication. As indicated earlier, the terms *cognitive processing* and *elaboration* in the ELM simply refer to active thinking by the person hearing a persuasive communication. In the case of counseling, persuasive communication could range from a single intervention by a counselor to all of the counselor's remarks about a particular topic. Central route attitude change occurs when a person is both able and motivated to cognitively process the topic. When these conditions are fulfilled, a person is more likely to think about the arguments presented in a persuasive communication. Central route attitude change is often heavily influenced by message factors such as the subjectively perceived strength of the persuasive arguments. If the person or client's predominant thoughts are favorable to the counselor's comments, then genuine and lasting attitude change can take place. If the person's predominant thoughts are unfavorable to the counselor's comments, then attitude change in the direction opposite to the message may take place. If neither favorable nor unfavorable thoughts predominate, central route attitude change is not likely to take place, but instead peripheral route change may occur. In order for successful central route attitude change to occur, consolidation of predominantly favorable or unfavorable thoughts into long-term memory is required; thus, central route attitude change is persistent, influences behavior, and is resistant to counterpersuasion.

Peripheral Route Attitude Change

If a person is not able or motivated to think carefully about a counselor's comments, or neither favorable or unfavorable thoughts predominate, or thoughts fail to be stored in long-term memory, then peripheral route attitude change may occur (corresponding to the right side of Figure 10.1, that is, items 7–9). Peripheral route attitude change is based on associations with positive or negative cues. For example, if a topic of counseling is associated with an expert's opinion or an attractive setting, these cues may act as triggers for peripheral route attitude change by the recipient. Peripheral route attitude change, however, is generally less persistent, less predictive of behavior, and less resistant to influence attempts in the opposite direction than is central route attitude change. Once a message is no longer associated with the persuasive cue, a person will usually return to the original attitude. If a person is not able or motivated to cognitively consider a persuasive message and no peripheral cues are present, then no attitude change is likely to take place.

When Initial Elaboration Likelihood Is Neither High Nor Low

The results of several studies (e.g., Heesacker, 1986a; Heesacker, Petty, & Cacioppo, 1984; Puckett, Petty, Cacioppo, & Fischer, 1983) suggest that when initial elaboration likelihood is neither high nor low, the effects of cues and thoughts about the topic interact. For example, if an individual is only marginally motivated to cognitively elaborate on a persuasive message, knowing that it is being presented by a source of high credibility may enhance motivation to the degree that the person will then have high elaboration likelihood. Some evidence suggests that some counseling clients may, indeed, initially possess moderate elaboration likelihood (Petty, Cacioppo, & Heesacker, 1984; Heesacker, 1986a, 1986b). So, it may be important to consider moderate elaboration likelihood, in addition to high and low elaboration likelihood, when considering attitude change processes in counseling.

Research on moderate elaboration likelihood suggests that in some circumstances, such as when the topic that the counselor and client are discussing is something the client feels favorable about, a counselor perceived as a relative inexpert may trigger more client thinking than a counselor of high credibility. This increased thinking about the counselor's message may result in more attitude change if the counselor's comments are perceived by the client as cogent. This unusual result can be understood using Heider's (1958) balance theory. The inconsistency between a proattitudinal message presented by a source of low credibility and a counterattitudinal message presented by a source of high credibility can be thought to represent imbalance and to result in increased elaboration likelihood because imbalance, according to Heider, is an uncomfortable state that calls forth additional action from the person experiencing it.

Research Findings

Basic Research and the ELM

To summarize the results of hundreds of basic research studies that have formed the scholarly foundation for the ELM and its various aspects would be inappropriate in this discussion of counseling applications. Nonetheless, several points from the research should be made. Every major aspect of the model has been supported by empirical research. In line with ELM predictions, central route attitudes have been shown to require the following: (1) motivation (e.g., Petty, Cacioppo, & Goldman, 1981) and ability (e.g., Cacioppo & Petty, 1979) to think about the topic; (2) mediation by participants' topic-relevant thinking (e.g., Petty, Cacioppo, & Heesacker, 1981); (3) thoughts based on message content and not on reactions to cues (e.g., Petty, Cacioppi, & Goldman, 1981); (4) persistence over time (e.g., Heesacker, Petty, Cacioppo, & Haugtvedt, 1988); (5) prediction of behavior (e.g., Gilbert, Heesacker, & Gannon, 1991; Neimeyer, Guy, & Metzler, 1989); and (6) resistance to counterpersuasion (e.g., Haugtvedt, 1988; Haugtvedt & Petty, 1992), relative to peripheral route attitudes. Peripheral route attitudes have been shown to require (1) low motivation (e.g., Petty & Cacioppo, 1979) or low ability (e.g., Petty, Cacioppo, & Goldman, 1981) to think about the topic; (2) mediation by participants' perceptions of cues (e.g., Petty, Cacioppo, & Schumann, 1983); (3) reactions based on cues and not on thoughts about message content (e.g., Petty & Cacioppo, 1984); (4) decay over time (e.g., Haugtvedt & Petty, 1992; Heesacker et al., 1988); (5) lack of behavior prediction (e.g., Gilbert et al., 1991; Neimeyer et al., 1989); and (6) less resistance to counterpersuasion (e.g., Haugtvedt, 1988; Haugtvedt & Petty, 1992), relative to central route attitudes. For specific details of much of this foundational research, readers are referred to Petty and Cacioppo's (1986) monograph, which contains an exhaustive, although now somewhat dated, literature review.

Research on the Role of Affect in the ELM

In such a cognitively oriented model of attitude change as the ELM, what, if any, is the place of affect or emotion? There are several ways in which people's emotion can influence attitude change processes according to the ELM (Wegener & Petty, 1996). Two of these can occur in central route processing. The first way is by affecting motivation to process. Topics about which people have strong feelings are likely to result in them being motivated to think about the topics or content of a counselor's remarks. The second way is by influencing the nature of cognitive processing made in response to a counselor's remarks (or any other potentially persuasive communication). Topics about which people have strong feelings are likely to cause biased (versus unbiased) processing. Biased processing occurs when people have a propensity to think more topic favorable thoughts or more topic unfavorable thoughts. Unbiased processing occurs when people are not predisposed to think one type of thought rather than another (Smith, Haugtvedt, & Petty, 1994; Petty, Schumann, Richman, & Strathman, 1993).

One way in which affect influences peripheral route attitude change processes is in people's attitudinal responses to cues. If a positive emotion, such as ecstasy or peacefulness, is associated with a cue, and the cue is associated with the topic, then the same positive emotion is likely to be associated with the topic, and it is likely to increase attitude favorability. Likewise, if a negative emotion, such as hopelessness or anger, is associated with a cue that is associated with the topic, a decrease in attitude favorability is likely to result.

Petty et al. (1993) conducted a study to demonstrate the different ways in which affect can change attitudes. They demonstrated that a person's emotional mood can directly influence attitudes under conditions of low elaboration likelihood. When elaboration likelihood was high, mood influenced attitudes differently than that suggested by Petty, Cacioppo, Sedikides, and Strathman (1988). Instead of mood having a direct affect on attitudes, the authors found that mood indirectly influences attitudes through the generation of positive thoughts.

In summary, affect can influence attitude change processes in three different ways: (1) by increasing motivation to think about the topic/content of a potentially persuasive communication, (2) by influencing the degree of bias with which someone thinks about an attitude topic, and (3) by influencing whether topic-associated cues are perceived favorably or unfavorably (Petty et al., 1988). The next section provides specific counseling examples of components that lead to high or low elaboration likelihood and of components that lead to attitude change under either high or low elaboration likelihood.

Applied Research and the Elaboration Likelihood Model

Research on the ELM and counseling is substantial and growing (see reviews by P. P. Heppner & Claiborn, 1989; P. P. Heppner & Frazier, 1992; Heesacker et al., 1995). A number of empirical investigations conducted in recent years demonstrate the benefits of drawing on ELM theory in counseling, specifically in preventative and psychoeducational interventions (e.g., Gilbert et al., 1991; M. J. Heppner, Neville, Smith, Kivlighan, & Gershuny, 1999; Rosenthal, Heesacker, & Neimeyer, 1995), as well as in structured group counseling for spouse abuse (Heesacker & Gilbert, 1997), and assertiveness (Ernst & Heesacker, 1993). Four studies are described to illustrate the ELM's utility for affecting counseling-relevant attitude and behavior change.

First, in their study of the effects of the ELM on decreasing sexual assault supportive attitudes in males, Gilbert et al. (1991) found that central route processing produced attitude change and that this attitude change endured for at least a month after the intervention. Using the ELM, the authors designed a psychoeducational intervention to encourage college males to reduce their attitudes supportive of sexual aggression. Males were divided into treatment and control groups, with the treatment group receiving the psychoeducational intervention. Because central route attitude change is enduring and resistant to counterpersuasion, the psychoeducational persuasive communication was designed to enhance the crucial central route components of motivation, ability, and favorable cognitive response. To enhance motivation, participants role-played vignettes (rather than passively listening to a message) and interacted with the facilitators. Ability was enhanced by using an audience-appropriate vocabulary, repeating key points, and summarizing the content at the end. Favorable cognitive responses were elicited by focusing on the negative intrapsychic consequences of sexual aggression supportive attitudes and on the societal sanctions associated with such beliefs. These two strategies also facilitated topically relevant thinking.

Results indicated that males who received the ELM-based psychoeducational intervention decreased significantly in their sexual aggression supportive attitudes compared to males in the control group. In an unrelated context, participants received phone calls regarding a women's safety project. Those from the intervention group showed more willingness to listen to the appeal and made more favorable comments. Measures of motivation, ability, and favorable cognitive response, or ELM variables, were also found to be predictive of attitude change. These initially encouraging findings have been replicated and extended (e.g., M. J. Heppner et al., 1999; Rosenthal et al., 1995).

Similarly encouraging results were reported by Ernst and Heesacker (1993), whose data demonstrated that assertiveness training workshops using the ELM increased attitude and behavior change more effectively than typical assertiveness training workshops. People who attend assertiveness training workshops often have difficulty transferring their training to natural situations. Ernst and Heesacker suggested that the failure of participants to behave assertively outside of workshop contexts may result, not from lack of a skill but from a lack of enduring assertion-related attitude and behavior change. They used the ELM as a guide for redesigning an assertiveness training workshop to maximize central route processing variables. College students who had registered for an assertiveness training workshop were assigned to either an ELM-based workshop or a traditional assertiveness workshop. To increase motivation to process, participants in the ELM-based workshop were asked to think of a time when failing to assert themselves hurt them. Ability and memory consolidation were enhanced by asking participants at the end of the workshop to recall assertion favorable thoughts that they had generated during the workshop. Assertion favorable cognitive responses were triggered by presenting participants with four arguments, which were pilot tested on similar participants, to elicit the most favorable cognitions. As predicted, ELM workshop participants showed greater attitude change regarding assertiveness, expressed greater intention to act assertively, evaluated the workshop content more favorably, and reported increased ability to think about the topic of assertiveness than participants in the traditional workshop. Two weeks later, roommates of those who participated in the ELM-based group rated participants as behaving more assertively than roommates of participants in the traditional assertiveness workshop.

Neimeyer et al. (1989) also employed the ELM, this time to facilitate eating-related cognitive restructuring among people with high levels of concern about dieting and eating. An ELM-based central route intervention resulted in significant improvement in both the quality of participants' cognitive restructuring homework (58% versus 40% relevant applications of cognitive restructuring) and the number of days across which participants engaged in cognitive restructuring (2.72 versus 1.56 days), compared to control group participants. This study demonstrates that the ELM can be used to enhance the quality of people's responses to a request to complete a specific therapeutic assignment. The study underscores the importance of the specific content a counselor uses to discuss a counseling assignment with a client in determining how well the client will do on the assignment. When participants in this study heard a persuasive communication that had been pilot tested to elicit favorable cognitive responses, they did their counseling assignments at a significantly higher level of quality than when they heard a less carefully crafted communication about completing the assignment.

Finally, Heesacker and Gilbert (1997) studied a one-year domestic violence counseling group that employed ELM-based principles. The widely used Duluth model curriculum (Pence & Paymer, 1993) was modified to include ELM central route processing components throughout the program. Use of this modified Duluth curriculum resulted in statistically significant reductions in scores on measures of aggression by the 55 convicted spouse batterers who participated and completed valid protocols. Program effectiveness did not differ as a function of race or marital status. The reduction in aggression scores was similar across several different aggression scales, including a scale that was developed specifically to differentiate those who do from those who do not engage in physical acts of aggression. Posttest aggression scores for this group were similar to and, in some cases, slightly lower than, that of norm samples of men not arrested for violence. This result suggests that the ELM can be useful in effecting therapeutic change even among clients traditionally viewed as reluctant to change and difficult to work with.

In summary, applied research suggests that the ELM has been effective at changing attitudes that are supportive of sexual assault, at improving the transfer of assertion training skills to natural settings, at enhancing the quality of participants' cognitive restructuring assignments, and at reducing the aggression levels of convicted spouse batterers, to name but four counseling-relevant examples. In each of these cases, the ELM served as a supplement to an existing technology or approach, one that enhanced the effectiveness of that technology or approach, rather than replacing it.

Practical Applications

This applications section first describes in practical- and counseling-relevant terms each of the components of the ELM. Second, this section presents a four-stage guide to implementing the ELM in counseling. Third, this section evaluates the ELM regarding its usefulness in counseling. Next, for each of the nine components of the ELM (items 1–9 in Figure 10.1), we provide a description, a section on implications for counseling, and a counseling-relevant example. The numbers next to component titles correspond to the components in Figure 10.1.

Central Route Processing

1. Persuasive Communication

Description. Persuasive communication refers to any verbal message, whether vocal or written, formal or informal, the intent of which is to influence someone to change an attitude. An attitude can be defined as a relatively enduring evaluation of a person, situation, or object along the positive–negative continuum (see Petty & Cacioppo, 1981). In this case, persuasive communication refers to the communication of a counselor to a client designed to change the attitude of the client, although, importantly, clients also communicate persuasively to counselors and often, as a result, facilitate a change in the counselor's attitude (Strong, 1986).

Implications for Counseling. The counselor who senses that a client, despite understanding an intervention, seems resistant to it, can use principles from the central route of Petty and Cacioppo's (1981) ELM to develop a counseling intervention or series of interventions akin to a persuasive communication, so as to put forth the strongest opportunity for clients to change their attitudes, thereby reducing resistance. This would involve the components discussed earlier regarding the ELM, such as making sure that clients are motivated to think about the content of the counselor's remarks, and that clients are able to think about the content. Importantly, counselors will need to implement these strategies cautiously, as they should any time they are making inferences about particular clients and their treatment, based on a general model of human behavior.

In general, counseling is an ideal setting for facilitating central route attitude change. Counselors are trained to be astute observers and should be able to detect when clients are motivated and able to think, when they are responding to counselor content with predominantly favorable thoughts, and when they have been able to consolidate those thoughts into memory. The counseling session can be tailored by the counselor to address these various issues in the way and to the degree that will optimally influence the client.

For the most part, we think that deliberately attempting to elicit peripheral route attitude change (by altering such cues as counseling expertness) will not particularly benefit the client or advance the goals of counseling. This is because the resulting attitude change does not last, is relatively easy to counterpersuade, and is not likely to result in behavior change. A related issue is the use of cues to increase motivation to process when involvement is only moderately high. In some cases, for example when motivation to process is neither high nor low, a counselor may wish to alter such cues as counselor expertness to improve motivation to process, and thus the degree to which clients will think about the counselor's remarks. Even when a client already has some positive feelings about a topic but could benefit from an increase in positivity, appearing somewhat less expert on the part of the counselor should result in a client's increased motivation to process because the client will increase scrutiny of a message. However, for a topic on which the client has some negative feelings that the counselor wants to shift in a positive direction, appearing somewhat more expert should result in increased motivation to process. One's level of expertness can be altered by such factors as attire, language, and setting (see Corrigan et al., 1980). Often, the client's prior attitude toward the topic (initially positive or negative) is not known. In these cases, it may be best to make the counselor's expertness–inexpertness nonsalient to avoid inadvertently producing reduced motivation to process. At the end of the previous section this moderate motivation issue was discussed in more detail.

The content of persuasive communication in counseling is not the same as instructional content, although at times a counselor may instruct a client on a particular technique or assignment. Instructional content involves what the counselor says about how to perform the behavior itself (for example, "Each member of the couple is to speak to the other member for five minutes, without interruptions, using 'I' statements and 'feelings' statements"). Persuasive communication content involves what the counselor says about justifying the performance of the behavior (for example, "Doing this particular homework assignment may reduce the likelihood of those open, loud fights that occur in front of the children").

Example.   Colleen is an experienced counselor skilled in basic attending skills, communication skills, and the fundamentals of counseling. When she is clear about her client's concerns, about the psychological processes underlying their concerns, about the preferred course of treatment, and when she senses or observes a resistant attitude opinion by the client regarding a particular therapeutic course of action, she deliberately engages in persuasive communication with the client. The purpose is to enhance the client's chances for successful counseling outcome by facilitating an attitude of openness and acceptance toward the therapeutically appropriate intervention. Often this involves sharing with the client reasons that, from the viewpoint of a client, not necessarily from a counselor's view, would be important in accepting the position of the counselor. These persuasive communications may be simply a sentence or two or may involve interaction throughout a session or over several sessions. For example, it was clear to Colleen that her client Norbert needed to participate in assertion training. But every time he was scheduled to join an assertion training group, he cancelled, each time with a different reason. Finally, Colleen realized that maybe Norbert's attitude about this was not sufficiently favorable to accept this intervention. During the course of two sessions she explained her position to Norbert, emphasizing points that she thought would elicit favorable cognitive responses from him.

2. Motivation to Process

Description.   Regarding motivation to process, the ELM holds that in order to be persuaded by the central route, the person must have had a thoughtful consideration of the topic or persuasive communication. In order to have this thoughtful consideration, the person must be motivated to do so, because such thoughtfulness requires effort. Motivation may be induced in several different ways, such as through personal involvement in the topic or the expectation that one will have to present one's views to others. Motivation may be increased or decreased by the situation, as described, but it also may be chronically higher or lower, depending on the person. So, some people are inherently motivated to think about all kinds of issues. Such people would be more likely, therefore, to engage in central route processing than those with less inherent motivation to think about attitude issues (Cacioppo & Petty, 1982; see Cacioppo, Petty, Feinstein, & Jarvis, 1996, for a review of research on the Need for Cognition scale, which measures trait motivation to cognitively process). Regardless of whether motivation is inherent or induced by the situation, persuasion will not follow the central route and enduring attitude change will not occur if the person is not sufficiently motivated.

Implications for Counseling.   In order for central route attitude change to occur, clients should be motivated to think about the meaning of the counselor's remarks. This is a far more modest criterion than clients being motivated to change, which is the focus of measures such as the Motivation subscale of Tinsley, Workman, and Kass's (1980) Expectations About Counseling Questionnaire (EAC). So initially, clients do not particularly have to express openness to change, but rather, simply openness to thinking about what the counselor is saying. If the client finds the counselor's remarks convincing, and responds with predominantly favorable thoughts, then at that point the client should be motivated to change. In short, one implication of the ELM is that the commitment to change would come as a consequence of counseling and being influenced by the counselor, rather than as a prerequisite for it, although this implication has not yet been tested empirically.

Interestingly, evidence by Harris and Heesacker (1989) suggests that some clients may actually be threatened by thinking about topics relevant to their problems because the clients are overinvolved. They found that clients possessing a very high degree of social anxiety thought less about a message about group counseling for dealing with these concerns than their less socially anxious peers. These data suggest that client overinvolvement may be as detrimental to motivation to process the counselor's remarks as underinvolvement. In such a case, it may be useful for counselors to attempt to reduce client involvement somewhat, in order to increase client motivation to think about counselor content.

Examples.   John exemplifies overinvolvement causing low motivation to process. He sought counseling because he was lonely. He wanted to get tips and helpful hints about how to get dates and be popular with his peers. He hoped the counselor would have a film to watch or some handouts. When she wanted to talk with him about his thoughts and feelings, however, John found himself really wanting to avoid the whole topic. He often found himself thinking about his loneliness and suffered so much as a result that he wanted to avoid discussing that topic with his counselor.

The counselor recognized that John was too consumed by his problems to think rationally about them and, therefore, could not be motivated to cognitively process her remarks about the topic. She decided instead to try different methods, such as progressive relaxation and systematic desensitization, to decrease John's anxiety and increase his ability to process.

Alternatively, Mark exemplified low motivation because of underinvolvement. He had similar concerns about dating and making friends, but when the counselor wanted to talk with him about his thoughts and feelings, he had the opposite of John's reaction. He had talked with his parents so much about the topic that he was bored with it. He felt numb to his problem and simply wanted things to be different.

In this case, the counselor wanted to increase Mark's ability to think about his problems. She felt that the best way to accomplish this was to get Mark to contemplate his loneliness by approaching it in a different, more relevant way. The counselor decided to provide a link between Mark's thoughtful consideration of his problems and an important outcome for him, being able to make friends.

Finally, Bill exemplifies optimal involvement and high motivation to process. He is concerned about his dating and friendship relationships but is not avoidant of the topic and certainly is not bored with it. He thinks very carefully about what the counselor says.

3. Ability to Process

Description.   Ability to process refers to the ELM contention that for central route attitude change to occur, the person must not only be motivated to consider thoughtfully the topic or message but must also have the cognitive capability to do so. Several factors can alter a person's ability to think about the topic and message, such as individual experiences, intelligence, distraction, and message comprehensibility. If the person does not have sufficient ability to think about the topic, attitude change will not follow the central route. For example, being distracted from thinking about a message they were hearing kept experimental participants in a study by Petty, Wells, and Brock (1976) from centrally processing the message they were hearing. In Petty et al.'s (1976) study, participants had to both listen to the message and look at a monitor and record when an "X" flashed in one of the corners of the screen. Those exposed to this distraction showed clear signs of reduced central route attitude change, relative to their undistracted counterparts.

Implications for Counseling.   Clients must be able to think about the counselor's remarks for central route attitude change to occur. There are two important components of this. The first is that the counselor's remarks have to be understandable to the client. For example, less verbal or psychologically minded clients may have difficulty understanding the psychological jargon that counselors frequently use. If clients do not understand it, they cannot think about it. The second component is that they have to have the ability to think about the content they have heard. The room must be free of distracting stimuli. The pace of the session must not be so hectic after a counselor's influence attempt is made that the client does not have time to think about it. The counselor can assess, and perhaps foster, the client's ability by saying such things as, "What did you think of what I just said?"

Example.   Robin was trying to think about what her counselor, Gerry, was saying to her. Robin came in concerned about her preoccupation with issues related to eating. It had "really gotten out of control," but she resisted Gerry's idea that she needed to see a physician and a dietician to assess possible health effects of her eating habits and to explore ways of improving her diet. It was a very busy time for Gerry's counseling agency, as well as for Gerry, herself. Because the agency was so busy, Gerry could see each client for only 30 minutes. So Gerry talked quickly to make the most of their time together and didn't take time to simplify or explain the terms she used. She simply did not have time to slow down for that. Because the agency was short staffed, Gerry had to answer her own phone so counseling was often interrupted two or three times per session with brief phone calls. The speed of Gerry's speech, with no quiet time for Robin to think, plus the use of terms that she did not understand, and the phone calls made it very hard for Robin to really collect her own thoughts about what Gerry was saying. If factors of time, jargon, and interruptions could have been changed, Gerry's impact on Robin's attitude toward visiting the physician and dietician would have been much greater.

4. Nature of Cognitive Processing

Description. The nature of cognitive processing refers to the ELM idea that people motivated and able to think about the topic or content of a persuasive communication will respond with thoughts of various kinds. The nature of the thoughts that predominate determines if attitude change occurs and in what direction. Relevant thoughts that are either favorable or unfavorable toward the topic must predominate for the occurrence of central route attitude change. Central route attitude change cannot occur if neutral or irrelevant thoughts predominate.

There are no general rules about what kinds of content will elicit favorable, unfavorable, and neutral or irrelevant thoughts. Some studies, however, have identified noncontent factors that influence how positive topic-related thoughts are. For example, Wells and Petty (1980) conducted a study to find the effects of positive actions, such as vertical head nodding, as opposed to movements that conjure up negative associations, such as horizontal head shaking, on proattitudinal and counterattitudinal messages. They found that vertical head nodding (a gesture typically denoting agreement) elicited more favorable thoughts and attitudes than horizontal head movements (a gesture typically denoting disagreement). To identify content that is persuasive, ELM scholars typically employ the method of pilot testing various persuasive arguments to find ones that elicit the most favorable thoughts from a sample of people similar to those who are the target of a persuasive communication.

Implications for Counseling. Clients will differ in what they find convincing. The thoughts one client generates to form the basis for central route attitudes can range from cold, dispassionate ones to very emotionally intense ones, so the model clearly allows for emotions in the attitude change process. Most importantly, the remarks of the counselor must elicit predominantly favorable thoughts from the client. In order to do this, the counselor's remarks should fit the cognitive structures of the client. If these structures can be tapped by the counselor's remarks, the counselor will have a much better chance of eliciting favorable thoughts from the clients regarding the desired behavior change.

In a study by Cacioppo, Petty, and Sidera (1982) participants were pretested so that their attitudes on certain issues could be obtained and also so that they could be classified as having either a "religious" or "legalistic" self-schema. Then these participants were exposed to proattitudinal messages from either a religious or a legalistic perspective. The authors found that when the schema and the message matched, message processing was facilitated.

Experimental research has shown that people can have attitude change in the opposite direction to that desired (a condition known as "boomerang" attitude change) when the arguments they hear elicit predominantly unfavorable thoughts. How can the counselor decide what will be convincing to the client? In the extensive laboratory research about the ELM, both using counseling topics and other topics, researchers have been able to change people's attitudes when the main points of the message were designed or pilot tested to strike a responsive chord in people similar to those who participated in the studies. For example, in Ernst and Heesacker's (1993) article on assertion training workshops and the ELM, students who participated in these workshops were placed in either typical assertion training workshops, or workshops that used the central route process to encourage assertive attitude change. Before the study began, a different group of students were pilot tested to find out which of 19 arguments would persuade them of the importance of being assertive. Then the top four arguments from the pilot tests were used as persuasive arguments for the central route processing group. The authors found that participants in the central route processing group responded more favorably and behaved more assertively than participants in the typical workshop group.

Example.   Tom and Mary Ellen have come in for marital counseling, and the counselor, Florence, has decided to have them engage in a communication exercise, which they are resisting. If Florence can relate persuasive remarks about this communication task to thoughts that she has learned are important to this couple, Tom and Mary Ellen's chances of changing their attitudes to accept the counselor's viewpoint about the utility of the communication exercise will be increased. The couple has come in with a concern very important to them: they dislike the fact that they argue openly and loudly in front of their children, because it distresses the children and makes the couple feel ashamed. If Florence could link performing this particular communication task with reducing the likelihood of these open, loud fights, Tom and Mary Ellen are more likely to respond with topic favorable thinking, which will increase the chance that they will engage in the assignment.

5. Cognitive Structure Change

Description.   Cognitive structure change refers to the ELM contention that central route attitude change cannot occur without the person consolidating into memory the new cognitions generated as a consequence of the topic or persuasive communication. For a person who has consolidated predominantly favorable thoughts into memory, enduring attitude change in the desired direction will result. If the persuasive communication triggers unintended, predominantly topic-negative thoughts that are consolidated into memory, the result could be central route persuasion in the reverse direction (or boomerang change). Harris, Heesacker, Chapin, and Gilbert (1989) demonstrated improvement in central route attitude change as a result of experimentally manipulating consolidation. When people who were already processing the persuasive message centrally were asked to rehearse or consolidate their own thoughts about the message, there was stronger evidence of central route attitudes than when they had a similar amount of time to think, but were not asked to rehearse. It is important to emphasize that these people were not memorizing what the counselor said, but rather their own thoughts about what was said. Central route attitude change will be reduced with cognitive structure change interference. Thoughtful consideration of the attitude topic often results in cognitive structure change "automatically," that is, without intentional effort to consolidate attitude-relevant thoughts into memory.

Implications for Counseling.   Based on Harris et al. (1989), counselors can improve consolidation by saying things to their clients such as, "Before we leave please take a minute to review in your own mind the important thoughts you had during today's session." Indeed, some persuasive improvement may occur if clients are instructed to focus on the topic favorable thoughts they had, but not on the topic unfavorable ones. This is based on the idea that the recalled thoughts (in this case the one's supporting the counselor's view) will be remembered longer and so are more likely to change the client's attitude and behavior than the unrecalled ones (in this case the thoughts that do not support the counselor's view).

Example.   Leland, the counselor, had been working with Tony whose presenting concern focused on selecting a career. Tony had initially been resistant to computerized career guidance, even though the system available was quite "user friendly" and the other available career resources were very limited. After Leland's remarks to Tony, which were designed to elicit favorable thoughts about computerized guidance, and after it was clear to Leland that Tony had responded with favorable thoughts to his point, Leland asked Tony to take a minute to think about the various thoughts he had about Leland's remarks about computerized guidance, so that he could clearly remember his own reactions to Leland's points. Tony went over these points one by one, in effect rehearsing mentally and making more memorable his thoughts that support his use of computerized guidance.

Results of Central Route Processing

6. Enduring Central Positive or Negative Attitude Change

Description.   When the person has been motivated to think about the counselor's attitude-relevant comments, has been able to think about them, and has elicited predominantly favorable thoughts that were consolidated into memory, then an enduring positive attitude, one consistent with the counselor's position, should result. Such attitudes should also be resistant to attitude change attempts in the opposite direction and should influence behavior. The same is true of negative central route attitude change (or boomerang), except that this occurs when the counselor's comments or thoughts about the topic result in predominantly negative thoughts.

Implications for Counseling.   One very important point suggested by the ELM in illuminating social influence processes in counseling is the notion that attitude change attempts can be for better or for worse. In the case of central route processes where predominantly unfavorable thoughts are elicited and incorporated into memory, what can result is boomerang change. In the case of central route boomerang, this change is difficult to reverse, is likely to persist, and is likely to lead to boomerang-related behaviors, precisely what the counselor wishes to avoid. This notion is potentially one of the most important ones for counselors to take from a discussion of the ELM. Certainly, the ethical maxim of nonmalfeasance ("Do no harm") is appropriate here. It is important for counselors to consider boomerang as one of the possible outcomes of an attitude change attempt. Central route boomerang is most likely when the counselor is not aware of the kind of persuasive arguments that are and are not likely to elicit topic unfavorable thoughts in the client.

Examples.   Ed's counselor, Amy, advocated that Ed join a counseling group as an adjunct to his individual counseling. Ed was not sure about group counseling and asked Amy why she wanted him to participate. She provided Ed with reasons from her viewpoint, such as her belief that Ed needed to be challenged by peers and that he needed honest feedback from others who could relate to him as a peer, rather than as a client. When Ed thought about Amy's reasons for him to join group counseling, he responded negatively, because her reasons did not address the issues that were important to him. Instead, her points implied to him that she was critical of what he said and of the roles he played with others. In reaction, Ed generated thoughts that counterargued Amy's and that supported him not joining the group. The outcome was that Ed's attitude about joining the group, once neutral, is now firmly negative and thought based, so his attitude is likely to endure, to resist additional persuasion, and to be reflected in his behavior. Predictably, he elected not to participate in the group.

An example of enduring positive attitude change for Ed would be quite different. In this case Amy works diligently to ensure that Ed is motivated and able to think about the persuasive communication that she is making, that she is able to elicit predominantly favorable responses in Ed (by employing arguments reflecting rather than antagonizing his perceived needs and his patterns of thinking), and that there were opportunities for topic favorable thoughts of Ed's to be consolidated into memory. Following this different approach of Amy's, the result of the conversation between Amy and Ed is quite different from before: an enduring attitude change toward joining the counseling group. This attitude change will be resistant to counterpersuasion (for example Ed's friends saying that participating in the group will take up too much time) and will be likely to result in therapeutically relevant behavior change, in this case, in Ed joining the group and being receptive to his experiences there.

Peripheral Route Processing

7. Peripheral Cue Present?

Description.   If cognitive responding to the topic or message is hindered in any of the ways noted, central route attitude change will not occur. Instead, what may occur is peripheral route attitude change, which is based on cues. A persuasion cue is any stimulus in the persuasion situation that is associated with the attitude topic and that elicits a favorable or unfavorable reaction in the person. For example, a female fashion model posed next to a new car in an advertisement may act as a positive cue to some people, who perhaps associate her with a glamorous lifestyle, or as a negative cue to others, who perhaps associate her with the degradation of women.

Implications for Counseling.   The problem of boomerang can also occur for peripheral route attitude processes, although because peripheral route attitudes are more elastic, less enduring, and less influential on behavior, the long-term implications are much less dramatic than for central route persuasion. If a client is using cues to influence attitudes and those provided by or associated with the counselor are negative, relative to the position advocated by the counselor, boomerang attitude change will result.

Example.   If Ed is not motivated to think about the topic, but instead relies on a cue on which to base his attitude and sees that the position is advocated by the counselor, Amy, whom he is angry with at this point in counseling, then Ed will have a negative attitude toward the group. Importantly, this negative attitude should not be as difficult to change as its central route boomerang counterpart. If the salient cue is changed, Ed's attitude could also change. Alternatively, if a change in motivation, ability, positivity of thoughts, or memory consolidation results in central route processing, then topic- and message-relevant thoughts could also change Ed's attitude to a favorable one, if the resulting thoughts are topic favorable.

Results of Peripheral Route Processing

8. Peripheral Attitude Shift

Description. The attitude change that is achieved is not likely to last a long time. When the cue is no longer associated with the attitude topic, the client's attitude should return to the original position. In laboratory research, this decay of attitude change occurred in two days (Haugtvedt & Petty, 1992).

Implications for Counseling. The implication for counseling is that temporary attitude shift is not a particularly useful strategy for counselors to employ. Although increasing client-perceived expertness, attractiveness, and trustworthiness of the counselor can result in attitude change, this change is not likely to endure and not likely to result in therapeutically relevant attitude change.

Example. A counselor decides to wear a business suit to see clients because such clothing will indicate to clients that the counselor is a professional. On counseling issues about which the client does not feel particularly interested, the client accepts the position advocated by the counselor, because the client perceives the counselor as an expert. On issues more personally relevant to the client, the client is unlikely to employ the counselor's expertise as an important factor in determining the client's attitude, relying instead on a more thoughtfully derived attitude.

9. Retain or Regain Initial Attitude

Description. When neither thoughtful (central route) or economical (peripheral route) attitude processes have been invoked, the client's attitude is not likely to change. It is likely to be exactly what it was before. This lack of change can occur for several reasons, according to the ELM: insufficient motivation to think about the counselor's communication, insufficient ability to think about the communication, predominantly neutral thoughts about the attitude topic, thoughts about the topic that are balanced with respect to positivity–negativity, insufficient consolidation of attitude-relevant thoughts into memory, an absence of topic linked cues, or a balance of positive and negative cues.

Implications for Counseling. There may be several reasons why a client's attitudes do not change following an influence attempt by the counselor. In these cases, detection of what part or parts of the process were not occurring is important to achieving greater success in future attempts. Once the counselor has made an assessment of where breakdowns in the process occurred in the prior attitude change attempt, future attempts can be tailored to address those breakdowns. The focus should be on central, not peripheral, route attitude change, because peripheral route attitude change is not as long lasting and is not as likely to influence behavior.

It is important to note that some attitudes cannot be changed. For many people, some opinions are so centrally important and so well thought through that no amount of outside influence will alter that attitude. If these highly resistant attitudes hinder therapy, there may be little for a counselor to do but recognize this, share this observation with the client, if appropriate, and alter or end treatment. By employing the ELM, counselors are much better able to discriminate an intractable attitude from attitudes that are open to change, but have not yet been effectively influenced.

Example.   A counselor, Florence, has become convinced that her client, Peggy, is in a physically and psychologically abusive relationship with her husband, Matt. The condition appears to be chronic and unchanging. No children are involved, and Peggy is financially independent. Florence has attempted to urge Peggy to move in with friends or seek shelter in a battered women's center, especially in times of crisis and violence. Despite the counselor's attitude change attempts, Peggy is not convinced that this is a good plan and does not leave the home, even when she has been physically assaulted. Florence's next step is to assess Peggy's motivation to think about the counselor's message, Peggy's ability to do so, especially given the turbulent nature of her life, whether Florence is eliciting predominantly favorable thoughts from Peggy about the content of her interventions, and whether Peggy's thoughts are being consolidated into memory. Through informal verbal assessment, or perhaps through brief written assessment based on laboratory manipulation check items and dependent measures, Florence could assess which aspects need additional attention.

In summary, the components required for and the consequences of both central route and peripheral route attitude change have been described. Implications for counseling and counseling examples have also been detailed for each component. What follows is the description of a step-by-step guide for using the ELM in counseling practice.

A Four-Stage Guide to Implementing the ELM in Counseling Practice

Heesacker and Mejia-Millan (1996) described a general approach to applying the ELM to counseling with 11 practical steps. Heesacker and Harris (1993) reported that a group of practicing psychotherapists taking a continuing education seminar gave a similar ELM-based approach to counseling high marks for understandability and usefulness for practice. Next, we describe Heesacker and Mejia-Millan's 11-step approach in a modified format. We have grouped their 11 steps into 4 stages. The first stage contains the steps designed to understand the attitudes and attitude position in question. The second stage delineates the process for influencing attitudes. The third stage entails delivering a persuasive communication and evaluating the immediate results. The final stage involves assessing the success of the change and whether the process needs revisiting.

Stage 1: Assess Attitudes and Attitude Elaboration Route

The first step involves assessing a client's attitudes, which can be done through the use of formal assessment instruments, such as an alcohol scale, or informal techniques consisting of clinical interviews or observations of behavior. We prefer the use of formal assessment procedures, because informal procedures are more susceptible to demand characteristics or reactivity on the part of the client and interpretation biases coupled with inaccurate measurement on the part of the counselor.

Next, attitudes being assessed are evaluated as soliciting central or peripheral routes. This is an important step because of the differences in attitudinal endurance between central and peripheral routes. Central route attitudes require more motivation and ability and are harder to change; however, once attitude change is achieved, the attitude is more resistant to counterpersuasion and results in greater attitude–behavior consistency than the peripheral route. Peripheral routes require less motivation and ability to think about the topic but are also less predictive of behavior and less resistant to counterpersuasion.

Assessing attitude elaboration can again be done formally or informally. Formal assessment includes Cacioppo and Petty's (1982) thought-listing technique, which instructs people to list their thoughts and ideas while listening to persuasive communications, then rating the list generated as reflecting either positively, negatively, or neutrally on the attitude topic. Moderate to high correlations between thoughts and attitudes suggest central route attitudes, whereas low correlations suggest peripheral route attitudes. Informal assessment of attitude routes includes direct inquiry or indirect observation of the degree to which the attitude is thought based. This process can be tricky because of the potential of encouraging greater adherence to the attitudes currently held, which the counselor is often interested in changing.

Stage 2: Determine the Desired Attitude Position, Desired Attitude Route, and Route Component Needs

Before an attitude can be changed, the counselor must decide what an appropriate new attitude might be, based on a synthesis of clinical training and situation-specific information. The counselor may find it helpful to determine whether the new attitude is specific or general, given that general attitudes tend to predict general behaviors and specific attitudes predict specific behaviors (Fishbein & Ajzen, 1974). It may be counterproductive to spend time encouraging the adoption of a general attitude concerning healthy lifestyles, when a counselor and client are working on a specific behavior of eating only at mealtimes.

In addition to determining the desired attitude, the counselor must also determine which route will be used to achieve the change. As mentioned earlier, central route attitudes last longer, have greater influence on behavior, but are harder to change, whereas peripheral route attitudes are easier to change but do not endure or hold much influence on behavior. Much of this decision will be governed by whether the existing or old attitude is a central or peripheral route attitude and whether the new attitude needs to endure or influence behavior. If the existing attitude is a central route attitude, then central route change is required. In all likelihood, counselors will be interested in central route attitudes because of counseling's emphasis on enduring behavior change.

Central route change requires motivation, ability, cognitive response, and memory consolidation (see central route change versus peripheral route change discussed earlier in this chapter). At this point, a counselor needs to assess to what extent these various components are present if central route attitudes are the focus. As in Stage 1, these components can be assessed using formal or informal procedures.

Motivation can be assessed using both trait and state perspectives. For example, the Need for Cognition Scale (NCS; Cacioppo & Petty, 1982) measures people's trait motivation to engage in effortful thought, with high need for cognition signaling high motivation. State motivation is frequently measured using a rating scale, which measures a topic's importance or personal meaningfulness to a client (see Petty & Cacioppo, 1986, chapter 2).

Ability can also be assessed using both trait and state perspectives. Trait perspectives assess a client's intellectual ability (through the use of cognitive ability tests) to understand and reflect on the content of a persuasive communication. State perspectives use rating scales to determine a person's ability to be free from distraction and to feel capable of careful thought.

Cognitive response may be assessed with the thought-listing technique previously described. In addition to focusing on the valence of a client's thoughts (positive, negative, or neutral), a counselor should also attend to a client's style so as to make use of this style in the development of persuasive communications. For example, attending to a client's response style might reveal cultural and religious orientations, a preference for deductive versus inductive reasoning, and so on. Using a person's cognitive response style as a framework for persuasive communication has been shown to be more effective than other approaches (Cacioppo et al., 1982).

Memory consolidation may be evaluated using immediate and delayed free-recall techniques, with greater accuracy of one's recall of one's topic relevant thoughts being suggestive of greater consolidation. Through interviews and observation, a counselor can also informally assess route components. Informal assessment techniques are usually preferred by counselors because of their flexibility; however, informal techniques are more susceptible to reliability problems and counselor biases.

Peripheral route change requires cue valence and cue association. Cue valence refers to whether the cue is positive or negative, such as whether the attitude object is associated with a likeable versus an unlikable counselor. Cue association refers to the link between the cue and the attitude object. We have uncovered no formal measures of cue valence and cue association. These route components can, however, be evaluated informally by interviewing and observation.

Stage 3: Prepare and Give Persuasive Communication and Then Reassess Attitudes

Persuasive communication may occur during a single setting, such as in a speech, or over time, for example, through ongoing individual or group psychotherapy. We recommend that counselors prepare what they plan to say and present a review of the previous steps. Once the communication has been delivered, the counselor needs to reevaluate a client's attitudes, using procedures outlined in Stage 1, taking care not to evoke socially desirable responses from the client. This may mean not proceeding with an immediate evaluation.

Stage 4: Assess Success of Change and Modify the Intervention as Needed

If attitude change does not correspond to the target attitudes, the counselor must assess where in the process there were difficulties. This determination can be made by revisiting Stages 1 through 3 and ascertaining whether the appropriate assessments tools were used, whether the appropriate route was chosen, whether the communication was persuasive, and to what extent reactivity, consistency motivation, or socially desirable responding are occurring. If necessary, a counselor can repeat the process with a revised persuasive communication based on an analysis of the process.

Evaluation of the ELM for Use in Counseling

A four-stage model for applying the ELM to counseling has been detailed. What follows is an evaluation of the ELM with regard to its usefulness in counseling contexts. The ELM has many strengths. First, its metatheoretical framework is based on cognitive science and includes propositions regarding processes that mediate successful outcomes, in this case counseling outcomes. Second, the ELM is based on a large body of basic research that has confirmed the model's validity. Third, a growing number of studies have demonstrated that the ELM has potential for improving counseling. Finally, the ELM continues to enliven a very strong and active area of traditional counseling research, the social influence area.

Despite these strengths, scholars have also identified areas of concern. For example, Strong (1995) has argued that the ELM was not explicitly designed for counseling, so researchers working at the ELM-counseling interface have had to develop specific ways to implement the ELM in counseling that have gone mostly undescribed. For example, Strong might suggest that the ELM does not provide clarity regarding exactly what kind of interventions elicit favorable cognitive responding in a particular client. For the ELM to be useful in counseling, Strong would contend, these kinds of details need to be made more clear. We hope that our descriptions of two approaches to using the ELM in counseling, as a general model for intervention and via the use of specific ELM components, addresses some aspects of this concern and reduces confusion for counselors who are interested in using the ELM.

Strong (1995) has also shown concern because in his view the ELM's reflects a dysfunctional trend in mainstream social psychology, generally, away from interpersonal and social processes and toward intrapsychic and cognitive processes. This cognitive focus, Strong argues, reduces the utility of social psychological theories, including the ELM, for counseling practice. Our perspective is that the intrapsychic and interpersonal foci are both necessary for optimal counseling effectiveness. The ELM's focus on client thought processes that are related to attitude and behavior change provides a blueprint that can guide, and indeed has guided, effective counseling interventions, though certainly other perspectives can enhance social influence processes in counseling as well.

Frazier, Gonzales, and Rudman (1995) have pointed out that although several studies have shown the ELM's effectiveness in counseling and psychoeducational settings, there have been no published reports of research on the ELM's effectiveness in traditional one-to-one counseling. We applaud their call for additional research and hope that it serves as an incentive for researchers and practitioners of individual counseling to cooperate in what we agree is a worthy endeavor.

Frazier et al. (1995) have also expressed concern regarding whether an ELM approach might fail to interest practitioners who do not conceptualize counseling interventions as persuasive communications. This is a very useful hypothesis to evaluate empirically, because if research supports their concern, care will need to be taken to discuss the ELM with practitioners in ways that are consistent with their conceptualizations of counseling interventions.

A final concern raised by Frazier and her colleagues (1995) is that ELM researchers may be overlooking a rich resource for effective attitude and behavior change interventions by not paying greater attention to the influence strategies that practitioners already use and find effective. This is another excellent point that we hope will motivate researchers to do additional social influence research. Combining a "top-down" (or theory-driven) approach, such as the ELM, with a "bottom-up" (or experience-driven) approach, such as that suggested by Frazier et al. may provide a most effective overall package for enhancing counseling-relevant attitude and behavior change.

Summary

Petty and Cacioppo's (1986) elaboration likelihood model of attitude change and its implications for counseling have been described, along with counseling-relevant examples, and a four-stage approach to using the ELM with counseling clients. The ELM is an empirically validated theoretical perspective on social influence processes in counseling that can improve a counselor's understanding of counseling as a social influence process and can enhance counseling effectiveness. Its principle contribution to improved understanding of social influence processes in counseling is the distinction between two types of attitude change: central route change, which is thought based, enduring, and influential on behavior; and peripheral route change, which is cue based, transitory, and less influential on behavior.

In basic research on attitude change, the ELM has proven to be an important theoretical approach for integrating and understanding a wide array of studies and phenomena. Likewise, the ELM is proving useful in facilitating the integration and understanding of research in social influence processes in counseling. Equally important is the contribution that the ELM can make to counseling practice. We believe that the ELM can provide counselors with a powerful, clear, and useful framework from which to understand the influence process between clients and counselors, as well as with guidelines for effectively influencing clients to engage in the therapeutic behaviors that are necessary for therapeutic change. This chapter is part of an active and ongoing collaboration with counselors and counseling researchers regarding the most effective ways social influence theory and research can be implemented to improve counseling outcome.

References

Cacioppo, J. T., Claiborn, C. D., Petty, R. E., & Heesacker, M. (1991). A general framework for the study of attitude change in psychotherapy. In C. R. Snyder & D. R. Forsyth (Eds.), *Handbook of social and clinical psychology: A health perspective* (pp. 523–539). Hillsdale, NJ: Erlbaum.

Cacioppo, J. T., & Petty, R. E. (1979). Effects of message repetition and position on cognitive response, recall, and persuasion. *Journal of Personality and Social Psychology, 37,* 97–109.

Cacioppo, J. T., & Petty, R. E. (1982). The need for cognition. *Journal of Personality and Social Psychology, 42,* 116–131.

Cacioppo, J. T., Petty, R. E., Feinstein, J., & Jarvis, B. (1996). Individual differences in cognitive motivation: The life and times of people varying in need for cognition. *Psychological Bulletin, 119,* 197–253.

Cacioppo, J. T., Petty, R. E., & Sidera, J. A. (1982). The effects of a salient self-schema on the evaluation of proattitudinal editorials: Top-down versus bottom-up message processing. *Journal of Experimental Social Psychology, 18,* 324–337.

Cacioppo, J. T., & Petty, R. E., & Stoltenberg, C. D. (1985). Processes of social influence: The elaboration likelihood model of persuasion. *Advances in Cognitive-Behavioral Research and Therapy, 4,* 215–274.

Claiborn, C. D. (1986). Social influence: Toward a general theory of change. In F. J. Dorn (Ed.), *The social influence process in counseling and psychotherapy* (pp. 31–41). Springfield, IL: Charles C Thomas.

Corrigan, J. D., Dell, D. M., Lewis, K. N., & Schmidt, L. D. (1980). Counseling as a social influence process: A review. *Journal of Counseling Psychology, 27,* 395–441.

Eagly, A. H., & Chaiken, S. (1993). *The psychology of attitudes.* Fort Worth, TX: Harcourt.

Ernst, J. M., & Heesacker, M. (1993). Application of the elaboration likelihood model of attitude change to assertion training. *Journal of Counseling Psychology, 40,* 37–45.

Fishbein, M., & Ajzen, I. (1975). *Belief, attitude, intention, and behavior: An introduction to theory and research.* Reading, MA: Addison-Wesley.

Frazier, P., Gonzales, M. H., & Rudman, L. A. (1995). Evaluating the effectiveness of applying social psychological theory to counseling. *Counseling Psychologist, 23,* 691–696.

Gilbert, B. J., Heesacker, M., & Gannon, L. J. (1991). Changing the sexual aggression-supportive attitudes of men: A psychoeducational intervention. *Journal of Counseling Psychology, 38,* 197–203.

Harris, J. E., & Heesacker, M. (1989, May). *Does the need for counseling hinder counseling-relevant attitude change processes?* Paper presented at the meeting of the Midwestern Psychological Association, Chicago, IL.

Harris, J. E., Heesacker, M., Chapin, J. L., & Gilbert, B. J. (1989, May). *Cognitive consolidation and need for cognition influence cognition-attitude consistency.* Paper presented at the meeting of the Midwestern Psychological Association, Chicago, IL.

Haugtvedt, C. P. (1988). Persistence and resistance of communication-induced attitude changes. In D. W. Schumann (Ed.), *Proceedings of the Society for Consumer Psychology* (pp. 111–114). Madison, WI: Omnipress.

Haugtvedt, C. P., & Petty, R. E. (1992). Personality and persuasion: Need for cognition moderates the persistence and resistance of attitude changes. *Journal of Personality and Social Psychology, 63,* 308–319.

Heesacker, M. (1986a). Counseling pretreatment and the elaboration likelihood model of attitude change to counseling. In F. J. Dorn (Ed.), *The social influence process in counseling and psychotherapy* (pp. 43–53). Springfield, IL: Charles C. Thomas.

Heesacker, M. (1986b). Counseling pretreatment and the elaboration likelihood model of attitude change. *Journal of Counseling Psychology, 33,* 107–114.

Heesacker, M., Conner, K., & Prichard, S. T. (1995). Individual counseling and psychotherapy: Applications from the social psychology of attitude change. *The Counseling Psychologist, 23,* 611–632.

Heesacker, M., & Gilbert, B. G. (1997, October). *Batterer intervention: Does it work?* Paper presented at the fifth annual conference "Ending Family Violence: A Community Challenge," Santa Clara County Domestic Violence Council, Santa Jose, CA.

Heesacker, M., & Harris, J. E. (1993). Cognitive processes in counseling: A decision tree integrating two theoretical approaches. *The Counseling Psychologist, 20,* 687–711.

Heesacker, M., & Mejia-Millan, C. (1996). A research program on attitude change processes and their applications to counseling. In W. Dryden (Ed.), *Research in counselling and psychotherapy: Practical applications* (pp. 49–78). London, England: Sage.

Heesacker, M., Petty, R. E., & Cacioppo, J. T. (1984). Field dependence and attitude change: Source credibility can alter persuasion by affecting message-relevant thinking. *Journal of Personality, 51,* 653–666.

Heesacker, M., Petty, R. E., Cacioppo, J. T., Haugtvedt, C. P. (1988, May). *Persistence of persuasion and boomerang effects.* Paper presented at the annual meeting of the Midwestern Psychological Association, Chicago.

Heider, F. (1958). *The psychology of interpersonal relations.* New York: Wiley.

Heppner, M. J., Neville, H. A., Smith, K., Kivlighan, D. M., & Gershuny, B. S. (1999). Examining immediate and long-term efficacy of rape prevention programming with racially diverse college men. *Journal of Counseling Psychology, 46,* 16–26.

Heppner, P. P., & Claiborn, C. D. (1989). Social influence research in counseling: A review and critique. *Journal of Counseling Psychology, 36,* 365–387.

Heppner, P. P., & Frazier, P. A. (1992). Social psychological processes in psychotherapy: Extrapolating basic research to counseling psychology. In S. D. Brown & R. W. Lent (Eds.), *Handbook of counseling psychology* (2nd ed., pp. 141–175). New York: Wiley.

Janis, I. L. (1968). Attitude change via role playing. In R. Abelson, E. Aronson, W. McGuire, T. Newcomb, M. Rosenberg, & P. Tannenbaum (Eds.), *Theories of cognitive consistency: A sourcebook.* Chicago: Rand McNally.

McNeill, B. W., & Stoltenberg, C. D. (1989). Social influence in counseling: A reconceptualization of the data. *Journal of Counseling Psychology, 36,* 24–33.

Milgram, S. (1974). *Obedience to authority.* New York: Harper & Row.

Neimeyer, G. J., Guy, J., & Metzler, A. (1989). Changing attitudes regarding the treatment of disordered eating: An application of the elaboration likelihood model. *Journal of Social and Clinical Psychology, 8,* 70–86.

Pence, E., & Paymar, M. (1993). *Education groups for men who batter: The Duluth model.* New York: Springer.

Petty, R. E., & Cacioppo, J. T. (1979). Issue involvement can increase or decrease persuasion by enhancing message-relevant cognitive responses. *Journal of Personality and Social Psychology, 37,* 1915–1926.

Petty, R. E., & Cacioppo, J. T. (1981). *Attitudes and persuasion: Classic and contemporary approaches.* Dubuque, IA: William C Brown.

Petty, R. E., & Cacioppo, J. T. (1984). The effects of involvement on responses to argument quantity and quality: Central and peripheral routes to persuasion. *Journal of Personality and Social Psychology, 46,* 69–81.

Petty, R. E., & Cacioppo, J. T. (1986). *Communication and persuasion: Central and peripheral routes to attitude change.* New York: Springer.

Petty, R. E., Cacioppo, J. T., & Goldman, R. (1981). Personal involvement as a determinant of argument-based persuasion. *Journal of Personality and Social Psychology, 41,* 847–855.

Petty, R. E., Cacioppo, J. T., & Heesacker, M. (1981). The use of rhetorical questions in persuasion: A cognitive response analysis. *Journal of Personality and Social Psychology, 40,* 432–440.

Petty, R. E., Cacioppo, J. T., & Heesacker, M. (1984). Central and peripheral routes to persuasion: Application to counseling. In R. P. McGlynn, J. E. Maddux, C. D. Stoltenberg, & J. H. Harvey (Eds.), *Social perceptions in clinical and counseling psychology* (pp. 59–89). Lubbock, TX: Texas Tech Press.

Petty, R. E., Cacioppo, J. T., Sedikides, C., & Strathman, A. (1988). Affect and persuasion: A contemporary perspective. *American Behavioral Scientist, 31,* 355–371.

Petty, R. E., Cacioppo, J. T., & Schumann, D. (1983). Central and peripheral routes to advertising effectiveness: The moderating role of involvement. *Journal of Consumer Research, 10,* 135–146.

Petty, R. E., Ostrom, T. M., & Brock, T. C. (1981). Historical foundations of the cognitive response approach to attitudes and persuasion. In R. E. Petty, T. M. Ostrom, & T. C. Brock (Eds.), *Cognitive responses in persuasion.* Hillsdale, NJ: Erlbaum.

Petty, R. E., Schumann, D. W., Richman, S. A., & Strathman, A. J. (1993). Positive mood and persuasion: Different roles for affect under high- and low-elaboration conditions. *Journal of Personality and Social Psychology, 64,* 5–20.

Petty, R. E., & Wegener, D. T. (1999). Attitude change: Multiple roles for persuasion variables. In S. Chaiken & Y. Trope (Eds.), *Dual-process theories in social psychology* (pp. 323–390). New York: Guilford Press.

Petty, R. E., Wells, G. L., & Brock, T. C. (1976). Distraction can enhance or reduce yielding to propaganda: Thought disruption versus effort justification. *Journal of Personality and Social Psychology, 34,* 874–884.

Puckett, J. M., Petty, R. E., Cacioppo, J. T., & Fischer, D. L. (1983). The relative impact of age and attractiveness stereotypes on persuasion. *Journal of Gerontology, 38,* 340–343.

Rosenthal, E. H., Heesacker, M., & Neimeyer, G. J. (1995). Changing the rape supportive attitudes of traditional and nontraditional males and females. *Journal of Counseling Psychology, 42,* 171–177.

Smith, S. M., Haugtvedt, C. P., & Petty, R. E. (1994). Attitudes and recycling: Does the measurement of affect enhance behavioral prediction? *Psychology and Marketing, 11,* 359–374.

Stoltenberg, C. D. (1986). Elaboration likelihood and the counseling process. In F. J. Dorn (Ed.), *The social influence process in counseling and psychotherapy* (pp. 55–64). Springfield, IL: Charles C Thomas.

Strong, S. R. (1968). Counseling: An interpersonal influence process. *Journal of Counseling Psychology, 15,* 215–224.

Strong, S. R. (1986). Interpersonal influence theory and therapeutic interactions. In F. J. Dorn (Ed.), *The social influence process in counseling and psychotherapy* (pp. 17–30). Springfield, IL: Charles C Thomas.

Strong, S. R. (1995). From social psychology: What? *The Counseling Psychologist, 23,* 686–690.

Tesser, A., & Leone, C. (1977). Cognitive schemes and thought as determinants of attitude change. *Journal of Experimental Social Psychology, 13,* 340–356.

Tinsley, H. E. A., Workman, K. R., & Kass, R. A. (1980). Factor analysis of the domain of client expectancies about counseling. *Journal of Counseling Psychology, 27,* 561–570.

Wegener, D. T., & Petty, R. E. (1996). Effects of mood on persuasion processes: Enhancing, reducing, or biasing scrutiny of attitude-relevant information. In L. L. Martin & A. Tesser (Eds.), *Striving and feeling: Interactions between goals and affect* (pp. 329–362). Mahwah, NJ: Erlbaum.

Wells, G. L., & Petty, R. E. (1980). The effects of overt head movements on persuasion: Compatibility and incompatibility of responses. *Basic and Applied Social Psychology, 1,* 219–230.

Session Evaluation and the Session Evaluation Questionnaire

William B. Stiles, Lisa E. Gordon, and James A. Lani

Miami University

Most therapists would indicate an interest in how their clients evaluate sessions. Consumer feedback is important in obtaining, retaining, and assisting clients. This chapter presents an instrument, the Session Evaluation Questionnaire, that is both brief and comprehensive for after-session administration to clients, therapists, or both.

Chapter Questions

- What dimensions are assessed by the Session Evaluation Questionnaire (SEQ)?
- What is the relationship between therapist and client SEQ ratings?
- How do SEQ ratings relate to theoretical orientation?
- How do SEQ rating relate to therapy outcome?
- What are the implications of SEQ research for clinical practice?

This chapter concerns how participants evaluate counseling or psychotherapy sessions—or other sorts of sessions. We focus on one instrument that measures people's evaluations of sessions: the Session Evaluation Questionnaire (SEQ; Stiles, 1980; Stiles & Snow, 1984a, 1984b; Stiles et al., 1994). After noting some basic concepts in session evaluation, we describe the scales of the SEQ, how they were constructed, their reliability, and their psychological meaning. We then review research on the relations of SEQ-measured session evaluations with other evaluative measures; with participants' in-session behaviors; with characteristics of clients, counselors, and treatment approaches; and with treatment outcomes. Evaluations of counseling session have been measured by many other instruments besides the SEQ, such as the Therapy Session Report (Orlinsky & Howard, 1975, 1977, 1986), the Session Impacts Scale (Elliott & Wexler, 1994; Mallinckrodt, 1994), the Counselor Rating Form (Barak & LaCrosse, 1975), and the Important Events Questionnaire (Cummings, Hallberg, Slemon, & Martin, 1992). Insofar as all of these share the SEQ's evaluative focus—assessing whether and how the session was good or bad—much of what we say about the SEQ would apply to these instruments as well.

Basic Concepts and Scales

Evaluations, Session Evaluations, and Session Impact

Evaluations concern whether things are good or bad. Theorists from Allport (1946) to Zajonc (1980) and from Skinner (1953) to Rogers (1951, 1959) have agreed that people's evaluations are universal, automatic, and adaptive. People assign some degree of positive or negative valence to most, or perhaps all, of the events they encounter. They work for positive events, and they work to avoid negative ones. Evaluations require no training or experience—as Zajonc (1980) put it, "preferences need no inferences" (p. 151)—though evaluations may be powerfully affected by training or experience.

In particular, participants in counseling or psychotherapy evaluate their sessions. Participants' session evaluations offer an immediate index of the interpersonal climate, sense of progress, and consumer satisfaction. Session impact is important also because clients' internal reactions to sessions logically must intervene between in-session events and the long-term effects of treatment. The SEQ was designed to measure these session evaluations.

Whereas descriptions concern properties of objects and events, evaluations concern a relation between the evaluator and the objects or events being evaluated. Insofar as people's requirements change over time, their relations to events change, and their evaluations also change. Thus, food that tastes good when one is hungry may be unappealing or even disgusting when one has overeaten. A relationship that feels fulfilling and rewarding at one stage of life may feel boring or exploitative at another stage.

Session evaluations too must be understood in the context of participants' requirements. It may be that sessions experienced as good in some circumstances (e.g., late in therapy, or when the client is working hard on difficult material, or with an elderly client) would be experienced as bad in other circumstances (e.g., early in therapy, or when the client is upset, or with an adolescent client).

Session impact refers to a session's immediate subjective effects (Stiles, 1980). The concept of session impact is broader than session evaluation; it includes participants' assessments of the session's specific (descriptive) character, specific internal reactions, and participants' postsession affective state (Stiles et al., 1994). In our review linking SEQ scores with other indexes of counseling and psychotherapy, we distinguish among impact, process, and outcome on the basis of the time and scope of measurement. *Impact measures,* such as the SEQ, were taken after sessions and refer to whole sessions (or to events anywhere in sessions). *Process measures* are those that refer to moment-by-moment observations of participants behaviors within sessions (typically based on rating or coding of tape recordings or transcripts). *Outcome measures* are those that are taken at or after the end of treatment and typically refer to the effects of the whole treatment. We also review research linking SEQ scores with personal characteristics of clients and of counselors and broad characteristics of the treatment itself (e.g., theoretical approach).

Structure of the SEQ

Counseling and psychotherapy sessions are judged as good or bad in at least two distinct ways simultaneously: (1) as powerful and valuable versus weak and worthless and (2) as relaxed and comfortable versus tense and distressing. On the SEQ, these two session evaluation dimensions are called Depth and Smoothness, respectively. The SEQ was designed to measure these two dimensions through several iterations, using factor analysis to obtain robust, internally consistent sets of items (Stiles, 1980; Stiles, et al., 1994; Stiles & Snow, 1984b; Stiles, Tupler, & Carpenter, 1982). These analyses have found the same factors (i.e., the same groupings of items) in ratings by counselors and clients, suggesting that they use the adjectives in similar ways (i.e., the adjectives' meanings overlap to about the same degree from both perspectives), and allowing researchers to use the same scales to study both participants. Depth and Smoothness vary independently; sessions may be perceived as deep and smooth ("smooth sailing" in Orlinsky & Howard's, 1977, nautical metaphor), as deep and rough ("heavy going"), as shallow and smooth ("coasting"), or as shallow and rough ("foundering").

In addition to session evaluation, the SEQ measures two dimensions of participants' postsession mood, Positivity and Arousal (Stiles & Snow, 1984b, Stiles et al., 1994). These are widely considered as basic theoretical dimensions of mood and emotion (Larsen & Diener, 1992; Reisenzein, 1994), and they account for most of the rating variance on a wide variety of measures of mood and emotion in a wide variety of circumstances (Russell, 1978, 1979). Because this chapter's focus is on session evaluation, however, we do not review results concerning the SEQ's Positivity and Arousal scales.

The SEQ, Form 5, includes 21 items in a 7-point bipolar adjective format, as shown in Appendix 1. Respondents are instructed, "Please circle the appropriate number to show how you feel about this session." The items are divided into two sections, session evaluation (the focus of this chapter) and postsession mood. The stem "This session was:" precedes the first 11 items (session evaluation): bad–good, difficult–easy, valuable–worthless, shallow–deep, relaxed–tense, unpleasant–pleasant, full–empty, weak–powerful, special–ordinary, rough–smooth, and comfortable–uncomfortable. The stem "Right now I feel:" precedes the second 10 items (postsession mood): happy–sad, angry–pleased, moving–still, uncertain–definite, calm–excited, confident–afraid, friendly–unfriendly, slow–fast, energetic–peaceful, and quiet–aroused. The adjective scales within each section were selected to clearly represent the two evaluative and two mood dimensions, respectively, and to avoid skew in the distribution of ratings.

Each item is scored from 1 to 7, reversed as appropriate, with higher scores indicating greater Depth, Smoothness, Positivity, or Arousal. An index for each dimension is calculated as the mean rating on the items that have had the highest and most consistent loadings in factor analyses. Assignment of items to scales is discussed later in the chapter in sections dealing with each dimension in turn. Unit-weighted item ratings are used, rather than factor scores, for simplicity and for generality across perspectives and levels of analysis (exact values of factor loadings have varied across analyses, but the items loading highest on each dimension have been consistent).

A score for each of the dimensions is calculated as the mean of the constituent item ratings, rather than the sum of the item ratings. Consequently, the dimension scores lie on the same 7-point scale as the individual items, making interpretation easier. The midpoint of each SEQ scale is 4.00, and the possible range (e.g., from maximum Shallowness to maximum Depth) is 1.00 to 7.00.

The SEQ Form 5 in Appendix 1 is identical to Form 4 (Dill-Standiford, Stiles, & Rorer, 1988; Stiles et al., 1994) except that three unused items were deleted to save space (safe–dangerous from the session evaluation section and wakeful–sleepy and involved–detached from the postsession mood section). The items used in scoring Depth, Smoothness, and Positivity are identical on Forms 3, 4 and 5. Form 4 differed from Form 3 (Stiles & Snow, 1984a, 1984b) only in that some of the adjective pairs were added or changed to construct the Arousal mood factor. Form 1 (Stiles et al., 1982) and Form 2 (Stiles, 1980) used somewhat different sets of adjectives, but results involving corresponding scales should be comparable.

From time to time, additional items and sections have been added to or removed from the SEQ. For example, Form 1 included a Stability dimension (Stiles et al., 1982) and Form 2 included a small Activity–Excitement dimension (Stiles, 1980). Early studies suggested that Depth and Smoothness were by far the most prominent session evaluation dimensions; however, subsequent versions have focused on these two session evaluation factors. In one study, a group of three items was added to assess evaluation of the therapist: The stem, "Today I feel my therapist was" preceded the items, skillful–unskillful, cold–warm, and trustworthy–untrustworthy (Stiles et al., 1994).

The SEQ has been applied to many types of individual counseling sessions, to group therapy and encounter group sessions, to family and marital sessions, and to supervision sessions. It has been translated into French (Lecompte & Tremblay, 1983), Chinese (Lin, 1999), and Greek (Nestoros & Zgantzouri, 1999). It is typically completed by participants immediately following the session to be evaluated, but it can be (and has been, in some studies) completed by participants at a later time or completed by external raters based on tape recordings. The SEQ's content and format make it appropriate for assessing anything that could be called a session. The psychological phenomena that it measures—evaluation and mood—appear to be components of essentially all human activity.

Reliability: Internal Consistency, Agreement, and Stability of SEQ Indexes

In discussing the reliability of SEQ indexes, one must distinguish among (1) *internal consistency,* the degree to which each index's items measure the same thing; (2) *interperspective agreement,* the degree to which individuals from different perspectives (e.g., counselor, client, observer) give similar ratings; and (3) *stability,* the degree to which respondents give the same ratings on different occasions.

Internal consistency, measured by coefficient alpha, has been high for all SEQ indexes across a wide variety of conditions and settings (e.g., .90 for Depth, .93 for Smoothness; Reynolds et al., 1996; see also Bunce & West, 1996; Gregory & Leslie, 1996; Millar & Brotherton, 1996; Stiles, et al., 1994; Stiles, Shapiro, & Firth-Cozens, 1988; Stiles &

Snow, 1984a). This is to be expected of scales constructed from robust factors, as the SEQ has been.

Interperspective agreement about the evaluation of a session is more complex. It is operationally parallel to interrater reliability (i.e., it compares different raters' ratings of a target). There are important and valid reasons, however, why counselors, clients, and external observers might evaluate sessions differently, so low interperspective agreement is not necessarily a drawback. On the contrary, it may have important substantive interpretations and consequences, as discussed later.

According to a framework proposed by Dill-Standiford et al., (1988), *consensus,* the similarity of clients' and counselors' own session evaluations, should be distinguished from other types of interperspective agreement based on participants' estimates of each other's session ratings. *Counselor awareness* involves comparing counselors' estimates of their clients' ratings with their clients' actual ratings. *Client awareness* involves comparing clients' estimates of their counselors' ratings with their counselors' actual ratings. In principle, participants might disagree about how to evaluate a session (low consensus) but be aware of how they disagreed. (As reviewed later, however, even counselor and client awareness of session evaluations are far lower than might be expected.)

Though operationally similar to test–retest reliability, stability across sessions should not be considered as reliability at all because the target of each rating is different. SEQ ratings vary from session to session (because sessions are not all alike), so that a single session rating is a poor measure of a respondent's typical experience. The stability of ratings by a particular client depends on the proportion of the rating's variance that is at the client level, as explained in the next section. Usually, however, the mean rating across four to six sessions gives a reasonably stable index of Depth or Smoothness (see Stiles & Snow, 1984a, especially footnote 1).

Hierarchical Organization of Session Evaluation Data

Session evaluation data often have a hierarchical structure, because sessions ratings are collected on several of each counselor's clients and several of each client's sessions. In such a hierarchical data set, treating raw session ratings as independent observations in statistical tests would fail to discriminate among several distinct sources of variation: (1) differences among counselors, (2) differences among clients of each counselor, and (3) differences among sessions of each client (Dill-Standiford et al., 1988; Stiles et al., 1994; Stiles & Snow, 1984a).

To ameliorate this problem, some investigators make statistical adjustments and conduct separate analyses at different levels: *Session-level* analyses use ratings of multiple sessions from each case that have been statistically adjusted for differences among cases (e.g., by using deviation scores, which are the differences between the observed session scores and the mean for that client) or that are averaged across cases. *Client-level* analyses use mean ratings across each client's sessions that have been adjusted for differences among counselors (i.e., one adjusted mean per client) or that are averaged across counselors. *Counselor-level* analyses use mean ratings across each counselor's clients (i.e., one mean per counselor). There is a good deal of variability in SEQ scores at both the session and client levels (but less at the counselor level), so it is interesting to study relations with other variables at both levels. For example, comparisons of session evaluations with measures of counseling process are typically made at the session level, whereas comparisons of session evaluations with measures of counseling outcomes or individual differences are typically made at the client level.

Because data sets typically contain observations on more sessions than clients, session-level statistical tests are typically more powerful than are client-level tests. Because few studies have gathered data on enough counselors to conduct meaningful statistical tests, counselor-level findings are rare and relatively unreliable. Some SEQ studies have not systematically distinguished among these levels, and they risk misinterpreting effects at one level for effects at another.

Separate factor analyses at the session and client levels have confirmed that the items on the Depth and Smoothness scales (and on the Positivity and Arousal scales) form the same factors at both levels (Stiles et al., 1994; Stiles & Snow, 1984b), suggesting that the constituent adjectives have similar meanings when used to distinguish among sessions as when used to distinguish among clients. Nevertheless, variables at these different levels have different interpretations, and they can (and sometimes do) have different relations with each other and with other variables (Dill-Standiford et al., 1988; Norman, 1967).

Research on Depth

Meaning of Depth

Session Depth is the quality described by respondents as deep, powerful, valuable, full, and special. The opposite, Session Shallowness, is the quality described as shallow, weak, worthless, empty, and ordinary. The core meaning of the Depth versus Shallowness dimension can be understood as the combination or overlap of these adjectives' common meanings. As explained in Appendix 1, the Depth scale score is the mean rating on the constituent items, scored from 1 to 7 and reversed as appropriate, so that high scores represent relatively Deep sessions and low scores represent relatively Shallow ones. (We capitalize these adjectives to indicate that we are referring to the Depth scale score rather than to judgments on the item, shallow–deep.) Conceptually, then, Depth seems to estimate the effectiveness of an ongoing treatment—its value and its power, and Depth scores have sometimes been considered as a measure of "session outcome." Their relation to treatment outcome is not clear or simple, however, as reviewed later.

Counselors seem to equate Depth with good sessions; however, clients give more equal weight to Smoothness. In factor analytic studies, for example, the bad–good item loaded highly on Depth for counselors at both session and client levels and for clients at the client level, but it is loaded equally on Depth and Smoothness for clients at the session level (Stiles & Snow, 1984b; Stiles et al., 1994). That is, in comparing their sessions, clients tended to rate smooth, easy, comfortable ones as "good," whereas counselors considered this aspect more neutrally. For this reason, the bad–good item is not included in the Depth scale, though the item is retained on the SEQ, Form 5, because of its intrinsic interest as a global evaluation item (see Stiles et al., 1994).

Incidentally, in contrast to clients' considering session Smoothness as good, some counselors may associate a degree of client discomfort with a session's power and value.

Some research has found small but significant negative correlations between counselor Depth ratings and client Smoothness ratings (Stiles, 1980; Stiles & Snow, 1984a).

Mean Depth Scores and Interperspective Agreement

Mean Depth scores have usually been comfortably above the 4.0 midpoint of the scale. Clients' Depth scores have tended to be higher than counselors' by half a point or more, with means frequently well over 5.0 for clients and a bit below 5.0 for counselors (Cummings, Slemon, & Hallberg, 1993; Dill-Standiford et al., 1988; Friedlander, Siegel, & Brenock, 1989; Stiles, 1980; Stiles et al., 1988; Stiles & Snow, 1984a). Counselors may feel some relief in knowing that their clients are likely to have rated their sessions as relatively Deeper (i.e., more powerful and valuable). There may be a selection bias in these means, however. In one study, clients who dropped out of treatment had lower Depth ratings (Samstag, Batchelder, Muran, Safran, & Winston, 1998).

Surprisingly, consensus on Depth is usually weak to negligible, particularly at the session level (Dill-Standiford et al., 1988; Hill, Helms, Tichenor, et al., 1988; Mallinckrodt, 1993; Stiles et al., 1988; Stiles & Snow, 1984a; Sumerel & Borders, 1996). Some studies that confounded all three levels, however, have reported moderate consensus on Depth (Horvath & Marx, 1990; Kelly, Hall, & Miller, 1989; Stiles, 1980).

In principle, counselors might be aware of their clients' evaluations of sessions even though their own evaluations differ. In one study that asked counselors to guess their clients' ratings, however, counselor awareness of client Depth was just as low at the session level (.19), though it was moderate at the client level (.42), suggesting that the counselors had some idea of which of their clients tended to have Deeper sessions, even though they had little idea of which sessions were the Deep ones (Dill-Standiford et al., 1988).

This pattern yields an important clinical message. Dyads engaged in counseling and psychotherapy do not agree about which sessions are Deeper or Shallower—more powerful and valuable or less powerful and valuable—and they do not know which sessions their partner considers Deeper or Shallower. Counselors should beware of assuming they know how their clients evaluate sessions on this dimension. The lack of agreement is in sharp contrast to the conviction with which individuals can assert their own sense of a session's value.

Relation of Depth to Other Impact Variables

Depth overlaps substantially with other evaluative indexes. Within the client perspective, Depth has shown consistently strong correlations with many other evaluative ratings drawn from a variety of instruments, including SEQ Positivity (Hanson, Claiborn, & Kerr, 1997; Horvath & Marx, 1990; Stiles et al., 1994; Stiles & Snow, 1984a), client assessment of counselors' expertness, trustworthiness, and attractiveness on the Counselor Rating Form (Hanson et al., 1997), satisfaction with treatment (Thompson & Hill, 1993), ratings of session helpfulness (Cummings, Barak, & Hallberg, 1995), Helpful Impacts and Relationship Impacts on the Session Impact Scale (Elliott & Wexler, 1994; Stiles et al., 1994), presession positive mood (Hill et al., 1994), and ratings of counselors' facilitative style (Thompson & Hill, 1993). Relations of Depth to other evaluative indexes within the counselor perspective have been less studied, but appear equally strong (Hill et al., 1994; Horvath & Marx, 1990; Stiles & Snow, 1984a).

The overlap is confined, however, to within-perspective comparisons. As might be expected from the weak consensus about Depth, correlations of client's Depth ratings with other evaluative measures by counselors, and vice-versa, have been weak or negligible.

The relation of session Depth to the alliance between client and counselor (therapeutic alliance, working alliance) is particularly interesting because of the replicated association of alliance measures with treatment outcome (Horvath & Symonds, 1991; Orlinsky, Grawe, & Parks, 1994). Measures of the alliance are evaluative and may be regarded as session-level measures (insofar as they are typically gathered during the course of treatment); however, the target of the evaluation is a relationship that extends over multiple, possibly heterogeneous sessions. Existing evidence suggests that Depth-alliance relations tend to follow the already-noted pattern of stronger within-perspective correlations and weaker between-perspective correlations (Heatherington & Friedlander, 1990; Horvath & Marx, 1990; Mallinckrodt, 1993; Raue, Goldfried, & Barkham, 1997). However, the correlations are somewhat weaker and less consistent, and this issue deserves more research.

Relation of Depth to Session Process

Comparisons with ratings of the counseling process (from tape recordings) have suggested that Depth is judged as relatively greater in sessions (1) where emotions are more focused on by counselors or stirred in clients—whether or not they are actually expressed in the sessions (Hill, Helms, Spiegel, & Tichenor, 1988; Regan & Hill, 1992), and (2) where the dialogue is more marked by clarity, definiteness, and sophistication by clients or counselors (Diemer, Lobell, Vivino, & Hill, 1996; Friedlander, Thibodeau, & Ward, 1985; Fuller & Hill, 1985; Hill, Helms, Tichenor et al., 1988; Kelly et al., 1989; McLennan, Twigg, & Bezant, 1993; Stiles, Shankland, Wright, & Field, 1997). Of course, such qualities are also evaluative, but they point beyond global evaluations to more specific descriptions of Deep sessions.

There is some evidence that Depth is negatively correlated with a focus on information transfer within sessions—giving and receiving facts, as contrasted with exploring feelings—and with confrontation of clients by counselors (Fuller & Hill, 1985; Hill, Helms, Tichenor et al., 1988). Such findings might reflect client dissatisfaction with an overcognitive or overcritical counselor, or, alternatively, a pattern of responsiveness (Stiles, Honos-Webb, & Surko, 1998) in which counselors seek information or confront difficulties in response to session Shallowness (e.g., sessions early in treatment or periods of floundering or resistance). For counselors, Depth has also appeared negatively associated with difficulties in the therapeutic relationship (Fuller & Hill, 1985; Hill, Helms, Tichenor et al., 1988).

Depth has a general tendency to increase across sessions, at least in successful treatments (Kivlighan, Angelone, & Swafford, 1991; Reynolds et al., 1996); however, within this general trend, there is a great deal of session-to-session change in both directions, reflecting developmental vicissitudes of life events, the therapeutic relationship, and the process of treatment (e.g., Friedlander et al., 1989; Stiles et al., 1982).

Relation of Depth to Person Variables

The Depth of sessions does not appear to depend very much on the stable personal characteristics of the client or counselor (demographics, personality, psychopathology). Correlations and significant differences have been sparse, small, and inconsistent (e.g., Gregory & Leslie, 1996; Herman, 1997; Jordan & Quinn, 1997; Kivlighan & Angelone, 1991; Nocita & Stiles, 1986). Depth may best be considered an interactively developed quality of the counselor–client relationship, depending on specific circumstances, context, and interpersonal events, rather than on stable characteristics of either person.

Even though Deep sessions are not restricted to particular classes of people, Depth may reflect complex interactions with treatment variables. For example, Hardy, Stiles, Barkman, and Startup (1998) found no main effects on SEQ ratings of whether clients were classified as interpersonally overinvolved, underinvolved, or neither, but they did find that underinvolved clients reported relatively Deeper sessions if they were assigned to cognitive behavioral treatment, whereas overinvolved clients reported relatively Deeper sessions if they were assigned to psychodynamic-interpersonal treatment. Counselors, who usually have a very clear evaluation of their own, should beware of assuming they know how their clients evaluate sessions on this dimension.

Relation of Depth to Treatment Approach

From the client perspective, investigators have most often reported little or no mean difference in the Depth of sessions of contrasting treatment approaches—for example, psychodynamic-interpersonal versus cognitive-behavioral (Reynolds et al., 1996; Stiles et al., 1988), or dream interpretation sessions versus event interpretation sessions versus unstructured sessions (Diemer et al., 1996), or termination sessions of time-limited versus brief time-limited group therapy (Sells & Hays, 1997). Under some circumstances, however, clients seem to make distinctions. Jordan and Quinn (1994) reported that family members gave higher Depth ratings to solution-focused family therapy sessions (which focused on developing a clear goal, reinvigorating problem-solving strategies, and planning the solution) than to problem-focused sessions (which focused on understanding the maladaptive problem-solving strategies), and Reynolds, Taylor, and Shapiro (1993) reported that workers gave higher Depth ratings to psychologically exploratory sessions than to structured stress management therapy.

The treatment conditions that lead to client-rated Depth thus remain unclear and may reflect implementations of the treatments in particular studies, rather than reliable features of the named treatment. As one contribution, clients' Depth scores may be increased by techniques aimed at actively involving clients, such as giving personality and vocational test interpretations in an interactive style (Hanson et al., 1997), or facilitated (rather than self-directed) dream interpretation sessions (Heaton, Hill, Petersen, Rochlen, & Zack, 1998), or drug abuse counseling that used a visual representation system (Dansereau, Dees, Greener, & Simpson, 1995).

Theoretical differences may sometimes have more affect on counselors who have been reported to rate psychodynamic-interpersonal sessions as Deeper than cognitive-behavioral sessions (Stiles et al., 1988), which is consistent with the former's theoretical "depth therapy" approach. Psychiatric day hospital patients who were not the targets of the therapeutic interventions, however, gave higher Depth ratings to videotapes of cognitive-behavioral therapy than to videotapes of psychodynamic or humanistic therapy, external locus of control instruction, or friendly reassurance and advice (Wanigaratne & Barker, 1995).

Relation of Depth to Outcome

There is evidence that clients who drop out of therapy have lower Depth scores than those who return (Samstag et al., 1998; Tryon, 1990). Considering that Depth explicitly measures participants' estimates of session value, however, evidence linking it with treatment outcome is modest. Thompson and Hill (1993) reported that client-rated Depth of third counseling sessions predicted treatment satisfaction and treatment outcome on a composite measure. Mallinckrodt (1993) found a multiple correlation of treatment outcome with SEQ scores, though the reported analyses did not separate the effect of Depth from Smoothness. Stiles, Shapiro, & Firth-Cozens (1990) reported that mean Depth ratings by clients and by external audiotape raters were not significantly correlated with outcome. Mean Depth ratings by one of the two principal therapists (but not the other) did correlate with client improvement, raising the possibility that evaluative criteria may differ across individuals in ways that only sometimes coincide with the sorts of changes assessed by standard symptom intensity outcome instruments. More generally, it is not clear whether the sparse evidence on the relation of Depth to treatment outcome reflects the absence of a stable link (investigators may fail to report null relations) or simply a failure to examine the question.

Research on Smoothness

Meaning of Smoothness

Smoothness is the quality described by respondents as smooth, relaxed, pleasant, easy, and comfortable. The opposite, session Roughness, is the quality described as rough, tense, unpleasant, difficult, and uncomfortable. As explained in Appendix 1, the Smoothness score is the mean rating on the constituent items, reversed as appropriate, so that high scores represent relatively Smooth sessions and low scores represent relatively Rough ones (again, we capitalize these adjectives to indicate that we are referring to the Smoothness scale score rather than to judgments on the item, rough–smooth).

Mean Smoothness and Interperspective Agreement

Some studies have found that sessions were rated as Smoother by clients than by counselors (Cummings et al., 1993; Friedlander et al., 1989; Stiles et al., 1988). This pattern has not been consistent, however, with other, larger studies reporting approximately equal mean Smoothness for clients and counselors (Dill-Standiford et al., 1988; Samstag et al., 1998).

In contrast to the general lack of agreement about Depth, client–counselor consensus about Smoothness appears at least moderate (typically .3 to .6; Dill-Standiford et al., 1988; Stiles & Snow, 1984a; Stiles et al., 1988). Client and counselor awareness were similar (Dill-Standiford et al., 1988). Smaller studies that have mixed levels of analysis have returned more mixed Smoothness consensus ranging from moderate to negligible (Hill, Helms, Tichenor et al., 1988; Horvath & Marx, 1990; Mallinckrodt, 1993; Stiles, 1980). It appears that, perceptions of whether a session was easy, comfortable, and relaxed—or difficult, uncomfortable, and tense—is shared to a much greater degree than are perceptions of a session's power and value.

Relation of Smoothness to Other Impact Variables

Even though Smoothness has usually been essentially uncorrelated with Depth, both have been strongly correlated with postsession positive mood, as measured by SEQ Positivity, within both client and counselor perspectives (Hanson et al., 1997; Horvath & Marx, 1990; Stiles & Snow, 1984a; Stiles et al., 1994). As a way of understanding this, both the Smoothness and Depth of a session may contribute to clients' and counselors' emotional state afterward.

Between perspectives, Smoothness-Positivity, correlations have been asymmetrical, with moderate correlations of counselor-rated Smoothness with client postsession Positivity but negligible correlations of client-rated Smoothness with counselor Positivity (Stiles, 1980; Stiles & Snow, 1984a). Presumably, this reflects the asymmetry of participants' knowledge about each other.

Correlations of Smoothness have been lower than those of Depth with evaluative scales drawn from some other session impact measures, such as Helpful Impacts and Relationship Impacts, as measured by the Session Impacts Scale (Elliott & Wexler, 1994; Stiles et al., 1994). Evidently, the other evaluative measures with which the SEQ has been compared have assessed mainly sessions' power and value rather than their comfort and relaxation. The Therapy Session Report (Orlinsky & Howard, 1975, 1977, 1986) appears to include indexes related to Smoothness; however, comparisons with the SEQ have not yet been reported. Measures of the counselor–client alliance evidently incorporate both evaluative aspects. Correlations of Smoothness with measures of the alliance, like those of Depth, have generally been significant and moderate (Heatherington & Friedlander, 1990; Horvath & Marx, 1990; Mallinckrodt, 1993; Raue et al., 1997).

Relation of Smoothness to Session Process

Not surprisingly, clients feel relaxed and comfortable when they are supported but tense and uncomfortable when they are challenged. Client-rated Smoothness has been associated positively with counselors' actively supportive interventions in sessions, measured as counselors' reported intentions (i.e., types of interventions that counselors said they used, based on reviewing their own videotapes), and negatively with challenging interventions (Fuller & Hill, 1985; Kivlighan & Angelone, 1991; Kivlighan et al., 1991). Convergently, counselor-rated Smoothness was related positively with counselors' giving direct guidance and information and negatively with confrontation as rated from tapes by observers (Hill, Helms, Tichenor et al., 1988).

Relatively few studies have linked client behaviors to Smoothness, but Stiles (1984) reported that client self-disclosure (percentage of client utterances) was negatively correlated with Smoothness as rated by clients, therapists, and an external rater. Presumably, high-disclosure sessions tended to be those in which clients examined difficult or painful feelings. Hill, Helms, Spiegel, & Tichenor (1988) reported that client-rated Smoothness was correlated positively with the *educated* index and, in some cases, negatively with *negative thoughts and behaviors, scared, feeling worse,* and *lack direction.*

Reynolds et al. (1996) reported that client-rated Smoothness increased across sessions in both 8-session and 16-session time-limited therapy. Interestingly, the rate of increase in

Smoothness was accelerated in the shorter (8-session) treatments, so that by termination, Smoothness was approximately equal in both treatment duration conditions. Sells and Hays (1997), however, compared the termination sessions of time-limited and brief time-limited group therapy and reported that the former was Smoother than the latter, presumably reflecting the relatively rushed schedule. Other, smaller studies have noted patterns of systematic fluctuations across time that may depend on particular sorts of in-session activities (Gregory & Leslie, 1996; Kivlighan et al., 1991; Reynolds et al., 1993; Stiles et al., 1982). For example, Reynolds et al. (1993) reported that sessions devoted to an introduction to stress management and a focus on relaxation exercises were rated as Smoother than sessions that focused on relationships at home and work, on rational thinking and attributions for stressful events, or on emotions and seeking social support.

Relation of Smoothness to Person Variables

Relatively shy, introverted clients tend to report Rougher sessions (introversion negatively correlated with Smoothness; Kivlighan & Angelone, 1991; Nocita & Stiles, 1986). Perhaps this can be considered as a specific manifestation of a general tendency to feel tense and uncomfortable in interpersonal encounters. In a perhaps related finding, Stiles et al. (1997) reported that Smoothness was negatively correlated with client internality (attribution of problems to personal qualities rather than external circumstances) and distress.

Except for the relation with introversion, associations of Smoothness with client characteristics have been sparse and inconsistent. For example, Gregory and Leslie (1996) reported that African American females had Smoother first sessions of family or marital therapy if their counselor was African American rather than White, and that African American males had Smoother first sessions than did White males, regardless of their counselor's race. Neither of these effects, however, appeared in SEQ ratings of their fourth session. Similarly, there is little evidence that Smoothness is a simple function of *counselors'* personal or profession characteristics, including their training and experience (e.g., Kivligan, 1989; Sumerel & Borders, 1996).

Relation of Smoothness to Treatment Approach

Sessions of structured, prescriptive treatments tend to be rated as Smoother than sessions of unstructured, exploratory treatments. This is one of the best replicated effects in SEQ research. Clients, counselors, and external raters rated cognitive-behavioral sessions as Smoother than psychodynamic-interpersonal sessions (Stiles et al., 1988). Psychiatric day hospital patients gave higher Smoothness ratings to videotapes of cognitive-behavioral therapy and external locus of control instruction than to tapes of psychodynamic or humanistic therapy or friendly reassurance and advice (Wanigaratne & Barker, 1995). Family members gave higher Smoothness ratings to solution-focused sessions than to problem-focused sessions (Jordan & Quinn, 1994). Workers gave higher Smoothness ratings to structured session stress management workshops than to exploratory counseling dealing with the same sorts of stress (Reynolds et al., 1993). A plausible interpretation of this clear pattern is that psychological exploration is experienced as difficult and uncomfortable, whereas counselor-provided structure and direction makes the client's job easier and more comfortable.

In a perhaps related finding, trainees who received videotaped supervision in psychodynamic-interpersonal therapy subsequently rated their own sessions as Smoother than did trainees who received live supervision (Kivlighan et al., 1991). The live supervision may have encouraged (uncomfortable) personal exploration. Dansereau, Dees, Greener, and Simpson (1995) reported that the use of a visual representation system called Node-link mapping decreased Smoothness scores in drug abuse counseling sessions; unmapped sessions were rated as Smoother than mapped sessions by both counselors and clients. The mapping may have intensified the exploration.

Importantly, the Roughness of unstructured treatments may be mitigated as treatment proceeds. Reynolds et al. (1996) reported that early sessions of cognitive-behavioral therapy were Smoother than early sessions of psychodynamic-interpersonal therapy. Smoothness tended to increase across sessions in both treatments, but it increased more rapidly in the psychodynamic-interpersonal therapy, so that there was no difference between the two therapies by the end of treatment. Clients' initial discomfort in the psychodynamic-interpersonal therapy may have reflected the early exploration of psychologically painful material, which was overcome as the material was dealt with in later sessions.

Relation of Smoothness to Outcome

There is some evidence that session Smoothness as rated by counselors and perhaps by external raters (but not by clients) may be correlated with treatment outcome. Samstag et al. (1998) reported that therapists' Smoothness ratings were highest for clients categorized as having good outcomes, followed by poor outcomes, and dropouts. As noted earlier, Mallinckrodt's (1993) multiple regression analyses showed that Depth and Smoothness considered together contributed significantly to therapy outcome. Stiles et al. (1990) reported that Smoothness scores given by raters who listened to tape-recorded sessions were correlated with client improvement from pretreatment to three-month follow-up on standard measures. Improvement was also correlated with therapist-rated Smoothness; however, this result reflected strong correlations with ratings by one of two principal therapists, whereas the other's were uncorrelated with outcome.

Summary

Research on session evaluation using the SEQ does not yield prescriptions for treatment, but it has produced several replicated findings that practitioners might wish to consider and integrate into their thinking about what they do.

1. Evaluations of counseling and psychotherapy sessions are made on at least two different and independent dimensions. Depth concerns the session's power and value; Smoothness concerns the session's comfort and relaxation. The same dimensions are used by clients and counselors, both to distinguish among a client's sessions and to characterize a client's typical session (i.e., at both session and client levels). When a client or a counselor describes a session or a course of treatment as "good," it may mean Deep or Smooth or both. Undifferentiated evaluative terms or scales run the risk of mixing these two aspects in unspecified proportions and, thus, overlooking their distinct contributions. Clinically, there is a danger that clients and counselors may misunderstand what the other means in describing a session as good or bad.

2. Both clients and counselors form clear opinions about their sessions on both dimensions, as shown, for example by high internal consistency of the Depth and Smoothness scales. Clients tend to consider their sessions as Deeper (but not necessarily Smoother) than do their counselors

3. Clients and counselors do not agree reliably about the Depth of sessions in which they both participated. For example, a session that the counselor considers to be powerful and valuable is as likely as not to be considered relatively weak and worthless by the client. Moreover, in the one study that examined the issue (Dill-Standiford et al., 1988), participants did not know when they disagreed. This stubborn lack of agreement may be surprising to participants, particularly in view of the conviction with which they hold their evaluations. Agreement is better for Smoothness, though it is still only moderate. That is, clients and counselors are usually more in accord about the degree to which a session was pleasant, comfortable, and relaxed.

Because client–counselor agreement is so weak, counselors should not presume to know how clients evaluated sessions they have shared. Asking the client to complete the SEQ is one way to obtain better information.

4. Even though Depth and Smoothness are independent dimensions, both contribute strongly to participants more global evaluations of sessions within perspectives. For example, within client and counselor perspectives, both session Depth and Smoothness are associated with postsession positive mood. In other words, both power/value and comfort/relaxation play a part in making a session good and in feeling good afterwards. There is some evidence that counselors tend to emphasize Depth whereas clients tend to emphasize Smoothness. These different emphases are a potential source of misunderstanding.

5. Both Depth and Smoothness are empirically associated with the client–counselor alliance (which is, after all, evaluative); however, the alliance has a longer time frame, at least conceptually. One might have an occasional Rough or Shallow session within a strong alliance. Research on the relations between the alliance and session evaluation might fruitfully explore such issues as ruptures in the alliances and the systematic development of the relationship. Insofar as such things are not synchronized across clients, such research may require examining temporal sequences within individual cases.

6. Depth is positively associated with an in-session focus on emotions and with clarity and sophistication in the session dialogue. Sessions that involve simple information exchange or confrontation, however, tend to be rated as relatively Shallow. Of course, such process features may be a result of the Depth or Shallowness of sessions as well as a cause. It appears that Depth ratings can be increased by systematic techniques aimed at actively involving clients in the session process.

7. Smoothness is positively related to active support from the counselor and negatively related to challenging, confronting interventions. Again, it may be best to consider such counselor interventions as responsive to context and the state of the relationship rather than as independent causal agents (Stiles et al., 1998).

8. With one exception, stable personal characteristics of clients and counselors (e.g., demographics, personality, diagnosis, training, experience) seem to have little consistent, predictable affect on session evaluations. All sorts of people can have all sorts of sessions. This is not to say that personal characteristics are unimportant, but rather that their influence on session Depth and Smoothness may depend on how they are responded to (Stiles et al., 1998). The exception is that shy, introverted clients tend to experience sessions as Rough—difficult and uncomfortable (as, indeed, they experience social encounters generally).

9. Depth is not associated with particular treatment approaches, at least from the client's perspective (some counselors may consider exploratory treatments as Deeper than prescriptive treatments). Again, all sorts of treatments may include powerful, valuable sessions.

10. Smoothness, however, is clearly related to treatment approach. Clients, counselors, and external observers tend to consider structured, prescriptive approaches, such as cognitive and behavioral therapies, as Smoother than unstructured, exploratory approaches, such as psychodynamic or experiential therapies. Presumably, a focus on exploring psychologically painful material can make some sessions difficult and tense. In the one study that examined this difference longitudinally, the Rougher sessions of the exploratory therapy occurred early in treatment, presumably when difficult material was being encountered, whereas later, the exploratory and prescriptive treatments were equivalent in Smoothness (Reynolds et al., 1996).

11. Depth and Smoothness tend to increase somewhat across sessions in successful treatment, but there are large fluctuations, which depend on many factors, including the developmental sequence, stated time limits for the treatment, and the specific within-session activities.

12. Shallow early sessions seem to predict dropout rate (clients who find early sessions worthless may not return), but beyond that, the association of session evaluations with outcome has been surprisingly weak and inconsistent. In particular, clients' session evaluations have not predicted long-term symptom change. Further research may modify this conclusion, but the weakness should be kept in mind in using "session outcome" as a proxy for therapeutic progress. Some (but not all) counselors may evaluate sessions in relation to an estimate of progress to date, and so predict outcome (Stiles et al., 1990). Interestingly, for session ratings by counselors and external raters, the (sparse) evidence suggests that mean session Smoothness, rather than Depth, is associated with long-term improvement. Counselors may wish to attend to the degree to which their clients feel comfortable and relaxed within sessions.

Appendix: Scoring the SEQ (Form 5)[1]

Indexes of session Depth, session Smoothness, postsession Positivity, and postsession Arousal are calculated as the mean ratings on the appropriate items, as indicated in the following formulas. On the form, item order is mixed within each section (session evaluation and postsession mood), and item directionality is approximately balanced. Each item is scored from 1 to 7, reversed as appropriate, with higher scores indicating greater Depth, Smoothness, Positivity, or Arousal. The mean is used as an index, rather than the sum of the item scores, so that the scores lie on the same 7-point scale as the individual items,

[1]*Source:* Copyright © William B. Stiles. Reprinted with permission.

making interpretation easier. Specifically, using the adjective on the right side of the form as the name of each item:

Depth = [(8-worthless) + deep + (8-empty) + powerful + (8-ordinary)]/5.

Smoothness = [easy + (8-tense) + pleasant + smooth + (8-uncomfortable)]/5.

Positivity = [(8-sad) + pleased + definite + (8-afraid) + (8-unfriendly)]/5.

Arousal = [(8-still) + excited + fast + (8-peaceful) + aroused]/5.

Note that only 20 of the 21 SEQ items are used in these indexes. The remaining one is the first-session evaluation item, Bad–Good, which tends to be used differently by clients than by counselors (Stiles, 1980; Stiles & Snow, 1984b). For counselors, Bad–Good has loaded on the Depth factor, but for clients it has often been split between Depth and Smoothness. The Bad–Good item has been retained on Form 5 because of its intrinsic interest as a global evaluation item (see Stiles et al., 1994).

ID: _____   Date: _____

Session Evaluation Questionnaire (Form 5)

Please circle the appropriate number to show how you feel about this session.

This session was:

Bad	1	2	3	4	5	6	7	Good
Difficult	1	2	3	4	5	6	7	Easy
Valuable	1	2	3	4	5	6	7	Worthless
Shallow	1	2	3	4	5	6	7	Deep
Relaxed	1	2	3	4	5	6	7	Tense
Unpleasant	1	2	3	4	5	6	7	Pleasant
Full	1	2	3	4	5	6	7	Empty
Weak	1	2	3	4	5	6	7	Powerful
Special	1	2	3	4	5	6	7	Ordinary
Rough	1	2	3	4	5	6	7	Smooth
Comfortable	1	2	3	4	5	6	7	Uncomfortable

Right now I feel:

Happy	1	2	3	4	5	6	7	Sad
Angry	1	2	3	4	5	6	7	Pleased
Moving	1	2	3	4	5	6	7	Still
Uncertain	1	2	3	4	5	6	7	Definite
Calm	1	2	3	4	5	6	7	Excited
Confident	1	2	3	4	5	6	7	Afraid
Friendly	1	2	3	4	5	6	7	Unfriendly
Slow	1	2	3	4	5	6	7	Fast
Energetic	1	2	3	4	5	6	7	Peaceful
Quiet	1	2	3	4	5	6	7	Aroused

References

Allport, G. W. (1946). Effect: A secondary principle of learning. *Psychological Review, 53,* 335–347.

Barak, A., & LaCrosse, M. (1975). Multidimensional perception of counselor behavior. *Journal of Counseling Psychology, 22,* 471–476.

Bunce, D., & West, M. A. (1996). Stress management and innovation interventions at work. *Human Relations, 49,* 209–232.

Cummings, A. L., Barak, A., & Hallberg, E. T. (1995). Session helpfulness and session evaluation in short-term counselling. *Counselling Psychology Quarterly, 8,* 325–332.

Cummings, A. L., Hallberg, E. T., Slemon, A., & Martin, J. (1992). Participants' memories for therapeutic events and ratings of session effectiveness. *Journal of Cognitive Psychotherapy, 6,* 113–124.

Cummings, A. L., Slemon, A. G., & Hallberg, E. T. (1993). Session evaluation and recall of important events as a function of counselor experience. *Journal of Counseling Psychology, 40,* 156–165.

Dansereau, D. F., Dees, S. M., Greener, J. M., & Simpson, D. D. (1995). Node-link mapping and the evaluation of drug abuse counseling sessions. *Psychology of Addictive Behaviors, 9,* 195–203.

Diemer, R. A., Lobell, L. K., Vivino, B. L., & Hill, C. E. (1996). Comparison of dream interpretation, event interpretation, and unstructured sessions in brief therapy. *Journal of Counseling Psychology, 43,* 99–112.

Dill-Standiford, T. J., Stiles, W. B., & Rorer, L. G. (1988). Counselor–client agreement on session impact. *Journal of Counseling Psychology, 35,* 47–55.

Elliott, R., & Wexler, M. M. (1994). Measuring the impact of treatment sessions: The Session Impacts Scale. *Journal of Counseling Psychology, 41,* 166–174.

Friedlander, M. L., Siegel, S. M., & Brenock, K. (1989). Parallel processes in counseling and supervision: A case study. *Journal of Counseling Psychology, 36,* 149–157.

Friedlander, M. L., Thibodeau, J. R., & Ward, L. G. (1985). Discriminating the "good" from the "bad" therapy hour: A study of dyadic interaction. *Psychotherapy, 22,* 631–642.

Fuller, F., & Hill, C. E. (1985). Counselor and helpee perceptions of counselor intentions in relation to outcome in a single counseling session. *Journal of Counseling Psychology, 32,* 329–338.

Grace, M., Kivlighan, D. M., & Kunce, J. (1995). The effect of nonverbal skills training on counselor trainee nonverbal sensitivity and responsiveness and on session impact and working alliance ratings. *Journal of Counseling and Development, 73,* 547–552.

Gregory, M. A., & Leslie, L. A. (1996). Different lenses: Variations in clients' perception of family therapy by race and gender. *Journal of Marital and Family Therapy, 22,* 239–251.

Hanson, W. E., Claiborn, C. D., & Kerr, B. (1997). Differential effects of two test-interpretation styles in counseling: A field study. *Journal of Counseling Psychology, 44,* 400–405.

Hardy, G. E., Stiles, W. B., Barkham, M., & Startup, M. (1998). Therapist responsiveness to client interpersonal styles during time-limited treatments for depression. *Journal of Consulting and Clinical Psychology, 66,* 304–312.

Heatherington, L., & Friedlander, M. L. (1990). Couple and Family Therapy Alliance Scales: Empirical considerations. *Journal of Marital and Family Therapy, 16,* 299–306.

Heaton, K. J., Hill, C. E., Petersen, D. A., Rochlen, A. B., & Zack, J. S. (1998). A comparison of therapist-facilitated and self-guided dream interpretation sessions. *Journal of Counseling Psychology, 45,* 115–122.

Herman, S. M. (1997). Therapist–client similarity on the multimodal structural profile inventory as a predictor of early session impact. *Journal of Psychotherapy Practice and Research, 6,* 139–144.

Hill, A. L., & Spokane, A. R. (1995). Career counseling and possible selves: A case study. *Career Development Quarterly, 43,* 221–232.

Hill, C. E., Helms, J. E., Spiegel, S. B., & Tichenor, V. (1988). Development of a system for categorizing client reactions to therapist interventions. *Journal of Counseling Psychology, 35,* 27–36.

Hill, C. E., Helms, J. E., Tichenor, V., Spiegel, S. B., O'Grady, K. E., & Perry, E. S. (1988). Effects of therapist response modes in brief psychotherapy. *Journal of Counseling Psychology, 35,* 222–233.

Hill, C. E., O'Grady, K. E., Balenger, V., Busse, W., Falk, D. R., Hill, M., Rios, M., & Taffe, R. (1994). Methodological examination of videotape-assisted reviews in brief therapy: Helplessness ratings, therapist intentions, client reactions, mood, and session evaluation. *Journal of Counseling Psychology, 41,* 236–247.

Horvath, A. O., & Marx, R. W. (1990). The development and decay of the working alliance during time-limited counseling. *Canadian Journal of Counseling, 24,* 240–259.

Horvath, A. O., & Symonds, B. D. (1991). Relation between working alliance and outcome in psychotherapy: A meta-analysis. *Journal of Counseling Psychology, 38,* 139–149.

Jordan, K., & Quinn, W. H. (1994). Session two outcome of the formula first session task in problem- and solution-focused approaches. *American Journal of Family Therapy, 22,* 3–16.

Jordan, K. B., & Quinn, W. H. (1997). Male and female client perception of session two outcome of the problem- and solution-focused approaches. *Family Therapy, 24,* 25–37.

Kelly, K. R., Hall, A. S., & Miller, K. L. (1989). Relation of counselor intention and anxiety to brief counseling outcome. *Journal of Counseling Psychology, 36,* 158–162.

Kivlighan, D. M., Jr. (1989). Changes in counselor intentions and response modes and in session evaluations after training. *Journal of Counseling Psychology, 36,* 471–476.

Kivlighan, D. M., Jr., & Angelone, E. O. (1991). Helpee introversion, novice counselor intention use, and helpee-rated session impact. *Journal of Counseling Psychology, 38,* 25–29.

Kivlighan, D. M., Jr., Angelone, E. O., & Swafford, K. G. (1991). Live supervision in individual psychotherapy: Effects on therapist's intention use and client's evaluation of session effect and working alliance. *Professional Psychology: Research and Practice, 22,* 489–495.

Larsen, R. J., & Diener, E. (1992). Promises and problems with the circumplex model of emotion. In M. Clark (Ed.), *Emotion (Review of personality and social psychology, Vol. 13,* pp. 25–59). Thousand Oaks, CA: Sage.

Lecompte, C., & Tremblay, L. (Trans.). (1983). *Questionnaire d'évaluation d'entrevue* [Session Evaluation Questionnaire]. Départment de Psychologie, Université de Montréal, Montréal, Québec, Canada.

Lin, M. -J. (Trans.). (1999). *SEQ in Chinese.* Counseling Center, National Hualien Teachers College, Hualien, Taiwan.

Mallinckrodt, B. (1993). Session impact, working alliance, and treatment outcome in brief counseling. *Journal of Counseling Psychology, 40,* 25–32.

Mallinckrodt, B. (1994). Session impact in counseling process research: Comment on Elliott and Wexler (1994) and Stiles et al. (1994). *Journal of Counseling Psychology, 41,* 186–190.

McLennan, J., Twigg, K., & Bezant, B. (1993). Therapist construct systems in use during psychotherapy interviews. *Journal of Clinical Psychology, 49,* 543–550.

Millar, R., & Brotherton, C. (1996). Measuring the effects of career interviews on young people: A preliminary study. *Psychological Reports, 79,* 1207–1215.

Nestoros, J. N., & Zgantzouri, K. (1999, August). The Greek version of the Session Evaluation Questionnaire. Paper presented at the fifth European Conference on Psychological Assessment, University of Patras, Greece.

Nocita, A., & Stiles, W. B. (1986). Client introversion and counseling session impact. *Journal of Counseling Psychology, 33,* 235–241.

Norman, W. T. (1967). On estimating psychological relationships: Social desirability and self-report. *Psychological Bulletin, 67,* 273–293.

Orlinsky, D. E., Grawe, K., & Parks, B. K. (1994). Process and outcome in psychotherapy—Noch einmal. In A. E. Bergin & S. L. Garfield (Eds.), *Handbook of psychotherapy and behavior change* (4th ed., pp. 270–376). New York: Wiley.

Orlinsky, D. E., & Howard, K. I. (1975). *Varieties of psychotherapeutic experience: Multivariate analyses of patients' and therapists' reports.* New York: Teachers College Press.

Orlinsky, D. E., & Howard, K. I. (1977). The therapist's experience of psychotherapy. In A. S. Gurman & A. M. Razin (Eds.), *Effective psychotherapy: A handbook of research* (pp. 566–590). Oxford: Pergamon Press.

Orlinsky, D. E., & Howard, K. I. (1986). The psychological interior of psychotherapy: Explorations with the Therapy Session Reports. In L. S. Greenberg & W. M. Pinsof (Eds.), *The psychotherapeutic process: A research handbook* (pp. 477–501). New York: Guilford Press.

Raue, P. J., Goldfried, M. R., & Barkham, M. (1997). The therapeutic alliance in psychodynamic-interpersonal and cognitive-behavioral therapy. *Journal of Consulting and Clinical Psychology, 65,* 582–587.

Regan, A. M., & Hill, C. E. (1992). Investigation of what clients and counselors do not say in brief therapy. *Journal of Counseling Psychology, 39,* 168–174.

Reisenzein, R. (1994). Pleasure-Arousal Theory and the intensity of emotions. *Journal of Personality and Social Psychology, 67,* 525–539.

Reynolds, S., Stiles, W. B., Barkham, M., Shapiro, D. A., Hardy, G. E., & Rees, A. (1996). Acceleration of changes in session impact during contrasting time-limited psychotherapies. *Journal of Consulting and Clinical Psychology, 64,* 577–586.

Reynolds, S., Taylor, E., & Shapiro, D. A. (1993). Session impact in stress management training. *Journal of Occupational and Organizational Psychology, 66,* 99–113.

Rogers, C. R. (1951). *Client-centered therapy.* Boston: Houghton-Mifflin.

Rogers, C. R. (1959). A theory of therapy, personality, and interpersonal relationships as developed by the client-centered framework. In S. Koch (Ed.), *Psychology: A study of a science: Volume III. Formulations of a person and the social context* (pp. 184–256). New York: McGraw-Hill.

Russell, J. A. (1978). Evidence of convergent validity on dimensions of affect. *Journal of Personality and Social Psychology, 36,* 1152–1168.

Russell, J. A. (1979). Affective space is bipolar. *Journal of Personality and Social Psychology, 37,* 345–356.

Samstag, L. W., Batchelder, S. T., Muran, J. C., Safran, J. D., & Winston, A. (1998). Early identification of treatment failures in short-term psychotherapy: An assessment of therapeutic alliance and interpersonal behavior. *Journal of Psychotherapy Practice and Research, 7,* 126–143.

Sells, J. N., & Hays, K. A. (1997). A comparison of time-limited and brief time-limited group therapy at termination. *Journal of College Student Development, 38,* 136–142.

Skinner, B. F. (1953). *Science and human behavior.* New York: Macmillan.

Stiles, W. B. (1980). Measurement of the impact of psychotherapy sessions. *Journal of Consulting and Clinical Psychology, 48,* 176–185.

Stiles, W. B. (1984). Client disclosure and psychotherapy session evaluations. *British Journal of Clinical Psychology, 23,* 311–312.

Stiles, W. B., Honos-Webb, L., & Surko, M. (1998). Responsiveness in psychotherapy. *Clinical Psychology: Science and Practice, 5,* 539–558.

Stiles, W. B., Reynolds, S., Hardy, G. E., Rees, A., Barkham, M., & Shapiro, D. A. (1994). Evaluation and description of psychotherapy sessions by clients using the Session Evaluation Questionnaire and the Session Impacts Scale. *Journal of Counseling Psychology, 41,* 175–185.

Stiles, W. B., Shankland, M. C., Wright, J., & Field, S. D. (1997). Dimensions of clients' initial presentation of problems in psychotherapy: The Early Assimilation Research Scale. *Psychotherapy Research, 7,* 155–171.

Stiles, W. B., Shapiro, D. A., & Firth-Cozens, J. A. (1988). Do sessions of different treatments have different impacts? *Journal of Counseling Psychology, 35,* 391–396.

Stiles, W. B., Shapiro, D. A., & Firth-Cozens, J. A. (1990). Correlations of session evaluations with treatment outcome. *British Journal of Clinical Psychology, 29,* 13–21.

Stiles, W. B., & Snow, J. S. (1984a). Counseling session impact as viewed by novice counselors and their clients. *Journal of Counseling Psychology, 31,* 3–12.

Stiles, W. B., & Snow, J. S. (1984b). Dimensions of psychotherapy session impact across sessions and across clients. *British Journal of Clinical Psychology, 23,* 59–63.

Stiles, W. B., Tupler, L. A., & Carpenter, J. C. (1982). Participants' perceptions of self-analytic group sessions. *Small Group Behavior, 13,* 237–254.

Sumerel, M. B., & Borders, L. D. (1996). Addressing personal issues in supervision: Impact of counselors' experience level on various aspects of the supervisory relationship. *Counselor Education and Supervision, 35,* 268–286.

Thompson, B. J., & Hill, C. E. (1993). Client perceptions of therapist competence. *Psychotherapy Research, 3,* 124–130.

Tryon, G. S. (1990). Session depth and smoothness in relation to the concept of engagement in counseling. *Journal of Counseling Psychology, 37,* 248–253.

Wanigaratne, S., & Barker, C. (1995). Clients' preferences for styles of therapy. *British Journal of Clinical Psychology, 34,* 215–222.

Zajonc, R. B. (1980). Feeling and thinking: Preferences need no inferences. *American Psychologist, 35,* 151–175.

The Termination of Psychotherapy

What Research Tells Us About the Process of Ending Treatment

Charles J. Gelso and Susan S. Woodhouse

University of Maryland

All therapy must end, but surprisingly little attention has been given to termination in the research literature. This chapter summarizes the extant research and offers suggestions to therapists of all orientations about how to terminate with clients. As a stage of counseling, termination requires the same careful attention to good practice as any other aspect of therapy. How client and therapist end their relationship may influence how the client continues or does not continue to apply the lessons learned in therapy. The way termination is handled may also influence the client's feelings about reentering therapy in the future.

Chapter Questions

- What typically happens during therapy termination?
- How do client and therapist react to termination?
- What client, therapist, and treatment factors influence termination?
- How and by whom is termination initiated?

Life may be thought of as an ongoing series of hellos and good-byes, of beginnings and endings. It "begins with our first hello at birth and ends with our last good-bye at death" (Goodyear, 1981. p. 349). Psychologists naturally have empirically investigated these beginnings and endings of life, but they have devoted a great deal more energy to the former. In fact, the experience of ending life was essentially ignored by researchers until Kübler-Ross's (1967) groundbreaking conception. Still, for a variety of reasons, the study of the beginnings of life continues to be much more vigorously pursued than that of life's ending. One reason is that we may find it more personally agreeable, even uplifting, to study hellos or beginnings than to investigate endings.

Psychotherapy, too, has a beginning and an ending. And researchers have devoted a great deal of time to studying the beginning of counseling, while neglecting its ending phase. In fact, most of the articles on termination begin by discussing how infrequently the process is addressed. This is so despite the fact that there appears to be agreement among observers that termination is a highly significant topic and that how termination is handled by the therapist probably affects the entire treatment, including the gains made by the client. Effectively handled termination, it is often maintained, can consolidate gains as well as help clients work through issues (some universal) concerning endings. Conversely, mishandled terminations (which includes ignoring the process) may sabotage the gains that emerge during therapy and deepen clients' conflicts about endings.

If there is relatively little theoretical work on the termination process, there is even less empirical research. The likely culprit for the meager amount of research is the great complexity of termination. Literally, termination includes everything in treatment that has preceded it. To this, one may add the complexity of how the so-called termination phase of counseling is defined. It is difficult to ascertain what is meant by a termination phase and what the boundaries of this phase are. Another reason for the lack of empirical attention to termination is because, just as with studying the ending of life, investigating the ending of the treatment relationship is emotionally conflictual and is likely to emote issues around separations and endings in the researcher. Endings of relationships are more difficult for most of us to examine than are beginnings.

Although the empirical neglect of the topic of therapy termination continues to this day, there has been a gradual accretion of research during the past two decades. Qualitative and quantitative studies have been conducted that examine the characteristics of the termination phase, client and therapist reactions to ending, and qualities within the participants that influence how they deal with and react to termination. This small body of research is clearly in its infancy, but enough findings have accumulated to offer some provisional guidance to the practitioner.

In this chapter, we review selectively the empirical work on the process of termination in counseling, psychotherapy, and psychoanalysis. Our aim is to educe how the research can help guide clinical practice with respect to termination of individual therapy, both brief and long term. The terms *counseling* and *therapy* are used interchangeably, whereas the term *psychoanalysis* is used in the traditional sense (e.g., meeting several times a week over a period of several years [see Gelso & Fretz, 1992, chapter 7]). In preparing for this review, we read all the empirical research that has been published in refereed journals in psychology, psychiatry, and social work. We focus on the research studies that have the greatest implications for counseling practice.

Our emphasis is on the process of termination, regardless of whether the ending is brought about by the client, the therapist, or both (mutual termination). The primary questions we address are

1. What transpires during the termination phase of counseling?
2. How is termination dealt with and reacted to by therapist and client?

3. What client, counselor, and treatment factors influence termination behavior and reactions?
4. How do we know when to bring therapy to an end?

In addressing these questions, we focus on termination as a distinctive and identifiable phase, stage, or part of counseling. It should be noted at the outset that we do not examine the issues of premature, early, or unilateral termination when the therapy
participants have never involved themselves in the counseling process to begin with (e.g.,
when the client drops out after one or two sessions) or have terminated abruptly and unilaterally without a termination phase, even after what may have been a considerable time in
treatment.

The working definition of termination that will guide this review is simply *the per-
manent or temporary ending of counseling.* We define a termination phase as *the last phase
of counseling, during which therapist and client consciously or unconsciously work toward
bringing treatment to an end.* This phase may be entered regardless of whether a termination date has been set. Usually, it is initiated by one or both of the participants suggesting
the idea of ending, an ending date, or, at a more subtle and less explicit level, experiencing
a growing awareness that termination is near. In treatment situations where a duration limit
is established at the beginning, the termination phase is that portion of counseling in which
one or both of the participants believes that the end is approaching and that termination
issues must be addressed. For example, if the counseling occurs at an agency that requires
an eight-session duration limit, the counselor or client may want to examine the process of
ending at, say, the seventh session. The point at which the participants feel moved to explore termination will vary, depending on the client's needs and, to an extent, the therapist's inclinations.

The time devoted to the termination phase, as implied in the preceding paragraph,
will vary widely, depending on treatment, client, and therapist considerations. In Mann's
(1973) 12-session, time-limited psychotherapy, for example, the last three sessions are
suggested as the termination phase. In counseling that lasts only a few sessions, the termination phase may be the last session, whereas in long-term therapy, this phase may encompass a two- or three-month period (e.g., Langs, 1974). As long-term therapy gets longer,
the termination phase may extend. For example, in psychoanalytically oriented therapy
lasting several years, the first author sets a termination date with his clients six months to a
year in advance, and the time between setting the data and the actual ending becomes the
termination phase. Similarly, in very long cases of psychoanalysis, the termination phase
may cover two years of work (Firestein, 1978).

Some therapists suggest that a certain proportion of the therapy be devoted to the termination phase. For example, Shulman (1979) suggests as a rule of thumb, that termination should constitute one-sixth of the treatment. Mann (1973) suggests that one-fourth of
his time-limited therapy constitute the termination phase.

We begin our review by examining the research on the process of termination. Who
usually initiates termination? What therapist and client behaviors are typical of the ending
phase? How do the participants react to ending? Is there a predictable process to the ending
phase? We examine the research that deals with these questions.

The Process of Termination

Who Initiates Termination?

In the time-limited therapy practiced at many agencies, the duration limit is established by the agency and is applied to all or most clients. The common practice is for the counselor to inform the client of the limit (either in the form of a date, a session number, or both) during the intake session or the first therapy session (e.g., Gelso & Johnson, 1983). However, this is not always the case. In a disquieting, qualitative study of 10 social work students who ended therapy because they were completing their placements, Gould (1978) found that only five of these therapists told their patients within the first few sessions when they would be leaving. Other therapist–trainees did not mention impending departure until four to seven weeks before the last session of therapy that usually lasted for nearly a year. These student practitioners were usually following guidance from their supervisors, who worried that telling patients of the ending date early in the work would impede their emotional involvement.

There are essentially no data on who initiates termination in brief therapy that is not time limited. Our clinically based impression is that the client and therapist are equally likely to do so. The few studies (see below) that address the question of who initiates termination suggest that the more extended the treatment, the more likely it is that the therapist will wait for the client to initiate the topic. Typically, once the client brings up the topic, the therapist will follow the client's lead if the therapist believes that the topic is being broached for the right reasons, for example, not as a defensive reaction by the client (Firestein, 1978; Fortune, Pearlingi, & Rochelle, 1992; Kramer, 1986). At times, though, therapists do bring up the topic first, for example, when therapists feel clients are avoiding ending or when additional gains are not expected (Firestein, 1978; Fortune et al., 1992; Kramer, 1986).

What Transpires During the Termination Phase?

The research evidence suggests that counselors typically do devote some session time to termination and address termination issues in a range of ways. In studies of short-term therapy (averaging about 10 sessions) at university counseling centers, both clients' reports (Marx & Gelso, 1987) and counselors' reports (Quintana & Holahan, 1992) indicate that time is devoted to this topic and that both client and counselor engaged in a range of behaviors.

Just how much time and how many sessions are devoted to termination issues has been rarely researched. Mann (1973) proposed that approximately the last quarter of his 12-session, time-limited psychotherapy should be focused on termination issues. In a study at a counseling center that relied heavily on Mann's conceptualization, however, it was found that issues of termination were raised during an average of only 1.3 sessions in therapy with a 12-session limit (Miller et al., 1983). It is not clear just how much time was devoted to termination issues during these sessions. Assuming that the clients in this study averaged 11 sessions (an unspecified number had between 8 and 12 sessions), the average percentage of sessions in which termination was discussed would be 11.8%. Interestingly, this is nearly identical to the 11.6% reported by de Bosset and Styrsky (1986) in their study of therapy conducted by psychiatric residents where "natural" rather than "forced" (e.g., because of residents' departures) terminations occurred, and the average duration of treatment was close to 50 sessions. Thus, in therapy that is brief as well as moderate, it appears that the time devoted to termination is considerably less than that suggested in Mann's theory but closer to the one-sixth rule of thumb suggested by Shulman (1979). Is the amount of time and effort that is customarily devoted to termination sufficient? We shall have more to say about that subsequently.

Two studies conducted at university counseling centers offer a picture of what typically transpires during the termination phase of brief therapy (generally 5 to 15 sessions). Marx and Gelso (1987) surveyed clients seen at one center, whereas Quintana and Holahan (1992) asked counselors from 31 different centers about the termination process with two clients with whom they had recently terminated (one successful and one unsuccessful case). Table 12.1 presents figures adapted from these two studies. It gives the frequencies and percentages of clients (Marx & Gelso, 1987) and counselors (Quintana & Holahan, 1992) who indicated that each termination behavior occurred during the termination process. Note that the figures in the Quintana and Holahan study are only those for the cases judged to be successful by the counselors. (These should provide the most comparable data to Marx and Gelso.)

As may be seen in the table, there is considerable agreement on what transpires during the termination phase, and the data are very similar to what is often suggested in the clinical literature (e.g., Lamb, 1985; Pinkerton & Rockwell, 1990; Ward, 1984). Typically, a final date is set by one or both participants and the work is summarized, including the extent to which goals have been accomplished. The client shares what he or she has liked about counseling, and, to a lesser extent, what he or she has disliked. Client and therapist examine the client's plans for the future, which, based on clinical experience, we assume includes the conflicts and problems that remain unresolved. The counselor typically invites the client to return if and when the client feels the need.

Finally, during this phase the counselor and client seek to bring closure to their relationship. Both share feelings about the work and its ending. The client thanks the counselor, they shake hands or hug, and the client departs.

Although there is great similarity between client and counselor reports of what happens during termination (Quintana & Holahan, 1992, report a .90 correlation between their rankings of counselor reports with Marx and Gelso's rankings of client reports), there is surely not total agreement. For example, therapists are more than twice as likely as clients to believe that therapists share more of their own reactions with their clients during termination. Conversely, clients are more likely than therapists to believe that clients ask therapists personal questions about their lives and that the two participants relate more as equals during this phase than others.

As we have noted, the data reported for the Quintana and Holahan (1992) study are for a successful client of each of the therapists. When the therapists made the same ratings of clients whose treatment was not deemed as successful, it was found that in the unsuccessful cases there was less often a review of the course of counseling, an attempt to bring closure to the relationship, and an examination of the clients' feelings about ending. Perhaps reflecting their anxiety, counselors with the unsuccessful cases were tremendously less likely than with successful cases (5% versus 68%, respectively) to self-disclose during

TABLE 12.1 *Number and Percentage of Clients (Marx & Gelso, 1987) and Counselors (Quintana & Holahan, 1992) Checking Each Item*

Termination Component/Item	Clients (n = 72)		Counselors (n = 85)	
	No.	%	No.	%
Ending Procedures				
Final date was set	50	69	52	61
Frequency of sessions tapered off	13	18	27	32
Review of Counseling and Goal Attainment				
Counselor/client summarized work	52	72	76	89
Assessed extent to which goals were attained	51	72	77	91
Clients stated things liked about counseling	—	—	65	76
Client stated things disliked about counseling	—	—	26	31
Client stated things liked *and* disliked	39	54	—	—
Client asked about how counseling works	13	18	12	14
Discussion of Plans for Future				
Discussed client's plans for future	51	71	76	89
Counselor invited client to return	48	67	64	75
Counselor suggested other help	34	47	47	55
Closure in Client–Counselor Relationship				
Client thanked counselor	58	81	79	93
Counselor shared feelings about therapy	51	71	69	81
Client shared feelings about ending	49	68	66	78
Counselor/client shook hands or hugged	40	56	56	66
Counselor talked more about self	22	31	58	68
Counselor and client related like equals	35	49	28	33
Client asked counselor personal questions	29	40	14	16
Client gave gifts	9	13	3	4

Note: The Counselor column includes counselors responses only in reference to a successful case.

termination. Unsuccessful clients, too, were much less likely to share their feelings about ending (42% versus 78%). These clients in comparison to the successful cases, however, were more likely (51% versus 31%) to share what they disliked about counseling. They did not express appreciation to the counselor as often (i.e, a smaller percentage thanked the counselor—54% versus 93%). It is noteworthy, though, that counselors focused on future planning with nearly all cases, and they did so equally with those they viewed as successful and unsuccessful. We shall have more to say about the relation of treatment success to termination behaviors and reactions when we discuss therapist variables.

In sum, there does appear to be a measurable set of what we would call "termination behaviors" that predictably occur during the termination phase of counseling. The participants typically look back on what has been accomplished, look forward to what is yet to be accomplished and to the client's plans, share feelings about the work and the relationship, and do the work of saying good-bye, while at the same time leaving the door open for future counseling. When cases are seen by the counselor as unsuccessful, though, fewer of the desired termination behaviors seem to occur, although in the majority of the cases, the work is still summarized, goal attainment is assessed, and plans for the future are discussed.

How do clients feel about this termination work? In the Marx and Gelso (1987) study, most felt it was important for them to discuss their reactions to ending (e.g., 69% rated doing so as either "important" or "very important"), and about two-thirds were satisfied or very satisfied with this ending phase. Thus, even in brief counseling (e.g., 10 sessions), it is important to most clients that there be an ending phase in which counselor and client do the work of termination, and, in fact, most clients feel satisfied with how this was handled. It should be noted that these findings about client importance and satisfaction ratings regarding termination have been replicated in a quantitative study of therapists' importance and satisfaction ratings conducted at one counseling center (Martinez, 1986). Interestingly, in a study of group therapy, it was found that clients who received a pretherapy handout discussing the termination process and how to best handle it felt more resolved after termination than did clients who received no such information (Corazzini, Heppner, & Young, 1980). Later we explore counselor and client factors that mediate how effectively termination is handled and how satisfied the participants are with termination.

How Do Clients and Therapists React to Ending Treatment?

Prior to the 1980s, the literature on termination largely stemmed from psychoanalysis and long-term analytic therapy, and empirical research was almost nonexistent. Perhaps because of the very long term, uncovering nature of the treatment on which clinical speculation was based, termination was seen as a "difficult and perilous period darkened by inevitable loss and mourning" (Fortune et al., 1992, p. 171). Ending was viewed as a largely painful experience in which a range of negative states and defensive processes predominated. Kauff (1977), for example, commented that "the effects most commonly associated with termination seem to span a short, bleak continuum that ranges from sad to downright morbid" (p. 4). As Quintana (1993) notes, this "termination as loss" (p. 426) model that predominated in psychoanalysis and long-term analytic therapy was also adopted in some conceptions of brief and time-limited therapy (e.g., Bauer & Kobos, 1987; Mann, 1973; Strupp & Binder, 1984).

At the same time, not all clinicians have shared this termination-as-loss viewpoint. Psychoanalytic therapists, such as Malan (1976), Davanloo (1980), and Sifneos (1992), note that in brief analytic therapy, termination is rarely experienced as a painful loss experience. Although patients will naturally experience some sadness and subsequently express feelings of missing their therapists, feelings about ending are much more positive than what is implied in the termination-as-loss model. This applies even to patients for whom loss and unresolved grief reactions have been a central issue, although such patients will need a few extra sessions to deal with ending issues. Similarly, nonanalytic therapists who practice brief therapy do not focus a great deal on termination, and they certainly do not subscribe to the termination-as-loss model (e.g., Budman & Gurman, 1988; Garfield, 1989).

What does the research tell us about the termination process? Is the process as pervaded by painful affects as the termination-as-loss literature suggests? Are there more positive affects associated with this process than has been implied? Are the positive affects little more than defenses against facing painful separation and loss issues?

Studies of therapies of varying durations suggest a far more positive picture than one would suspect based on the termination-as-loss model. For example, the studies of brief therapy by Marx and Gelso (1987) and Quintana and Holahan (1992) indicate that among clients at university counseling centers, positive feelings during and about termination far outweigh more painful, negative, or defensive reactions. This experience of predominantly positive reactions has also been documented in studies on moderate-length therapy (e.g., 37 sessions) conducted in agencies and private practice (Fortune, 1987; Fortune et al., 1992). It is instructive to look at some of the data from these studies.

Marx and Gelso (1987) found that the following adjectives were checked by half or more of their former clients regarding their feelings about ending counseling: cooperative, calm, alive, agreeable, friendly, good, healthy, thoughtful, and satisfied. Conversely, items checked by fewer than 3% of the respondents included destroyed, miserable, sunk, forlorn, terrible, tormented, bitter, cruel, disagreeable, enraged, furious, irritated, mean, stormy, hostile, incensed, indignant, jealous, and rough. On the whole these former clients checked more than three times as many positive adjectives as negative when describing their feelings about ending. There were almost no indications of depressed or hostile feelings in these participants' responses. Similarly, Quintana and Holahan's (1992) counselors, when responding in terms of successful clients' reactions to termination, typically noted the expression of feeling healthy (79%), proud (68%), and calm (59%). Many fewer clients expressed feelings of concern (26%), frustration (13%), or fear (21%).

In the qualitative research of Fortune and her colleagues (Fortune, 1987; Fortune et al., 1992), the most positive client reactions during termination, according to their therapists, were evaluation of progress and success in treatment; and feelings of pride, self-accomplishment, and independence. According to Fortune (1987), "the client's reexperiencing of losses, often considered inevitable and an important therapeutic process, was relatively infrequent" (p. 164). Fortune's therapists, too, experienced largely positive reactions during termination (i.e., the period shortly before actual ending). The most common reactions were pride in the client's successes and in the therapist's therapeutic skill. The least common reactions were reexperiencing previous losses, doubt about therapeutic skill, disappointment in the client, and relief. It is noteworthy that even when counselors were asked to respond to a grief questionnaire about the termination during the last year that resulted in the most intense feelings of loss (Swords, 1985), the grief response was only mild, and not disruptive of the therapists' lives.

Although positive feelings predominate during the termination phase in both therapists and clients, it would be a mistake to conclude that termination is a totally uplifting, rosy experience. It is not, and both therapist and client responses reveal this. In successful work, there is naturally some degree of sadness about ending a good experience and a good relationship. For example, more than half of Fortune's (1987) therapists mentioned feelings of sadness and loss in half or more of their terminated cases. Marx and Gelso (1987) also note that a substantial minority of former clients checked items such as afraid (38%), alone (32%), nervous (31%), and shaky (25%) to describe their feelings about ending counseling. In putting these two studies together, it appears that some degree of anxiety and sadness about ending is fairly common on the client's part, and therapists often feel some sadness, too.

One additional finding from Marx and Gelso (1987) deserves note. Recall that the counseling they studied was brief (10 sessions). This raised the question of whether the preponderantly positive reactions they observed were because of the brevity of the work and the lesser degree of emotional attachment that occurs in brief as compared to longer work. To address this question, Marx and Gelso correlated the number of sessions clients reported with the number of negative adjectives (revolving around anxiety, depression, and hostility) these clients checked. The correlation ($r = .35$, $p < .01$), although modest, does indicate that as therapy is extended, negative affective reactions may slightly increase. The longer therapy studied by Fortune and her colleagues (1987; Fortune et al., 1992), however, does not bespeak anything like a preponderance of negative reactions. Instead, because the longer-term work probably entails deeper attachments between the participants, clients are more likely to experience higher degrees of sadness and anxiety about ending their work, along with a preponderance of positive reactions and the range of such feelings as we have described.

Finally, note that much of the information in this section applies to clients who terminated successful treatment. The picture may be quite different when treatment is unsuccessful. For example, Quintana and Holahan (1992) found that counselors, when rating termination reactions of unsuccessful cases, reported very few expressions of health, pride, or calmness by these clients during termination. Yet, few (less than 20%) expressed negative reactions about the termination, although a greater percentage of these unsuccessful cases than successful cases (34% versus 13%, $p < .05$) did express feelings of frustration regarding the ending of their work.

We have examined the process of termination—what occurs during the termination phase and how clients and therapists react to the ending of treatment. Apart from considerations of treatment length and whether therapy is successful, termination has been discussed as if the process is the same for everyone. Nothing could be further from the truth, however, as client and therapist factors weigh heavily in how termination is conducted and the ways in which the participants react to the ending of treatment. In the following sections, we examine the research literature on how client, therapist, and treatment factors affect the termination equation.

Client Factors That Affect Termination

Much more is known about therapist factors that affect the process of termination than is known about client factors. Nevertheless, research does suggest that client diagnoses, client issues concerning loss, and client gender have some bearing on how termination unfolds and how clients and their therapists respond to the ending of therapy.

First, we consider how client diagnosis may be an important factor in termination. It is clear from the qualitative studies of brief psychoanalytic therapy (Malan, 1979) and psychoanalysis (Firestein, 1978) that individual differences among clients in terms of dynamics and life situations are enormously important in the events and meanings of termination—how the client feels, the underlying issues that emerge, and the attention that must be devoted to the termination process. Similarly, as Malan notes, the main themes of therapy are most likely to reflect the main themes of termination.

Many clinicians have special concerns about termination with clients who have borderline personality dynamics because of their affective and behavioral instability and because frequently such clients are eager to avoid real or imagined abandonments. Sansone, Fine, and Dennis (1991) surveyed therapists who treat clients who show borderline personality dynamics. Sansone et al. wanted to learn more about therapists' termination experiences with this population. In setting goals to achieve prior to termination, therapists in this study reported that 76% work toward character change but do not expect "normality," whereas 13% only work to stabilize self-destructive behaviors. Eleven percent work toward "normality."

Sansone et al. (1991) found that therapists of clients with borderline personality dynamics had the same concerns as other therapists about termination: Has the client had successfully completed treatment? Most therapists were worried about clients regressing to previous levels of functioning, acting out, and behaving in a self-destructive manner. Unfortunately, the most frequently cited reasons for termination in this sample were "patient does not see the purpose of treatment" and "patient terminates through acting out behaviors" (p. 176). Fair and Bressler (1992) found in their sample of 33 trainees that for therapists of clients with certain personality disorders (e.g., borderline personality disorder and narcissistic personality disorder), termination planning was less thorough than for therapists of clients with less severe diagnoses (e.g., dysthymic disorder, generalized anxiety disorder, and adjustment disorders). Thus, therapists may tend to find termination difficult with clients with certain personality disorders.

Research has also shown that client issues about loss have an important influence on termination. Client issues about loss can make the loss of the relationship with the therapist more complex and require that therapists spend more time processing the termination. Marx and Gelso (1987) found that loss as a theme in counseling and a history of losses were the best predictors of clients' ratings of the importance of discussing reactions to termination. Clients will tend to want to explore termination more when they have a history of losses, or when loss has been important in the therapy.

However, Marx and Gelso (1987) found that loss as a theme in counseling and loss history were unrelated to clients' satisfaction with termination. The sole predictor of clients' satisfaction with termination was the amount of termination work done in the therapy. This finding is particularly interesting in light of the fact that Martinez (1986) found that the degree of termination work strongly predicted therapists' satisfaction with termination. Thus, both clients and therapists (particularly therapists) tend to be more satisfied with termination when more time is spent on the termination process. Neither clients' history of loss nor the degree to which loss is a theme in counseling, however, affect clients' satisfaction with termination. They merely influence the degree to which clients feel it is important to process reactions to termination.

A third, and final, client factor that has received some attention in the research on termination is client gender. Although client gender per se may be unrelated to either client or therapist reactions to termination (Fortune et al., 1992), certain psychological aspects of gender may, indeed, be related. Paster (1983) found that clients with an undifferentiated sex-role orientation, both male and female, appeared to show the highest degrees of anxiety, depression, and hostility in response to termination, as compared to clients with either male sex-typed or female sex-typed role orientation. It may be that clients with an undifferentiated sex-role orientation experience greater conflicts, which in some way make termination a more difficult experience for them. There is no evidence, however, that male or female clients respond to termination differently from one another.

Therapist Factors That Affect Termination

Research on therapist factors that affect termination reveals a number of important areas. First we consider therapists' personal factors. For example, therapists' issues concerning loss and separation show an important relation to therapists' affective reactions to termination. Additionally, aspects of therapists' personalities and therapists' experiences in their own personal therapy may also affect how therapists end treatment with their clients.

Second, we examine whether the therapist's theoretical orientation may be related to differences in termination. Next, we highlight research findings that show that therapists' beliefs and perceptiveness about clients' issues of loss are importantly related to the work of termination, as well as to therapists' reactions to ending therapy with particular clients. Perceptions of treatment outcome are the fourth factor to be explored. Perceptions of treatment outcome have been found to be related to client reactions, therapist termination behavior patterns, therapist affective reactions, the degree to which termination is discussed, and therapist ratings of satisfaction with termination.

Finally, the complexities of the relation between therapist gender and termination is examined. Although no relation has been found between therapist gender per se and termination, sex-role-related behavior and sex-role orientation in the therapist may be related to termination.

Therapist Personal Factors

Because much of the research in this section refers to therapists' affective reactions to termination, it is important to clarify the terminology that is used to refer to these therapist feelings, in particular therapist depression and therapist anxiety (Boyer & Hoffman, 1993; Greene, 1980; Martinez, 1986). An understanding of Greene's definitions of therapist depression and anxiety at termination may help therapists (and supervisors) to better monitor their own affective reactions to the ending of treatment and heighten awareness of the manifestations of anxiety and depression, given that these terms are not meant strictly in the clinical sense. *Depression,* as defined by Greene, reflects therapists' dysphoric reactions to termination and the degree to which the therapist withdraws from the client before the treatment is actually concluded. Signs of therapist depression at termination may include enjoying being with clients less, finding sessions less rewarding, experiencing sessions as passing more slowly, feeling less concentration on therapeutic tasks, or feeling the urge to withdraw emotionally. *Anxiety,* according to Greene, reflects therapists' experiences of termination as stormy and affectively intense. Although some of Greene's indicators of anxiety do not seem to be reasonable signs of therapists' anxiety about termination (e.g., experiencing more intimate moments of communication or feeling more emotionally involved), others do seem to have some value (e.g., thinking more about clients outside of sessions or feeling increasingly upset).

Therapists' issues concerning both separation and loss have been tied to therapists' affective responses to termination. Boyer and Hoffman (1993), in a study of licensed practicing psychologists, found a significant relation between therapist loss history and therapist anxiety and depression during termination. Relatedly, in a qualitative study, Parkerton (1987) found that analysts who were traumatically separated from their mothers during latency tended to struggle more with issues concerning termination and have a harder time after terminating with a client.

Boyer and Hoffman (1993), in studying the relation between therapists' history of loss and therapists' affective reactions during termination, examined both past grief reactions, that is, the degree to which life had been disrupted when the loss initially occurred, and present grief reactions. Present grief reactions concerned how much the individual's life was currently disrupted by reactions to the same (past) loss. Specifically, Boyer and Hoffman found that past and present grief reactions were related to therapist anxiety at termination. Only past grief reactions, however, were related to therapist depression at termination. These findings support the idea that countertransference seems to result when unresolved feelings about old losses are stimulated by the impending loss through termination.

It is important to note that it is not the number of losses per se that are significant in determining therapists' affective reactions to termination. Rather, it is the degree to which therapists have experienced disruptive grief reactions in response to those losses that is related to countertransference reactions of depression and anxiety when concluding therapy (Boyer & Hoffman, 1993). The number of losses a therapist has experienced, however, is related to the number of sessions a therapist spends working on termination, as well as on the number of termination behaviors the therapist tends to exhibit. It appears that when therapists have experienced numerous losses, they tend to believe in the need to work through termination more completely, perhaps because they have become more sensitized to loss issues (Martinez, 1986).

In addition to specific issues regarding loss, one study examined general therapist personality traits and how these influence the process of termination. Martinez (1986) explored how therapist interpersonal needs may moderate termination reactions. She found only the therapist's need for dominance to be an important moderator and not the need for affiliation or the need for nurturance. Therapists who have a greater need for dominance are less likely to shift to an egalitarian stance to bring closure to the therapy than therapists with a lower need for dominance.

Finally, therapists' experiences in their own personal therapies are likely to affect the way they handle termination with their clients. Parkerton (1987) and Porter (1987/1988) each found that therapists model their style of termination on the way their own therapists' managed their terminations. Alternatively, Parkerton found that therapists may attempt to adjust for what they felt their own therapist did wrong in handling their own terminations. Martinez (1986) found no significant differences among the terminations of therapists who had received treatment and those who had not undergone counseling of their own. However, among clinicians who had been in their own personal therapy, those who had been in therapy longer were more likely to shift toward an informal stance during termination.

Therapist Theoretical Orientation

The theoretical orientation of the therapist appears to have no relation either to therapist reactions to termination (Fortune, 1987; Fortune et al., 1992; Martinez, 1986; Swords, 1985) or to client reactions to termination (Fortune et al., 1992). However, Greene (1980) found that nonanalytic therapists in a hospital setting were more likely to have an open-door policy with their clients after termination than were analytic therapists, who tended to end treatment with greater finality. Analytically oriented therapists in this sample, in comparison to nonanalytically oriented therapists, tended to ascribe mostly positive affects to their clients during termination. Greene's findings concerning differences in termination behaviors and attributions of client affect based on differences in theoretical orientation, however, were not confirmed in a study of counseling center therapists (Martinez, 1986).

Therapist Beliefs About and Perceptiveness Regarding Loss Issues

A number of research studies have found that, unsurprisingly, therapists tend to become aware that loss may be an important issue for their clients when loss or separation are an important theme in therapy (Boyer & Hoffman, 1993, Gould, 1978; Marx & Gelso, 1987). Research has also shown that therapists tend to be aware that loss may be important to attend to with their clients during the ending phase of therapy when therapists perceive that clients are particularly sensitive to loss and, at the same time, lack the capacity to mourn. Additionally, data suggest that issues concerning loss should be explored when termination seems to be happening at an inopportune time with respect to other factors in their clients' lives, such as a move or a relationship ending (Boyer & Hoffman, 1993; Gould, 1978).

Research findings indicate that therapists tend to believe that termination will be difficult for clients whom they perceive to be sensitive to loss (Gould, 1978; Martinez, 1986; Marx & Gelso, 1987) and thus tend to spend more time discussing termination with such clients (Martinez, 1986; Marx & Gelso, 1987). Boyer and Hoffman (1993) found that therapists' perceptions of clients' sensitivity to loss were significantly related to therapist anxiety about termination. It makes sense that therapists notice strong feelings about loss that a client might have and that the therapist would feel anxious about termination with that client.

Therapist Perceptions of Treatment Outcome and the Quality of the Relationship

Therapists' perceptions of treatment outcome are significantly related to a number of termination variables, including client reactions, therapist termination behavior patterns, therapist affective reactions, the degree to which termination is discussed, and therapist ratings of satisfaction with termination. Earlier in the chapter, we discussed research findings that indicated that clients' reactions tend to differ depending on therapists' perceptions of treatment outcome. Clients who successfully completed therapy were more likely to express their own feelings about termination than clients who ended unsuccessful treatment, and the successful clients tended to experience more positive affect (Fortune et al., 1992; Quintana & Holahan, 1992). However, there are additional findings that add to an understanding of the relation between outcome and client reactions to termination. In unsuccessful cases, clients tended to frequently engage in problematic behaviors at termination, such as devaluing counseling, attacking the therapist, and missing sessions (Fortune et al., 1992; Quintana & Holahan, 1992). When therapists perceived treatment to be successful, however, clients tended to be able to make an appropriate shift to positive activities in their lives in place of therapy (Fortune et al., 1992).

We also described Quintana and Holahan's (1992) findings that suggest that the process of termination itself, particularly therapists' behavior patterns at termination, is related to how successful treatment is, as perceived by therapists. Quintana and Holahan found that therapists whose clients were finishing successful therapy tended to engage in a wider variety of helpful termination behaviors than did therapists whose clients were ending unsuccessful therapy.

We turn now to other findings that shed further light on the relation between outcome and therapists' management of and reactions toward termination. When therapists perceive treatment to be successful, they tend to have a positive affective reaction to termination and feel greater pride (Fortune, 1987; Fortune et al., 1992). They also tend to feel less doubt, both about their own work and their clients' progress, and to feel less relief about ending (Fortune et al., 1992). The more successful therapy is, the less likely therapists are to rate termination as difficult. Difficulty in termination is significantly associated with client negative affect, ambivalence, regression, and expression of a need for further treatment. Also, when there is a greater difficulty in termination, clinicians report feeling more sadness and reexperiencing previous losses. Of course, it is important to note that there is no way to know what the causal relationships between these factors are (Fortune et al., 1992).

The degree to which termination is discussed is related to therapists' perceptions of treatment outcome. As mentioned earlier, Quintana and Holahan (1992) found that therapists tended to discuss termination more in cases they judged to be successful than in cases deemed unsuccessful. Another variable that research has found to be related to the degree to which termination is discussed, however, is the client and therapist focus on the therapeutic relationship in general during the course of therapy. Thus, Martinez (1986) found that if client and therapist tended to discuss the therapeutic relationship to a greater degree, they also tended to discuss termination issues more as well.

Therapists' perceptions of the quality of the relationship between client and therapist were also correlated with therapists' self-disclosure about their own affective reactions to termination. Therapists who were more likely to self-disclose, were also more likely to feel close to their clients and like them (Martinez, 1986). Finally, therapists' ratings of satisfaction with termination related to their perceptions of the quality of the therapeutic relationship. Martinez found that perceived closeness with the client was the best moderator of therapist termination responses. For example, closeness with the client was positively correlated with satisfaction about how the work ended. Because closeness was also associated with therapist feelings of anxiety and emotionality about termination, these findings together imply that when the therapeutic relationship feels close, termination may feel more difficult for therapists in certain ways, but that it will be satisfying in the end. As mentioned earlier, Martinez found that therapists were more likely to be satisfied with the termination phase of therapy when more time was spent processing the termination with the client.

Therapist Gender and Termination

Therapist gender per se is not an important factor in predicting therapists' affective or behavioral reactions to termination (Fortune et al., 1992; Martinez, 1986; Swords, 1985). Greene (1980), however, explored how therapist sex might interact with theoretical orientation to result in differences in role shift during termination, anxiety about termination, or denial of termination issues. He found that analytically oriented males, analytically oriented females, and nonanalytically oriented males were not significantly different from each other in terms of the three termination variables. Nonanalytically oriented female therapists, however, reported more anxiety, a shift toward a more egalitarian therapeutic relationship, and showed less denial and behavioral rigidity compared to nonanalytically oriented male therapists, as well as analytically oriented therapists of both sexes. Greene thought that these findings might reflect a tendency for nonanalytical therapists to follow traditional sex-role prescriptions for more emotional expressiveness and availability in females, and less emotional expressiveness and availability in males. He suggested that the nonanalytical therapists might be substituting sex-roles for therapeutic roles. Further, Greene argued that the analytically oriented male and female therapists did not differ from one another, because their behavior was guided by psychoanalytical theory. Psychoanalytical theory may dictate a set of behaviors, including greater emotional restraint and neutrality, which could be seen as consistent with masculine sex-role norms.

Paster (1983) found that the sex-role orientation of the therapist is important in how clients experience therapy and in the emotions that clients express during termination. Clients of male sex-typed therapists were more hostile than clients of female sex-typed therapists, and hostility appeared to be the dominant emotion exhibited by the clients of male sex-typed therapists. Paster argued that masculine therapists may encourage the expression of affect by clients that is sex-role consonant for the therapist (i.e., hostility) but discourage others. However, it would appear just as likely that female sex-typed therapists tend to discourage client hostility, because such affect may not be consonant with the female sex-role. Further, sex-role orientation may distort either the emotions therapists see in or report about their clients. More research is needed to examine the process whereby clients of male sex-typed and female sex-typed therapists may come to have different affective experiences of termination.

Treatment Factors That Affect Termination

There are two main groupings of treatment factors that have received attention in the research on termination. The first group of treatment factors involves specific practices in the process of termination, whereas the second group of treatment factors centers around whether the termination was the planned end to a successful therapy or forced by outside circumstances.

Some Specific Termination Practices

Therapists vary in the termination practices they use. When therapy is not time-limited, therapists may vary in the termination criteria they select. Therapists may also differ with respect to whether and how clients are prepared for termination. Research has shown that most therapists include an invitation to the client to return to therapy if needed, and there are some data on how this is done and what clients do with this invitation. Finally, there are some data on who suggests termination and how this affects the termination process, as well as data on different styles therapists use to review progress at termination.

If therapy is not time-limited, knowing when to end treatment is of great importance. Bywaters's (1975) study may be somewhat dated since the advent of managed care and, consequently, the greater inclination to specify client goals for treatment. He found that most social workers did not have clearly delineated goals, however, and so were not able to make rational decisions about when to terminate with clients. Thus, personal bias and agency needs influenced termination too often. He argued for the importance of determining clear goals in the context of needing to ration care for a large number of potential clients.

Kramer (1986) surveyed therapists about the types of termination cues they tended to rely on in their own practice. Therapists described four termination cues: (1) Clients no longer idealize or depreciate their therapists, but rather begin to relate to them more as equals; (2) clients seem to need less input, evaluation, and interpretation from the therapist, and seem to have internalized the therapist; (3) clients start to expand the time between sessions; and (4) clients have less to talk about in sessions, not simply in one or two sessions, but during a long period of time.

In Kramer's (1986) qualitative study of 20 psychotherapists who were each interviewed about two recent terminations, it was rare to find cases in which the therapist wanted to terminate but the client disagreed, because in all but two cases it was the client who initiated termination. It was much more common for disagreements about termination to involve a client who wanted to terminate, whereas the therapist believed the client was merely avoiding dealing with clinical material. The question remains, of course, of how such disagreements are best resolved.

One intriguing area that awaits further research is that of whether clients benefit from some kind of formal or informal preparation for termination. We have noted that Corazzini et al. (1980) found that clients who were formally prepared for the termination of group therapy by a written handout discussing the process of termination and suggesting ways to deal with termination felt more resolved after the end of treatment than clients who did not receive the handout. No research has been done on the effects of preparation for termination in individual therapy. Kramer's (1986) qualitative study of termination in long-term therapy in private practice settings, however, revealed that most therapists had no procedure for informing their clients about what to expect in termination or how to determine when to end treatment. Kramer suggested that therapists could inform their clients at the beginning of therapy about their expectations regarding termination. For example, therapists who wait until clients bring up termination may want to tell those clients such, whereas therapists who believe that they themselves will initiate termination could inform their clients that this is how they work. However, there are currently no research data regarding this suggestion.

Most therapists invite clients to return if needed (de Bosset & Styrsky, 1986; Kramer, 1986; Marx & Gelso, 1987; Quintana & Holahan, 1992). In fact, de Bosset and Styrsky found that most of the psychiatric residents in their study invited clients to contact them for further therapy if needed, despite the fact that this would likely be impossible because many residents were terminating therapy because of a change in assigned setting. Kramer found that therapists were using two styles in implementing an open-door policy: (1) Some therapists emphasized that clients could return to therapy whenever desired, and little attention is put on the end of therapy itself; and (2) some therapists placed emphasis on the end of therapy, but let the clients know that the therapist would continue to be available to the client if needed.

The only research on what clients do once they recontact their therapists involves a qualitative study with psychoanalysts. Hartlaub, Martin, and Rhine (1986) surveyed psychoanalysts regarding recontact with the analyst after the completion of analysis. Of those who had successfully completed their analyses, two-thirds of the patients recontacted their analysts. Half of those who recontacted their analysts came in to see the analyst in person, most often for a brief office visit or for brief psychotherapy. The other half of patients who recontacted their analyst did so by letter or by telephone. The rate of recontact was unrelated to age, diagnosis, or length of analysis. Women were more likely to recontact than men. The researcher found that recontact was usually not an indication of the analysis having been incomplete, but rather that patients were working through posttermination issues. Posttermination issues might include (1) continuing to move away from an idealized view of the analyst, (2) restructuring inner representations of self and of others by telling the analyst about important developmental accomplishments the patient had achieved after termination, and (3) strengthening the self-analytic function that allows the individual to be independent of the analyst. These finding support the conclusions of Firestein (1978) that the termination work of psychoanalysis does not end when the formal analysis ends. For most analysands, termination work continues well after treatment has ended (Firestein, 1978).

Whether it is the client or the therapist who initiates the subject of termination in therapy may have some effect on the process of termination. Although it is unclear what the causal relations between the various factors may be, Fortune et al. (1992) found that client reactions and therapist reactions to termination were significantly related to which member had suggested the termination. When the therapist intiated termination, the client was less likely to evaluate the progress made in treatment and was more apt to change the therapeutic relationship toward greater equality and comfort. Meanwhile, when the client initiated termination, the client tended to evaluate the progress of therapy to a greater degree. Clients were more likely to begin or increase constructive activities outside of therapy. It appears then that whether it is the therapist or the client who iniates termination, either path to the end of therapy can be positive. However, clients tend to review therapy to a greater extent and transition to new constructive activities quickly if it is the client who suggests termination rather than the therapist.

Finally, Kramer (1986) found two styles for handling the process of review of the therapy during termination. Some therapists believed that a structured review of the therapy was required. Other therapists thought instead that review should only happen in an unstructured way, without preconceptions as to what it should look like, and that it should develop naturally, following the client's lead.

Planned Versus Forced Terminations

When factors outside the therapy influence termination, such as the therapist's move to a new training setting, the termination is known as a *forced termination.* Forced terminations are fairly common, particularly among trainees, but also in counseling centers, in hospitals, and in private practice under managed care. Thus, research on forced terminations is of great interest to many practitioners.

In a study of psychiatric residents by de Bosset and Styrsky (1986), the most common reason cited for terminating therapy was a change in setting for the therapist (35.53%). Change of setting, however, coincided with the attainment of mutual therapeutic goals in only 3.85% of the cases. Natural terminations occurred in only 15.38% of cases. Interestingly, this study also found that residents were likely to receive the most extensive supervision on termination in cases of natural termination but less extensive supervision when terminations were considered premature. The reasons for these differences in supervision, however, were not explored.

The data suggest that forced terminations tend to be harder for clients than natural terminations (Fortune et al., 1992; Goldthwaite, 1985; Saad, 1983). Saad found that clients in forced terminations may experience increased levels of anger, mourning, and mood disturbance, and Fortune et al. found that such clients may exhibit a decreased ability to engage in positive activities outside of therapy. Research findings also suggest that therapists tend to respond to forced termination with increased sadness, helplessness, anger, or frustration, or they may pull away from clients prematurely (Cicchitto, 1982; Fortune et al., 1992; Gould, 1978). Fortune et al. found that forced terminations were associated with clients being less able to move toward positive activities outside of therapy.

Earlier in the chapter we mentioned Gould's (1978) qualitative finding that some trainee supervisors believed that clients should not be told about the forced end of therapy at the end of the school year because they were concerned that clients would fail to engage in therapy if they knew there was a time limit. However, the supervisors' fears were not realized in the data. Gould found that clients whose therapists informed them they would be leaving at the end of the school year appeared relieved to know there would be a time limit and that they would not be in therapy indefinitely. Informed clients did not appear to have difficulty investing in the therapeutic work. All clients who were informed stayed in treatment for the duration. Some clients who were informed near the end of the therapy, however, did not return to sessions once they were told, which made the therapist feel frustrated and guilty. Therapists who did not inform their clients near the beginning felt more guilt, expressed more discomfort in the research interview, and generally experienced termination as more unpleasant than therapists who did inform their clients within the first three sessions.

Implications for Training and Practice

In this section, we discuss the ways in which the research findings that have been presented may be relevant to therapists and trainers. Before discussing implications for practice, however, we offer two comments about the research on termination. These comments are made with the aim of placing the subsequent material in a context that reflects key methodological issues in the research. We also present a viewpoint about how the termination research may be effectively used by therapists.

Our first comment on the research pertains to its quantity and quality. That is, in this review we are drawing on a small number of studies and a meager number of methodologically sound ones. Although we do not seek to provide a methodological critique here, we do believe it important to underscore the fact that there are only a handful of studies that incorporate sufficient methodological rigor (regardless of whether they are quantitative or qualitative studies) to be replicable and to permit reliable conclusions. This, of course, affects the degree of confidence we can have in drawing implications for practice. At the same time, we believe some valuable implications may be deduced, provided that the very tentative nature of the findings and the implications are understood from the outset.

Our second point follows from the first. That is, research has not thus far sought to link termination phenomena to treatment outcome (e.g., the actual gains made by clients during treatment). Because we do not know how termination factors are related to outcomes, the certitude with which we can offer recommendations for practice is reduced. Yet some studies have, indeed, examined variables that would appear to be highly relevant to outcome, for example, client satisfaction with termination. Thus, as noted previously, tentative implications are viable.

The viewpoint we wish to present pertains to how research may best be used in formulating implications for practice. In our view, research is most relevant to practice when that research is melded with clinical experience and theory. Likewise, this melding allows the practitioner to derive the most meaningful implications for practice. In essence, research findings are most helpful when placed in the context of theory and clinical experience. We do not believe that any findings should be applied directly to practice, given the inevitable differences that occur between the research setting and the individual case being treated. Instead, research is most clinically meaningful when it is used to inform the practitioner's explicit or implicit personal theory and applied to individual cases after being filtered through the lens of that theory (as the theory is applied to and altered by the individual case). Based on these views of how to develop implications for practice from research, we have sought to blend research findings with our own clinical experience and with existing clinical theory as we organized the implications presented in the following sections. In addition, we formulated implications with the idea that research is most relevant to practice through theory rather than being directly applicable to individual cases (see Gelso & Fretz, 1992, p. 113).

Termination Activities—What Is and Should Be Done

Taken together, the studies we have reviewed suggest that it is important to have a termination phase of treatment. Clients' reports indicate that they want and need such a phase (e.g., Marx & Gelso, 1987), and clinical theory and experience support its value. This statement may seem so obvious as to not need stating, and yet most experienced practitioners have likely heard stories of treatments that were abruptly ended by therapists without anything resembling a termination phase and with no attention to termination issues. The first author, for example, has learned, over the years, of cases in which treatment that had lasted for several months was terminated by the therapist in a single session, without prior warning to the patient. Research has yet to study the effects on patients of such abruptly terminated treatments, but our clinical observations suggest that abruptly ended terminations can have traumatic and enduring effects on clients.

Fortunately, research clearly indicates that therapists usually do allow for an ending phase and do engage clients in termination activities. In extrapolating from the few studies that have examined how much time is devoted to termination (de Bosset & Styrsky, 1986; Miller et al., 1983), we would speculate that typically about 10% to 12% of treatment time involves termination activities. This is far less than the time suggested by some theoreticians. For example, Mann's (1973) time-limited psychoanalytic therapy, as noted earlier, devotes about one-quarter of the treatment to termination issues. What does the research say about who is "right?" Although there is no clear answer to this question, we would suggest that, Mann's extensive focus on termination may be highly effective, but the devotion of less time and energy to termination may also be effective. Thus, the therapist may focus a great deal on termination or may focus significantly less (closer to our 10%) and still be equally efficacious. The bottom-line implication of our findings, however, is that enough time should be allowed for the work of termination to occur.

The work of termination, as suggested in theory and some of the studies we have reviewed (Fortune, 1987; Fortune et al., 1992; Marx & Gelso, 1987; Quintana & Holahan, 1992), involves looking back, looking forward, and saying good-bye. In looking back, therapist and client review the work. Together they explore the issues that have been examined, resolved, and unresolved. The ways in which the client has grown and the remaining impediments to growth are explored. In looking forward, the participants discuss what issues remain to be resolved and the direction in which the client believes he or she is heading. Plans and hopes for the future are examined. Finally, in saying good-bye, the participants focus on their relationship, what it has meant, feelings surrounding its ending, and, of course, feelings surrounding the ending of treatment. Based on the research, it appears that these activities are typically involved during the ending phase; however, the extensiveness of termination activities will vary with particular clients, therapists, and treatments.

The invitation for clients to return to counseling if they feel they need further work is common, and it seems to make sense, provided the invitation does not dilute to too great an extent the client's dealing with issues around ending (Mann, 1973). At the same time, there is no research on the efficacy of such invitations. Thus, clinical guidance must await future empirical work on this topic.

Generally, clients are satisfied with the termination work that is done, just as they tend to be satisfied with and helped by their therapy (see the outcome review by Lambert & Bergin, 1994). To this extent, the implications of research for practice are that practitioners should continue to do what is usually done. It tends to be effective, on the whole. Later we examine implications beyond this "on the whole" statement.

Reactions to Ending—Beyond Termination as Loss

Naturally, clients who have been in successful therapy and have formed an attachment with their therapists will experience some sadness about ending, as will therapists. It is also expected that there will be a degree of anxiety resulting from giving up the support of therapy and "facing the world" on one's own. These emotional reactions, sadness and anxiety, are particularly predictable the longer therapy lasts, because as the duration increases, the client's emotional attachment to the therapist becomes stronger (Marx & Gelso, 1987). A clinical implication of this empirically supported increase of sadness and anxiety at termination as therapy extends is that therapists need to devote more time to the termination phase in longer-term cases (see the earlier section about the proportion of therapy time devoted to termination issues). On the whole, though, the research clearly suggests that positive feelings outweigh negative ones—pride, pleasure, excitement, eagerness, and gratitude are much more evident than feelings revolving around depression, anxiety, and anger. A case presented by Malan (1979), from his qualitative study of brief analytic therapy, perhaps best illustrates our clinical observations, as well as the quantitative research findings.

> The patient was a 32-year-old woman who was in her 17th and last session with a male therapist. The therapy had been quite successful in a range of ways. In the final session, after offering the therapist a gift which he admired and accepted with thanks, "Miss D." discussed her feelings about the death of the mother of Arthur, the man she planned to marry. She then gave an example of how the therapy had helped her be able to speak up for herself. Miss D. "went on to say that things were very different from how they had been before she started the therapy with me. She realized now that she had not been able to grieve about the end of her previous, group therapy, whereas plainly she had been able to be sad about finishing the work with me. She was not depressed and she was struck by my remark of last week that there was a considerable difference between sadness and depression. She was quite sure that what she was feeling was sadness.
>
> "At about this point Miss D. sort of settled back in her chair, looked at her watch, and then said that it was odd that she felt she had nothing more to say, but that it was different—she could be quiet and didn't feel she had to rattle on. After a bit she said she thought it would be best if we ended the session now. I said of course it was her decision to do as she wished, but I'd be very happy if she'd come back in the summer and tell me how things had gone. 'Oh,' she said, 'How nice. You've really made my day. I'd love to do that. Thank you very much.' We agreed that she should get in touch with me after Easter, and we parted on very good terms." (pp. 207–208)

What are the clinical implications of the findings about clients' emotional reactions to ending? Given that the large majority of clients experience substantially more positive than negative affect at termination, it may be wise to move away from the "termination-as-loss" model that seems to have pervaded clinical theory. The repeated finding of positive affect at termination may be the single most important development in our understanding of the significance of termination for clients. We agree with Fortune et al. (1992), who suggest that therapists savor, rather than question and interpret, their own and their clients' sense of pride and accomplishment, and that such an approach may actually help to reinforce clients' sense of mastery.

We have discussed implications of research findings for clients and treatments *on the whole*. Let us now consider implications as related to client, therapist, and treatment factors.

The Client Factor—Individual Differences Matter

Given the empirically documented importance of client factors in all of psychotherapy (see reviews by Garfield, 1994; Hill & Williams, 2000), it is striking to see how little research has been done on client factors in termination. There are few replicated findings in this area.

Earlier we mentioned Malan's (1979) and Firestein's (1978) qualitative studies, which found that the individual client's dynamics are an important factor in determining the way in which termination may unfold and the meaning termination may have. The rule of thumb suggested by Malan's data is that the therapist look for continuity of themes during termination rather than qualitatively different content. A clinical implication of Malan's and Firestein's findings is that the therapist needs to work hard to grasp the unique meaning of termination for each individual client.

Can any particular client individual difference factors be culled from the few studies that have been done? The factor that stands out most pertains to clients' experiences with losses in their lives. In essence, it appears that loss themes in the client's life are associated with, and probably influence, the amount of termination work done in therapy, and the amount of termination work relates to clients' satisfaction with the termination process (Martinez, 1986; Marx & Gelso, 1987). These findings suggest that therapists and trainers need to attend carefully to the client's history of losses. When the client has experienced emotionally significant losses (and here we would recommend looking at both the number of losses and the psychological impact of those losses), the issue of loss is more likely to be evidenced in the work. In such cases, more attention needs to be given to the termination process and how issues of loss may be revived during termination. Regarding therapist training, supervisors may need to assist therapist–trainees in developing their sensitivity to loss issues in their clients and to deepen their understanding of how these issues may lead to difficulties in facing the loss of the therapeutic relationship.

The Therapist Factor—A Key Influence

Research suggests that therapists who experience greater than usual increases in anxiety and depression during termination are likely to have experienced past grief reactions. Depressed therapist affect during termination also signals continued grief reactions (Boyer & Hoffman, 1993). An implication of this finding is that therapists who experience elevated anxiety and depression during termination should determine whether their own issues concerning loss are interfering with their comfort and effectiveness in managing the termination process. At the same time, the increase in depressed and anxious feelings of the therapist may reflect the therapist's sensitivity to the client's loss issues, as is also suggested by Boyer and Hoffman's important study. Finally, it should be remembered that therapists tend to feel more emotional about termination when they feel close to their client (Martinez, 1986), so supervisors may want to normalize trainees' affective reactions to termination, assuming that reactions are relatively free of countertransference problems.

The fact that therapists tend to be influenced by the termination they experienced in their own personal therapy (Parkerton, 1987; Porter, 1987/1988) emphasizes the importance of therapists' reflecting on their feelings during the ending phase of their own therapy. Such an examination should include a consideration of what they liked and disliked about the process.

Research also suggests that it is important for therapists to understand how sex-role prescriptions (Greene, 1980) and sex-role orientation (Paster, 1983) may affect their behavior with clients during termination and the kinds of feelings they attend to or avoid during this process. Therapists must be aware of the various ways that culture-based, gender-role expectations and the internalization of these roles impact termination work. Sex roles may affect which feelings therapists experience as comfortable or alien. Of course, assuming that we all have gender-cultural scripts as part of our intrapsychic world, it seems worthwhile to examine how our scripts, as therapists, interact in unexpected ways with client scripts when clients are from different cultures than our own.

It is important to note that researchers have not examined the roles of culture, ethnicity, and race in the termination process. These factors have received some attention in the research on premature termination; however, because our focus has been on the termination process itself, we do not address these studies. Cultural, ethnic, and racial factors may have significant implications for termination. For example, collectivist cultures and individualistic cultures may hold different beliefs about saying good-bye and may have different values about the nature of ties after the ending of a helping relationship. More research in this area would be useful to therapists attempting to navigate the complexities of termination.

Perhaps the bottom-line implication for therapists based on the research on therapist factors that have been reviewed is that the importance of self-inspection, self-understanding, and self-monitoring cannot be overestimated. Attention to countertransference and other therapist experiences (Gelso & Hayes, 1998) is an important, if not vital, part of all of psychotherapy, including issues concerning termination. Such attention is equally, or perhaps more, pertinent when the work has not gone well, a situation we now discuss.

Treatment Factors—Unsuccessful Cases and Forced Terminations

Quintana and Holahan (1992) found that therapists appear to engage in fewer of the desired termination behaviors with unsuccessful than with successful cases. These researchers suggest that therapists may profit from examining their reactions to termination with clients whose therapy has not gone well and that therapists pay special attention to reviewing the course of therapy and discussing termination with these clients. This suggestion makes sense because of the finding that clients feel greater satisfaction when more, rather than less, termination work is done. Also, clinical experience suggests that avoidance of therapist–client relationship issues may have resulted in the lack of success of the treatment. Thus, avoidance of reviewing the course of therapy with these clients, as often happens, may be "more of the same."

At the same time, there is a temptation to overprescribe to therapists, and clinicians may refrain from exploring the course of therapy with unsuccessful cases for clinical reasons. For instance, in certain cases, it may be unnecessarily painful for the client (and therapist) to review an unsuccessful experience; in other instances, the client will resist such a review to the extent that the therapist would need to "force" the issue, which would not be helpful. Perhaps the most that can be said about termination with unsuccessful cases is that the therapist should sort through carefully the pros and cons of exploring what has happened in the work and the relationship during the termination phase. Part of this exploration will entail assessing the extent to which the therapist's tendency to avoid is countertransference based and the extent to which it may be truly helpful to the client to review what has happened during therapy.

Regarding the phenomenon of so-called forced terminations, it seems empirically clear that such endings tend to be harder than natural terminations for both clients (Fortune et al., 1992; Goldthwaite, 1985; Saad, 1983) and therapists (Cicchitto, 1982; Fortune et al., 1992; Gould, 1978). This being the case, it makes sense for therapists to attempt to transform therapies that will be forced terminations into time-limited therapies. The client is told at the outset when therapy will end. Such a transformation seems especially called for when the therapist knows the work will be ending at a particular time, for example, when practicum or residency ends. The limited research evidence (e.g., Gould, 1978) suggests that time-limited therapy works better for both clients and therapists than a forced termination announced late in the work. Based on clinical experience and research (e.g., Gelso & Johnson, 1983), it seems wise to focus the therapy on particular goals that realistically can be accomplished within the time limits available rather than essentially working as if the treatment were open ended.

Knowing When to End

Unless the therapy is time-limited or planned for the short-term, it is not easy to decide when it should end. Of course, at times clients force the decision by a geographic move or a life decision that necessitates ending therapy. This circumstance aside, there are no clear rules about when to end. As we have noted, Kramer (1986) found a number of cues to termination that therapists may find helpful. These bear repeating: (1) Clients no longer idealize or depreciate their therapists, but rather relate to them more as equals; (2) clients seem to need less input, evaluation, and interpretation from their therapist, and seem to have internalized the therapist; (3) clients start to expand the time between sessions (either deliberately or unconsciously, we would add); and (4) clients seem to have less to talk about in sessions, not only for one or two sessions, but during a long period of time.

Our own clinical experience suggests that about the time these cues occur, the client either directly or indirectly (e.g., through metaphors or dreams) suggests termination. When the cues occur, it is probably time for the therapist, as Kramer (1986) notes, to begin dialogues with the client about ending therapy, including the thoughts and feelings the client has about that possibility. Further, therapists may find it helpful to consider the termination criteria they hold for each individual client they work with, especially because research in different settings suggests that therapists tend not to have fully considered the therapeutic goals for each client (Bywaters, 1975; Kramer, 1986). General criteria for termination found in the literature concern sufficient improvement on the client's part (in terms of the goals the therapist and client established), client understanding of the problem and its source (in the terms the client and therapist use), and stability of change in the client (i.e., the change should not be transitory but rather stabilized). At the same time, these general criteria need to be translated for each unique client–therapist relationship.

Summary

The process of termination in counseling and psychotherapy has been given relatively little attention by theoreticians and especially by researchers. However, enough research has accumulated over the years to permit us to draw tentative implications for therapy practice. We have sought to paint an empirically based picture of the termination process, while at the same time addressing client, therapist, and treatment factors that moderate such a picture. Numerous questions about termination await empirical scrutiny. An increase in research activity is needed if we are to draw richer and firmer clinical implications.

References

Bauer, G. P., & Kobos, J. C. (1987). *Brief therapy.* New Jersey: Aronson.

Boyer, S. P., & Hoffman, M. A. (1993). Counselor affective reactions to termination: Impact of counselor loss history and perceived client sensitivity to loss. *Journal of Counseling Psychology, 40,* 271–277.

Budman, S. H., & Gurman, A. S. (1988). *Theory and practice of brief therapy.* New York: Guilford Press.

Bywaters, P. (1975). Ending casework relationships: 1. The closure decision. *Social Work Today, 6,* 301–304.

Cicchitto, F. R. (1982). Countertransference reactions to forced and natural termination of psychotherapy. (Doctoral dissertation, California School of Profession Psychology, 1982) *Dissertation Abstracts International, 43,* 3727B–3728B.

Corazzini, J. G., Heppner, P. P., & Young, M. D. (1980). The effects of cognitive information on termination from group counseling. *Journal of College Student Personnel, 21,* 553–557.

Davanloo, H. (1980). (Ed.), *Short-term dynamic psychotherapy.* New York: Spectrum.

de Bosset, F., & Styrsky, E. (1986). Termination in individual psychotherapy: A survey of residents' experience. *Canadian Journal of Psychiatry, 31,* 636–642.

Fair, S. M., & Bressler, J. M. (1992). Therapist-initiated termination of psychotherapy. *The Clinical Supervisor, 10,* 171–189.

Firestein, S. K. (1978). *Termination in psychoanalysis.* New York: International Universities Press.

Fortune, A. E. (1987). Grief only? Client and social worker reactions to termination. *Clinical Social Work Journal, 15,* 159–171.

Fortune, A. E., Pearlingi, B., & Rochelle, C. D. (1992). Reactions to termination of individual treatment. *Social Work, 37,* 171–178.

Garfield, S. L. (1989). *The practice of brief psychotherapy.* New York: Pergamon.

Garfield, S. L. (1994). Research on client variables in psychotherapy. In A. Bergin & S. Garfield (Eds.), *Handbook of psychotherapy and behavior change* (4th ed., pp. 190–228). New York: Wiley.

Gelso, C. J., & Fretz, B. R. (1992). *Counseling psychology.* Fort Worth, TX: Harcourt.

Gelso, C. J., & Hayes, J. A. (1998). *The psychotherapy relationship: Theory, research, practice.* New York: Wiley.

Gelso, C. J., & Johnson, D. H. (1983). *Explorations in time-limited counseling and psychotherapy.* New York: Columbia University, Teachers College Press.

Goldthwaite, D. E. (1985). The client's perspective on the forced termination of psychotherapy. (Doctorate dissertation, Boston College, 1985) *Dissertation Abstracts International, 47,* 2164B.

Goodyear, R. K. (1981). Termination as a loss experience for the counselor. *Personnel and Guidance Journal, 59,* 347–350.

Gould, R. P. (1978). Students' experience with the termination phase of individual treatment. *Smith College Studies in Social Work, 48,* 235–269.

Greene, L. R. (1980). On terminating psychotherapy: More evidence of sex-role related countertransference. *Psychology of Women Quarterly, 4,* 548–557.

Hartlaub, G. H., Martin, G. C., & Rhine, M. W. (1986). Recontact with the analyst following termination: A survey of 71 cases. *Journal of the American Psychoanalytic Association, 34,* 895–910.

Hill, C. E., & Williams, E. N. (2000). The process of individual psychotherapy. In R. Lent & S. Brown (Eds.), *Handbook of counseling psychology* (3rd ed.). New York: Wiley.

Kauff, P. F. (1977). The termination process: Its relationship to the separation-individuation phase of development. *International Journal of Group Psychotherapy, 27,* 3–18.

Kramer, S. A. (1986). The termination process in open-ended psychotherapy: Guidelines for clinical practice. *Psychotherapy, 33,* 526–531.

Kübler-Ross, E. (1967). *On death and dying.* New York: Macmillan.

Lamb, D. H. (1985). A time-frame model of termination in psychotherapy. *Psychotherapy, 22,* 604–609.

Lambert, M., & Bergin, A. (1994). The effectiveness of psychotherapy. In A. Bergin & S. Garfield (Eds.), *Handbook of psychotherapy and behavior change* (4th ed., pp. 143–189). New York: Wiley.

Langs, R. (1974). *The technique and practice of psychoanalytic psychotherapy.* New York: Jason Aronson.

Malan, D. H. (1976). *Frontiers of brief psychotherapy.* New York: Plenum Press.

Malan, D. H. (1979). *Individual psychotherapy and the science of psychodynamics.* London: Butterworth.

Mann, J. (1973). *Time-limited psychotherapy.* Cambridge, MA: Harvard University Press.

Martinez, A. C. (1986). Counselor responses to the termination of individual counseling in a university counseling center. *Dissertation Abstracts International, 48,* 268B.

Marx, J. A., & Gelso, C. J. (1987). Termination of individual counseling in a university center. *Journal of Counseling Psychology, 34,* 3–9.

Miller, J. M., Courtois, C. A., Pelham, J. P., Riddle, P. E., Spiegel, S. P., Gelso, C. J., & Johnson, D. H. (1983). The process of time-limited therapy. In C. Gelso & D. Johnson (Eds.), *Explorations in time-limited counseling and psychotherapy* (pp. 153–162). New York: Columbia University, Teachers College Press.

Parkerton, K. (1987). When psychoanalysis is over: An exploration of the psychoanalyst's subjective experience and actual behavior related to the loss of patients at termination and afterward. *Dissertation Abstracts International, 48,* 2790B. (University Microfilms No. 87-27, 129)

Paster, L. F. (1983). The influence of the gender and sex role of the patient and psychotherapist on the termination of psychotherapy. (Doctoral dissertation, St. John's University, 1983) *Dissertation Abstracts International, 44,* 320B.

Pinkerton, R. S., & Rockwell, W. J. K. (1990). Termination in brief psychotherapy: the case for an eclectic approach. *Psychotherapy, 27,* 362–365.

Porter, J. E. (1987/1988). The role of intimacy status, boundary style, and personal therapy in therapists' experiences of termination. *Dissertation Abstracts International, 48,* 2106B. (University Microfilms No. 87-20, 715)

Quintana, S. M. (1993). Toward an expanded and updated conceptualization of termination. *Professional Psychology: Research and Practice, 24,* 426–432.

Quintana, S. M., & Holahan, W. (1992). Termination in short-term counseling: Comparison of successful and unsuccessful cases. *Journal of Counseling Psychology, 39,* 299–305.

Saad, J. R. (1983). After ending long-term psychotherapy: Patient reaction to planned and forced termination. (Doctoral dissertation, St. Johns's University, 1983) *Dissertation Abstracts International, 44,* 3541B.

Sansone, R. A., Fine, M. A., & Dennis, A. B. (1991). Treatment impressions and termination experiences with borderline patients. *American Journal of Psychotherapy, 45,* 173–180.

Shulman, L. (1979). *The skills of helping individuals and groups.* Itasca, IL: Peacock.

Sifneos, P. E. (1992). *Short-term anxiety-provoking psychotherapy: A treatment manual.* New York: Basic Books.

Strupp, H. H., & Binder, J. L. (1984). *Psychotherapy in a new key.* New York: Basic Books.

Swords, M. J. (1985). Counselors' grief responses to termination. (Doctoral dissertation, University of Wisconsin–Madison, 1985) *Dissertation Abstracts International, 46,* 3607.

Ward, D. E. (1984). Termination of individual counseling: Concepts and strategies. *Journal of Counseling and Development, 63,* 21–25.

Name Index

Subject Index

Ability to process, 301–305, 307, 309, 312–313, 320
  by central route, 312–313, 315, 319
  by peripheral route and, 305, 309, 317, 319
Abstract cognitive techniques, 91
Acceptance, 30–32, 84–85, 102, 208, 215
Acceptance scale, 41, 42, 48, 49, 54
  EAC scales, 32, 33, 38, 50, 59
  gender differences in expectancy of, 30, 39, 43, 48, 57, 58
Acculturation, 40, 41, 42, 44, 60
Acculturation Rating Scale for Mexican Americans (ARSMA), 41
Acculturation Scale, 40
Accuracy, 180, 181, 238, 255, 301
  of empathetic knowing, 200, 201, 210, 215, 217, 218, 255
  of therapist interpretation, 167–169, 174, 179–181, 191–192
Acomplementary level, 283
Acting out behavior, 353, 357
Action stage, 10, 52, 53, 254, 255
Adherence, forms of, 273, 274
Adjustment disorders, 353
Adlerian therapy, 207–208, 209, 245
Administrative factors, nonengagement and, 6–7, 8
Adult Attachment Interview (AAI), 187, 188, 191
Adult Attachment Scale (AAS), 187, 188, 191
Advisement mode (directives), 18, 235, 236
Affect. *See* Emotional experience
Affective empathy, 201–205, 209–210
Affective mode, 223, 241–243, 252–253, 275, 293
Affective Process Scale, 49
Affiliation, control and, 94, 279, 286, 292
Affirmation, by therapist, 94, 102, 114, 117
African American clients, 42, 43, 122, 149, 152, 336
Africans, counseling of, 39, 40
Age, 8, 12, 98–99, 112, 150
  counseling expectations, 32, 41, 44–46, 51, 60
Aggressive behavior, 157, 298, 299, 307, 308

Alcohol expectancy, definition, 28
Alcoholism counseling, 57, 92, 111, 245
Alliance. *See* Client-therapist relationship, Therapeutic alliance, Working alliance
Alliance-as-a-by-product argument, 94
Ambiguity, of role expectations, 137, 138, 146
American Psychological Association Membership Register, 33
Amount/level, transference pattern of, 174, 176, 191
Analyses of variances (ANOVA), 31, 50
  expectancy about counseling, 50, 57, 59
ANCOVA, 55
Anger, 115, 116, 218, 298, 361
Anglo American clients, 41, 42, 44, 237
Anticomplementarity level, 283
Antisocial personality disorder, 9
Anxiety, 43, 138, 156, 178, 311, 354
  alliance and outcome, 111, 116, 120
  of client, 69–70, 72, 352, 353, 363
  self-talk component of, 251, 252, 253
  of therapist, 72, 354–358, 365
  therapist techniques to relieve, 248
Approach-avoidance conflict, 173
Approval, 15, 235, 238, 244, 246, 249
Arousal scale, postsession, 327–328, 330, 339–340
Asian American clients, 41, 122, 149, 237, 239, 256
Asians, counseling of, 39, 40
As if boundary, 216, 218, 219, 226
Assertiveness training, 307–308, 310, 311
Assessment, 117, 118, 120, 150, 185–190
Assessment instruments/devices, 136, 186, 187, 318
Assessment measures
  pretreatment, 186, 187, 188, 191
  process, 186, 187, 191
Assessment of Career Decision-Making Styles Scale (ACDMSS), 54
Assimilation, definition, 40
Assimilation scale, 41
Attitude, 7, 144, 298–299, 306, 309, 318–319

Attitude change, 298–299, 300, 306, 313–316
  central route processing, 301, 302, 304, 307, 309, 315–316
  long-term, 302–305, 307, 314–317
  peripheral route, 302, 303
Attitude change model, 299
Attractiveness, 28, 152, 157, 255
  of candidate for counseling, 9, 10, 11
  as cue variable, 301, 303, 304, 317
  supervisor's judgment and, 139, 140, 144
  therapist characteristic of, 28, 32, 35, 47, 54–57, 59, 72
Attractiveness scale, 32–34, 38, 41–43, 46, 48–49, 58–59
Autonomous vs. dominant behavior, 286
Autonomous vs. submissive behavior, 286
Autonomy scale, 43, 44
Avoidance maneuvers, 94, 100, 112–113, 116, 189, 353
Awareness exercises, 221–225, 226

Bad–Good evaluation item, 340
Behavior change, 317, 320, 367
  attitude change, 298, 299, 307, 309, 313, 322
Barrett-Lennard Relationship Inventory (BLRI), 29, 36, 138, 149
Barriers to treatment, 21, 52
Barriers to treatment model, 20
Barriers to Treatment Participation Scale (BTPS), 20, 21
Beck Anxiety Inventory (BAI), 170
Beck Depression Inventory (BDI), 170
Behavioral change, 235, 266, 274–278
Behavioral interchanges, complementary/symmetrical, 268
Behavioral therapy, 31–32, 73, 82, 92, 96, 107, 110
  empathy in, 203, 207
  stage process of change, 265, 278
Bem Sex Role Inventory (BSRI), 39
Bereavement, 92, 111
Bias in cognitive processing, 182–183, 301, 306, 319–320, 331, 359
Bigotry, 152
Biofeedback exercises, 223